RETHINKING VALUATION AND PRICING MODELS

EDITOR'S DISCLAIMERS

To avoid misunderstandings, we would like to emphasise, that all opinions expressed herein are the authors' and should not be cited as being those of their affiliated institutions. None of the methods described herein is claimed to be in actual use.

Neither the editors nor the publisher is responsible for the content of each chapter. The contributors are solely responsible for their work.

And
"We would like to thank executive editor J.S.Bentley and Kathleen Paoni at Elsevier."

RETHINKING VALUATION AND PRICING MODELS

Lessons Learned from the Crisis and Future Challenges

Edited by

CARSTEN S. WEHN
CHRISTIAN HOPPE
GREG N. GREGORIOU

AMSTERDAM • BOSTON • HEIDELBERG • LONDON
NEW YORK • OXFORD • PARIS • SAN DIEGO
SAN FRANCISCO • SINGAPORE • SYDNEY • TOKYO
Academic Press is an Imprint of Elsevier

Academic Press is an imprint of Elsevier
The Boulevard, Langford Lane, Kidlington, Oxford, OX5 1GB, UK
225 Wyman Street, Waltham, MA 02451, USA

First published 2013

Notices
Knowledge and best practice in this field are constantly changing. As new research and experience
broaden our understanding, changes in research methods, professional practices, or medical
treatment may become necessary.

Practitioners and researchers must always rely on their own experience and knowledge in evaluating
and using any information, methods, compounds, or experiments described herein. In using such
information or methods they should be mindful of their own safety and the safety of others,
including parties for whom they have a professional responsibility.

To the fullest extent of the law, neither the Publisher nor the authors, contributors, or editors, assume
any liability for any injury and/or damage to persons or property as a matter of products liability,
negligence or otherwise, or from any use or operation of any methods, products, instructions, or
ideas contained in the material herein.

British Library Cataloguing in Publication Data
A catalogue record for this book is available from the British Library

Library of Congress Cataloguing in Publication Data
A catalog record for this book is available from the Library of Congress

ISBN: 978-0-12-415875-7

For information on all Academic Press publications visit
our website at store.elsevier.com

Printed and bound in the United States
12 13 14 15 10 9 8 7 6 5 4 3 2 1

Working together to grow
libraries in developing countries

www.elsevier.com | www.bookaid.org | www.sabre.org

ELSEVIER | BOOK AID International | Sabre Foundation

CONTENTS

**Chapter 22 A Maximum Entropy Approach to the Measurement
of Event Risk** **375**

Marco Bee

**Chapter 23 Quantifying the Unquantifiable: Risks Not in Value
at Risk**...**387**

Carsten S. Wehn

FOREWORD

By the editors

The recent years were characterized by first the financial crisis and then the sovereign crisis that created many pitfalls for the valuation and risk management of financial products. The unprecedented financial losses both in the private and institutional sectors around the world aling with the near collapse of the global banking industry have occurred despite highly praised advances in risk management methodologies, such as regulatory developments meant to safeguard the financial system. On the other hand, during the last decade, the volume of financial derivatives increased dramatically and thus the related valuation methods and risk management processes were further developed. Even the theory of blaming "the models" on the crisis appeared. The 2008-2009 crisis has pushed us aside and further perform additional reengineering on problems thought to be previously solved such as the valuation of plain vanilla derivatives.

As any other model, valuation and risk measurement models are seen as an approximation to the real world. One could possibly consider, for instance, of a "model" of the world. In ancient times, people thought of earth as being a flat disk in the centre of the universe. But, due to the exploration of larger horizons the flat world model was challenged. Galileo's geocentric model of the world was replaced by a heliocentric model consistent with Newton's theory of gravitation. Last not least, the relativity theory by Einstein replaced Newton's model with an abstract version where time was not kept constant.

The example demonstrates that every approximation and illustration of reality will be challenged by "real world observations" from time to time and then potentially be modified to incorporate new observations. While the root causes of the global financial crisis were numerous and convoluted, it is certain that the failure of some financial pricing models have catalyzed the spiraling events as they triggered investors' loss of confidence in the very financial models they were hailed as "best in class" and "best practices" only a few years ago.

As a consequence, it is perhaps more imperative for any participant in financial markets to grasp the importance of modeling financial products and assessing the strengths, but also the weaknesses of the models employed in valuing financial assets and risk management.

Thus, there could be no better timing for a comprehensive and deep compendium on assessing the challenges of valuing derivatives, revisiting valuation and risk models. The authors have done a superb job in compounding the relevant contributory articles in an all-encompassing effort to gather the most recent industry and academic progress in the field. The book stands out for its exclusivity of chapters and ability to match the theoretical thoroughness with the high level of practicality in a "post subprime crisis" economic environment.

The handbook draws the line between classical, well established models and new issues that have come to the forefront when using valuation models, calculating risk, and managing portfolios. The book focuses on the current state of derivatives pricing and risk management in cases where the financial crisis revealed the need to improve valuation models.

The handbook addresses observations made during the crisis as well as the current state of solutions by different aspects: First, the needs to readjust valuation models even for plain vanilla derivatives (but not only) are revisited. This touches the pricing of derivatives and hybrid products as well as the incorporation of counterparty risk in the models. Second, different models for valuation of equities and markets are analyzed. There are several challenges for risk management that will be reflected in the third part comprising estimation of default probabilities, correlation, and distributional assumptions and so on. This all flows into investment decisions, treated in the fourth part. Also, the requirements by regulation and accounting have increased and are reflecting the observations made during the crisis, which treated in the fifth section of the book. Finally, a part on empirical observations completes the picture.

The handbook addresses issues relevant for upper-division undergraduates, graduate students, junior academics and professionals worldwide working in asset management, trading, risk control of banks and insurance companies, consultancy firms, auditing, regulation, applied mathematics and finance or other applied academic working fields. The contributors to the compendium are some of the most prominent academics and practitioners in the field of modern risk management and have distinguished themselves over decades with seminal articles that have taken the financial risk management profession into the twenty-first century. We have attempted to provide the most appropriate articles pertaining to each subject in a flawlessly structured manner.

The book will hopefully become a key reference in the shelves of any modern financial professional and will likely contribute to elucidate the continuing shaded areas of valuation and risk models, especially in light of the recent happenings in financial markets. We hope the readers will share our opinion that the challenges to valuation and risk management models posed by the crisis are a subject worth being studied in-depth.

Greg N. Gregoriou

Christian Hoppe

Carsten S. Wehn

EDITORS

Dr. Carsten S. Wehn is head of the risk modelling team at DekaBank, Frankfurt, where he is responsible for the risk methods for market and credit risks in a portfolio context. Risk modelling also is responsible for validation the risk models and the regular development with respect to new regulatory or business requirements. The team is also responsible for the operational controlling of credit risks in the ICAAP framework. In his career, he administered several different roles like the heading of the market risk control team where he was responsible for the measurement of market and liquidity risk of the bank and the development of risk methods and models as well as the validation of the adequacy of the respective risk models. Before joining DekaBank, he worked at Deutsche Bundesbank as an auditor and audit supervisor for regulatory examinations of banks' quantitative models for risk measurement and management. He holds a Ph.D. in mathematics and gives lectures at universities. He regularly publishes in well known industrial magazines as well as in books, mainly about quantitative aspects of risk modelling.

Christian Hoppe works as head of credit solutions in the credit portfolio management in the corporate banking division of Commerzbank AG Frankfurt. His main focus is on structured credit transactions to actively manage the corporate credit portfolio. Christian is also co-founder and CEO of the Anleihen Finder GmbH in Frankfurt, an information platform for mezzanine and debt capital. Prior to this he was credit portfolio manager at Dresdner Kleinwort, the Investment Bank arm of Dresdner Bank AG in Frankfurt. He started his career as a Business and Financial Controller for Dresdner Bank in Frankfurt responsible for the corporate client business in Germany. He completed his economics degree at the University of Essen-Duisburg in 2003. Whilst writing his master thesis, Christian worked in the Institutional Research Department of Benchmark Alternative Strategies GmbH in Frankfurt. Christian is the co-author of several articles as well as books, author of the German book "*Derivate auf Alternative Investments — Konstruktion und Bewertungsmöglichkeiten*" published by Gabler and co-editor of the "*Handbook of Credit Portfolio Management*" and "*Risk Modeling — The Evaluation Handbook*" published by McGraw Hill.

Greg N. Gregoriou a native of Montreal, Professor Gregoriou obtained his joint PhD at the University of Quebec at Montreal in Finance which merges the resources of Montreal's four major universities UQAM, McGill, Concordia, and HEC. Professor Gregoriou has published 45 books, 60 refereed publications in peer-reviewed journals and 20 book chapters since his arrival at SUNY (Plattsburgh) in August 2003. Professor Gregoriou's books have been published by McGraw-Hill, John Wiley & Sons, Elsevier-Butterworth/Heinemann, Taylor and Francis/CRC Press, Palgrave-MacMillan and Risk Books. His articles have appeared in the Review of Asset Pricing Studies, Journal of Portfolio Management, Journal of Futures Markets, European Journal of Operational Research, Annals of Operations Research, Computers and Operations Research, etc. He has also been quoted several times in the New York Times and the Financial Times of London. Professor Gregoriou is hedge fund editor and editorial board member for the *Journal of Derivatives and Hedge Funds*, as well as editorial board member for the *Journal of Wealth Management*, the *Journal of Risk Management in Financial Institutions*,

Market Integrity, IEB International Journal of Finance, The Journal of Quantitative Methods for Social Sciences, and the *Brazilian Business Review.* Professor Gregoriou's interests focus on hedge funds, funds of funds, and CTAs. He is an EDHEC Research Associate in Nice, France, a Research Associate at the Caisse de Dépôt et placement du Québec Endowed Chair in Portfolio Management at the University of Quebec at Montreal and also teaches finance courses in graduate program at McGill University.

THE EDITORS AND PUBLISHER ARE NOT RESPONSIBLE AND CANNOT GUARENTEE THE ACCURACY FOR EACH CHAPTER PROVIDED BY EACH CONTRIBUTOR!

CONTRIBUTORS

Numbers in parentheses indicate the chapter the contributor has written.

Camillo Lento (1) is Assistant Professor in the Faculty of Business Administration at Lakehead University, Thunder Bay, Ontario, Canada. He holds a PhD from the University of Southern Queensland (Australia) and holds an M.Sc. (Management) and BComm (Honours) from Lakehead University. In addition, he is a Chartered Accountant (Canada), Certified Fraud Examiner and a student of the Canadian Institute of Chartered Business Valuators. Before embarking on his PhD, he worked in a variety of positions in accounting, auditing, and asset valuation with both Ernst and Young LLP and Grant Thornton LLP. He has authored several book chapters, journal articles, and practitioner magazine articles. Noteworthy, his financial planning commentary has been featured in the Globe and Mail's Report on Business, MoneySense Magazine, MoneySaver Magazine, and Canadian Business (online).

Nikola Gradojevic (1) earned a PhD degree in financial economics from the University of British Columbia, Vancouver, BC, Canada, in 2003. Currently, he is an Associate Professor of Finance at the Faculty of Business Administration, Lakehead University, Thunder Bay, Ontario, Canada. During his career he took positions at the University of British Columbia, Bank of Canada, Federal Reserve Bank of St. Louis, and in the private sector as a consultant. He has held visiting appointments at Rouen Business School in France and University of Novi Sad, Faculty of Technical Sciences, Serbia. He is a Research Fellow at the Rimini Center for Economic Analysis in Italy. His research interests include international finance (market microstructure), empirical asset pricing (option pricing), technical trading, non-extensive entropy, asset price volatility and bubbles, and artificial intelligence (neural networks, fuzzy logic, etc.). He has published his research in journals such as Journal of Banking and Finance, Journal of Empirical Finance, Quantitative Finance, Journal of Economic Dynamics and Control, IEEE Signal Processing Magazine, IEEE Transactions on Neural Networks, Physica D and Journal of Forecasting.

Messaoud Chibane (2) has been working as a quant since 1997. He has held various senior quant positons at Merril Lynch and Bank Of America specializing in Interest Rates and long dated FX modelling. He currently runs Shinsei Bank Quantitative Analytics team globally. He holds an engineering degree from Ecole Centrale Paris and a DEA in financial mathematics from La Sorbonne University.

Yi-Chen Huang (2) joined Shinsei Bank Quantitative Analytics team in 2011. Prior to that he worked in the field of credit derivative modeling in Credit Portfolio Management group. He holds a financial engineering degree from University of California Berkeley and a finance degree from Imperial College London.

Jayaprakash Selvaraj (2) has been a Senior Quant at Shinsei Bank since 2007. His focus is on single currency pricing and hedging issues. He holds an Engineering Degree from Visvesvaraya Technological University, Bangalore.

Péter Dobránszky (3) manages a team being responsible for the independent review of the internal risk methodologies related to capital markets. Earlier, he was validating equity, commodity and energy pricing models. As a consultant, he helped banks to develop and implement financial models and pricing engines. As part of his academic researches, he focused on credit derivatives, on capturing the asset price and volatility dynamics and on advanced numerical techniques.

Rosa Cocozza (4) is Full Professor of Financial Risk Management and Financial Engineering at the Università di Napoli Federico II; she holds an M.A. in Banking and Finance and a PhD in Business Administration. She presently runs the Finance Course (undergraduate and post-graduate degree) and the Ph.D. in Mathematics for Finance and Economics at Federico II. Her research focuses on quantitative management modelling for financial intermediaries. Her publications have been selected by major editors and publishing companies and her activity is recorded into main citation databases. Author of many articles on risk management process and techniques, she also published two main monographs and an insurance management textbook. In her professional capacity, she is author of expert reports in litigations about financial derivatives and portfolio management.

Antonio De Simone (4) is PhD candidate in Mathematics for Economics and Finance at the University of Napoli Federico II. His main research field focuses on financial markets and derivatives, financial risk management, with particular reference to market and liquidity risk, board structure and corporate governance in financial institutions. He published scholarly articles and proceedings on pricing interest rate derivatives and participating policies.

Marcus R.W. Martin (5) is professor of financial mathematics and stochastics at the University of Applied Sciences in Darmstadt (Germany) since September 2008. Before, he has been with Deutsche Bundesbank since 2002 where he headed the Quantitative Risk Model Examination Group at Hauptverwaltung Frankfurt of Deutsche Bundesbank since November 2004. In this position he was responsible for conducting regulatory audits of IRBA, IMM, IAA, internal market risk and liquidity risk models in German banks. His main research interests currently spin around modeling counterparty risk as well as asset liability, liquidity risk, and commodity risk modeling.

Stefan Reitz (5) holds a PhD degree in mathematics and is professor for financial mathematics at the University of Applied Sciences in Stuttgart, Germany. He also works as a consultant in the financial industry in various projects (risk controlling, risk management, pricing of derivatives). Prior to his current position he was an auditor and audit supervisor within the banking examination department, Deutsche Bundesbank, regional office Frankfurt. He conducted international audits at major and regional banks in the areas portfolio risk models, pricing of derivatives, risk management, minimum requirements for trading activities, Basel implementation.

Birgitta Drwenski (6) is Head of the Pricing & Analysis Team in the FIC CVA Trading & Risk Optimisation group at Commerzbank Corporate & Markets. Working both in London and Frankfurt, she previously headed the Pricing Team in Dresdner Bank's Investment Banking Counterparty Portfolio Management Department. She started her working life as an interest rate option trader at WestLB in Düsseldorf. Birgitta holds a Diplom (equivalent to a Masters) in economics from the University of Heidelberg and is a CFA charterholder.

Jochen Beißer (6) received his PhD in Finance from Johannes Gutenberg-University in Mainz. He also holds an MSc in Mathematics as well as an MSc in Economics. As Head of Dresdner Bank AG's Group Audit Risk&Models team he was responsible for the audits of the bank's various risk models. Currently, he is Professor of Finance at the University of Applied Sciences in Wiesbaden. His research interests focus on financial derivatives and banking regulation.

Lutz Mangels (6) is a Vice President of Commerzbank's Group Treasury and is covering strategic Asset/Liability Management matters of European subsidiaries and branches. He started his career at Dresdner Kleinwort Investment Bank in the Counterparty Risk Management area, later he managed teams of the Global Audit department while focusing on the Front-Office's Risk Management practices. His academic background includes an Executive MBA degree of the Goethe Business School in alliance with Duke University, Durham and a Bachelor degree of the Frankfurt School of Finance and Management. Furthermore he is a Financial Risk Manager charterholder. He also regularly teaches Financial Risk Management courses at the House of Finance.

Matthieu Maurice (7) is Head CVA Management, Commerzbank AG - Mittelstandsbank. He built the CVA Management desk of the Mittelstandsbank at Commerzbank AG in August 2010 with the focus of pricing, monitoring and hedging the counterparty risk inherent to OTC derivatives. A current activity of his team is the development of cutting-edge portfolio solutions to mitigate the counterparty risk of illiquid names, particularly under the coming regulatory framework. From 2002 to 2010, he had various positions at Dresdner Kleinwort within the Loan Asset Management Unit and the CVA Trading Desk. Before 2002, he worked at BNP Paribas. Matthieu Maurice studied Financial Mathematics at the Ecole des Mines.

Sami Attaoui (8) is an Associate Professor at Rouen Business School, France. He holds an MS in financial engineering from Toulouse University, an MA and a PhD in finance from the University of Paris Panthéon-Sorbonne. His research interests include interest rate modeling and credit risk. His research is published in peer-reviewed journals such as Financial Management, Applied Financial Economics and Bankers, Markets and Investors.

Pierre Six (8) is an Assistant Professor in Finance at Rouen Business School, France. He holds an engineering degree from Ecole Centrale de Nantes as well as an MA and a PhD in finance from the University of Paris Panthéon-Sorbonne. His research interests cover asset pricing and asset allocation. His research is published in peer-reviewed journals such as the Financial Review, Revue Finance and Bankers, Markets and Investors.

Fabio Mercurio (9) is head of Quant Business Managers at Bloomberg LP, New York. Previously, he was head of Financial Engineering at Banca IMI, Milan. He is also adjunct professor at NYU. Fabio has jointly authored the book *Interest rate models: theory and practice* and published extensively in books and international journals, including 12 cutting-edge articles in Risk Magazine. Fabio holds a BSc in Applied Mathematics from the University of Padua and a PhD in Mathematical Finance from the Erasmus University of Rotterdam.

Jean-Claude Gabillon (10) is Professor of Finance at Toulouse Business School. His research interests are credit risk modeling and credit derivatives, Corporate risk management, real options, risk premium and monetary macroeconomics. In these fields he has published numerous articles in peer-reviewed journals. He got his PhD from Toulouse School of Economics.

Laurent Germain (10) is Professor of Finance and the Head of the Finance Group at Toulouse Business School. He teaches also at ISAE. His research interests are Market Microstructure, Behavioral Finance and Corporate Finance. He is graduated from Toulouse Business School, Toulouse School of Economics, New York University and University Paris Dauphine. After a Post doctorate at London Business School in 1996 financed by the European Commission he got a position of Assistant Professor of Finance at London Business School. He left LBS in 2000 to join TBS. He was one of the Director of the European Financial Management Association and published articles in leading journals such as Review of Financial Studies, Journal of Financial and Quantitative Analysis, Journal of Financial Intermediation, European Financial Management.

Nicolas Nalpas (10) is Professor of Finance at Toulouse Business School (France). He also teaches Finance at the Universities of Paris Sorbonne and Aix-Marseille as well as at ISAE (Engineering School). He obtained his PhD in financial economics at the University of Paris Sorbonne (France) in 2003. He got scholarships to visit the Economics Department of the Ohio State University (USA) and the Canada Research Chair in Risk Management at HEC Montreal (Canada). Before joining Toulouse Business School, he was an Assistant Professor of Finance at HEC Montreal from 2001 to 2004. His research focuses on decision making under risk, asset pricing, and empirical finance.

Tao Jiao (11) received her PhD in accounting degree from Rotterdam School of Management, Erasmus University. Her research interests include valuation, earnings quality and corporate governance. Her paper has been published in International Review of Financial Analysis and Shanghai Accounting Research. From 2008 to 2009, she worked as a valuation consultant at Duff and Phelps Amsterdam office.

Gerard Mertens (11) is Dean of the School of Management, Open University Netherlands and Professor of Financial Management & Governance. He held previous appointment at the Rotterdam School of Management, Erasmus University, Tilburg University and was visiting professor at the University of Leuven. His research interests include financial accounting and (corporate) governance. His work has been published in ABACUS, the Journal of Corporate Finance, Journal of Accounting and Public Policy, European Accounting Review, International Journal of Accounting and the Journal of Management & Governance among others. He contributed to numerous chapters to various books on financial reporting and corporate governance.

Peter Roosenboom (11) is Endowed Professor in Entrpreneurial Finance and Private Equity at the Rotterdam School of Management, Erasmus University and member of ERIM. He holds a PhD in finance from Tilburg University. His research interests include corporate governance, venture capital, private equity and initial public offerings.

Wolfgang Breuer (12), born in 1966. Since March 2000, he has been a full professor of Finance at the RWTH Aachen University, one of Germany's leading Technical Universities. From October 1995 to February 2000 he was a full professor of Finance at the University of Bonn. He earned his PhD degree in February 1993 and his habilitation degree in July 1995, both at the

University of Cologne. After his diploma in 1989 he worked one year in Frankfurt as a consultant at McKinsey & Co., Inc., before he continued his academic career. His current research interests focus on portfolio management and asset valuation issues as well as behavioral corporate finance and international financial management.

Klaus Mark (12), currently works in the credit analysis of KfW IPEX Bank in Frankfurt, Germany. Before he joined IPEX, he held positions in the international economic policy-division of the Chancellery of the Federal Republic of Germany and the economic research department of KFW Banking Group. After receiving his PhD-degree in Finance from Aachen University of Technology, Mr Mark started his career as a consultant in a leading German auditing company focusing on corporate finance. He earned his master degree in economics at University of Bonn. His research interests comprise valuation-topics, venture capital, credit analysis.

John Simpson (13) is an Associate Professor in the School of Economics and Finance at Curtin University in Western Australia. His PhD in economics and finance was gained from the University of Western Australia in the areas of international banking, finance and country risk. These areas continue to be his focus of research. He has published over 50 book chapters and journal articles with well respected international publishers and journals, as well as a co-edited book and a forthcoming co-authored book, all in the broad area of financial economics.

Goknur Buyukkara (13) is a candidate Professor of the University of Hacettepe in Ankara, Turkey. Her Doctorate in financial economics has been developed with numerous journal articles and book chapters specifically about international finance, risk models and energy economics with particular expertise in applied time series analysis and dynamic approaches.

Roberto Savona (14) is Associate Professor of Financial Markets and Institutions at the University of Brescia (Italy). He received his PhD in Finance from University of Udine (Italy). He is a member of the Board of Directors on the European of Financial Management Association and his works have been published in Applied Financial Economics, Economic Notes, European Journal of Finance and some international books in finance.

Marika Vezzoli (14) is Research Fellow of Statistics at the University of Brescia (Italy). She received her PhD in Methodological and Applied Statistics, University of Milano Bicocca (Italy). Her works have been published in Electronic Journal of Applied Statistical Analysis and some international books in classification and data analysis.

Dean Fantazzini (15) is an Associate Professor in econometrics and risk management at the Moscow School of Economics – Moscow State University. The author has to his credit more than 30 publications, including three monographs. On the 28/04/2009 he was awarded for fruitful scientific research and teaching activities by the former USSR president and Nobel Peace Prize winner Mikhail S. Gorbachev and by the MSU rector prof. Viktor A. Sadovnichy.

Mario Maggi (15) is Assistant Professor of mathematical finance at the University of Pavia. He holds a MS in Economics from the University of Pavia and a PhD in Mathematical Finance from the University of Brescia. He held positions at the Universities of Insubria (Varese), Piemonte Orientale (Alessandria), Bologna (Rimini) and Bocconi (Milano). His research interests are mathematical finance, decision theory and numerical methods. He is author of research chapter published on international reviews, textbooks.

Pu Chen (16), is an economist, has a Bachelor in Science at University of Technology Shandong, China, 1982; Diploma in Business and Management, 1991; PhD in Economics, Bielefeld University, Germany, 1995. Worked as Mining Engineer at Yanzhou Mining Group, China, 1982−86; was lecturer at Department of Economics, Bielefeld University. 1996−2001, senior lecturer, 2002−06; and Theodor-Heuss lecturer at the New School University, New York, 2006. He was Visiting Professor for statistics at Rostock University, Germany, 2007−08; senior research fellow at Melbourne University, Australia, 2008-2010, and since 2011 he is Researcher at Melbourne Institute of Technology.

Willi Semmler (16) is Professor of Economics at New School University, at the Center for Empirical Macroeconomics at Bielefeld University, and Research Fellow at the Bernard Schwartz Center for Economic Policy Analysis. He also evaluates research projects for the European Union, serves as a consultant for the World Bank, and regularly writes columns for the German "Spiegel". He is author or co-author of more than 85 refereed articles in international journals and is author or co-author of 11 books. His recent publications include the third edition of his book "Asset prices, Booms and Recessions" (Springer Publishing House, 2011) and a co-edited book "Foundations of Credit Risk Analysis" (Elgar, 2007). He is a member of the New York Academy of Sciences and has been a visitor of Columbia University, Stanford University and the Cepremap in Paris.

Kasirga Yildirak (17, 18) is an Associate Professor at Trakya University and affiliated with the Institute of Applied Mathematics of Middle East Technical University (METU). He holds a M.A. in Economics from North Carolina State University and a PhD with dissertation in financial mathematics from METU. He is specialized in risk modeling and has been supervising Financial Institutions and United Nations on risk modeling and programming the necessary algorithms.

Cumhur Ekinci (17, 18) is an Assistant Professor of finance at Istanbul Technical University (ITU). He studied economics and finance at Bogazici, Paris I Pantheon-Sorbonne and Aix-Marseille III. Dr. Ekinci established and worked in a trading room at CNAM in Paris. He has been teaching financial markets, investment, corporate finance and accounting at ITU, CNAM, Aix-Marseille II and ENPC. His research interests include market microstructure and behavioral finance.

Ali Sabri Taylan (18) is with the Dept. of Market Oversight at Turkish Derivatives Exchange (TURKDEX). He holds a MSc. from Hacettepe U and pursues a PhD in statistics at Dokuz Eylul U. He is specialized in probability theory, time series, financial risk modelling, multivariate statistics and portfolio optimization. Priorly, Mr. Taylan was a teaching assistant at Anadolu U and conducted research on financial econometrics, risk management and derivatives pricing.

Riadh Aloui (19) is a researcher at the Research Laboratory of Quantitative Economics of Development at Tunis El Manar University where he obtained his PhD in Economics in 2011.

His research areas cover various fields of financial economics and econometrics. He has published several chapters in referred journals such as Journal of Banking and Finance, and Journal of Times Series Econometrics.

Mohamed Safouane Ben Aïssa (19) is a Professor of Macroeconometrics and Head of the Research Laboratory of Quantitative Economics of Development at Tunis El Manar University. He holds an MSc and a PhD in Economics from the University of Aix Marseille II (France) in 2004. His principal research areas concern monetary policy, business cycles, economic integration, trade, volatility modeling and risk management in international capital markets. His most recent articles are forthcoming and published in refereed journals such as Journal of Banking and Finance, Bulletin of Economic Research, Journal of Times Series Econometrics, Journal of Empirical Finance.

Duc Khuong Nguyen (19) is a Professor of Finance and Head of the Department of Finance and Information Systems at ISC Paris School of Management. He holds an MSc and a PhD in Finance from the University of Grenoble II (France). He is also an Associate Researcher at the Department of Finance, Centre d'Economie de la Sorbonne (CES), University Paris 1 Panthéon-Sorbonne. His research articles have appeared in refereed journals such as Energy Economics, Economic Modelling, Energy Policy, Journal of Banking and Finance, Journal of International Money and Finance, and Macroeconomic Dynamics.

Massimo Morini (20) is Head of Fixed Income Models and Coordinator of Model Research at IMI Bank of Intesa San Paolo. He is Professor of Fixed Income at Bocconi University. He regularly delivers advanced training on financial models and model risk management, he leads workshops in the main international conferences, and his papers appeared on Risk Magazine, Mathematical Finance, the Journal of Derivatives. He is the author of "Understanding and Managing Model Risk. A practical guide for Quants, Traders and Validators". He holds a PhD in Mathematics.

Sergei Esipov (21) has been working in reinsurance and financial industry (Centre Solutions, Bear Stearns, Banc of America Securities and major hedge funds). He heads a company, Quant Isle, Ltd, which offers financial services. Mr. Esipov holds a PhD in theoretical physics from the Landau Institute.

Marco Bee (22) is Associate Professor in Economic Statistics at the University of Trento (Italy). After spending one year as a visiting scholar at the Department of Mathematics of the Indiana University and receiving a PhD in Mathematical Statistics from the University of Trento in 1998, from 1999 to 2005 he has held positions at the Risk Management department of Banca Intesa in Milan, where he has been developing quantitative models in the areas of operational and credit risk. His current research interests focus on quantitative risk management and applied statistics, with particular emphasis on the analysis of the computational aspects of the models.

Ralph Karels (24) is a Senior Consultant on Barra portfolio management and risk analytics at MSCI for clients across German speaking Europe and the Scandinavia region. Ralph joined MSCI in 2009. Prior to that, he worked as a Quant Equity Portfolio Manager at Invesco and as a Product Manager for Quant Products at Deka Investment. He holds a diploma in Theoretical Mathematics from the Technical University in Munich and a Master of Arts in Banking and Finance from the Frankfurt School of Finance and Management.

Michael Sun (24) is a consultant on the Barra portfolio management and risk analytics team based for asset management clients across the UK and Benelux region. Michael holds a PhD in Mathematical Science with specialization of copula modeling. He joined MSCI in 2010.

Massimiliano Caporin (25) is Associate Professor of Econometrics at the University of Padova. He received a doctorate in Quantitative Economics from the University of Venice. His research interests include volatility modelling, quantitative asset allocation, portfolio risk management, performance measurement and evaluation, long range dependence in finance, high frequency data modelling, quantitative trading rules development, financial contagion analysis, and model based weather and energy derivative pricing. Some of his works have been published in the Journal of Financial Econometrics, Econometric Reviews, the Journal of Forecasting, Computational Statistics and Data Analysis, the Journal of Economic Surveys, the European Journal of Finance, and the Journal of Risk.

Loriana Pelizzon (25) is Associate Professor of Economics at the University of Venice and Research Affiliate at MIT Sloan. She graduated from the London Business School with a doctorate in Finance. She was Assistant Professor in Economics at the University of Padova from 2000 till 2004 and recently Visiting Associate Professor at MIT Sloan. Her research interests are on risk measurement and management, asset allocation and household portfolios, hedge funds, financial institutions, systemic risk and financial crisis. Her work includes papers published in the Journal of Financial Economics, Journal of Financial and Quantitative Analysis, Journal of Financial Intermediation, and Journal of Banking and Finance. Pelizzon has been awarded the EFA 2005 − Barclays Global Investor Award for the Best Symposium chapter, FMA European Conference for the best conference chapter and the Award for the Most Significant Paper published in the Journal of Financial Intermediation 2008.

Manuel Moreno (26) is PhD in Economics from University Carlos III. He is Associate Professor of Finance at University of Castilla-La Mancha. He has held teaching and research positions at Warwick Business School, Universidad Carlos III, Universidad Pompeu Fabra, IESE Business School, and IE Business School. He has published articles in *European Journal of Operational Research, Review of Derivatives Research*, and *Journal of Futures Markets*, among other academic journals.

Javier F. Navas (26) is PhD in Management from Purdue University. He is Associate Professor of Finance at Pablo de Olavide University. He has held teaching and research positions at Purdue University, RCC at Harvard University, Universidad Carlos III, Universidad Pompeu Fabra, and IE Business School. He has published articles in *The Journal of Fixed Income, The Journal of Derivatives*, and *The Review of Derivatives Research*, among other academic journals.

David E. Allen (27) has a PhD in Finance from the University of Western Australia, plus an M.Phil in Economics from the University of Leicester. In the course of the last 35 years he has been employed by De-Montfort University and the University of Edinburgh in the UK, and the University of Western Australia, Curtin University and Edith Cowan University in Western Australia where he is currently Professor of Finance. He has published 3 books, and over 100 other contributions to books and refereed journal publications.

Abhay Kumar Singh (27) is a Post-Doctoral Research Fellow in the School of Accounting Finance & Economics at Edith Cowan University (ECU) Australia. He holds a PhD in finance from ECU Australia and an Integrated Post Graduate degree with B. Tech in Information Technology and an MBA from ABV-IIITM India. His research interests are focused primarily on Financial Risk modeling including quantification and analysis of various market and credit risk models.

Robert J. Powell (27) has 20 years banking experience in South Africa, New Zealand and Australia. He has been involved in the development and implementation of several credit and financial analysis models in Banks. He has a PhD from Edith Cowan University, where he currently works as a researcher and Associate Professor in banking and finance.

Lerby M. Ergun (28) is a PhD student at Tinbergen Institute in Amsterdam. He holds a Master degree in Economics and a Master degree in Finance, both from VU University Amsterdam. He is member of the Educational Board of Tinbergen Institute and he is affiliated with Duisenberg School of Finance. His research won him the "Grote Financiën Prijs" in 2007 and a Mozaiek PhD scholarship by NWO.

Philip A. Stork (28) is Professor of Financial Markets and Instruments at VU University Amsterdam and Visiting Professor at Duisenberg School of Finance in Amsterdam. He has worked in various roles for banks and market makers in Europe, Australia and the US. Recently, he has been an advisor to the European Parliament and to the Banking Code Monitoring Committee in the Netherlands. His academic work has been published in major international journals.

Pankaj K. Jain (P.K.) (29) is an Associate Professor of Finance at the Fogelman College of Business & Economics at the University of Memphis. He recently served as the President of the CFA society of Memphis and one of the Directors of the Memphis Center of International Business Education and Research. He is an Associate Editor of the Financial Review and has published in Journal of Finance, Journal of Financial and Quantitative Analysis, Financial Management, Journal of Banking and Finance, and Journal of Financial Research.

Ajay K. Mishra (29) is a PhD candidate at IBS, Hyderabad the IFHE University, AP, India. He holds a master's degree in electronics and telecommunication. He joined PhD (Finance) program in year 2009. He has been visiting research scholar during 2011-2012 at Fogelman College of Business and Economics, University of Memphis TN (US). His area of interests are market microstructure, assets pricing and international finance.

Thomas H. McInish (29), CFA, PhD, has published more than 110 articles in leading academic journals. Dr. McInish's path-breaking article published in the Journal of Finance has been recognized as a "critical writing" in market microstructure. Another article dealing with price discovery led to a special issue of the Journal of Financial Markets. Dr. McInish's book, Capital Markets: A Global Perspective published by Blackwell in 2000 has both an international and microstructure perspective. Dr. McInish's book, Corporate Spin-Offs, was cited as an outstanding academic book. He is an Associate Editor of the Financial Review.

Marco Rossi (30) received his PhD in Quantitative Economics jointly from the Catholic University of Louvain and the London School of Economics. He is currently Senior Economist at the International Monetary Fund (IMF). Prior to joining the IMF, he worked at the Bank of England as economist in its Research Department. He has published on a wide range of topics in monetary and financial economics and international finance. He is the author of Payment Systems in the Financial Markets (MacMillan Press and St. Martin's Press).

Gabriele Zinna (30) received his PhD from University of Tor Vergata in Rome, Italy. Gabriele has worked at the Bank of England. He was Visiting Scholar at the Warwick Business School, Marie Curie fellow at the Manchester Business School, and Summer Intern at the International Monetary Fund.

Matthias Muck (31) is the holder of the Chair of Banking and Financial Control at University of Bamberg. His research fields are derivatives pricing, asset management, and term structure models. From 2003-2006 he was Assistant Professor at the WHU — Otto Beisheim School of Management. He graduated in 2000 and earned his PhD degree in 2003 at WHU as well.

Stefan Weisheit (31), MSc. is a PhD student and assistant at the Chair of Banking and Financial Control at University of Bamberg. He focusses on the research fields derivatives pricing and asset allocation. He graduated in 2009 at University of Bamberg as well.

Christopher Kullmann (32) is an Executive Director at Nomura based in Frankfurt, Germany and working in Fixed Income Structuring. Besides his structuring work, he analyses accounting and regulatory developments from a transactions point of view and has published various articles on the impact of regulation changes on institutional investors. Prior to joining Nomura in 2010 he spent nine years at PricewaterhouseCoopers in Frankfurt, Hamburg and Washington, DC. At PwC Christopher's focus was the regulatory and accounting impact of structured capital markets transactions. Christopher holds a degree in business from the Deutsche Bundesbank's University of Applied Sciences.

Abraham Lioui (33) is a Professor of Finance at EDHEC Business School. He teaches courses related to portfolio choice, asset pricing and derivatives; he has also extensively published in academic as well as professional journals on these themes.

Michelle Sisto (33) is a Professor of Statistics and Mathematics at the International University of Monaco. She is also currently a PhD candidate in Finance at EDHEC Business School in France. Her current research interests are asset pricing and statistics education.

Modena Matteo (34) holds a degree in Economics from the University of Milan-Bicocca, a M.Sc. in Economics and Finance from the University of Edinburgh, and a PhD in Economics from the University of Glasgow where his studies have been supervised by Prof. Ronnie MacDonald. Modena worked as risk manager in the hedge funds industry. He is currently Research Fellow at the the Catholic University of Milan. While completing his PhD studies, he attended some editions of the Summer School of Econometrics (CIDE Bertinoro, Italy); his research interests cover the fields of macroeconomics, monetary policy, financial markets, and applied econometrics.

Lossani Marco (34) is a Full Professor of International Economics at the Catholic University of Milan. Visiting professor at Universidad Catolica Argentina de Buenos Aires, Chulalongkorn

University at Bangkok, Vietnamese Science Academy at Hanoi and Saint Joseph University at Beirut where he gave lectures on the process of European monetary unification. He is currently Director of the Monetary Lab (a joint initiative of the Catholic University of Milan and the Association for the Studies on Banking and Finance) and editor of Osservatorio Monetario, a quarterly review on the current economic outlook. His research has been focussed on the process of economic and monetary integration in Europe, the institutional design of Central Banks and the role of emerging market economies in the current process of globalization.

Borello Giuliana (34) is Research Fellow at the Catholic University of Milan. She holds a PhD in Markets and Financial Intermediation from the Catholic University of Milan. Her research interests focus on Asset Allocation Strategies, Portfolio Management, and Financial Economics. She is currently working on a project with the aim of assessing the efficiency of Asset Management Companies.

Rituparna Das (35) is Associate Professor and Executive Director in the Centre of Risk Management and Derivatives at National Law University Jodhpur. He is specialized in Econometrics, Market Risk, Asset Liability Management and Project Finance.

Michael C. S. Wong (35) is an Associate Professor of Finance of City University of Hong Kong, specialized in financial markets, risk management, and bank management. Dr. Wong advised many banks on risk modeling and risk process reengineering, and founded CTRISKS, one of the five licensed credit ratings agencies in Hong Kong. He published more than 60 academic work and was awarded Teaching Excellence Award by the university.

Jonathan Penm (36, 37) is currently a PhD candidate at the Faculty of Pharmacy, the University of Sydney; and a hospital pharmacist at the Sydney & Sydney Eye Hospital. He won the International Pharmacy Federation's 2010 Young Pharmacists Group Grant for Professional Innovation. His main research interests are in sparse patterned neural networks and vector time-series modelling in pharmacy.

Betty Chaar (36, 37) is currently a lecturer at the Faculty of Pharmacy, the University of Sydney. Her main research interests are in promoting moral reasoning in the delivery of healthcare services by pharmacists, in particular developing a psychometric measure of moral reasoning. She is an author/co-author of more than thirty chapters published in various internationally recognised journals.

Rebekah Moles (36, 37) is currently a senior lecturer at the Faculty of Pharmacy, the University of Sydney. Dr. Moles is also Vice President Australasia of the Hospital Pharmacy Section of the International Pharmacy Federation. She is an Applied Pharmacist with international recognition for her involvement in hospital pharmacy. She has published more than thirty research papers in leading journals.

Jack Penm (37) is currently the Managing Director of Evergreen Publishing and Investment Research, Australia. He has an excellent research record in the two disciplines in which he earned his two PhDs, one in electrical engineering from University of Pittsburgh, USA, and the other in finance from ANU. He is an author/co-author of more than eighty chapters published in various internationally respectful journals.

THE EFFECTIVENESS OF OPTION PRICING MODELS DURING FINANCIAL CRISES

Camillo Lento* and Nikola Gradojevic**

*Lakehead University, **Lakehead University and The Rimini Centre for Economic Analysis

CHAPTER OUTLINE

1.1 Introduction

Options can play an important role in an investment strategy. For example, options can be used to limit an investor's downside risk or be employed as part of a hedging strategy. Accordingly, the pricing of options is important for the overall efficiency of capital markets.[1] The purpose of this chapter is to explore the effectiveness of the original Black and Scholes (1973) option pricing model (BS model) against a more complicated non-parametric neural network option pricing model with a hint (NN model). Specifically, this chapter compares the effectiveness of the BS model versus the NN model during periods of stable economic conditions and economic crisis conditions.

Past literature suggests that the standard assumptions of the BS model are rarely satisfied. For instance, the well-documented "volatility smile" and "volatility smirk" (Bakshi *et al.*, 1997) pricing biases violate the BS model assumption of

---

[1] Readers interested in a detailed survey of the literature on option pricing are encouraged to review Garcia *et al.* (2010) and Renault (2010).

constant volatility. Additionally, stock returns have been shown to exhibit non-normality and jumps. Finally, biases also occur across option maturities, as options with less than three months to expiration tend to be overpriced by the Black–Scholes formula (Black, 1975).

In order to address the biases of the BS model, research efforts have focused on developing parametric and non-parametric models. With regard to parametric models, the research has mainly focused on three models: The stochastic volatility (SV), stochastic volatility random jump (SVJ) and stochastic interest rate (SI) parametric models. All three models have been shown to be superior to the BS model in out-of-sample pricing and hedging exercises (Bakshi *et al.*, 1997). Specifically, the SV model has been shown to have first-order importance over the BS model (Gencay and Gibson, 2009). The SVJ model further enhances the SV model for pricing short-term options, while the SI model extends the SVJ model in regards to the pricing of long-term options (Gencay and Gibson, 2009).

Although parametric models appear to be a panacea with regard to relaxing the assumptions that underlie the BS model, while simultaneously improving pricing accuracy, these models exhibit some moneyness-related biases for short-term options. In addition, the pricing improvements produced by these parametric models are generally not robust (Gencay and Gibson, 2009; Gradojevic *et al.*, 2009). Accordingly, research also explores non-parametric models as an alternative, (Wu, 2005). The non-parametric approaches to option pricing have been used by Hutchinson *et al.* (1994), Garcia and Gencay (2000), Gencay and Altay-Salih (2003), Gencay and Gibson (2009), and Gradojevic *et al.* (2009).

Non-parametric models, which lack the theoretical appeal of parametric models, are also known as data-driven approaches because they do not constrain the distribution of the underlying returns (Gradojevic *et al.*, 2011). Non-parametric models are superior to parametric models at dealing with jumps, non-stationarity and negative skewness because they rely upon flexible function forms and adaptive learning capabilities (Agliardi and Agliardi, 2009; Yoshida, 2003). Generally, non-parametric models are based on a difficult tradeoff between rightness of fit and smoothness, which is controlled by the choice of parameters in the estimation procedure. This tradeoff may result in a lack of stability, impeding the out-of-sample performance of the model. Regardless, non-parametric models have been shown to be more effective than parametric models at relaxing BS model assumptions (Gencay and Gibson,

2009; Gradojevic and Kukolj, 2011; Gradojevic *et al.*, 2009). Accordingly, the BS model is compared against a non-parametric option pricing model in this chapter.

Given its currency, little research has been conducted on the effectiveness of option pricing during the 2008 financial crisis. However, the 1987 stock market crash has proved to be fertile grounds for research with regard to option pricing during periods of financial distress. For example, Bates (1991, 2000) identified an option pricing anomaly just prior to the October 1987 crash. Specifically, out-of-the-money American put options on S&P 500 Index futures were unusually expensive relative to out-of-the-money calls. In a similar line of research, Gencay and Gradojevic (2010) used the skewness premium of European options to develop a framework to identify aggregate market fears to predict the 1987 market crash.

This chapter expands the option pricing literature by comparing the accuracy of the BS model against NN models during the normal, pre-crisis economic conditions of 1987 and 2008 (the first quarter of each respective year) against the crisis conditions of 1987 and 2008 (the fourth quarter of each respective year). Therefore, this work also provides new and novel insights into the accuracy of option pricing models during the recent 2008 credit crisis.

The results suggest that the more complicated NN models are more accurate during stable markets than the BS model. This result is consistent with the past literature that suggest non-parametric models are superior to the BS model (e.g. Gencay and Gibson, 2009; Gradojevic *et al.*, 2009). However, the results during the periods of high volatility are counterintuitive as they suggest that the simpler BS model is superior to the NN model. These results suggest that a regime switch from stable economic conditions to periods of excessively volatile conditions impedes the estimation and the pricing ability of non-parametric models. In addition to the regime shift explanation, considerations should be given to the fact that the BS model is a pre-specified non-linearity and its structure (shape) does not depend on the estimation dataset. This lack of flexibility and adaptability appears to be beneficial when pricing options in crisis periods. It conclusion, it appears as if the learning ability and flexibility of non-parametric models largely contributes to their poor performance relative to parametric models when markets are highly volatile and experience a regime shift.

The results make a contribution that is relevant to academic and practitioners alike. With the recent financial crisis of 2007−2009 creating pitfalls for various asset valuation models, this chapter provides practical advice to investors and traders with regard to the most effective model for option pricing during times of economic turbulence. In addition, the results make a contribution to the theoretical literature that investigates the BS model versus its parametric and non-parametric counterparts by suggesting that the efficacy of the option pricing model depends on the economic conditions.

The remainder of this chapter is organized as follows: Section 1.2 outlines the methodology, Section 1.3 discusses the data, Section 1.4 presents the results and Section 1.5 provides concluding remarks.

1.2 Methodology

The option pricing formula is defined as in Hutchinson *et al.* (1994) and Garcia and Gençay (2000):

$$C_t = \phi(S_t, K, \tau), \tag{1.1}$$

where C_t is the call option price, S_t is the price of the underlying asset, K is the strike price and τ is the time to maturity (number of days). Assuming the homogeneity of degree one of the pricing function ϕ with respect to S_t and K, one can write the option pricing function as follows:

$$\underbrace{\frac{C_t}{K}}_{C_t} = f\left(\underbrace{\frac{S_t}{K}}_{x_1}, 1, \underbrace{\tau}_{x_2}\right) = f(x_1, x_2). \tag{1.2}$$

We extend the model in Equation (1.2) with two additional inputs—the implied volatility and the risk-free interest rate:

$$c_t = f\left(\frac{S_t}{K}, \tau, \sigma_1, r\right) = f(x_1, x_2, x_3, x_4) \tag{1.3}$$

We estimate Equation (1.3) non-parametrically using a feedforward NN model with the "hint" from Garcia and Gençay (2000). This model is an improvement on the standard feedforward NN methodology that provides superior pricing accuracy. Moreover, when Gençay and Gibson (2009) compared the out-of-sample performance of the NN model to standard parametric approaches (SV, SVJ and SI models) for the S&P 500 Index, they found that the NN model with the generalized autoregressive conditional heteroskedasticity GARCH(1,1) volatility dominates the parametric models over various moneyness and maturity ranges. The superiority of the NN model can be explained by its adaptive learning and the fact that it does not constrain the distribution of the underlying returns.

The "hint" involves utilizing additional prior information about the properties of an unknown (pricing) function that is used to guide the learning process. This means breaking up the pricing function into four parts, controlled by x_1, x_2, x_3 and x_4. Each part contains a cumulative distribution function which is estimated non-parametrically through NN models:

$$f(x_1, x_2, x_3, x_4; \theta) = \beta_0 + x_1 \left(\sum_{j=1}^{d} \beta_j^1 \frac{1}{1 + \exp(-\gamma_{j0}^1 - \gamma_{j1}^1 x_1 - \gamma_{j2}^1 x_2 - \gamma_{j3}^1 x_3 - \gamma_{j4}^1 x_4)} \right)$$

$$+ x_2 \left(\sum_{j=1}^{d} \beta_j^2 \frac{1}{1 + \exp(-\gamma_{j0}^2 - \gamma_{j1}^2 x_1 - \gamma_{j2}^2 x_2 - \gamma_{j3}^2 x_3 - \gamma_{j4}^2 x_4)} \right)$$

$$+ x_3 \left(\sum_{j=1}^{d} \beta_j^3 \frac{1}{1 + \exp(-\gamma_{j0}^3 - \gamma_{j1}^3 x_1 - \gamma_{j2}^3 x_2 - \gamma_{j3}^3 x_3 - \gamma_{j4}^3 x_4)} \right)$$

$$+ x_4 \left(\sum_{j=1}^{d} \beta_j^4 \frac{1}{1 + \exp(-\gamma_{j0}^4 - \gamma_{j1}^4 x_1 - \gamma_{j2}^4 x_2 - \gamma_{j3}^4 x_3 - \gamma_{j4}^4 x_4)} \right),$$

$$(1.4)$$

where θ denotes the parameters of the NN model that are to be estimated (β and γ) and d is the number of hidden units in the NN model, which is set according to the best performing NN model in terms of the magnitude of the mean-squared prediction error (MSPE) on the validation data. To control for possible sensitivity of the NNs to the initial parameter values, the estimation is performed from ten different random seeds and the average MSPE values are reported.

The out-of-sample pricing performance of the NN model is first compared to the well-known benchmark—the BS model. The Black–Scholes call prices (C_t) are computed using the standard formula:

$$C_t = S_t \mathcal{N}(d) - K e^{-r\tau} \mathcal{N}(d - \sigma\sqrt{\tau}),$$

where :

$$d = \frac{\ln(S_t/K) + (r + 0.5\sigma^2)\tau}{\sigma\sqrt{\tau}}$$

$$(1.5)$$

where $\mathcal{N}$ is the cumulative normal distribution, S_t is the price of the underlying asset, K is the strike price, τ is the time to maturity, r is the risk-free interest rate and σ is the volatility of the underlying asset's continuously compounded returns.[2] The risk-free rate is approximated using the monthly yield of US Treasury bills.

The statistical significance of the difference in the out-of-sample (testing set) performance of alternative models is tested using the Diebold–Mariano test (Diebold and Mariano, 1995). We test the null hypothesis that there is no difference in the MSPE of the two alternative models. The Diebold–Mariano test statistic for the equivalence of forecast errors is given by:

$$DM = \frac{\frac{1}{M} \sum_{t=1}^{M} d_t}{\sqrt{\frac{2\pi f(0)}{M}}} \qquad (1.6)$$

where M is the testing set size and $f(0)$ is the spectral density of d_t (the forecast error is defined as the difference between the actual and the forecasted output value) at frequency zero. Diebold and Mariano (1995) show that DM is asymptotically distributed in a $N(0,1)$ distribution.

1.3 Data

The data options data for 1987 and 2008 were provided by DeltaNeutral and represent the daily S&P 500 Index European call option prices, taken from the Chicago Board Options Exchange. Call options across different strike prices and maturities are considered. Being one of the deepest and the most liquid option markets in the United States, the S&P 500 Index option market is sufficiently close to the theoretical setting of the BS model. Options with zero volume are not used in the estimation. The risk-free interest rate (r) is approximated by the monthly yield of the US Treasury bills. The implied volatility (σ_I) is a proprietary mean estimate provided by DeltaNeutral.

The data for each year are divided into three parts: First (last) two quarters (estimation data), third (second) quarter (validation data) and fourth (first) quarter (testing data). Our first exercise prices options on the fourth quarter of the year that includes the market crisis periods. The second pricing exercise focuses on the performance of the models on the first quarter of each year that represents the out-of-sample data. In 1987, there are 1710

---

[2] In order to be consistent and not provide an informational advantage to any model, we also use the implied volatility in the BS model.

observations in the first quarter, 1900 observations in the second quarter, 2010 observations in the third quarter and 2239 observations in the fourth quarter. To reduce the size of the dataset for 2008, we also eliminated options with low volume (that traded below 100 contracts on a given day) and, due to theoretical considerations, focused only on the close to at-the-money options (with strike prices between 95% and 105% of the underlying S&P 500 Index). This resulted in 14,838 observations of which 3904 were in the first quarter, 4572 were in the second quarter, 4088 were in the third quarter and 2274 were in the fourth quarter of 2008.

1.4 Results

Table 1.1 displays the out-of-sample pricing performance of the NN model with the hint (Garcia and Gençay, 2000) relative to the BS model. The NN model is estimated using the early stopping technique. As mentioned before, the optimal NN architecture was determined from the out-of-sample performance on the validation set with respect to the MSPE. To control for potential data snooping biases, as in Garcia and Gençay (2000), the estimation is repeated 10 times from 10 different sets of starting values and the average MSPEs are reported.

First, it can be observed that the BS model performs similarly for each out-of-sample dataset. As expected, the pricing performance is worse for the crisis periods (the fourth quarter), but the forecast improvements in the first quarter are roughly 50%. In

Table 1.1. Prediction performance of the option pricing models for 1987 and 2008

	NN with hint	BS model	MSPE ratio	DM
2008				
MSPE-Q4	17.34×10^{-4}	3.05×10^{-4}	5.68	4.54
MSPE-Q1	4.17×10^{-5}	1.50×10^{-4}	0.27	−6.68
1987				
MSPE-Q4	6.67×10^{-4}	4.87×10^{-4}	1.37	2.39
MSPE-Q1	8.68×10^{-6}	2.16×10^{-4}	0.04	−27.52

The out-of-sample average mean MSPE of the Garcia and Gençay's (2000) feedforward NN model with the hint and the BS model. The pricing error for a non-parametric model with four inputs (S_t/K, τ, r, σ_l) was calculated. Suffix "Q1" ("Q4") denotes that the S&P 500 Index call options were priced in the first (fourth) quarter that was kept as out-of-sample observations. MSPE ratio is the ratio between the corresponding statistics between the NN with hint model and the BS model. DM denotes the Diebold and Mariano (1995) test statistic. This test is used to assess the statistical significance of the MSPE forecast gains of the NN with the hint model relative to the BS model.

contrast, non-parametric models exhibit more substantial differences in their pricing accuracy. In 1987, the average MSPE for the NN with the hint model is about 77 times smaller for the first quarter than for the fourth quarter. The average MSPE improvement in the first quarter of 2008 is about 42-fold. This results in the average MSPE ratios of 4 and 27% in 1987 and 2008, respectively. In other words, in terms of their pricing accuracy, non-parametric models are dominant in stable markets. The pricing improvements offered by such models are statistically significant at the 1% significance according to the Diebold and Mariano (1995) test statistic, which is illustrated by large negative values in the last column of Table 1.1.

A striking result is the inaccuracy of the NN with the hint model in the crash periods. Specifically, the BS model significantly improves upon the NN model in both years. This is more apparent in the fourth quarter of 2008, whereas the MSPE difference in the pricing performance in 1987 is statistically significant at the 5% significance level. The values for the *DM* statistic are positive for the fourth quarters of both years, which is interpreted as the rejection of the null hypothesis that the forecast errors are equal in favor of the BS model. To investigate the puzzling pricing performance of the NN with the hint model further, we plot the squared difference between the actual option price (c_t) and the price estimated by the NN with the hint model $(\hat{c}_t)$: $MSPE_t = (\hat{c}_t - c_t)^2$, where $t = 1, ..., M$ (size of the testing set). The top panel of Figure 1.1 displays data along with option prices estimated by the NN with the hint model over the first quarter of 2008. Clearly, the estimates follow the actual prices very closely and there are no major outbursts in the prices as well as in the $MSPE_t$, except for the two outliers between the 500th and the 1000th observation.

Figure 1.2 is similar to Figure 1.1 and it concerns the fourth quarter of 2008, which includes the climax of the subprime mortgage crisis. When compared to the options in the first quarter, Figure 1.2 indicates excessive movements in the option prices traded over the last quarter. This regime switch limits learning and generalization abilities of non-parametric models and results in pricing inaccuracy. Essentially, the NN with the hint model is estimated (trained) based on a different market regime from the one that it is expected to forecast. As can be seen in the top panel of Figure 1.2, the model frequently misprices options that fluctuate in a much wider range than observed in the first quarter. Consequently, pricing errors $MSPE_t$ are much larger with numerous outliers, especially in the second part of the testing data (Figure 1.2, bottom panel).

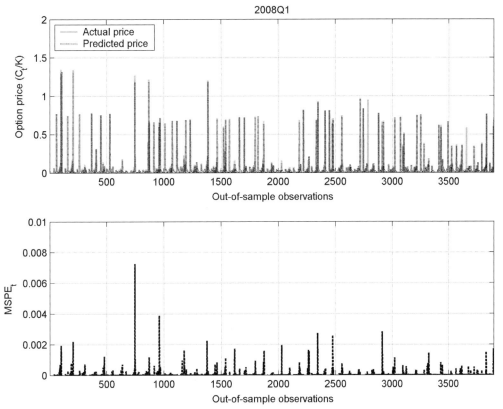

Figure 1.1 Pricing performance of the NN with the hint model in the first quarter of 2008. (Top) Out-of-sample predictions of c_t (black, dotted line) and the actual data (gray, solid line) are plotted for 2008. First, the NN model with the hint is estimated using the data from the last three quarters of the year and, then, 3904 out-of-sample estimates of c_t are generated for the first quarter. (Bottom) The pricing error $MSPE_t = (\hat{c}_t - c_t)^2$ across the testing data is shown on the vertical axis (dashed line).

In addition to the regime shift explanation for the poor performance of the non-parametric model, one should also consider the fact that the BS model incorporates information from the third quarter (and the second quarter) that is used for validation and not for the estimation of the NN with the hint model. Also, the BS model is a pre-specified non-linearity and its structure (shape) does not depend on the estimation dataset. This lack of flexibility and adaptability appears to be beneficial when pricing options in crisis periods. To conclude, the very advantages of non-parametric models over their parametric counterparts such as the learning ability and the flexibility of functional forms largely contribute to the poor performance of non-parametric models when markets are highly volatile and experience a regime shift.

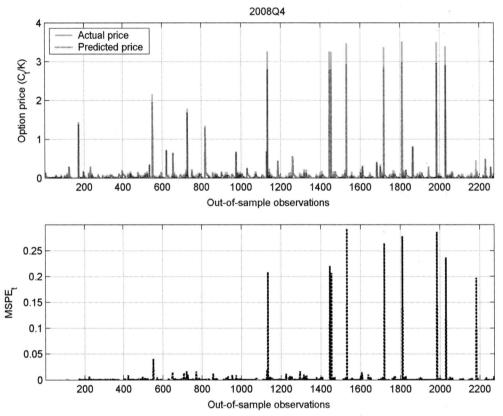

Figure 1.2 Pricing performance of the NN with the hint model in the last quarter of 2008. (Top) Out-of-sample predictions of c_t (black, dotted line) and the actual data (gray, solid line) are plotted for 2008. First, the NN model with the hint is estimated using the data from the first three quarters of the year and, then, 2274 out-of-sample estimates of c_t are generated for the fourth quarter. (Bottom) The pricing error $MSPE_t = (\hat{c}_t - c_t)^2$ across the testing data is shown on the vertical axis (dashed line).

1.5 Concluding Remarks

In summary, this chapter provides new and novel insights into the accuracy of option pricing models during periods of financial crisis relative to stable economic conditions. Specifically, this paper suggests that NN models are more accurate than the BS model during stable markets, while the BS model is shown to be superior to the NN model during periods of excess volatility (i.e. the stock market crash of 1987 and the credit crisis of 2008). This conclusion may result from the estimation and the pricing ability of non-parametric models being impeded by a regime switch from stable economic conditions to periods of excessive volatility. The BS model features, such as being pre-specified, non-linear and non-dependent on the estimation dataset, appear to be optimal during crisis periods. Conversely, the main advantages of the NN model (e.g. learning abilities) largely contribute to their poor performance relative to parametric models when markets experience a regime shift from stable to crisis conditions.

References

Agliardi, E., Agliardi, R., 2009. Fuzzy defaultable bonds. Fuzzy Sets and Systems 160, 2597–2607.

Bakshi, G., Cao, C., Chen, Z., 1997. Empirical performance of alternative option pricing models. Journal of Finance 52, 2003–2049.

Bates, D.S., 1991. The crash of '87 – was it expected? The evidence from options markets. Journal of Finance 46, 1009–1044.

Bates, D.S., 2000. Post-'87 crash fears in the S&P 500 futures option market. Journal of Econometrics 94, 181–238.

Black, F., Scholes, M., 1973. The pricing of options and corporate liabilities. Journal of Political Economy 81, 637–659.

Black, F., 1975. Fact and fantasy in the use of options. Financial Analysts Journal 31 (36–41), 61–72.

Diebold, F.X., Mariano, R.S., 1995. Comparing predictive accuracy. Journal of Business and Economic Statistics 13, 253–263.

Garcia, R., Gencay, R., 2000. Pricing and hedging derivative securities with neural networks and a homogeneity hint. Journal of Econometrics 94, 93–115.

Garcia, R., Ghysels, E., Renault, E., 2010. The econometrics of option pricing. In: Ait-Sahalia, Y., Hansen, L.P. (Eds), Handbook of Financial Econometrics. volume 1. Amsterdam, North-Holland, pp. 479–552.

Gencay, R., Altay-Salih, A., 2003. Degree of mispricing with the Black–Scholes model and nonparametric cures. Annals of Economics and Finance 4, 73–101.

Gencay, R., Gibson, R., 2009. Model risk for European-style stock index options. IEEE Transactions on Neural Networks 18, 193–202.

Gencay, R., Gradojevic, N., 2010. Crash of '87-was it expected? Aggregate market fears and long-range dependence. Journal of Empirical Finance 17, 270–282.

Gradojevic, N., Gencay, R., Kukolj, D., 2009. Option pricing with modular neural networks. IEEE Transactions on Neural Networks 20, 626–637.

Gradojevic, N., Kukolj, D., 2011. Parametric option pricing: a divide-and-conquer approach. Physica D: Nonlinear Phenomena 240, 1528–1535.

Gradojevic, N., Kukolj, D., Gencay, R., 2011. Clustering and classification in option pricing. Review of Economic Analysis 3, 1–20.

Hutchinson, J.M., Lo, A.W., Poggio, T., 1994. A nonparametric approach to pricing and hedging derivative securities via learning networks. Journal of Finance 49, 851–889.

Renault, E., 2010. Econometrics of option pricing. In: Cont, R. (Ed), Encyclopedia of Quantitative Finance, volume 2. Wiley, New York, pp. 518–528.

Yoshida, Y., 2003. The valuation of European options in uncertain environment. European Journal of Operational Research 145, 221–229.

2

TAKING COLLATERAL INTO ACCOUNT

Messaoud Chibane, Yi-Chen Huang and Jayaprakash Selvaraj
Shinsei Bank

CHAPTER OUTLINE

2.1 Introduction

With the start of the credit crunch in summer 2007 and the subsequent upheavals in market conditions, all the basic assumptions used in derivatives pricing, such as infinite liquidity and no counterparty default risk, have been called into question. Practitioners first started to regard the basis spread effect on discount curve construction as a substantial parameter, as stressed in Chibane (2009) or Mercurio (2009). Since then, a number of derivative pricing frameworks have moved from a naïve single-curve system to a dual-curve one, clearly separating the discounting curve and the Libor forecasting curve. Following this change, practitioners started wondering what should be the ideal discount curve when transactions were collateralized, as is customary between dealers in order to mitigate counterparty credit risk.

Groundbreaking work in investigating the effect of collateral on derivatives pricing was done by Piterbarg (2010). In the current

Rethinking Valuation and Pricing Models. http://dx.doi.org/10.1016/B978-0-12-415875-7.00002-6

13

chapter, we pursue the same kind of approach, but we investigate its applicability to fixed-income markets and focus our analysis on swap derivatives and swaptions, and show how a classic dual-curve framework can be adapted to the presence of collateral. This chapter is organized as follows. In Section 2.2 we introduce the problem setting and notations. We then build a pricing framework that incorporates the posting of collateral in Section 2.3. In Section 2.4, under these assumptions, we use the overnight index swap (OIS) market to produce an adequate collateral discount curve. In Section 2.5, we show how to keep the entire framework consistent with the market of interest rate (IR) vanilla swaps. We then investigate the impact of collateral on market European swaptions in Section 2.6. Finally, in Section 2.7, we show a possible way of extending the framework to term structure models. We conclude in Section 2.8 by stating a few extensions to this approach.

2.2 Notations and Problem

We assume the existence of a risk-neutral measure and set ourselves in the usual setting with a probability space $(\Omega, \mathscr{F}, Q)$ equipped with the standard filtration $(\mathscr{F}_t)_{t \geq 0}$ generated by a standard Brownian motion W. We will refer to calendar time as t where $t = 0$ will coincide with the current trading date. The expectation operator conditional on time t under the risk-neutral measure will be denoted by $E_t[\ ]$. The expectation conditional on time 0 will simply be denoted as $E[\ ]$.

We consider a transaction between two counterparties A and B. We assume that the net present value of the transaction is positive to counterparty A and that to mitigate B's default risk, the transaction imposes on B to post collateral. We will restrict ourselves to the case where the transaction involves only one currency and where collateral is posted in cash of the same currency. Furthermore, A has a duty to remunerate the posted collateral at an overnight rate that we call r_C. Let us assume that counterparty A funds itself at a rate r_F. We will denote the associated discount bond price at time t for delivery at time T by $P_F(t, T)$ defined by:

$$P_F(t, T) = E_t\left[\exp\left(-\int_t^T r_F(s)\mathrm{d}s\right)\right].$$

Now let us consider an asset price which dynamics under the real measure can be written as:

$$\frac{\mathrm{d}S(t)}{S(t)} = \mu(t)\mathrm{d}t + \sigma(t)\mathrm{d}W(t), \tag{2.1}$$

where we make no assumptions on μ and σ other than they be adapted processes.

We assume for the time being that collateral funding rates are deterministic. From here on, we investigate the construction of a pricing framework for collateralized transactions whose price is contingent on the underlying price process S.

2.3 Black—Scholes Partial Differential Equation in the Presence of Collateral

First, we would like to build a risk-free portfolio made of the derivative transaction and the underlying asset. At any time t we hold a notional $-\Delta(t)$ of this asset. We denote the value of this portfolio at time t by $\pi(t)$, which can be written as:

$$\pi(t) = V(t) - \Delta(t)S(t).$$

Between time t and $t + \mathrm{d}t$, the portfolio is risk free so its value changes by a quantity:

$$\mathrm{d}\pi(t) = r_\mathrm{F}(t)\pi(t)\mathrm{d}t. \tag{2.2}$$

If the transaction were not collateralized, using Itô's lemma the instantaneous variation of the portfolio would be:

$$\mathrm{d}\pi(t) = \left(\frac{\partial V}{\partial t} + \frac{1}{2}\frac{\partial^2 V}{\partial S^2}\sigma_\mathrm{S}^2(t)S^2(t)\right)\mathrm{d}t + \frac{\partial V}{\partial S}\mathrm{d}S(t) - \Delta(t)\frac{\partial V}{\partial S}\mathrm{d}S(t).$$
$$\tag{2.3}$$

However, under collateralization agreement, counterparty A gets funding on the collateral at funding rate $r_\mathrm{F}(t)$ and must pay collateral rate to counterparty B at rate $r_\mathrm{C}(t)$ on cash amount. Therefore, variation (3) must add the cash flow $(r_\mathrm{F}(t) - r_\mathrm{C}(t))C(t)$ to the right-hand side.

First, for this portfolio to be riskless we need to impose $\Delta(t) = \partial V/\partial S$ in order to eliminate risky components. Furthermore, equating drifts imposes:

$$\frac{\partial V}{\partial t} + \frac{1}{2}\frac{\partial^2 V}{\partial S^2}\sigma_\mathrm{S}^2(t)S^2 + r_\mathrm{F}(t)S\frac{\partial V}{\partial S} = r_\mathrm{F}(t)V(t) + (r_\mathrm{C}(t) - r_\mathrm{F}(t))C(t).$$
$$\tag{2.4}$$

In the case of full collateralization then $C(t) = V(t)$, the Black—Scholes partial differential equation becomes:

$$\frac{\partial V}{\partial t} + \frac{1}{2}\frac{\partial^2 V}{\partial S^2}\sigma_\mathrm{S}^2(t) + r_\mathrm{F}(t)S(t)\frac{\partial V}{\partial S} = r_\mathrm{C}(t)V(t). \tag{2.5}$$

Using the Feynman–Kac theorem we know that the solution to this problem is:

$$V(t) = E_t\left[\exp\left(-\int_t^T r_C(s)ds\right)V(T)\right].$$

Thus, in the presence of full collateralization, which is our assumption from now on, the discounting formalism is the same as in the Black–Scholes case, but discounting should be performed using the collateral rate rather than the short rate. It is also worth noting that, as in Karatzas and Shreve (1991), even if short rate and collateral rate are both stochastic, the result still holds. We now introduce the collateral discount factor denoted by $P_C(t, T)$ and defined by:

$$P_C(t, T) = E_t\left[\exp\left(-\int_t^T r(s)ds\right)\right].$$

Then by using the classic change of numéraire technique, we can rewrite the present value as:

$$V(t) = P_C(t, T)E_t^{C,T}[V(T)], \tag{2.6}$$

where $E_t^{C,T}[\ ]$ refers to the expectation operator under the T forward collateral measure. This is the measure where the collateral bond price associated with expiry T, i.e. $P_C(\cdot, T)$, is the numéraire. The first step to using this discounting framework is to obtain the value of the initial discount curve $(P_C(0,T))$. That is what we set to do in Section 2.4.

2.4 Collateral Discount Curve Bootstrapping

In practice, the collateral rate boils down to the overnight rate plus a fixed spread. For simplicity and without loss of generality we will assume that this spread is set to zero. Now let us consider the market of OIS swaps, which are transactions where counterparties exchange a fixed coupon payment against the compounded overnight rate over the same period. The market quotes par swaps through the fixed coupon rate called the OIS rate. We denote the OIS rate for the tenor τ by $S(\tau)$. We assume the payment schedule is given by the dates $(T_i)_{1 \le i \le N}$ and that the first fixing date is denoted by T_0 while the last payment date relates to the tenor of the swap so that $T_N - T_0 = \tau$. Also we will denote the accrual periods for the fixed leg and for the floating leg, respectively, by Δ_i^{Fx} and Δ_i^{Fl}.

Using the arbitrage arguments developed in the previous section, it is easy to prove that the value of the par payer OIS swap at initial time is:

$$V(0) = P_C(0, T_0) - P_C(0, T_N) - S(\tau) \sum_{i=1}^{N} P_C(0, T_i)\Delta_i^{\text{Fx}}.$$

Remembering that its initial value must be zero, we get the following bootstrapping formula:

$$P_C(0, T_N) = \frac{P_C(0, T_0) - S(\tau) \sum_{i=1}^{N-1} P_C(0, T_i)\Delta_i^{\text{Fx}}}{1 + S(\tau)\Delta_N^{\text{Fx}}}. \qquad (2.7)$$

Assuming that the market gives us a set of OIS rates $(S(\tau_i))_{i \in I}$ for respective tenors $(\tau_i)_{i \in I}$, then bootstrapping the OIS swap market boils down to finding a set of discount factors $(P_C(0, T_0 + \tau_i))_{i \in I}$, so that:

$$\forall i \in I : P_C(0, T_0 + \tau_i) = \frac{P_C(0, T_0) - S(\tau_i) \sum_{j=1}^{N-1} P_C(0, T_j)\Delta_j^{\text{Fx}}}{1 + S(\tau_i)\Delta_N^{\text{Fx}}},$$

$$(2.8)$$

where $P_C(0, T_j)$ are discount factors that coincide with a regular schedule, but values might have to be interpolated from the sparse discount factor $(P_C(0, T_0 + \tau_i))_{i \in I}$.

Once the discount curve has been constructed, we can use it to price off market OIS swaps by simple interpolation of the discount factors. Figure 2.1 illustrates the numerical impact on discount factors of using the JPY OIS market as opposed to the standard bootstrapping method based on IR vanilla swaps as

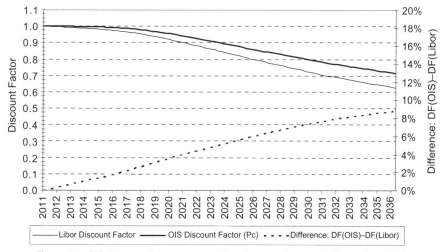

Figure 2.1 OIS discount factor versus Libor discount factor (25 November 2011).

described in Chibane and Sheldon (2009). The discount factors bootstrapped from OIS swaps are substantially higher than in the Libor framework. It means that under this new discounting framework, single positive cash flows will have a higher net present value. This is intuitively satisfactory since using OIS discounting reflects the fact that we have mitigated counterparty default risk which a Libor-based curve does not account for.

So far the OIS market gives information about how to discount future cash flows. What it does not tell us about is how we should estimate forward Libor rates. It seems natural to use the market of IR vanilla swaps to achieve this goal. We describe how to do this in practice in Section 2.5.

2.5 Pricing and Bootstrapping of the IR Vanilla Swap Term Structure

Here, we adopt the terminology and notation presented in Chibane and Sheldon (2009) where we denote the Libor rate fixing at time T_{i-1} and spanning the period $[T_{i-1}, T_i]$ as $L(T_{i-1}, T_i)$ and the associated forward rate agreement (FRA) rate as $F^*(t, T_{i-1}, T_i)$. By definition, we have:

$$F^*(t, T_{i-1}, T_i) = E_t^{C,T_i}[L(T_i, T_{i+1})].$$

FRA rates relate to the forecast curve $(P^*(t,.))$ through the identity:

$$F^*(t, T_i, T_{i+1}) = \frac{1}{\delta_i}\left(\frac{P^*(t, T_{i-1})}{P^*(t, T_i)} - 1\right)$$

$$\delta_i = T_i - T_{i-1}.$$

The initial value of a payer vanilla swap fixing at time T_0, with maturity T_N and strike K, is:

$$V(0) = \sum_{k=1}^{N} P_C(0, T_k)(F^*(0, T_{k-1}, T_k) - K)\delta_k. \qquad (2.9)$$

Let us assume that the market provides us with a term structure of vanilla par swap rates $(S_i)_{1 \le i \le N}$ for maturities $(T_i)_{1 \le i \le N}$. Then bootstrapping the vanilla swap rate term structure boils down to solving the following program:

$$\forall i \in \{1, ..., N\}$$

$$F^*(0, T_{i-1}, T_i) = \frac{S_i \sum_{j=1}^{i} P_C(0, T_j)\delta_j - \sum_{j=1}^{i-1} P_C(0, T_j)F^*(0, T_{j-1}, T_j)\delta_j}{P_C(0, T_i)\delta_i}$$

$$P^*(0, T_i) = \frac{P^*(0, T_{i-1})}{1 + F^*(0, T_{i-1}, T_i)\delta_i}.$$

$$(2.10)$$

This bootstrapping can be done quasi-instantaneously. However.
a few remarks need to be added on to the assumptions. (i) The
first swap being a single-period swap, it should really be understood as a FRA, although the latter differs from a theoretical
single-period swap by some technicalities. (ii) Par swap rates
might not be available for all maturities so the bootstrapping
algorithm should be changed in the spirit of (2.8) to cope with
sparse maturities. A numerical example of the impact of different
curve methodologies on JPY forward swap rates is given in
Figure 2.2, where we display the changes in forward swap rates
obtained in an OIS discounting framework compared to a Libor
discounting framework. We find that forward rates obtained in
the OIS discounting framework are consistently lower than in the
Libor framework. This arises from the fact that in the OIS
framework the swap annuity increases, causing an increase in the
IR vanilla swap fixed leg net present value. For par swaps, the
floating leg net present value must increase equally, therefore
pushing forward swap rates down.

After examining the impact of curve methodology on forward
swap rates, this begs the next question: How should we price
European swaptions. We investigate this in Section 2.6.

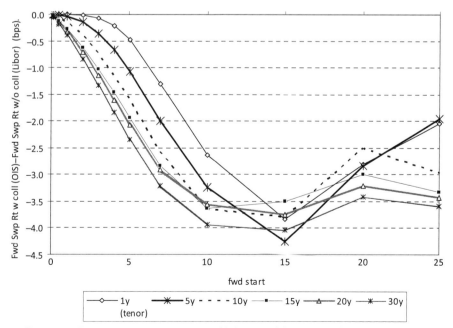

Figure 2.2 Forward swap rate difference (OIS − Libor) (basis points) (21 October 2011).

2.6 European Swaption Pricing Framework

Our favored solution for pricing European swaption is the SABR expansion based on the model specified in Hagan and Al (2002), and recalled below:

$$dS(t) = \sigma(t)S(t)^\beta dW^1(t)$$
$$d\sigma(t) = v\sigma(t)dW^2(t)$$
$$S(0) = F$$
$$\sigma_0 = \alpha$$
$$\langle dW^1(t), dW^2(t) \rangle = \rho dt$$
$$\beta \in [0, 1],$$

where $S(t)$ denotes the forward swap rate associated with fixing date T_i and strike K, paying on the schedule T_{i+1}, ..., T_N, and W^1, W^2 are correlated Brownian motions under the collateral annuity measure. The collateral annuity measure is associated with the collateral annuity numéraire defined by:

$$A_C(t) = \sum_{j=i+1}^{N} P_C(t, T_j)\delta_j.$$

Indeed the value of a forward starting swap with strike K at time $t \le T_i$ as induced by (2.6) is given by:

$$V(t) = A_C(t)(S(t) - K).$$

Now let us consider the deflated value of this swap:

$$\frac{V(t)}{A_C(t)} = S(t) - K.$$

The deflated value process, as a tradable price over the numéraire value must be a martingale. Therefore, so is the forward swap rate. Under this framework we can apply the entire improved SABR arsenal as described in Obloj (2008). This boils down to computing the SABR implied volatility $I^{BS}(K, T_i)$ for expiry T_i and strike according to the following expansion:

$$I^{BS}(K, \tau) = I^0(K, \tau)(1 + I^1(K, \tau)\tau) + O(\tau^2)$$

$$I^0(K, \tau) = \frac{v\ln\left(\frac{F}{K}\right)}{\ln\left(\frac{\sqrt{1 - 2\rho z + z^2} + z - \rho}{1 - \rho}\right)}$$

$$z = \frac{v \ln\left(\frac{F}{K}\right)}{\alpha} \quad \text{if } \beta = 1$$

$$z = \frac{v}{\alpha} \frac{F^{1-\beta} - K^{1-\beta}}{1 - \beta} \quad \text{if } \beta \in [0, 1[$$

$$I^1(K, \tau) = \frac{(1-\beta)^2}{24} \frac{\alpha^2}{(FK)^{1-\beta}} + \frac{1}{4} \frac{\rho\beta v\alpha}{(FK)^{\frac{(1-\beta)}{2}}} + \frac{2 - 3\rho^2}{24}v^2.$$

(2.11)

As is well known, expansion (2.11) can be used in an optimization routine to imply SABR parameters from quoted volatilities for a particular swaption expiry and tenor. The SABR expansion is then used to interpolate volatility in the strike direction. Then the price of a European payer swaption is given by the Black formula such that:

$$V(0) = A_C(0)(S(0)N(\mathrm{d}_1) - KN(\mathrm{d}_2))$$

$$\mathrm{d}_1 = \frac{\ln\left(\frac{S(0)}{K}\right)}{I^{BS}(K,T_i)\sqrt{T_i}} + \frac{1}{2}I^{BS}(K,T_i)\sqrt{T_i}$$

$$\mathrm{d}_2 = \mathrm{d}_1 - I^{BS}(K,T_i)\sqrt{T_i}.$$

The price of a receiver swaption can of course be obtained by put-call parity. We now examine the potential impact of moving from Libor to OIS discounting on SABR swaption pricing. Table 2.1 shows the differences for market at-the-money (ATM) swaption prices under two discounting systems assuming we

Table 2.1. ATM swaption price difference (OIS−Libor)/OIS annuity (basis points) (12 January 2012)

Expiry	1Y	3Y	5Y	7Y	10Y	15Y	20Y	25Y	30Y
1M	0.0	0.0	0.0	0.0	0.1	0.1	0.2	0.2	0.3
3M	0.0	0.0	0.0	0.1	0.1	0.2	0.3	0.4	0.5
6M	0.0	0.0	0.1	0.1	0.2	0.3	0.5	0.6	0.8
1Y	0.0	0.1	0.1	0.2	0.3	0.5	0.7	1.0	1.2
2Y	0.1	0.2	0.3	0.4	0.6	0.9	1.2	1.6	1.9
3Y	0.2	0.3	0.5	0.6	0.8	1.2	1.6	2.1	2.5
4Y	0.3	0.5	0.7	0.8	1.1	1.5	2.0	2.5	3.0
5Y	0.5	0.7	0.9	1.1	1.4	2.0	2.5	3.0	3.6
7Y	1.1	1.2	1.5	1.7	2.0	2.7	3.4	4.0	4.6
10Y	2.0	2.3	2.6	2.9	3.4	4.3	5.1	6.0	7.0
15Y	3.9	4.6	5.4	5.8	6.5	7.8	8.9	10.2	11.5
20Y	7.6	8.7	9.6	10.1	10.8	12.2	13.8	15.4	17.0
25Y	12.7	13.8	14.5	14.6	15.4	17.5	19.3	21.2	22.7
30Y	16.8	17.9	18.8	19.5	21.0	23.4	25.5	27.2	28.8

M = month(s); Y = year(s).

use the same OIS consistent Black volatilities as quoted by the market. For ease of comparison between expiries and tenors we rescaled the results by the underlying OIS consistent annuities. Results in Table 2.1 show that the error in JPY swaption pricing due to not using the OIS consistent swap rate/discounting is significant, and is an increasing function of expiry and tenor—the maximum error being 28 basis points for the 30Y into 30Y swaption.

The next natural question is: Can this framework be easily adapted to term structure models to incorporate collateral posting? In Section 2.7, we take the example of the Cheyette model and describe the different steps of this adjustment.

2.7 Collateral Effect and Term-Structure Models

In this work, our favored term structure model to price path-dependent IR exotic options is the one-factor linear Cheyette model as introduced in Chibane (2012). In this work, we content ourselves in describing the specifics of the model, but we refer to Chibane (2012) for a complete account of calibration procedures. Here, we focus on describing how to adapt the Cheyette model so that it is consistent with collateral posting. We first introduce the collateral instantaneous forward rates f_C defined by:

$$P_C(t,T) = \exp\left(-\int_t^T f_C(t,s)\mathrm{d}s\right) \Leftrightarrow f_C(t,T) = -\frac{\partial \ln P_C(t,T)}{\partial T}.$$

The Cheyette model in its full generality guarantees the absence of arbitrage through the Heath–Jarrow–Morton (HJM) drift condition and assumes separability of volatility. This can be written in mathematical form through the following dynamics:

$$\mathrm{d}f_C(t,T) = v(t,T)\left(\int_t^T v(t,s)\mathrm{d}s\right)\mathrm{d}t + v(t,T)\mathrm{d}W(t)$$

$$v(t,T) = \frac{\alpha(T)}{\alpha(t)}\beta(t,\theta),$$

where W is a one-dimensional Brownian motion under the collateral risk-neutral measure, α is a deterministic function of time, and β is a function of the forward curve and possibly other stochastic factors.

In the linear Cheyette model we assume the following functional form for the forward rate volatility:

$$\alpha(t) = \exp(-\kappa t)$$
$$\beta(t, \theta) = a(t)x(t) + b(t)$$
$$x(t) = r_{\mathrm{C}}(t) - f_{\mathrm{C}}(0, t),$$

where κ is a positive constant, and a and b are deterministic functions of time. The dynamics of the collateral discount curve are fully defined. However, for most trades we also need to define the FRA rate dynamics. To do so we use the conventional assumption that forward basis swap spreads are not stochastic; this translates into the following preservation rule:

$$\forall t : F^*(t, T, T + \delta) - F_{\mathrm{C}}(t, T, T + \delta)$$
$$= F^*(0, T, T + \delta) - F_{\mathrm{C}}(0, T, T + \delta) \qquad (2.12)$$

$$F^*(t, T, T + \delta) = \frac{1}{\delta}\left(\frac{P^*(t, T)}{P^*(t, T + \delta)} - 1\right)$$

$$F_{\mathrm{C}}(t, T, T + \delta) = \frac{1}{\delta}\left(\frac{P_{\mathrm{C}}(t, T)}{P_{\mathrm{C}}(t, T + \delta)} - 1\right),$$

where δ is the Libor tenor.

Under assumption (2.12), the model dynamics are perfectly determined and path-dependent exotics can be priced under standard Monte Carlo or finite difference methods. In Figures 2.3 and 2.4 we show the impact, in relative difference, of switching from Libor discounting to the OIS discounting framework on

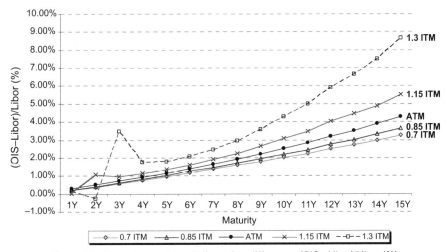

Figure 2.3 Payer Bermudan relative price difference (OIS−Libor)/Libor (%).

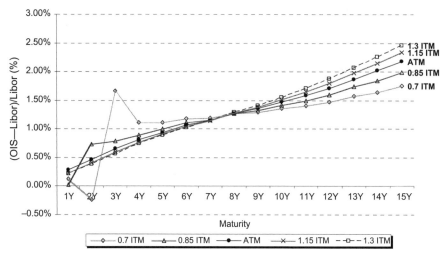

Figure 2.4 Receiver Bermudan relative price difference (OIS—Libor)/Libor (%).

fixed strike Bermudan prices for various "in the moneyness" (ITM) and Bermudan maturities assuming that input SABR volatilities are OIS consistent. Here, in the moneyness is with respect to the OIS consistent forward swap rates underlying the first core swaption. We see that switching to the OIS framework broadly increases the value of Bermudan prices. This makes intuitive sense since forward rates slightly decrease under the OIS framework while discount factors increase significantly.

2.8 Conclusion

We have shown how the standard dual-curve framework can be extended to account for collateral posting in the context of derivatives pricing. Our approach consisted in transferring the usual non-arbitrage assumptions onto the appropriate collateral measure. This has significant practical impact since the classic pricing framework can still be reused provided that the discount curve is changed appropriately to account for collateral. However, there are still practical issues at hand. (i) Different transactions/counterparties yield different collateral policies, i.e. different collateral rates or different levels of collateralization. This implies maintaining many curve systems, which may prove hard to manage. (ii) Collateral policies may include several currencies giving birth to, "cheapest to deliver" collateral types of issues. The latter is still to be investigated and is left for further research.

References

Chibane, M., Sheldon, G., 2009. Building curve on a good basis. Shinsei Bank Working paper Available at http://papers.ssrn.com/sol3/papers.cfm?abstract_id=1394267.

Chibane, M., 2012. Explicit Volatility Specification for the Linear Cheyette Model Available at http://papers.ssrn.com/sol3/papers.cfm?abstract_id=1995214.

Hagan, P.S., Kumar, D., Lesniewski, A.S., Woodward, D.E., 2002. Managing smile risk. Wilmott Magazine, 84–108. September.

Karatzas, I., Shreve, S.R., 1991. Brownian Motion and Stochastic Calculus, second edn). Springer, Berlin.

Mercurio, F., 2009. Interest rates and the credit crunch: new formulas and market models Available at http://papers.ssrn.com/sol3/papers.cfm?abstract_id=1332205.

Piterbarg, V., 2010. collateral agreements and derivatives pricing. Risk, Funding beyond discounting February, 42–48.

Obloj, J., 2008. Fine tune your smile Available at http://arxiv.org/pdf/0708.0998.pdf.

SCENARIO ANALYSIS IN CHARGE OF MODEL SELECTION

Péter Dobránszky

BNP Paribas and Katholieke Universiteit Leuven, Belgium

CHAPTER OUTLINE

3.1 Introduction to Model Risk

In this chapter, we need to distinguish models and rules-of-thumb, the latter of which are often considered as actually being models in the literature. We may build models or apply rules-of-thumb for various reasons. In the following paragraphs we list various cases.

In some cases we know the price of a financial instrument, but we would like to know the risks of holding a given position for a given time horizon. One example is the long-only portfolio of liquid stocks. Although the price of such a portfolio is directly available on the market, answering the question of how much the portfolio may lose from its value on a 10-day horizon with a given probability requires the construction of models. Such value at risk models are widely discussed in the literature. Another example is the trading of listed futures, in which case the valuation does not, but the liquidity management does, require sophisticated models.

In other cases, we know the theoretical price of some instruments, but we need to apply a credit valuation adjustment (CVA) to the theoretical price. This may happen, for instance, when we

Rethinking Valuation and Pricing Models. http://dx.doi.org/10.1016/B978-0-12-415875-7.00003-8

move from listed options to over-the-counter options. For the required price adjustment, we may need to know the future dynamics of the derivatives' theoretical price, which may require building models for the underlying price movements.

In the third category of our classification, we do not know the price of an instrument, but a very close market is available, thus we intend to apply rules-of-thumb to mark our position. For instance, the foreign exchange risk reversals traded today become bespoke by tomorrow. Furthermore, not all strikes and maturities of options are equally traded on other markets. In practice, rules-of-thumb are used to mark the options with bespoke strike or maturity. Rules-of-thumb can mean, for instance, the marking of bespoke vanilla options based on the parameterization of the implied volatility surface or marking bespoke commodity futures based on the parameterization of the futures curve. Such parameterizations may incorporate basic intuitions like mean-reversion effect and shall comply with arbitrage rules. However, rules-of-thumb usually do not say anything about the dynamics of the market and they do not answer the question of how the prices may evolve in the future. For instance, the vanna–volga method presented by Castagna and Mercurio (2007) may help to price options with different strikes. However, the method hardly helps in identifying the market dynamics and calculating risks of holding a position on a given horizon.

In the fourth category of our classification, we do not know the price, but following some rules we would like to find a replication strategy and mark the given instrument to the chosen model. This is the case, for instance, when we intend to mark forward start or barrier options based on the vanilla option market. In these cases, it is important that we choose a model that can describe the market dynamics well or which is equal to the market standard. Otherwise, the replication strategy given by the model will not be efficient and we may realize significant cumulative losses during the life of the product. The Venn diagram of Whitehead (2010) in Figure 3.1 shows the level of model risk in various cases.

If we use the market standard model for pricing our derivatives and this model captures the market dynamics well, then the model risk is low. If we use the market standard model for pricing our derivatives, assuming that this model does not properly capture the market dynamics, we bear moderate model risk. Nevertheless, we may decide to use a model that differs from the market standard. However, even if our model captures the market dynamics well, but the market standard model does not, then we bear high model risk by trading the instrument. We may realize significant losses if we must close our position before expiry.

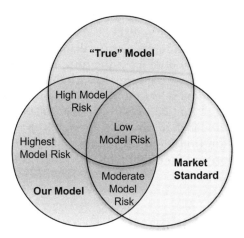

Figure 3.1 Model risk diagram.

Obviously, if our model is neither the market standard model nor the "true" model that captures the market dynamics, then we bear the highest model risk.

Before the recent subprime crisis, the trading of exotic products, such as barrier options on oil prices, was increasing. The pricing of these products was more than challenging. With regard to trading vanilla options on oil, not only are the volatilities and the implied volatility skews stochastic, but also the spot price of oil products is mean-reverting, and the implied volatility skew may have a different sign for short-term and long-term maturities. Furthermore, since the liquidity of these products was always low, the market standard model for pricing them has never existed. In other cases, there may exist a market standard model. For instance, in many markets local stochastic volatility models are used. However, the calibration of these models is definitively non-standard, i.e. the various institutions calibrate these models differently.

With the lack of a market standard model, the task of a quant is often to find a model that best describes the market dynamics and that ensures consistent pricing of vanilla instruments. We may think that, since the recent subprime crisis, the market has significantly reduced the trade of sophisticated structured products. Therefore, the development of sophisticated pricing models and the proper understanding of market dynamics is not so important anymore. However, as the credit default swap spreads systematically widened on the markets, even the fair valuation of some vanilla products became sophisticated. For many fixed-income products the CVA became an important component of the fair value. For example, from a modeling point of view, while the calculation of a risk reversal's theoretical value requires only the vanilla option prices today, i.e. the current implied volatility skew, the potential future exposure calculation of the same risk reversal requires the modeling of the future volatility skew.

The purpose of this chapter is to introduce a technique that can be used for model selection in cases when the objective is to identify the model that can best describe the market dynamics and thus the model that can best approach the "true" model. Nevertheless, the presented technique can also be applied for model validation and for quantifying model uncertainty in many cases.

3.2 Classical Calibration Procedure

In practice, the various stochastic volatility and Lévy models are usually calibrated to the implied volatility surface on a given date (see, e.g. Schoutens *et al.*, 2004). As an example, we consider here the calibration of the stochastic volatility jump-diffusion model of Bates (1996), of which the dynamics can be described by the following differential equations:

$$dS_t/S_t = \mu dt + \sigma_S \sqrt{\nu_t} dW_t^S + Q dN$$
$$d\nu_t = \kappa_\nu(\theta - \nu_t)dt + \sigma_\nu \sqrt{\nu_t} dW_t^\nu$$
$$\langle dW_t^S, dW_t^\nu \rangle = \rho dt, \Pr(dN = 1) = \lambda dt, Q \sim LN(\eta, \gamma).$$

We chose 30 September 2009 as the calibration date for our example and we calibrated the parameters of the Bates model to a set of 15 options written on the S&P 500 Index by minimizing the squared distance between the market implied and model implied volatilities. We chose the 15 vanilla options to represent the implied volatility surface. Therefore, we chose three maturities (one month, one year and two years) and five relative strikes (10Δ, 25Δ, 50Δ, 75Δ and 90Δ). Figure 3.2 shows that the result of the calibration seems to be satisfactory, because the difference between market and model option prices is always below one vega in each of the 15 cases.

However, one should not be misled by the impression of the good fit in terms of price differences, because once looking at the calibrated model parameters, one will realize that the calibrated model parameters can hardly be accepted, i.e. the result of the calibration in terms of implied market dynamics is against normal intuition. As a result of the blind calibration, the correlation between log-spot moves and instantaneous variance moves turned to be -100%, and the calibrated volatility mean-reversion rate is also very high. The perfect negative correlation

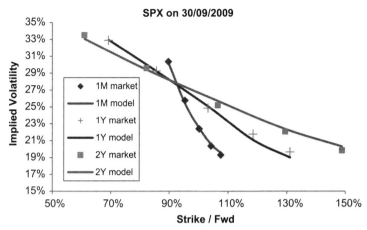

Figure 3.2 Calibration of the Bates model.

between the spot and variance terms would mean that only one stochastic factor would drive the whole asset price and volatility dynamics. Furthermore, the high mean-reversion rate implies that even if short-term implied volatilities are volatile, the long-term implied volatilities are expected to be stable. However, as Figure 3.3 highlights, the long-term implied volatilities are nearly as volatile as the short-term implied volatilities.

The Bates model has many model parameters, but it has only two state variables, i.e. the spot price and the instantaneous variance. Based on the construction of the model, the

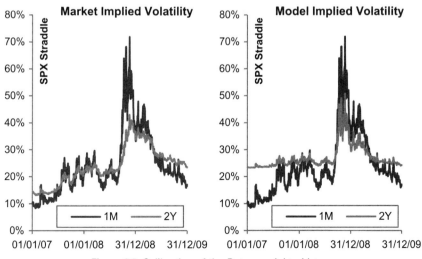

Figure 3.3 Calibration of the Bates model to history.

level of the spot price does not influence the level and shape of the implied volatility surface. Therefore, in theory, the daily change in the instantaneous variance ν should explain the dynamics of the implied volatility surface. Keeping fixed the model parameters calibrated earlier, we recalibrated the instantaneous variance ν for each day in order to match the level of the one-month at-the-money implied volatility. Figure 3.3 shows that, indeed, keeping the model parameters fixed, the results of the above-mentioned calibration imply that the long-term implied volatility should be stable. However, as we see in figure 3.3, the two-year implied volatilities were highly volatile during the analyzed period.

3.3 Processes, Dynamics and Model Definition

In our definition, the model is a set of:
- *State variables* (risk factors) that stochastically change over time.
- *Equations* that describe the dynamics of state variable changes.
- *Model parameters* that parameterize the equations.

For instance, the stochastic volatility model introduced by Heston (1993) has two state variables (S and ν), four model parameters (σ_S, σ_ν, κ and ρ) and the following stochastic differential equations (SDEs) to describe the dynamics:

$$dS_t/S_t = \mu dt + \sigma_S \sqrt{\nu_t} dW_t^S$$
$$d\nu_t = \kappa(1 - \nu_t)dt + \sigma_\nu \sqrt{\nu_t} dW_t^\nu$$
$$\langle dW_t^S, dW_t^\nu \rangle = \rho dt.$$

The model is as valuable (1) as many risk factors it has and (2) as rich the description of the dynamics of the risk factors is. For instance, the Heston model has a spot and a volatility risk factor; accordingly, it will not be able to capture the risks in a product that makes a bet on the evolution of the implied volatility skew, while the product with its hedge is delta and vega neutral. By building models, we need at least as many risk factors as there are properties of the dynamics we intend to capture.

With regard to the example in Section 3.2, if we want to capture not only the variation in the level of the implied volatilities, but also the variation in the slope of the volatility term structure, then we need at least two volatility risk factors. Furthermore, if we also want to capture the dynamics of the implied volatility skew, which may move independently from the volatility level and volatility term structure, then we need at least a third volatility risk factor.

The model is a simplified version of the reality. With a finite set of risk factors that we choose for our model, we will always underestimate the risk profile of the reality. In practice, we see that models need to be recalibrated from time to time; thus model parameters are changing, although by theory they should be permanent. We consider a model as being well defined if the model parameters remain stable over the course of recalibrations. A model, in our definition, should explain the price of basic market instruments (quoted liquid instruments) not only on one day, but on each day.

We should find risk factors that drive the daily price movements of basic market instruments and for the exotic products they should explain the largest possible proportion of the profit and loss fluctuation. Marking-to-model means that the theoretical price of derivatives is given by the replication strategy implied by the model. However, if the model parameters must be changed every day to match the price of basic market instruments, then the dynamics of asset prices and volatilities are not captured well and, accordingly, we fail to price derivatives.

Our key assumption in this chapter is that there is a unique equivalent martingale measure that does not change from one day to another, i.e. the market dynamics and the model parameters are stable. Obviously, such assumptions are not always true. For instance, when there is a new regulation or there is a significant market event, the market dynamics may change. However, in general terms we may assume that some liquid markets have stable dynamics and, accordingly, the market dynamics observed in the past few years are representative for the market dynamics in the following few years. Nevertheless, we do not mean that the statistical and risk-neutral measures are equal. We shall make the link between the two measures and the measure change shall be part of the model.

3.4 Importance of Risk Premia

In this chapter, we assume that the dynamics of the risk factors, i.e. the equations and the model parameters, are stable over time; nonetheless, the levels of state variables are continuously changing. When we calibrate our models to time a series of market prices, e.g. to time a series of implied volatility surfaces, then we look for the best combination of equations and model parameters that allows the best fit to the historical market prices. Furthermore, we look for the combination that ensures that the dynamics of the calibrated state variables correspond to the dynamics implied by the equations and model parameters.

On the one hand, when we calibrate our model to historical time series of derivatives prices, the combination of equations and model parameters defines the dynamics of the state variables in the risk-neutral measure. On the other hand, the calibrated daily evolution of the state variables defines the dynamics in the physical measure. The dynamics of the state variables in the risk-neutral and physical measures are not necessarily the same. However, the difference between the two dynamics must be limited to differences in model parameters as implied by risk premia.

According to portfolio theories, only non-diversifiable risks are compensated. For instance, if asset prices and volatilities are strongly negatively correlated, then in the case that assets are priced with positive risk premium, volatilities should be priced with negative premium, i.e. the implied volatilities are greater than the realized ones.

It is important to clarify where risk premia may enter the model definition. If a model contains diffusion processes, a risk premium may enter the model in a drift component as required for the change of measure. Furthermore, since jumps cannot be hedged, in the case that the model contains jump components, then a risk premium may enter the model by implying different jump parameters in the physical and risk-neutral measures.

However, risk premia may not enter the model in other forms. For instance, it is wrong to assume that the correlation between two diffusion processes, which is assumed to be a constant model parameter, such as the ρ in the Heston model, may differ in the physical and risk-neutral measures.

Therefore, if we observe after calibration that the physical and risk-neutral dynamics of the state variables differ in more aspects than allowed by the concept of risk premia, then it means that our model is wrongly defined and some components may be missing from our model or the assumption of comovements between risk factors may be inappropriate.

Often, in practice, the models are chosen based on the availability of a closed-form solution or fast pricer. However, the constraints on the calculation side should not mislead and force us to choose a model that fails to capture the market dynamics. Although models, if they are widely applied, may to some extent drive the markets, we assumed earlier in this chapter that with the lack of a market standard model we look for the best representation of the "true" model.

Applying scenario analyses techniques for model selection and model validation will mean investigating whether the dynamics of the calibrated state variables correspond to the dynamics implied by the equations and model parameters. In the case that we observe differences between the two, we will look for ways to improve our models and to better capture the market dynamics.

3.5 Equity Volatility Modeling

Let us now consider the pricing of cliquet spread options, which are sets of forward starting options. The vanilla option market tells us the possible asset price evolution from today to a future date, but it does not tell us anything about the evolution between two future dates. Therefore, based only on the price of vanilla options, we do not know what the market expects about the forward volatility and what the risks are of cliquet spread options.

In order to mark-to-model cliquet spread options, we consider first using the stochastic volatility jump-diffusion model that was introduced by Bates (1996). In Section 3.2, we have already calibrated this model to the implied volatility surface observed on 30 September 2009 and we concluded that the calibrated asset–volatility correlation was unrealistic (-100%) and that, in spite of empirical observations, the calibrated volatility mean-reversion rate was very high.

In the first step, we overcome the deficiencies of the Bates model by incorporating a new risk factor into the model, which provides volatility also for long-term implied volatilities. Similar to the model presented by Carr and Wu (2007), we have chosen the stochastic central tendency approach. The dynamics of this extended Bates model can be described by:

$$dS_t/S_t = \mu dt + \sigma_S \sqrt{v_t} dW_t^S + Q dN$$
$$dv_t = \kappa_v(\theta_t - v_t)dt + \sigma_v \sqrt{v_t} dW_t^v$$
$$d\theta_t = \kappa_\theta(1 - \theta_t)dt + \sigma_\theta \sqrt{\theta_t} dW_t^\theta$$
$$\langle dW_t^S, dW_t^v \rangle = \rho dt, \Pr(dN = 1) = \lambda dt, Q \sim LN(\eta, \gamma).$$

Unlike the classic calibration procedure described in Section 3.2, we calibrate the extended Bates model to the time series of the S&P 500 implied volatility surface over a three-year period. In order to avoid that the calibration results in local optima, we capture the characteristics of the implied volatility surface on each day by the same kind of 15 options (one month, one year and two years, 10Δ, 25Δ, 50Δ, 75Δ and 90Δ).

In terms of scenario analyses, we first obtain the time series of the state variables by carrying out the historical calibration above. Afterwards, based on the SDEs, we approximate the time series of the error terms (dW terms). At the end, we check whether the distribution properties and the correlation of the error terms are in line with the risk factor dynamics implied by the calibration results.

According to the calibration results, the model implied correlation is −80%, which is acceptable considering that the empirical correlation between dS_t/S_t and dv_t was −60% for the analyzed period, and considering that jumps decorrelate the two processes. Furthermore, according to the calibration results, the instantaneous variance is volatile and highly mean-reverting ($\kappa = 2.2$), while the stochastic central tendency has low mean-reversion rate ($\kappa = 0.3$).

Figure 3.4 shows that, after introducing a new risk factor, the model not only captures the short-term, but also the long-term, implied volatility dynamics. It is not surprising considering that, after introducing a new risk factor, the number of objectives and the number of instruments became equal.

Nonetheless, when we extended the Bates model, we assumed that the correlation between the stochastic central tendency and variance error terms is zero. We assumed this because, as a result,

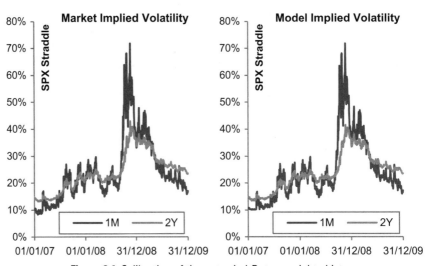

Figure 3.4 Calibration of the extended Bates model to history.

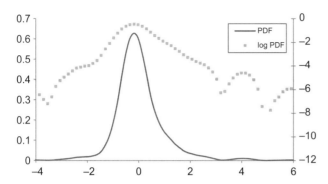

Figure 3.5 Variance error term distribution.

the model stayed in the affine class of Duffie *et al.* (2000), and therefore, the option pricing remained simple and fast. However, the empirical correlation between the stochastic central tendency and variance error terms is −28%, which invalidates our original model assumption about the independence of the variance and stochastic central tendency processes. Moreover, as shown in Figure 3.5, the distribution of the variance error terms is leptokurtic, which suggests that the model should be extended with jumps in the variance.

Although we defined a stochastic volatility model that can reproduce the heteroskedasticity of the asset price return, the model is not advanced enough to capture the heteroskedasticity in the various error terms. Figure 3.6 shows the exponentially weighted moving average (EWMA) of the various error terms. The

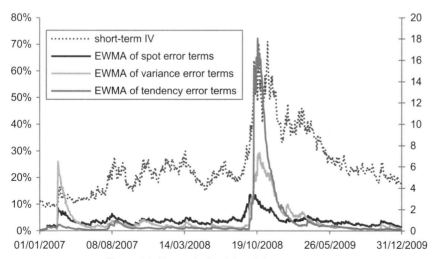

Figure 3.6 Heteroskedasticity of the error terms.

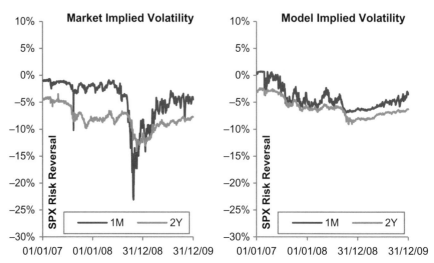

Figure 3.7 Calibration of the extended Bates model to history.

graph suggests that our model misses a special link between the risk factors.

Since the variance error terms were more volatile when the volatility level was higher, Figure 3.6 suggests that for the variance process we should have used a different exponent, i.e. a log-normal process instead of a square-root process. However, we have chosen the square root process for our model, because otherwise the pricing of the vanilla options could have been difficult, preventing us from performing an efficient calibration. Again, this highlights that we should be cautious with the model assumptions, because any model restrictions may result in the failure of the model to capture the market dynamics.

Last, but not least, in Figure 3.7 we show that by having only two volatility risk factors in the model we can capture the dynamics of the volatility term structure's slope, but we are unable to capture the dynamics of the implied volatility skew. That would require the inclusion of further risk factors into our model.

3.6 Foreign Exchange Volatility Modeling

When we consider the extension of our model to capture the dynamics of the implied volatility skew, we turn our attention to the foreign exchange derivatives market, because unlike equities in the case of foreign exchanges the implied volatility skew is not only volatile, but it even often changes sign. Therefore, as a second case study, we consider the modeling of foreign exchange rates. A sophisticated model may be required to analyze the risks in delta-hedged risk reversals and butterflies.

In this section, we further extend the Bates model and, as a special case of the stochastic skew model of Carr and Wu (2007), we separate the variance processes of the left-side moves and of the right-side moves. When the left-side moves are more volatile, the model implies that the terminal densities of the spot price moves are skewed to the left, while when the right-side moves are more volatile, skewness to the right is assumed. The dynamics of the twice-extended Bates model can be described by:

$$dy_t = \mu dt + \sigma_y \left(\sqrt{v_t^{L}} + \sqrt{v_t^{R}} \right) dW_t^{y} - Q^{L}dN^{L} + Q^{R}dN^{R}$$

$$dv_t^{j} = \kappa_v (\theta_t - v_t) dt + \sigma_v \sqrt{v_t} dW_t^{j}$$

$$d\theta_t = \kappa_\theta (1 - \theta_t) dt + \sigma_\theta \sqrt{\theta_t} dW_t^{\theta}$$

$$\langle dW_t^{y}, dW_t^{j} \rangle = \rho^{j} dt, \Pr(dN^{j} = 1) = \lambda v_t^{j} dt, Q^{j} \sim \exp(\eta).$$

In Figures 3.8 and 3.9 we show that the twice-extended Bates model is not only capable of capturing the volatility term structure dynamics, but in most cases the implied volatility skew dynamics also. There is only a short period during which the model was unable to explain the traded implied volatility skew of the EUR/USD exchange rate. However, this short period coincides with the stressed period after Lehman's default when many traders marked the implied volatility skew based on some rules-of-thumb using some unrealistic, extreme parameters.

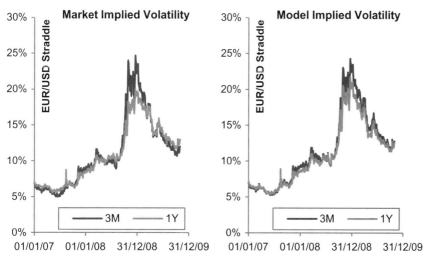

Figure 3.8 Calibration of the stochastic skew model to history.

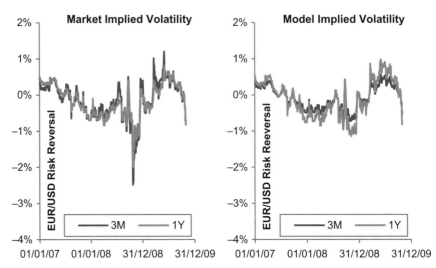

Figure 3.9 Calibration of the stochastic skew model to history.

According to the calibration results, jumps in the EUR/USD exchange rates are infrequent and they have only a small amplitude. Therefore, in this specific example, nearly the same calibration performance could have been achieved by assuming that the model contains no jumps, but only correlated diffusion processes. With regard to the central tendency component, it is highly volatile and it has a low mean-reversion rate. These two choices are required to be able to capture the fact that in the past the foreign exchange implied volatilities were highly volatile, while the volatility term structure was most often flat.

Furthermore, not only the calibrated jump parameters suggest that jumps can be removed from our model for this specific example, but also the very strong normality of the error terms' distributions gives the same message. However, this twice-extended Bates model struggles to match the empirical correlations of the error terms, similarly to the extended Bates model of the previous section. The implied correlations between the spot price moves and the two types of variance moves are −26 and 24%, while the empirical correlations are significantly stronger, being −64 and 58%, respectively.

Finally, there is a strong negative empirical correlation of −39% between the error terms of the two variance processes, while the constructed model assumed zero correlation between these two terms. Again, when constructing the model, we restricted the correlation between the two variance error terms to zero, because in this way the model stayed in the affine class, allowing efficient pricing and calibration. However, thanks to the applied scenario analysis technique, we could identify, for instance, that the zero correlation assumption is too restrictive, and therefore the model should be further extended in the direction of linear quadratic jump-diffusion models of Cheng and Scaillet (2007).

As the models are simplified versions of reality, obviously we will never be able to capture the full market dynamics. This is especially true because as we go into finer and finer modeling details, we question more and more the stability of the market dynamics. Nevertheless, we must find a pragmatic limit until we proceed with the refinement of our model. Usually, the limit is product dependent. For each exotic product in our scope and for their portfolio we have to identify which property of the market dynamics they make a bet on. Accordingly, our model has to capture at least those properties. Afterwards, scenario analyses techniques should be further used to assess the calibration and valuation uncertainties. Often, model backtesting based on trading strategies may help to identify which model components the products are sensitive to and what the price of using a simplified model may be.

3.7 Conclusions

In this chapter, via two case studies, we explained how scenario analyses techniques can be used to discover model deficiencies and to propose further enhancements.

We proposed not to calibrate the sophisticated models to a single day implied volatility surface, but, for instance, to the time series of implied volatility surfaces. Applying scenario analyses techniques for model selection and model validation means investigating whether the dynamics of the calibrated state variables correspond to the dynamics implied by the equations and model parameters. Scenario analyses may incorporate checking the distribution properties of the error terms, the correlation of the error terms or, for instance, the heteroskedasticity of the state variables. In the case that we observe differences between the empirical dynamics of the state variables and the dynamics implied by the model, we shall look for ways to improve our models and to better capture the market dynamics.

While applying the risk premium adjusted empirical dynamics of the error terms for future simulations, one may assess the model risk and quantify valuation uncertainty. Furthermore, a good understanding of the risk factors' dynamics in the physical and risk-neutral measures may help to better measure and manage market and counterparty credit risks.

Although scenario analyses techniques may help to continuously improve our models to better describe the market dynamics, it is important to keep in mind that these models will never have a perfect match to the prices of the various vanilla instruments. The reason for this phenomenon is that traders do not use sophisticated models for marking, but they often use rules-of-thumb. In this manner, as long as we hedge our derivatives with instruments that are marked based on rules-of-thumb, the challenge is to model the dynamics of how rules-of-thumb or their parameters are changing.

Nonetheless, when a sophisticated model is required for marking exotic products, after capturing the market dynamics on a satisfactory level, one may apply valuation adjustment techniques as presented by Castagna and Mercurio (2007) and Ekstrand (2010) in order to ensure full consistency with the pricing of vanilla instruments when pricing exotic products. In this way, the model developer can ensure consistency with the vanilla markets while retaining the captured market dynamics that determines the replication strategy.

Note

The contents of this chapter represent the author's views only and are not intended to represent the opinions of any firm or institution. None of the methods described herein is claimed to be in actual use.

References

Bates, D.S., 1996. Jumps and stochastic volatility: exchange rate processes implicit in Deutsche Mark options. Review of Financial Studies 9 (1), 69–107.

Carr, P., Wu, L., 2007. Stochastic skew in currency options. Journal of Financial Economics 86 (1), 213–247.

Castagna, A., Mercurio, F., 2007. The vanna–volga method for implied volatilities. Risk, January, 106–111.

Cheng, P., Scaillet, O., 2007. Linear-quadratic jump-diffusion modeling. Mathematical Finance 17 (4), 575–598.

Duffie, D., Pan, J., Singleton, K., 2000. Transform analysis and asset pricing for affine jump-diffusions. Econometrica 68 (6), 1343–1376.

Ekstrand, C., 2010. Calibrating exotic models to vanilla models. Wilmott Journal 2 (2), 109–116.

Heston, S.L., 1993. A closed-form solution for options with stochastic volatility with applications to bond and currency options. Review of Financial Studies 6 (2), 327–344.

Schoutens, W., Simons, E., Tistaert, J., 2004. A perfect calibration! Now what? Wilmott Magazine, March, 66–78.

Whitehead, P., 2010. Techniques for Mitigating Model Risk. In: Gregoriou, G., Hoppe, C., Wehn, C. (Eds.), The Risk Modeling Evaluation Handbook. McGraw-Hill, New York, pp. 271–286.

4

AN "ECONOMICAL" PRICING MODEL FOR HYBRID PRODUCTS

Rosa Cocozza and Antonio De Simone
Università degli Studi di Napoli Federico II

CHAPTER OUTLINE

4.1 Introduction

Convertible bonds are hybrid products very common in the financial industry. A fundamental role played by such securities is to provide funding for firms at lower costs with respect to other financial contracts, such as ordinary bonds, mainly because they bear a lower interest coupon payment. However, such advantages are offset by the right, granted to the bondholder, to modify their "status," switching from creditor to shareholder, if they find it convenient. Moreover, it can be noticed that convertibles are commonly adopted by management to enhance the capital structure of the firm. This is the case because the exercise of the conversion privilege makes it possible to contemporaneously reduce the debt exposure and to increase the common equity of the issuer. This latter can doubtless be a desirable feature, especially during the periods characterized by increasing interest rates and by the necessity for deleveraging.

If, on the one hand, convertible bonds may be considered as an important tool for capital structure management, it can, on the other hand, be noticed that these securities are considerably more complex with respect to other financial instruments; such as ordinary bonds, options and warrants, and their pricing implies accounting for many sources of risk and dealing with complex evaluation frameworks and models.

Many contributions in the literature may be recognized, beginning from the seminal papers by Ingersoll (1977) and Brennan and Schwartz (1977, 1980) where, for the first time, a replicating strategy and numerical approximation methods for convertible bond pricing are proposed. In particular, Brennan and Schwartz (1980) develop a pricing framework for convertible bonds that accounts for two sources of risk: The firm value and the interest rate. Furthermore, the approach adopted by Brennan and Schwartz in credit risk modeling is somewhat similar to that adopted by Merton (1974), sometimes defined as the "structural approach," where the default event is endogenously defined by the case of an asset value lower than the liability value. The Brennan and Schwartz model suffers from the main drawback, generally related to the structural approach, that the firm value and volatility are not directly observable. For this reason, a different approach, sometimes defined as "reduced-form approach," has been successively developed, first by Jarrow and Turnbull (1994) and then by of Duffie and Singleton (1999). The main idea of this new approach is that the default risk is exogenously characterized by a jump–diffusion process and that the probability of default is inferred by financial market data.

Finally, very relevant are the contributions by Tsiveriotis and Fernandes (1998), where partial differential equations are concerned within a reduced-form approach, and by Hung and Wang (2002), where the dynamics of the risk factors are described by means of binomial trees.

This chapter proceeds as follows. Section 4.2 offers a brief review of the convertible bond pricing theory as well as of the basic methodology, based on binomial trees, without interest rate risk and default risk. Section 4.3 shows the mechanics of an innovative numerical procedure (Cocozza and De Simone, 2011a, 2011b) with the aim of computing the arbitrage-free price of convertible bonds within a reduced-form approach. Such a procedure accounts for two sources of risk: The underlying asset and the spot interest Libor rate. Section 4.4 illustrates how to compute the default probabilities, starting from the observed market prices, while Section 4.5 reports a numerical example of convertible bond pricing. Section 4.6 concludes by reporting some final remarks.

4.2 Pricing Convertible Bonds

A convertible bond is a hybrid security allowing the bondholder to convert the nature of his/her investment from bond to equity, at particular conditions and maturities defined by the contract. Very often the faculty will opt for an equivalent sum of money instead of receiving the shares granted to the bondholder. Anyway, such instruments combine typical features of ordinary bonds with the upside potential of an investment in common equity shares. The conversion privilege can be seen as an American (or sometimes Bermudan) option that the bondholder can exercise at their discretion. However, such discretion is commonly limited by the fact that the issuer retains the right to call the convertible for redemption; even if, very often, such a right cannot be exercised before a certain period of time has expired. When the call provision is exercised, the bondholder can decide to convert the bond in common equity shares, at a pre-defined conversion ratio, or to redeem it at a pre-defined call price. It is worth noticing that the conversion strategy set by the bondholder will depend on the call strategy set by the issuer and *vice versa*, and that the equilibrium value of the convertible is the value that offers no arbitrage opportunity to both the parties. For this reason, the value of the convertible cannot be determined until the two strategies are simultaneously set.

It is worth noting that to determine the arbitrage-free value of the convertible it is necessary to set the optimal conversion strategy followed by the bondholder and the optimal call strategy followed by the issuer. In addition, it is important to consider that the issuer and bondholder have conflicting interests because, the market value of the firm being the same,[1] the strategy of maximizing the value of the common equity can be pursued only by minimizing the value of the convertibles and *vice versa*.

---

[1] This assumption implies that the issue of convertibles does not influence the market value of the firm. The assumption is a consequence of the Miller and Modigliani theorem, and appears to be quite restrictive, especially if we consider the role played by convertibles in optimizing the capital structure with the aim of value creation.

4.2.1 Optimal conversion strategy

In general, it is noticeable that the bondholder will always find it optimal to exercise the conversion privilege if the price of the convertible falls below the conversion value (i.e. the value of the shares the bondholder receives as result of the conversion). This way the bondholder renounces the market value of the convertible to obtain its conversion value. On the contrary, if the price of the convertible is above the conversion value, the bondholder never finds it optimal to convert since this would imply renouncing a value (the price of the convertible) that the market considers higher than the conversion value. Therefore, the optimal conversion strategy imposes a constraint on the bondholder to convert as soon as the price of the convertible equals the conversion value.

Moreover, it can be proved that the bondholder never finds it optimal to convert an uncalled convertible bond except immediately prior the dividend date or the date at which a change in the term condition occurs; or, finally, at the expiration date.[2] Intuitively, this is the case because only in the above-mentioned cases may the price of the convertible be equal or less the conversion value. Otherwise, the bondholder prefers to sell the bond on the market instead of converting it, implying the following lower bound condition:

$$C \geq CV, \tag{4.1}$$

where C is the market value of the convertible and CV is the conversion value, and it is equal to the value of the shares the bondholder receives if he or she exercises the conversion privilege.

Since it is never optimal to convert an uncalled convertible bond (except in the above-mentioned cases) a call provision can therefore be included in the contract in order to force the conversion before the expiration date.

4.2.2 Optimal call strategy

The call provision implies that, if the bond is called for redemption by the issuer, the bondholder has the option to choose whether to exercise the conversion privilege and receive the conversion value, or to redeem it and receive the call price (CP).

---

[2] The reason for this is similar to the reason why the holder of an American call option, written on a non-paying dividend asset, will never find it optimal to exercise the option before the expiration (see Merton, 1973).

Bearing in mind that the issuer's objective is to minimize the value of the convertible, an optimal call strategy implies to call the convertible bond as soon as the value if called (*VIC*) is equal to the value if not called. This is the case because, if the convertible bond were left uncalled at a market price higher than the value if called, the issuer would maximize the stock value by calling it. On the contrary, if the convertible bond were called at a market price lower than the value if called, an extra profit would be offered to bondholders so that the issuer would minimize the value of the convertible by leaving it uncalled. The first result is therefore that:

$$C \geq VIC. \tag{4.2}$$

Moreover, the value of the convertible if called is:

$$VIC = \max\{CV, CP\}, \tag{4.3}$$

and it is clear that *VIC* reaches the minimum value of *CP* when $CV = CP$. The logical consequence is that the issuer will call the bond as soon as the conversion value is at least equal to the call price. Moreover, after the convertible becomes callable, if the conversion value were higher than the call price, the issuer will decide to call the bond because, by condition (4.1), it would be sold at a price higher than (or at least equal to) the conversion value that, in this case, is the value if called.

For this reason, an optimal call strategy is to call the convertible as soon as $C = CP$ and the following upper bound condition can be recognized:

$$C \leq CP. \tag{4.4}$$

4.2.3 Basic model

In evaluating the arbitrage-free value of a convertible bond the need for cash flow mapping arises. With this aim, at least four elements should be considered: The stock price, the equity component of the convertible (i.e. the expectation about the conversion), the debt component (the expectation in case of no conversion) and, finally, the total value of the convertible bond. This last is therefore given by the sum of the two components, if lower than the call price. Otherwise, the issuer will find it optimal to call the convertible bond and its value is equal to the conversion value. Many pricing models describe the dynamics of such components by means of binomial trees. Following this approach, it is first necessary to determine the payoff of the convertible at maturity and then to roll back the tree structure till the evaluation date, checking at each time step if the optimal conversion and call strategies are respected (i.e. to check if conditions (4.1) and (4.4) are respected).

At maturity date T, if the conversion value (that in this case is the equity component) is higher than the face value of the convertible bond, the bondholder decides to convert. In this case the debt component of the convertible bond is equal to zero, while the equity component is equal to the number of shares offered in conversion for each convertible bond, times the stock price at the expiration date. On the contrary, if the face value of the convertible bond is higher than the conversion value, the bondholder does not decide to convert, and the payoff is equal to the face value of the convertible bond. Rolling back the tree, it should be necessary to check if the sum of the equity component and of the debt component is greater than the call price, if the convertible is already callable. A numerical example can simplify the explanation. In this framework, it is assumed that the interest rate term structure is flat and not stochastic. Furthermore, the event of default is for the moment not explicitly considered, even if the discount rate applied to the debt part of the convertible bond is a risky rate.

Figure 4.1 shows a binomial tree of the four components of the convertible bond. It is assumed that the risk-free rate (r) is constant over time and is equal to 3%, while the risky yield is equal to 6% (i.e. to fix a spread $s = 3\%$). The risk-free yield is adopted to

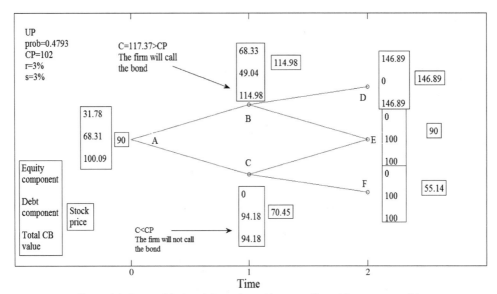

Figure 4.1 Convertible bond dynamics without credit and interest rate risk.

construct the implied binomial stock tree, while the risky yield is adopted to discount the debt part of the convertible bond.

Note that, since the risk-free rate is constant over time, the up probability of the stock price is constant too and in this case is equal to 0.4793. For simplicity, it is assumed that each convertible bond can be converted into one share (i.e. the conversion ratio is 1), whose price at $t=0$ (the evaluation date) is equal to 90. For simplicity, we assume that the convertible bond pays no coupons, has a two-year maturity and can be immediately called by the firm at a price of 102. Finally, the stock pays no dividend during the following two years. From Figure 4.1 it can be noticed that, at node D, the stock price is equal to 146.89. This is the equity component at time $t=2$ and the bondholder decides to convert. Since the conversion occurs, the debt component of the convertible falls to zero. On the contrary, at node E and F, the stock price is equal to 90 and 55.14, respectively, and is in both cases lower than the face value of the convertible. The bondholder decides to not convert it, so that the equity component falls to zero and the convertible bond value is given from the debt component only.

Proceeding backward, at node B there is a probability of 47.93% that the equity component will rise to 146.89 in the next period and a probability of 52.17% that it will fall to zero. The equity component is therefore equal to $(0.4793 \times 146.98 + 0.5217 \times 0)\exp\{-0.03\} = 68.33$. Moreover, at the same node, there is a probability of 52.17% that the debt part will rise to 100 and a 47.93% of probability that it falls to zero. The debt component is therefore equal to $(100 \times 0.5217)\exp\{-0.06\} = 49.04$. At node B we notice that the convertible bond value, that is equal to the sum of the two components (117.37), is greater than the call price (102). Condition (4.4) is violated so that the firm decides to call the bond, forcing the conversion. In turn, the bondholder decides to convert the bond because he or she receives a stock whose value (114.98) is higher than the call price. On the contrary, at node C it can be noticed that the equity component is equal to zero because there is no chance to convert the bond at maturity. The debt part is equal to $100\exp\{-0.06\} = 94.18$. Since the value if not called is lower than the value if called, the firm will decide to not call the bond. Therefore, at node C, the value of the convertible is 94.18.

Rolling back the tree, it is possible to determine the value of the convertible at $t=0$ just by computing the sum of the equity and of the debt part, and checking for conditions (4.1) and (4.4).

4.3 Two-Factor Numerical Procedure

The procedure described in this section was thought to determine the arbitrage-free value of structured products, such as participating policies (Cocozza *et al.*, 2011), under two-risk-factor modeling and it is here extended to determine the arbitrage-free value of convertible bonds. The procedure accounts for two sources of risk: The stock price and the interest rate.

4.3.1 Interest rate modeling

The interest rate considered as a risk factor is the spot inter-bank offered rate, such as the Libor or Euribor rate, and its dynamics is described according to the one-factor Black–Derman–Toy (BDT; Black *et al.*, 1990) model. Such a model determines the arbitrage-free price of securities whose dynamics depends on the interest rate's levels, by means of binomial trees. It is therefore useful to determine the stochastic risk-free rate and the relative discount factor. The advantages in using this model are that the price of a straight bond is exogenously determined so that the observed term structure of the interest rate can be reproduced perfectly. Moreover, the model can be satisfactorily calibrated by using the implied volatilities from caps, floors and swap option markets.

To sketch the mechanics of the model, a numerical example is provided. Let $L(t,t+\delta)$ be the spot Libor rate observed at time t and tenor δ, usually expressed as fraction of the year according to the relevant market conventions. Assuming a tenor equal to one year ($\delta = 1$), an example of the BDT arbitrage-free dynamics of the one-year Libor rate and of a corresponding risk-free bond are illustrated in Figure 4.2 (a and b, respectively).[3]

Notice that the spot Libor rate at time $t = 0$, $L(0,1)$ is equal to 2% and it is not a random variable. Moreover, an important feature of the BDT model is that the risk of neutral increasing probability is constant over time and is equal to $1/2$. Therefore, at time $t = 1$ the one-year Libor rate, $L(1,2)$, is a random variable assuming the values of 2.9% or 5.2% with equal risk-neutral probability.

At time $t = 2$, the Libor rate $L(2,3)$ can rise from 5.2 to 12.9% or drop to 5% with equal probability and so on. Since the tree is recombining, at time $t = 2$ the Libor rate can reach the value of 5% following two different paths (2% → 5.2% → 5% or 2% → 2.9% → 5%). As for the interest rate, the value of the risk-free

---

[3] For a detailed explanation about the construction of the interest rate tree and of the bond tree, see Neftci (2008).

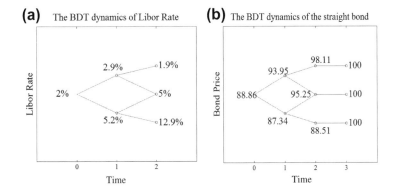

(a) The BDT dynamics of Libor Rate

(b) The BDT dynamics of the straight bond

Figure 4.2 (a) BDT dynamics of Libor rate. (b) BDT dynamics of the straight bond.

bond can be determined using an appropriate discount rate according to the interest rate dynamics.

As it can be easily seen from Figure 4.2(b), the risk-free bond is assumed to have a par value equal to 100 and the maturity is set at time $t = 3$. According to the interest rate tree, the bond price at time $t = 2$ will be equal to 98.11, 95.25 and 88.51 if the interest rate at time $t = 2$ is equal to 1.9, 5 and 12.5%, respectively. Proceeding backward, at each node, the bond price will be equal to the expected value of the bond at the successive node (children node), discounted with the appropriate interest rate. For instance, at time $t = 2$ the bond value can be equal to $(98.11 \times 0.5 + 95.25 \times 0.5)/(1 + 0.029) = 93.95$ or to $(88.51 \times 0.5 + 95.25 \times 0.5)/(1 + 0.052) = 87.34$ when the Libor rate is equal to 2.9 and 5.2% respectively. Similarly, the current observed market price of the bond is equal to $(93.95 \times 0.5 + 87.34 \times 0.5)/(1 + 0.02) = 88.86$.

4.3.2 Stock price dynamics under a stochastic interest rate

The other risk factor considered is the stock price. The main assumption of the numerical procedure is that its risk-free dynamics is described, by means of an implied binomial tree, according to the Cox–Ross–Rubinstein (CRR; Cox *et al.*, 1979) model. At each time step, stock price (S) can increase to $u \cdot S$ with probability p or decrease to $d \cdot S$ with probability $1 - p$.

It is worth noticing that the probability distribution function (PDF) is in the limit log-normal, so that the tree can efficiently been calibrated by adopting the implied stock volatility derived by means of the Black and Scholes (1973) formula. Moreover, the risk neutral probability p^* of an up movement of the stock price is equal to:

$$p^* = \frac{m - d}{u - d} \qquad (4.5)$$

where $m = 1 + L(t, t + \delta)\delta$. This implies that, at each time step, the up probability changes according to the changes of the Libor rate. To understand this point, consider that the stock price dynamics can be approximated by the following stochastic differential equation:

$$\Delta S_t = r S_t \Delta + \sigma S_t \sqrt{\Delta} \varepsilon_t, \qquad (4.6)$$

where S_t is the stock price at time t, r is the risk-free rate, Δ is the time distance between two observations, σ is the instantaneous volatility coefficient and ε_t can be interpreted as the outcome of a binomial random variable under the risk neutral probability p^*. Notice that as $\Delta \to 0$, ε_t tends, in distribution, to a standard normal random variable so that $\sqrt{\Delta}\varepsilon_t$ can be interpreted as a Wiener increment. As a result, the final stock price tends in distribution to a log-normal random variable. The key assumption is that the risk-free rate changes according to the BDT model described above. As the risk-free changes, the drift of Equation (4.8) also changes, but this effect is captured by the binomial tree only by means of the risk neutral probability p^* while the level of the stock price at each node depends only on the observed stock market price and on the volatility (that affects the value of u and d).

However, to decide the probability associated with each couple of possible stock price and interest rate, it is necessary to specify at each node of the tree the joint PDF of the two risk factors. An easy and "naïve" way to accomplish this task is by setting the hypothesis of independence (zero correlation) between the marginal PDFs of the two risk factors.[4] In this case, the probability of each state of the world is equal to the product of the (marginal) up or down probabilities of the stock price (p^*) and of the interest rate (q^*). Figure 4.3(a) shows an example of the joint PDF of the two risk factors at time $t = 1$.

At node A the stock price is equal to $S(0)$ and the Libor rate is equal to $L(0,1)$, while at nodes B and C the stock price increase to $S(1)u$ or decrease to $S(1)d$, respectively, whilst the Libor rate can increase to $L(1,2)u$ or decrease to $L(1,2)d$. Take for instance the

---

[4] Notice that the BDT and CRR model are adopted to extract the marginal PDF of the two risk factors.

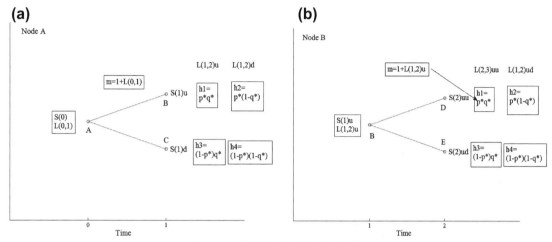

Figure 4.3 (a) Node A. (b) Node B.

case of a contemporaneous up movement of both risk factors. Under the hypothesis of zero correlation, the probability of such a state of the world is equal to $h_1 = p^*q^*$, where $q^* = 0.5$ according to the BDT model and where p^* is defined by (4.7) with $m = 1 + L(0,1)$. Figure 4(b) shows what happen when the stock price reach node B and the Libor rate increases to $L(1,2)u$.

It is, however, remarkable that the correlation between interest rate and stock price can be different from zero. Such a restrictive assumption can be released by "redistributing;" in other words, the joint probabilities calculated in the case of independency that are exposed in Figure 4.3(a and b), among the possible states of the world.

At each node, we can set the hypothesis, for instance, that the stock price and the interest rate show perfectly negative correlation by equally distributing the probabilities (in the case of independence) of contemporaneously up movements and down movements of the stock price and rate to the other two states of the world, according to Figure 4.4.

If in general one decides to equally redistribute to the other two states of the world only a percentage γ of the probability of contemporaneous up and down movements, it will result in a correlation equal to $-\gamma$. For instance, if one decides to equally redistribute only 10% of the probability of contemporaneously up and down movement to the other states of the world, it will result in a correlation of -0.1. On the contrary, if one decides to equally distribute a percentage γ of the probability of opposite movements of the considered risk factors to the other two states of the world, it will result in a correlation equal to γ.

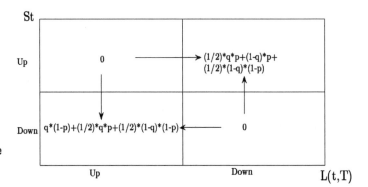

Figure 4.4 The joint PDF of the stock price and of the interest rate in case of perfectly negative correlation.

4.4 Default Risk

From Section 4.2, it is possible to notice that the interest rate adopted to discount the equity part is the risk-free yield, while for the debt part the risky yield is concerned. However, the event of default has not properly been considered. It is possible to account for the default risk by inferring the default probability from the market prices of risky bonds having an equivalent credit rating of the convertible bond or of the issuer. Let $v(t,T_i)$ and $\gamma(t,T_i)$ be the market prices, observed at time t and maturing at time T_i, with $i=1,2$ of a risk-free bond and of a risky bond respectively, having a face value equal to 1, and let RR be the recovery rate in case of default. The probability that the default occurs between time t and T_1, λ_1, can be estimated as:

$$g(t,T_1) = (1 - \lambda_1)\cdot v(t,T_1) + \lambda_1\cdot RR\cdot v(t,T_1) \qquad (4.7a)$$

$$\lambda_1 = \frac{g(t,T_1)v(t,T_1)^{-1} - 1}{RR - 1}. \qquad (4.7b)$$

Once λ_1 has been estimated and assuming that the dynamics of the risk-free bond is described according to the BDT model, it is possible to infer the probability that the default occurs between time T_1 and time T_2, λ_2, as:

$$g(t,T_2) = v(t,T_1)\left\{ \begin{array}{l} q^*(1 - \lambda_1)v(T_1,T_2)^{\mathrm{u}}[(1 - \lambda_2) + \lambda_2 RR] \\ +(1 - q^*)(1 - \lambda_1)v(T_1,T_2)^{\mathrm{d}}[(1 - \lambda_2) + \lambda_2 RR] \\ +q^*\lambda_1 RRv(T_1,T_2)^{\mathrm{u}} + (1 - q^*)\lambda_1 RRv(T_1,T_2)^{\mathrm{d}} \end{array} \right\}$$
$$= v(t,T_2)\{\lambda_1 RR + (1 - \lambda_1)[\lambda_2 RR + (1 - \lambda_2)]\}$$

$$(4.8a)$$

$$\lambda_2 = \left(\frac{g(t, T_2) v(t, T_2)^{-1} - \lambda_1 RR}{1 - \lambda_1} - 1 \right) \Big/ (RR - 1). \qquad (4.8b)$$

4.5 Pricing Convertible Bonds Subject to Interest Rate Risk and Default Risk

In this section, a numerical example is reported to describe how the arbitrage-free price of a convertible bond can be determined. Assume that the convertible pays no coupon and that the underlying stock pays no dividend during the entire period. Moreover, the convertible has a maturity of two years and a par value (F) of 100, it is immediately callable at the price of 102, and the conversion ratio is one (meaning that each convertible bond can be converted to one share of common stock). The arbitrage-free dynamics of the Libor rate is described by Figure 4.2(a) while the spread is of 3% and is constant over time. Table 4.1 reports the parameters employed to determine the price of the convertible. It is worth noting that the up probability from $t = 1$ to $t = 2$ depends on the value of the Libor rate that, at $t = 1$, stochastic. Therefore, four states of the world are considered, each of probability h_i, with $i = 1, \ldots, 4$.

More specifically, h_1 and h_3 are, respectively, the probabilities of a contemporaneous up and down movement of stock price and Libor rate, while h_2 and h_4 are the probabilities of opposite movements of the two risk factors (the stock price increases—the Libor rate decreases and *vice versa*), respectively. Since at time $t = 0$ the Libor rate is not a random variable, only two states of the world are concerned, so that p^* represents the probability of an up movement of the stock price from $t = 0$ to $t = 1$.

Table 4.1. Parameters

$S(0)$	90	CP	102	p^*	0.52
$L(0,1)$	2%	$v(0,1)$	0.98	q^*	0.5
$L(0,2)$	3%	$v(0,2)$	0.94	h_1	0.23
$S(0,1)$	3%	$\phi(0,1)$	0.95	h_2	0.29
$S(0,2)$	3%	$\phi(0,2)$	0.89	h_3	0.22
$\sigma(S)$	30%	$\gamma(L,S)$	−0.1	h_4	0.26
$\sigma[L(0,2)]$	20%	F	100		

To begin with, as in the basic model explained in Section 4.2.3, it is necessary to start by constructing the stock tree and by setting the payoff of the convertible at time $t = 2$. In doing this, it is necessary to pay attention to the default event. For this reason, we have two basic scenarios for each state of the world—one where the default occurs between $t = 1$ and $t = 2$, and the other where the default does not occur. The convertible bond tree is shown in Figure 4.5.

Since the event of default is included in the model, we have tree columns at each node: The first column is the payoff in the case the default does not occur; the second is the payoff in case of default; the third is the "certain equivalent" of the two states. For example, when using node D, E and B, at node D the stock price is 146.98 and, if default does not occur, the bondholder will decide to convert. The convertible bond value is thus formed only by the equity part that is equal to 146.98.

On the contrary, if the default occurs, the bondholder will receive only the face value times the recovery rate, the convertible bond value is formed only by the equity part and is equal to 30. The certain equivalent is the expected value of the two cases, calculated by means of the default probability λ_2. More precisely, the certain equivalent of the equity part and of the bond part are $0\lambda_2 + 146.98(1 - \lambda_2) = 140.93$ and $30\lambda_2 + 0(1 - \lambda_2) = 1.22$, respectively. At the same time, the payoff at node E can be calculated. In this case, the equity part is zero

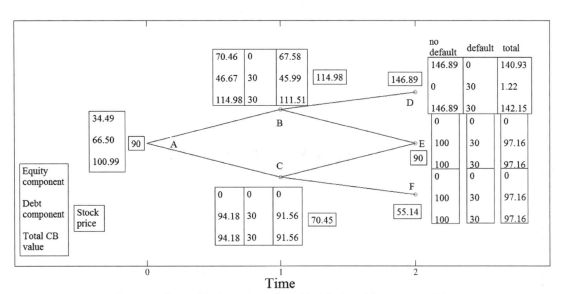

Figure 4.5 Convertible bond dynamics with default and interest rate risk.

irrespective of the default event, while the debt part will be 100 or 30 if the default occurs.

Once the certain equivalent has been calculated for the equity and the debt part and for the convertible bond value, it is necessary to discount it using as (stochastic) discount rate, the Libor rate for both the equity and the debt part. In particular, notice that node E corresponds to an up movement of the stock price. Thus, the discount rate is 5.2 and 2.9 with probability equal to h_1 and h_2, respectively. On the contrary, node D corresponds to a down movement of the stock price, and for this reason, the discount rate is 5.2 and 2.9 with probability h_3 and h_4, respectively. At node B the equity part is therefore equal to $(140.93/1.052)h_1 + (140.93/1.029)h_2 + (0/1.052)h_3 + (0/1.029)$ $h_4 = 70.46$, while the debt part is $(1.22/1.052)h_1 + (1.22/1.029)$ $h_2 + (97.16/1.052)h_3 + (97.16/1.029)h_4 = 45.42$. The convertible bond value at node B is therefore equal to the sum of the two parts (115.88) and, if default does not occur between $t = 0$ and $t = 1$, the issuer will decide to call the convertible bond, whose total value is therefore given by the stock price. This is the value of the convertible bond at node B (if default does not occur) because the bondholder decides to convert because the conversion value is higher than the call price. Rolling back the tree, it is possible to get the $t = 0$ value of the convertible. Notice that calculating the present value of the certain equivalent from $t = 1$ to $t = 0$ is similar to the basic case because the interest rate between these two dates is not a random variable.

4.6 Conclusion

This paper illustrates how to apply an innovative numerical procedure for pricing convertible bonds. Such a procedure accounts for two sources of risk: The stock price and the spot Libor rate. Moreover, it takes into account the default of the issuer, not simply discounting the bond part at a risky rate, but considering the event of default as a possible state of the world. The main drawback of the procedure proposed is that it does not take into account the possible correlation between the two risk factors and the default probability. In fact, it can be noticed that as the stock price decreases, the default is more likely to occur, while the opposite can be said about the relationship between the interest rate and the stock price. This point is, on the contrary, captured by pricing models within a structural approach, where the default is characterized by a market value of the firm lower than the market value of its liabilities.

Nevertheless, it is worth noting that such a procedure represents a good compromise between the computational burden that in general characterizes convertible bond pricing and calibration efficiency. This way it is possible to combine the main features of the CRR model for stock price modeling and the BDT model to describe the Libor rate dynamics, so that an efficient calibration to the observed market data can be performed. Moreover, the correlation between interest rate and stock price, that is neglected very often when binomial trees are concerned, is also taken into account, even if in this case the issue of computing such a parameter arises.

Note

Although the paper is the result of a joint effort of the authors, Section 4.1 is due to R.C., whilst Sections 4.2–4.6 are due to A.De S.

References

Black, F., Derman, E., Toy, W., 1990. A one-factor model of interest rates and its application to treasury bond options. Financial Analysts Journal 46 (1), 33–39.

Black, F., Scholes, M., 1973. The pricing of options and corporate liabilities. The Journal of Political Economy 81 (3), 637–654.

Brennan, M.J., Schwartz, E.S., 1977. Convertible bonds: valuation and optimal strategies for call and conversion. Journal of Finance 32 (5), 1699–1715.

Brennan, M.J., Schwartz, E.S., 1980. Analyzing convertible bonds. Journal of Financial and Quantitative Analysis 15 (4), 907–929.

Cocozza, R., De Simone, A., 2011a. One numerical procedure for two risk factors modeling Munich Personal RePEc Archive. http://mpra.ub.uni-muenchen.de/30859/.

Cocozza, R., De Simone, A., 2011b. The pricing of equity-linked contingent claims under a lognormal short rate dynamics. Presented at the International Conference on Applied Financial Economics Samos.

Cocozza, R., De Simone, A., Di Lorenzo, E., Sibillo, M., 2011. Participating policies: Risk and value drivers in a financial management perspectives. Presented at the 14th Applied Stochastic Models and Data Analysis Conference Rome.

Cox, J.C., Ross, S.A., Rubinstein, M., 1979. Option pricing: a simplified approach. Journal of Financial Economics 7 (3), 229–263.

Duffie, D., Singleton, K.J., 1999. Modeling term structure of defaultable bonds. Review of Financial Studies 12 (4), 687–720.

Hull, J.C., 2009. Options, futures and other derivatives. Prentice-Hall, Englewood Cliffs, NJ.

Hung, M.-W., Wang, J.-Y., 2002. Pricing convertible bonds subject to default risk. The Journal of Derivatives 10 (2), 75–87.

Ingersoll Jr., J.E., 1977. A contingent-claims valuation of convertible securities. Journal of Financial Economics 4 (3), 289–321.

Jarrow, R.A., Turnbull, S.M., 1995. Pricing derivatives on financial securities subject to credit risk. The Journal of Finance 50 (1), 53–85.

Merton, R.C., 1973. Theory of rational option pricing. The Bell Journal of Economics and Management Science 4 (1), 141–183.

Merton, R.C., 1974. On the pricing of corporate debt: the risk structure of interest rates. The Journal of Finance 29 (2), 449–470.

Neftci, S., 2008. Principles of Financial Engineering. Academic Press, New York.

Tsiveriotis, K., Fernandes, C., 1998. Valuing convertible bonds with credit risk. The Journal of Fixed Income 8 (2), 95–102.

CREDIT VALUATION ADJUSTMENTS— MATHEMATICAL FOUNDATIONS, PRACTICAL IMPLEMENTATION AND WRONG WAY RISKS

Marcus R. W. Martin* and Stefan Reitz**

*Darmstadt University of Applied Sciences, Competence Center Stochastics and Operations Research (CCSOR),
**University of Applied Sciences, Stuttgart

CHAPTER OUTLINE

5.1 Introduction

According to the Basel Committee, counterparty credit risk (CCR) resulting from migrations rather than defaults accounted for more than two-thirds of losses during the credit crunch of 2007–2008 (Basel Committee on Banking Supervision, 2009, 2011).

Rethinking Valuation and Pricing Models. http://dx.doi.org/10.1016/B978-0-12-415875-7.00005-1

Since then the market practice of pricing over-the-counter (OTC) derivatives has changed dramatically, forcing the industry to include credit valuation adjustments (CVAs) as an essential pricing component: In particular, 2011 can for sure be called "the year of CVAs" as proposed by *Risk* magazine (Carver, 2011). While the search for a consistent theoretical pricing framework—including bilateral CVAs as well as liquidity and funding constraints—is still ongoing (Castagna, 2011), we aim at reporting the mathematical foundations of CVA calculation and discuss some current issues in implementing it, also addressing potential model risks arising in this context. We will have a closer look at the impact of wrong way risk (WWR) on future exposures focusing on a simple "working example." Thereby, we demonstrate that the alpha multiplier, a former International Swaps and Derivatives Association proposal adapted by the Basel Committee in the Basel regulations to capture the impact of WWRs, might be too low in certain stylized cases.

Therefore, we will provide the mathematical foundations for measuring unilateral as well as bilateral CVAs in Section 5.2. Furthermore, we discuss open problems in efficiently calculating and practically implementing CVA in Section 5.3 where we will also have a closer look at WWRs in a case study. Finally, we will also discuss aspects of model risks occurring in CVA calculations in Section 5.4, before we conclude with some outlooks and prospects in Section 5.5.

5.2 Mathematical Foundations of CVA

5.2.1 Notation and basics from derivatives pricing theory

In arbitrage-free markets the price of a derivative is the expected value of future cash flows, where the expected value is calculated using an appropriate probability measure, the so-called martingale measure or pricing measure (Brigo and Mercurio, 2006). More precisely, for every numéraire, i.e. the price process (N_t) of a traded asset with positive value and without any coupon or dividend payments, there exists a (unique) probability measure, the martingale measure Q_N, such that the fair value (price) of a (derivatives) payment X without default risk at future time $T > 0$ can be calculated as:

$$PV_0 = N_0 \cdot E_{Q_N}\left(\frac{X}{N_T}\right),$$

where $E_{Q_N}(\cdot)$ denotes the expected value operator.

A popular numéraire is given by $N_t = B(t, T)$, i.e. the price at time t of a risk-free zero bond with face value 1 and expiry date T. The martingale measure belonging to this numéraire is called the time T forward measure and denoted by Q_T. It is easy to see that under the measure Q_T we can calculate the time T forward value of a traded asset with price S_t (without coupon or dividend payments) as $E_{Q_T}(S_T)$: The forward value is defined as the strike-price K, which makes the price of a T maturing forward contract with payoff $S_t - K$ to zero:

$$0 = N_0 \cdot E_{Q_T}\left(\frac{S_T - K}{N_T}\right) = B(0, T) \cdot E_{Q_T}\left(\frac{S_T - K}{1}\right) \Leftrightarrow K = E_{Q_T}(S_T).$$

For calculating $E_{Q_T}(S_T)$ it is important to understand that in an arbitrage-free market the discounted price processes of tradable assets (without coupons or dividends) are martingales, i.e. their expected value as seen from time t equals their value at time t. This implies the relation:

$$E_{Q_N}(S_t/N_t) = S_0/N_0,$$

for every chosen numéraire (N_t). If we apply this statement to time T forward value, we can write:

$$E_{Q_T}(S_T) = E_{Q_T}(S_T/B(T, T)) = S_0/B(0, T).$$

Hence, we have found an expression for the time T forward value:

$$S_0^{fwd} := S_0/B(0, T).$$

An important property of the time T forward measure is that even in case of stochastic interest rates, we can separate the expression $1/N_t = 1/B(t, T)$ from the expected value operator. The price of payoff X without default risk at T under the measure Q_T is:

$$PV_0 = N_0 \cdot E_{Q_N}\left(\frac{X}{N_T}\right) = B(0, T) \cdot E_{Q_T}\left(\frac{X}{1}\right) = B(0, T) \cdot E_{Q_T}(X).$$

5.2.2 CCR and CVA

Up to now we have considered the pricing of future cash flows without any default risk, i.e. CCR. The CCR is defined in the Basel rules as the risk that the counterparty to a transaction could default before the final settlement of the transaction's cash flows. An economic loss would occur if the transactions or portfolio of transactions with the counterparty has a positive economic value at the time of default.

Accounting for CCR in derivatives pricing is done via a CVA, which is a price adjustment. The CVA is obtained by pricing the counterparty risk component of an over-the-counter deal or a securities financing transaction (SFT), similarly to how one would price a credit derivative.

The CVA for an OTC or SFT contract depends on the volatility of the underlying risk factors, the correlation between the underlying risk factors and default of the counterparty, and the counterparty credit which spreads volatility. Thus, it is model dependent and impacted by model risks (as we will discuss in Section 5.4).

In case the references underlying and the counterparty are (strongly) correlated in the wrong direction we speak of "WWR," which can severely impact the expected exposure and, hence, the CVA. We will discuss the implications and study the impact in a case study in Section 5.3 in more detail.

The calculation of CVA depends on the presence of collateral or netting agreements since counterparty risk is reduced in theses situations. In general, collateral is a guarantee (liquid and secure asset or cash) that is deposited in a collateral account in favor of the investor party facing the exposure. A netting agreement is the agreement to net all positions towards a counterparty in the event of the counterparty default. This way positions with negative present value can be offset by positions with positive present value and counterparty risk is reduced.

Here, we will consider only a case without collateral or netting agreements.

Investors, who considers themselves to be default-free (unilateral case), price future cash flows in an OTC contract reflecting the CCR (indicated by D) under the time T forward measure as:

$$PV_0^D = PV_0 - E_{Q_T}\left(LGD \cdot 1_{\{0 < \tau_C \leq T\}} \cdot B(0, \tau_C) \cdot \max(PV_{\tau_C}, 0)\right), \quad (5.1)$$

where the counterparty's default time is denoted by τ_C and the loss rate for unsecured claims by LGD (loss given default). Furthermore, PV_t denotes the present value of all future cash flows between t and the final maturity T without default risk and $1_{\{0 < \tau_C \leq T\}}$ is the default indicator function. So the above formula states that the present value with CCR $\left(PV_0^D\right)$ is the difference between the risk-free present value (PV_0) and the expression:

$$CVA := E_{Q_T}\left(LGD \cdot 1_{\{0 < \tau_C \leq T\}} \cdot B(0, \tau_C) \cdot \max(PV_{\tau_C}, 0)\right), \quad (5.2)$$

which measures the present value of the realized loss in case of a counterparty default event at time τ_C.

From the formula it becomes clear that the inclusion of counterparty risk adds a level of optionality to the payoff. In particular, model-independent products like swaps become model-dependent also in the underlying market.

We suppose now that we allow for both parties to default (bilateral case). Then we have:

$$PV_0^D = PV_0 - CVA + DVA,$$

where:

$$CVA = E_{Q_T}\left(LGD_C \cdot 1_{A_1 \cup A_2} \cdot B(0, \tau_C) \cdot \max(PV_{\tau_C}, 0)\right),$$

and:

$$DVA = E_{Q_T}\left(LGD_I \cdot 1_{A_3 \cup A_4} \cdot B(0, \tau_I) \cdot \max(-PV_{\tau_I}, 0)\right).$$

Within these formulas, C refers to the counterparty and I refers to the investor who deals with the counterparty. The term *DVA* is the debit valuation adjustment, which is positive to the investor. The events A_1-A_4 in the indicator functions are defined as follows and describe the possible order of the counterpart's and the investor's default time and the maturity, respectively (Brigo, 2010):

$$A_1 := \{\tau_C \leq \tau_I \leq T\}, \quad A_2 := \{\tau_C \leq T \leq \tau_I\},$$
$$A_3 := \{\tau_I \leq \tau_C \leq T\}, \quad A_4 := \{\tau_I \leq T \leq \tau_C\}.$$

We observe that in the bilateral case the present value increases if the credit quality of the investor worsens and *vice versa* (the credit quality of the counterparty being unchanged). Pricing derivatives in the bilateral case is very complex, since two credit spreads are involved together with their correlations and the correlations to the underlying asset.

In the unilateral case, in order to calculate PV_0^D we have to come up with a model for the counterparty default time τ_C as well as the underlying of the contract (including correlation among these variables).

A typical approach might be to use a short-rate model for modeling the interest rate dynamics (in the case of interest rate derivatives) or a Black–Scholes dynamics for an equity deriva-tive and, for example, a Cox–Ingersoll–Ross process (CIR process) for modeling stochastic intensity rates $\lambda(t)$, which is defined by:

$$\lambda(t) = y(t) + \theta(t),$$
$$dy(t) = \alpha \cdot (\mu - y(t)) \cdot dt + \sigma \cdot \sqrt{y(t)} dW_t.$$

We then have:

$$Q_T(\tau_C \le t) = 1 - E_{Q_T}\left(\exp\left(-\int_0^t \lambda(u)du\right)\right).$$

The calibration of the CIR process is done by fitting model default probabilities to default probabilities stripped from counterparty credit default swaps (CDS) quotes assuming deterministic interest rates; $\theta(t)$ is necessary to match the given CDS curve. In fact, we will review some important issues regarding the practical implementation of the CIR process in Section 5.3.

An approximation of Formula (1) is realized via default bucketing (where still a joint model for τ_C and the underlying variable of the contract is needed, but the *LGD* is already assumed to be deterministic and, hence, decoupled from the loss and the asset value process(es) driving the present value of the counterparty's portfolio):

$$PV_0^D \approx PV_0 - LGD \cdot \sum_{j=1}^{n} B(0, T_j) \cdot E_{Q_T}\left(1_{\{T_{j-1} \le \tau_C \le T_j\}} \cdot \max(PV_{T_j}, 0)\right),$$

(5.3)

where $T_n = T$.

Assuming independence between the default events and the underlying variable of the contract (i.e. ignoring potential WWR), we obtain:

$$PV_0^D \approx PV_0$$

$$- LGD \cdot \sum_{j=1}^{n} B(0, T_j) \cdot Q_T\left(1_{\{T_{j-1} \le \tau_C \le T_j\}}\right) \cdot E_{Q_T}\left(\max(PV_{T_j}, 0)\right). \quad (5.4)$$

Here, only default probabilities are needed for pricing, but no stochastic model for default events is necessary. Note that in both Formulas (3) and (4) there is still an optionality involved which is applied to the risk factors driving the underlying process.

5.3 Practical Implementation: Issues and (Wrong Way) Risks

The implementation of CVA calculation faces several practical challenges that will be discussed in Section 5.3.1 before we have an in-depth look on the impact of WWR on capital and (unilateral) CVA calculations in Section 5.3.2.

5.3.1 Practical implementation—open issues and risks

Implementing a system for calculating CVA means extending existing front- and mid-office systems according to the increasing level of complexity as introduced above. This leads to several challenging issues that start at the very generic level: The definition of CVA was still not consistent among market participants, as one can see from the latest annual reports of different financial institutions. For example, some institutions still use a credit risk-type approach via reserves instead of actively hedging CVA. A particular facet of this discussion is still the question whether unilateral or bilateral CVA (i.e. CVA and DVA) has to be implemented.

Some of the most challenging issues from a practical point of view are market data availability and calibration of the CVA models. As a price component, risk-neutral or market-implied parameters (e.g. drifts, volatilities and correlations) have to be used as long as these are available while historic market data is typically used as a fallback solution. In this context, the question of having liquid market data plays a crucial role and goes along with a segmentation of counterparties since market information, e.g. for small and mid cap corporates, might be rather scarce: CDS spreads will, in general, not be available for all counterparties or all maturities, such that a mapping with regard to sector and rating of the counterparty might be necessary. Furthermore, as bond spreads may serve as fallback, these might introduce a certain bias due to the fact that these spreads carry funding and tax components.

The way of managing CCRs and CVAs has also seen significant changes in recent years: While prior to the financial crisis the widely used practice to deal with CVAs was more of an accounting- or reserve-based approach, recent years have seen an increasing set-up of CVA trading desks that actively manage CVAs centrally for their institution.

Technically, recent years brought along an ever-increasing complexity of pricing models even for collateralized plain vanilla products due to a multiple-curve interest rate framework in CVA calculations (Crépey, 2011), the impact of close-out conventions on CVAs (Brigo and Morini, 2011), and the current and future role of central counterparties and, more generally, multiparty collateralization and margining structures (Albanese et al., 2012). Even ignoring these advanced topics and resorting to the comparatively simple pre-crisis approaches, the problems of adequately capturing all products (e.g. exotic options) for real-time pricing and hedging CVAs is still evolving (Capriotti *et al.*, 2011). Beside pricing models and market data supply, validating and back-testing CCR systems (on risk factor, trade, portfolio and netting set level) and stress testing clearly show that an efficient data model and IT architecture is inevitable (Albanese *et al.*, 2011; Cesari *et al.*, 2009; Schlener 2011).

The effect of positive correlation between exposure and default probability is usually called WWR and was introduced by the International Swaps and Derivatives Association Working Group on Counterparty Risk in 2001 (International Swaps and Derivatives Association, 2001):

> *The ISDA working group distinguish between specific WWR, which arises through poorly structured transactions, for example those collateralized by own or related party shares; and general or conjectural WWR, where the credit quality of the counterparty may for non-specific reasons be held to be correlated with a macroeconomic factor which also affects the value of derivatives transactions.*

According to Basel III, specific WWR positions have to be carved out from netting sets, have to be closely monitored by counter-party risk management and are charged with extra regulatory capital, while general WWR is still assumed to be captured applying the so-called alpha multiplier to the expected positive exposure in the regulatory internal model method; for an overview, we refer to Cesari *et al.* (2009), Gregory (2010), and Hahn and Reitz (2011).

For the mathematical foundations and different approaches to include WWR in exposure and CVA calculations, we refer to Cesari *et al.* (2009), Hull and White (2011), and Rosen (2011).

5.3.2 Case study on the impact of WWR

As a simple example for demonstrating the impact of (specific) WWR on counterparty exposure and CVA, we consider as counterparty a company that sells puts and calls on its own stock to a financial institution. We consider this transaction from the perspective of the financial institution that buys the derivative. We closely follow Martin (2012) in this section and refer to that paper for further details.

5.3.2.1 Scenario generation—with and without WWR

For an integrated modeling of equity and default dynamics to capture WWR, let us assume that the default of the firm c is modeled according to the classical Merton model. Therefore, starting from today's firm value FV_0 let the firm value evolve according to:

$$dFV_t = r \cdot FV_t \cdot dt + \sigma \cdot FV_t \cdot dW_t, \tag{5.5}$$

i.e. following a geometric Brownian motion with risk-neutral drift given by a risk-neutral rate r and firm value volatility σ. A default event occurs whenever the firm value FV_T at a pre-specified time horizon T falls below the firm's total liabilities which is comprised by equity S_t and by its debt modeled as a zero bond with face value N and maturity T. Since, under these assumptions, equity represents a call option on the firm's assets with maturity T and strike price of N we can derive the corresponding stock price:

$$S_t = (FV_t - N)^+, \tag{5.6}$$

at each $t \in [0, T]$. In particular, in case of a default, the stock is worth zero which directly impacts the present value of the put or call option of the firm which is given by the Black–Scholes formula, under the assumption of constant equity volatility σ_S:

$$
PV_t = Ke^{-r(T-t)}\Phi\left(-\frac{\log\left(\frac{S_t}{K}\right) + \left(r - \frac{\sigma_S^2}{2}\right)(T-t)}{\sigma_S^2\sqrt{T-t}}\right)
$$

$$
- S_t\Phi\left(-\frac{\log\left(\frac{S_t}{K}\right) + \left(r + \frac{\sigma_S^2}{2}\right)(T-t)}{\sigma_S^2\sqrt{T-t}}\right) \tag{5.7}
$$

for $t \in [0, T)$ and $PV_T = (K - S_T)^+$ for $t = T$.

The firm value model is to be calibrated to market data, e.g. specifying the risk-neutral dynamics of the firm value process from two implied volatilities of liquidly traded options on that company (for details, see Hull *et al.*, 2005; Stamicar and Finger, 2005). For demonstration purposes it suffices to consider, as a working example, a firm with today's equity price $S_0 = 100$, a face value of debt of $N = 200$, an implied 1-year equity volatility $\sigma_S = 40\%$ and risk-neutral interest rate $r = 3\%$ such that we can infer today's firm value $FV_0 = 294.0985$ and an annual firm value volatility $\sigma = 13.6\%$.

Based on these settings, we generate $M = 5000$ scenarios of the firm value $FV_t = FV_{t_k}(\ell)$, $\ell \in \{1, ..., M\}$, at each point of the equidistant time grid $t_k := k \cdot \Delta t$, $k \in \left\{1, ..., \frac{T}{\Delta t} = n\right\}$, by discretizing Equation (5.5) using monthly time steps $\Delta t = 1/12$ according to the Euler Maruyama scheme for $T = 5$ years (for details, see Kloeden *et al.*, 2003). For each of these scenarios we derive the corresponding equity values $S_{t_k}(\ell) = (FV_{t_k}(\ell) - N)^+$ of the firm per grid point and scenario according to Equation (5.6), and revalue the respective put and call options for these applying well-known Black–Scholes Formula (5.7) obtaining the future market values $PV_{t_k}(\ell)$ at a point of the equidistant time grid.

In the classical setting, i.e. stand-alone calculation of the counterparty's exposure and CVA without recognition of WWR, the equity process is modeled directly through a geometric Brownian motion with risk-neutral drift and constant equity volatility σ_S by:

$$dS_t = r \cdot S_t \cdot dt + \sigma_S \cdot S_t \cdot dW_t^S, \qquad (5.8)$$

starting from $S_0 = 100$. The future market values are then derived applying the Black–Scholes Formula (7). Here, the future equity values $S_t = S_{t_k}(\ell)$ are generated for $M = 5000$ scenarios $\ell \in \{1, ..., M\}$ per bucket of the equidistant time grid $t_k := k \cdot \Delta t, \quad k \in \left\{1, ..., \frac{T}{\Delta t} = n\right\}$, by discretizing Equation (5.8) using monthly time steps $\Delta t = 1/12$ according to the Euler Maruyama scheme for $T = 5$ years, and the future market values $PV_t = PV_{t_k}(\ell)$ of the put option are calculated according to Black–Scholes Formula (7) for each scenario $\ell \in \{1, ..., M\}$.

5.3.2.2 Expected positive exposure, alpha and (unilateral) CVA

First, we want to compare the exposure profiles visualized by the 5 and 95% quantiles of the future market values (which are called potential future exposures at confidence level 5 and 95%, respectively) and the expected value of the non-negative future market values (which is called expected exposure) of the at-the-market (ATM) equity put option on the company's stock with maturity $T = 5$ years and a strike $K = S_0 = 100$ per time step.

Figure 5.1 displays the resulting exposure profiles due to classical implementation as dashed graphs (potential future exposure at 5 and 95% confidence level (thin) and expected exposure (thick)), i.e. without taking into account that the counterparty and the underlying ATM make the equity option identical, while the solid graphs display the exposure profile (potential future exposure at 5 and 95% confidence level (thin) and expected exposure (thick)) in the case of integrated modeling of the stock price and the default of the counterparty as described above, i.e. including the specific WWR.

We observe that in at least 5% of all scenarios the counterparty defaults after 22 months, which yields the present value of the put

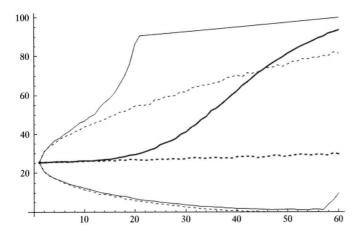

Figure 5.1 Exposure profiles (5 and 95% quantiles of the future market values as well as the expected values of the positive future market values) of the ATM put option where the WWR is recognized (solid graphs) and the WWR is not recognized (dashed graphs).

option as potential future exposure at a confidence level of 95% in the case of default of the counterparty, i.e.:

$$PV_{\tau_C} = e^{-r(T-\tau_C)} \cdot (K - S_T)^+ = e^{-r(T-\tau_C)} \cdot (K - 0)^+ = e^{-r(T-\tau_C)} \cdot K,$$

since if the counterparty defaults at time $\tau_C \in (0, T]$ we obtain $S_t = S_{\tau_C} = 0$ for all $t \in [\tau_C, T]$. Consequently, the expected exposure is a strictly monotonically increasing function that severely increases the regulatory and economic capital in comparison to the case where the specific WWR is neglected. For calculating regulatory or economic capital, typically the time-weighted expected exposure is chosen, which is called the expected positive exposure, i.e.:[1]

$$EPE_T = \frac{1}{T} \cdot \int_0^T \max(0, PV_t) \mathrm{d}t \approx \sum_{k=1}^{T/\Delta t} \max(0, PV_{k \cdot \Delta t}) \cdot \frac{\Delta t}{T}.$$

Overall, the ratio of integrated expected positive exposure EPE_T^{WWR}, i.e. fully capturing WWR, versus WWR-neglecting expected positive exposure EPE_T^{woWWR} for the put option is approximately given by $\tilde{\alpha} \approx \left(EPE_T^{WWR} / EPE_T^{woWWR} \right) = (50.6468/27.6292) = 1.8331$, which exceeds the regulatory alpha multiplier $\alpha = 1.4$ by about 31%.

While this calculation already indicates that economic and regulatory capital for absorbing counterparty default risks could

---

[1] The definition of the expected positive exposure for regulatory capital needs to be modified according to a capital horizon of one year, and certain conservative rollover assumptions and an "effective" maturity adjustment (Hahn and Reitz, 2011).

be seriously underestimated, a similar effect can be observed for unilateral CVA capturing WWR. Here, we will only consider the unilateral case and calculate it approximately by means of Equation (5.3) for the scenarios and equidistant time grid $T_k := t_k = k \cdot \Delta t$ generated as described above, i.e. we have:

$$CVA \approx LGD \cdot \sum_{k=1}^{n} B(0, t_k) \cdot E_{Q_T} \left(1_{\{t_{k-1} < \tau_C \leq t_k\}} \cdot \max(PV_{t_k}, 0) \right),$$

with $LGD = 60\% = 1 - 40\%$, $B(0, t_k) = e^{-r \cdot t_k}$ and:

$$E_{Q_T} \left(1_{\{t_{k-1} < \tau_C \leq t_k\}} \cdot \max(PV_{t_k}, 0) \right)$$

$$\approx \frac{1}{M} \cdot \sum_{\ell=1}^{M} 1_{\{t_{k-1} \leq \tau_C(\ell) \leq t_k\}} \cdot \max \left(PV_{t_k}(\ell), 0 \right) \text{ for all } k \in \{1, ..., n\},$$

where the default time is given by:

$$\tau_C(\ell) = \inf\{t \quad : \quad FV_t(\ell) < N, \quad t \in \{1, ..., n\}\}.$$

Without recognizing WWR we arrive at $CVA^{\text{woWWR}} \approx 0.4349$ while taking it into account yields $CVA^{\text{WWR}} \approx 0.5878$ which exceeds the former by 30% too.

Summarizing the above results, (specific) WWRs need to be captured adequately since simple approximations may be misleading and may underestimate the total impact.

5.3.2.3 Outlook

Similarly, the corresponding call option significantly reduces the expected positive exposure and, hence, the regulatory or economic capital for absorbing the default of the counterparty.

In the case of a default event at $\tau_C \in (0, T]$ the call will expire with a zero exposure and, hence, reduce the exposure, as can

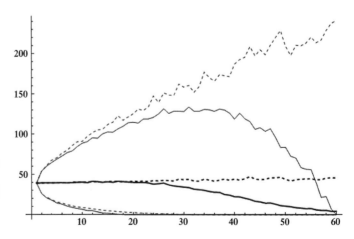

Figure 5.2 Exposure profiles (5 and 95% quantiles of the future market values as well as the expected values of the positive future market values) of the ATM call option where the WWR is recognized (solid graphs) and the WWR is not recognized (dashed graphs).

be seen Figure 5.2. In this case we obtain $\tilde{\alpha} = (EPE_T^{\mathrm{WWR}}/EPE_T^{\mathrm{woWWR}}) = (28.2997/42.7415) = 0.6621$, which is significantly lower than the regulatory alpha factor $\alpha = 1.4$ and indicates the right way risk character of a call option issued by the counterparty.

More details—including details on the regulatory capital charges—as well as the calculation of bilateral CVA can be found in the working paper of Martin (2012).

5.4 Model Risks in CVA Calculation

Calculating CVAs is even more complex than simply calculating the market value or even the future exposure of the counterparty's portfolio of transactions. For CVAs we can start with the basic three categories described in Martin (2010a, 2010b) for exposure models:

  (i) *Scenario generation risks* as those model risks (including all aspects of specification, estimation and implementation risks) as defined in the well-known model risk theory that occur by specifying the evolution of risk factors and all relevant assumptions on the choice of risk factors and time buckets as well as generating overall consistent future market scenarios.

 (ii) *Pricing model risks* as those model risks (including all aspects of specification, estimation and implementation risks) inherent to the specific requirements on instrument model pricing routines that are needed to evaluate the counterparty's positions in a fast but adequate manner.

(iii) *Aggregation risks* as those model risks (including all aspects of specification, estimation and implementation risks) occurring in the process of aggregating the counterparty's exposures, recognizing any eligible netting agreements and modeling the margin process including collateral valuations and so on. We will consider these risks in forthcoming publications in more detail, and focus on pricing and scenario generation risks here only.

In principle, calculating CVAs would just add two additional layers of model complexity on top of these three basic components as is evident from (5.2): The loss given default (or recovery rate) and the default event of the counterparty (and the investor for bilateral CVA) have to be modeled consistently with the asset value, default event and recovery rate processes already implemented for measuring the future exposure. Apart from the WWR issues outlined in Section 5.3, the resulting of model risks can be included in the scenario generation of model risks and aggregation model risks from a universal point of view. Hence, existing counterparty risk systems and model risk management processes have only to be extended with regard to these particular issues.

Recall that model weaknesses and risks have to be identified, analyzed and quantified in the model review process and stress testing process. For example, some implementations of interest or commodity scenario generators relying on CIR processes pose some severe numerical issues with particular impact on counterparty exposure and CVAs (for details, see Noé, 2011). Furthermore, Haase *et al.* (2010) provide model-free bounds for unilateral and bilateral CVA calculations that can be obtained by separately modeling the default events and market values of the counterparty's portfolio. Even stress testing itself needs to be implemented with caution as Fries (2011) points out for Monte Carlo simulations in general. These methods need to be applied, in particular, to exposure and CVA calculation models.

5.5 Summary and Prospects

Here, we have provided the mathematical foundations as well as practical implementation issues for calculating unilateral and bilateral CVAs. In a case study we took a closer look at the impact of WWR, and indicated the importance of model risks for exposure and CVA calculation. In any case, efficient IT implementation and infrastructure, and adequate management processes, in particular for complex derivatives, raise several open questions. Finally, a fully integrated theoretical framework including liquidity, funding and CCR adjustments is outstanding.

Notes

All opinions within this text are the authors' and should not be considered as being the opinions of their respective employers. None of the methods described herein is claimed to be in actual use.

References

Albanese, C., Bellaj, T., Gimonet, G., Pietronero, G., 2011. Coherent global market simulations and securization measures for counterparty credit risk. Quantitative Finance 11 (1), 1−20. Avaialble on. http://frank-oertel-math.de/Paper_of_CA_DB_and_FO_FV_31_10_2011.pdf.

Albanese, C., Brigo, D., Oertel, F., 2012. Restructuring counterparty credit risk. Working Paper. Global Valuation Ltd. Available online: http://frank-oertel-math.de/Paper_of_CA_DB_and_FO_FV_31_10_2011.pdf, August, 9th, 2012.

Basel Committee on Banking Supervision, 2009. Consultative Document: Strengthening the Resilience of the Banking Sector. Basel Committee on Banking Supervision, Basel. Revised version June 2011.

Basel Committee on Banking Supervision, 2011. Basel III: A Global Regulatory Framework for More Resilient Banks and Banking Systems. Basel Committee on Banking Supervision, Basel. Revised version June 2011.

Brigo, D., 2010. Counterparty risk pricing: intro to unilateral and bilateral CVA across asset classes with netting and collateral. Presentation at *Credit and Counterparty Risk Quant Congress Europe* London.

Brigo, D., Mercurio, F., 2006. Interest Rate Models — Theory and Practice: With Smile, Inflation and Credit. Springer, Berlin.

Brigo, D., Morini, M., 2011. Close-out convention tensions. Risk 24 (12), 74–78.

Capriotti, L., Lee, J., Peacock, M., 2011. Real time counterparty credit risk management in Monte Carlo. Risk 24 (12), 82–86.

Carver, L., 2011. The year of CVA. Risk 24 (12), 70–73.

Castagna, A., 2011. Pricing of derivatives contracts under collateral agreements: liquidity and funding value adjustments. Working Paper. Iason Ltd. Available online: http://www.iasonltd.com/FileUpload/files/pricing%20with%20collateral%202.0.pdf, August 9th, 2012.

Cesari, G., Aquilina, J., Charpillon, N., Filiopvic, Z., Lee, G., Manda, I., 2009. Modelling, Pricing, and Hedging Counterparty Credit Exposure — A Technical Guide. Springer, Berlin.

Crépey, S., 2011. A BSDE approach to counterparty risk under funding constraints. Working Paper. Laboratoire Analyse et Probabilités, Université d'Évry Val d'Essonne.

Fries, C., 2011. Stressed in Monte Carlo. Risk April, 75–70.

Gregory, J., 2010. Counterparty Credit Risk: The New Challenge for Global Financial Markets. Wiley, New York.

Haase, J., Ilg, M., Werner, R., 2010. Model-free bounds on bilateral counterparty valuation adjustment. Working Paper. Available online: http://www.defaultrisk.com/pp_other201.htm, August 9th, 2012.

Hahn, R., Reitz, S., 2011. Possibilities of estimating exposures. In: Engelmann, B., Rauhmeier, R. (Eds), The Basel II Risk Parameters. Springer, Berlin, pp. 185–200.

Hull, J.C., 2011. Options, Futures, and Other Derivatives, 8th edn). Prentice Hall, Englewood Cliffs, NJ.

Hull, J.C., White, A., 2011. CVA and wrong way risk. Working Paper. J.L. Rotman School of Management, University of Toronto.

Hull, J.C., Nelken, I., White, A., 2005. Merton's model, credit risk, and volatility skews. Journal of Credit Risk 1 (1) 1–27.

International Swaps and Derivatives Association, 2001. Letter to the Chairman of the Counterparty Risk sub-group of the Models Task Force. Basel Committee on Banking Supervision, Basel.

Kloeden, P.E., Platen, E., Schurz, H., 2003. Numerical Solution of SDE Through Computer Experiments. Springer, Berlin.

Martin, M.R.W., 2010a. Model Risk in Counterparty Exposure Modeling. In: Hoppe, Ch., Gregoriou, G.N., S.Wehn, C. (Eds), Model Risk Evaluation Handbook. McGraw-Hill, New York, pp. 365–378.

Martin, M.R.W., 2010b. Identification and classification of model risks in counterparty credit risk measurement systems. In: Rösch, D., Scheule, H. (Eds), Model Risk — Challenges and Solutions for Financial Risk Models. RISK Books/Incisive Media, London, pp. 91–110.

Martin, M.R.W., 2012. Don't take it the wrong way. Working Paper. University of Applied Sciences, Darmstadt.

Noé, M., 2011. Valuation of counterparty risk for commodity derivatives. Master Thesis. University of Applied Sciences, Darmstadt.

Rosen, D., 2011. CVA, Basel III and wrong-way risk. Presentation at *IX Risk-Lab Madrid Meeting on Financial Risks – Post Crisis Risk Management*. Madrid. Available online: http://www.risklab.es/es/jornadas/2012/Rosen%20Models%20-%20RiskLab%20Madrid%20May%202012.pdf, August 9th, 2012.

Schlener, M., 2011. Implementation und Praxis. Presentation at *PRMIA Credit Valuation Adjustments (CVA) Congress* Frankfurt.

Stamicar, R., Finger, C.C., 2005. Incorporating Equity Derivatives Into the CreditGrades Model. Risk Metrics Group, New York.

6

COUNTERPARTY CREDIT RISK AND CREDIT VALUATION ADJUSTMENTS (CVAS) FOR INTEREST RATE DERIVATIVES—CURRENT CHALLENGES FOR CVA DESKS

Birgitta Drwenski*, **Jochen Beißer****, and **Lutz Mangels*****
*CFA, Diplom Volkswirtin, **Department of Business Administration, University of Applied Sciences RheinMain, ***FRM, Master of Business Administration

CHAPTER OUTLINE

Rethinking Valuation and Pricing Models. http://dx.doi.org/10.1016/B978-0-12-415875-7.00006-3

6.1 Introduction

The current financial crisis started with the US subprime mortgage crisis. The first prominent institution to require support was Bear Stearns. Other institutions got caught in the subsequent turmoil. These bailouts and the actual default of Lehman Brothers dramatically raised the awareness of counterparty credit risk (CCR).

The fact that Lehman Brothers was not rescued caused serious concerns and the realization that other market players could fail as well. This created pressure on international interbank markets and caused a severe loss of trust between banks. Exposure to US mortgages was suddenly deemed as toxic and banks with any such exposure were regarded as "infected." Since only a handful of European banks had direct on-balance cash loan exposure to the United States, the focus swiftly shifted to indirect exposure via securitizations and credit derivatives. At this time market participants realized that the interbank market contained considerable credit risk. As a result, widening spreads between overnight rates and three-month rates were observed.

The crisis then shifted to sovereign states like Ireland, with an urgent need to recapitalize their banking systems. The amount of capital injected to strengthen banks' balance sheets jeopardized the financial stability of the sovereign itself. Still grappling with the realization that the too-big-to-fail paradigm had lost its validity, the market started to question the ability of all highly indebted European countries, not merely those recapitalizing their banking system. Credit default swap (CDS) spreads of most EU sovereigns and yield spreads to German Government bonds widened significantly in 2011. Italy, for example, did not have to bail out significant local financial institutions. Nevertheless, and despite this well-known fact, the market reassessed Italy's high debt-to-GDP ratio in autumn 2011. As a response to stressed funding conditions the European Central Bank (ECB) allotted unlimited liquidity up to three years to all European Banks that provided the needed collateral in December 2011 and again in early 2012.

The credit crisis led to a situation in which bank defaults and near defaults increased dramatically. The former belief in the too-big-to-fail concept is not valid any longer since states lose the capacity to bail out their banks. Consequently, the credit risk represented by banks is critical. Now, more than ever, it is important to adequately price default risk into derivatives contracts. Credit valuation adjustments (CVAs) are a fair value adjustment and hence also a general reserve for CCR. Changes in this domain therefore have a direct impact on the bottom line: a bank's profit and loss (P&L) account. Moreover, the introduction of Basel II CVA drives risk-weighted assets (RWAs) and regulatory capital requirements. This chapter focuses on CCR and CVA of interest rate derivatives (IRDs).

6.2 Traditional Counterparty Risk Management Approaches

High-quality counterparties were the first to trade IRDs. The decision to trade was generally based on Risk Management's approval. Then it was up to the trader's ability to price the respective derivative by taking into account all market risk factors. Trades with riskier clients generated larger profits as they allowed for wider margins. Often it was left to a sales person's experience to decide on the exact scope for wider margins. By how much one counterpart was riskier than another was merely estimated.

Trading lines were therefore pure notional limits. However, during the 1990s more experienced banks quickly changed to probability-driven approaches. Limit utilization, i.e. exposure, of interest rate swaps (IRS) was calculated by adding a factor that took account of the most severe possible changes under a given confidence interval to the trade's present value. This add-on factor was based on the observed volatility of underlying market rates.

Master agreements gained importance after the Asian and Russian crises (1997 and 1998). These agreements allow for payment netting on particular settlement dates. Master agreements published by industry organizations, such as the International Swap Dealer Association (ISDA), allow for the netting of present values across all governed trades at bankruptcy. Enforcing such agreements depends on the counterparty's jurisdiction and applicable law. Alongside international master agreements, local agreements were also established.

Additional termination events were introduced to the trade's documentation to allow counterparts to shorten the original maturity of a trade. In such events, the swap's present value is determined and exchanged. In addition, strong counterparts negotiated early termination events linked to the counterparty's rating (downgrade triggers).

Since the late 1990s, trading books suffered losses from prominent defaults that resulted in forced closeouts of derivatives contracts. Banks realized that a significant driver of IRD profitability was linked to events that could not be managed by traders: Their counterparty's credit quality. It became clear that a link between the trader's ability to value and manage market risk and Risk Management's ability to assess credit risk had been missing. This recognition led to the establishment of dedicated CVA desks, first in the United States, then in Europe.

6.3 Modeling Credit Exposure and Pricing CCR

6.3.1 Credit exposure on a derivative

CCR of a derivative is more complex to determine than credit risk of a loan because credit exposure on a derivative is bilateral, uncertain and fluctuates over time with changing market variables. In the following, we describe how credit exposure of a derivative depends on its current and future market values assuming derivatives are uncollateralized and option premiums are paid upfront.

A long position in an interest rate option constitutes an asset and always has a positive market value. If the counterparty defaults, the contract needs to be replaced in the market and the bank faces a loss. A short position in an interest rate option is a liability and the bank is not negatively affected by default of the counterparty. Depending on the value of the underlying market variables, derivatives like IRSs or forward rate agreements (FRAs) may have a positive or a negative market value for the bank.

Let $V_i(t)$ denote the time t market value of derivative i, $i = 1, ...,$ n. In the case of counterparty default, two possible outcomes can be distinguished:

- $V_i(t) \leq 0$: The bank has no credit exposure because it is not negatively affected by counterparty default.
- $V_i(t) > 0$: The bank has credit exposure and incurs a loss if the counterparty is not able to fulfill its obligations.[1]

---

[1] See Pykhtin and Zhu (2007) for the corresponding trading strategy that the bank follows in each case.

If the bank has only one derivative contract with the counterparty, the bank's credit exposure on the contract level is given by:

$$EX_i(t) = \max\{V_i(t), 0\}. \tag{6.1}$$

The bank's credit exposure for a portfolio of derivatives on the counterparty level is given by the sum of all contract-level exposures:

$$EX(t) = \sum_{i=1}^{n} EX_i(t) = \sum_{i=1}^{n} \max\{V_i(t), 0\}. \tag{6.2}$$

If m master agreements $MA_j, j = 1, \dots, m$, that allow for cash flow netting are in place, the credit exposure is given by:

$$EX(t) = \sum_{j=1}^{m} \max\left\{ \sum_{i \in MA_j} V_i(t), 0 \right\}$$
$$+ \sum_{i \notin MA_1 \cup \dots \cup MA_m} \max\{V_i(t), 0\}. \tag{6.3}$$

The first term in Equation (6.3) includes all trades belonging to a master agreement, whereas the second term includes all trades not covered by any master agreement. Comparing Equations (6.2) and (6.3) shows that master agreements reduce credit exposure on the counterparty level.

6.3.2 Determination of future credit exposure

Using Formulas (6.1) or (6.3), current credit exposure on the contract or counterparty level, respectively, is straightforward to calculate. Current exposure can be interpreted as the replacement cost of the derivative in the case the counterparty defaults. Even more important than the current replacement cost is the potential replacement cost of the derivative at each time point until maturity. Banks need to know future credit exposure for pricing, hedging, risk management and regulatory purposes. However, future credit exposure is more difficult to determine than current credit exposure because the future value of a derivative is unknown at present. To emphasize the uncertainty of future credit exposure, it is often called potential credit exposure. In order to assess potential credit exposure, probabilistic methods have to be applied. Monte Carlo simulation, historical simulation and approximation methods using option valuation are among the most common approaches. We briefly outline the simulation approach following De Prisco and Rosen (2005) and

Pykhtin and Zhu (2007), and the idea behind the approximation method.

The simulation approach determines the distribution of potential credit exposure on counterparty level. Based on the distribution, various estimates of potential credit exposure can be calculated. The simulation algorithm includes three steps.

6.3.2.1 Step 1: Scenario generation

All risk factors influencing the value of the derivatives have to be identified first. Typical examples for risk factors of IRDs are interest rates and foreign exchange (FX) rates. For each risk factor, a process for its evolution has to be specified. Consistent modeling of interest rates requires a term structure model like the Heath–Jarrow–Morton model, while FX rates can be modeled using a (generalized) geometric Brownian motion. Using an appropriate stochastic model for each risk factor and calibrating the model to market data, various future market scenarios are generated for a set of simulation dates. For pricing and hedging purposes scenarios are generated under the risk-neutral probability measure by calibrating risk factor models to implied market data. For regulatory purposes the real-world probability measure is used calibrating risk factor processes to historical data.

6.3.2.2 Step 2: Instrument valuation and exposure profiles

Next, each derivative is valued at each future simulation date using the realizations of the corresponding risk factors generated in Step 1. In contrast to front office pricing, instrument valuation in this context is more difficult. Pykhtin and Zhu (2007) mention as an example that path-dependent derivatives, such as American, Asian or Barrier Options, are more difficult to value at future dates as information about the entire path of the underlying up to the valuation date is necessary to price them.

For each simulation of a risk factor we get a future value of the derivative, which, inserted into Formula (6.1), results in the corresponding potential credit exposure on the contract level. Various simulation runs yield the distribution of potential credit exposure. Figure 6.1 illustrates possible values of the derivative and the corresponding density functions of the distribution of potential credit exposure after six and 12 months. Note that for negative values of the derivative credit exposure is zero.

Based on the probability distribution of potential exposure, various measures of potential credit exposure can be calculated.

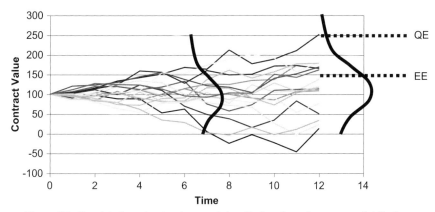

Figure 6.1 Simulated contract values and density function of exposure distribution.

Common measures are expected exposure (EE) or quantile exposure (QE). At each simulation date EE is computed as the mean of simulated exposure values, whereas QE is calculated as a specific quantile of the exposure distribution. Often a 95 or 99% quantile is used.

Future exposure can be visualized in so-called exposure profiles (Figure 6.2). The shape of the exposure profile depends on the derivative's cash flow pattern and is characteristic for each derivative, regardless of whether exposure values are based on EE or QE. Whereas exposure profiles of multi-cash-flow products without principal exchange at maturity like IRSs typically have a hump-backed form, exposure profiles of single-cash-flow products like FRAs, options, zero coupon structures or multi-cash-flow products with principal exchange at maturity like cross-currency swaps are upward sloping and peak at the maturity of the transaction.

Two offsetting effects influence the exposure profile of multi-cash-flow trades: Diffusion and amortization. Looking further

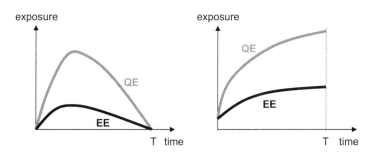

Figure 6.2 Exposure profile of IRS (left) and option (right).

into the future, risk factors are less predictable as their variability increases. Outstanding cash flows become more uncertain. Thus, the diffusion effect tends to increase the credit exposure of a trade. The amortization effect works in the opposite direction. Over time, some cash flows are realized and the amount of outstanding cash flows decreases. Thus, uncertainty and exposure are reduced.

6.3.2.3 Step 3: Portfolio aggregation

After all instruments are valued, at each simulation date potential credit exposure on the counterparty level is computed using Formula (6.3). Figure 6.3 illustrates the counterparty exposure based on 10 different risk factor scenarios. Each path represents a possible evolution of the bank's potential credit exposure on the counterparty level over time for a specific risk factor scenario. For each simulation date we get a distribution of potential credit exposure. As in Step 2, it is possible to calculate different measures of potential credit exposure based on the simulated distribution.

Using a simulation approach to determine potential credit exposure is very time consuming and requires considerable IT resources. Approximation methods based on option pricing theory are an alternative to compute potential credit exposure. However, these apply only to single trades and do not allow for netting. For example, the current value of the exposure of a 10-year swap in three years equals the premium of a three-year swaption to enter into a swap with a maturity of seven years.

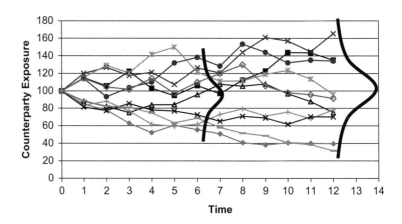

Figure 6.3 Potential credit exposure distribution on the counterparty level.

6.3.3 Calculation of CVAs

Apart from market risk, the fair value of a derivative should also reflect CCR. A CVA is defined as the difference of the value of the derivative without and with CCR (see e.g. Assefa et al (2011)):

$$CVA := V^{\text{default–free}} - V^{\text{risky}}.$$

The CVA is the fair value of CCR and represents the cost of hedging against default. As a hedging cost, the CVA should be included in the derivative's premium charged to the counterparty. The CVA is also interpreted as the expected loss arising from counterparty default. We determine the CVA using risk-neutral valuation and the following notation: R denotes the expected recovery rate, $B(0,\cdot)$ is the discount factor, $EX(\cdot)$ is the stochastic counterparty credit exposure taking into account netting agreements, $F(\cdot)$ is the cumulative density function of the risk-neutral probability of counterparty default, T is the longest maturity of all derivatives with the counterparty and $E_Q[\cdot]$ is the expectation under a risk-neutral probability measure Q.

If the counterparty defaults at a random time $\tau \in (0,T)$, the bank's expected discounted exposure at default under a risk-neutral probability measure Q is given by:

$$E_Q[B(0,\tau)\cdot EX(\tau)].$$

In the case of counterparty default, the bank recovers a certain percentage R of the outstanding exposure, so that the bank's loss given default in τ is:

$$(1-R)\cdot E_Q[B(0,\tau)\cdot EX(\tau)].$$

As counterparty default is possible at any point in time in the interval $[0,T]$, all products of expected discounted exposure given default and probability of default are added to yield the following formula for the unilateral CVA:

$$CVA^{\text{unilateral}} = \underbrace{(1-R)}_{LGD} \int_0^T \underbrace{E_Q[B(0,u)\cdot EX(u)|u=\tau]}_{EAD} \ \underbrace{\mathrm{d}F(u)}_{PD}\ .$$

$$(6.4)$$

Taking into consideration that loss given default $LGD = 1 - R$, Formula (6.4) resembles the expected loss calculation for a loan $EL = LGD \cdot EAD \cdot PD$.

If credit exposure and probability of counterparty default in τ are independent from one another, we can neglect the conditioning on default in (6.4) and get:

$$CVA^{\text{unilateral}} = (1 - R) \int_0^T E_Q[B(0, u) \cdot EX(u)] \ dF(u) . \qquad (6.5)$$

For a fixed set of simulation dates $\{t_j\}, j = 1, ..., m$, the integral in (6.5) can be approximated by the following sum:

$$CVA^{\text{unilateral}} \approx (1 - R) \sum_{j=1}^m E_Q[B(0, t_j) \cdot EX(t_j)] \cdot [F(t_j) - F(t_{j-1})].$$

$$(6.6)$$

The risk-neutral expected discounted exposure is computed using either a simulation approach or an approximation method (see Section 6.3.2).

So far, we have assumed that only the counterparty might default and that the bank itself is default-free. Banks that trade with corporates might successfully include a unilateral CVA into the premium of the derivative. However, two banks trading with each other will not agree on a fair premium if both of them incorporate a unilateral CVA into the derivative's premium. In order to agree on a price, both banks have to consider their own default risk as well. A bilateral CVA considers the possibility of default of both counterparts. Taking the perspective of counterparty 2, the bilateral CVA is calculated as:

$$CVA^{\text{bilateral}}$$

$$= \underbrace{(1 - R_1)}_{\text{LGD of CP1}} \int_0^T \underbrace{E_Q[B(0, u) \cdot EX_1(u)|u = \tau_1]}_{\text{expected exposure of CP1}} \cdot \underbrace{P[\tau_2 > u|u = \tau_1]}_{\text{survival probability of CP2}} \quad \underbrace{dF_1(u)}_{\text{default probability of CP1}} \quad \underbrace{- (1 - R_2)}_{\text{LGD of CP2}}$$

$$\int_0^T \underbrace{E_Q[B(0, u) \cdot EX_2(u)|u = \tau_2]}_{\text{expected exposure of CP2 = negative expected exposure of CP1}} \cdot \underbrace{P[\tau_1 > u|u = \tau_2]}_{\text{survival probability of CP1}} \quad \underbrace{dF_2(u)}_{\text{default probability of CP2}} \quad .$$

The formula to calculate bilateral CVA consists of two parts. The first term is the CVA that accounts for the possibility of counterparty default. The second term is called the debt value adjustment (DVA) and is the adjustment for the possibility of own default.

6.3.4 Wrong way risk

So far, no correlation between exposure and counterparty default probability has been assumed. This reflected market consensus for the majority of interest rate derivatives prior to the current financial crisis. However, the ongoing financial crisis has shown that such a systematic relationship exists. The term "wrong way risk" (WWR) denotes a negative correlation between a market value and a counterpart's credit quality.

The most obvious example is a self-referencing CDS: A corporate purchases protection against the default of a bank from this same bank. Such a hedge is evidently inadequate. If the credit quality of the counterparty deteriorates, the present value of the CDS rises at the same time.

For interest rate derivatives the concept of WWR is not as straightforward. Under normal conditions interest rates rise, if the economy recovers. The number of corporate bankruptcies decreases. Hence, positions under which corporate counterparts receive a fixed rate, increase in values for their bank counterparts while the likelihood of receiving this value grows as well ("right way risk"). However, consider the case of a highly leveraged institution like a hedge fund funding itself short-term via a three-month Euribor and paying a floating interest rate payment to the bank. Clearly, a raise in short-term interest rates significantly increases the default risk of that fund. Another example of less obvious WWR could be observed during summer 2011: German long-term interest rates were at a historically low level and short-term rates were also very low. This apparent support of the creditworthiness of large German banks was deceptive, since these banks held most of their risky assets outside of the German economy.

6.3.5 Parameter availability

Different sources can be used to determine the counterparty default probability (PD) and the expected recovery rate or LGD:

- Market-implied PDs can be bootstrapped from information available in the capital markets. Credit spreads are easily quantifiable in CDSs, bonds and loans.[2] Implied LGD is a component of credit derivative pricing, but is generally not traded separately.[3] The advantage of marked-implied PDs is

---

[2] It should be noted that bond and loan spreads contain elements of funding, due diligence costs, etc., whereas credit derivative spreads can include illiquidity premiums for rarely traded names.

[3] The same LGD is frequently used for bootstrapping PDs and calculating CVAs. Before the financial crisis, a market for exotic credit derivatives that allowed for the setting of pre-agreed recovery rates existed. With increasing general skepticism towards exotic products, these niche products have almost ceased to be traded.

that they are measureable, and can thus be traded and hedged. However, their major disadvantage is that the CDS market does not include every potential counterparty. It is therefore unlikely that an institution's entire counterparty universe can be mapped to observable credit spreads. For illiquid credit risks, generic credit spread indices based on rating, jurisdiction and industry class are helpful. Changes of such indices can only be hedged with significant basis risk[4]—they are not a reliable indicator for a specific counterparty default. They should be determined at "arm's length."

- Internal model-based PDs and LGDs do not have the shortcomings mentioned above as they can be determined for all counterparts. They are based on internal rating methods that are agreed with regulators and external auditors. A significant disadvantage is that they are based on non-observable parameters (some of which are backward looking) and thus cannot be hedged completely. While they are adjusted at regular intervals, the frequency of review may only be annual. CVA changes due to newly calibrated LGDs or reviewed PDs will result in P&L volatility.
- Empirical data, be it internal or acquired from rating agencies, is backward looking and heavily dependent on the business cycle. The recent crisis demonstrates that relying on historic information to predict future developments is not sufficient to allow for early recognition of paradigm changes. Such paradigm changes will profoundly modify fundamental beliefs, pricing methods and assumed relationships between parameters. Although empirical data can provide useful information when forecasting losses for certain asset classes, it is of limited use for pricing purposes.

The choice of source depends on the setup and mandate of the CVA desk, and is subject to the approval of external auditors.

6.4 New Challenges and Reactions

6.4.1 Accounting standards

As a result of the financial crisis, assessing CCR and refining fair market valuation of derivatives have become important requirements requested by accounting boards and regulators. Accounting standards now require a valuation adjustment to

---

[4] See Section 6.4.5 on CVA hedging.

ensure that CCR is appropriately reflected in the reported value of derivatives. Specific accounting rules are:

- International Accounting Standards Board (IASB): IAS 39 AG.73, AG.82 required to consider the possible default of both counterparts in a derivative contract.
- Financial Accounting Standards Board (FASB): Statement of Financial Accounting Standards No. 157 "Fair Value Measurements," appendix B, paragraph B5, refers to US Generally Accepted Accounting Principles and requires that "a fair value measurement should include a risk premium reflecting the amount market participants would demand because of the risk (uncertainty) in the cash flows."

The fair value of over-the-counter (OTC) derivatives has to be adjusted by CVAs in order to reflect potential counterparty default. Economically, a CVA creates a counterparty credit loss reserve for derivative transactions.

6.4.2 Capital requirements

The financial crisis also triggered new banking regulation such as Basel III, the Dodd−Frank Act or the European Market Infrastructure Regulation (EMIR). The main objective of the new regulations is to raise the resilience of the banking sector. The Basel III framework represents the center of all regulatory efforts regarding capital requirements. With respect to CCR, the Basel III regulations (see Basel Committee on Banking Supervision, 2010a) reform and extend the previous Basel II rules in two respects:

- The capital charge for CCR previously introduced by Basel II now has to be calculated using stressed input variables.
- To enhance the risk coverage a new capital charge that is supposed to measure the volatility of CVAs is introduced. According to Basel III, paragraph 14 (b), "banks will be subject to a capital charge for potential mark-to-market losses [CVA risk] associated with a deterioration in the credit worthiness of a counterparty. While the Basel II standard covers the risk of a counterparty default, it does not address such CVA risk...."

During the financial crisis the greatest CCR losses were not caused by defaults, but from increasing CVAs due to deterioration in the creditworthiness of counterparts. Basel III introduces the new capital charge to protect banks from these rises in CVAs and the resulting losses. The new regulations are set out in paragraph 99, which adds the new section VIII "Treatment of mark-to-market counterparty risk losses (CVA capital charge)," consisting of nine paragraphs (paragraphs 97−105), to annex 4 of the Basel II framework. The new CVA capital charge for OTC derivatives is introduced in paragraph 97: "In addition to the default risk capital requirements for counterparty credit risk ..., a bank must add a capital charge to cover the risk of mark-to-market losses on the expected counterparty risk [CVAs] to OTC derivatives." Basel III distinguishes two different approaches to quantify the CVA capital charge: The standard approach (paragraph 104) and the more advanced bond equivalent approach (paragraphs 98–103).

- *Standard approach.* This approach provides for the capital charge to be calculated using a formula furnished by the regulator. Here, the main drivers of the capital charge are fixed regulatory counterparty risk weights, exposure at default and the effective maturity of the transaction. Market volatility is not part of the input parameters.
- *Advanced approach.* Banks with internal market model (IMM) approval and specific interest rate risk "value at risk" (VaR) model approval for bonds may use the bond-equivalent approach to calculate the CVA capital charge. They do this "by modeling the impact of changes in the counterparts" credit spreads on the CVAs of all OTC derivative counterparts ... using the bank's VaR model for bonds" (see paragraph 98). The capital charge is then calculated in a two-step procedure. (i) The CVA of each counterparty or the credit spread sensitivity of the CVA is calculated using formulas provided by the regulator (paragraphs 98 and 99). The main input variables into these formulas are CDS spreads, market implied LGD and EE. (ii) CVA or credit spread sensitivities are input into the bank's VaR model for bonds treating CVA as a bond, sensitive to credit spread changes only (and not to changes in other market risk factors). As specified in paragraph 100, the CVA capital charge is the sum of the non-stressed VaR component (using current parameter calibrations for EE) and the stressed VaR component (using futures EE profiles and stressed credit spread parameters).

Basel III regulation may have the following direct effects on banks:

- Incentives to trade with central counterparts (CCPs) will decrease bilateral OTC transactions and increase centrally cleared transactions.
- The new capital requirements will increase the capital charge for CCR (stressed inputs and CVA capital charge). Estimates envisage a doubling of the charge or more.
- Increasing cost of capital due to the CVA capital charge will have repercussions on the pricing and hedging of derivatives.

- Credit derivatives [CDS, contingent CDS (CCDS) or index CDS] are being used as the only eligible instruments to hedge the CVA capital charge.
- Other indirect effects such as product standardization and an increased requirement to hedge CVA movements are described below.

Although the new regulatory rules are welcomed by the general public, some aspects, especially the method to determine the CVA capital charge, have raised concern:

- Current regulation does not allow banks to use their own internal risk models to calculate the CVA capital charge.
- The CVA capital charge is only sensitive to changes in the credit spread of the counterparty. Thus, only the credit spread volatility risk of CVA is accounted for. Although fluctuations of other market parameters (e.g. interest rates, FX, etc.) have an impact on counterparty exposure and CVA, the current regulatory methodology does not model the sensitivity of CVA to variations in those factors.
- Regulation allows banks to mitigate the CVA capital charge by hedging against a deterioration of the counterparty's credit quality using CDS or similar instruments. On the other hand, hedges against adverse movements of market risk factors are not deemed eligible to mitigate CVA risk. On the contrary, Basel III, paragraph 99, requires the latter hedges to be treated "as any other instrument in the bank's inventory for regulatory capital purposes."
- The use of CDS spreads in the regulatory modeling approach has a procyclical effect. Since banks buy CDS protection in order to reduce the CVA capital charge, the volume of CVA risk hedges is expected to increase. Demand for protection raises credit spreads because of insufficient depth of the CDS market. Higher CDS spreads, however, will increase the CVA capital charge, potentially creating a vicious circle. In such a scenario, credit spreads would increase for regulatory reasons, even though the creditworthiness of the counterparty has not changed.
- Banks can reduce the CVA capital charge by moving bilateral OTC derivative contracts to the CCPs. RWAs for the latter are calculated using a proposed risk weight of 2%, i.e. RWA = 2% * EAD. Although the CCR is reduced, the concentration risk increases.[5]

---

[5] In Basel Committee on Banking Supervision (2010b), annex A, the Basel Committee on Banking Supervision proposes to add a new section on central counterparts to annex 4 of the Basel II regulation. The proposed risk weight of 2% is stated in paragraph 114. Gregory (2010) provides a detailed discussion about advantages and disadvantages of central clearing.

6.4.3 CCPs and customer clearing

In order to reduce CCR in the financial sector, both the Dodd–Frank Act in the US and its European counterpart EMIR require a larger proportion of derivatives with financial counterparts to be cleared centrally by exchanges or clearinghouses. Moreover, this legislation introduces higher reporting standards for OTC derivatives. Regulators penalize bilateral trades by means of higher capital requirements. Depending on the legislation in each jurisdiction, specific products or counterparts are exempt from those regulatory requirements. Bilateral collateral agreements are likely to change as well. A standardized Credit Support Annex (CSA) that mirrors some CCP collateral details is currently being discussed by ISDA members. The effects of these elements on the OTC market are a likely standardization of trade features and an industrialization of derivative trading via electronic trading platforms and automatic trade confirmations. Larger banks now offer customer clearing services to those of their bank counterparts who cannot or will not become a member of a clearer themselves. In addition to LCH.Clearnet, both CME Clearing and the International Derivatives Clearing Group (IDCG) in the United States and EUREX in Europe already offer or plan to provide clearing services for interest rate derivatives.[6] The handling of closeouts by CCPs following the Lehman bankruptcy successfully tested procedures and processes that thus far had remained untested. Trading via CCPs does not create positions without credit risk as concentration risk rises. The necessity to clear will reduce the numbers of institutions trading IRDs to include only those who can generate profits through efficient handling of mass business and niche players with specialized product or client franchises.[7]

6.4.4 Derivative pricing—no such thing as "plain vanilla"

In the last 10–15 years, derivatives' pricing has undergone fundamental changes and this is set to continue. There is no such thing as a "plain vanilla" IRS at present. The days of all market participants trading at identical screen prices are gone and are not set to return.

---

[6] Details for products and service ranges can be found at www.lchclearnet.com, www.cmegroup.com, www.idcg.com and www.eurexchange.com.
[7] See Böhme *et al.* (2011).

It started with the differentiation between alternative payment frequencies, such as three- or six-month floating indices. An increasing number of counterparts then started taking account of their counterparts' and/ or their own credit quality (uni- or bilateral CVA). A relatively recent development is the inclusion of banks' funding costs to price derivatives.[8] This change was caused by banks' rising funding costs and the increased basis between overnight indices and Libor or Euribor rates. LCH.Clearnet set a visible marker for the new market standard by changing their valuation method to discounting with overnight index swaps (OISs). All major swap dealers now apply this method.

If funding costs are a component of the derivative's price, banks that use bilateral CVAs need to be careful to avoid double-counting these costs since funding and CVA are closely connected.[9] The latest development in derivative pricing is to incorporate costs for required capital and balance sheet usage. Both are impacted by recent or future regulatory changes in the United States and Europe. As a result, the costs of trading derivatives have already increased.

6.4.5 Active risk cost pricing and management

Banks are at different stages when mitigating costs associated with their incumbent OTC portfolio caused by additional regulation. While some institutions are advanced users of mitigating techniques, such as transferring eligible trades to a CCP and actively terminating trades by multiparty trade compression or through bilateral closeouts, some still struggle to come to terms with the P&L effects of transferring trades from their books to a CCP. In addition to managing legacy trades, banks need to consider the new regulatory framework when pricing new transactions. While some IRSs will remain profitable cross-sell products, other proposed transactions will not even break even. Banks need to decide whether they are willing to provide these products to their clients as part of a comprehensive banking service. Clients, on the other hand, need to understand that the operating landscape of their bank counterparts has changed. The obligation to evaluate the profitability of entire client relationships is accelerated by rising expected costs of derivatives positions to maturity. "Best Practice" is a moving target. The

---

[8] These costs are: costs/benefits of (i) expected collateral balances if a trade is collateralized—taking account of all details of the governing collateral agreement—or of (ii) expected cash flows if a trade is uncollateralized.
[9] For more details, see Tang and Williams (2009).

authors believe that institutions currently not actively managing these cost parameters will face problems in the future when higher costs will apply to their non-optimized derivative portfolios.

6.4.6 CVA hedging

The aim of CVA desks is to manage the P&L fluctuation caused by CVA changes. CVA is generally calculated at regular intervals by independent divisions within a bank, such as Risk Management or Finance. These divisions will then charge the risk owner(s) with their respective CVA or CVA changes. The two main reasons for variations in CVA are changes of exposure or counterparty credit quality. Other reasons include model changes and changes in regulatory requirements.

6.4.6.1 Exposure changes

Counterparty exposure may change for a variety of reasons. Exposure is not only affected by new, amended, prematurely terminated trades or fluctuating market parameters, but also by factors such as netting rules and collateralization agreements. Hedging the impact of changes in market parameters requires regular calculations of the CVA's sensitivity to each specific risk factor. A variety of instruments is used to hedge specific risk factors, such as IRS or FX transactions, neither of which requires any upfront payments. Due to the volume of transactions affected by major risk parameters, CVA desks themselves have become a driver of market movements.

6.4.6.2 Credit spread and default risk changes

Counterparty credit quality may change during a business cycle for industry- or company-specific reasons. With the exception of hedging default risk, which is always hedged via CDS or insurance-type products, the CVA spread hedge strategy depends on the PD source used in the CVA calculation.

Internal-model PDs cannot be hedged explicitly. A CVA desk might choose to proxy these PDs with single-name CDSs or indices, although this may result in significant P&L volatility. If market-observed PDs are used to calculate CVAs, it will be necessary to hedge credit spread movements. Such a hedge is easily executed, if the counterparty name trades in the CDS market. However, as mentioned above, not all counterparty names are represented in the CDS market. For illiquid names, a meaningful proxy spread needs to be found to provide a hedge.

Correlation changes affect the validity of these proxies, regular reviews are therefore essential.

CVA desks may decide to fund protection premiums by selling protection via relevant indices on a wider range of names. This strategy introduces a further basis risk to the CVA P&L, since the hedge is approximate and spread developments for specific names need not always follow the development of an index. CVA theta can be seen as a funding source.

6.4.6.3 Cross gamma

Links between the CVA's different driving factors sometimes cause significant cross-gamma effects. For example, it will become necessary to increase interest rate hedge notionals when CVA rises as a result of spread widening or counterparty downgrades, even though the actual exposure remains unchanged.

CVA for OTC positions with severely distressed but not yet defaulted counterparts need to be hedged differently. Reliable data, extensive legal netting opinions and a sound collateral negotiation process are vital and cannot be replaced by hedging alone.

6.5 Practical Problems

Practical problems encountered in CVA management fall into the following categories.

6.5.1 Data quality

The amount of data required is substantial and diverse. Different divisions are responsible for different datasets. Inaccurate or outdated information has direct economic implications on CVA and other risk charges. Not all data owners fully understand their responsibility.

6.5.2 Methodology

A consistent valuation framework across all risk charges is essential. Since models for funding, accounting, capital and derivative pricing are owned and developed by different departments, this consistency is difficult to achieve. CVA desks face the challenge of comprehensively identifying WWR, deciding whether and how to hedge it, but most importantly, attaching a fair price tag to trades incorporating WWR. Due to the complexity involved, model-based solutions will always need to be accompanied by qualitative case-by-case analysis.

6.5.3 Infrastructure and data dependencies

The CVA calculation requires data from different sources within an organization. Thus the CVA calculation engine needs to interface with diverse sources such as Front Office tools, collateral systems, and Legal, Risk Management and Finance databases. Connectivity between systems that were often developed in isolation from each other is always difficult to achieve. Once the vast amount of data, different identifiers, responsibilities and P&L volatility are added on top, it soon becomes clear how complex the information flow in a CVA process is likely to be.

Computations can easily get very time consuming. In a simple example, a bank with 100 counterparts and 25 trades per counterparty using 100 future simulation dates and 4000 market scenarios has to compute 1 billion trade values. A full Monte Carlo simulation on complex Front Office pricing routines is often not possible at all. In such cases it is reasonable to refer to less accurate but faster pricing algorithms (e.g. approximation methods). Too much simplification does, however, harbor dangers.

An efficient and targeted IT infrastructure is of the utmost importance. Pre-deal CVA pricing is difficult to introduce into Front Office systems in isolation. Apart from their inability to consider netting across different systems or asset classes, Front Office systems often lack counterparty-specific information such as details of available collateral agreements.[10]

6.5.4 Organizational setup

Most banks take account of CCR in their balance sheet by either regularly calculating CVA or setting aside a provision. Currently, an almost equal split between CVA desks as profit centers and cost centers exists, with CVA groups either situated in Risk Management, Trading or Central Management areas. There is currently no industry standard.

Setting up a CVA desk should start with finding out (i) who calculates CVA and (ii) who owns a trade's specific CCR, i.e. who takes the loss if the counterparty defaults. CVA is usually calculated by Risk Management, while CCR was traditionally owned by those taking a trade's benefit, i.e. its profit. This was either the Relationship Manager or the original Trading Desk. The financial crisis highlighted that in addition to specialist technical knowledge, cross-sector expertise is vital. The impact of parameter changes on CVA and cost of capital must be quantified and the

---

[10] However, the later is now required to correctly price derivatives (see Section 6.4.4).

necessary tools must be chosen to accomplish desired changes or mitigate undesired developments. Since different departments are responsible for the various parameters driving CVA, it is imperative for the CVA group to have access to all necessary information.

6.5.5 Mandate

A CVA desk's mandates range from cost center functions in Risk Management, where risk is warehoused, to profit centers in trading areas where CCR is traded alongside other hybrid products. The financial crisis has put a focus on funding, capital and balance sheet usage. Since funding profiles, RWA (i.e. capital) and balance sheet usage are driven by the same or very similar parameters as the CVA, a CVA desk's mandate might be extended to include managing these risk charges. The extent to which risk charges are transferred to clients will steer new business as some trades may not meet internal cost hurdles. If the CVA desk sits outside Risk Management, there may be methodology disputes or problems with access rights to simulation engines.

6.6 Conclusions and Lessons Learned

During the recent crisis, the banking industry briskly woke to the fact that CCR from derivatives cannot be ignored and should be given adequate attention. Banks are faced with the challenge of first understanding the impact of the new regulation on their business profile and then adjusting to the new environment. It is likely that market participants will cease to offer certain product types and that certain business activities will be discontinued, while it is not yet known whether or how their revenue stream can be replaced. Banks need to take a holistic view of derivative trading, and jointly consider effects such as funding, capital costs and pricing, which were previously evaluated separately. Banks are at different stages with respect to adjusting to new operational frameworks. This process requires a review of the existing business profile and substantial investments in infrastructure. With new regulation already in place or set to take effect shortly, time is running out for banks that have thus far ignored the sweeping changes.

References

Assefa, S., Bielecki, T.R., Crépey, S., Jeanblanc, M., 2011. CVA computation for counterparty risk assessment in credit portfolios. In: Bielecki, T.R., Brigo, D., Patras, F. (Eds), Credit Risk Frontiers. Wiley, Hoboken NJ., 397–436.

Basel Committee on Banking Supervision, 2006. International Convergence of Capital Measurement and Capital Standards: A Revised Framework. Basel Committee on Banking Supervision, Basel.

Basel Committee on Banking Supervision, 2010a. Basel III: A Global Regulatory Framework for More Resilient Banks and Banking Systems. Revised version June 2011. Basel Committee on Banking Supervision, Basel.

Basel Committee on Banking Supervision, 2010b. Consultative Document: Capitalisation of Bank Exposures to Central Counterparts. Basel Committee on Banking Supervision, Basel.

Böhme, M., Chiarella, D., Härle, P., Neukirchen, M., Poppensieker, T., Raufuss, A., 2011. Day of reckoning? New regulation and its impact on capital-markets businesses. In: McKinsey Working Papers on Risk, 29. McKinsey, Atlanta, GA.

Carver, L., 2011. A recipe for disaster? Risk 16–21.

Cesari, G., Acquilina, J., Charpillon, N., Filipovic, Z., Lee, G., Manda, I., 2009. Modelling, Pricing and Hedging Counterparty Credit Exposure—A Technical Guide. Springer, Berlin.

De Prisco, B., Rosen, D., 2005. Modeling stochastic counterparty credit exposure for derivatives portfolios. In: Pykhtin, M. (Ed.), Counterparty Credit Risk Modeling. Risk Books, London, 3–47.

Financial Accounting Standards Board, 2006. Statement of Financial Accounting Standards No. 157—Fair Value Measurements. Financial Accounting Standards Board, Norwalk, CT.

Gregory, J., 2009. Counterparty Credit Risk: The New Challenge for Global Financial Markets. Wiley, Chichester.

Gregory, J., 2010. Are we building the foundations for the next crisis already? The case of central clearing. DefaultRisk.com available at. http://www.defaultrisk.com/pp_other192.htm.

Pykhtin, M., Zhu, S.H., 2007. A guide to modelling counterparty credit risk. Global Association of Risk Professionals 37 (July/August), 16–22.

Tang, Y., Williams, A., 2009. Funding benefit and funding cost. In: Canabarro, E. (Ed.), Counterparty Credit Risk: Measurement, Pricing and Hedging. Risk Books, London, 185–198.

7

DESIGNING A COUNTERPARTY RISK MANAGEMENT INFRASTRUCTURE FOR DERIVATIVES

Matthieu Maurice

Commerzbank

CHAPTER OUTLINE

Rethinking Valuation and Pricing Models. http://dx.doi.org/10.1016/B978-0-12-415875-7.00007-5

99

7.1 Need for an Integrated Counterparty Risk Management

7.1.1 Trade workflow pre-crisis

In this section, we will trace the typical workflow within a bank before and after the financial crisis. We first examine the workflow from a corporate treasury perspective hedging its business risk with the typical derivative instruments. Note that a corporate treasury can also enter into a derivative transaction for speculative purpose. Nevertheless, we trace the lifecycle of the trade within the bank providing the hedge from pre-deal pricing to internal risk management and regulatory reporting.

The business risk may be related to foreign exchange (FX), interest rate risk, commodities, inflation or equity. For instance, the corporate treasury may want to lock in a forward price of a commodity, to hedge future cash flows in a foreign currency or even enter into an interest rate swap to convert fixed-rate payments into floating payments in order to mitigate interest rate risk. In each case, the corporate treasurer explains his hedging objectives to the bank derivatives salesperson that structures the derivatives hedge (it could be either plain vanilla or even structured, i.e. tailormade). The salesperson requests the adequate market price of the hedge from the relevant derivatives trading desk. At this time either the funding or liquidity costs associated to the trade are usually included. In the pre-crisis time, many banks did not even consider, in this upfront pricing, the credit and capital add-ons to cover the risk of losses due to deterioration of the credit quality of the counterparty or even due to default. See Figure 7.1.

7.1.2 Review of the process during the financial crisis

The trader then liaises with the risk control group, which checks exposure limits and even in some cases provides the credit and capital charges. The credit and capital charges are based on internal quantitative and qualitative assessments of the credit quality of the counterparty. The credit portion of this charge is for the expected loss (EL, i.e. the cost of running business). The capital portion is for the potential unexpected loss. These charges go into reserves that can be used to reimburse the trading desk for counterparty credit losses. The risk control provides exposure reports, checks limit breaches and calculates the capital measures as required by the bank's regulator, which approves the

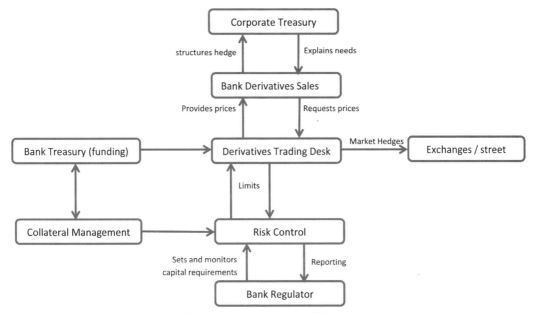

Figure 7.1 Derivatives pricing workflow pre-crisis.

capital calculation methodology and monitors the ongoing exposure according the Basel guidelines. Therefore, the counterparty risk is managed through credit and capital reserves. The market risk of the transaction is fully hedged by the desk on the exchange or with other market participants, as the derivatives trading desk mostly does not want or is not allowed to hold open positions. On an uncollateralized basis, the funding for the transaction is brought by the treasury. This represents a loan to a customer in the form of a derivatives line of credit. For most financial clients and for specific corporate customers, the portfolio can be fully or at least partially collateralized. This definitely increases the size of the operational workflow by adding other entities such as collateral management.

As highlighted by Kelly (2011), one of the drivers for the setup of a credit valuation adjustment (CVA) desk within a bank and subsequently of a CVA infrastructure is the need to reduce credit risk in an efficient way, and to centralize the quantification, pricing and management of their counterparty credit risk (CCR). Some front-runners started establishing CVA desks in the aftermath of the Asian crisis to lay off counterparty risk. Numerous large Swiss and American banks attempted to securitize it, i.e. to transfer it to external investors. The most common way was the active use of the new market for credit default swaps (CDSs) to hedge the counterparty risk. The US accounting rules (FAS 157) mandate the inclusion of the CVA in the mark-to-market valuation of financial derivatives, highlighting not only the requirement for CVA infra-structure to quantify with accuracy the counterparty risk, but also the need to actively manage this risk. One can consider the counterparty risk like market risk and hedge all the underlying risk factors inherent to the CVA to avoid any dramatic profit and loss swings. The complexity of CVA pricing and hedging is exacerbated by the new regulatory framework hitting the derivatives market with an increased capital charge requirement for counterparty default risk and with the additional CVA "value at risk" (VaR) charge covering the CVA losses. See Figure 7.2.

Adding a dedicated CVA desk consolidating the above-mentioned activities to the previous workflows does not change the overall picture, in the sense that the CVA desk is only an additional intermediary between the derivatives trading desk and risk control. Whereas the derivatives traders were used to asking directly about risk control for the credit and capital

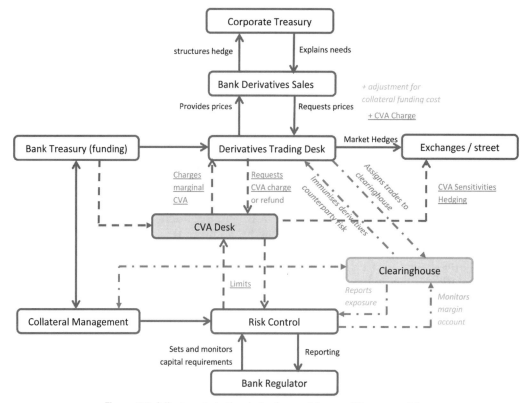

Figure 7.2 Adjustments to the derivatives pricing workflow pre-crisis.

charges (consider that not all risk controls want or are able to provide the front office with such a calculation), they now ask the CVA desk to run a marginal CVA calculation to assess the marginal impact of a new transaction on the current portfolio. Some CVA desks take ownership of the counterparty risk, receiving the CVA upfront and selling credit protection to the derivatives desk. The CVA desk then actively manages the counterparty risk, hedging both credit and market sensitivities inherent to counterparty risk.

The main problem of CVA desks is that they insert an additional participant to the workflow, also inducing an extreme analytical complexity because all risk quantifications usually have to be done on a simulation basis due to the stochastic nature of the potential loss in the case of a default. All risk factors of the underlying derivatives plus the credit risk of the counterparty have to be incorporated in the CVA model. Even the counterparty risk of an FX forward is complex because the counterparty risk on the derivatives is analogous to the pricing of an American-style FX option; by the way, this representation allows an easy benchmark with a closed-form solution to the results of the simulation presented in the forthcoming sections. In addition to the difficult task of assessing the correct exposure profile of the risk, the CVA desk needs to retrieve all market information to quantify the default probability of the counterparty, and to take the correlation between exposure and credit quality of the counterparty into account, i.e. the so-called "wrong way risk" (WWR).

Even if margining could be difficult to setup, its quantification is quite simple and transparent, and the new regulation appears to provide an incentive for banks to fully collateralize derivatives transactions or even mandate the transfer of plain vanilla products to a clearing platform. A clearing house effectively replaces the CVA desk in the workflow for a cleared transaction. The clearing house becomes the counterparty to both sides of the trade. In this case, the CVA charge is replaced by the collateral funding cost, which is typically based on overnight rates. Counterparty risk is mitigated as the exposure is fully collateralized and backed by the clearing house and its members. Nevertheless, there is still the risk that the clearing house fails.

Not all trades can be cleared; focus is first on standardized products and the new regulations of the Dodd–Frank Act, or the European Market Infrastructure Regulation (EMIR), in their latest definition explicitly excluding corporate hedging transactions from mandatory clearing, so banks need to maintain the CVA desk and the according workflow. There is definitely a need to unify this dual system as both CVAs and clearing houses have a significant operative impact on the derivatives workflows. The advent of Basel III requires a huge change in the way financial institutions have to address CCR and CVA. As highlighted in this chapter, the complexity and the associated costs of such an infrastructure are daunting for most financial institutions.

7.2 Building Blocks for an Adequate Infrastructure

7.2.1 Data management

CCR management workflows require excessive amounts of data as well as scalable high-performance technology and infrastructure. An integrated risk management infrastructure to support CVA and clearing house workflows is very challenging and requires a specific design covering the following areas as presented by Gregory (2009).

7.2.1.1 Trade data

An efficient and precise assessment of the impact of a trade on an existing portfolio can only be based on a complete disclosure of all trade details such as product type, cash flow, optionality, or any specific feature associated to a specific transaction.

Over-the-counter (OTC) derivatives account for the biggest portion of counterparty risk in a usual portfolio of a corporate or investment bank. Securities financing transactions may also make up another significant share, but they are definitively less risky due to their short maturity. Standard hedging instruments used to actively manage the counterparty risk inherent either to a derivatives book or to a liquid loan book have also to be taken into account.

7.2.1.2 Market data

Market data gives the adequate framework to price a derivative transaction with the current market dataset or with market datasets resulting from simulation (using specific curve calibration and pricing models). A market dataset usually covers all risk assets such as interest rate products, FX, commodity, equity and credit. Without giving an exhaustive list of all possible items, the most significant elements for the required infrastructure are:
- Interest rate products (IR): yield curves, basis and volatility surface.
- Inflation (IN): zero and year-on-year swap curves, seasonality, and volatility.

- FX: e.g. spot rates, forward curves, volatility surface and currency basis spread.
- Commodity (CO): spot, forward rate, volatility.
- Equity (EQ): spot, volatility, dividend.
- Credit (CS): CDS spread (specific, index, tranche), bond spread or any proxy curve.

Information such as correlation or historical volatility can also be derived from the above-mentioned information and be stored in order to be reused in the following stages. In particular, correlation between the counterparty's default probability and each risk factor within the simulation is needed to properly assess the right and wrong way risks.

7.2.1.3 Counterparty data

All specific information relative to the counterparty has gained a massive emphasis over the past decade due to its requirement in multiple calculations of risk quantities. This information could have an economic nature (such as probability of default and recovery rate), an organizational nature (credit hierarchy and seniority within a group), a legal nature (presence of master agreement, cross-product netting agreement) or even some aspect of risk mitigation [credit support annex (CSA), downgrade trigger or break clause].

7.2.2 Usage of markup languages

During the latest decade, OTC markets have evolved very quickly, not only in terms of volume, but also in terms of complexity. The focus has been on building tools for pricing and risk managing transactions. With the emergence of massive electronic trading, market practitioners decided to build standard electronic mechanisms for interchanging details of the transactions between participating companies, implying some cost-efficient standards for communication, for the structuring and execution of trades, confirmation, and settlement of these transactions; this could also be extended to a communication with a firm offering a service related to that transaction (e.g. a central clearing or an independent valuation agent).

From a counterparty risk perspective, an even more important aspect should be analyzed, as most banks have multiple systems for reference data, market data and transactions. A counterparty risk system needs to integrate all these systems to generate a comprehensive set of counterparty risk metrics. As presented in Cesari (2009), there are some tremendous infrastructure challenges here, as the systems involved could use different technologies (.NET, Java or C++), so there is a need for a common language to standardize and facilitate communication between different systems. The Financial Products Markup Language (FpML®) has been established as the current business information exchange standard for electronic dealing and the processing of financial products. This language is recommended by the International Swaps and Derivatives Association (ISDA). FpML is recognized as an extension of the broadly used meta-language XML (extensible markup language) for describing data shared between applications. FpML allows market practitioners to automate the flow of information within the derivatives community, avoiding the constraints from different underlying back/front office pricing software or hardware infrastructures. For instance, real-time analytics and market data providers allow for the storing of any derivatives entered in their front office system in an FpML format, facilitating integration in the proposed framework.

7.2.3 Application of cubes

The infrastructure briefly introduced so far relies on complex calculations on very significant datasets. The stochastic processes underlying the derivative business lead to massive data storage from simulation that needs to be combined in order to assess the relevant key risk figures. By nature, these computations have to be made in a very quick and dynamic environment, underlying the fundamental usage of BI (business intelligence) or OLAP (online analytical processing) solutions. The latest developments in this area brought the "in-memory analytics" that avoid the latency boundary of the usual OLAP solutions. Such in-memory object-oriented OLAP engines can aggregate and perform in-memory analytics on massive flows on data, enabling tailored business logic—for our purpose, the computation of counter-party exposure. The in-memory analytics is based on multi-threaded algorithms using high data compression to significantly reduce the memory consumption and to allow real-time BI.

7.2.4 Grid computing

The most important possibility to accelerate a simulation lies in its technological implementation. One of the most usual concepts is "grid computing," i.e. the systematic distribution of computation on multiple computers. This is an infrastructure that allows the coordinated and optimized usage of distributed resources, and a tremendous increase in computing speed can be achieved. In the case of Monte Carlo processes, the terms "threaded Monte Carlo" or "grid Monte Carlo" are commonly used; the simulation time is significantly reduced. A threaded Monte Carlo will distribute the simulation on a multi-CPU machine in parallel threads and a grid Monte Carlo will distribute the simulation on a grid node of multiple machines. An optimal performance could first be reached as soon as the architecture of the underlying simulation software is based on grid computing; a performing programming language needs to be used for this, usually C++, and on top of this, the deployment of a robust hardware is the best complement.

7.3 General Computing Approach

A required infrastructure was defined Section 7.2 and this will now be the basis to run any simulation needed to compute the various counterparty risk metrics.

7.3.1 Scenario generation

The first step in the process of computing CVA or any CCR relevant figures is to generate market scenarios at a pre-defined set of futures dates. Although they are of course dependent on market data, scenarios cannot be generated each time a CCR or CVA computation is required. A scenario generation will be considered valid for a certain time, which should remain scalable upon market conditions or user-defined parameters (typically four or five daily runs, but the target model should handle on-demand intra-day reruns).

We now present different ways to run such simulations and examine the different issues that could arise in the implementation of these processes. Models can take correlation into account if required and can be calibrated using historical data or market prices depending on whether users want to use historical (real) or market-implied (risk-neutral) probabilities. As explained by Pykhtin (2005), the *path-dependent simulation (PDS)* implies that each state at each specific time node should contain the previous state and the following one so the full path can be rebuilt during the pricing process for path-dependent product like Asian options or Look-Back options. This specificity should be depicted in the data model of the solution. This can be done using a full Monte Carlo simulation. Unfortunately, all products cannot be priced analytically, but rather using partial differential equations or a Monte Carlo approach. An embedded Monte Carlo simulation within an exposure calculation through Monte Carlo simulation will lead to difficulties in the computation power required, such as in calibration of the model. The American Monte Carlo AMC algorithm is, in this case, a viable and performing alternative using a pricing algorithm relying on backward induction to compute counterparty exposure. The *direct-jump to simulation date (DJS)* implies that the prevailing scenarios at previous simulation dates are fully unrelated to the current scenarios. This allows a quick computation of the counterparty risk exposure as proposed by Jamshidian (1996) in a quasi-Monte Carlo framework, but is not suited to path-dependent, Bermudan/American style or even asset-settle derivatives. The mandatory input data for the scenario generator engine are as follow:

- *Market data*: Risk factors will be deduced from the list of market data used for pricing the portfolio (FX, IR, EQ, CS, CO, etc.); volatility and correlations are also needed in case the user wants to correlate scenarios across risk factors and not to consider each risk factor from a segmental perspective.
- *Portfolio data*: Especially for building the time buckets usually based on different frequencies for the respective building segments of the curves.
- *Current credit exposure*: Depending on the method used for generating scenarios or on the risk figure to be computed, the scenario generator may require credit exposure of the entire portfolio.

The model must provide a reasonable distribution of the possible risk of the transactions and thus account for a large fraction of future plausible scenarios. The first step in the simulation is the definition of the time buckets to be used. As previously mentioned, the bucketing should be user-defined and captured through the scenario generator. These data should be considered as static and will not change often. In case the portfolio requires additional points due to optionality or early termination events, intermediate points are calculated by backward induction. The second step is the definition of the risk factor types for the scenario generation. This procedure is definitely dependent on the underlying portfolio and on the pricing algorithms. Calibration of the following models is very important since future scenarios will be determined by this process: Models calibrated to market prices tend to be more forward-looking, but contain components such as risk premiums and storage costs that introduce bias. Based on this list of risk factor types, the scenario generation engine will either run a full (brute force) Monte Carlo or an optimized quasi-Monte Carlo simulation. In the latter, in order to optimize performance, the system should provide numerical techniques like principal component analysis (PCA) to reduce the full universe of random paths to those statistically relevant for a portfolio. Scenario plausibility criteria can be used separately upon definition of the Mahalanobis distance or concurrently with numerical receipts like PCA. There are two different approaches to scenario analysis that should provide an efficient complementary framework:

- *Classic generic scenario framework*: Usage of macroeconomic scenarios and/or specific historical periods. The focus is on flexibility to reproduce a large variety of scenarios. Additionally, there is a regulatory requirement with specific stress testing constraints.
- *Systemic scenario framework*: This is based on the identification of the most severe and most plausible scenarios given the existing exposures in the portfolio, and on the analysis of the key concentration and idiosyncratic risk within a given scenario.

In both cases, we should define a plausibility measure for scenarios to identify the most likely scenarios and rule out non-sensible scenarios. Choosing a level of plausibility is a key step in systematic stress testing as it defines entirely the set of admissible scenarios: A simple and meaningful choice is the Mahalanobis distance.[1]

The output of the scenario generator engine is a cube of scenarios where each trade of the portfolio can be further priced on each state on each time bucket, therefore generating empirical price distributions. The cube of scenarios is typically built upon the following components: Risk factors (list of all risk factors defined for a specific portfolio), scenarios (list of Monte Carlo simulations used) and time buckets (list of pre-defined time nodes). See Figure 7.3.

7.3.2 Pricing and analytics

Returning to the CCR framework, the second step in the credit exposure calculation is to value instruments at different future times using the simulated scenarios generated in the previous step. Whereas credit exposure management should generally focus on real parameters, pricing should more generally focus on risk-neutral market-implied parameters, especially where

---

[1] In statistics, Mahalanobis distance is a distance measure introduced by P. C. Mahalanobis in 1936. It is based on correlations between variables by which different patterns can be identified and analyzed. It gauges the *similarity* of an unknown sample set to a known one. It differs from Euclidean distance in that it takes into account the correlations of the dataset and is scale-invariant.

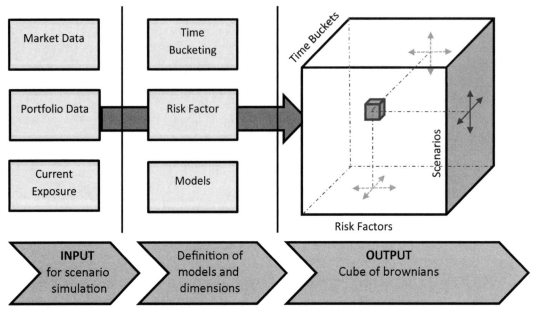

Figure 7.3 Core of the scenario generation: cube of Brownians.

counterparty risk is actively managed. As the general framework is Monte Carlo based, it is preferable for performance purposes not to use Monte Carlo-based pricing models. As a result, proxy pricing models are probably worth developing to reach the optimal tradeoff between performance and accuracy. One requires pricing a trade on each node—a node being defined by a date and a path. As a result, the amount of unit pricings is very large so that the use of GPU (grid performance unit) or grid techniques should be investigated.

A CVA/CCR system must be able to deal with the aging of positions by resolving cash flows, exercise options, and resets at multiple future time nodes. The incorporation of new pricing models must definitely be facilitated.

Additionally, the analytical gap that widened between the front office and usual support units such as finance or risk control during the past decades needs to be filled as both sides have to collaborate efficiently to assess and work out the new regulatory landscape. In other words, the financial crisis added emphasis to the disjunction between these parallel pillars in the financial industry as the support unit could not really follow and properly assess the risks inherent to the positions taken by the front office. Due to the tremendous technological and analytical challenges underlying the new regulatory landscape, only a bank-wide unified framework could be supported.

7.3.3 Portfolio aggregation engines

Isolated counterparty risk for a single transaction could be done easily using the framework presented before. However, credit exposure needs to be computed on the counterparty level, and then requires a computational platform across all assets and also aggregation algorithms.

Risk mitigation techniques often do not change the probability of suffering a loss, but do reduce the resulting credit exposure. As a consequence, the system should retrieve all relevant information for computing the resulting exposure. This part is probably the most insidious to implement since there exist many different ways for institutions to mitigate their counterparty risk. Various forms of risk mitigation focus on controlling credit exposure, with the most important being netting agreements, CSA, break clauses or even hedging activities.

The aggregation engine should retrieve information from the pricing cube, collateral data from the collateral management systems and many static data related to the trades, so that an efficient netting process can take place. The aggregation engine may also enrich the pricing cube in order to provide credit-related statistics at the trade level. Apart from these "internal" mitigation techniques, central counterparty (CCP) is a master-piece of the banking framework since banks will be obliged by the regulator to trade through these systems in order to limit their credit exposure. Furthermore, the distinction between bilateral and CCP-cleared OTC transactions is recognized under the Basel II framework, which gives a 0% weighting of exposure to a CCP. Even if the risk weight for a CCP will only slightly increase to 2%, significant capital reserve will have to be built for transactions cleared by a CCP. See Figure 7.4.

7.3.3.1 Mitigation process phase 1: netting agreements

From a computational point of view, netting and no-netting agreements will determine how aggregation is performed within a pool of transactions. The main challenge is the requirement of being scenario-consistent across trades. This means that the price distribution of all transactions has to be computed together in order to choose the correct risk measurement of the whole port-folio together with the correct netting agreements. The aggregation engine should support cross-product netting, specific to the transaction, that can have both positive and negative values such as derivatives. A netting agreement is a legally binding contract that allows the aggregation of transactions without agreement; the agreement that the purpose of a trade was to cancel a previous one

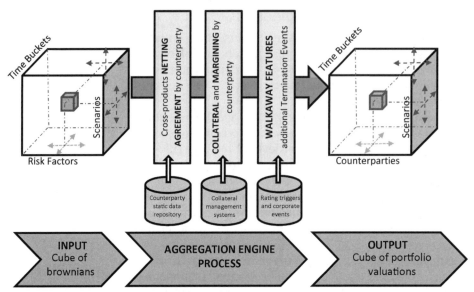

Figure 7.4 Output of the scenario generation engine: cube of portfolio valuations.

does not justify the netting of their values in a case when the counterparty is in default. This kind of netting is called payment netting as counterparties agree to combine payments occurring the same day into a single net payment. Payment netting reduces settlement risk and enhances operational efficiency.

Bilateral netting is recognized for OTC derivatives, repo-style transactions, and on-balance-sheet loans and deposits. However, netting across these product categories is often not allowed and may not be recognized for regulatory capital purposes. The efficiency of netting is directly dependant on the correlation between the mark-to-market (MtM) values of the transactions involved in the process: Negative correlation will tend to better offset netted expected exposure and therefore netting efficiency will be higher. Netting efficiency could be computed by counterparty under a specific assumption of distributed random variables.

7.3.3.2 Mitigation process phase 2: collateralization (under CSA agreement)

Collateral is intended to offset the exposure of the margined portfolio over time. Even after the netting process occurs, there might be a remaining big positive exposure with the counterparty: A collateral agreement limits this exposure by specifying that collateral must be posted by one counterparty against the other to support such an exposure. Sources of

remaining non-zero exposure despite collateralization to be taken into account in the model are:
- Grace period (in case of counterparty default, the remargining process stops: until the defaulted trades have been replaced/ rehedged, the replacement costs will evolve unmargined).
- Remargining frequency (delta between the MtM and the margin settlement time).
- Agreement details such as thresholds (level of exposure below which collateral will not be posted, i.e. amount of uncollateralized exposure).
- Independent and minimum transfer amounts (MTA) and funding rate[2] for cash collateral.
- Haircut for reflecting collateral quality.
- Amount rounding for posting the collateral.
- Liquidity of the collateral.
- Time to liquidate the collateral on the market.
- Correlation between the value of the transaction being pledged and the value of the underlying collateral.
- Collateral currency that could lead to an FX risk.
- Rehypothecation criteria (non-cash collateral may be sold, used in repos or, more commonly, passed on as collateral to another counterparty).

The following time periods are essential for margin agreements and should be made available (or mapped) in the system accordingly:
- *Call period*: The period that defines the frequency at which the collateral is monitored and called for.
- *Cure period*: The time interval necessary to close out the counterparty and rehedge the resulting market risk; this period generates the so-called close-out risk, which is the amount by which the value of a transaction could change during this period until the collateral has been liquidated and used to fund, at current market conditions, the replacement of the default counterparty in the transaction.
- *Margin period of risk*: The time interval from the last exchange of collateral until the defaulting counterparty is closed out and the resulting market risk is rehedged; it is usually assumed to be the sum of the call period and cure period, typically it can be assumed to be 10 days, but it can be shorter or longer depending on the liquidity of the collateral being sold out.
- Reconciliation period: Computing the difference between the credit exposure and the MtM of the underlying collateral

---

[2] There is a common practice now for paying the overnight risk-free rate plus a spread in line with the collateral giver's credit quality.

posted so any dispute can be avoided during the collateralization process.

A collateral management Application Programming Interface (API) will be called on each counterparty credit exposure in order to apply the logic to determine, at each point of the cube, how much of the exposure would be actually collateralized.

7.3.3.3 Mitigation process phase 3: break clauses (additional termination events)

Typically, rating-based additional termination event (RB-ATE) clauses give a counterparty the right to close out one or all derivative contracts with a given counterparty if its rating falls below a specified rating level. The break clause will usually only be possible after a certain period and normally at pre-specified dates, so the system must be able to retrieve the break clause schedule. As part of the potential data representation in the system, FpML uses the tag "MutualOrOptionalEarlyTermination" for specifying whether the Mutual Early Termination Right that is detailed in the Master Confirmation will apply.

Since the financial crisis of 2008, derivative participants have been stepping up their negotiation of RB-ATEs to mitigate their risk against credit quality deteriorations. The aggregation engine should adjust the valuation of a derivative contract under an ISDA agreement that contains a unilateral RB-ATE clause against the bank. The downgrade intensity is calibrated to historical credit rating transition matrices for financial institutions or corporates over a specific period of time. In practice, to keep good relationships with specific counterparties, these ATEs will be partially or totally ignored by the front office; therefore, a specific flag may or may not be implemented to weight these clauses at the counterparty level, thus avoiding overestimating the break clause protection. Additionally, downgrade triggers are also defined with some financial institutions or supranationals.

7.3.3.4 Hedges

Due to the stochastic processes underlying any exposure profile calculation, a key driver of CVAs is the sensitivity to volatility and this means that a CVA desk has to buy volatility in different asset classes.

The new regulatory framework that will come into place from 1 January 2013 onwards highlights the relevance and benefits of credit risk hedging instruments. For instance, a CDS can be used to hedge the regulatory exposure according the Basel III regulation;

Table 7.1. Eligible hedges for CVA and CCR capital management

	Regulatory (capital)		Economic (P&L)	
	Basel II	Basel III	Basel II	Basel III
Market hedges				
FX			×	×
IR			×	×
COM			×	×
EQ			×	×
Credit hedges				
CDS		×	×	×
Contingent CDS (CCDS)		×	×	×
Index CDS		×	×	×

depending on the approach followed by the bank, this hedging instrument needs also to be incorporated within the simulation process, representing *de facto* additional risk mitigants.

Table 7.1 gives an overview of some current products used to actively manage the counterparty risk within a bank and their eligibility for capital and profit and loss (P&L) purposes.

7.4 Trade Assessment

On the basis of the presented framework, the toolbox is now prepared to compute the following credit risk quantifications. See Figure 7.5.

The aggregation engine provides a cube of portfolio valuations using either economic or regulatory relevant risk mitigants. A slicer can easily select the relevant scenarios necessary to compute the different counterparty risk measure:

- *Potential future exposure (PFE)* is the typical measure used in the financial industry to characterize and monitor credit exposure. This is a high-level quantile of the price distribution. A PFE is typically generated for many future dates up until the longest maturity date of transactions in the netting set.
- *Expected positive exposure (EPE)* is another fundamental measure used in the financial industry, corresponding to the mean of the positive part of the price distribution. This measure can run on risk-neutral scenarios (used in practice

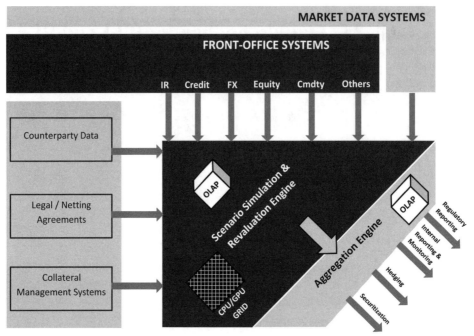

Figure 7.5 Overview of a CCR/CVA framework.

for the hedging of counterparty exposure) or on risk-mean scenarios (usually used for the calculation of risk weighted assets and capital).

- *Expected negative exposure (ENE)* is defined as the mean of the negative part of the price distribution and is equivalent to the EPE from the perspective of the counterparty.

All these exposure profiles are the necessary masterpieces to assess the profitability of a trade. For this, the following incremental costs relative to the counterparty risk will be calculated on the basis of the previous outputs of the models:

- *CVA (credit valuation adjustment)*: The cost of buying protection on the counterparty that pays the portfolio value in case of default, this is based on the EPE (expected value under the risk neutral measure). It is a significant part of the P&L of any financial institution, and most of banks are hedging CVA actively.
- *DVA (debt valuation adjustment)*: The cost for the counterparty of buying protection on the bank that pays the portfolio value from his perspective in case of default, this is based on the ENE (expected liability under the risk neutral measure).
- *FVA (funding valuation adjustment)*: In any derivatives contract future cash flows need to be funded. In a bilateral

transaction, an open negative MtM position can be seen as an overnight loan granted by the counterparty; logically, this funding benefit is financed at the cost of funds. In the case of a positive MtM, this is represents a funding cost, i.e. by unwinding the trade and investing this amount with the treasury, which is the rate the desk should get. For a single contract, DVA is equal to the funding benefit.

- *Capital costs*: Associated to the regulatory capital requirements over the lifetime of the trade. This is based on the regulatory exposure. Under Basel III, they are split into two components: capital costs for default risk and capital costs for CVA risk.
- *Bank levy*: Tax to be paid on balance sheet usage. This is currently in place in France, Germany and the United Kingdom. For instance, the calculation is made on the expected liability and on the notional of the trade in Germany.

The first effect of the new regulation will be directly assessed in the upfront pricing of a new deal on a marginal basis. The inclusion of a new transaction within an existing portfolio for a counterparty and also within the overall derivatives portfolio of the bank also triggers some additional adjustments for risk quantifications and for hedging positions. Through the computation of prices of complex transactions in potential futures scenarios for a counterparty risk purpose, we can get definitive insights on price distributions relevant for values at risk and stress testing. Whereas the market risk of the new transaction is directly hedged by the trading desk, the incremental counterparty risk (spread risk, CVA capital charge and even the market inherent to the counterparty risk) will be adjusted dynamically. For instance, the presented framework can also provide CVA sensitivities to allow an active management of the P&L-relevant CVA reserve. The usual sensitivities calculated are the credit spread sensitivities and the market risk sensitivities associated with the risk factors simulated previously.

Notes

The opinions expressed in this article are those of the author and do not necessarily reflect the views of Commerzbank.

References

Basel Committee on Banking Supervision, 2010. Basel III: A Global Regulatory Framework for More Resilient Banks and Banking Systems. Basel Committee on Banking Supervision, Basel.

Cesari, G., Acquilina, J., Charpillon, N., Filipovic, Z., Lee, G., Manda, I., 2009. Modelling, Pricing and Hedging Counterparty Credit Exposure—A Technical Guide. In: Berlin. Springer, 101−109.

Financial Accounting Standards Board, 2006. Statement of Financial Accounting Standards No. 157—Fair Value Measurements. Financial Accounting Standards Board, Norwalk, CT.

Gregory, J., 2009. Counterparty Credit Risk: The New Challenge for Global Financial Markets. Wiley, Chichester, 41−74.

Kelly, D., 2011. How the credit crisis has changed counterparty risk management. Risk Professional 18 (6), 27−31.

Jamshidian, F., Zhu, Y., 1996. Scenario simulation: theory and methodology. Finance and Stochastics 1 (1), 43−67.

Pykhtin, M., 2005. Counterparty Risk Modelling. Risk Books, London, 97−125.

8

A JUMP—DIFFUSION NOMINAL SHORT RATE MODEL

Sami Attaoui and Pierre Six
Rouen Business School

CHAPTER OUTLINE

8.1 Introduction

Modeling interest rates has been achieved through two different approaches: The arbitrage-free framework[1] and the equilibrium approach.[2] The equilibrium setting is very useful to gain insights into the economic background of the model and to understand the interplay between variables. In addition, equilibrium models explicitly specify the risk premia.

Lioui and Poncet (2004) build a general equilibrium model where a monetary economy affected by both real and monetary shocks is considered. Relying on the money-in-the-utility function where the investor holds money in addition to consumption, Lioui and Poncet (2004) investigate money non-neutrality, and show that money cannot be neutral due to the important role monetary parameters play within various financial and economic quantities. In addition to specifying the endogenous expressions

---

[1] See, e.g. Heath *et al.* (1992) and Brace *et al.* (1997).
[2] In the finance literature, one of the most used equilibrium framework is the seminal work of Cox *et al.* (1985a, 1985b).

Rethinking Valuation and Pricing Models. http://dx.doi.org/10.1016/B978-0-12-415875-7.00008-7

for the drift and diffusion terms of the general price level, Lioui and Poncet (2004) focus on deriving, under specific assumptions, different dynamics of the real and nominal interest rates. Nevertheless, since Lioui and Poncet (2004) consider the case of pure diffusion processes, the obtained dynamics of the various short-term interest rates do not meet the empirical evidence on the presence of discontinuities in the processes of the interest rates. For instance, Das (2002) and Johannes (2004) show that jumps are present in the dynamics of interest rates. Similarly, Guan *et al.* (2005) find that a jump–diffusion setting is required to efficiently explain the innovations in Libor rates.

The goal of this chapter is to derive a jump–diffusion model for the nominal interest rate based on economic arguments. Indeed, Lu and Wu (2009) highlight the importance of inflation-related and output-related releases on the shape of the term structure of interest rates, in particular for the short rate. We extend the monetary economy of Lioui and Poncet (2004) to a jump–diffusion setting. Thus, the inflation rate process incorporates jumps, in addition to its diffusion component. This feature is very likely since the inflation rate can be subject to jumps on macroeconomic data release. Indeed, Johannes (2004) finds that jumps are a consequence of unanticipated news about the macroeconomy. We also analyze the impact of introducing jumps on various financial entities such as the expected excess return on a nominal bond and the inflation risk premium.

This chapter is organized as follows. Section 8.2 presents the general setting and derives the dynamics of the general price level. Section 8.3 obtains the expressions for the real and nominal short–term interest rates as well as the inflation risk premium. Section 8.4 derives, under specific assumptions for the dynamics of the state variables, the production and the monetary supply, the dynamics of the nominal short-term interest rate. Section 8.5 concludes.

8.2 The Economy

We consider, as in Lioui and Poncet (2004), an economy with real and monetary sectors. In the real sector, there is a single good, which may be allocated to either consumption or investment, produced by a single technology. In the monetary sector, the central bank, based on economic targets, sets the money supply. We, therefore, assume an exogenous money supply process. We differ from the framework of Lioui and Poncet (2004) by introducing jumps in the dynamics of all the processes involved. That is, the production, the state variables[3] and the money supply follow jump–diffusion processes.

A.1 There are K state variables whose dynamics obey to the system of stochastic differential equations (SDE):

$$dY(t) = \mu(t, Y)dt + \sigma(t, Y)'dZ(t) + \gamma(t-, Y)'dN(t), \qquad (8.1)$$

where $\mu(t, Y)$ is a bounded $K \times 1$ vector function of drifts, $\sigma(t, Y)'$ is a bounded $K \times (Q + K)$ diffusion matrix function and the jump amplitudes $\gamma(t, Y)'$ is a $K \times (Q + K)$ matrix of mutually independent random variables.[4] $N(t) = (N_1(t), \ldots, N_{Q+K}(t))'$ is the $(Q + K) \times 1$ vector of independent Poisson processes with $(K + Q) \times 1$ vector of constant intensity λ. $Z(t)$ is a $(K + Q) \times 1$ vector of independent Wiener processes. The Poisson and Wiener processes are independent and defined on the complete filtered probability space $(\Omega, \mathbb{F}, P)$, where $\mathbb{F} = \{\mathcal{F}_t, t \geq 0\}$ and $\mathbf{P}$ is the historical probability measure.

A.2 The production of the good is governed by the SDE:

$$\frac{d\eta(t)}{\eta(t-)} = \mu_\eta(t, Y)dt + \sigma_\eta(t, Y)'dZ(t) + \sum_{j=1}^{Q+K} \gamma_{\eta,j}(t, Y)dN_j(t), \quad (8.2)$$

where $\eta(t)$ denotes the amount of the good invested at date t in the technology, $\mu_\eta(t, Y)$ is a bounded function, $\sigma_\eta(t, Y)$ is a bounded $(Q + K) \times 1$ vector valued function and $\gamma_\eta(t, Y) = (\gamma_{\eta,1}(t, Y), \ldots, \gamma_{\eta,K+Q}(t, Y))'$ denotes the $(Q + K) \times 1$ vector of mutually independent random jump amplitudes.

A.3 The money issued by the central bank, $M(t)$, has the following dynamics:

$$\frac{dM(t)}{M(t-)} = \mu_M(t, Y)dt + \sigma_M(t, Y)'dZ(t) + \sum_{j=1}^{Q+K} \gamma_{M,j}(t, Y)dN_j(t),$$

$$(8.3)$$

where $\mu_M(t, Y)$ is a bounded function, $\sigma_M(t, Y)$ is a $(Q + K) \times 1$ vector valued function of volatilities and $\gamma_M(t, Y) = (\gamma_{M,1}(t, Y), \ldots, \gamma_{M,K+Q}(t, Y))'$ denotes a $(Q + K) \times 1$ vector of mutually independent random jump amplitudes.

---

[3] See Ahn and Thomson (1988) who extend the framework of Cox *et al.* (1985a, 1985b) to a jump–diffusion setting.

[4] This is, for ease of exposition and tractability, a standard assumption in the literature. It also is in line with economic intuition since magnitudes related to independent shocks should not *a priori* be linked by random events.

It will be shown that the general price level, $P(t)$, expressed in units of the consumption/investment good, obeys the dynamics:

$$\frac{\mathrm{d}P(t)}{P(t-)} = \mu_p(t,Y)\mathrm{d}t + \sigma_p(t,Y)'\mathrm{d}Z(t) + \sum_{j=1}^{Q+K} \gamma_{p,j}(t,Y)\mathrm{d}N_j(t), \quad (8.4)$$

where $\gamma_p(t,Y) = (\gamma_{p,1}(t,Y),...,\gamma_{p,K+Q}(t,Y))'$ and $\sigma_p(t,Y)$ are two $(Q+K) \times 1$ vector valued functions, and $\mu_p(t,Y)$ is a bounded function. The quantities $\mu_p(t,Y)$, $\sigma_p(t,Y)$ and $\gamma_p(t,Y)$ will be determined endogenously.

A.4 Real and nominal money market accounts exist. The real one has a riskless, in real terms, instantaneous real return equal to the real interest rate $r(t)$. The nominal savings, which is also riskless but in nominal terms,[5] has an instantaneous nominal return equal to the nominal interest rate $R(t)$.

A.5 There is a competitive market for a real default-free zero-coupon bond $b(t,T,w,Y)$ whose dynamics are:

$$\frac{\mathrm{d}b(t,T,w,Y)}{b(t-,T,w,Y)} = \mu_b(t,T,w,Y)\mathrm{d}t + \sigma_b(t,T,w,Y)'\mathrm{d}Z(t)$$

$$+ \sum_{j=1}^{Q+K} \gamma_{b,j}(t,T,w,Y)\mathrm{d}N_j(t), \quad (8.5)$$

where w denotes the investor real wealth, $\mu_b(t,T,w,Y)$ is the expected rate of return on the real zero-coupon bond and $\sigma_b(t,T,w,Y)$ and $\gamma_b(t,T,w,Y)$ are two $(Q+K) \times 1$ vectors.

Applying Itô's lemma to the real zero-coupon bond price, we determine the values of the diffusion and jump components, i.e. $\sigma_b(t,T,w,Y) = \frac{b_w}{b}\sigma_w + \frac{b_Y}{b}\sigma$ and $\gamma_b(t,T,w,Y) = \frac{1}{b}[b(t,T,w+\gamma_w,Y+\gamma) - b(t,T,w,Y)]$, respectively. Note that μ_b will be determined endogenously in the sequel. Furthermore, b_w and b_Y are the first derivatives of $b(t,T,w,Y)$ with respect to w and Y, respectively. σ_w and γ_w are the diffusion and the jump amplitude, respectively, of the real wealth w (their precise expressions will be given in Proposition (1) below).

A.6 We finally assume that continuous trading in all financial and monetary assets and in the technology takes place in frictionless and arbitrage-free markets and at equilibrium prices only.

---

[5] The nominal money market account is a risky asset in real terms.

We consider a representative agent that aims to maximize, over an infinite horizon, his or her expected utility function:

$$\max_{c,m,\alpha,\theta,\delta} \left(\int_0^\infty U(t,c(t),m(t))dt \right), \qquad (8.6)$$

subject to the following budget constraint:[6]

$$
\begin{aligned}
dw = &\left[\alpha w(\mu_\eta - r) + w \sum_{i=1}^{K+Q} \theta_i(\mu_{b_i} - r) + \delta w \left(R - \left(\mu_p - \sigma'_p \sigma_p \right) - r \right) \right. \\
&\left. + wr - c - m \left(\mu_p - \sigma'_p \sigma_p + r \right) \right] dt \qquad + \left[\alpha w \sigma'_\eta + \theta' w \Sigma_b \right. \\
&\left. - (\delta w + m) \sigma'_p \right] dZ(t) + \sum_{j=1}^{Q+K} \left[\alpha w \gamma_{\eta,j} + w \sum_{i=1}^{K+Q} \theta_i \gamma_{b_i,j} \right. \\
&\left. - (\delta w + m) \left(\frac{\gamma_{p,j}}{1 + \gamma_{p,j}} \right) \right] dN_j(t), \qquad (8.7)
\end{aligned}
$$

where $U(t,c,m)$ is the standard money-in-the-utility function, θ represents a vector of proportions of real wealth invested in discount bonds, δ denotes the proportion of real wealth invested in the nominal money market account and α is the ratio[7] of investment to real wealth. Moreover, w is the investor's time t real wealth, c is the time t consumption rate and m denotes real money balances holdings.

The equilibrium of the economy is characterized by the following market clearing conditions. (i) Total wealth must be equal to the total amount invested in the technology plus the holdings of real value money balances, i.e. $\kappa \eta + m = w$. Hence, we have $m = w(1 - \alpha)$. (ii) Net holdings in the nominal money market account and in bonds must be nil, i.e. $\delta = 0$ and $\theta = 0$,

---

[6] For ease of notation, we drop the explicit dependence on time.

[7] More precisely, let κ be the number, at time t, of units held in the technology. Therefore, $\alpha \equiv \kappa \eta / w$. For the sequel, we consider the dynamics of α as:

$$\frac{d\alpha(t)}{\alpha(t-)} = \mu_\alpha dt + \sigma'_\alpha dZ(t) + \sum_{j=1}^{Q+K} \gamma_{\alpha,j} dN_j(t).$$

respectively. (iii) Money supply must equal money demand, i.e., $M/P = m$.

Under the above equilibrium conditions, Equation (8.7) becomes:

$$\frac{dw}{w} = \left[\alpha\mu_\eta - \frac{c}{w} - (1-\alpha)\left(\mu_p - \sigma'_p\sigma_p\right)\right]dt$$

$$+ \left[\alpha\sigma'_\eta - (1-\alpha)\sigma'_p\right]dZ(t) \qquad (8.8)$$

$$+ \sum_{j=1}^{Q+K}\left[\alpha\gamma_{\eta,j} - (1-\alpha)\frac{\gamma_{p,j}}{1+\gamma_{p,j}}\right]dN_j(t).$$

In addition, since at equilibrium we have $P = M/m = M/w(1-\alpha)$, we derive[8] the dynamics of the price level and real wealth as stated by the following proposition.

Proposition 1 *At equilibrium, the dynamics of the price level and the wealth are:*

$$\frac{dP(t)}{P(t-)} = \mu_p dt + \sigma'_p dZ(t) + \sum_{j=1}^{Q+K}\gamma_{p,j}dN_j(t), \qquad (8.9)$$

where:

$$\mu_p = \frac{1}{1-\alpha}\mu_\alpha + \frac{1}{\alpha}\mu_M + \frac{c}{w\alpha} - \mu_\eta + \frac{\alpha}{(1-\alpha)^2}\sigma'_\alpha\sigma_\alpha$$

$$+ \sigma'_\eta\sigma_\eta - \frac{1}{\alpha}\sigma'_M\sigma_\eta + \frac{1}{1-\alpha}\sigma'_M\sigma_\alpha - \frac{1}{1-\alpha}\sigma'_\alpha\sigma_\eta \qquad (8.10)$$

$$\sigma_p = \frac{1}{1-\alpha}\sigma_\alpha + \frac{1}{\alpha}\sigma_M - \sigma_\eta \qquad (8.11)$$

$$\gamma_{p,j} = \frac{1}{1+\gamma_{\eta,j}}\left[\frac{\gamma_{\alpha,j}}{1-\alpha\left(1+\gamma_{\alpha,j}\right)} + \frac{1-\alpha}{\alpha}\frac{\gamma_{M,j}}{1-\alpha\left(1+\gamma_{\alpha,j}\right)} - \gamma_{\eta,j}\right],$$

$$\qquad (8.12)$$

and:

$$\frac{dw(t)}{w(t-)} = \mu_w dt + \sigma'_w dZ(t) + \sum_{j=1}^{Q+K}\gamma_{w,j}dN_j(t), \qquad (8.13)$$

---

[8] This is achieved by applying Ito's lemma to $M/w(1-\alpha)$.

where:

$$\mu_w = \mu_\eta - \frac{c}{\alpha w} - \mu_\alpha - \frac{1-\alpha}{\alpha}\mu_M + \sigma'_\alpha\sigma_\alpha - \frac{1-\alpha}{\alpha}\sigma'_M\sigma_\eta$$

$$+ \frac{2-\alpha}{\alpha}\sigma'_M\sigma_\alpha + \frac{1-\alpha}{\alpha^2}\sigma'_M\sigma_M - \sigma'_\alpha\sigma_\eta$$

(8.14)

$$\sigma_w = \sigma_\eta - \sigma_\alpha - \frac{1-\alpha}{\alpha}\sigma_M \qquad (8.15)$$

$$\gamma_{w,j} = \frac{\alpha\gamma_{\eta,j} - \alpha\gamma_{\alpha,j} + \alpha\gamma_{M,j}\gamma_{\eta,j} - (1-\alpha)\gamma_{M,j}}{\gamma_{M,j} + \alpha\left(1 + \gamma_{\alpha,j}\right)}, \qquad (8.16)$$

Where μ_α, σ_α and γ_α denote the drift, diffusion and jump amplitude of α (see Footnote 7).

Equations (8.10), (8.11), (8.14) and (8.15) are similar to those obtained by Lioui and Poncet (2004) in the pure diffusion case. We, therefore, focus our attention to the discussion of the jump-related equations, i.e. Equations (8.12) and (8.16). First, one can notice that the jump component in the wealth dynamics is affected by both monetary and real parameters. The presence of a monetary component indicates that money non-neutrality is preserved in the presence of jumps. Furthermore, Equation (8.12) shows that the jump amplitude in the general price level is a function of monetary and real parameters, and it has the same sign as that in the money supply γ_M. A positive (negative) jump in the money supply yields an increase (decrease) in the inflation rate. Moreover, a positive (negative) jump in the production leads to a negative (positive) jump in the general price level. Finally, Equation (8.12) provides a theoretical ground of the econometric modeling of Kim (1993), who finds a regime switching and an heteroskedasticity in the variance of the inflation.

8.3 Equilibrium Interest Rates and Monetary Policy

We assume, for tractability, a log-separable utility function:

$$U(t, c(t), m(t)) = e^{-\rho t}(\beta\log(c(t)) + (1 - \beta)\log(m(t))), \quad (8.17)$$

where ρ is the rate of impatience and $\beta \in [0, 1]$ is a weighting factor.

The indirect utility function is state independent and has the form:

$$J(t, w(t)) = \frac{1}{\rho} e^{-\rho t} \log(Aw(t)), \qquad (8.18)$$

where A is a constant. We provide below equilibrium expressions for the real and nominal rates, the expected excess returns and the inflation risk premium.

Proposition 2   *At equilibrium and given (8.17) and (8.18) the real and nominal interest rates are given by:*

$$r = \mu_\eta - \sigma'_\eta \sigma_\eta + \sigma'_\alpha \sigma_\eta + \frac{1-\alpha}{\alpha} \sigma'_M \sigma_\eta$$

$$+ \sum_{j=1}^{Q+K} \lambda_j \mathbb{E} \left[\frac{\gamma_{\eta,j} \gamma_{M,j}}{\alpha \left(1 + \gamma_{\eta,j}\right)\left(1 + \gamma_{M,j}\right)} + \frac{1}{1 + \gamma_{M,j}} \right.$$

$$\left. + \frac{\gamma_{\eta,j} \gamma_{\alpha,j} - 1}{\left(1 + \gamma_{\eta,j}\right)\left(1 + \gamma_{M,j}\right)} \right], \qquad (8.19)$$

and:

$$R = \rho + \frac{\alpha}{1-\alpha} \mu_\alpha + \mu_M - \sigma'_M \sigma_M - \frac{\alpha}{1-\alpha} \sigma'_\alpha \sigma_M$$

$$+ \sum_{j=1}^{Q+K} \lambda_j \mathbb{E} \left[\frac{\gamma_{M,j}}{1 + \gamma_{M,j}} + \frac{\alpha}{1-\alpha} \frac{\gamma_{\alpha,j}}{1 + \gamma_{M,j}} \right], \qquad (8.20)$$

respectively.

Proof. See the Appendix.   □

With respect to the results of Lioui and Poncet (2004) in the pure diffusion case, the Expressions (8.19) and (8.20) contain additional jump-related terms. They are the fifth and sixth terms in Equations (8.19) and (8.20), respectively. We reach, when introducing jumps, similar conclusions as in the pure diffusion case, i.e. the real interest rate is affected by both monetary and technological parameters, whereas the nominal interest rate is solely determined by monetary factors.[9] Actually, jumps in technology play a crucial role since if we set γ_η to zero then jumps disappear from Equation (8.19). However, when we suppose that $\gamma_M = 0$, then the expression between brackets in Equation (8.19) becomes $1 - 1/1 + \gamma_{\eta,j}$. Moreover, from Equation (8.20), a positive (negative) jump in money supply is related to higher (lower) interest rates.

At equilibrium, the expected excess return on a real discount bond is given by:

---

[9] In addition to the utility function parameters.

$$\mu_b - r = \sigma_b' \left(\sigma_\eta - \sigma_\alpha - \frac{1-\alpha}{\alpha} \sigma_M \right) - \sum_{j=1}^{Q+K} \lambda_j \mathbb{E} \left[\frac{\gamma_{b,j}}{1 + \gamma_{w,j}} \right]. \quad (8.21)$$

The expected excess return depends, in addition to the covariance between the bond and the real wealth, on the sign of jump amplitude of the bond price. Specifically, for negative jumps, the expected excess return increases and inversely. This is a well-known result: When the bond price rises, its yield decreases.

The nominal price of the real discount bond, B, can be obtained by applying Ito's lemma to $B = bP$. Thus, the nominal expected return of the discount bond is given by:

$$\mu_B - R = \sigma_B' \left(\frac{\alpha}{1-\alpha} \sigma_\alpha + \frac{1}{\alpha} \sigma_M \right)$$
$$- \sum_{j=1}^{Q+K} \lambda_j \mathbb{E} \left[\frac{1 - \alpha \left(1 + \gamma_{\alpha,j} \right)}{(1 - \alpha) \left(1 + \gamma_{M,j} \right)} \gamma_{B,j} \right], \quad (8.22)$$

where $\sigma_B = \sigma_b + \sigma_p$ and $\gamma_{B,j} = \gamma_{b,j}(1 + \gamma_{p,j}) + \gamma_{p,j}$. As in the case of the real bond, the expected excess return on the nominal bond decreases when jumps in the bond price are positive.

Another important quantity is the inflation risk premium, ε, defined by $\varepsilon = R - r + \mathbb{E}_t[dP^{-1}/P^{-1}]$. When investing in a nominal money market account, instead of a real one, the investor takes a risk, due to inflation uncertainty, which is compensated by the inflation risk premium.

From Equations (8.19), (8.20) and (8.9), one obtains, after rearrangement, the expression:

$$\varepsilon = \frac{\alpha - \beta}{\alpha} \rho - \mu_\alpha - \frac{1-\alpha}{\alpha} \mu_M + \frac{1-\alpha^2}{\alpha^2} \sigma_M' \sigma_M$$
$$- \frac{1}{\alpha(1-\alpha)} \sigma_\alpha' \sigma_M \left(\alpha^2 + \alpha - 2 \right) + \sigma_\eta' \sigma_\eta$$
$$- \frac{2-\alpha}{1-\alpha} \sigma_\alpha' \sigma_\eta - \frac{2-\alpha}{\alpha} \sigma_M' \sigma_\eta + \frac{1}{1-\alpha} \sigma_\alpha' \sigma_\alpha$$
$$+ \sum_{j=1}^{Q+K} \lambda_j \mathbb{E} \left[\frac{(1-\alpha)\left(\gamma_{M,j} - 1 \right) + \alpha \gamma_{\alpha,j}}{(1-\alpha)\left(1 + \gamma_{M,j} \right)} - \frac{\gamma_{M,j} + \alpha \left(1 - \gamma_{\eta,j} \gamma_{\alpha,j} \right)}{\alpha \left(1 + \gamma_{M,j} \right) \left(1 + \gamma_{\eta,j} \right)} \right.$$
$$\left. - \frac{\alpha \gamma_{\alpha,j} \left(\gamma_{M,j} + 1 \right) + \left(1 - \alpha \left(1 + \gamma_{\alpha,j} \right) \right) \left(\gamma_{M,j} - \alpha \gamma_{\eta,j} \right)}{(1-\alpha)\gamma_{M,j} + \alpha(1-\alpha)\left(1 + \gamma_{\eta,j} \right)} \right].$$

$$(8.23)$$

We focus our analysis on the jump component. We notice that it is impacted by both real and monetary parameters. This indicates that the equilibrium value of the inflation risk premium is still affected by monetary policy in the presence of jumps. Moreover, a positive jump in the production leads to a decrease in the inflation risk premia. This is due to the fact that there is, as we mentioned above, an inverse relationship between jumps in the production and those occurring at the inflation rate level.

We also derive, in equilibrium, the dynamics of the real and nominal pricing kernels under the jump–diffusion framework.[10] The real pricing kernel is defined to be the investor's marginal utility of consumption (U_c) which is equal, in our specific case, to $e^{-\rho t}\beta\dfrac{1}{c}$. Thus, the expression of the optimal consumption in terms of real wealth obtains:[11]

$$c = \rho\beta w. \tag{8.25}$$

The real pricing kernel is given by $\xi(t) = \dfrac{1}{\rho}e^{-\rho t}\dfrac{1}{w(t)}$. We apply Ito's lemma to $\xi(t)$ and obtain:

$$\frac{d\xi(t)}{\xi(t-)} = -r dt - \sum_{j=1}^{Q+K} \lambda_j \mathbb{E}\Big[\gamma_{\xi,j}\Big] dt + \sigma'_\xi dZ(t) + \sum_{j=1}^{Q+K} \gamma_{\xi,j} dN_j(t),$$

$$\tag{8.26}$$

where:

$$\sigma_\xi = -\sigma_w \text{ and } \gamma_{\xi,j} = -\frac{\gamma_{w,j}}{1 + \gamma_{w,j}}.$$

One can notice that the market price of jump volatility risk, $\gamma_{\xi,j}$ is affected by monetary parameters. Therefore, the money non-neutrality is preserved under the jump–diffusion extension.

Once the real pricing kernel is known, we can derive the dynamics of the nominal one, $\zeta(t) = \xi(t)P^{-1}(t)$, as:

---

[10] The pricing kernel approach gives the time t price of a claim delivering a certain payoff at a given maturity.

[11] Equation (8.25) deserves the following comment. Assuming a smooth function of consumption (see Campbell and Deaton, 1989), i.e. its dynamics is not affected by a jump component ($\gamma_c = 0$), yields (it is obtained from Equation (8.16) by setting $\gamma_w = 0$) the following relationship between jumps in the money supply and in the technology:

$$\alpha\gamma_{\eta,j} - \alpha\gamma_{\alpha,j} + \alpha\gamma_{M,j}\gamma_{\eta,j} - (1-\alpha)\gamma_{M,j} = 0, \quad j = 1,...,Q+K. \tag{8.24}$$

Equation (8.24) confirms that the money supply is not independent of the economic activity. Indeed, a shock in the money supply is negatively related to shocks occurring at the technology level. This result is in line with central bank policy, which is likely to reduce its money supply in fear of increasing inflation, and *vice versa*.

$$\frac{d\zeta(t)}{\zeta(t-)} = -Rdt - \sum_{j=1}^{Q+K} \lambda_j \mathbb{E}\left[\gamma_{\zeta,j}\right]dt + \sigma_\zeta' dZ(t) + \sum_{j=1}^{Q+K} \gamma_{\zeta,j} dN_j(t),$$

$$(8.27)$$

where:

$$\sigma_\zeta = -\sigma_M - \frac{\alpha}{1-\alpha}\sigma_\alpha \text{ and } \gamma_{\zeta,j} = -\frac{\gamma_{M,j}}{1+\gamma_{M,j}} - \frac{\alpha}{1-\alpha}\frac{\gamma_{\alpha,j}}{1+\gamma_{M,j}}.$$

The jump volatility risk of the nominal pricing kernel depends, as expected, on monetary parameters. As we will show below, the investment to real wealth ratio terms depend, in fact, on the monetary state variable and monetary policy parameters. This is due to the log-separable assumption of the utility function.

8.4 A Nominal Interest Rate Model

In order to derive the dynamics of the nominal interest rate further specification of the dynamics of the state variables as well as those of the production and money supply are needed. We consider, in the following, the case of two state variables, one real and one nominal whose dynamics are given by:

$$\frac{dY_\eta(t)}{Y_\eta(t-)} = \mu_{Y_\eta}dt + \sigma_{Y_\eta}' dZ(t) + \sum_{j=1}^{Q+2} \gamma_{Y_{\eta,j}} dN_j(t), \qquad (8.28)$$

and:

$$\frac{dY_M(t)}{Y_M(t-)} = \mu_{Y_M}dt + \sigma_{Y_M}' dZ(t) + \sum_{j=1}^{Q+2} \gamma_{Y_{M,j}} dN_j(t), \qquad (8.29)$$

respectively. μ_{Y_η} and μ_{Y_M} are positive constants, σ_{Y_η} and σ_{Y_M} are $(Q+2) \times 1$ vectors of constants describing volatilities, and $\gamma_{Y_\eta} = (\gamma_{Y_{\eta,1}}, \ldots \gamma_{Y_{\eta,Q+2}})'$ and $\gamma_{Y_M} = (\gamma_{Y_{M,1}}, \ldots \gamma_{Y_{M,Q+2}})'$ are $(Q+2) \times 1$ vectors of mutually independent random jump amplitudes. $Z(t)$ is a $(Q+2) \times 1$ - dimensional Wiener process and $N(t)$ is a $(Q+2) \times 1$ - dimensional Poisson process. The Wiener, the Poisson and the jump amplitudes are independent.

Furthermore, Equations (8.2) and (8.3) are assumed to have the forms:

$$\frac{d\eta(t)}{\eta(t-)} = \mu_\eta Y_\eta(t)dt + \sqrt{Y_\eta(t)}\sigma_\eta' dZ(t) + \sum_{j=1}^{Q+2} Y_\eta(t-)\gamma_{\eta,j} dN_j(t),$$

$$(8.30)$$

and:

$$\frac{dM(t)}{M(t-)} = \mu_M Y_M(t) dt + \sqrt{Y_M(t)} \sigma'_M dZ(t)$$

$$+ \sum_{j=1}^{Q+2} Y_M(t-) \gamma_{M,j} dN_j(t), \tag{8.31}$$

respectively. μ_η and μ_M are positive constants, σ_η and σ_M are $(Q+2) \times 1$ vectors of positive constant volatilities, and γ_η denotes a $(Q+2) \times 1$ vector of mutually independent jump amplitudes.

To determine the dynamics of the nominal short-term interest rate $R(t)$, we rely on a standard result,[12] i.e. the nominal interest rate is equal, in equilibrium, to the ratio of marginal rates of substitution between real money balances and consumption, $R = U_\mathrm{m}/U_\mathrm{c}$, which gives in our separable utility function case:

$$R = \frac{1-\beta}{1-\alpha} \rho. \tag{8.32}$$

The presence of a monetary state variable implies a stochastic behavior of the investment to wealth ratio α. This stems from the fact, as it will be shown below, that α can be written as a function of Y_M. Therefore, α will be constant if we no longer assume a monetary state variable in our framework. This feature results in a constant nominal interest rate, which is, of course, a non-realistic assumption.

First, using Equations (8.32) and (8.20), we straightforwardly obtain:

$$\beta\rho + \mu_M Y_M - Y_M \sigma'_M \sigma_M + \sum_{j=1}^{Q+2} \lambda_j \mathbb{E} \left[\frac{Y_M \gamma_{M,j}}{1 + Y_M \gamma_{M,j}} \right]$$

$$= \alpha \left(\rho - \mu_\alpha + Y_M \mu_M - Y_M \sigma'_M \sigma_M + \sqrt{Y_M} \sigma'_\alpha \sigma_M \right.$$

$$\left. + \sum_{j=1}^{Q+2} \lambda_j \mathbb{E} \left[\frac{Y_M \gamma_{M,j}}{1 + Y_M \gamma_{M,j}} - \frac{\gamma_{\alpha,j}}{1 + Y_M \gamma_{M,j}} \right] \right), \tag{8.33}$$

---

[12] See proposition 5 in Lioui and Poncet (2004).

which can be rewritten in a compact form as $\alpha = f(Y_M)$. Applying Ito's lemma to $f(Y_M)$ yields the SDE that governs changes in α:

$$
\frac{d\alpha}{\alpha} = \underbrace{\left(\frac{f'_{Y_M}}{f} \mu_{Y_M} Y_M + \frac{1}{2} \frac{f'_{Y_M}}{f} Y_M^2 \sigma'_{Y_M} \sigma_{Y_M} \right)}_{=\mu_\alpha} dt + \underbrace{\frac{f'_{Y_M}}{f} Y_M \sigma'_{Y_M}}_{=\sigma'_\alpha} dZ
$$

$$
+ \left(\sum_{j=1}^{Q+2} \underbrace{\frac{f\left(Y_M \left(1 + \gamma_{Y_{M,j}} \right) \right)}{f} - 1}_{=\gamma_{\alpha,j}} \right) dN_j. \tag{8.34}
$$

Substituting the expressions of μ_α, σ_α and γ_α in Equation (8.33) and rearranging terms gives:

$$
\frac{\beta\rho + Y_M \left(\mu_M - \sigma'_M \sigma_M \right) + \sum_{j=1}^{Q+2} \lambda_j \mathbb{E} \left[\dfrac{Y_M \gamma_{M,j} + f\left(Y_M \left(1 + \gamma_{Y_{M,j}} \right) \right) - f}{1 + \gamma_{M,j} Y_M} \right]}{\rho + Y_M \left(\mu_M - \sigma'_M \sigma_M \right) + \sum_{j=1}^{Q+2} \lambda_j \mathbb{E} \left[\dfrac{Y_M \gamma_{M,j}}{1 + Y_M \gamma_{M,j}} \right]}
$$

$$
= f - f'_{Y_M} \frac{Y_M \mu_{Y_M} - Y_M^{\frac{3}{2}} \sigma'_{Y_M} \sigma_M}{\rho + \mu_M Y_M - \sigma_M^2 Y_M^2 + \sum_{j=1}^{Q+2} \lambda_j \mathbb{E} \left[\dfrac{\gamma_{M,j} Y_M}{1 + \gamma_{M,j} Y_M} \right]}
$$

$$
- \frac{1}{2} f'_{Y_M} \frac{\sigma_{Y_M}^2 Y_M^2}{\rho + \mu_M Y_M - \sigma_M^2 Y_M + \sum_{j=1}^{Q+2} \lambda_j \mathbb{E} \left[\dfrac{\gamma_{M,j} Y_M}{1 + \gamma_{M,j} Y_M} \right]}. \tag{8.35}
$$

One can notice that, due to the log separable utility function, the investment-to-real wealth ratio depends solely on the nominal state variable. Therefore, in the case of state variables occurring only at the real level, the expression of α reduces down to:

$$
\alpha = \frac{\beta\rho + \mu_M - \sigma'_M \sigma_M + \sum_{j=1}^{Q+2} \lambda_j \mathbb{E} \left[\dfrac{\gamma_{M,j}}{1 + \gamma_{M,j}} \right]}{\rho + \mu_M - \sigma'_M \sigma_M + \sum_{j=1}^{Q+2} \lambda_j \mathbb{E} \left[\dfrac{\gamma_{M,j}}{1 + \gamma_{M,j}} \right]}, \tag{8.36}
$$

leading to a constant α whose is only affected by monetary quantities.

An explicit solution for $f(Y_M)$ may not be obtained since the coefficients (Equation 8.35) depend themselves on the monetary state variable. Nevertheless, following Lioui and Poncet (2004), α can be approximated as:

$$\alpha \approx \frac{\beta\rho + Y_M\left(\mu_M - \sigma'_M\sigma_M\right) + \kappa_1}{\rho + Y_M\left(\mu_M - \sigma'_M\sigma_M\right) + \kappa_2}, \qquad (8.37)$$

where $\kappa_1 = \sum_{j=1}^{Q+2}\lambda_j\mathbb{E}\left[\dfrac{Y_M\gamma_{M,j} + f(Y_M(1 + \gamma_{Y_{M,j}})) - f}{1 + Y_M\gamma_{M,j}}\right]$ and $\kappa_2 = \sum_{j=1}^{Q+2}\lambda_j\mathbb{E}\left[\dfrac{Y_M\gamma_{M,j}}{1 + Y_M\gamma_{M,j}}\right]$.

Using Equation (8.37) and applying Ito's lemma to Equation (8.32) yields, under the jump–diffusion setting, the dynamics of the nominal short interest rate.

Proposition 3   *In the special economy, the nominal interest rate evolves, under the jump-diffusion framework, according to the following SDE:*

$$dR(t) = (R(t) - \overline{\pi})\mu_R dt + (R(t) - \overline{\pi})\sigma_R dz(t) + (R(t-)$$
$$- \overline{\pi})\gamma_R dn(t), \qquad (8.38)$$

where we have introduced the one-dimensional Wiener process, $dz(t)$, *and the Poisson process,* $dn(t)$. *Also, we define* $\overline{\pi} = \dfrac{\rho + \kappa_2}{1 + \pi}$ *with* $\pi = \dfrac{\kappa_2 - \kappa_1}{\rho(1 - \beta)}$, $\mu_R \equiv \mu_{Y_M}$, $\sigma_R \equiv \sigma_{Y_M}$ *and* $\gamma_R \equiv \gamma_{Y_M}$, *and is chosen so that the nominal interest rate remains positive.*

Proof.   From Equations (8.37) and (8.32), we write:

$$R(Y_M) = \overline{\pi} + \frac{1}{1 + \pi}\left(\mu_M - \sigma'_M\sigma_M\right)Y_M \qquad (8.39)$$

Applying Ito's lemma to Equation (8.39) and rearranging terms completes the proof.   □

Equation (8.38) provides the dynamics of a shifted short nominal interest rate process of a mixed jump–diffusion type. The model can be considered as an extension of a shifted-log-normal model where $\overline{\pi}$ is the shift parameter. Brigo and Mercurio (2001) provide a deterministic shift extension in the pure diffusion case for various interest rate models such as the mean-reverting model of Vasicek (1977) and the log-normal model of Dothan (1978). In our model, the sign of the shift parameter $\overline{\pi}$ depends on that of $\kappa_2 - \kappa_1$, which is actually the jump occurring at the investment to wealth ratio. A positive (negative) shift implies a decrease (increase) in the level of the nominal interest rate.

The solution of Equation (8.38) is:

$$R(t) = \bar{\pi} + (R(0) - \bar{\pi})e^{\left(\mu_R - \frac{1}{2}\sigma_R^2\right)t + \sigma_R z(t) + \ln(1 + \gamma_R)n(t)}.$$

$$(8.40)$$

Other jump–diffusion models of interest rates include those of Das and Foresi (1996) and Ahn and Thomson (1988). Our model, however, incorporates monetary variables. The implication of our richer dynamics lies in the implementation of the model that would require both economic and market data. The model would thus provide a high forecasting power of the level of nominal interest rates.

8.5 Conclusion

This paper extends to a jump–diffusion setting the monetary equilibrium of Lioui and Poncet (2004). Assuming a particular dynamics of the state variables as well as a log-separable utility function, we obtain a model of the short-term nominal interest rate that follows a mixed process of diffusion and jumps. Empirical evidence in the literature shows that introducing jumps is a desired feature to capture the dynamics of changes in interest rates. Moreover, we determine the inflation risk premium and derive the dynamics of the general price level. A future line of research may focus on estimating the model's parameters from market data on treasury bills and bonds and money supply data. In addition, relying on the jump–diffusion dynamics of the inflation rate we can price various contingent claims from the fast growing inflation-linked derivatives market.

Appendix: Proof of Proposition 2

Let $J(t, w, Y)$ be the indirect utility function that satisfies the Hamilton–Jacobi–Bellman jump–diffusion equation:

$$0 = \max_{c,m,\alpha,\theta,\delta} \left(U + J_w w \mu_w + \frac{1}{2} J_{ww} w^2 \sigma_w' \sigma_w + J_Y \mu + \frac{1}{2} J_{YY} \sigma' \sigma \right.$$

$$\left. + J_{wY} \sigma_w' \sigma + \sum_{j=1}^{Q+K} \lambda_j \mathbb{E}\left[J\left(t, w + \gamma_{w,j}, Y + \gamma_j\right) - J(t, w, Y) \right] \right).$$

$$(A8.1)$$

The first-order conditions for the investor's optimization are:

$$U_c - J_w = 0 \tag{A8.2}$$

$$U_m - J_w\left(\mu_p - \sigma_p'\sigma_p + r\right)$$

$$+ J_{ww}\left(m\sigma_p'\sigma_p + \delta w\sigma_p'\sigma_p - w\theta\sigma_b'\sigma_p - \alpha w\sigma_\eta'\sigma_p\right) - J_{wY}\sigma_p'\sigma \tag{A8.3}$$

$$- \sum_{j=1}^{Q+K} \lambda_j \mathbb{E}\left[J_w\left(w + \gamma_{w,j}, Y + \gamma_j\right) \frac{\gamma_{p,j}}{1 + \gamma_{p,j}}\right] = 0$$

$$J_w w(\mu_\eta - r) + J_{ww}\left(\alpha w^2 \sigma_\eta + \theta w^2 \sigma_\eta'\sigma_b - \delta w^2 \sigma_p'\sigma_\eta - m w\sigma_p'\sigma_\eta\right)$$

$$+ wJ_{wY}\sigma_\eta'\sigma + \sum_{j=1}^{Q+K} \lambda_j \mathbb{E}\left[J_w\left(w + \gamma_{w,j}, Y + \gamma_j\right) w\gamma_{\eta,j}\right] = 0 \tag{A8.4}$$

$$J_w w\left(R - \left(\mu_p - \sigma_p'\sigma_p\right) - r\right)$$

$$+ \frac{1}{2}J_{ww}\left(2\delta w^2 \sigma_p'\sigma_p + 2m w\sigma_p'\sigma_p - 2w^2\alpha\sigma_p'\sigma_\eta - 2w^2\theta\sigma_b'\sigma_p\right)$$

$$- wJ_{wY}\sigma_p'\sigma - \sum_{j=1}^{Q+K} \lambda_j \mathbb{E}\left[J_w\left(w + \gamma_{w,j}, Y + \gamma_j\right) w\frac{\gamma_{p,j}}{1 + \gamma_{p,j}}\right] = 0$$

$$J_w w(\mu_b - r) + J_{ww}\left(\theta w^2 \sigma_b'\sigma_b' + \alpha w^2 \sigma_b'\sigma_\eta - \delta w^2 \sigma_p'\sigma_b - m w\sigma_p'\sigma_b\right)$$

$$+ wJ_{wY}\sigma_b'\sigma + \sum_{j=1}^{Q+K} \lambda_j \mathbb{E}\left[J_w\left(w + \gamma_{w,j}, Y + \gamma_j\right) w\gamma_{b,j}\right] = 0. \tag{A8.5}$$

Equations (8.19) and (8.20) are obtained from applying market clearing conditions to Equations (A8.4) and (A8.5), respectively.

Acknowledgments

We are deeply indebted to Abraham Lioui and Patrice Poncet for helpful discussions and suggestions on previous drafts of the chapter. We also thank Jean-Luc Prigent and participants at the AFFI 2008 Conference in Paris as well as participants at the QMF 2009 Conference in Sydney for comments. We bear sole responsibility for any remaining errors.

References

Ahn, C.M., Thomson, H.E., 1988. Jump diffusion and the term structure of interest rates. Journal of Finance 43 (1), 155—174.

Brace, A., Gatarek, D., Musiela, M., 1997. The market model of interest rate dynamics. Mathematical Finance 7 (2), 127—155.

Brigo, D., Mercurio, F., 2001. A deterministic-shift extension of analytically-tractable and time-homogeneous short-rate models. Finance and Stochastics 5 (3), 369—387.

Campbell, J., Deaton, A., 1989. Why is consumption so smooth? Review of Economic Studies 56, 357—373.

Cox, J., Ingersoll, J., Ross, S., 1985a. An intertemporal general equilibrium model of asset prices. Econometrica 53 (2), 363—384.

Cox, J., Ingersoll, J., Ross, S., 1985b. A theory of the term structure of interest rates. Econometrica 53 (2), 385—407.

Das, S., 2002. The surprise element: jumps in interest rates. Journal of Econometrics 106 (1), 27—65.

Das, S.R., Foresi, S., 1996. exact solutions for bond and option prices with systematic jump risk. Review of Derivatives Research 1 (1), 7—24.

Dothan, L., 1978. On the term structure of interest rates. Journal of Financial Economics 6, 59—69.

Guan, L.K., Ting, C., Warachka, M., 2005. The implied jump risk of Libor rates. Journal of Banking and Finance 29 (10), 2503—2522.

Heath, D., Jarrow, R., Morton, A., 1992. Bond pricing and the term structure of interest rates: a new methodology. Econometrica 60, 77—105.

Johannes, M., 2004. The statistical and economics role of jumps in continuous-time interest rate models. Journal of Finance 59 (1), 227—260.

Kim, C.-J., 1993. Unobserved-component time series models with Markov-switching heteroscedasticity: changes in regime and the link between inflation rates and inflation uncertainty. Journal of Business & Economic Statistics 11 (3), 341—349.

Lioui, A., Poncet, P., 2004. General equilibrium real and nominal interest rates. Journal of Banking and Finance 28 (7), 1163—1180.

Lu, B., Wu, L., 2009. Macroeconomic releases and the term structure of interest rates. Journal of Monetary Economics 56, 872—884.

Vasicek, O., 1977. An equilibrium characterization of the term structure. Journal of Financial Economics 5 (2), 177—188.

9

THE WIDENING OF THE BASIS: NEW MARKET FORMULAS FOR SWAPS, CAPS AND SWAPTIONS

Fabio Mercurio
731 Lexington Avenue, New York, NY 10022, Bloomberg

CHAPTER OUTLINE

9.1 Introduction

The 2007 liquidity crisis widened the Libor–overnight indexed swap (OIS) basis. Market rates that used to be consistent with each other suddenly diverged. For instance, the forward rates implied by two consecutive deposits became different than the corresponding quoted forward rate agreement (FRA) rates or forward rates implied by OIS quotes. As an example, a swap rate based on semiannual payments of the six-month Libor rate can be different (and higher) than the same-maturity swap rate based on quarterly payments of the three-month Libor rate.

Practitioners have addressed this issue by forsaking the traditional concept of a single yield curve and by constructing as many forward curves as market rate tenors (e.g. one month, three months, six months, one year). Future cash flows are generated through the curves associated to the underlying rates and then discounted by another curve, which we term the

Rethinking Valuation and Pricing Models. http://dx.doi.org/10.1016/B978-0-12-415875-7.00009-9

137

"discount curve." This chapter shows how to generalize the main (interest rate) market models so as to account for the new market practice of using multiple curves for each given currency.

The valuation of interest rate derivatives under different curves for generating future rates and for discounting, in non-credit−related applications, was first applied by Henrard (2007), whereas Bianchetti (2010) and Mercurio (2009) are the first to deal with the post-subprime crisis environment. Other developments in the same direction are the works by Chibane and Sheldon (2009), Henrard (2009), and Kijima *et al.* (2009).

The chapter is organized as follows. Sections 9.2 and 9.3 introduce the main definitions and notations. Section 9.4 shows how to value interest rate swaps (IRSs) when future Libor rates are generated with one yield curve, but discounted with another. Section 9.5 extends the market Black formulas for caplets and swaptions to the dual-curve case. Section 9.6 concludes the chapter.

9.2 Assumptions on the Discount Curve

It is current market practice to value interest rate swaps and other derivatives with OIS discounting (see, e.g. Whittall, 2010). Consistently with this market practice, we assume that the discount curve is the OIS zero-coupon curve:

$$P_D(0, T) = P^{OIS}(0, T),$$

for each T, where $P^{OIS}(0, T)$ denotes the OIS-implied discount factor at time 0 for maturity T and $P_D(t, T)$ denotes the discount factor at time t for maturity T for the discount curve D.

The rationale for assuming the OIS curve as a discount curve is that the swap rates quoted by the market refer to a transaction for which a collateral agreement (credit support annex) is typically negotiated between the two counterparties. Given that both parties' positions are marked to market daily, the collateral is also revalued at a rate equal (or close) to the overnight rate, which can thus justify the use of the OIS rates for discounting.

The OIS curve can be stripped from OIS swap rates using standard (single-curve) bootstrapping methods. For currencies where OIS rates are quoted only up to a relatively short maturity, one has to resort to alternative constructions, by modeling, for instance, the spread between OIS (forward) rates and corresponding (forward) Libor rates or by using OIS basis swaps (versus Libor).

9.3 Fra Rates: Definition and Pricing

Definition 1 *Consider times T_1 and T_2. The time-t FRA rate* **FRA**$(t; T_1, T_2)$ *is defined as the fixed rate to be exchanged at time T_2 for the Libor rate $L(T_1, T_2)$ so that the swap has zero value at time t.*

This FRA rate slightly differs from that defined by the market. This slight abuse of terminology is justified by the definition that applies when payments occur at the end of the application period (like in this case).

Denoting by Q_D^T the generic T-forward measure with numéraire the zero-coupon bond $P_D(t, T)$, by no-arbitrage pricing we define:

$$\textbf{FRA}(t; T_1, T_2) = E_D^{T_2}[L(T_1, T_2)|\mathcal{F}_t], \qquad (9.1)$$

where $E_D^{T_2}$ denotes expectation under $Q_D^{T_2}$ and $\mathcal{F}_t$ denotes the "information" available in the market at time t.[1]

In the classic single-curve valuation, i.e. when the Libor curve corresponding to tenor $T_2 - T_1$ coincides with the discount curve, the FRA rate **FRA**$(t; T_1, T_2)$ coincides with the forward rate:

$$F(t; T_1, T_2) = \frac{1}{T_2 - T_1}\left[\frac{P_D(t, T_1)}{P_D(t, T_2)} - 1\right]. \qquad (9.2)$$

In fact, the Libor rate $L(T_1, T_2)$ can be defined by the classic relation:

$$L(T_1, T_2) = \frac{1}{T_2 - T_1}\left[\frac{1}{P_D(T_1, T_2)} - 1\right] = F(T_1; T_1, T_2), \qquad (9.3)$$

so that we can write:

$$\textbf{FRA}(t; T_1, T_2) = E_D^{T_2}[F(T_1; T_1, T_2)|\mathcal{F}_t].$$

Since $F(t; T_1, T_2)$ is a martingale under $Q_D^{T_2}$, we can then conclude that:

$$\textbf{FRA}(t; T_1, T_2) = F(t; T_1, T_2).$$

In a dual-curve setting, however, (9.3) does not hold any more, since the simply-compounded rates defined by the discount curve are different, in general, from the corresponding Libor fixings.

---

[1] As in Kijima *et al.* (2009), the pricing measures we will consider are those associated to the discount curve D.

The FRA rate $\mathbf{FRA}(t; T_1, T_2)$ is the natural generalization of the forward rate $F(t; T_1, T_2)$ to the dual-curve case. In fact:

  (i) $\mathbf{FRA}(t; T_1, T_2)$ coincides with $F(t; T_1, T_2)$ in the limit case of a single interest rate curve.

  (ii) At its reset time $t = T_1$, it coincides with the Libor rate $L(T_1, T_2)$.

(iii) Its time-0 value can be stripped from market data.

In addition, the FRA rate is a martingale under the corresponding forward measure and it is the proper building block for pricing interest rate derivatives in a market model set-up, (see Mercurio, 2010a, 2010b).

9.4 IRS Valuation

Here, we show how to value IRSs under the assumption of distinct forward and discount curves. To this end, let us consider a set of times T_a^i, ..., T_b^i compatible with a given tenor i^2 and an IRS where the floating leg pays at each time T_k^i the Libor rate $L^i(T_{k-1}^i, T_k^i)$ of curve i set at the previous time T_{k-1}^i, $k = a+1$, ..., b. In formulas, the time-T_k^i payoff of the floating leg is:

$$\mathbf{FL}\left(T_k^i; T_{k-1}^i, T_k^i\right) = \tau_k^i L^i\left(T_{k-1}^i, T_k^i\right), \qquad (9.4)$$

where τ_k^i denotes the floating-leg year fraction for the interval (T_{k-1}^i, T_k^i).

The time-t value, $\mathbf{FL}(t; T_{k-1}^i, T_k^i)$, of such a payoff can be obtained by taking the discounted expectation under the forward measure $Q_D^{T_k^i}$:

$$\mathbf{FL}\left(t; T_{k-1}^i, T_k^i\right) = \tau_k^i P_D\left(t, T_k^i\right) E_D^{T_k^i}\left[L^i\left(T_{k-1}^i, T_k^i\right)|\mathcal{F}_t\right].$$

Applying Definition 1 and setting:

$$L_k^i(t) := \mathbf{FRA}\left(t; T_{k-1}^i, T_k^i\right) = E_D^{T_k^i}\left[L^i\left(T_{k-1}^i, T_k^i\right)|\mathcal{F}_t\right],$$

we can write:

$$\mathbf{FL}\left(t; T_{k-1}^i, T_k^i\right) = \tau_k^i P_D\left(t, T_k^i\right) L_k^i(t). \qquad (9.5)$$

---

[2] For instance, if i denotes the three-month curve, the times T_k^i must be three-month spaced.

The net present value of the swap's floating leg is simply given by summing the values (9.5) of single payments:

$$
\begin{aligned}
\mathbf{FL}\left(t; T_a^i, ..., T_b^i\right) &= \sum_{k=a+1}^{b} \mathbf{FL}\left(t; T_{k-1}^i, T_k^i\right) \\
&= \sum_{k=a+1}^{b} \tau_k^i P_D\left(t, T_k^i\right) L_k^i(t),
\end{aligned}
\qquad (9.6)
$$

which will be different in general than $P_D(t, T_a^i) - P_D(t, T_b^i)$.

Let us then consider the swap's fixed leg and denote by K the fixed rate paid on the fixed leg's dates $T_c^S, ..., T_d^S$. The present value of these payments is immediately obtained by discounting them with the discount curve D:

$$
\mathbf{FxL}\left(t; T_c^S, ..., T_d^S\right) = \sum_{j=c+1}^{d} \tau_j^S K P_D\left(t, T_j^S\right) = K \sum_{j=c+1}^{d} \tau_j^S P_D\left(t, T_j^S\right),
$$

where τ_j^S denotes the year fraction for the fixed leg.

Therefore, the time-t IRS value, to the fixed-rate payer, is given by:

$$
\begin{aligned}
\mathbf{IRS}\left(t, K; T_a^i, ..., T_b^i, T_c^S, ..., T_c^S\right) &= \sum_{k=a+1}^{b} \tau_k^i P_D\left(t, T_k^i\right) L_k^i(t) \\
&\quad - K \sum_{j=c+1}^{d} \tau_j^S P_D\left(t, T_j^S\right).
\end{aligned}
$$

We can then calculate the corresponding forward swap rate as the fixed rate K that makes the IRS value equal to zero at time t. We get:

$$
S_{a,b,c,d}^i(t) = \frac{\sum_{k=a+1}^{b} \tau_k^i P_D\left(t, T_k^i\right) L_k^i(t)}{\sum_{j=c+1}^{d} \tau_j^S P_D\left(t, T_j^S\right)}.
\qquad (9.7)
$$

This is the forward swap rate of an IRS where cash flows are generated through curve i and discounted with curve D.

9.5 Pricing of Caplets and Swaptions

The purpose of this section is to derive pricing formulas for options on the main interest rates under a dual-curve paradigm.

The formal justifications for the use of Black-like formulas for caps and swaptions come, respectively, from the log-normal Libor market model of Brace *et al.* (1997) and Miltersen *et al.* (1997), and the log-normal swap model of Jamshidian (1997). To be able to adapt such formulas to our dual-curve case, we will have to reformulate accordingly the corresponding market models.

9.5.1 Market formula for caplets and floorlets

We first consider the case of a caplet paying out at time T_k^i:

$$\tau_k^i \left[L^i \left(T_{k-1}^i, T_k^i \right) - K \right]^+, \tag{9.8}$$

whose time-t price is given by:

$$\mathbf{Cplt}\left(t, K; T_{k-1}^i, T_k^i \right) = \tau_k^i P_D\left(t, T_k^i \right) E_D^{T_k^i} \left\{ \left[L^i \left(T_{k-1}^i, T_k^i \right) - K \right]^+ \Big| \mathcal{F}_t \right\}.$$

Since, at the reset time T_{k-1}^i:

$$L_k^i \left(T_{k-1}^i \right) = L^i \left(T_{k-1}^i, T_k^i \right),$$

we can replace the payoff (9.8) with:

$$\tau_k^i \left[L_k^i \left(T_{k-1}^i \right) - K \right]^+, \tag{9.9}$$

and view the caplet as a call option on $L_k^i(T_{k-1}^i)$. This leads to:

$$\mathbf{Cplt}\left(t, K; T_{k-1}^i, T_k^i \right) = \tau_k^i P_D\left(t, T_k^i \right) E_D^{T_k^i} \left\{ \left[L_k^i \left(T_{k-1}^i \right) - K \right]^+ \Big| \mathcal{F}_t \right\}. \tag{9.10}$$

The FRA rate $L_k^i(t)$ is, by definition, a martingale under the measure $Q_D^{T_k^i}$. Assuming:

$$dL_k^i(t) = v_k L_k^i(t) dZ_k(t), \quad t \le T_{k-1}^i,$$

where v_k is a constant and Z_k is a $Q_D^{T_k^i}$-Brownian motion, leads to the following pricing formula:

$$\mathbf{Cplt}\left(t, K; T_{k-1}^i, T_k^i \right) = \tau_k^i P_D\left(t, T_k^i \right) \mathrm{Bl}\left(K, L_k^i(t), v_k \sqrt{T_{k-1}^i - t}, 1 \right),$$

where:

$$\mathrm{Bl}(K, F, v, w) = wF\Phi\left(w \frac{\ln(F/K) + v^2/2}{v} \right)$$
$$- wK\Phi\left(w \frac{\ln(F/K) - v^2/2}{v} \right),$$

and Φ denotes the standard normal distribution function.

Therefore, under log-normal dynamics for the rate L_k^i, the caplet price is again given by Black's formula with an implied volatility v_k.

The price of a floorlet paying out at time T_k^i:

$$\tau_k^i \left[K - L^i \left(T_{k-1}^i, T_k^i \right) \right]^+, \tag{9.11}$$

can be derived in a similar fashion. We get:

$$\mathbf{Flt}\left(t, K; T_{k-1}^i, T_k^i \right) = \tau_k^i P_D\left(t, T_k^i \right) \mathrm{Bl}\left(K, L_k^i(t), v_k \sqrt{T_{k-1}^i - t}, -1 \right).$$

9.5.2 Market formula for swaptions

The other plain vanilla option in the interest rate market is the European swaption. A payer swaption gives the right to enter at time $T_a^i = T_c^S$ an IRS with payment times for the floating and fixed legs given, respectively, by $T_{a+1}^i, ..., T_b^i$ and $T_{c+1}^S, ..., T_d^S$, with $T_b^i = T_d^S$ and where the fixed rate is K. Its payoff at time $T_a^i = T_c^S$ is therefore:

$$\left[S_{a,b,c,d}^i \left(T_a^i \right) - K \right]^+ \sum_{j=c+1}^{d} \tau_j^S P_D\left(T_c^S, T_j^S \right), \tag{9.12}$$

where, see (9.7):

$$S_{a,b,c,d}^i(t) = \frac{\sum_{k=a+1}^{b} \tau_k^i P_D\left(t, T_k^i \right) L_k^i(t)}{\sum_{j=c+1}^{d} \tau_j^S P_D\left(t, T_j^S \right)}.$$

Setting:

$$C_D^{c,d}(t) = \sum_{j=c+1}^{d} \tau_j^S P_D\left(t, T_j^S \right),$$

the payoff (9.12) is conveniently priced under the swap measure $Q_D^{c,d}$, whose associated numéraire is the annuity $C_D^{c,d}(t)$. In fact, we get:

$$\mathbf{PS}(t, K; T_{a+1}^i, ..., T_b^i, T_{c+1}^S, ..., T_d^S)$$

$$= \sum_{j=c+1}^{d} \tau_j^S P_D\left(t, T_j^S \right) E^{Q_D^{c,d}} \left\{ \left. \frac{\left[S_{a,b,c,d}^i\left(T_a^i \right) - K \right]^+ \sum_{j=c+1}^{d} \tau_j^S P_D\left(T_c^S, T_j^S \right)}{C_D^{c,d}\left(T_c^S \right)} \right| \mathcal{F}_t \right\}$$

$$= \sum_{j=c+1}^{d} \tau_j^S P_D\left(t, T_j^S \right) E^{Q_D^{c,d}} \left\{ \left[S_{a,b,c,d}^i\left(T_a^i \right) - K \right]^+ \middle| \mathcal{F}_t \right\}.$$

$$\tag{9.13}$$

As in the single-curve case, the forward swap rate $S_{a,b,c,d}^i(t)$ is a martingale under the swap measure $Q_D^{c,d}$. Assuming that the swap rate $S_{a,b,c,d}^i$ evolves, under $Q_D^{c,d}$, according to a driftless geometric Brownian motion:

$$dS_{a,b,c,d}^i(t) = v_{a,b,c,d} S_{a,b,c,d}^i(t) dZ_{a,b,c,d}(t), \quad t \le T_a^i,$$

where $v_{a,b,c,d}$ is a constant and $Z_{a,b,c,d}$ is a $Q_D^{c,d}$-Brownian motion, the expectation in (9.13) can be explicitly calculated as in the caplet case, leading to the generalized Black formula:

$$\mathbf{PS}\left(t, K; T_{a+1}^i, ..., T_b^i, T_{c+1}^S, ..., T_d^S\right)$$

$$= \sum_{j=c+1}^{d} \tau_j^S P_D\left(t, T_j^S\right) \mathrm{Bl}\left(K, S_{a,b,c,d}^i(t), v_{a,b,c,d}\sqrt{T_a^i - t}, 1\right).$$

Therefore, the dual-curve swaption price is still given by a Black-like formula, with the only differences with respect to the basic case that discounting is done through curve D and that the swap rate $S_{a,b,c,d}^i(t)$ has a more general definition.

Analogously, the price of a receiver swaption paying out at time $T_a^i = T_c^S$:

$$\left[K - S_{a,b,c,d}^i\left(T_a^i\right)\right]^+ \sum_{j=c+1}^{d} \tau_j^S P_D\left(T_c^S, T_j^S\right),$$

is given by:

$$\mathbf{PS}\left(t, K; T_{a+1}^i, ..., T_b^i, T_{c+1}^S, ..., T_d^S\right)$$

$$= \sum_{j=c+1}^{d} \tau_j^S P_D\left(t, T_j^S\right) \mathrm{Bl}\left(K, S_{a,b,c,d}^i(t), v_{a,b,c,d}\sqrt{T_a^i - t}, -1\right).$$

9.6 Conclusions

We have shown how to price the main (linear and plain vanilla) interest rate derivatives under the assumption of two distinct curves for generating future Libor rates and for discounting. The pricing formulas for caps and swaptions result in a simple modification of the corresponding Black formulas used by the market in the single-curve setting.

Exotic derivatives can then be priced by extending classic interest rate models. Extensions of the Libor market model to the multicurve (single currency) setting can be found in Mercurio (2010a, 2010b).

References

Bianchetti, M., 2010. Two curves, one price. Risk, August, 74–80.

Brace, A., Gatarek, D., Musiela, M., 1997. The market model of interest rate dynamics. Mathematical Finance 7, 127–154.

Chibane, M., Sheldon, G., 2009. Building curves on a good basis. Technical report. Shinsei Bank. Available at http://papers.ssrn.com/sol3/papers.cfm?abstract_id=1394267.

Henrard, M., 2007. The irony in the derivatives discounting. Wilmott Magazine, July, 92–98.

Henrard, M., 2009. The Irony in the Derivatives Discounting. Part II: The Crisis. Dexia Bank, Brussels.

Kijima, M., Tanaka, K., Wong, T., 2009. A multi-quality model of interest rates. Quantitative Finance 9, 133–145.

Jamshidian, F., 1997. LIBOR and swap market models and measures. Finance and Stochastics 1, 293–330.

Mercurio, F., 2009. Interest rates and the credit crunch: new formulas and market model. Available at http://papers.ssrn.com/sol3/papers.cfm?abstract_id=1332205.

Mercurio, F., 2010a. Modern LIBOR market models: using different curves for projecting rates and for discounting. International Journal of Theoretical and Applied Finance 13, 1–25.

Mercurio, F., 2010b. A Libor market model with a stochastic basis. Risk, December, 96–101.

Miltersen, K.R., Sandmann, K., Sondermann, D., 1997. Closed form solutions for term structure derivatives with log-normal interest rates. The Journal of Finance 52, 409–430.

Whittall, C., 2010. The price is wrong. Risk, March, online.

10

THE FINANCIAL CRISIS AND THE CREDIT DERIVATIVES PRICING MODELS

Jean-Claude Gabillon, Laurent Germain and Nicolas Nalpas
Toulouse Business School

CHAPTER OUTLINE

10.1 Introduction

The economic and financial crisis of 2007–2008 cannot be reduced to the crisis that affected the subprime loans from 2007; the latter being triggered by the drop in property prices in the United States that began in late 2006. However, this is

Rethinking Valuation and Pricing Models. http://dx.doi.org/10.1016/B978-0-12-415875-7.00010-5

147

undoubtedly the first milestone and it constitutes the initial shock that has upset first the entire US financial system and then those of all of the industrialized countries. This crisis raises many questions and we must recognize that we still far from fully understand the complete series of events, despite the tremendous academic literature published on the subject. The media and politicians often convey a caricature of this crisis and the role played by the different market participants, and it is always tempting to look for scapegoats. Credit derivatives, credit default swaps (CDSs) and collateralized debt obligations (CDOs) that have been considered as far too complex and abstruse appear as good candidates. They are widely suspected of wild speculation, especially because their intrinsic mechanism is poorly understood and because the huge outstanding amounts traded seem unreasonable. The failure of pricing models have been hastily denounced since they have led to overly optimistic ratings and also because high CDS spreads seem not to reflect the actual defaults that can be observed thereafter. Does the crisis question the models currently used?

In Section 10.2, we provide a short description of the main credit derivatives and structured credit products, by highlighting their similarities.

In Section 10.3, we are thus able to review the CDO pricing models used in subprime securitization. It shows that the reference model, i.e. the Gaussian copula (or its one-factor subcase), suffers from multiple inconsistencies that can be partially rubbed out by passing from the "compound correlation" framework to that of "basis correlation." Even if the use of non-Gaussian copulas can change the distribution of losses by expanding its tails or by creating "dependence tails," they remain inconsistent and fundamentally static, atheoretical and purely computational. Dynamic models have been explored, well before the crisis. They aim to define a dynamic and stochastic framework. However, being more complex, at least in the "bottom-up" versions, they do not always support satisfactory calibration properties.

On the eve of the financial crisis there were no dominant models. However, the large variety of models and approaches indeed allowed to test variants and to better estimate risks. Using different copulas, Hull and White (2010) investigate whether the rating agencies have been complacent in awarding ratings of CDO tranches or if, given the available information, they have provided acceptable assessments. In fact, when different models are calibrated to the same market data, they necessarily produce close prices. However, models differ on the sensitivity coefficients and then on the hedging policies they suggest. In this context during the crisis, their performances were poor overall. The assessment methods vary from one author to another and, thus, it appears difficult to select the "best models." We therefore suggest a unified approach for testing a model towards its own assumptions.

That being said, the apparent poor performance of pricing models, which seemed to have been way too optimistic with regard to what has been observed *ex post*, does not come from their intrinsic properties, but is due to the blindness of market participants. The literature on CDO pricing models has been almost exclusively focused on the technical issues related to the correlation of loan portfolios. However, this technical characteristic remained relatively secondary in the sequence of the subprime mortgage crisis.

A poor understanding of correlations affects the shape of the distribution of losses, but not the expected overall losses of the portfolio on the different investment horizons. In other words, an underestimation of the correlations leads to an undervaluation of certain tranches and overvaluation of others, but does not affect all tranches in the same direction. However, during the subprime crisis, the prices of all tranches were downgraded irrespective of their original ratings. Therefore, the issue is not to better model the correlations in the portfolio, but to provide a better assessment of unconditional survival probabilities, which are affected by market correlations. We solve this apparent paradox by using a two-factor model. The correlations of a portfolio combine two distinct components: A market component whose changes affect the marginal risk-neutral probabilities of survival, and a specific component that remains without influence on them and which only affects the shape of the distribution of losses, leaving the mean unchanged.

Finally, Section 10.4 concludes this chapter by examining the contagion mechanisms of the crisis in the spirit of Longstaff (2010). He showed the essential role played by higher risk premia. Unfortunately, changes in risk premia are not well measured.

10.2 Brief Description of Credit Derivatives

The seller of credit derivatives (CDS, CDS index, CDO, CDO or CDS index tranches) covers losses recorded on a security, a portfolio or a specific part of a portfolio and receives in return the regular payment of a spread expressed as an annual rate.

The "par spread" (or break-even spread), which is, in general, the quoted spread of the contract, is the annual amount of the periodic spread whose present value equals the present value of future benefits. At inception and based on the "par spread" these contracts are worth zero:

$$\delta_0^* | v_0 \left[CDS(0, T; \delta_0^*) \right] = 0 \tag{10.1}$$

where δ_0^* is the "par spread" of a CDS contract that starts today at (0) and whose maturity is T.

The notional amount allows the calculation of the periodic spread.[1] It decreases each time a loss is recorded. In the case of a single-name CDS, it disappears completely once the reference entity defaults before the contract expires. The payment of the spread then stops and the compensation is paid to the buyer of the CDS. Otherwise, the payment of the spread continues until the term T of the contract. In the case of a CDS, the equation that determines the spread is:

$$\delta_0^* \sum_{m=1}^{M} (t_m - t_{m-1}) B(0, t_m)(1 - Q(0, t_m))$$

$$= \sum_{m=1}^{M} B(0, t_m) \left(E_0^Q L_{t_m} - E_0^Q L_{t_{m-1}} \right),$$

with:

$$E_0^Q L_t = Q(0, t)(1 - R). \tag{10.2}$$

where $t_1, t_2, ..., t_m, ..., t_M = T$ are the dates where the payments of the spreads are made (usually every quarter), $Q(0, t)$ is the cumulative marginal probability of default under the risk-neutral measure, $B(0, t)$ is the current price of a zero coupon bond with maturity t, $E_0^Q L_t$ is the expected cumulative loss at time t under the risk-neutral measure Q, $t_m - t_{m-1}$ represents the time length of the quarterly (under the usual conventions) payments expressed as a fraction of a year, and R is the recovery given default.

The present value of the "premium leg" is on the left-hand side of Equation (10.2), whereas its right-hand side is the present value of the "protection leg." It is assumed here that default and rates are independent.

---

[1] Since 2009, we must distinguish the "quoted spread," which makes null the value of the CDS, and the "effective spread" paid periodically until maturity or upon the occurrence of the credit event, s_0. In the United States, there are two possible levels for the actual CDS spread: 100 or 500 basis points (the first associated to investment grades and the second for speculative grades, but it is not compulsory). The difference $v_0[CDS(0, T; s_0^*)] - v_0[CDS(0, T; s_0)]$ results in an upfront payment at settlement. This is also the case for the equity tranche of a CDO.

In the case of a multiname CDS (CDS index) such as the swap CDX.NA.IG (North American Investment grade) in the United States, the benchmark portfolio is an equally weighted portfolio of 125 corporate names. In other words, the notional of the contract, that we will always assume equal to 1, is divided into 125 individual notionals of size 1/125. In the contingent leg (default leg), the CDS index coincides with the protection that would be provided by 125 individual CDS, each with a notional of 1/125. If one of the 125 names defaults, the compensation paid by the seller of the protection is therefore: $(1-R)/125$.

The residual notional with which the following spreads will be calculated is reduced by 1/125, i.e. the notional amount of the defaulted entity. However, a portfolio combining 125 individual CDS would lead initially to the payment of 125 different spreads, while the spread of the CDX contract is unique. For theoretical reasons, its value does not correspond to the arithmetic average of the 125 individual spreads; it is actually lower.[2] The equivalent of the Equation (10.2) for a CDS index with n names is:

$$\delta_0^* \sum_{m=1}^{M} (t_m - t_{m-1})B(0,t_m)\left[1 - \frac{E_0^Q L_t}{1-R}\right]$$

$$= \sum_{m=1}^{M} B(0,t_m)\left(E_0^Q L_{t_m} - E_0^Q L_{t_{m-1}}\right),$$

with:

$$E_0^Q L_t = \sum_{i=1}^{n} E_0^Q L_{it}$$

$$E_0^Q L_{it} = Q_i(0,t)(1-R). \tag{10.3}$$

The right-hand side of the first equation expresses the present value of the expected sequence of quarterly losses covered by the protection seller. It is determined by the evolution of the expected loss on the portfolio. The latter is only the sum of expected losses $E_0^Q L_{it}$ on individual entities making up the index. The spread of a CDS index does not depend on correlations between the components of the index. It is entirely determined by the marginal probabilities of default under the risk-neutral measure. Clearly, the expected loss is independent of the correlations

---

[2] The "par spread" of the CDS index is a weighted average of individual CDS spreads. The weights are all different since they depend on survival probabilities. The weights are low on high spreads (low survival probabilities) and high on moderate spreads, resulting in a weighted average less than the simple arithmetic mean.

between credits. We will see, however, that this conclusion is only true to some extent. The left-hand side of the equation defined on the level of the "par spread" corresponds to the present value of the spreads' sequence paid by the buyers of protection for each date on the expected notional residual $\left[1 - \dfrac{E_0^Q L_t}{1 - R}\right]$.[3]

In mid-2003, an interdealer market appeared for standardized CDO tranches of index CDX, which is a corporate index.[4] It corresponds to swaps on index tranches. A tranche is characterized by an attachment point and detachment point ([0, 3%], [3%, 7%], ...). The protection seller in a swap on a tranche bears losses only when their cumulative amount will enter into the tranche defined by the contract. The first losses are deducted from the equity tranche. Any loss is covered by the seller of the equity tranche as long as its notional $0.03 - L_t$ has not disappeared. Initially, the notional of the equity tranche is indeed 0.03, but it is reduced by the accumulated losses, L_t, on date $t \leq T$. If we note $K_0 = 0, K_1, K_2, ..., K_K = 1$, the sequence of attachment–detachment points, the loss attributed to a date $t \leq T$ on the tranche $k = 1, 2, ..., K$ is:

$$L_{kt} = \max(L_t - K_{k-1}, 0) - \max(L_t - K_k, 0) \qquad (10.4)$$

and the notional of the tranche k becomes: $K_k - K_{k-1} - L_{kt}$.

The spread, fixed at the start of the contract, applies on this reduced notional.

In terms of allocation mechanism of losses and spread determinants, the CDS index tranche is a type of CDO written on a simple benchmark.

The simplified formula for determining the spread of a CDS on the tranche k of an index, δ_{k0}^*, is then:

$$\delta_{k0}^* \sum_{m=1}^{M} (t_m - t_{m-1}) B(0, t_m) \left[K_k - K_{k-1} - E_0^Q L_{kt_m}\right]$$

$$= \sum_{m=1}^{M} B(0, t_m) \left(E_0^Q L_{kt_m} - E_0^Q L_{kt_{m-1}}\right),$$

with:

$$ETL_{kt} = E_0^Q L_{kt} = \int_{K_{k-1}}^{K_k} (L_t - K_{k-1}) f_t^Q (L_t) \mathrm{d}L_t. \qquad (10.5)$$

---

[3] For the sake of simplicity, we assume a common recovery rate for all the entities of the index, typically $R = 40\%$.
[4] iTraxx for Europe.

The main novelty is that the expected loss tranche (ETL), $ETL_{kt} = E_0^Q L_{kt}$, does not only depend on the expected losses (EL) of the portfolio, but on the shape of the risk-neutral distribution of the losses. The ETL is obtained from a tranche of the probability density function of losses, $f_t^Q(L_t)$ as shown in the second Equation of (10.5). However, a crucial determinant of the shape of the distribution of losses (but without any effect, at first glance, on the EL) is the correlation[5] between defaulted entities in the index. Strengthening the correlation between defaults of a portfolio thickens the tails of the distribution of losses. The standardized CDO tranches of the CDX index are therefore "correlation products" as the CDOs. Of course, a consistency property of the pricing model used (no-arbitrage prices: Price of CDS, on one hand, and index tranche prices, on the other) is the sum of the ETL of all tranches being equal to the EL of the portfolio as a whole, hence:

$$\sum_{k=1}^{K} ETL_{kt} = \sum_{k=1}^{K} E_0^Q L_{kt} = EL_t \; ; \forall t \in [0, T]. \qquad (10.6)$$

Technically, the correlation between defaults in the portfolio distributes the EL of the portfolio into the tranches; the former being itself determined by the marginal distributions of a default under the risk-neutral measure.

Asset-backed securities (ABSs) and CDOs are securitized structured products, in which a portfolio is formed, housed within a special purpose vehicle (SPV). It is tranched in a similar manner. Building a CDO comes to the simple superposition of two layers: The protection layer comparable to CDS on tranches and the collateral layer built with an investment at Libor sufficient to cover the losses.

CDOs were responsible for $542 billion in losses suffered by financial institutions in 2007. Perhaps most disturbing about these losses is that most of the securities being marked down were initially given a rating of AAA by one or more of the three nationally recognized credit rating agencies.

CDOs with a high level of exposure to residential mortgage securities, specifically those backed by subprime and adjustable-rate mortgages, consistently underperformed other CDOs. ABS CDOs accounted for more than 90% of the US CDOs downgraded in 2007. Lastly, the original credit ratings assigned to

[5] It is in fact a correlation matrix of $n(n-1)/2$ distinct terms. However, it is often represented by a unique (common) coefficient that can be estimated implicitly as the implied volatility in option pricing.

CDOs failed to capture the true risks of these securities. On the whole, the original credit ratings of CDO bonds, most notably those given to the senior tranches, appear, *ex post*, grossly inflated.

10.3 CDO Pricing Models and the Financial Crisis

The performance appraisal of financial models is a complex task. The vocation of a "pricing model" is to provide a price for a financial security that is acceptable for the market, and thus is consistent with its expectations and requirements (current risk premia). There is thus a close interaction between modeling and market, underlined by the so-called calibration procedure.

CDO pricing models suffered from weaknesses that were not ignored by market participants even if active research had begun well before the crisis tried to overcome them. However, the failures of models themselves do not explain the crisis. The exclusive focus on instantaneous market data and the lack of historical statistical evidence are its dominant cause.

10.3.1 CDO pricing and correlation

As O'Kane (2008) notices, "the Gaussian latent variable model"[6] has been the standard model for most of the pricing and risk management of the products traded in the credit correlation market. It is the Black–Scholes model of the correlation market and continues to be widely used.

We have a random variable V_i associate with credit i, drawn from a Gaussian distribution with mean 0 and unit standard deviation. In the approximate spirit of the Merton structural model, the default occurs before date $t \in \{t_1, t_2, ..., t_M\}$ if the value of V_i is less than a time-dependant threshold κ_{it}.

We write:

$$Q_i(0, t) = \text{Prob}_0^Q(V_i \le \kappa_{it}) = N(\kappa_{it})$$
$$\Leftrightarrow \kappa_{it} = N^{-1}(Q_i(0, t)) \tag{10.7}$$

where $Q_i(0, t)$ is the marginal default probability implied by the CDS market. κ_{it} grow with t and are often negative if $Q_i(0, t)$ are small.

[6] Or Vasicek's portfolio model.

It is then used as a unifactorial model where the factor V_i depends on two sources of risk: A market-like one symbolized by V, and another that is idiosyncratic and denoted by ε_i:

$$V_i = \sqrt{\rho}V + \sqrt{1 - \rho}\varepsilon_i. \tag{10.8}$$

The variables V and ε_i are independent. If they are distributed according to standard normal distributions, we are dealing with a standard Gaussian model. If one of them is distributed according to a Student law, we are dealing with the Student-t copula. When both have Student distributions, we refer to a double-t copula distribution.[7] We have $\rho = \text{cov}(V_i, V_{i'}) = \rho_{ii'}$ if $i \neq i'$. Conditionally on V, the default times are independent.

10.3.1.1 Failure of the "compound correlation" model

The single-factor copula model is in general not able to match the market quotes directly. It was soon observed that the spreads obtained, e.g. on CDS index tranches, could not coincide with the spreads quoted for a given level of correlation.

Loosely speaking, the main idea behind compound correlation is to compute the correlation that reprices each tranche to fit market prices, i.e. obtain the credit default dependence from liquid market data. One would expect that such a calculation could be very complicated if the underlying assets were all different, and so the homogeneity of the reference portfolio is assumed in the first crack at the problem. This means that all assets share the same pair-wise correlation, default probability and recovery rate.

The calibration of the model consists to extract the implied correlation $\rho = \rho_k$ with $k = 1, 2, ..., K$ compatible with the market spread for each tranche separately. This set of correlations appropriate to each tranche is called "compound correlation."

Implied correlation has been widely used to communicate "tranche correlation" between traders and investors using the Gaussian copula as a common framework.

It turned out that it was not always possible to extract such a compound correlation, especially for the mezzanine tranches intermediate between the equity tranches for which the spread is a decreasing function of the correlation level and senior tranches where this relationship is reversed. For some tranches, none or two solutions can be obtained (the curve of the spread is

[7] To get unit variances, the Student variables are scaled by the multiplicative factor $\sqrt{\dfrac{d-2}{d}}$ where d is the chosen degree of liberty. Since the sum of two Student laws does not follow a Student, V_i is not distributed according to a Student law.

concave with respect to the compound correlation of the tranche).

Nevertheless, this model has many other inconsistencies. As the level of correlation determines the shape of the distribution of losses, using separated and related levels of correlations for the various tranches is equivalent to using a distinct distribution of losses for every tranche. There is no reason that the aggregation of these distribution functions for the different tranches can be consistent with the distribution of losses for the entire portfolio. The simple no-arbitrage property requiring the keeping unchanged of the expected loss in Equation (10.6) is therefore not met: The sum of the losses on the different tranches differs from the total loss on the portfolio.[8]

Moreover, it was difficult to interpolate–extrapolate the correlation curve of standard tranches in order to price non-standard tranches traded on the over-the-counter (OTC) market. Indeed, the compound correlation of the tranche k does not correspond to a specific point, but belongs to the interval $[K_{k-1}, K_k]$ defining the tranche k.

As these "compound correlations" continue to be calculated and used, a new framework for extracting implied correlations known as "basis correlations" has been developed.

10.3.1.2 Failures of the "basis correlation" model

The "basis correlation" method consists of extracting implied correlations from market spreads to preserve the property of aggregation of the expected losses in Equation (10.6). The approach looks for the correlations that are implicit to "equity tranches" $\{(0, K_1), (0, K_2), ..., (0, K_K)\}$ and that can be defined from the set of attachment–detachment points $\{0, K_1, K_2, ..., K_K\}$ of standard tranches. The first "basis correlation" ρ_{K_1} coincides with the "compound correlation" ρ_1 of the standard equity tranche that produces the same distribution of losses on that tranche and then the same ETL. The second "basis correlation" ρ_{K_2} applicable to the non-standard equity tranche $(0, K_2)$ is extracted so that the spread obtained for the standard tranche (K_1, K_2) corresponds to that of the market:

$$\rho_{K_2} | ETL_{K_1, K_2} = ETL_{0, K_2}^{\rho_{K_2}} - ETL_{0, K_1}^{\rho_{K_1}}. \tag{10.9}$$

The ETL of the first equity tranche, $ETL_{0, K_1}^{\rho_{K_1}}$, is determined by the choice of ρ_{K_1}. The choice of ρ_{K_2} allows for obtaining the expected

---

[8] In practice, this problem has long been obscured by the lack of reliable quotations for the last tranche.

ETL, $ETL_{0,K_2}^{\rho_{K_2}}$, providing the required ETL for the tranche (K_1, K_2), i.e. ETL_{K_1,K_2}.

The property of "conservation of expected loss" is then restored since:

$$\sum_{k=1}^{K} ETL_{kt} = \sum_{k=1}^{K} \left[E_0^Q L_{(0,K_k)t}^{\rho_{K_k}} - E_0^Q L_{(0,K_{k-1})t}^{\rho_{K_{k-1}}} \right] = E_0^Q L_{(0,K_K)t}^{\rho_{K_K}}$$

$$= EL_t^\rho \quad ; \forall t \in [0, T].$$

The instantaneous arbitrage then disappears: The sum of the losses on the different tranches corresponds to the total loss on the portfolio, which constitutes a minimum requirement of consistency. As proved by Burtschell *et al.* (2009), in the Gaussian copula case, equity tranche premiums are decreasing with respect to the correlation parameter. This guarantees the uniqueness of base correlations whatever the maturity of the CDO or the marginal distributions of default times.[9]

However, this approach is not fully satisfactory. Base correlation is inconsistent at the level of a single tranche. We value the same payout with different models: In Equation (10.9), the loss ETL_{K_1,K_2} is valued with two different models, $E_0^Q L_{(0,K_k)t}^{\rho_{K_k}}$ and $E_0^Q L_{(0,K_{k-1})t}^{\rho_{K_{k-1}}}$ with two different correlation levels.

O'Kane (2008) defines the no-arbitrage conditions of the expected ETL curve:

$$\psi(K, t) = ETL_{(0,K)}(t) = E_0^Q[\min(L_t, K)].$$

The function is increasing in each of its two arguments, concave with respect to K, with a positive second cross-derivative:

$$\psi_K' > 0; \quad \psi_t' > 0; \quad \psi_{KK}'' < 0; \quad \psi_{Kt}'' > 0.$$

The concavity condition states that the successive enlargements of the tranche imply an increasing loss of a decreasing amount. However, the additional loss due to an enlargement of the tranche increases with the horizon, as is stated in the last condition.

The extraction of the implied "basis correlations" provides points (ρ_{K_k}, K_k) with $k = 1, 2, ..., K$ that allow the extrapolation–interpolation of the curves $\psi(K,t)$ for each $t \in \{t_1, t_2, ..., t_M\}$. Unfortunately, it turns out that it is not always possible to meet the above conditions, including the concavity of

---

[9] Such a result also holds for the Student-*t*, Clayton and Marshall–Olkin copulas with respect to the corresponding dependence parameter.

the ETL with respect to K or its growth with respect to t. In practice, the obtained ETL curves may have points of convexity, which affects the credibility of the pricing of non-standard tranches and tranchelets. The prices that are obtained this way theoretically open arbitrage opportunities:

- *Some arbitrage in the direction of the strikes.* The ETL function of tranchelets of the same width (0.01) is not decreasing in the strikes. The curve of spreads is then partly increasing
- *Some arbitrage in the time direction.* The function of the expected losses from a tranche is not always increasing with respect to time when CDO indexes of distinct expiry dates are considered. So far the reasoning has been conducted on the basis of spreads on a set of index tranches with a given maturity T.[10] However, some standard tranches were quoted for different maturities by imposing constraints on the calibration of the ETL for these maturities. The calibration then defines a correlation surface $\{\rho_{K_k, T_h}\}$, $k = 1, 2, ..., K, h = 1, 2, ..., H$.

The research, well before the crisis, was oriented in various directions to improve a benchmark model in the market that suffered from obvious weaknesses.

10.3.1.3 Non-Gaussian copulas

The first direction taken was to make changes in the characteristics of the Gaussian latent variable model. While convenient and intuitive, the Gaussian copula has a number of obvious shortcomings as a model of the real world. For instance, common formulations of the model (Li, 2000) make the assumption that recovery rates on default are known firm-specific constants. Empirical recovery rate distributions have a high variance and tend to be inversely related to default rates; in a bad year, not only are there many defaults; but recoveries are also low (for a review, see Altman *et al.*, 2003).

In one extension, recovery rates are randomized, explicitly allowing for the empirically well-established effect of inverse correlation between recovery rates and default frequencies. The existence of a correlation smile (which is rather a correlation skew on basis correlations) suggests a stochastic correlation extension of the Gaussian copula allowing default correlations to be higher in bear markets than in bull markets (Andersen and Sidenius, 2004). Research suggests that correlations increase in stressed market conditions. For example, Servigny and Renault (2002), who look at

---

[10] Usually of five years.

historical data on defaults and ratings transitions to estimate default correlations, find that the correlations are higher in recessions than in expansion periods. Das *et al.* (2006) employ a reduced-form approach and compute the correlation between default intensities. They conclude that default correlations increase when default rates are high. Ang and Chen (2002) find that the correlation between equity returns is higher during a market downturn.

In a crisis, correlations typically increase. Hence, it would be desirable to apply a correlation model with high comovements in the lower tail of the joint distribution. Remaining within a static model, an active research proposed the use of non-Gaussian copulas defining another structure of dependence between the marginal probabilities of default.[11]

Equation (10.8) defines the more general special case of a bivariate Gaussian copula that is characterized by a symmetric matrix of correlation ($n \times n$) whose elements outside the diagonal are different. We can generalize the Equation (10.8) to define bivariate copulas: The Student-*t* copula or the double-*t* copula.

Laurent and Gregory (2005) tested among the most used in practice: The Student-*t* extension of the Gaussian copula, a double-*t* one-factor model as introduced by Hull *et al.* (2004), the Clayton copula model, that can also be seen as a frailty model with a Gamma distribution, and a multivariate exponential model associated with multiple defaults. The associated copula is then the Marshall–Olkin copula.

Hull *et al.* (2004), in calibrating the Gaussian model and the double-*t* distribution copula model with four degrees of freedom on prices for iTraxx EUR index tranches (4 August 2004), show that the first requires implied basis correlations ranging from 0.204 to 0.448, while on the second they remain in a fairly narrow range [0.266, 0.241] between the equity and the super senior tranches. In the Gaussian model, correlation allows to thicken the tails of distributions.

In a crisis correlations typically increase. Hence, it would be desirable to use a correlation model with high comovements in the lower tail of the joint distribution. A bivariate copula has lower tail dependence if:

$$d_{\mathrm{L}}(X_i, X_j) = \lim_{u \to 1}\left[\Pr\left(X_i > F_{X_i}^{-1}(u)\middle|X_j > F_{X_j}^{-1}(u)\right)\right] > 0.$$

While in the Gaussian case, the two variables are asymptotically independent (for $\rho < 1$). The dependence is obtained with a bivariate Gumbel copula, for instance.

---

[11] Another objective was to thicken the tails of the distributions.

However, the 2007 crisis was less a matter of a particular copula model, but rather an issue of irrational unaware optimism. In the period that preceded it, a satisfactory organization of risk control and hedging processes were sometimes neglected. The case of AIG is probably a very vivid illustration.

The use of copulas to price CDOs has its pitfalls, but these were recognized before the "crisis" occurred. The analytic copula framework does not guarantee arbitrage-free prices in the strike and in the time dimensions.

The "implied copula" concept was introduced by Hull and White (2006) as a non-parametric model, to deduce, from a set of market CDO spreads, the shape of the risk-neutral pool loss distribution. This is essentially a numerical method, relatively easy to implement in the simplified framework of large homogeneous portfolios where the marginal probabilities[12] of default entities are equal, the correlation is unique and the portfolio equally weighted. This approach is, for example, exposed in Brigo *et al.* (2010) who concluded:

> *The Implied Copula can calibrate consistently across the capital structure but not across maturities, as it is a model that is inherently static. When CDO tranche quotes for more than one maturity are available, we cannot account consistently for them with an implied copula model. We need a arbitrage-free dynamic loss model, implying future distributions of losses at different times that are consistent with the tranche quotes at each maturity.*

The next step of the academic research thus consists in building dynamic loss models.

10.3.1.4 Dynamic loss models

The more recent approaches use dynamic models in which it is conventional to distinguish between bottom-up[13] and top-down dynamic models.

In principle, the dynamic approaches should allow a calibration on a correlation surface and give consistent expectations of losses. In copula models, loss distributions at different time horizons are built using the same specification for the default

---

[12] In the implied copula approach, the starting point is to deal with marginal probabilities of default. In this respect, this approach is a classic "bottom-up" method. In Brigo *et al.* (2010), the direct extraction of the ETL surface $\{E_0^Q L(K_k, t)\}$, $k = 1, 2, ..., K$, $t = t_1, t_2, ..., t_M = T_H$, that is consistent with the spreads of standard index tranches with different maturities $T_1, T_2, ..., T_H$. This contrasts with a "top-down" approach that has the disadvantage of breaking the link with the marginal probabilities and that thus loses the information included in the CDS spreads.

[13] Static models are usually models of bottom-up type.

variables, V_i, but using different default boundaries (increasing with the horizon). For each name, the default boundary, κ_{it}, is derived from the marginal risk-neutral default probabilities implied from a term structure of single-name CDS spreads. It looks like an *ad hoc* procedure of which any economic or financial interpretation is unclear, even if it advocates an approximate reference to the structural model of Merton. They are atheoretical models intended to formally produce a distribution of losses, but without any explanation of the process associated with default. Between 0 and T, there is no stochastic path, nor for CDS spreads or spreads for CDOs, which prohibits the use of the model to price for options on CDO[14] or CDS spread.[15] The concept of volatility is virtually absent, making the calculation of sensitivity coefficients such as the vega without much meaning.

In the top-down approach, one starts directly from the dynamics of the global loss function itself. Even if it looks simpler, this shortcut has an obvious drawback: The hedge ratios associated to the spreads of entities[16] in the portfolio cannot be computed. We can refer to O'Kane (2008) for some illustrations of this approach.

The bottom-up approach is obviously more cumbersome to implement. The affine jump–diffusion (AJD) model of Duffie and Gârleanu (2001), for example, is based on the modeling of the stochastic evolution of the default intensity in term of $n + 1$ AJD process $(X(t), \{X_i(t)\}_{i=1,\dots,n})$:

$$\mathrm{d}X(t) = v(\theta - X(t))\mathrm{d}t + \sigma\sqrt{X(t)}\mathrm{d}W(t) + J\mathrm{d}N(t).$$

It is similar to the CIR model where jumps occur when $\mathrm{d}N(t) = 1$ and whose intensity l is introduced. The size of the jump J is, itself, an exponential random variable (positive jumps) of given mean μ.

The AJD for $\{X_i(t)\}$, $i = 1, \dots, n$, have identical structures. They are mutually independent (idiosyncratic risk) and independent of $X(t)$, which represents the market risk. Following Mortensen (2006) we can write:

$$\lambda_i(t) = \alpha_i X(t) + X_i(t).$$

---

[14] A model very similar to the CDS market model can be used. See, e.g. Hull and White (2007).

[15] The reference model for options on CDS spread is the CDS market model or log-normal forward-CDS model that postulates the process followed by the forward spread and that allows finding the closed-form formula of the Black type.

[16] Measures such as the delta spread or the PV01. However, there are complementary techniques for overcoming this difficulty. See Bick and Kraft (2012).

The presence of common jumps in $X(t)$ allows creating a sufficiently strong correlation between the intensities of default of various credits that would not have been possible with a simple diffusion process. The dependency structure is defined by the parameters $(\{\alpha_i\}_{i=1,2,\ldots,n}, l, \mu)$.

The long-run variance and expected value of $X(t)$ are known, as well as the closed form of the survival probabilities. To compute the distributions of losses in the model, we define the common factor Z as the cumulated common process:

$$Z(t) = \int_0^t X(s)\mathrm{d}s.$$

Given the common factor, defaults occur independently across entities.

In the expression of the cumulative marginal probabilities of default (calibrated on the term structure of CDS spreads) only $Z(t)$ intervenes and not the path of $X(t)$. According to Cox's formula:

$$Q_{i0}(t) = E_0^Q\left[\exp\left(-\int_0^t \lambda(s)\mathrm{d}s\right)\right] = E_0^Q\left[e^{-\alpha Z(t) - Z_i(t)}\right].$$

Consequently, conditional on $Z(t)$, these marginal probabilities are independent, which allows one to easily obtain the joint conditional probabilities. These steps are similar in the copula methods.

Unconditional joint default probabilities can be written as integrals of the conditional probabilities over the common factor distribution. Once the density has been found (see Mortensen, 2006), numerical integration can be done.

It is an elegant model, but the calibration of the model by Mortensen (2006) on the CDX.NA.IG August 2004 is not in the bid-offer spread. There are sometimes significant discrepancies.

It appears from this brief overview that at the eve of the crisis, financial theory was well aware that the design of the models commonly used in the pricing of CDOs was affected by various imperfections or inconsistencies. When models are calibrated to market spreads they obviously produce prices that are always very close. They may differ in the pricing of tranches or non-standard portfolios as well as in their sensitivity measures. It is then, in that way, we may appreciate their respective performances.

However, these imperfections are by no means the cause of the crisis. They explain only marginally the alleged failures of models. Moreover, Hull and White (2010) use different pricing models to examine whether the ratings attributed by the rating agencies to ABS-CDO subprimes may seem reasonable based on the data available at that time.

10.3.2 CDO pricing models and ratings

The rating agencies came under sharp criticism after the financial crisis and the downgrading of many notes associated to ABS-CDO mortgage tranches. They cannot be compared in any way with the movements observed on corporate bonds. Losses on ABS or CDO tranches, for each level of initial rating, were unprecedented and far exceeded the average losses recorded on corporate bonds of the same level of rating.

In the period just before the crisis, rating agencies seemed more and more optimistic, and lowered attachment points for AAA-rated tranches. Thus, in 2002, the AAA tranches were protected by equity and mezzanine tranches that could absorb losses of 25%, while in 2006 this pillow of protection was reduced to 15% on average (source: Lehman Live). It is true that, at the same time, spreads on subprime loans and the default rate on these loans were decreasing.

The ability of rating agencies to grade sovereign bonds is based on long experience and extensive data with a great historical depth. They use a mixture of methods that combine qualitative and quantitative judgment. However, their expertise in the evaluation of ABS-CDO was much more recent and was mostly based on models.

Hull and White (2010) seek to determine whether the scores for the various tranches in the ABS-CDO arrangements were well justified, based on the information accepted at the grant date, or could appear unusually complacent. They use two criteria, themselves employed by rating agencies:[17]

- *Probability of default*: A tranche has received an appropriate rating if the probability that it recorded at least one default should not exceed the probability of loss of a corporate bond. (the probability of default in a tranche is equal to the probability that the loss of the portfolio exceeds the attachment point of the tranche)
- *Expected loss*: The expected loss on ABS-CDO bonds of a given rating should not exceed the expected loss of a corporate bond whose rating is the same.

Note that the first criterion seems particularly severe, since a loss on a ABS tranche of about 1000 credits, with a recovery rate

---

[17] Models that were widely known and publicized, so that the sometimes addressed charges claiming their opacity seem unfounded in this case.

of 50% represents a fraction of $1/1000 \cdot 50\% = 1/2000$ of the nominal of the corresponding bond, while the first and last loss on a senior corporate bond represents about 60% of its principal amount. Losses on ABS tranches occur according to a succession of defaults, each of a small scale, gradually eroding the tranche, while a corporate bond is significantly affected by a single credit event. The criterion of the expected loss seems more appropriate to make comparable the ratings of ABS-CDO tranches and corporate bonds. See Table 10.1.

Their tests are simultaneously based on two basic models: The Gaussian copula model and the double-t copula model, with different variants whose central assumptions are generally used (constant recovery rate of 75% or stochastic ones varying between 50 and 100%, marginal probabilities of default 5, 10 and 20% over a period of five years, a correlation coefficient between 0.05 and 0.30). The authors conclude that the AAA ratings assigned to the ABS tranches were not unreasonable, in contrast to those awarded to ABS-CDOs that were much less justified. The variety of available models are allowed to multiply variants, showing that to grant an AAA rating, they would have needed safety requirements much stronger than those in existence. It should be noted that the approach is subject to criticism, since it uses risk-neutral probabilities equal to the true probabilities. Searching for attachment points that provide probabilities of losses or expectations of losses similar to those that have historically been observed constitutes a severe criterion as long as the ratio of risk-neutral probabilities over true ones has not been computed. Overall, it

Table 10.1. Cumulative probability of default over 5 years for bonds initially rated AAA and BBB taken from Moody's statistics for the 1970–2007 period (expected loss calculated by assuming a recovery rate of 40%)

Rating corporate	Probability of loss (%)	Expected loss (%)
AAA	0.1	0.06
BBB	1.8	1.08

Source: Hull and White (2010).

does not appear that the rating agencies have seriously failed in their grading process.

10.3.3 CDO pricing models and risk management

The recent financial crisis has revealed inefficiencies of methods used in credit risk management. In fact, there are no clear criteria for assessing the performance of models. There are at least three levels of analysis for a model:

- The pricing includes a calibration on market data, transposing it to the pricing of non-standard products.
- The calculation of sensitivity coefficients and the hedging policy.
- The risk analysis that uses the model in different variants and extreme scenarios.

There is a great deal of heterogeneity of approaches, and it would undoubtedly be desirable to move towards a more consistent and unified measurement methodology for the performance appraisal of a model in terms of stability and hedging.

10.3.3.1 Studies on hedging efficiency

Bick and Kraft (2012) show that in terms of hedging efficiency of idiosyncratic as well as systematic risks, the performance of CDO models was poor during the financial crisis. This confirms previous studies of Cont and Kan (2011) and Cousin *et al.* (2012).

They study several static bottom-up and dynamic top-down credit portfolio models,[18] and compute the resulting delta hedging strategies using either index contracts or a portfolio of single-name CDS contracts as hedging instruments. The particular models are tested in realistic settings using market data from April and September 2008. They compute the residual profit-and-loss profiles after hedging and assess the performances of these hedging strategies. The interesting conclusions are:

- The average calibrations error of top-down models are bigger.
- Delta hedging with Gaussian copulas works very poorly.
- Among all 10 pricing models that they consider, the Student-t copula model performs the best.

---

[18] Gaussian copula, Student-t copula, double-t copula and Clayton copula, all with compound and basis correlation, dynamical generalized-Poisson loss model of Brigo *et al.* (2007), Longstaff and Rajan (2008) model, and Errais *et al.* (2010) model.

However, the overall hedge performances of all models are poor. Even for the best models, the biggest daily losses can exceed 5% of the tranche notional.[19]

10.3.3.2 Towards a concept of structural stability

In the literature on the pricing of CDOs, various articles have been devoted to studying the properties of any particular model or copula. The focus and the properties studied are different, so that some confusion exists due to the lack of a systematic process for comparing models. The following section does not pretend to fill this gap, but it is a first simple attempt in this direction.

If we consider a valuation model calibrated on market data at date t, we can write:

$$v_t^* = v(\Theta_t, X_t, t) + e_t, \qquad (10.10)$$

where v_t^* represents the market price, $v(\Theta_t, X_t, t)$ the price produced by the model based on exogenous variables such that the yield curve and the CDS spreads curves on portfolio entities directly incorporated into the model, parameter values $\Theta_t = [\theta_{1t}, .., \theta_{Ct}]'$ induced by the calibration procedure, as the correlation coefficient in the Gaussian pricing model, or the implied volatility in the Black–Scholes model. e_t represents the calibration error.

In terms of CDOs, note that the X variables are common to all models;[20] however, the calibrated parameters Θ are often unique to each model.

It is also worth noting that among the calibrated parameters, we can distinguish:

- Those subject to a point estimate (as, in general, the correlation coefficient in the pricing of CDOs).
- Those that are written as deterministic functions of time, such as the long-term rate in the stochastic interest rates model of Hull and White (1990), which allows to adjust the Vasicek's model, any sort of yield curve.

In the latter case, the successive calibration procedure generally creates a problem of intertemporal inconsistency, since the deterministic dynamics of one day is contradicted the next day. Θ_t^{t+1} denotes the set of all calibration parameters at date t adjusted on the date $t+1$ based on their assumed dynamics. If no parameter is a function of time, we will of course have $\Theta_t^{t+1} = \Theta_t$.

---

[19] These are severe numbers with respect to the market value of the position, which is much smaller than the tranche notional.

[20] With the notable exception of top-down models, which do not directly use data on CDS.

The next day, the market data has changed and the model is calibrated again so that:

$$v_{t+1}^* = v(\Theta_{t+1}, X_{t+1}, t+1) + e_{t+1}. \qquad (10.11)$$

If the model is "perfect," we should have $\Theta_t^{t+1} = \Theta_{t+1}$. However, this is not generally the case.

The daily profit and loss (P&L) with no hedging is then:

$$PL_{t+1}^{NH} = v_{t+1}^* - v_t^*$$

$$= [v(\Theta_{t+1}, X_{t+1}, t+1) - v(\Theta_t^{t+1}, X_{t+1}, t+1)]$$

$$+ [v(\Theta_t^{t+1}, X_{t+1}, t+1) - v(\Theta_t, X_t, t)] + [e_{t+1} - e_t]. \qquad (10.12)$$

There are three components (each in brackets) in the right-hand side of the Equation (10.12). The P&L resulting from the calibration adjustment (model imperfections), the P&L resulting from the modification of the financial environment and finally the P&L resulting from calibration errors.

Hedging is primarily intended to cancel the second term (the P&L resulting from changes in the financial environment and the passage of time). These hedges are not perfect. Deltas and other measures of sensitivity are, in principle, the partial derivatives with respect to X and t. A jump on some variable belonging to X creates a hedging error in case of non-linearity.[21]

The delta hedging corresponds to a partial hedging of some of the variables belonging to X. In terms of CDOs, we can consider the delta spreads, which measure the effect of a variation of one basis point of the spread on the value of the CDO.[22]

However, it is also possible to set up a hedging procedure seeking to cancel the first component that is similar to a vega-neutral strategy in the case of an option. We shall leave aside this type of hedging in this first approach. The P&L after hedging the X variables becomes:

$$PL_{t+1}^{HX} = [v(\Theta_{t+1}, X_{t+1}, t+1) - v(\Theta_t^{t+1}, X_{t+1}, t+1)]$$

$$+ \left[v(\Theta_t^{t+1}, X_{t+1}, t+1) - v(\Theta_t, X_t, t) - \nabla_X'(X_{t+1} - X_t)\right]$$

$$+ [e_{t+1} - e_t],$$

where $\nabla_X' = \nabla_X' v(\Theta_t^{t+1}, X_{t+1}, t+1)$ is the row vector of partial derivatives with respect to the variables belonging to X.

---

[21] We do not consider here the hedging of the gamma type, involving the calculus of a second derivative.

[22] We can talk about specific delta if only the spread of a single CDS varies or systematic delta if all the CDS spreads move of one basis point.

The hedged P&L represents a hedging error due to three factors:

- The imperfection of the model due to the first factor in brackets.
- Jumps in the variables due to non-linearities in the model that make the hedging procedure imperfect. In a crisis, it is likely that this factor is significant and interferes with the model assessment, if we do not isolate it.
- Calibration errors traceable to the imperfections of the model that fail to reproduce some market conditions.

To the best of our knowledge there is no study adopting such an approach, so that, for pricing a CDO, there is no reference model, but rather some disorderly profusion of models.

10.3.4 Failure of pricing models has another origin: the calibration procedure

The development of pricing models for CDOs has been almost exclusively focused on technical issues of the modeling of the correlation of the credits portfolio representing the CDO. However, this characteristic is obviously secondary in the sequence of the subprime crisis.

It is not the subprime portfolio correlations that have been particularly poorly appreciated, but the risk-neutral survival probabilities extracted from instant adjustments of market data (CDS spreads).

A poor understanding of correlations affects the shape of the distribution of losses, not the expectation of the overall losses of the portfolio on the various horizons, as has been noticed previously. In other words, an underestimation of the correlations of the portfolio led to the undervaluation of certain tranches and overvaluation of other tranches, but does not affect all tranches in the same direction. However, during the subprime crisis and more broadly the CDO crisis, we have observed a drop in the price of all tranches irrespective of their original rating. The correlations are then not involved in this process, but the unconditional survival probabilities are. However, the latter are affected by market correlations.

A pricing model is not intrinsically a predictive model, although it is used to assess a financial product that produces cash flows over time. However, market practice is to calibrate it to liquid market data. The model should then be consistent with market data that reflect the current expectations of investors. If sudden changes occur in prices, it means that previous expectations were inaccurate and, therefore, the model calibration was as well.

What, in this case, has modified expectations?

The change of the trajectory of housing prices was the trigger for the subprime crisis. It was a segment of the housing market fueled almost exclusively by credit and whose growth was well above the overall real estate market. In such a market a reversal is inevitable.

The increasing share of these credits in the portfolio of creditors pushes it to diversify and to restrict the distribution of credits. The deterioration of the solvency ratios of borrowers (prices going down faster than their income) can only temporarily be offset by the increase in the duration of loans, deferred repayment and the narrowing of spreads. Demand from borrowers fatally dropped.

Once the price path is reversed, price expectations change dramatically and change the behavior of borrowers.

The decrease in the ABS-CDO prices, from the moment it became general, were affecting all the tranches (equity, mezzanine and senior) irrespective to the technical question of correlations between specific components of ABS-CDO portfolios.

The increase of risk-neutral marginal probabilities of default due to environmental factors that upset the behavior of the real estate market was the transmission channel of the crisis. Four factors played in the same direction and produced cumulative effects:
• Increase of market correlations.
• Increase of risk aversion independently of risk premia.
• Increase in effective probabilities of default.
• Drop of market liquidity that strengthens liquidity risk premia.

10.3.4.1 Increase of market correlations

Empirical research suggests that correlations increase in stressed market conditions. For given effective probabilities of default, the increase in market correlations thickens the tails of the distributions of losses and the likelihood of bad states for the world. This leads to an increase in risk premia that expands the CDS spreads and pushes the risk-neutral probabilities of default well beyond the true ones. Marginal probabilities of default are not sensitive to the correlation that characterizes the benchmark portfolio of the CDO. They are affected by the market correlations. In this sense, the CDS and CDS index products are correlation products. However, it is not the case for given marginal probabilities. These risk-neutral probabilities depend on changes in risk premia, themselves partly determined by changes in correlations. We can easily highlight this duality by considering a simple model with two factors (e.g. Hull and White, 2009).

Consider a homogeneous CDO pool (e.g. built with subprime mortgage types). We expand the standard two-factor Gaussian model of Equation (10.8):

$$V_i = \sqrt{\rho}V + \sqrt{\rho'}Z + \sqrt{1 - (\rho + \rho')}\varepsilon_i, \qquad (10.13)$$

with:

$$V \perp Z \perp \varepsilon_i.$$

The parameter $\rho + \rho'$ is the total within-pool correlation. From the perspective of CDO pricing on this pool, the relevant correlation is the one that combines the correlation factor created by the market, V, and the correlation created by a sectoral factor, Z. However, in fact, these two components of the correlation of the pool have distinct effects. A change in ρ' does not affect CDS spreads and single-name CDS indexes. It does not affect the expected loss of the pool. It simply changes the distribution of losses and therefore the ETL, and has ultimately opposite effects on the spreads of the different tranches.

However, an increase of ρ will have wider and more fundamental consequences. By broadening the tails of the distributions of losses and by enhancing the likelihood of bad states of nature, it increases the risk premia on loans, which are components of the credit spreads.[23] Risk-neutral probabilities of default increase with respect to the true ones. Spreads on single-name CDS, CDS indexes and CDOs evolve in the same direction.

It is clear that the use of pricing models for measuring and monitoring risk as well as in scenario analyses should carefully distinguish these two components of the correlation of a pool of credits. Moreover, the contagion can strengthen the risk premia.

For example, Azizpour *et al.* (2011) estimate reduced-form models of correlated default timing under actual and risk-neutral probabilities, using data on corporate default experienced in the United States, and time series of market rates of index and tranche swaps referenced on the CDX North American High Yield and Investment Grade portfolios. It is a top-down model. The default intensity applies to the pool as a whole. They also relax the doubly stochastic assumption of (10.8), where conditionally on the evolution of the common factors, defaults are independent, by incorporating the impact of defaults on a portfolio intensity,

---

[23] Conceptually, it is convenient to distinguish two components in a credit spread: The default premium, which is actually not a premium, but simply the compensation of the expected loss given default for a risk-neutral agent, and the risk premium, which is the additional expected remuneration borne by a security (risky bond or CDS) and which reflects the risk aversion of investors.

i.e. self-exciting effects. Das *et al.* (2007) and Azizpour *et al.* (2011) find strong evidence of the violation of the doubly stochastic hypothesis under the actual measure.[24] Owing to the impact of a new default on default intensity, correlated default risk is not conditionally diversifiable.[25] Therefore, a default event may command a premium even in well-diversified portfolios of credit-sensitive positions.

In addition, their estimates indicate the presence of substantial premia for default event risk. The gap between actual intensity and risk-neutral intensity is substantial for the swaps on CDX, and their paths can diverge sharply. Such was the case during the financial crisis. The actual intensity reached a low point in November 2007 (following the frequency of corporate defaults observed in the economy) while the risk-neutral intensity increased sharply in February 2007. Any security whose price drop is closely associated with a crisis situation will incur enhanced risk premia.

10.3.4.2 Independent variation in risk premia

In addition, there may be increases of risk premia that are independent of correlation changes or of contagion effects that will widen the gap between the risk-neutral probabilities of default and the true ones. The mere prospect of a crisis can strengthen risk aversion as shown, for example, by Brunnermeier and Nagel (2008).

10.3.4.3 Changes in the frequency of defaults

On the subprime market, the default rates on mortgages have increased significantly. So, it is clear that the actual default intensities had changed in response to the change in the trajectory of the real estate market.

10.3.4.4 Liquidity drop

During the crisis, the market liquidity profoundly deteriorated, starting with the ABS-CDO subprime market and beyond for all

---

[24] Result challenged by Kramer and Löffler (2010) and Lando and Nielsen (2010). The question is the following: For companies, business cycles or stock market valuations (as expressed through macro variables) influence the probability of default; however, are defaults conditionally independent given the state of the business cycle?

[25] We should qualify this statement. If the contagion is limited to a sector (e.g. automotive industry or the internet sector), we can not, *ipso facto*, give it a systematic character. However, in the case of banks themselves linked by contractual relationships, the contagion effect may take a different turn and affect the economy as a whole.

structured credit products. The new securitization operations have completely disappeared: Measured by issuance, non-mortgage securitization exceeded the issuance of all US corporate debt starting in 2004. The effects of the crisis on issuance were radical. This market was essentially dying in 2008. Global CDO issuance in the fourth quarter of 2007 was $47.5 billion— a nearly 74% decline from the $180 billion issued in the fourth quarter of 2006. First quarter 2008 issuance of $11.7 billion was nearly 94% lower than the $186 billion issued in the first quarter of 2007.

This lack of liquidity distorts prices, which consequently do not necessarily reflect their fundamental values. No CDO pricing models incorporate this risk factor, probably amplified by the excessive complexity of these products.

Liquidity of the market or of a portfolio of assets during good times is not the same as liquidity during an economic downturn or a financial crisis. Assets that are easy to sell when economic agents share a sense of optimism about their profitability, liquidity and safety, often turn out to be unwanted and expensive bundles of "illiquid" debt when the sense of optimism evaporates. Hence, liquidity can evaporate literally overnight.

Apart from the pricing models, regulators and risk managers had other modeling tools. However, they did not have any historical perspective (as for corporate bonds). The subprime market was new and experienced only the upswing of the business cycle. This led to difficulties in measuring actual risks out of a more detailed and a more economic analysis of the behavior of borrowers.

The scoring models (see Demyanyk and van Hemert, 2011), themselves estimated from a single phase of the business cycle, failed to fully detect the deterioration of credit ratings. Furthermore, they poorly capture non-linearities that affect behavior, where equity becomes negative.

However, Shiller (2007), based on a fundamental analysis, claimed early that the US real estate market suffered a speculative bubble. He also announced a potential risk of collapse. A legal analysis of contracts as well as an economic study of these markets and their incentives could also have helped to identify the extreme fragility of the foundations of this new market whose growth should have attracted extreme vigilance.

However, here again, we find the illustration of not the failure of a model that is intrinsically an imperfect tool, but of the necessity to adopt diversified approaches in at least three levels, i.e. pricing and hedging, risk measurement and monitoring, and lastly an economic analysis, often overlooked, that should be more integrated within the banking organization than they actually are.

10.4 Conclusion: Risk Premia and Asset Pricing Models

During the years 2007–2009 the banking system and financial markets experienced massive losses. The diffusion of losses in the markets was triggered by the subprime crisis of 2007, itself caused by an inevitable reversal of housing prices on a segment fueled almost exclusively by credits. This deterioration in the quality of mortgages has profoundly changed expectations about future defaults and has led to massive reductions in the market value of large portfolios of ABSs or CDOs despite their flattering ratings. This resulted in a general distrust of this type of product and the paralysis of almost all the structured finance sector whatever the quality of the collateral, and a drop of liquidity in these markets. Various financial institutions faced liquidity problems and numerous businesses were experiencing a sudden credit crunch.

Meanwhile, the securitization market suffered a dramatic drop that made it virtually disappear. In 2008, the crisis was spreading again and clearly took the appearance of a global financial crisis. Numerous financial institutions were in financial distress and some were saved *in extremis* thanks to protective measures (e.g. forced mergers/bailouts). The US Treasury intervened massively to provide financial guarantees at the risk of spoiling its own financial stability. The central objective of the government was undoubtedly to contain the crisis, to avoid a broader spillover to other markets and other sectors or a deep decline in markets already shaken.

Longstaff (2010) analyzes the pricing of subprime CDOs and their contagion effects on the market. Longstaff assumes that reported ABX.HE prices are proxies for subprime CDO market prices and found strong contagion effects from lower-rated subprime CDOs to the higher-rated subprime CDOs, and finally to the stock market.

As recalled by Longstaff (2010), the literature on the diffusion of financial crises identifies three mechanisms by which a shock in one market tends to spill over to other markets:

- *Informational contagion*: A shock in one market conveys new information and leads agents to change their expectations. It implies a gradual discovery of the price level adjusted to new environmental factors in evolution. On the most liquid markets, the discovery mechanism is usually faster. So, we should observe its diffusion from the most liquid markets to the less liquid markets. Contrary to this scheme, it seems that the subprime crisis has completed a reverse path, since the liquidity in this market remained poor.

- *Contagion through the lack of liquidity*: Investors who suffer losses in one market are seen as insolvent and are excluded from funding on other markets, spreading the contraction of trade and triggering a flight to quality. In this mechanism, the contagion spreads through a liquidity shock in the direction of all other markets. Bank runs or phenomena that suddenly deteriorate bank liquidity can be ranked in this category.
- *Contagion through risk premia*: A negative shock in one market, surrounded by uncertainties about its size and its potential effects, increases the risk premia required on all other markets. The time-varying risk premia increase emphasizes the price drop of main assets.

Longstaff (2010) shows that despite its low liquidity, the ABS-CDO market (through the measure of the return of the ABX index) shows a significant predictive power (Granger causality) on stock returns, treasury yield changes, corporate bond changes and changes in the VIX volatility index. At the height of the subprime crisis in 2007, the movements of the ABX index seem to anticipate up to three weeks in advance the variations of these variables. This predictive power faded thereafter. In his study, contagion through liquidity and risk premia appear to be the main factors in the diffusion of the financial crisis.

Various authors have shown that the subprime crisis resulted in a rather general increase of CDS spreads that do not correspond to changes in true probabilities of default. In most cases, the increase in these spreads has resulted in an enhancement of risk premia from: A strengthening of correlations, an increase in the marginal probabilities of default or a standalone reinforcement of risk premia.

However, it is striking to note the low number of academic studies devoted to the evolution of risk premia during the financial crisis. Estimating risk premia is not an easy task. Butler *et al.* (2005) and Goyal and Welch (2008) show that performance in out-of-the-sample forecasting power of the different regression models was generally poor and does not outweigh the simple model of the historical risk premium (calculated as the average excess return at the beginning of the forecasted month). To state this conclusion, Goyal and Welch (2008) examine the out-of-the-sample predictive performance of most predictive variables used so far in the literature. This may mean that the correlations detected "in the sample" come from either data snooping, errors in the estimation of regression coefficients as sources of forecasting errors or time-varying regression coefficients. Moreover, the realized excess returns are at best very noisy measures of the risk premia. These findings lead Goyal and Welch (2007) to conclude "the profession has yet to find some variable that has meaningful and robust empirical equity premium forecasting power." However, large financial institutions, financial information providers (Bloomberg, FactSet, BARRA, etc.) adopting various methodologies converge in their estimation of a sharp rise in risk premia during the crisis. The level of the risk premium closely tracks both market volatility (reflected in the VIX index) and credit spreads. Surveys such as the one conducted by Graham and Harvey (2010) yielded the same conclusions.

References

Ang, A., Chen, J., 2002. Asymmetric correlations of equity portfolios. Journal of Financial Economics 63, 443–494.

Andersen, L.B., Sidenius, J., 2004. Extensions to the Gaussian copula: random recovery and random factor loadings. Journal of Credit Risk 1, 29–70.

Azizpour, S., Giesecke, K., Kim, B., 2010. Premia for correlated default risk. Journal of Economic Dynamics & Control 35, 1340–1357.

Bick, B., Kraft, H., 2012. Hedging Structured Credit Products During the Credit Crunch: A Horse Race of 10 Models. Goethe University Working Paper, Germany, pp. 50.

Brunnermeier, M.K., Nagel, S., 2008. Do wealth fluctuations generate time-varying risk aversion? Micro-evidence on individuals. American Economic Review 98, 713–736.

Brigo, D., Pallavicini, A., Torresetti, R., 2007. Calibration of CDO tranches with the dynamical generalized-poisson loss model. Risk 20, 70–75.

Brigo, D., Pallavicini, A., Torresetti, R., 2010. Credit Models and the Crisis: A Journey into CDOs, Copulas, Correlations and Dynamic Models. John Wiley & Sons, Chichester (U.K), pp. 176.

Burtschell, X., Gregory, J., Laurent, J.-P., 2009. A comparative analysis of CDO pricing models under the factor copula framework. Journal of Derivatives 16, 9–37.

Butler, A.W., Grullon, G., Weston, J., 2005. Can managers forecast aggregate market returns? Journal of Finance 60, 963–986.

Cont, R., Kan, Y.H., 2011. Dynamic hedging of portfolio credit derivatives. SIAM Journal on Financial Mathematics 2, 112–140.

Cousin, A., Crepey, S., Kan, Y., 2012. Delta-hedging correlation risk? Review of Derivatives Research 15, 25–56.

Das, S.R., Freed, L., Geng, G., Kapadia, N., 2006. Correlated default risk. Journal of Fixed Income 16, 7–32.

Das, S., Duffie, D., Kapadia, N., Saita, L., 2007. Common failings: how corporate defaults are correlated. Journal of Finance 62, 93–117.

Demyanyk, Y., Van Hemert, O., 2011. Understanding the subprime mortgage crisis. Review of Financial Studies 24, 1848–1880.

Duffie, D., Gârleanu, N., 2001. Risk and the valuation of collateralized debt obligations. Financial Analysts Journal 57, 41–59.

Goyal, A., Welch, I., 2008. A comprehensive look at the empirical performance of equity premium prediction. Review of Financial Studies 21, 1455–1508.

Graham, J.R., Harvey, C.R., 2010. The equity risk premium amid a global financial crisis. In: Kolb, R. (Ed.), Lessons from the Financial Crisis, Hoboken. John Wiley and Sons, New Jersey, pp. 525–536.

Hull, J., Predescu, M., White, A., 2004. The relationship between credit default swap spreads, bond yields, and credit rating announcements. Journal of Banking and Finance 28, 2789–2811.

Hull, J., White, A., 1990. Pricing interest-rate-derivative securities. Review of Financial Studies 3, 573–592.

Hull, J., White, A., 2006. Valuing credit derivatives using an implied copula approach. Journal of Derivatives 14, 8–28.

Hull, J., White, A., 2007. Forwards and European options on CDO tranches. Journal of Credit Risk 3, 63–73.

Hull, J.C., White, A., 2010. The risk of tranches created from mortgages. Financial Analysts Journal 66, 54–67.

Kramer, F., Löffler, G., 2010. Corporate bond defaults are consistent with conditional independence. Journal of Credit Risk 6, 3–35.

Lando, D., Nielsen, M.S., 2010. Correlation in corporate defaults: contagion or conditional independence? Journal of Financial Intermediation 19, 355–372.

Laurent, J.P., Gregory, J., 2005. Basket default swaps, CDOs and factor copulas. Journal of Risk 7, 103–122.

Longstaff, F.A., 2010. The subprime credit crisis and contagion in financial markets. Journal of Financial Economics 97, 436–450.

Longstaff, F.A., Rajan, A., 2008. An empirical analysis of the pricing of collateralized debt obligations. Journal of Finance 63, 529–563.

Mortensen, A., 2006. Semi-analytical valuation of basket credit derivatives in intensity-based models. Journal of Derivatives 13, 8–26.

O'Kane, D., 2008. Modelling Single-Name and Multi-Name Credit Derivatives. Wiley Finance, pp. 514.

Servigny, A., de Renault, O., 2002. Default Correlation: Empirical Evidence. Standard & Poor's Risk Solution Research Paper, pp. 27.

Shiller, R.J., 2007. Understanding Recent Trends in House Prices and Home Ownership. NBER Working Paper # 13553, pp. 34.

11

INDUSTRY VALUATION-DRIVEN EARNINGS MANAGEMENT

Tao Jiao,* Gerard Mertens** and Peter Roosenboom***

*University of California, Irvine, **Open University, Heerlen, ***Erasmus University*

11.1 Introduction

The current earnings management literature has examined earnings management from either a transaction-specific or a firm-specific point of view. In their review of earnings management literature, Healy and Wahlen (1999) mention that firms manage their earnings when they raise capital or when they need to meet analyst expectations or performance targets related to executive compensation schemes. However, these studies disregard the fact that market conditions, like economic growth and industry valuation, are not constant over time. Focusing on the latter, we hypothesize that industry valuation will influence managers' decisions to engage in earnings management. This can

Rethinking Valuation and Pricing Models. http://dx.doi.org/10.1016/B978-0-12-415875-7.00011-7

provide an explanation as to why earnings management occurs more frequently in some periods than in others.

Jensen (2005) argues that overvalued firms have incentives to sustain their overvaluation. Kothari *et al.* (2006) empirically test Jensen's argument and find that overvalued firms' discretionary accruals are much higher than those of firms with lower valuations. However, we differ from Kothari *et al.* (2006) in arguing that the level of industry valuation can influence the earnings management decisions of all firms in that industry, not only overvalued ones. This is because industry valuation level can change the benefits and costs of managing earnings for all firms in that industry.

We employ a large sample of US firms taken from Compustat. The sample period covers 20 years, from 1985 to 2005. We test our hypothesis by examining the association between industry valuation and the aggregate current discretionary accruals in the industry. Following the behavioral finance literature (Baker *et al.*, 2007), we use market-to-book ratio to proxy for the valuation level.

First, we find that after including the usual explanatory factors for earnings management, such as leverage, size, and performance, our measure for industry aggregate earnings management of each quarter remains significantly positively associated with the lagged industry market-to-book ratio. This result holds for both current and total discretionary accruals. In economic terms, this implies that one standard deviation increase in the industry valuation is associated with a significant increase of 2.4 cents in an average firm's quarterly earnings per share due to earnings management. Second, to exclude alternative explanations, we run several robust analyses and continue to find a significant, positive association between aggregate current discretionary accruals and the industry market-to-book ratio.

This chapter is organized as follows. Section 11.2 discusses related literature and develops our hypotheses. Section 11.3 describes our data and variables. Section 11.4 presents our results.

11.2 Literature Review and Hypotheses Development

Firms make earnings management decisions after balancing the associated benefits with costs. We briefly discuss these benefits and costs in the next two subsections.

11.2.1 Benefits of earnings management

The positive association between earnings surprises and stock returns motivates managers to use earnings management to influence stock price. Managers have strong incentives to increase their firms' earnings because their personal wealth, such as equity-based compensation and human capital, is closely linked with the stock price (Murphy, 1999). Graham *et al.* (2005) report that chief financial officers (CFOs) recognize stock price as one of their main motivations for earnings management. Stock price will decline if firms miss their analyst forecasts (Skinner and Sloan, 2002).

Although incentives to use earnings management to influence stock price always exist, we argue that the extent to which stock prices react to earnings is positively associated with industry valuation. Veronesi (1999) shows that investors will over-react to bad news when the market is performing well, but under-react to good news when the stock market is performing poorly. When this argument is applied at the industry level, it implies there is more severe punishment for releasing disappointing earnings when the industry is expected to perform well than when it is expected to perform poorly. In addition, the benefits of meeting or exceeding earnings expectations are higher in good times than in bad. Therefore, earnings management has more appeal to managers when the industry valuation is higher.

11.2.2 Costs of earnings management

11.2.2.1 Accruals reversal

Accruals cannot artificially boost earnings forever, but have to reverse at some point in time. We argue that the costs of accrual reversal decrease in case of higher or increasing industry valuation and increase in case of lower or decreasing industry valuation. Prior studies (e.g. Lee, 1992) find that stock prices can predict future economic performance. Based on this finding, we expect that managers tend to have an optimistic outlook on economic prospects and expect an industry to have increasing future cash flows when its average stock price increases. As a consequence, it is more likely for managers to believe that earnings management imposes fewer constraints on future reporting flexibility, because the reversal of accruals will be covered, at least partially, by increasing cash flows in the future. Hence, the negative influence from accrual reversal will be mitigated. In the case of lower or decreasing average industry stock prices, the problem with reporting flexibility will be more severe if managers engage in earnings management. Large amounts of accruals applied in the current period will mean greater difficulty in avoiding the negative consequences of an accrual reversal (i.e. a decrease of future earnings), since cash flow will decrease during an economic downturn or recession. Therefore, we conclude that the costs associated with reporting flexibility change with industry valuation. High industry valuation and an optimistic outlook offer managers greater reporting flexibility.

11.2.2.2 Probability of detecting earnings management

A challenge to our argument about accrual reversal might be that stock market participants can see through the components of earnings and thus detect accounting discretion. However, we claim that this probability is likely to be lower in the case of higher industry valuation.

First, investors, especially individual investors, lack the ability to see through earnings management. Sloan (1996) examines the information content of both accruals and cash flow. He finds that investors react to earnings rather than to either of these components. This result implies that investors might not be able to see through earnings management immediately. Hence, we argue that a high industry valuation predicts growing future cash flow and thus leads investors to be (more) optimistic about a firm's performance. In this case, it is easier for investors to believe a firm's performance results are plausible even if they can be attributed to a higher level of earnings management. Conversely, a low industry valuation increases investors' skepticism and makes them more suspicious of firms' performance.

Second, several studies find that the probability for journalists to see through firms' discretion is low when an industry performs well (e.g. Dyck and Zingales, 2002). We argue that industry valuation impacts the media's effectiveness in communicating information and monitoring firms. Periods of high industry valuation make it less likely that the media will alert investors about negative information, such as earnings management. Hence, we propose that the probability that investors will detect earnings management is lower when stock market valuation is high.

Combining the above arguments about the influence of industry valuation on the costs and benefits of earnings management, as well as the likelihood that earnings management will be detected, we predict that the incentives to engage in earnings management vary across time and are associated with aggregate levels of industry valuation: Earnings management is expected to occur more frequently when industry valuation is high. Therefore, we hypothesize that industry valuation has a positive impact on the degree of earnings management in that industry.

11.3 Data and Variables

11.3.1 Sample selection

We collect quarterly accounting data of non financial US firms from Compustat, and the initial public offering (IPOs) and seasoned equity offerings (SEOs) information of these firms from the Securities Depository Center (SDC). Table 11.1 shows how we constructed our sample.

11.3.2 Earnings management measurement

We use current discretionary accruals as the proxy for earnings management because current discretionary accruals are "the component most easily subject to successful managerial manipulation" (Teoh *et al.*, 1998c, p. 195). We compute the quarterly current discretionary accruals (DCA_{jtq}) based on the method used by Matsumoto (2002). The only difference between Mastsumoto (2002) and the modified Jones Model is

Table 11.1. Steps to screen our initial sample

Screening steps	No. of observations in sample	No. of firms in sample	Sample period
Initial sample	1,871,232	22,382	1970.1−2005.4
Less:	1,475,632	17,524	1970.1−2005.4
Financial firms	1,475,632	17,524	1970.1−2005.4
Observations with less than necessary data for modified Jones model	498,315	15,601	1972.3−2005.4
Less than 10 observations	382,012	15,267	1975.1−2005.4
Missing control variables	178,683	9354	1985.3−2004.4
Top and bottom 1% outliers	164,320	9065	1985.3−2004.4

First, we screen this initial sample by eliminating non-US stocks and financial companies (those with an SIC code beginning with 6). Second, we delete the observations that do not have enough data to estimate discretionary current accruals. Third, we drop observations if there are fewer than 10 observations to estimate the coefficients of total accruals. Fourth, we exclude observations that have a missing market value and book value, and other missing control variables. Finally, we delete the outliers by excluding the bottom and top 1% of every variable.

the fourth-quarter dummy added to control the fourth-quarter difference. Industry current discretionary accruals are measured as the lagged asset weighted average of discretionary accruals of all firms in an industry. Equation (11.1) presents the way to calculate industry current discretionary accruals:

$$DCA_{jtq} = \frac{\sum_i DCA_{ijtq} \times A_{ijtq-1}}{\sum_i A_{ijtq-1}}, \tag{11.1}$$

where DCA_{jtq} is the industry current discretionary accruals in quarter q of year t in industry j.

11.3.3 Stock valuation measurement

In their review of behavioral corporate finance, Baker *et al.* (2007) suggest that the market-to-book ratio is the most often used proxy for stock valuation.

We use the industry market-to-book ratio (MB_{jtq}) as our proxy for industry valuation. It is calculated as the ratio of the sum of the market capitalization of all stocks in quarter q of year t in industry j to the sum of the book value of these stocks in the same period and same industry:

$$MB_{jtq} = \frac{\sum_i M_{ijtq}}{\sum_i B_{ijtq}}, \tag{11.2}$$

where M_{ijtq} is the market value of firm i in quarter q of year t in industry j, B_{ijtq} is the book value of firm i in quarter q of year t in industry j and MB_{jtq} is the industry market-to-book ratio in quarter q of year t in industry j.

11.3.4 Control variables

Prior studies on earnings management have identified several factors that can influence earnings management decisions, so it is important for our study to control for these variables as well.

- *Firm valuation* (VAL_{ijtq-4}). Several studies (e.g. Degeorge *et al.*, 1999) argue that firms manage their earnings to meet stock market expectations and hence to sustain or increase their stock price. Jensen (2005) and Kothari *et al.* (2006) argue that overvalued equities count on their earnings to keep up the already-high valuation. Therefore, we include firm valuation as a control variable and use market-to-book ratio as the proxy.

- *Demand for external financing* ($FreeC_{ijtq-4}$). An *ex ante* measure of the demand for external financing ($FreeC_{ijtq-4}$) developed by Dechow *et al.* (1996) is included as a control variable. It measures the level of free funds within a firm. When firms have less "stock" of funds, there is a higher demand for external financing and, hence, more incentives to manage earnings. Our study follows the definition of Dechow *et al.* (1996). The expected relationship between earnings management and $FreeC_{ijtq-4}$ is positive.
- *Leverage* (LEV_{ijtq-4}). Prior studies (e.g. Dechow *et al.*, 1996) use leverage to measure the debt covenant motivation for earnings management. Assuming that firms with more leverage are closer to debt covenant violation, these firms are more inclined to engage in earnings management. We use leverage to measure firms' closeness to their potential debt covenant violation. Leverage is defined as total long-term debt scaled by total assets.
- *Size* ($SIZE_{ijtq-4}$). Several studies (e.g. Watts and Zimmerman, 1990) find that larger firms have more potential for earnings management. We also expect the sign of firm size to be positive. We use the natural logarithm of sales as the proxy of firm size.
- *Performance* (ROA_{ijtq-4}). Several studies (e.g. Bowen *et al.*, 2008) show that the modified Jones model can be misspecified without controlling firms' performance. Following Bowen *et al.* (2008), we include return on assets (ROA_{ijtq}) as a control variable. ROA_{ijtq} is defined as income before extraordinary items scaled by lagged total assets.
- *Equity issue* (IPO_{ijtq+m}, SEO_{ijtq+m}). Several studies (e.g. Teoh *et al.*, 1998a) find that firms manage earnings upward before going public to attract investors. Similar income-increasing earnings management is found before seasoned equity offerings (Teoh *et al.*, 1998b). Consistent with these studies, we include IPOs (IPO_{ijtq+m}) and seasoned equity offers (SEO_{ijtq+m}) dummies to control the effects of equity offerings on earnings management. These dummies equal one for the four quarters before (m is the $[-4,0]$) and after (m is the $[0,4]$) the quarter of either IPOs or seasoned equity offerings.
- *Industry and quarter dummies* (D_{in}, D_{qtr}). To control for unobservable factors, which are related to industry characteristics and might influence firms' earnings management decisions, we introduce industry [two-digit Standard Industrial Classification (SIC) code] and quarter dummies.

11.3.5 Descriptive statistics

Descriptive statistics of the final sample appear in Tables 11.2 and 11.3. To avoid the influence of outliers, we trim each variable at the first and 99th percentile. The mean of discretionary current accruals is 0.58%, and its median is 0.46%. The individual market-to-book ratio has a mean of 1.9875 and a median of 1.4189. The mean of the industry market-to-book ratio is 1.8712 and the median is 1.637.

Table 11.2. **Descriptive statistics of the sample**

Variable	Firm quarters	Mean	Median	Standard deviation	Minimum	Maximum
DCA_{ijtq}	164,320	0.0058	0.0046	0.0879	−0.5254	0.6222
MB_{ijtq-4}	164,320	1.8712	1.6370	0.7479	0.7520	6.0992
VAL_{ijtq-4}	164,320	1.9875	1.4189	1.6869	0.5518	15.3904
LEV_{ijtq-4}	164,320	0.1745	0.1228	0.1856	0	0.9055
$FreeC_{ijtq-4}$	164,320	0.0753	0	0.2707	0	1
$SIZE_{ijtq-4}$	164,320	3.1286	3.1361	2.1979	−3.2968	8.3825
ROA_{ijtq-4}	164,320	−0.0088	0.0078	0.0638	−0.4764	0.1065

DCA_{ijt} is quarterly current discretionary accruals. MB_{ijtq-4} is industry market-to-book ratio with a four-quarter lag behind the quarter of DCA_{ijt}. VAL_{ijtq-4}, LEV_{ijtq-4}, $FreeC_{ijtq-4}$, $SIZE_{ijtq-4}$ and ROA_{ijtq-4} represent individual firms' market-to-book ratio, leverage, demand for external capital, size and performance respectively. All have a four-quarter lag behind the quarter when the DCA is estimated.

Table 11.3. **Correlation matrix of variables of the final sample**

	DCA_{ijtq}	MB_{ijtq-4}	VAL_{ijtq-4}	LEV_{ijtq-4}	$FreeC_{ijtq-4}$	$SIZE_{ijtq-4}$	ROA_{ijtq-4}
DCA_{ijtq}	1						
MB_{ijtq-4}	−0.0101	1					
VAL_{ijtq-4}	0.0124	0.2661	1				
LEV_{ijtq-4}	−0.0083	−0.1624	−0.2085	1			
$FreeC_{ijtq-4}$	0.0059	−0.0515	0.0247	0.1653	1		
$SIZE_{ijtq-4}$	0.0173	−0.0917	−0.2131	0.2433	−0.1285	1	
ROA_{ijtq-4}	0.0478	−0.1397	−0.2191	0.0305	−0.2267	0.4042	1

11.4 Empirical Tests and Results

This section presents the results of our empirical analyses that test whether there is a relationship between industry market-to-book ratio and magnitude of earnings management at the industry level. In addition to controlling for the identifiable variables that affect firms' earnings management decisions, we include time dummies to control for all time-related factors. To minimize the collinearity between time dummy and industry valuation, this study uses a two-stage analysis. The first stage explains earnings management by regressing it on the control variables, including leverage, size, performance, demand for external financing, equity issue dummies, time dummies and industry dummies. Control variables, excluding dummy variables (equity issue, time and industry dummies), have a four-quarter lag behind the period of earnings management. As a result, the error terms from the first-step regression contain the component of earnings management that is not explained by the variables in the first-stage regression. We then aggregate the error terms for each industry quarter. The aggregation is a proxy for the unexplained portion of earnings management at the industry level and thus the dependent variable in our second-stage regression. The second stage uses a univariate regression to examine the association between unexplained earnings management in industry quarters and the four-quarter lagged industry market-to-book ratio. The coefficient estimated from this regression provides us with an estimate of industry valuation's effect on that industry's degree of earnings management.

Equation (11.3) (see below) is the model we used in the first step of the regression with current discretionary accruals as the dependent variable. The left-hand panel of Table 11.4 shows the results based on this model. The coefficients of firm valuation, demand of external finance and firm performance are in line with expectations. The signs of these coefficients are positive and significant. The coefficient of firm size is significantly positive and is consistent with the argument that larger firms have more resources to manage earnings. In order to conserve space, we do not report the coefficients of quarter and industry dummies. The overall R^2 of Model 3 is 1.40%, suggesting that much of the variation in discretionary accruals remains unexplained. However, we should bear in mind that this low R^2 is not surprising because our sample is not constructed to be conditional on special events, as, for example, in the case of equity offerings. Moreover, prior studies on earnings management

Table 11.4. Results of regression based on Equation (11.3) (the coefficients for quarter and industry dummies are also included in the regression but not reported here) and results of the second-stage regression based on Equation (11.4)

Results of first-stage analysis

Variable	Coefficient	p-value
VAL_{ijtq-4}	0.001	0.0001
LEV_{ijtq-4}	−0.0052	0.0001
$FreeC_{ijtq-4}$	0.0061	0.0001
$SIZE_{ijtq-4}$	0.0002	0.092
ROA_{ijtq-4}	0.0725	0.0001
IPO_{ijtq-4}	0.0002	0.979
IPO_{ijtq-3}	−0.0075	−0.0417
IPO_{ijtq-2}	0.0199	−0.015
IPO_{ijtq-1}	0.0035	−0.0322
IPO_{ijtq}	−0.0017	−0.0432
IPO_{ijtq+1}	−0.0242	−0.0646
IPO_{ijtq+2}	0.0178	−0.0226
IPO_{ijtq+3}	0.0039	−0.0389
IPO_{ijtq+4}	0.0264	−0.0178
SEO_{ijtq-4}	0.0039	0.0003
SEO_{ijtq-3}	0.0043	0.0005
SEO_{ijtq-2}	0.0085	0.0047
SEO_{ijtq-1}	0.0118	0.008
SEO_{ijtq}	0.0126	0.0087
SEO_{ijtq+1}	0.0091	0.0051
SEO_{ijtq+2}	0.0042	0.0002
SEO_{ijtq+3}	0.0015	−0.0026
SEO_{ijtq+4}	0.0052	0.0011
Intercept	0.0433	0.39
Overall R^2	0.014	
No. of Observations	164320	

Result of second-stage analysis

Variable	Predicted Sign	Coefficient	p-value
MB_{ijtq-4}	+	0.0014	0.0001
Intercept		0.0053	0.0001
Adjusted R^2		0.007	
No. of observations		4549	

report similar levels of explanatory power in their models (e.g. Kasznik, 1999):

$$DCA_{ijtq} = \alpha_0 + \alpha_1 VAL_{ijtq-4} + \alpha_2 LEV_{ijtq-4} + \alpha_3 FreeC_{ijtq-4}$$

$$+ \alpha_4 SIZE_{ijtq-4} + \alpha_5 ROA_{ijtq-4}$$

$$+ \sum_{n=6,m=-4}^{n=14,m=4} \alpha_n IPO_{ijtq+m} + \sum_{n=15,m=-4}^{n=23,m=4} \alpha_n SEO_{ijtq+m}$$

$$+ D_{\mathrm{qtr}} + D_{\mathrm{in}} + \varepsilon_{ijtq}, \tag{11.3}$$

where VAL_{ijtq-4} is the market-to-book ratio of individual firms, LEV_{ijtq-4} is the leverage (the ratio of long-term debt to total assets), $FreeC_{ijtq-4}$ is the demand for external financing, $SIZE_{ijtq-4}$ is the firm size measured as ln(sales), ROA_{ijtq-4} is the firm performance measured as return on assets, IPO_{ijtq+m} is the IPO dummy, SEO_{ijtq+m} is the seasoned equity offer dummy, D_{qtr} is the quarter dummy and D_{in} is the industry dummy.

After the first stage analysis, we aggregate the error term of each industry by quarter and regress the aggregated error terms on the industry market-to-book ratio:

$$\sum_i \varepsilon_{ijtq} = \lambda_0 + \lambda_1 MB_{jtq-4} + v_{jtq}, \tag{11.4}$$

where $\sum_i \varepsilon_{ijtq}$ is the aggregated error terms from the first-stage analysis per industry and MB_{jtq-4} is the lagged aggregate industry market-to-book ratio.

Descriptive statistics of the variables used in the second stage are presented in Table 11.5. The right-hand panel of Table 11.4 presents the results of the second-stage analysis. The coefficient of the industry valuation from the second step is significantly positive, which is consistent with our hypothesis. These results show that the industry average valuation has a positive relationship with earnings management, after controlling for the usual suspects. The coefficient of the industry valuation is 0.0014 and highly significant. This result implies that one standard deviation increase in industry valuation leads to an increase of 0.08 percentage points in aggregated error terms, which is about 11% of its average value. To translate this result into earnings per share, we first calculate the quarterly average assets per share within each industry, which is the ratio of the sum of total assets to the sum of outstanding shares in each industry quarter. The mean assets per share in our sample is $30.06 per share, which

Table 11.5. Statistics of variables in the second-stage analysis

Variable	Industry quarters	Mean	Standard deviation	Minimum	Maximum
MB_{jtq-4}	4549	1.5957	0.5361	0.752	6.0992
$\sum_i \varepsilon_{jtq-4}$	4549	0.0075	0.0086	−0.0335	0.0608

indicates that one standard deviation increase in industry market-to-book ratio will lead to an increase of about 2.4 cents (0.08% *30.06 = 2.4) earnings per share. This result indicates that firms on average inflate their earnings per share by 2.4 cents when the standard deviation of the industry market-to-book ratio increases by one. In sum, our result suggests that industry valuation influences the degree of earnings management.

We have done several robustness checks. In the first test, to be consistent with most earnings management studies, we use total discretionary accruals instead of current discretionary accruals as the proxy for earnings management. Second, it is possible that our results are driven by high-tech firms because they use more stock-based compensation than other firms. To control for these effects, we exclude high-tech firms from our sample. Third, because the likelihood of committing earnings management during the stock market boom of the late 1990s was higher than other periods, we run our tests without the observations in 1999 and 2000. Last, to examine this assumption's sensitivity in our results, we also test the relationship between earnings management and industry valuation for three quarters, two quarters and one quarter ago. The results of all these robustness tests still show that a positive relation between industry valuation and earnings management.

11.5 Conclusion

This study investigates the relationship between industry valuation and earnings management behavior. Previous academic research has investigated several capital market motivations for earnings management. However, most of these studies take the industry environment as constant and focus on earnings management motivated by firm-specific and transaction-specific factors. We argue that the industry valuation affects the expected.

payoff and cost of earnings management, and thus has an impact on earnings management. Our main hypothesis is that industry valuation has a positive impact on the degree of earnings management in an industry.

We apply a two-stage empirical model to explore the association between industry aggregate earnings management and industry valuation. We use current discretionary accruals as our proxy for earnings management. After controlling for several incentives for earnings management, such as leverage, firm size and firm performance, we find a significant positive relationship both between industry valuation and aggregate discretionary current accruals. We conclude that industry valuation is another motivation for earnings management.

References

Baker, M., Ruback, R., Wurgler, J., 2007. Behavioral corporate finance: a survey. In: Eckbo, E. (Ed.), Handbook of Corporate Finance: Empirical Corporate Finance. Elsevier, New York, pp. 145–188.

Bowen, R.M., Rajgopal, S., Venkatachalam, M., 2008. Accounting discretion, corporate governance and firm performance. Contemporary Accounting Research 25 (2), 351–405.

Dechow, P., Sloan, R., Sweeney, A., 1996. Causes and consequences of earnings manipulation: an analysis of firms subject to enforcement actions by the SEC. Contemporary Accounting Research 13 (1), 1–36.

Degeorge, F., Patel, J., Zeckhauser, R., 1999. Earnings management to exceed thresholds. Journal of Business 72 (1), 1–33.

Dyck, A., Zingales, L., 2002. The Bubble and the Media. In: Cornelius, P., Kogut, B. (Eds.), Corporate, Governance and Capital Flow in a Global Economy, Volume 1. Oxford University Press, New York, pp. 83–104.

Graham, J.R., Campbell, H.R., Rajgopal, S., 2005. The economic implications of corporate financial reporting. Journal of Accounting and Economics 40 (1-3), 3–73.

Healy, P., Wahlen, J., 1999. A review of the earnings management literature and its implication for standard setting. Accounting Horizons 13 (4), 365–383.

Kasznik, R., 1999. On the association between voluntary disclosure and earnings management. Journal of Accounting Research 37 (1), 57–81.

Kothari, R., Loutskina, E., Nikolaev, V., 2006. Agency theory of overvalued equity as an explanation for the accrual anomaly. University of Chicago. Working Paper. http://faculty.chicagobooth.edu/valeri.nikolaev/PDF/Kothari% 20Loutskina%20Nikolaev%202009%20Agency%20Theory%20of% 20Overvalued%20Equity%20as%20an%20Explanation%20for%20Accrual% 20Anomaly.pdf.

Lee, B.S., 1992. Casual relations among stock returns, interest rates, real activity and inflation. Journal of Finance 47 (4), 1591–1603.

Jensen, M., 2005. Agency costs of overvalued equity. Financial Management 34 (1), 5–19.

Matsumoto, D., 2002. Management's incentives to avoid negative earnings surprises. The Accounting Review 77 (3), 483–514.

Murphy, K., 1999. Executive Compensation. In: Ashenfelter, O.C., Card, D. (Eds.), Handbook of Labor Economics, Volume 3. Elsevier, Amsterdam, pp. 2485–2563.

Skinner, D.J., Sloan, R.G., 2002. Earnings surprises, growth expectations, and stock returns or don't let an earnings torpedo sink your portfolio. Review of Accounting Studies 7 (2-3), 289–312.

Sloan, R.G., 1996. Do stock prices fully reflect information in accruals and cash flow in future earnings. The Accounting Review 71 (3), 289–315.

Teoh, S., Welch, I., Wong, T., 1998a. Earnings management and the long-run market performance of initial public offerings. Journal of Finance 53 (6), 1935–1974.

Teoh, S., Welch, I., Wong, T., 1998b. Earnings management and the underpeformance of seasoned equity offerings. Journal of Financial Economics 50 (1), 63–99.

Teoh, S., Wong, T., Rao, G., 1998c. Are accruals during initial public offerings opportunistic? Review of Accounting Studies 3 (1-2), 175–208.

Veronesi, P., 1999. Stock market overreaction to bad news in good times: a rational expectation equilibrium model. Review of Financial Studies 12 (5), 975–1007.

Watts, R.L., Zimmerman, J.L., 1990. Positive accounting theory: a ten year perspective. The Accounting Review 65 (1), 131–156.

VALUATION OF YOUNG GROWTH FIRMS AND FIRMS IN EMERGING ECONOMIES

Wolfgang Breuer* and Klaus Mark**

*RWTH Aachen University, **KfW Banking Group

CHAPTER OUTLINE

12.1 Introduction

One of the main factors increasing the danger of financial crises is the formation of an asset price bubble. That is, prices paid on the market or in transactions for an asset which has lost the linkage to fundamentals. As we observed after the internet hype in 2000 or after the heavily credit financed housing boom in the United States, the burst of a price bubble can not only have adverse effects on investor confidence, but can also result in a crisis of the real sector with a massive downturn of economic activity. Thus, an important contribution of financial theory to reduce risk of financial crises is to endow investors with valuation models that are carefully calibrated to avoid excessive over-valuation. In this paper, we focus on the valuation of firms with the widely used discounted cash flow (DCF) methodology. It is well known in the literature that the bias associated with the estimation of future cost of capital utilizing historical rates of return can cause substantial overvaluation effects in a DCF model (see, e.g. Butler and Schachter, 1989; Cooper, 1996). In this chapter, we illustrate that the danger of overvaluation, due to estimation risk regarding the cost of capital, is particularly high

Rethinking Valuation and Pricing Models. http://dx.doi.org/10.1016/B978-0-12-415875-7.00012-9

when valuation parameters are optimistic and the prediction of future parameters is more uncertain anyway, i.e. when valuing young growth and technology firms or firms in emerging economies. Using a bootstrap simulation, we show that with the help of simple heuristics that can easily be adopted in the valuation process in practical settings, overvaluation effects due to an estimation bias can be considerably reduced. In particular, the heuristics are appropriate to substantially reduce overvaluation for young growth firms and emerging market firms which are heavily exposed to this problem.

When employing the DCF approach to determine firm values, there are generally two possible ways to compute adequate discount rates for expected cash flows. On the one hand, one may rely on analysts' estimates of future dividends and earnings. Combining these estimates with current stock market values makes it possible to calculate corresponding implied costs of capital as internal rates of return (see, e.g. Claus and Thomas, 2001; Gebhardt *et al.*, 2001). However, to this end analysts' forecasts must be both unbiased and representative for overall market expectations. Both conditions are typically not satisfied (see, e.g. Becker *et al.*, 2009). Therefore, practitioners often do not rely on the implied cost of capital approach (see, e.g. Wagner *et al.*, 2006). On the other hand, one may utilize historical return moments, if historical returns are—due to capital market efficiency—independently and identically distributed (i.i.d.) over time so that they are stationary. The most straightforward idea is then to compute the arithmetic mean of historical return realizations and to utilize it as a (time-invariant) discount rate for firm value estimation. However, even if it is possible to estimate expected one-period returns on this basis without a bias, by way of Jensen's inequality it can be shown that corresponding discount factor estimates are upwards biased. This implies that firm valuations based on arithmetic mean estimates of cost of capital are systematically too high. Breuer *et al.* (2011) suggest quite a simple remedy to address this problem: If one refrains from estimating firm value as a perpetual with eventually constant cash flow growth rates (as is the typical approach in practical applications), but instead truncates the number N of future cash flow years under consideration to, say, $N = 30$ or $N = 50$, estimation results can become better, not worse, although without the bias problem, estimates would now be too low due to the neglect of cash flows. This neglect, however, is just suited to reduce otherwise too high firm value estimates.

Among other things, Breuer *et al.* (2011) show that the problem of upwards biased estimates based on simple arithmetic mean estimators becomes more severe for firms with high annual growth rates of expected cash flows. As this may be in particular a problem for young growth companies and for companies in emerging economies, the authors conclude that for valuations regarding such clientele the utilization of a "truncated" arithmetic mean estimator might become even more helpful. The aim of this chapter is to analyze to what extent this conjecture holds. To this end, we follow Breuer *et al.* (2011) by performing a bootstrap analysis for several stock market indices. We refer to the S&P 500 and the Dow Jones from the United States, the DAX and the CDAX from Germany, the FTSE 100 from the United Kingdom, and the Nikkei from Japan as examples for well-established markets. Firm valuation results for these indices are contrasted with results for the NASDAQ from the United States as a typical market segment for young technology firms, and for the Hang Seng for Hong Kong (China), the Indian SENSEX and the South Korean KOSPI as examples for stock markets in emerging economies.

Our numerical results confirm the conjecture of Breuer *et al.* (2011) stated above. Particularly, the utilization of the simple arithmetic mean for firm valuation would lead to considerably upwards biased estimates for young growth companies and companies in emerging economies, possibly leading to price bubbles. Therefore, a more conservative firm valuation procedure based on truncated arithmetic means would not only result in more precise firm value estimates, but also help to avoid a possible source of bubbles. In addition, we also examine an estimator introduced by Cooper (1996) as an alternative to arithmetic mean truncation. Somewhat surprisingly, while we are able to confirm the finding of Breuer *et al.* (2011) of arithmetic mean truncation being superior even to the Cooper estimator for firms in developed markets, this does not necessarily hold true for companies from emerging economies. For them, average biases are often even smaller when applying the Cooper estimator. However, squared mean biases are lower for the truncated arithmetic mean estimator than for the Cooper estimator. Thus, both valuation approaches have their merits. In any case, the simple arithmetic mean is not suitable for firm value estimation and the overvaluation problem can be substantially reduced with quite simple techniques.

The chapter is organized as follows. In Section 12.2, we present some basics regarding the bias problem in discount factor estimation. Section 12.3 describes our data and numerical procedure. In Section 12.4, results are derived. Section 12.5 concludes.

12.2 The Basic Problem

Today's firm value V_0 may be determined as the expected future firm value $E[\tilde{V}_n]$ (at time n) discounted with the cost of capital $\bar{r}$ that is identical to the firm's expected one period-return:

$$V_0 = \frac{E[\tilde{V}_n]}{(1+\bar{r})^n}. \tag{12.1}$$

In practical valuation problems, however, it is not only necessary to estimate expected future market values (or underlying cash flows), but also expected future one-period returns in order to apply Equation (12.1). In what follows, we focus on the special problems connected with the determination of the discount factor $d_n := (1+\bar{r})^{-n}$ on the basis of historical return realizations. The most straightforward way to do so seems to be to compute the arithmetic mean $\hat{A}_T$ of historical return realizations $\tilde{r}_t$ ($t = 1, ..., T$) of T past periods:

$$\hat{A}_T := \frac{1}{T} \cdot \sum_{t=1}^{T} (1 + \tilde{r}_t). \tag{12.2}$$

Based on (12.2), one may define $\hat{D}_n = 1/(\hat{A}_T)^n$ as an estimator for d_n. However, even if $\hat{A}_T$ is an unbiased estimator for $1 + \bar{r}$, we will have $E[\hat{D}_n] = E[(\hat{A}_T)^{-n}] > (1+\bar{r})^{-n}$ because of Jensen's equality, as $1/(\hat{A}_T)^n$ is a strictly convex function of $\hat{A}_T$ (see Butler and Schachter, 1989; Cooper, 1996).

It is difficult to address this problem analytically in a general way. There are some approaches that try to resolve the bias problem under special distributional assumptions (see, once again, Butler and Schachter, 1989). Moreover, Cooper (1996) developed an estimator $\hat{C}_T$ based on a Taylor approximation and computed as a linear combination of the arithmetic mean and the corresponding geometric mean estimator $\hat{G}_T := \left[\prod_{t=1}^{T} (1 + \tilde{r}_t) \right]^{1/T}$. The weights for both the arithmetic and the geometric mean depend on sample length T and forecasting horizon n. In any case, we call such an approach that is directly based on historical equity return realizations a "total returns" approach. In contrast, one may also first rely on historical excess returns in order to estimate market risk premia, which then can be added to the current term structure of riskless interest rates (e.g. when employing the capital asset pricing model). Here, the same bias problem prevails and we speak of a "partial returns" approach.

Against this background, Breuer *et al.* (2011) derive several hypotheses with respect to the precision of various estimation procedures and these are examined numerically based on a bootstrap approach for 13 different developed countries. In order to do so, Breuer *et al.* (2011) consider the following full-fledged formula for firm valuation:

$$
\hat{V} = \sum_{n=1}^{N_1} \frac{\bar{c}_n}{(1+\hat{r}_{0,n})^n} + \sum_{n=N_1+1}^{N_2} \frac{\bar{c}_{N_1} \cdot (1+g)^{n-N_1}}{(1+\hat{r}_{0,n})^n}
$$
$$
+ \frac{\bar{c}_{N_1} \cdot (1+g)^{N_2-N_1+1}}{(\hat{r}_{0,N_2} - g) \cdot (1+\hat{r}_{0,N_2})^{N_2}}. \tag{12.3}
$$

It is assumed that expected future cash flows $\bar{c}_n$ up to a forecast horizon N_1 are explicitly estimated by decision makers. From N_1 on, expected cash flows are assumed to grow at a constant growth rate g per period. Moreover, up to a forecast horizon of $N_2 \geq N_1$, risk-adjusted zero bond discount rates $\hat{r}_{0,n}$ from time 0 to n may be explicitly estimated in the partial returns approach. From N_2 on, zero bond discount rates are assumed to be identical to the last one that has been explicitly estimated, i.e. $\hat{r}_{0,N_2}$. In contrast, when referring to the total returns approach based on the arithmetic mean or geometric mean estimator, it is not necessary to distinguish between N_1 and N_2. So we can simply set $N_2 = N_1$, because a flat term structure of risk-adjusted discount rates is implicitly assumed. Things are different with respect to the Cooper estimator, as resulting discount rates here are a function of the forecasting horizon n. In practical applications, there are hardly values for N_1 beyond five to ten years. However, in order to utilize as much information as possible, a choice of $N_2 = 30$ or even $N_2 = 50$ years should be generally preferable to settings with $N_1 = N_2 = 5$ or $N_1 = N_2 = 10$ when applying the Cooper estimator.

Based on (12.3) and different parameter settings, several results are obtained in Breuer *et al.* (2011). First of all, it is shown that all three estimators $\hat{A}_T$, $\hat{C}_T$ and $\hat{G}_T$ may lead to discount factor estimates greater than 1. Moreover, the Cooper estimator may even result in a *negative* discount factor estimate. The exclusion of such unreasonable discount factor estimates increases the average positive estimation considerably, particularly with respect to the Cooper estimator. Moreover, the geometric mean estimator cannot be recommended as it leads to unambiguously inferior results. A longer sample length T of historical return realizations mitigates the bias problem, while relative estimation errors increase for longer forecasting horizons n. Moreover, if historical sample returns used as estimation input have a lower standard deviation, estimation precision rises. Higher growth rates g of future firm cash flows worsens the bias problem. Last, but not least, terminal value computation, i.e. the last summand in Equation (12.3) is exposed to the most pronounced estimation problems.

As a consequence of the last two findings, Breuer *et al.* (2011) recommend to truncate at least the arithmetic mean estimator by simply neglecting the terminal value contribution to overall firm value while—at the same time—setting $N_1 = 30$ or $N_1 = 50$. Thereby, it is not necessary to explicitly estimate 30 or 50 different expected values. In contrast, after some point in time one may simply assume $\bar{c}_n$ to increase by a constant factor g. However, these summands do not enter terminal value computation (which is neglected), but they are explicitly computed. In what follows, we simply use the variable N to characterize the number of cash flow summands that are explicitly considered, as we do not have to distinguish between N_1 and N_2 due to the use of the total returns approach.

Breuer *et al.* (2011) show that the arithmetic mean estimator without truncation is simply dominated by the truncated arithmetic mean estimator and, without truncation, the arithmetic mean estimator would also be unconditionally inferior to the Cooper estimator. Moreover, the simple measure of cash flow truncation establishes the superiority of the arithmetic mean estimator also over the Cooper estimator for sufficiently high cash flow growth rates. Without truncation, situations with high annual growth rates of 4% or more could simply not be addressed adequately at all. Based on historical values for economic growth for the 13 industrialized countries under consideration, an average growth rate of 4% per year seems of most practical importance. Furthermore, Breuer *et al.* (2011), conjecture that for developing countries like China, India or South Korea with considerably higher growth rates of the nominal as well as the real GDP (used as a proxy for cash flow growth), the truncated arithmetic mean estimator for firm valuation may on average even be more important. In addition, historical sample returns for developing countries are typically more volatile so that there is another reason why the estimation problem regarding terminal value determination may cause extreme distortions which should be avoided by simply dropping the terminal value. A similar conclusion may be drawn with respect to young growth companies in industrialized countries.

12.3 Data and Numerical Procedure

The aim of this chapter is to examine the hypotheses of Breuer *et al.* (2011) as described in the last section somewhat more in depth by explicitly looking at capital market data of Hong Kong (Hang Seng index), India (SENSEX index) and South Korea (KOSPI index) as typical examples of Asian developing countries, and the NASDAQ as one (United States) market for faster growing technology companies. We contrast these markets with those of Germany (DAX and CDAX indices), Japan (Nikkei index) the United Kingdom (FTSE 100 index), and the United States (S&P 500 and Dow Jones indices). With the exception of the NASDAQ, the S&P 500, the CDAX, and the KOSPI, all indices represent the share market index of each country that only comprises the biggest firms in terms of market capitalization. While the NAS-DAQ addresses technology firms, the S&P 500, the CDAX and the KOSPI are broader indices irrespective of the industry sector (see the footnote of Table 12.1 for more details). We replicate the bootstrap approach by Breuer *et al.* (2011). According to the findings in this previous paper we are allowed to restrict ourselves to the total returns approach. We refrain from any tax consider-ations. Moreover, we restrict discount factor estimates to the interval [0.0001;1] as non-positive values and values greater than 1 are unreasonable. Estimates violating these restrictions are replaced by the lower or the upper bound of the interval of admissible discount factors.

Table 12.1 presents an overview of capital market data that are taken from Bloomberg. For all return time series we employed an Augmented Dickey–Fuller (ADF) test to confirm that rates of return follow an i.i.d. process. The lengths of the time series vary from country to country with the longest time series stemming from the United States and the shortest from the United Kingdom and South Korea. As can be seen in Table 12.1, standard deviations of stock market returns in developing countries are much higher than in developed countries. At the same time, the average rates of return in China, India and South Korea substantially exceed the corre-sponding values of the developed countries. The same holds true with respect to average growth rates of nominal GDP which are derived from the world economic outlook forecast (average forecast for 2011–2016) of the International Monetary Fund (IMF). Similarly to practitioners, we use them as a proxy for the average "sustain-able" growth rate of expected firm cash flows in the countries under consideration. The underlying idea is that in the DCF model, in some kind of steady state after the detailed planning period for firms, cannot generate cash flows that grow faster than the economy. However, for the NASDAQ, we deviate from this approach. Starting with a US nominal GDP growth rate of 3.9%, the assumed cash flow growth rate is increased by two percentage points, which roughly equals the difference between the arithmetic

Table 12.1. Characteristics of sample data that build the basis for the bootstrap approach

| | | Share index data | | | | ADF test | | Nominal GDP growth (average IMF forecast 2011—2016) (%) | Standard deviation of arithmetic sample means of the bootstrap simulation (percentage points) |
		Sample length (years)	Arithmetic mean (%)	Geometric mean (%)	Standard deviation (percentage points)	t-value	p-value		
United States	Dow Jones	109	8.92	6.51	22.32	−9.8168	0.0000	3.9	2.12
	S&P 500	83	11.11	9.05	20.35	−6.9204	0.0000	3.9	2.25
	NASDAQ	39	12.17	8.66	27.40	−5.1803	0.0001	5.9[a]	4.31
Germany	DAX	51	8.54	5.77	24.56	−5.8996	0.0000	2.5	3.40
	CDAX	40	9.88	7.47	22.13	−5.4319	0.0001	2.5	3.56
Japan	Nikkei	40	7.52	4.61	25.50	−3.6942	0.0082	1.2	4.10
United Kingdom	FTSE 100	26	10.17	8.89	16.28	−3.3559	0.0233	5.2	3.16
China	Hang Seng	42	23.44	15.19	44.47	−6.7737	0.0000	12.8	6.36
India	SENSEX	30	23.02	17.85	35.33	−4.5204	0.0013	14.0	6.34
Korea	KOSPI	28	17.76	11.35	38.20	−3.4061	0.0200	7.3	7.13

Characteristics of the historical return data of the share indices used in the bootstrap simulation. The Dow Jones Industrial index comprises the 30 biggest firms traded on the New York Stock Exchange in terms of market capitalization. The S&P 500 represents the share price movement of the 500 biggest US firms in terms of market capitalization. The NASDAQ composite index comprises 3000 technology firms. The DAX index is built by the 30 biggest German firms according to market capitalization traded on the Frankfurt Stock Exchange. The CDAX consists of all German companies listed on the General and the Prime Standard on the Frankfurt Stock Exchange. The Japanese Nikkei index represents the share price development of the 225 most important Japanese firms listed on the Tokyo Stock Exchange. The FTSE 100 (Financial Times Stock Exchange 100) entails the 100 biggest UK firms according to market share turnover. The Hang Seng index consists of 45 firms representing about 75% of the market capitalization on the Hong Kong Stock Exchange. The SENSEX index entails the 30 biggest Indian firms according to market capitalization in free float. The KOSPI index reflects the share price movement of all firms listed at the Korea Exchange. The nominal GDP growth rates are computed by the arithmetic mean of nominal GDP growth forecasts by the IMF 2011—2016 according to the World Economic Outlook, September 2011. The standard deviation of the arithmetic sample means of the bootstrap simulation is computed by the means of the 10 000 artificial return paths of the simulation.

[a]For the NASDAQ, firm cash flow growth is adjusted. Starting from US nominal GDP growth rate of 3.9%, the assumed cash flow growth rate is increased by 2 percentage points, which roughly equals the difference between the arithmetic mean return of the NASDAQ index and the mean of the two other US indices corresponding average returns.

Source: Bloomberg and IMF

mean return of the NASDAQ index and the middle of the two other US indices corresponding average returns. By doing so, the higher growth potential of young technology companies is taken into account, although it is clear that eventually cash flow growth rates even for this kind of firms have to go down.

Based on the data presented in Table 12.1, we perform a bootstrap approach in order to analyze the estimation goodness of the simple as well as the truncated arithmetic mean estimator and the Cooper estimator. To this end, we assume expected firm cash flows that are growing from time $t = 1$ on with a constant growth rate $g \geq 0$ per period until infinity. We are able to compute "true" firm values by assuming that the correct probability distribution of possible one-period returns is described by the historical time series of return realizations. For each stock index, we then generate 10,000 artificial time series of rates of returns of length T based on the extent of the original return time series according to Table 12.1. We derive estimates for the arithmetic mean of returns (and the other estimators under consideration) for each of our 10,000 artificial time series of rates of return and contrast average results for firm value estimates across all 10,000 simulation runs with the true firm value. Thereby, we are able to determine average (relative) estimation biases as well as the (relative) root mean squared errors in firm value estimations. The latter indicator avoids offsetting the effects of positive and negative deviations between estimated and true firm value.

12.4 Results

We start by a detailed comparison of estimation results for the Dow Jones, the DAX and the KOSPI based on the arithmetic mean of historical return realizations and the corresponding Cooper estimator according to Table 12.2. Regarding their basic structure, the results are quite similar for all three indices. In particular, the success of the arithmetic mean that the estimator does not depend much on the length N of the detailed planning period. In line with the theoretical considerations of Section 12.2, the arithmetic mean estimator is generally upwardly biased. However, the bias regarding the arithmetic mean estimator is much smaller for the Dow Jones than for the DAX and the KOSPI. This is a consequence of the considerably longer time series of returns available for the Dow Jones. A second reason is the smaller standard deviation of the Dow Jones yearly returns. For the same reasons, the bias regarding the arithmetic mean estimator is smaller for the DAX than for the KOSPI with differences, however, not as pronounced as in comparison to the Dow Jones.

Table 12.2. Relative average bias in firm values and relative root mean squared errors for detailed planning periods and terminal values for selected indices (cash flow growth 0%)

	N = 5			N = 10		
	Detailed planning	Terminal value	Total firm value	Detailed planning	Terminal value	Total firm value
Dow Jones						
Fraction of (true) total firm value	*34.56*	*65.44*	*100.00*	*57.47*	*42.53*	*100.00*
(Average) Bias						
Arithmetic mean	0.1	10.2	6.7	0.6	16.5	7.4
Cooper estimator	−0.1	7.4	4.8	−0.2	9.1	3.8
Root mean squared error						
Arithmetic mean	5.5	50.3	34.6	9.5	70.8	35.0
Cooper estimator	5.5	47.4	32.7	9.4	62.3	31.3
DAX						
Fraction of (true) total firm value	*33.39*	*66.61*	*100.00*	*55.79*	*44.21*	*100.00*
(Average) Bias						
Arithmetic mean	0.3	58.1	38.8	1.5	87.1	39.3
Cooper estimator	−0.4	46.5	30.8	−0.7	57.2	24.9
Root mean squared error						
Arithmetic mean	9.0	270.1	181.8	15.8	400.2	182.8
Cooper estimator	8.9	256.3	172.5	15.3	364.2	166.2
KOSPI						
Fraction of (true) total firm value	*55.16*	*44.84*	*100.00*	*80.04*	*19.96*	*100.00*
(Average) Bias						
Arithmetic mean	1.8	110.3	50.5	5.0	235.0	50.9
Cooper estimator	−0.9	78.3	34.6	−2.9	126.7	23.0
Root mean squared error						
Arithmetic mean	17.2	664.4	303.2	30.0	1454.2	305.2
Cooper estimator	16.4	631.6	287.6	26.5	1343.3	279.2

	N = 30			N = 50		
	Detailed planning	Terminal value	Total firm value	Detailed planning	Terminal value	Total firm value
Dow Jones						
Fraction of (true) total firm value	*92.30*	*7.70*	*100.00*	*98.63*	*1.37*	*100.00*
(Average) Bias						
Arithmetic mean	3.1	55.7	7.1	5.1	153.4	7.1
Cooper estimator	−1.5	−6.9	−2.0	−3.8	−84.7	−4.9
Root mean squared error						
Arithmetic mean	21.0	227.3	34.8	27.2	787.3	34.8
Cooper estimator	18.7	124.6	25.3	20.9	242.0	21.6
DAX						
Fraction of (true) total firm value	*91.30*	*8.70*	*100.00*	*98.33*	*1.67*	*100.00*
(Average) Bias						
Arithmetic mean	8.8	365.1	39.8	16.2	1.468.5	40.6
Cooper estimator	−5.1	100.4	4.1	−8.9	505.2	−0.3
Root mean squared error						
Arithmetic mean	40.5	1807.7	185.4	64.2	8295.9	191.3
Cooper estimator	32.9	1468.8	147.6	43.8	6402.9	139.9
KOSPI						
Fraction of (true) total firm value	*99.29*	*0.71*	*100.00*	*99.99*	*0.01*	*100.00*
(Average) Bias						
Arithmetic mean	20.5	4695.6	53.6	39.6	383,808.6	65.1
Cooper estimator	−9.9	2547.6	8.2	−8.1	228,323.0	7.1
Root mean squared error						
Arithmetic mean	133.2	36,477.3	333.3	839.6	3,458,629.9	928.5
Cooper estimator	50.4	32,163.7	263.9	71.5	3,016,369.4	261.8

Precision results for firm value estimation (in percent of the corresponding true value) based on the simple arithmetic mean and the Cooper estimator according to the average relative estimation bias and the root mean squared error for three different indices (Dow Jones, DAX and KOSPI) from three different countries (United States, Germany and South Korea).

In contrast, the correctness of the Cooper estimator critically depends on the length of the detailed planning period. There seems to be a country-specific inner optimum for N which is the greater the smaller is the time series of historical rates of return. Generally, values for N of 30−50 seem to be good choices.

Moreover, for $N = 30$ and $N = 50$, the contribution of the terminal value to overall firm value is limited. Thus, high values of N imply the advantage that severe distortions that can be observed especially regarding terminal value estimates have only minor relevance for total firm value estimation result. Moreover, this may also render 'truncation' a good idea to resolve the problem of the upwards biased arithmetic mean estimator. Without such a truncation, the Cooper estimator proves superior to the simple arithmetic mean of historical rates of return. Results are quite similar for all three countries. However, this conclusion is based on the assumption that expected firm cash flows per year are constant over time. We therefore take a closer look at possible consequences of variations in annual cash flow growth rates for bias problems.

According to Table 12.3, we confirm the finding in Breuer *et al.* (2011) that the value of the cash flow growth rate g is critical for the extent of the bias problem. The simple arithmetic mean reacts quite sensitively to variations of cash flow growth rates and is always dominated by an application of the Cooper estimator. Similarly to the findings in Breuer *et al.* (2011) for the Dow Jones and the DAX, cash flow growth rates beyond 4% lead to quite high estimation errors even for the Cooper estimator with $N = 30$ or $N = 50$. Rather unexpectedly, the bias regarding the Cooper estimator for the KOSPI index does not react much to variations of g, if $N = 30$ or $N = 50$. This means that, in this case the Cooper estimator, combined with long detailed planning periods, seems to offer an effective protection against estimation problems in the case of high expected cash flow growth rates.

The underlying reason is that the Cooper estimator slightly underestimates values in the detailed planning period. Although the bias of the Cooper estimator is often enormous for the terminal values on a stand-alone basis, this does not distort the overall firm value that much because the value contribution of the terminal value for $N = 30$ or $N = 50$ is very small, especially for the indices of the emerging market economies. Since the average index return rate is in the area of 20% for the KOSPI and the other emerging economies, this implies very small discount factors for longer time horizons. As a result, the moderate underestimation effect of the detailed planning period is a fairly appropriate offset

Table 12.3. Relative average bias of total firm value and cash flow growth for selected indices (%)

	Cash flow growth rate (%)	Arithmetic mean				Cooper estimator			
		N = 5	N = 10	N = 30	N = 50	N = 5	N = 10	N = 30	N = 50
Dow Jones	0	6.7	7.4	7.1	7.1	4.8	3.8	-2.0	-4.9
	1	9.5	10.3	10.0	10.1	7.1	5.7	-2.0	-6.4
	2	14.8	15.7	15.3	15.5	11.5	9.6	-1.6	-8.6
	3	24.6	25.7	25.2	25.6	19.6	16.4	-0.4	-11.7
	4	41.2	42.7	42.1	43.0	34.4	29.8	2.6	-15.9
	5	62.0	64.2	63.5	65.7	53.4	47.6	9.3	-21.9
	6	77.6	81.1	80.9	85.3	67.9	62.1	15.7	-30.7
DAX	0	38.8	39.3	39.8	40.6	30.8	24.9	4.1	-0.3
	1	56.6	57.2	57.9	59.8	45.1	36.4	6.4	-0.8
	2	77.2	77.9	79.1	83.1	61.0	48.6	6.3	-3.6
	3	101.2	102.1	103.9	111.1	80.0	62.5	3.3	-8.4
	4	119.3	120.6	123.3	135.1	96.5	76.8	-2.5	-16.0
	5	124.4	126.3	130.3	147.9	102.8	83.6	-11.4	-26.1
	6	104.3	107.2	112.4	136.0	86.9	72.1	-24.7	-39.2
KOSPI	0	50.5	50.9	53.6	65.1	34.6	23.0	8.2	7.1
	1	65.2	65.6	69.3	87.1	44.4	29.6	9.0	7.4
	2	81.7	82.1	87.3	114.5	55.6	36.4	9.2	7.4
	3	100.1	100.3	107.5	148.5	66.0	43.2	8.9	7.4
	4	120.8	120.9	130.5	191.4	78.3	48.0	7.4	7.4
	5	143.2	143.1	155.7	244.8	91.1	54.1	5.4	8.2
	6	166.9	166.6	183.0	311.6	104.5	59.6	2.6	10.0

Average relative estimation biases for three indices (Dow Jones, DAX and KOSPI) in three countries (United States, Germany and South Korea) for two different estimators. Simple arithmetic mean and Cooper estimator, give different lengths of the detailed planning period and different cash flow growth rates.

Table 12.4. Relative average bias and relative root mean squared errors in firm valuation based on simple and truncated arithmetic mean as well as on the Cooper estimator

Stock index (%) (1)	Simple arithmetic mean (2)	Truncated arithmetic mean (3)	Difference |(2)| − |(3)| (4)	Cooper estimator (5)
Bias				
Dow Jones	39.2 ($N = 5$)	*0.1* ($N = 50$)	39.1	2.1 ($N = 30$)
S&P 500	17.8 ($N = 30$)	4.8 ($N = 50$)	13.0	−1.4 ($N = 30$)
NASDAQ	138.8 ($N = 10$)	−0.6 ($N = 30$)	138.2	−14.4 ($N = 50$)
DAX	89.3 ($N = 5$)	−8.7 ($N = 30$)	80.6	*5.1* ($N = 30$)
CDAX	69.0 ($N = 5$)	−1.6 ($N = 30$)	67.4	−2.2 ($N = 30$)
Nikkei	118.6 ($N = 5$)	−0.9 ($N = 30$)	117.7	40.4 ($N = 50$)
FTSE 100	101.7 ($N = 10$)	15.4 ($N = 50$)	86.4	−8.1 ($N = 30$)
Hang Seng	156.5 ($N = 10$)	21.4 ($N = 30$)	135.1	−13.1 ($N = 50$)
SENSEX	183.5 ($N = 10$)	21.3 ($N = 30$)	162.2	−13.0 ($N = 50$)
KOSPI	196.3 ($N = 10$)	39.0 ($N = 30$)	157.3	−1.5 ($N = 30$)
Root mean squared errors				
Dow Jones	148.8 ($N = 5$)	38.5 ($N = 50$)	110.3	73.8 ($N = 30$)
S&P 500	86.9 ($N = 30$)	35.3 ($N = 50$)	51.6	38.1 ($N = 30$)
NASDAQ	370.1 ($N = 10$)	62.3 ($N = 30$)	307.8	183.6 ($N = 50$)
DAX	278.0 ($N = 5$)	39.8 ($N = 30$)	238.2	171.3 ($N = 30$)
CDAX	256.9 ($N = 5$)	43.2 ($N = 30$)	213.7	141.0 ($N = 30$)
Nikkei	338.9 ($N = 10$)	57.6 ($N = 30$)	281.3	286.4 ($N = 50$)
FTSE 100	279.4 ($N = 10$)	102.8 ($N = 50$)	239.1	97.5 ($N = 30$)
Hang Seng	486.0 ($N = 10$)	114.4 ($N = 30$)	371.6	384.5 ($N = 50$)
SENSEX	506.3 ($N = 10$)	121.5 ($N = 30$)	384.8	296.2 ($N = 50$)
KOSPI	565.6 ($N = 10$)	261.1 ($N = 30$)	304.5	266.2 ($N = 30$)

The top half presents relative estimation biases based on the simple arithmetic mean, the truncated arithmetic mean and the Cooper estimator. For each estimator, four different values of N are considered ($N = 5, 10, 30$ and 50) and the one with the smallest average estimation error is chosen. In columns (3) and (5), results printed in italic denote the overall smallest estimation errors, i.e. across all three estimation approaches for each stock index. The bottom half presents the relative root mean squared errors for the corresponding estimators and values for N.

of the overestimation effect of the terminal value that is heavily discounted.

With these findings in mind, in Table 12.4 we extend our analysis to the whole sample of countries under consideration. As the simple arithmetic mean estimator is dominated by the Cooper estimator, we follow Breuer *et al.* (2011) by applying the truncated arithmetic mean estimator. As already pointed out, such an approach will prove most useful in situations when the simple arithmetic mean is severely upwards biased due to high annual cash flow growth rates, which in turn should be typical for growth firms and firms in emerging economies. We thus come to the conclusion of Breuer *et al.* (2011) that in such situations estimator truncation can improve estimation results considerably.

Table 12.4 is based on firm value estimates via the arithmetic mean estimator, the Cooper estimator and the truncated arithmetic mean estimator for the cases $N = 5$, 10, 30 and 50. The upper part of Table 12.4 shows the respective relative bias results; the lower part presents the corresponding relative root mean squared errors. For each country, we presume a cash flow growth rate which equals the average annual nominal GDP growth from 2011 to 2016 according to the World Economic Outlook forecast by the IMF as of September 2011 (Table 12.1). As already pointed out, for the NASDAQ we assume a higher cash flow growth rate of 5.9% compared to the other US indices.

In column (2), we present the best arithmetic mean estimator with respect to the relative bias of all respective four values of N as well as the corresponding root mean squared errors. As the results are almost independent of N, the optimal value for N is not necessarily very high. The same does not hold true for the truncated arithmetic mean estimator and the Cooper estimator in columns (3) and (5). Here, the choice of $N = 30$ or $N = 50$ is optimal. In column (4), a comparison of columns (2) and (3) reveals the tremendous gain in precision that is achievable by switching from the simple to the truncated arithmetic mean estimator. Moreover, the results of Table 12.4 confirm the conjecture in Breuer *et al.* (2011) that estimator truncation is particularly useful for young growth companies and companies in emerging economies. In contrast to the situation for developed countries, the Cooper estimator seems to do an even better job with respect to developing countries as long as relative bias is concerned. However, the truncated arithmetic mean estimator is superior to the Cooper estimator, when referring to root mean squared errors. This implies that both approaches have their merits even with respect to firms in developing countries. However, estimation precision is generally considerably poorer for emerging economies than for well-developed and slowly growing economies. Summarizing, the conjecture of Breuer *et al.* (2011) regarding the usefulness of truncation of the arithmetic estimator is confirmed, although the Cooper estimator might be a potential alternative in developing countries.

12.5 Conclusion

Due to Jensen's inequality, estimations of discount factors based on statistics of expected one-period returns from historical return realizations are upwards biased even if unbiased estimates of one-period expected rates of return are possible. We have shown that this problem is most relevant for firms with high expected cash flow growth rates, which is typical for young growth companies and companies in emerging economies. To mitigate the problem of upwards biased firm value estimates it thus may pay to neglect terminal value computation beyond a certain time horizon of, for example, $N = 30$ or $N = 50$ years. Such a truncated estimation proves indeed superior if discount rates are computed by the simple arithmetic mean of historical returns. An alternative might be the so-called Cooper estimator. In any case, the simple arithmetic mean approach would imply much too high firm value estimates. The bias reducing measures we present are of an heuristic nature. However, as we show by way of a bootstrap simulation, these measures work quite well in practically relevant data constellations and can easily be employed in firm valuation settings, e.g. in mergers and acquisitions processes. Such techniques that reduce problems of the overvaluation of firm values or other assets are of high importance insofar as they can contribute to reducing the risk of the emergence of price bubbles, which are key triggers of financial crises.

References

Becker, F., Breuer, W., Gürtler, M., 2009. Analysts' dividend forecasts as a basis for portfolio selection and for the calculation of market risk premia. In: Ellison, G.I. (Ed.), Stock Returns: Cyclicity, Prediction and Economic Consequences. Hauppauge. Nova Science, pp. 69–90.

Breuer, W., Mark, K., Fuchs, D., 2011. Estimating cost of capital in firm valuations with arithmetic or geometric mean—or better use the Cooper estimator? SSRN Working Paper. Available at http://ssrn.com/abstract=1183003. http://dx.doi.org/10.2139/ssrn.1183003.

Butler, J.S., Schachter, B., 1989. The investment decision: Estimation risk and risk adjusted discount rates. Financial Management 18 (4), 13–22.

Claus, J., Thomas, J., 2001. Equity premia as low as three percent? Evidence from analysts' earnings forecasts for domestic and international stock markets. Journal of Finance 56, 1629–1666.

Cooper, I., 1996. Arithmetic versus geometric mean estimators: Setting discount rates for capital budgeting. European Financial Management 2, 157–167.

Gebhardt, W.R., Lee, C.M.C., Swaminathan, B., 2001. Toward an implied cost of capital. Journal of Accounting Research 39, 135–176.

Wagner, W., Jonas, M., Ballwieser, W., Tschöpel, A., 2006. Unternehmensbewertung in der Praxis—Empfehlungen und Hinweise zur Anwendung des IDW S1. Die Wirtschaftsprüfung 59, 1005–1028.

13

TOWARDS A REPLICATING MARKET MODEL FOR THE US OIL AND GAS SECTOR

John Simpson* and Goknur Buyukkara**

*Curtin University, **University of Hacettepe

CHAPTER OUTLINE

13.1 Introduction

Researchers often look to macroeconomics in supply and demand for shares and oil and macroeconomic variables, such as oil prices, interest rates, unemployment, growth rates and exchange rates, to help explain the movements in the globally powerful US oil and gas stock market sector. Another approach used in this chapter is to examine financial markets and risk ratings data.

The specific issues dealt with are:

- Are price movements in domestic and global stock market variables, together with financial risk ratings changes, robust in their role to substantially explain US oil and gas stock market price movements?
- Are these price movements positively or negatively related to US oil and gas sector movements?

Rethinking Valuation and Pricing Models. http://dx.doi.org/10.1016/B978-0-12-415875-7.00013-0

- Do all of these relationships alter when comparing periods of relative US oil and gas price stability and relative volatility?

The resolution of these issues should be of use to medium-term stock market investors in the energy sector. The theoretical base for the study reported in this chapter lies in the efficient markets hypothesis (Fama, 1970)—to explain the speed of information transfer; portfolio theory (Markowitz, 1959)—to explain risk and return relationships; and theories of asset pricing, such as the capital assets pricing model (e.g. Sharpe, 1964; Roll, 1977) and arbitrage pricing theory (Ross, 1976)—to explain sectoral asset pricing and market index replication.

The literature review draws on evidence of significant relationships between economic and financial information, stock markets and country risk (e.g. Holthausen and Leftwich, 1986; Hand *et al.*, 1992; Maltosky and Lianto, 1995;[1] Erb *et al.*, 1996;[2] Radelet and Sachs, 1998;[3] Ferri *et al.*, 1999;[4] Brooks *et al.*, 2004;[5] Hooper *et al.*, 2004[6]). Most evidence indicates that country/sovereign risk has a significant relationship with stock market price changes.

The literature relating oil and gas price movements to macro- and microeconomic variables is vast. This study narrows down that literature to studies that have some similarity in subject and methodology. For example, Sadorsky (1999) examined oil price shocks and stock market activity, recognizing that oil price movements are often indicative of inflation, which affects interest rates, as well as stock market investments. The findings were that oil price dynamics had altered since 1986. Oil prices were more important than interest rates in explaining movements in the stock market and that oil price shocks have asymmetric effects on the economy.

[1] Sovereign risk rating downgrades are informative to equity markets, but upgrades do not supply markets with new information.
[2] Country risk measures are correlated with future equity returns, but financial risk measures reflect greater information. They also found that country risk measures are also highly correlated with country equity valuation measures and that country equity value-oriented strategies generated higher returns.
[3] Country/sovereign risk ratings agencies were too slow to react to crises, and when they did react it was suggested that their ratings intensified and prolonged the crisis.
[4] Ratings agencies behaved in a procyclical manner by upgrading country/sovereign risk ratings during boom times and downgrading them during crises.
[5] Equity market responses to country/sovereign risk ratings changes revealed significant responses following downgrades.
[6] Ratings agencies provided stock markets and foreign exchange markets in the United States with new tradable information. Ratings upgrades increased stock markets returns and decreased volatility significantly.

Lescaroux (2011) is a more recent example, with the investigation of the relative importance of macro- and microeconomic variables in oil prices. The Lescaroux model, with application to the US economy, finds evidence to support the estimation of stable relationships between sectoral economic indicators, demonstrating that the oil price macroeconomy is weakening, but the oil price microeconomy is "alive and well."

Notwithstanding some similarities, this chapter uses an approach that posits those broad-based stock market indices, providing they are well constructed and representative of the market, may be viewed as macro- or microeconomic, and domestic or global economic indicators, depending on the indices selected. This study is also unique in that it takes a stock market domestic and global financial market sectoral approach, combined with the analysis of financial risk ratings to endeavor to account for sources of volatility in the US oil and gas stock market in a period of relative stability and in a period of relative instability. The methodology involves the analysis of data in an autoregressive conditional heteroskedasticity (ARCH) model.

Three periods are studied in monthly data. The full period is from the end of June 1998 to the end of August 2011. A subperiod of relative stability is studied from the end of June 1998 to the end of January 2004 and then a period of relative volatility from the end of January 2004 to the end of August 2011. Whilst the examination of subperiods loses impact in degrees of freedom, the advantage is that other problems associated with structural breaks and time-varying relationships may be alleviated. Nevertheless, structural break tests were initially run on all variables in the model over all periods and breaks are not evident. However, even if structural breaks are not problematic, a comparison of these subperiods is useful in testing the changes in the influence of the variables over relatively stable and relatively unstable oil and gas markets periods.

Section 13.2 deals with the model. This is followed by Section 13.3 on an explanation of the data. The preliminary results are reported in Section 13.4. Section 13.5 shows the results of the main analysis in each of the subperiods and over the full period. Section 13.6 provides the conclusion.

13.2 Model

The following unlagged model is specified in the percentage changes in the variables. Initially the model is tested in ordinary least square (OLS) regressions, over the full period of the study and over the two subperiods:

$$\%\Delta P_{\mathrm{USOG}_t} = \alpha_{\mathrm{USOG}_t} + \beta_{1_t}(\%\Delta P_{\mathrm{USSM}_t}) + \beta_{2_t}(\%\Delta P_{\mathrm{WOG}_t})$$
$$+ \beta_{3_t}(\%\Delta P_{\mathrm{WSM}_t}) + \beta_{4_t}(\%\Delta FR_{\mathrm{USFR}_t}) + e_{\mathrm{USOG}_t}$$

(13.1)

where $\%\Delta P_{\mathrm{USOG}_t}$ is the percentage change in US oil and gas market sector prices at time t, α_{USOG_t} is the regression intercept representing the base change in the prices in the US oil and gas market sector. $\%\Delta P_{\mathrm{USSM}_t}$, $\%\Delta P_{\mathrm{WOG}_t}$, $\%\Delta P_{\mathrm{WSM}_t}$ and $\%\Delta FR_{\mathrm{FRUS}_t}$ are the percentage change in US stock market prices, the percentage change in global oil and gas market prices, the percentage change in global stock market prices, and the percentage change in financial risk ratings respectively at time t, $\beta_{1_t}, \beta_{2_t}, \beta_{3_t}$ and β_{4_t} are the respective regression coefficients for the above named variables each at time t; and e_{USOG_t} is the regression residual and represents the contribution to the intertemporal percentage changes in the US oil and gas market prices not explained by the foregoing independent variables, at time t.

Percentage changes are deemed appropriate *in lieu* of returns, as the model includes a financial risk ratings variable. Percentage changes allow for a comparison of the values of the variables in the model and also produce stationary series according to unit root tests. Durbin–Watson (DW; Durbin and Watson, 1971) tests are used to test serial correlation in the errors of Equation (13.1) when percentage changes in variables are utilized. White tests (White, 1980) are also applied to test for heteroskedasticity in the errors and if discovered, Equation (13.1) is respecified from OLS into an ARCH model to control in part for any model misspecification and error volatility.

Bearing in mind that the US oil and gas sector is strongly represented in the US stock market, there is expected to be a positive relationship between those variables. However, the initial correlation testing in prices and price changes reveals a negative relationship between world stock markets and US oil and gas markets. This might be rationalized on the basis that US oil and gas companies are large enough to be influential in global markets, and that manufacturing companies make up a sizeable part of the world stock exchange index. In addition, US oil and gas markets are logically strongly positively related to world oil and gas markets. When world oil and gas markets (and therefore US oil and gas markets) increase in value, the world stock markets decrease in value, because of the drain in profits of manufacturing due to higher expenses.

13.3 Data

Reilly and Brown (2003) assert that stock market indices may be used in market models provided the constituents of the indices are representative of the market. The stock market indices considered in this chapter are US oil and gas, US stock market, world oil and gas, and world stock market. All stock market indices produced in the Datastream database are calculated for aggregate sector and market price indices with sector and market aggregations weighted by market value and calculated using a representative list of shares. The values are at the close of business each day in US dollars and the data are converted into monthly data for the close of business in each month.

Datastream global and country equity indices claim that they provide a comprehensive, independent standard for equity research and benchmarking (Thompson Financial Limited, 2007). For each financial market a representative sample of shares covering a minimum of 75–80% of total market capitalization enables the market indices to be calculated. By aggregating market indices for regional groupings, regional and world indices may be calculated. Within each market the allocation of stocks is made according to industrial sectors using the Industry Classification Benchmark created by the Financial Times Exchange and the Dow Jones organizations. Sector indices are then created. Full integration with other data available through Datastream enables detailed comparison with other market or user-created indices, rates, economic indicators and any of the large range of tradable securities held on the database. There is a quarterly review of indices to ensure that they continue to represent the top stocks by market capitalization, and reflect investment trends as new markets and sectors rise to prominence.

The indices are broken down into six levels. This study uses only Levels 1 and 2. Level 1 indices are used for the US stock market and the world stock market. The Level 1 index is the market index covering all sectors within each group in each region or country. Logically, it is expected that the US stock market and the world stock markets are strongly positively related. This chapter uses Level 2 indices for the oil and gas sector in the US and the world oil and gas sector. The Level 2 indices divide the market into industry sectors (e.g. oil and gas) and cover the industry sectors within each group in each region or country. The oil and gas sector index measures the performance of the oil and gas sector of the equity markets covering oil and gas producers, oil equipment, oil services, and oil and gas distribution companies.

The formula for indices (daily) calculation is:

$$I_t = I_{t-1} * \frac{\sum_1^n (P_t * N_t)}{\sum_j (P_{t-1} * N_t * f)},$$

where I_t is the index value on day t, I_{t-1} is the index value on the previous working day, P_t is the unadjusted price on day t, P_{t-1} is the unadjusted price on the previous working day, N_t is the number of shares in issue day t, f is the adjustment factor for a capital action on day t and n is the number of constituents in the index. Summations are performed on the constituents as they exist on day t.

The financial risk ratings are taken from the International Country Risk Guide (2011), which implies a definition of country risk as the risk that a country will be either unable or unwilling to service its international obligations. The components of country risk are economic and financial risk (indicating the ability to perform) and political risk (dealing with legal standing and indicating the willingness to perform). The component ratings are based on economic information (objectively assessed balance of payments current account data primarily demonstrating international trade performance), financial information (objectively assessed balance of payment capital account data demonstrating the ability to service international commitments) and political data (subjectively assessed, but providing an indication of collective expert opinion on a country's level of risk for political, legal and human factors).

The subperiods were decided as follows from Figure 13.1, which presents a graph of the level series of US oil and gas market prices that defines two subperiods of relative stability and volatility respectively broken at the point indicated at the end of January 2004.

13.4 Preliminary Analysis and Results

The study first tests all variables in each period studied for unknown structural breaks using the Quandt–Andrews breakpoint test (Quandt, 1988; Andrews, 1993). The test statistics, in the maximum likelihood ratio F statistic and the maximum Wald F statistic, were significant in every case at the 1% level, thus allowing the acceptance of the null hypothesis of no structural breaks. The default trimming level of 15% (where the first and last 7.5% of observations were excluded in each sample period) was used but tests were also run at other higher as well as lower trimming levels with the same results.

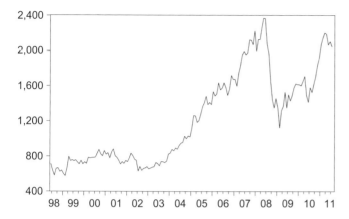

Figure 13.1 Prices of the US oil and gas market sector.

Then the study tests all variables in each period including the residuals of the Equation (13.1) relationship, for unit roots in both level series and first differences. Augmented Dickey–Fuller (ADF; Dickey and Fuller, 1981) and Phillips–Perron (PP; Phillips and Perron, 1988) unit root tests are applied to level series and to first differenced series, and to the errors of the relationships. The PP tests are deemed more reliable in their testing for series in which there may be structural breaks. It has been demonstrated in preliminary analysis, however, that structural breaks in any period are not problems. Nevertheless, both ADF and PP test results are retained as a confirmation of stationarity of the first differences (percentage changes) and the non-stationarity of levels (price index values), and these results are reported in Table 13.1. Due to evidence of heteroskedasticity (see Table 13.2) in the errors of the ordinary least squares regression of Equation (13.1) the model is respecified as an ARCH model in means. These results are reported in the main results section in Table 13.3.

In preliminary correlation analysis, it was evident that US oil prices and percentage price changes were not significantly related to economic and political risk ratings and changes, but that the ability of a country to perform in servicing international obligations (financial risk ratings) was related. This latter component of country risk is therefore included in the analysis in keeping with the study using financial variables to ascertain if they replicate or behave similarly to other macro- and micro-economic variables. The financial risk ratings (scores) are calculated out of 50 points. The higher the score, the lower the risk. The ratings are upgraded at the end of each month. In keeping with the risk/return maxim from portfolio theory the relationship with US oil and gas markets is expected to be negative, reflecting

Table 13.1. Unit root tests

Period	Variable	Level series t statistic ADF/PP	First differenced series t statistic ADF/PP
Subperiod 1	US oil and gas market	−2.4331/−2.4331	−9.3467***/−9.5299***
	Global oil and gas market	−1.3393/−1.3295	−8.7026***/−8.7026***
	US stock market	−1.2855/−1.2790	−8.2020***/−8.2070***
	Global stock market	−1.1562/−1.2384	−7.8268***/−7.8330***
	Financial risk ratings	−2.8975*/−3.0597**	−8.4061***/−9.1831***
	Errors of the US oil and gas markets regression	−4.1031**/−4.1287***	−10.9511***/−11.5889***
Subperiod 2	US oil and gas market	−1.7499/−1.8355	−9.0000***/−9.0234***
	Global oil and gas market	−1.8927/−2.0347	−8.2201***/−8.2685***
	US stock market	−1.5437/−1.6979	−8.3852***/−8.3728***
	Global stock market	−1.8927/−2.0347	−8.2201***/−8.2686***
	Financial risk ratings	−1.7331/−1.4055	−9.8424***/−10.5658***
	Errors of the US oil and gas markets regression	−3.0662**/−3.1495**	−9.4545***/−9.4563***
Full period	US oil and gas market	−0.6523/−0.8071	−12.1926***/−12.2497***
	Global oil and gas market	−0.8492/−1.0449	−11.0923***/−11.1658***
	US stock market	−1.9129/−2.7079	−11.8819***/−11.9443***
	Global stock market	−1.3157/−1.7650	−10.5702***/−10.8264***
	Financial risk ratings	−3.3892**/−3.2911**	−13.0514***/−17.6038***
	Errors of the US oil and gas markets regression	−4.1098***/−4.1510***	−13.6687***/−13.7845***

First subperiod critical values for ADF and PP tests are 1%: −3.5316; 5%: −2.9055; 10%: −2.5903. Second subperiod critical values for ADF and PP tests are 1%: −3.5056; 5%: −2.8943; 10%: −2.5843. Full period critical values for ADF and PP tests are 1%: −3.4723; 5%: −2.8799; 10%: −2.5766. Significance levels for the t statistic are denoted ***1%, **5% and *10%. For the first subperiod the level series t statistics for US financial risk ratings are accepted as non-stationary at the 1% critical value. For the full period the level series US financial risk rating is accepted as non-stationary at the 1% critical value.

higher returns (percentage price changes) for a higher amount of risk (lower risk rating score).

In both financial market and financial risk ratings data the full study period of the monthly data is from the end of June 1998 to the end of August 2011. Two subperiods are included for examination. They are a period of relative stability in US oil and gas markets from the end of June 1998 to the end of January 2004 and from the latter date, in a period of relative volatility, to August 2011. The former subperiod is the relatively stable period prior to the massive OPEC supply induced oil prices increases from early to mid-2004. The latter subperiod incorporates the rapid oil and

Table 13.2. White tests of US oil and gas price percentage changes

Period	F test statistics/observed R^2 test statistic
Subperiod 1	0.5991/9.3056
Subperiod 2	1.6515/21.2077
Full period	0.7053/10.2079

No asterisk against test statistics means not significant at the 5% level, so that the null hypothesis of homoskedasticity is rejected in those instances.

Table 13.3. ARCH model of US oil and gas percentage price changes

Period	Variable/indicator	Statistic	Value
Subperiod 1	US stock market	z	3.8883***
	World oil and gas market	z	19.0428***
	World stock market	z	−4.3844***
	US financial risk rating	z	−1.5283
	Explanatory power	Adjusted R^2 value	0.8868***
	Short-term effects	ARCH coefficient	−0.2239**
	Long-term effects	GARCH coefficient	1.1350***
	Serial correlation	DW statistic	2.6170***
Subperiod 2	US stock market	z	8.5821***
	World oil and gas market	z	17.3659***
	World stock market	z	−7.7466***
	US financial risk rating	z	−1.0860
	Explanatory power	Adjusted R^2 value	0.9275***
	Short-term effects	ARCH coefficient	−0.0296
	Long-term effects	GARCH coefficient	0.8603***
	Serial correlation	DW statistic	2.0888***
Full period	US stock market	z	7.4838***
	World oil and gas market	z	26.1656***
	World stock market	z	−8.1325***
	US financial risk rating	z	−2.3304**
	Explanatory power	Adjusted R^2 value	0.9108***
	Short-term effects	ARCH coefficient	−0.0582*
	Long-term effects	GARCH coefficient	1.0362***
	Serial correlation	DW statistic	2.4287***

Significance levels are denoted ***1%, **5% and *10%. No asterisks mean no significance.

gas price rises as well as the rapid falls during the global financial crisis and rises during the period of partial share market and oil price recovery from 2009 to the date of writing in August 2011.

Significance levels of 5% are accepted in this study due to the loss of degrees of freedom in the study of monthly data over two subperiods. It should also be noted, however, that generally the results reveal significance at the 1% level. Table 13.2 shows the results of tests for heteroskedasticity in the errors of that model over the full period and over subperiods 1 and 2. Prior to running the ARCH model, all variables in the model are tested for unit roots. The results of ADF/PP tests are shown in Table 13.1.

The results reveal that the level series are non-stationary and that the first differenced series, including the series of the errors of the first differenced relationships, are stationary.

13.5 Main Results

Evidence of heteroskedasticity in the errors in all periods leads to the specification of an ARCH model *in lieu* of OLS and the results of the testing of this model are shown in Table 13.3. The results are also reported for each period of the study.

13.5.1 Subperiod 1

Subperiod 1 is a period of relative stability in US oil and gas markets from the end of June 1998 to the end of January 2004. All variables are significant explanatory variables for US oil and gas market movements (at the 1% level), except the US financial risk rating movements. The explanatory power of the model is at 0.8868. The ARCH coefficient is significant at the 5% level. The generalized autoregressive conditional heteroskedasticity (GARCH) coefficient is significant at the 1% level. The sum of the ARCH and GARCH coefficients is less than 1, indicating that the model has controlled, in part, for heteroskedasticity and this indicates greater model stability. Serial correlation is not a problem, the regression is not spurious and the results are therefore deemed reliable with a DW statistic of 2.6170.

The US stock market movement is positively related to the US oil and gas market movements. This demonstrates that the US oil and gas sector is an important part of the US stock market. The world oil and gas market movements are logically strongly positively related to the movements in the US oil and gas market. The world stock market movements are negatively related to the US oil and gas market movements. It may be that as oil and gas sector prices in the US rise, there is a negative effect on the important manufacturing sector of the world stock market.

13.5.2 Subperiod 2

Subperiod 2, from the end of January 2004 until the end of August 2011, was a period of relative volatility in the US oil and gas market. The period was inclusive of the rapid increase in the prices of energy to early 2008; the subsequent collapse of stock markets from early to mid-March 2008 during the global financial crisis and the partial recovery of stock markets during late 2009 to the end of the full sample period. All independent variables remain significant in this subperiod, except the US financial risk rating variable. The explanatory power of the model is higher than in the first subperiod (see subperiod 2 adjusted R^2 value at 0.9275 significant at the 1% level). The ARCH and GARCH coefficients totaled remain less than 1. The ARCH coefficient is not significant, but the GARCH coefficient is significant at the 1% level. The DW statistic reveals no problem with serial correlation, with a value of 2.0888.

The movements in the US stock markets remain positively related to the US oil and gas markets at a significance level of 1%. The magnitude of the z statistic is higher than that in the first subperiod (see subperiod 2 value at 8.5821). The world oil and gas mark remains a significant variable at the 1% level and maintains a positive relationship, but this relationship is weaker than in the first subperiod (see subperiod 2 value at 17.3659). The strength of this relationship appears to slightly reduce in periods of volatility in US oil and gas markets. The world stock market movements remain negatively related at a significance level of 1%. This relationship is stronger during a period of US oil and gas market instability (see subperiod 2 value at −7.7466) than in the first subperiod of relative stability. The movements in the financial risk ratings variable are negatively related, but not significant in this period of volatility.

13.5.3 Full Period

The full period of the study is from the end of June 1998 to the end of August 2011, and includes both subperiods of relative stability and relative volatility. The specified explanatory variables have z statistics that are all statistically significant at the 5% level and the signs of the z statistics are similar to those in the first and second subperiods. The explanatory power of the model is strong, with an adjusted R^2 value of 0.9108, which is slightly higher than in the first subperiod, but slightly lower than in the second subperiod. It is evident that the explanatory power of the model is not vastly changed over the two subperiods of the study. The ARCH terms are not significant at the 5% level, but the GARCH coefficient is significant at the 1% level and some control for the stability is evident. The DW test (see full period statistic at 2.4287) reveals that there is not a problem with serial correlation in the errors.

The positive relationship of the US stock market movements to the US oil and gas movements over the full period is stronger than in the first subperiod, but slightly less strong than in the second subperiod (see full period z statistic value at 7.4838). It remains consistent with theory and evidence that as US stock markets rise, so do US oil and gas markets, thus reflecting the importance of the oil and gas sector in the US stock market, with the greatest effect observed in the second subperiod of volatility. Nevertheless, the effects over the two subperiods do not greatly vary. The positive movements in the world oil and gas market over the full period are stronger than in the first subperiod and in the second subperiod (see full period value of z statistic at 26.1656). The explanation of this is logically that, as global oil and gas markets rise, US oil and gas markets rise, again reflective of the important interaction between global and US stock markets, and the consistency of that relationship over the two subperiods.

The world stock market movements in the full period are negatively related to US oil and gas market movements, and the value of the full period z statistic, at -8.1325, is stronger than those values in the first and second subperiods. It appears that the strong effect of this variable in the second subperiod of volatility carries through over the full period. Over the full period the movements in the US financial risk ratings remain negatively related to the US oil and gas market movements, but this effect is only significant (at the 5% level) over the full period (see the full period z statistic value at -2.3304). The negative relationship results are explained in the measurement of risk ratings. The risk ratings show the higher the score the lower the risk. Therefore, higher risk (lower score) is associated with higher movements in the US oil and gas market. This is consistent with portfolio theory and the risk and return trade-off.

13.6 Conclusion

Overall, the specified variables in unlagged models show that conventional macro- and microeconomic indicators can be proxied by US and world financial market variables, and that a financial risk rating variable is useful in explaining financial market movements (significant over the full period of the study). The models are clearly effective in their explanatory power in the task of US oil and gas index replication, and therefore deemed useful in sectoral asset pricing. However, the models and analysis presented in this chapter are preliminary. Future study will expand the analysis to examine ARCH and GARCH models in variances as well as in means. Further research may also expand the analysis to the analysis of optimally lagged vector autoregressive and vector error correction models to investigate cointegration and exogeneity.

In the first subperiod of relatively stable US oil and gas prices, the most important variables are the world oil and gas market, world stock market, and US stock market, respectively. The US financial risk rating variable is not significant. In the second subperiod of relatively volatile US oil and gas prices the most important variables are the world oil and gas market, the US stock market, and the world stock market, in that order. The US financial risk rating variable is not significant. Over the full period the most important independent variables are the world oil and gas market, the world stock market, the US stock market, and the US financial risk ratings variables, respectively.

The relationships are demonstrated to be in accordance with theory and reality. The consistent positive relationship of US oil and gas markets with the world oil and gas markets is logical. The consistent positive relationship of US oil and gas with the US stock markets is understandable, given the strength of the representativeness of US oil and gas companies in the US stock market index. The consistent negative relationship between US oil and gas markets and the world stock market might be explained if higher world oil and gas prices (and thus higher US oil and gas prices) conspire to reduce global manufacturer profits with the manufacturing sector being a major part of the world stock market index. The consistent negative relationship with of US oil and gas markets with financial risk ratings, although significant only over the full period, is supportive of portfolio theory when the measurement of the ratings reflects lower risk for higher scores. This is consistent with the risk/return maxim where the higher the risk (lower the ratings score), the higher the price movements or returns.

This information should be useful to medium-term US oil and gas sector investors. The question remains as to whether or not the above relationships will continue to demonstrate the global influence of US oil and gas markets and US financial risk ratings in the face of bourgeoning US current account deficits and US public debt, and in light of the increasing potential debt spill-over problems from the European Monetary Union.

References

Andrews, D.W.K., 1993. Tests for parameter instability with unknown change points. Econometrica 61, 821–856.

Brooks, R., Faff, R., Hillier, D., Hillier, J., 2004. The national market impact of sovereign rating changes,. Journal of Energy and Finance 28, 233–250.

Dickey, D.A., Fuller, W.A., 1981. Likelihood ratio statistics for autoregressive time series within a unit root. Econometrica 49, 1022–1057.

Durbin, J., Watson, G.S., 1971. Testing for serial correlation in least squares regression-111. Biometrica 58, 1–42.

Fama, E.F., 1970. Efficient capital markets: a review of theory and empirical work. Journal of Finance 25, 383–417.

Erb, C.B., Harvey, C.R., Viskanta, T.E., 1996. Political risk, economic risk and financial risk. Fuqua School of Business Working Paper 9606. Fuqua School of Business, Durham, NC.

Ferri, G., Liu, L., Stiglitz, J., 1999. The pro-cyclical role of rating agencies: evidence from the East Asian crisis. Economic Notes 28, 335–355.

Hand, J., Holthausen, R., Leftwich, R., 1992. The effect of bond rating agency announcements on bond and stock prices. Journal of Finance 47, 733–752.

Holthausen, R., Leftwich, R., 1986. The effect of bond rating changes on common stock prices. Journal of Financial Economics 17, 57–89.

Hooper, V., Hume, T.P., Kim, S.-J., 2004. Sovereign rating changes—do they provide new information for stock markets? Working Paper. University of New South Wales, Sydney.

International Country Risk Guide, 2011. International Country Risk Guide. Political Risk Services Group, East Syracuse, NY.

Lescaroux, F., 2011. The oil price microeconomy relationship is alive and well. The Energy Journal 32, 25–48.

Maltosky, Z., Lianto, T., 1995. The incremental information content of bond rating revisions: the Australian evidence. Journal of Energy and Finance 19, 891–902.

Markowitz, H., 1959. Portfolio Selection – Efficient Diversification of Investments. Yale University Press, New Haven, CT.

Phillips, P.C.B., Perron, P., 1988. Testing for a unit root in a times series regression. Biometrika 75, 335–346.

Quandt, R.E., 1988. The Econometrics of Disequilibrium. Oxford, Blackwell.

Radelet, S., Sachs, J., 1998. The onset of the East Asian financial crisis. NBER Working Paper 6680. NBER, Cambridge, MA.

Reilly, F.K., Brown, K.C., 2003. Investment Analysis and Portfolio Management. Mason, OH: Thomson South Western, 176–285.

Roll, R., 1977. A critique of the asset pricing theory's tests. Journal of Financial Economics 4, 129–176.

Ross, S., 1976. The arbitrage theory of capital asset pricing. Journal of Economic Theory 13, 341–360.

Sadorsky, P., 1999. Oil price shocks and stock market activity. Energy Economics 21, 449–469.

Sharpe, W.F., 1964. Capital asset prices: a theory of market equilibrium under conditions of risk. Journal of Finance 19, 425–442.
Thompson Financial Limited, 2007. Datastream Global Equity Indices: User Guide, Issue 4. Thompson Reuters, New York.
White, H., 1980. A heteroskedasticity-consistent covariance matrix estimator and a direct test for heteroskedasticity. Econometrica 48, 817–838.

14

MEASURING SYSTEMIC RISK FROM COUNTRY FUNDAMENTALS: A DATA MINING APPROACH

Roberto Savona and Marika Vezzoli
University of Brescia

14.1 Introduction

The global financial turbulences that have occurred over the last 40 years have shown increasing interconnections among banking, sovereign, currency and inflation crises over time. The crises have become more and more complex to detect, due to the globalization and sophistication of financial markets, which have not been fully interiorized within traditional asset pricing models. Indeed, the recent global crisis that began in 2007 has shown up the limits of traditional approaches, which have been ineffective to price risks for most of financial assets.

Rethinking Valuation and Pricing Models. http://dx.doi.org/10.1016/B978-0-12-415875-7.00014-2

One of the main reasons of such a fallacy can be ascribed to the underlying "data modeling culture," through which economists (i) elaborate a theory, (ii) formalize a model, and (iii) validate theory and model looking at the empirical data. This philosophical approach dramatically failed in 2007–2010 essentially because of: (i) Complex and non-linear price dynamics, and (ii) the absence of a unified framework to model macro financial risk transmission in an integrated way. The objective of this chapter is to handle the two problems, focusing on the financial crises of Organization for Economic Cooperation and Development (OECD) countries that occurred over the period 1981–2010.

In more depth, we first focus on bank- currency-, inflation- and sovereign-type crises using macroeconomic fundamentals to such an extent to infer probability estimates that a crisis event could happen. Next, we try to infer the common risk source underlying the financial crises, which is our measure for the systemic risk. To do this we proceed as follows:

(i) We reverse the traditional data modeling culture, i.e. we democratically process the data in order to explain why and when a crisis could happen, no matter about *a priori* theories, and moving in a, potentially, highly non-linear world. The methodology pertains to regression trees (RTs), introduced in the statistical community by Breiman *et al.* (1984), and recently implemented in Manasse and Roubini (2009) and Savona and Vezzoli (2011).

(ii) After having inferred the probability estimates relative to single financial crises, we next extract the first principal component (PC) among these estimates. This is the unobservable common latent risk factor underlying global financial crises. Since PCs are essentially statistical artifacts that are difficult to understand, in order to obtain our proxy for the systemic risk we finally "mimic" this first PC using the same probability estimates. Specifically, we realize a mimicking systemic risk factor (MSRF) using the probability estimates of financial crises as covariates and the first PC as dependent variable, constraining the loadings to be non-negative and sum to unity. Such an approach allows the MSRF to be interpreted as the probability that a global financial crisis could happen.

(iii) In order to inspect the underlying mechanism of MSRF, we realize an early warning system (EWS) using RT analysis then providing a recursive partitioning of predictor space that allows us to endogenously identify different risk regimes conditional on observable macroeconomic covariates.

The structure of the chapter is as follows. In Section 14.2, we provide formal definition of various types of financial crises and discuss the potential predictors in signaling impending crisis events. We also present the dataset used in the empirical analysis. Section 14.3 discusses the methodology and Section 14.4 presents the results. Section 14.5 concludes.

14.2 Financial Crises and Leading Indicators

14.2.1 Crisis definition

The abundant empirical evidence on financial crises that occurred from 1970 to date proved that bank-, currency-, inflation- and sovereign debt-based problems interact in a lead–lag process also spreading across countries, and possibly culminating in global imbalances with extreme negative impacts on financial systems and the real economy. The definition of each type of financial crisis is essential to uncover the latent common risk source of global crises. To this end we followed the criteria used in Reinhart and Rogoff (2010) (RR), who classified the various types of crises as follows:

- *Banking crisis*: (i) Bank runs that lead to the closure, merging or takeover by the public sector of one or more financial institutions; or, in the absence of bank runs, (ii) closure, merging, takeover or large-scale government assistance of an important financial institution(s).
- *Currency crisis*: Following a variant of Frankel and Rose (1996), annual depreciations exceeding the threshold of 15% per annum.
- *Inflation crisis*: Whenever the annual inflation rate is of 20% or greater.
- *Sovereign debt crisis*: Defined according to the S&P's criteria together with additional information from Lindert and Morton (1989), Suter (1992), and Tomz (2006). The concept of sovereign default is relative to external debt and involves outright default on payment of debt obligations incurred under foreign legal jurisdiction, repudiation or the restructuring of debt into terms less favorable to the lender than in the original.

Based on these criteria and focusing on OECD countries, we selected 27 countries matched with the RR[1] database of financial crises. Table 14.1 reports the overall number of financial crises explored in this study over the period from 1981 to 2010 for each

[1] The data are available at http://www.carmenreinhart.com/data/browse-by-topic/topics/7/.

Table 14.1. Number of financial crises that occurred in each OECD country over the period 1981—2010

Country	Banking	Sovereign	Currency	Inflation
Australia	4	0	5	0
Austria	3	0	1	0
Belgium	3	0	2	0
Canada	3	0	1	0
Denmark	9	0	1	0
Finland	4	0	1	0
France	5	0	1	0
Germany	3	0	4	0
Greece	8	0	8	2
Hungary	4	0	3	1
Iceland	7	0	9	8
Ireland	6	0	2	0
Italy	10	0	0	0
Japan	11	0	2	1
South Korea	9	9	11	14
Mexico	3	0	1	0
Netherlands	4	0	4	0
New Zealand	7	0	3	0
Norway	5	14	17	13
Poland	3	0	5	3
Portugal	8	0	3	0
Spain	4	0	4	0
Sweden	2	0	2	0
Switzerland	7	2	22	23
Turkey	6	0	5	0
UK	8	0	8	6
US	12	0	2	0
Total	*158*	*25*	*127*	*71*

country. In total we analyzed 381 crisis events (158 banking crises, 127 currency crises, 71 inflation crises and 25 sovereign debt crises).

14.2.2 Economic and financial leading indicators

The literature on potential indicators for financial crises is ample, and mainly refers to empirical studies that tried to use economic and financial variables as signals of impending crises.

Some explanatory variables are exclusive for specific crises, while others are informative for more than one type of crisis.

A comprehensive list of crisis indicators is given in Kaminsky *et al.* (1998) who, notwithstanding focusing on currency crises, identify a list of potential covariates, classified within six homogeneous clusters according to their economic/financial nature, which can be used to realize EWSs also for the other types of crises (bank, inflation, sovereign):

- *Capital account* (e.g. international reserves, capital flows, foreign direct investment).
- *Debt profile* (e.g. public and total foreign debt, short-term debt).
- *Current account* (e.g. current account balance, exports and imports, terms of trade).
- *International variables* (e.g. foreign real GDP growth, interest rates).
- *Financial liberalization* (e.g. credit growth, spread between bank lending and deposit interest rates).
- *Other financial variables* (such as bond yields, domestic inflation and M2/international reserves).

The dataset used in our study is based on this list and derives from the OECD, International Monetary Fund, World Bank, Bank for International Settlements (BIS) and Datastream. In total, we selected 38 variables, reported below in Table 14.2, which have been chosen after removing those covariates having more than 30% of missed observations and controlling for severe multicollinearity.[2]

14.3 Financial Crises and Risk Signals

Most of the modeling approaches on financial crises reflects what Breiman (2001) referred to as the "data modeling culture"—a philosophical approach in which data are assumed to be generated by a given stochastic data model.

Instead, the "algorithmic modeling culture" processes the data democratically trying to speak about a specific event, not about *a priori* theories that are usually pre-specified in the data modeling approach. This philosophical perspective was first introduced in the context of financial crises by Kaminsky *et al.*

---

[2] We used the variance inflation factor (*VIF*) computed as $1/(1-R^2)$ with R^2 to denote the R squared obtained by regressing each variable one at time using the remaining ones as ones as covariates. Based on *VIF* values, we removed those variables showing values greater than five, which is the common "rule of thumb" used to detect high multicollinearity.

Table 14.2. Variables used as potential predictors of financial crises

Code	Description
ppcr	Private consumption expenditure at current market prices, as a percentage of GDP
gce	Government consumption expenditure at current market prices, as a percentage of GDP
inv_gdp	Gross fixed investment expenditure at current market prices, as a percentage of GDP
pstk	Stockbuilding at current market prices, as a percentage of GDP
exp_gdp	Value of exports at current market prices, as a percentage of GDP
pimp	Value of imports at current market prices, as a percentage of GDP
pddd	Total domestic expenditure (including stockbuilding) at current market prices, as a percentage of GDP
dagr	Change in real agricultural value-added, including livestock, forestry and fishing, over previous year (in %)
ind	Change in real mining, quarrying, manufacturing, construction and utilities value-added, over previous year (in %)
dser	Change in real services sector value-added, over previous year (in %)
psav	Aggregate national savings by the public and private sector, as a percentage of nominal GDP
dipi	Change in index of industrial production, over previous year (in %)
psbr	Central government receipts minus central government outlays, as a percentage of GDP
dcpi	Change in consumer price index in local currency (period average), over previous year (in %)
lrat	Commercial banks average lending rate to non-financial enterprises (in %)
bint	Debt interest payments, as a percentage of GDP
pbax	Primary balance, as a percentage of GDP
pudp	Total debt after consolidation (both local and foreign currency) expressed as a percentage of GDP
sodd	Change in bank lending to public and private sectors, plus bank lending in domestic currency overseas (in %)
dir	Average rate on all deposits excluding current accounts (in %)
unem	Recorded official unemployment as a percentage of total labor force (in %)
cara	Current-account balance, as a percentage of GDP
fras_gdp	Foreign assets held by domestic commercial banks at end-period, as a percentage of GDP
frpli_gdp	Foreign liabilities of domestic commercial banks at end-period, as a percentage of GDP
nfas_gdp	Foreign assets held by domestic commercial banks less their foreign liabilities at end-period, as a percentage of GDP
res_GDP	Stock of foreign reserves plus gold (national valuation), end-period, as a percentage of GDP
openess	Export plus Imports at market prices, as percentage of GDP
res_debt	Stock of foreign reserves plus gold over total public debt
res_interest	Stock of foreign reserves plus gold over debt interest payments
tdra	Trade balance, as a percentage of GDP
ifdi_gdp	Stock of direct investment by non-residents into the country, as a percentage of GDP
ofdi_gdp	Stock of direct investment capital by domestic residents out of the country, as a percentage of GDP

Table 14.2. *(Continued)*

Code	Description
tt	Terms of trade (1990 = 100)
ltir	Long-term interest rate (in %)
imr	Interest margin (lend minus deposit interest rate) (in %)
dyield	Dividend yield on S&P's 500
S&P	Annual rate of return of S&P's 500
ted	TED spread (3 months eurodollar deposit minus 3 months T-bill) (in %)

(1998), through which a crisis is signaled when pre-selected leading economic indicators exceed some thresholds to be estimated according to a minimization procedure of the false alarm-to-good signal ratio.

More recently, Manasse and Roubini (2009) and Savona and Vezzoli (2011) developed an EWS by using a RT approach that helped predict potential crises in the spirit of Kaminsky *et al.* (1998), while simultaneously using the preselected indicators.

In this study we rely on CRAGGING (CRoss-validation AGGregatING), which is the novel RT-based approach used in Savona and Vezzoli (2011), Vezzoli and Zuccolotto (2011), and introduced in Vezzoli and Stone (2007) in order to handle panel and/or hierarchical data structures.

14.3.1 RT approach

The methodological notations used to formalize our approach are based on a 0−1 dependent variable Y, which indicates the occurrence of a crisis event, and $\mathbf{X} = \{X_1, ..., X_R\}$ predictors. The relationship we envision is of the following form:

$$y = f(\mathbf{x}) + \varepsilon_t, \tag{14.1}$$

where $f(\mathbf{x})$ is an unknown functional form of predictors $\mathbf{X}$, and ε is the error term for which, differently from stochastic data-based models such as Logit and Probit, no distributional assumptions are specified. The statistical objective of the RT approach is to estimate $f(\mathbf{x})$ so as to obtain reliable forecasts for Y, i.e. accurate predictions of crisis.

The RT approach is a non-parametric approach introduced in Breiman *et al.* (1984) that looks for the best local prediction of a dependent variable Y which can be continuous, dichotomous (*regression tree*) or categorical (*classification tree*). To do this, RTs partition recursively the space of predictors in order to best approximate $f(\mathbf{x})$ using a non-linear function (or, more precisely, a piecewise constant function) $H(\mathbf{x}; \psi)$, where ψ is the vector of parameters. Such non-linear function reflects a binary tree that graphically depicts the topology of the predictor space by a series of subsequent nodes that collapse into distinct partitions, called regions or terminal nodes, and denoted by $\tilde{T}$, in which the distribution of Y is more homogeneous.

Hence, the output from such an approach produces a system that helps to classify and predict financial crises through a sequence of decision splitting rules. Computationally, the problem of finding the optimal tree is solved by minimizing

$$[Y - H(\mathbf{x}; \psi)]^2, \tag{14.2}$$

through the selection of the optimal number of regions $(|\tilde{T}|)$ and the corresponding splitting values. The approach delivers a risk stratification together with a variable selection through which impending crises are signaled by a series of splitting rules that act as risk thresholds.

RTs are conceived with the end of improving the out-of-sample predictability and to do this they are estimated through a rotational estimation procedure, the cross-validation, with which the sample is partitioned into subsets such that the analysis is initially performed on a single subset (the training sets), while the other subset(s) are retained for subsequent use in confirming and validating the initial analysis (the validation or testing sets).

14.3.2 CRAGGING

While RTs seem to be well suited to realize EWSs for financial crises in the spirit of Kaminsky *et al.* (1998), when dealing with hierarchical data structures (e.g. panel data) they do not pay attention to the intrinsic data structure, and this could be a serious drawback when autocorrelations and other latent dependencies and/or commonalities play a major role. To handle these issues, Vezzoli and Stone (2007) introduced a new algorithm that uses an increasing number of trees, combining them in order to obtain an accurate predictor. This is CRAGGING and it belongs to the family of the ensemble learning (Friedman and Popescu, 2003, 2005).

Mathematically, let us denote by $\mathcal{L}$ a panel data with n_j observations for each unit j and $j = 1, ..., J$, hence having a total of $N = \sum_{j=1}^{J} n_j$ observations. The J units are homogeneous groups exogenously or endogenously determined using some logical, natural or mathematical criteria. In Savona and Vezzoli (2011), the units are countries and as such the homogeneity is assumed at the country level. Alternatively, one can use different clustering procedures depending on the objective of the study. In our case, the perspective is systemic and therefore related to the cross-section of countries. As a result, the units are the single years of the time interval and n_j is the number of countries included in the dataset corresponding to the jth year. In doing this, we then assume a "risk homogeneity" across countries year by year, which is indeed the perspective to be used in order to infer the common latent systemic risk factor.

By denoting y_{jg} the dependent variable and $\mathbf{x}_{jg}$ the vector of predictors at time j for country g, the CRAGGING predictions are obtained as:

- The J units (years in our case) are partitioned at random in V subsets denoted by $\mathcal{L}_v$ with $v = 1, ..., V$, each one containing, if possible, the same number of units. Since we have $j = 1, ..., 30$ units (the dataset contains the years from 1981 to 2010) and we imposed $J_v = 3$ units for each v subset, we obtain $V = 10$ sets.
- We next remove the ℓth unit from a generic training set $\mathcal{L}_v^c = \mathcal{L} - \mathcal{L}_v$, and we denote it $\mathcal{L}_{v\backslash\ell}^c$. Using this $\mathcal{L}_{v\backslash\ell}^c$ training set we compute a RT based on a cost complexity parameter α,[3] obtaining the following fitted function:

$$\hat{y}_{jg,\alpha\ell} = \hat{f}_{\alpha,\mathcal{L}_{v\backslash\ell}^c}(\mathbf{x}_{jg}) \text{ with } j \in \mathcal{L}_v \text{ and } g = 1, ..., n_j, \quad (14.3)$$

which is the expectation of the dependent variable at time j for the country g in the test set L_v. In our analysis n_j is constant for each year and equal to 27 (the number of countries included in the dataset). The procedure is repeated for the all the units in the training set, obtaining the fitted functions $\hat{f}_{\alpha,\mathcal{L}_{v\backslash\ell}^c}(\cdot)$.

---

[3] The cost complexity α (≥ 0) is a parameter entering into a corresponding cost complexity function in the form of $LF_\alpha(T) = LF(T) + \alpha|\tilde{T}|$ in which $|\tilde{T}|$ denotes the number of the terminal nodes and $LF(\cdot)$ is a loss function (mean squared errors for RTs). Hence, α modulates the tradeoff between the size of the RT (number of terminal nodes) and its goodness of fit to the data: large values of α result in smaller trees and *vice versa*.

- We then compute the overall average of the expectations realized for each unit, i.e.:

$$\hat{y}_{jg,\alpha} = \frac{1}{J_v^c} \sum_{l \in \mathcal{L}_v^c} \hat{f}_{\alpha, \mathcal{L}_{vl}^c}(\mathbf{x}_{jg}) \text{ with } j \in \mathcal{L}_v \text{ and } g = 1, ..., n_j, \quad (14.4)$$

where J_v^c is the number of units in the training set.[4] In other words, (14.4) is the average of the functions (14.3) fitted over the units contained within the test set $\mathcal{L}_v$. This procedure is carried out for every test set $\mathcal{L}_v$.

- The procedure is repeated for different values of α and finally the algorithm chooses the optimal tuning parameter α^* that corresponds to that value for which the out-of-sample error estimation over all $\mathcal{L}_v$ is minimized. Consequently, the CRAGGING predictions are given by:

$$\tilde{y}_{jg}^{\text{crag}} = \hat{y}_{jg,\alpha^*} \text{ with } j \in \mathcal{L} \text{ and } g = 1, ..., n_j. \quad (14.5)$$

14.4 Analysis and Results

The next sections describe and comment on the main results obtained in our empirical analysis, in which (i) we used the CRAGGING algorithm for each type of crisis using the predictors lagged one year, (ii) we extracted the first PC from the CRAGGING predictions, then realizing a MSRF, and (iii) we run a RT on this MSRF in order to realize an EWS for the systemic risk.

14.4.1 Predicting financial crises

The methodology outlined in Section 14.3.2 was computed over the period 1981–2010 for banking, currency, inflation, and sovereign debt crises, obtaining the CRAGGING predictions to be next used in order to extract the first PC, as a measure of common latent systemic risk.

The ability of the CRAGGING probabilities to predict financial crises was evaluated using the area under the curve (AUC),[5] also computing the share of correctly classified crises and no-crises using a Youden-based threshold λ with $0 \leq \lambda \leq 1$. Specifically, the

---

[4] In our analysis, since we have $J_v = 3$ units in each test set, we obtain $J_v^c = J - J_v = 27$ units in each training sample.

[5] The AUC is the area under the receiver operating characteristic (ROC) curve, i.e. the function that maps the hit ratio (share of correctly classified crises) onto type II errors for each possible thresholds, then visualizing the tradeoff between type I and type II errors.

Table 14.3. **Diagnostics used to assess the model's accuracy over the entire period 1981–2010**

	Cutoff point	AUC	Correctly classified crises	Correctly classified no-crises
Banking crisis	0.1290	0.8006	0.7848	0.7761
Sovereign crisis	0.0490	0.8602	0.7200	0.9745
Currency crisis	0.3170	0.7092	0.4488	0.9575
Inflation crisis	0.0110	0.9672	0.9155	0.9242

"Cutoff point" is the best cutoff point that maximizes the Youden Index. "Correctly classified crises" and "Correctly classified no-crises" are the shares of correctly classified crisis events and tranquil times.

threshold λ is the cutoff point maximizing the Youden Index, which is a summary measure of the model accuracy both considering type I (incorrectly classified crises in percentage form a) and type II errors (incorrectly classified no-crises in percentage form b) and computed as $[(1 - a_\lambda) + (1 - b_\lambda) - 1]$.

The results are shown in Table 14.3 and confirm high power in predicting both crisis and no-crisis events for all types of financial crises except for currency crises. The predictive ability of these crises is 44.89%, while tranquil times are forecasted with a share of 95.75%, thus obtaining an AUC of 0.7092. Instead, other types of crises show values for AUC well above 0.8, then corroborating the robustness of the CRAGGING predictions.

14.4.2 MSRF

As discussed in Section 14.1, once we obtain the CRAGGING predictions we extract the first PC to proxy the common risk source among different financial crises. Next, we mimic the first PC using the CRAGGING predictions as covariates running the following regression:

$$PC_{1,jg} = \delta_{BA}\tilde{y}_{BA,jg}^{cragg} + \delta_{CU}\tilde{y}_{CU,jg}^{cragg} + \delta_{IN}\tilde{y}_{IN,jg}^{cragg} + \delta_{SO}\tilde{y}_{SO,jg}^{cragg} + e_{jg}$$

$s.t.:$

$$\sum_{i=1}^{4} \delta_i = 1; \ \delta_i > 0 \ \forall i$$

$$(14.6)$$

where $PC_{1,jg}$ is the first PC extracted from the CRAGGING predictions $\tilde{y}_{i,jg}^{cragg}$ with $i = 1, ..., 4$ to denote the four financial crises (*BA* for banking, *CU* for currency, *IN* for inflation, and *SO* for sovereign) and δ_i are the loadings constrained to be non-negative and sum to unity.

The MSRF is the expectation of Equation (14.6) and, given the constraints imposed on the loadings, it can be read as the country-specific probability that a systemic crisis could happen:

$$MSRF_{jg} \equiv E\left(PC_{1,jg}\right) = \delta_{BA}\tilde{y}_{BA,jg}^{\text{cragg}} + \delta_{CU}\tilde{y}_{CU,jg}^{\text{cragg}} + \delta_{IN}\tilde{y}_{IN,jg}^{\text{cragg}} + \delta_{SO}\tilde{y}_{SO,jg}^{\text{cragg}} \tag{14.7}$$

Computationally, we run Equation (14.6) year by year thus obtaining time-varying loadings. In so doing we inspected the contribution of each financial crisis in explaining the MSRF computed according to Equation (14.7).

Figure 14.1 depicts the time evolution of the δ coefficients. Currency and inflation risks assumed a major role until 1989, and next sovereign risk appeared as the major source of the systemic risk until 2001, when inflation risk was the unique driver, assuming a loading of 100%. More recently, the pattern changed significantly, exhibiting an increasing role of banking together with sovereign risks. Interestingly, the recent global crisis that

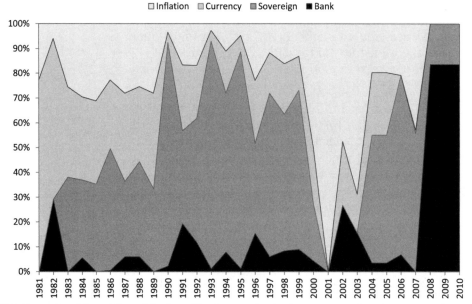

Figure 14.1 Systemic crisis and financial crises: The time-varying loadings computed each year over the period 1981−2010 according to Equation (14.6).

began in 2007 appears to be banking driven, also showing a significant role played by sovereign risk. Indeed, the financial turmoil that occurred in Greece in April–May 2010 highlighted the importance of monitoring the feedback between sovereign debt and bank risks (International Monetary Fund, 2010). Specifically, in many countries the intervention of the governments to bail out the banking system increased the concern about fiscal sustainability, translated into higher public sector indebtedness and resulted in sovereign funding difficulties.

In Figure 14.2, we analytically report the values of the MSRF for each country over the entire period 1981–2010. Interestingly, the data show that the recent global crisis would have been signaled for most of the OECD countries over the years 2008–2010. Values for MSRF exceeding the 90th percentile, which clearly denotes severe systemic crises, were reached for 18 out of 27 countries in 2010, while in 2008 there were four countries showing excess systemic risk.[6] Note also that the bank crises that started in 2007 (Iceland, Ireland, United Kingdom, United States) were associated with low MSRF values, while warning signals on impending systemic crises were launched in 2009 and, more severely, in 2010.

The period from 1981 to 2001 was not tranquil as it included the severe banking crises in the Nordic countries and Japan in the early 1990s as well as the Asian crisis of 1997–1998, together with the emerging market crises (in particular Argentina and Turkey in 2001). Also, in all these cases, the values for MSRF would been able to signal impending systemic crises, thus proving to be an effective measure of systemic risk.

14.4.3 Explaining systemic risk

To realize a risk mapping for the MSRF, thus inferring the inner causes underlying systemic risk, we finally run an RT using the MSRF as dependent variable and the 38 crisis predictors discussed in Section 14.2 as explanatory variables. In doing this, we recursively partition the predictor space, thus endogenously identifying different systemic risk regimes conditional on observable macroeconomic covariates.

The risk stratification is reported in Figure 14.3, which depicts an RT with nine final nodes. The leading indicators selected by the procedure are: Deposit interest rate (dir), government consumption (pgce), industry change (ind), TED spread (ted),

---

[6] However, many values of MSRF were at significant levels, thus sending the first alarm signals.

	1981	1982	1983	1984	1985	1986	1987	1988	1989	1990	1991	1992	1993	1994	1995	1996	1997	1998	1999	2000	2001	2002	2003	2004	2005	2006	2007	2008	2009	2010
Australia	19.47%	26.02%	7.85%	9.63%	3.67%	4.19%	7.18%	4.90%	4.40%	2.14%	8.83%	4.64%	0.51%	1.51%	0.98%	3.39%	2.03%	1.99%	1.87%	2.56%	0.20%	2.21%	2.14%	2.49%	2.48%	0.42%	0.36%	1.70%	1.71%	33.35%
Austria	19.61%	11.68%	2.72%	2.08%	2.70%	2.54%	2.63%	3.14%	2.93%	0.60%	3.65%	2.19%	0.41%	1.50%	0.80%	2.89%	1.57%	1.99%	1.06%	2.06%	0.20%	2.21%	1.44%	1.54%	1.54%	0.21%	0.20%	2.15%	43.16%	42.85%
Belgium	19.61%	8.76%	6.13%	2.22%	2.63%	2.54%	2.64%	3.14%	3.48%	0.60%	3.17%	2.23%	0.49%	5.39%	0.82%	3.02%	5.68%	2.07%	1.20%	2.06%	0.20%	2.30%	2.26%	2.08%	1.86%	0.21%	0.20%	1.70%	45.89%	60.22%
Canada	22.05%	12.94%	4.13%	3.90%	2.63%	2.81%	3.63%	3.14%	4.25%	0.79%	4.70%	3.84%	0.47%	1.96%	0.80%	2.94%	1.57%	1.99%	1.06%	2.06%	0.20%	3.49%	1.44%	1.55%	1.54%	0.21%	0.20%	5.12%	1.68%	39.75%
Denmark	19.61%	8.76%	7.10%	2.29%	2.63%	3.16%	5.45%	3.14%	3.46%	1.16%	7.31%	3.80%	0.70%	1.62%	0.80%	2.58%	2.80%	2.06%	1.06%	2.06%	0.20%	3.49%	1.46%	1.56%	1.57%	0.21%	0.20%	1.79%	9.59%	42.85%
Finland	23.33%	8.76%	2.91%	2.24%	2.63%	2.54%	2.74%	3.21%	3.46%	1.23%	7.81%	7.39%	1.49%	8.56%	0.89%	4.62%	1.56%	2.06%	1.06%	2.06%	0.20%	2.21%	1.43%	1.54%	1.57%	0.21%	0.20%	2.31%	1.03%	3.26%
France	19.61%	5.84%	2.72%	2.49%	2.63%	2.54%	3.37%	3.59%	2.93%	1.82%	3.99%	3.09%	0.52%	3.06%	0.81%	3.50%	5.37%	2.06%	1.06%	2.06%	0.20%	2.35%	6.46%	1.54%	1.57%	0.21%	0.18%	5.65%	30.43%	48.90%
Germany	19.61%	9.07%	2.72%	2.08%	2.63%	2.54%	2.63%	3.14%	2.93%	0.60%	4.86%	2.94%	0.44%	2.24%	0.80%	11.44%	1.59%	1.99%	1.06%	2.06%	0.20%	2.21%	1.44%	1.56%	1.54%	0.21%	0.20%	1.70%	1.71%	3.26%
Greece	22.13%	34.47%	19.01%	16.34%	16.10%	9.17%	6.18%	9.51%	20.34%	1.76%	17.47%	12.43%	2.84%	12.24%	1.70%	6.69%	6.05%	6.21%	2.02%	2.92%	0.20%	7.49%	2.57%	2.44%	2.41%	0.42%	0.29%	5.46%	52.60%	30.66%
Hungary	19.61%	8.96%	6.60%	3.01%	3.67%	3.67%	2.63%	3.14%	18.84%	0.77%	37.84%	43.08%	3.50%	14.11%	3.55%	20.47%	8.55%	6.44%	2.57%	2.57%	0.20%	4.73%	3.48%	2.34%	4.34%	0.36%	0.29%	3.54%	8.97%	48.01%
Iceland	90.01%	67.28%	58.20%	31.12%	21.54%	43.82%	5.99%	14.41%	57.43%	8.04%	5.69%	3.12%	0.51%	2.00%	0.80%	2.91%	4.54%	2.06%	1.66%	4.04%	0.20%	4.64%	1.43%	2.74%	2.85%	0.91%	0.36%	43.61%	55.52%	69.10%
Ireland	19.61%	19.84%	7.64%	3.87%	2.63%	2.91%	3.09%	3.12%	2.93%	0.60%	3.70%	2.18%	0.43%	1.86%	0.80%	5.74%	1.57%	2.02%	1.22%	2.32%	0.20%	3.13%	1.56%	1.56%	2.36%	0.42%	0.28%	46.73%	72.12%	44.50%
Italy	19.61%	13.34%	5.71%	2.94%	2.63%	2.55%	2.72%	3.44%	2.93%	1.44%	7.16%	3.38%	0.95%	5.39%	0.99%	6.35%	5.53%	2.00%	1.06%	2.06%	0.20%	2.21%	1.44%	1.56%	1.57%	0.21%	0.19%	1.70%	4.85%	3.26%
Japan	6.84%	6.34%	5.30%	6.23%	2.63%	2.60%	4.55%	3.73%	10.07%	0.73%	9.15%	6.15%	0.79%	8.62%	1.93%	16.10%	2.09%	2.70%	5.56%	4.14%	0.20%	13.33%	2.18%	2.82%	1.54%	2.55%	0.18%	2.15%	10.62%	12.31%
South Korea	21.03%	11.34%	4.76%	6.66%	2.63%	2.77%	3.79%	3.80%	2.93%	0.93%	9.22%	2.54%	0.44%	1.84%	1.10%	9.66%	2.38%	2.54%	6.15%	3.78%	0.20%	2.26%	1.97%	1.55%	1.66%	0.87%	0.18%	1.87%	10.82%	7.12%
Mexico	19.47%	47.46%	60.00%	94.28%	96.85%	77.55%	82.66%	90.16%	79.88%	8.35%	42.51%	-1.35%	1.40%	35.23%	1.32%	66.64%	46.57%	55.11%	44.09%	6.81%	3.03%	10.88%	1.44%	1.55%	1.78%	0.21%	1.53%	1.70%	1.71%	3.47%
Netherlands	19.61%	6.32%	5.30%	2.08%	2.63%	2.53%	2.65%	3.11%	3.46%	0.60%	3.21%	2.21%	0.41%	1.50%	0.80%	2.95%	1.57%	2.09%	1.22%	2.06%	0.20%	2.30%	1.39%	1.78%	1.57%	0.21%	0.20%	1.70%	44.11%	63.22%
New Zealand	19.61%	12.69%	6.77%	3.55%	2.63%	5.10%	7.47%	10.25%	6.56%	1.69%	7.38%	5.19%	0.51%	1.96%	0.98%	3.52%	1.61%	2.34%	1.17%	2.56%	0.20%	3.49%	2.14%	2.34%	2.33%	0.21%	0.36%	16.05%	29.00%	2.75%
Norway	19.61%	6.32%	5.30%	2.09%	2.63%	3.02%	10.45%	7.78%	3.72%	1.30%	6.86%	9.25%	0.80%	1.50%	0.80%	4.00%	1.56%	2.06%	1.19%	2.08%	0.20%	2.26%	1.66%	1.55%	1.57%	0.21%	0.25%	5.83%	1.71%	3.36%
Poland	79.04%	75.16%	91.95%	77.01%	77.57%	2.56%	74.04%	61.39%	59.81%	13.25%	58.52%	59.76%	6.28%	27.76%	10.03%	37.47%	10.01%	22.01%	2.06%	3.07%	0.20%	3.56%	1.44%	1.55%	10.69%	0.32%	0.20%	1.70%	1.71%	37.36%
Portugal	40.88%	16.79%	39.67%	47.49%	65.77%	33.11%	4.34%	3.16%	2.93%	0.64%	3.98%	2.92%	0.40%	3.96%	0.81%	2.91%	2.38%	2.31%	3.22%	4.05%	0.20%	3.73%	2.17%	2.35%	2.51%	0.33%	0.29%	1.70%	1.71%	42.85%
Spain	19.61%	29.09%	6.97%	3.01%	2.63%	2.82%	3.03%	3.29%	2.93%	1.27%	5.05%	3.54%	0.75%	2.16%	0.81%	3.84%	1.83%	1.99%	1.06%	2.06%	0.20%	3.60%	1.44%	2.28%	2.33%	0.87%	0.29%	1.70%	1.71%	39.75%
Sweden	19.61%	13.57%	2.72%	2.70%	2.63%	2.56%	3.22%	3.45%	3.13%	1.18%	9.05%	3.41%	1.25%	1.86%	0.89%	4.75%	1.56%	2.06%	1.06%	2.06%	0.20%	3.49%	1.43%	1.55%	1.57%	0.21%	0.20%	1.70%	37.83%	42.85%
Switzerland	23.33%	7.83%	2.91%	2.08%	2.63%	2.54%	2.88%	2.35%	2.93%	1.56%	3.62%	4.15%	0.57%	1.51%	0.80%	8.33%	3.70%	2.03%	1.04%	2.08%	0.20%	2.21%	1.63%	1.56%	1.53%	0.21%	0.20%	41.59%	39.63%	36.32%
Turkey	21.03%	47.92%	77.26%	61.24%	61.70%	49.19%	58.78%	56.80%	87.24%	9.57%	45.22%	33.32%	10.47%	31.77%	16.78%	53.06%	31.11%	42.07%	33.36%	57.02%	100.00%	84.56%	39.97%	22.19%	19.52%	1.09%		6.28%	6.87%	17.42%
UK	19.47%	9.63%	6.13%	2.37%	2.63%	2.60%	2.84%	3.20%	5.64%	1.07%	4.49%	3.58%	0.68%	3.40%	0.80%	8.75%	4.20%	2.08%	1.04%	2.18%	0.20%	3.49%	2.04%	1.56%	1.60%	0.21%	0.18%	1.70%	1.68%	42.85%
US	20.89%	21.68%	2.72%	4.69%	3.00%	3.00%	7.10%	7.06%	2.93%	2.22%	7.61%	4.82%	0.48%	3.34%	0.85%	7.80%	2.04%	2.20%	5.25%	2.17%	0.20%	15.09%	6.19%	2.51%	2.74%	1.47%	0.29%	30.50%	30.50%	30.88%

Figure 14.2 Values for the MSRF computed for each country over the period 1981–2010.

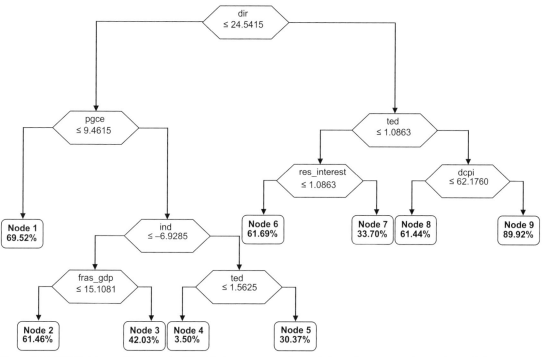

Figure 14.3 MSRF risk stratification: the RT with the corresponding splitting rules computed over the period 1981–2010. In each terminal node we report the arithmetic average computed using the MSRF values corresponding to each node.

international reserves over debt interest payment (res_interest) and consumer price change (dcpi).

An in-depth analysis of the tree structure provides interesting findings on systemic risk. In particular, we note that higher probabilities of having a systemic crisis are associated with high interest rate on deposits and TED spread together with significant consumer price changes (Node 9). This risk regime confirms the findings of many studies on banking and sovereign debt crises, which empirically proved the role played by these three leading indicators in predicting financial crises. Kaminsky and Reinhart (1998) indeed emphasized the signaling power of interest rates on deposits in capturing overlending cycles and the associated financial sector problems, due to the fact that some aggressive banks use high deposit interest rates to fund their risky lending strategies. The high inflation as a predictor of sovereign debt crises was instead proven in Manasse *et al.* (2003), while the impact of the TED spread on the pricing of sovereign risk was recently documented in Aizenman *et al.* (2011).

Focusing on Nodes 6–9 of Figure 14.3, we note that whenever we observe a high interest rate on deposits, the TED spread and the consumer price changes exacerbate the effect of systemic risk. Indeed, when TED spread is moderate (less than 1.0863%), the international reserves over debt interest payment discriminates between high (Node 6) and moderate (Node 7) risk, confirming the role of such a liquidity measure as a leading indicator used, in particular, to predict sovereign debt crises.

Although high interest rates on deposits essentially signal potential systemic crises, other indicators warn of impending risks as well. Specifically, we note that less government consumption (Node 1) and high foreign assets held by commercial banks together with a negative performance of the industry sector (Node 3) lead to significant systemic risk. Also, in these two cases, we have interesting linkages with the existing literature on economic growth and financial crises. In fact:

- We fist observe that, with no pressure on interest rate on deposits, government consumption seems to indicate a positive contribution in maintaining systemic risk at low levels, in particular when the performance of the industry sector is not strongly negative and the TED spread is kept down (Node 5). This finding seems coherent with Romer and Bernstein (2009), who provide estimates on the positive impact of an increase in government spending on GDP and employment in the United States.
- We note that a relatively high systemic risk probability is associated with foreign assets held by commercial banks greater than 15.1081% of GDP, which seems to denote possible spillover effects through which crises spread across countries via financial linkages.

The risk mapping proposed in this section thus completes the analysis of systemic risk. Indeed, through the MSRF we proposed a probabilistic measure for the systemic risk, while using RT analysis we provided a risk stratification for such an unobservable common latent factor. This is done by a series of splitting rules based on common macroeconomic variables. These rules represent not only a possible warning map to be used to predict impending systemic risk, but also to prevent global crises. Obviously, this could be the case if such rules were used to maintain the macroeconomic conditions within the safe zones traced by the tree (low MSRF values).

14.5 Conclusions

In this chapter, we have offered a new way to measure and inspect the systemic risk also developing a possible EWS for it based on observable macroeconomic variables. To do this we relied on a novel algorithm pertaining to RT analysis, which allows uncovering forms of non-linear and complex behaviors of financial crises. Using the probability estimates of financial crises as covariates and the first PC as dependent variable, we then realized the MSRF, i.e. the country-specific systemic crisis probability. The results of our empirical analysis carried out on 27 OECD countries over the period 1981−2010 and taking into account 381 crisis events (158 banking crises, 127 currency crises, 71 inflation crises and 25 sovereign debt crises) are as follows. (i) We provided convincing evidence on the reliability of our approach in predicting financial crises, in particular for banking, sovereign and inflation crises. (ii) We found that the pattern assumed by the systemic risk over the recent global crisis changed significantly, exhibiting an increasing role of banking together with sovereign risks. (iii) The higher probabilities of having a systemic crisis are primarily associated with high interest rate on deposits and TED spread, together with significant consumer price changes. However, having less government consumption and high foreign assets held by commercial banks together with a negative performance of the industry sector also lead to significant systemic risk.

References

Aizenman, J., Hutchison, M., Jinjarak, Y., 2011. What is the risk of European sovereign debt defaults? Fiscal space, CDS spreads and market pricing of risk. NBER Working Paper 17407. NBER, Cambridge, MA.

Breiman, L., 2001. Statistical modeling: the two cultures. Statistical Science 16 (3), 199−231.

Breiman, L., Friedman, J., Olshen, R., Stone, C., 1984. Classification and Regression Trees. Chapman & Hall/CRC, Boca Raton, FL.

Frankel, J., Rose, A., 1996. Currency crashes in emerging markets: an empirical treatment. Journal of International Economics 41 (3−4), 351−368.

Friedman, J., Popescu, B., 2003. Importance sampled earning ensembles. Technical Report, Department of Statistics. Stanford University, Stanford, CA.

Friedman, J., Popescu, B., 2005. Predictive learning via rule ensembles. Technical Report. Department of Statistics. Stanford University, Stanford, CA.

International Monetary Fund, 2010. Global Financial Stability Report—Sovereigns, Funding, and Systemic Liquidity. International Monetary Fund, Washington, DC.

Kaminsky, G., Reinhart, C., 1998. Financial crises in Asia and Latin America: then and now. The American Economic Review 88 (2), 444−448.

Kaminsky, G., Lizondo, S., Reinhart, C., 1998. Leading indicators of currency crises. International Monetary Fund Staff Papers 45. International Monetary Fund, Washington, DC.

Lindert, P., Morton, P., 1989. How sovereign debt has worked. In: Sachs, J. (Ed.), Developing Country Debt and Economic Performance, volume 1. University of Chicago Press, Chicago, IL, pp. 39−106.

Manasse, P., Roubini, N., 2009. Rules of thumb for sovereign debt crises. Journal of International Economics 78 (2), 192–205.

Manasse, P., Roubini, N., Schimmelpfennig, A., 2003. Predicting sovereign debt crises. International Monetary Fund Working Paper 03/221. International Monetary Fund, Washington, DC.

Reinhart, C., Rogoff, K., 2010. From financial crash to debt crisis. NBER Working Paper 15795. NBER, Cambridge, MA.

Romer, C., Bernstein, J., 2009. The Job Impact of the American Recovery and Reinvestment Plan. Executive Office of the President. Council of Economic Advisers, Washington, DC, WA.

Savona, R., Vezzoli, M., 2011. Fitting and forecasting sovereign defaults using multiple risk signals. Working Paper 364. Department of Quantitative Methods, University of Brescia, Brescia.

Suter, C., 1992. Debt Cycles in the World-Economy: Foreign Loans, Financial Crises, and Debt Settlements, 1820–1990. Westview Press, Boulder, CO.

Tomz, M., 2007. Reputation and International Cooperation, Sovereign Debt Across Three Centuries. Princeton University Press, Princeton, NJ.

Vezzoli, M., Stone, C., 2007. CRAGGING. Book of short papers of CLADAG 2007. University of Macerata.

Vezzoli, M., Zuccolotto, P., 2011. CRAGGING: measures of variable importance for data with hierarchical structure. In: Ingrassia, S., Rocci, R., Vichi, M. (Eds), New Perspectives in Statistical Modeling and Data Analysis. Springer, Berlin, pp. 393–400.

15

COMPUTING RELIABLE DEFAULT PROBABILITIES IN TURBULENT TIMES

Dean Fantazzini* and Mario Maggi**

*Moscow State University, **University of Pavia

CHAPTER OUTLINE

15.1 Introduction

The financial crisis that started in 2007 has clearly highlighted the importance of having robust and reliable methods to compute default probabilities. When Lehman Brothers filed for bankruptcy on 15 September 2008, marking the largest bankruptcy in US history, numerous analysts were almost caught by surprise: Two weeks prior to bankruptcy, the official Moody's KMV one-year estimated default frequency (EDF) for Lehman Brothers was only 0.62%; moreover, it decreased from 0.69% on 29 July 2008 to 0.62% on 31 August 2008 (see, e.g. Hovhannisyan, 2010). Similarly, Lehman Brothers still enjoyed an Λ2 (S&P equivalent) credit rating up to 10 September 2010.

However, if we look at Lehman's stock price, we notice that after reaching a maximum of $85.8 per share on 2 February 2007, it fell to $66 on 1 February 2008, to $16.13 on 2 September 2008 and finally to $0.21 when Lehman Brothers filed for bankruptcy. Such a price fall in 18 months should have alarmed any investor

Rethinking Valuation and Pricing Models. http://dx.doi.org/10.1016/B978-0-12-415875-7.00015-4

of a potential default event in the near term; unfortunately, this was not the case, and the domino effect that followed exposed publicly the limits of Merton-type models and rating agencies.

Merton-type models such as the one by KMV-Moody's are based on the assumption that the company accounting data represents a true picture of its financial situation—this approach may not be robust to "window dressing" policies made to improve the financial score of a company or, in the worst case, to financial fraud. In addition, KMV itself admits that "in practice the market leverage moves around far too much to provide reasonable results" and particular iterative methods have to be used instead (see Crosbie and Bohn, 2001). Therefore, the design of a credit default early warning system is not a lost cause.

Fantazzini *et al.* (2008) recently proposed a completely new approach called the zero price probability (ZPP) model, which only considers stock price data and is also able to model non-normalities of the price distribution. The authors justified the model by resorting to a vast literature demonstrating how quoted prices are mostly driven by private information and therefore should be closer to the "true" values than accounting data. Hausbrouck (1988), Madhavan and Smidt (1991), Hasbrouk and Sofianos (1993), and Madhavan and Sofianos (1997) showed the importance of asymmetric private information for stock prices and futures dynamics (for recent surveys about market micro-structure studies, see Biais *et al.* 2005; Hansbrouck, 2007). Starting from simple financial identities based on the "true" accounting figures, Fantazzini *et al.* (2008) show that, in a model allowing for non-positive prices, the null price can be used as a barrier to separate an operative firm from a defaulted one. Moreover, the default probability is computed as the probability of a non-positive price.

Su and Huang (2010), in the most recent and largest out-of-sample comparison so far, compared the discriminatory powers of Logit, KMV and ZPP models, and found that "… the KMV performs the worst" and "… it is clear to recognize that the ZPP type models perform much better."

In this chapter, we compare the probabilities of default (PDs) computed by using the KMV-Merton model with the ones implied in the official credit ratings assigned by rating agencies, together with the PDs estimated by using the ZPP model, using the list of acquired or bankrupt banks during the global financial crisis of 2007—2009, available at Wikipedia.[1]

---

[1] http://en.wikipedia.org/wiki/List_of_acquired_or_bankrupt_banks_in_the_late_2000s_financial_crisis.

In order to better highlight the limits of Merton-type models and to consider the importance of insider information, a range of alternatives is considered beyond the previous three models:

- The classic Merton model coupled with a generalized autoregressive conditional heteroskedasticity (GARCH) model for the volatility forecast, where the amount of total debt is multiplied by 0.97 to take into account the so-called "forbearance" allowed to banks (see Ronn and Verma, 1986).
- The classic Merton model estimated with a top management perspective, i.e. considering the case when the total debt amount is already known at the beginning of the year (and not at the end of the year, like for an external public investor).
- The classic Merton model estimated using the "net debt", i.e. short- and long-term debts but with all the cash and quasi-cash excluded.

The remainder of the chapter is organized as follows. In Section 15.2, we review the KMV-Merton model, whereas Section 15.3 presents the ZPP model. Section 15.4 discusses an empirical analysis with the acquired or bankrupt banks during the 2007–2009 financial crisis, comparing various models' PDs. Section 15.5 concludes.

15.2 Brief Review of the KMV-Merton Model

15.2.1 Classic Merton model

We briefly review below the classic structure of Merton-type models, following closely Fantazzini *et al.* (2008) and Fantazzini (2009). See Crosbie and Bohn, (2001) for the KMV technical document, as well as Crossen *et al.* (2011) for a recent validation of the Moody's Analytics Public EDF™ model for North American corporate firms during the last decade.

Merton-type models (see, e.g. Ingersoll, 1987; Mason and Merton, 1985; Merton, 1977) assume that the value A_t of the firm follows a geometric Brownian motion:

$$\mathrm{d}A_t = \mu_A A_t \mathrm{d}t + \sigma_A A_t \mathrm{d}W_t,$$

where W_t is a Wiener process, and the drift and volatility coefficients μ_A and σ_A do not depend on the capital structure, i.e. on how the assets' value A_t is split into equity (E_t) and bonds (B_t) values. This simply translates the Miller–Modigliani theorem (see Miller and Modigliani, 1958, 1961). Moreover, the assets' value is assumed to be exogenous, so it can be treated as the underlying in an option pricing framework, while the equity has a residual value at maturity (the model time horizon) T. Therefore the equity's market value E_t is given by:

$$E_t = A_t N(d_1) - e^{-rT} B_T N(d_2), \qquad (15.1)$$

where B_T is the face value of the firm debt, r is the risk free rate, $N(\cdot)$ is the cumulative standard normal distribution function, and d_1 and d_2 are given by:

$$d_1 = \frac{\log(A_t/B_T) + (r + 0.5\sigma_A^2)T}{\sigma_A \sqrt{T}}$$

$$d_2 = d_1 - \sigma_A \sqrt{T}.$$

Under the Merton model assumptions the volatility of the equity is:

$$\sigma_E = \frac{A_t}{E_t} N(d_1)\sigma_A. \qquad (15.2)$$

In the Merton model, the underlying variable A_t, and hence its volatility, cannot be directly observed. To overcome this problem, the KMV-Merton model (see also Ronn and Verma, 1986; Crosbie and Bohn, 2001) numerically solves, for A_t and σ_A, the nonlinear system given by Equations (15.1) and (15.2). Once the solution is approximated, the distance to default can be calculated as d_2, while the implied probability of default is $\Pr[A_t \le B_T] = N(-d_2)$.

15.2.2 Merton-type models: The iterative procedure by KMV

KMV affirms that solving Equations (15.1) and (15.2) simultaneously gives bad results, so that they use a modified version of the previous approach, where an iterative procedure is employed:
- Start with an initial σ_A.
- Solve the Black–Scholes equation for A_t, given E_t each day for the previous year, using σ_A.
- Take the resulting time-series of A_t and calculate a new σ_A and μ_A.
- Iterate until σ_A converges.
- Given the final estimates of A_t and σ_A, define the distance to default (DD) as:

$$DD = \frac{\log(A_t/B_T) + (\mu_A + 0.5\sigma_A^2)T}{\sigma_A \sqrt{T}},$$

hence, the probability of default (or EDF) is $\Pr_{(KMV-Merton)}[A_t \le B_T] = N(-DD)$.

Bharath and Shumway (2008) employed the same approach to compare the Merton model with several alternative models, finding that the Merton default probabilities are usually out-performed out of sample. Moreover, they also show that "the Merton DD model does not produce a sufficient statistic for the probability of default," but nevertheless "its functional form is still useful for forecasting defaults."

15.2.3 An extension: The Merton-GARCH model

In order to compare the classic models with the new ZPP approach, we try to improve the Merton model, obtaining a sort of hybrid model coupling a structural model with a market model. One of the main limitations of Merton-type models is the use of constant volatility. Moreover, even the above-presented KMV iterative method makes use of historical volatility values. In order to alleviate this strong restriction, we propose here for the first time an extension of the original Merton model that aims at incorporating a GARCH volatility forecast for the stock price. In this way, the volatility model exploits a relevant part of the risk information embedded in stock price dynamics. The volatility forecast σ_E is then employed in system (15.1) and (15.2) to obtain A_t and σ_A.

The practice of waiting before forcing the closure of an insolvent bank is called "forbearance." The common way to incorporate this feature into a Merton model is to multiply the amount of total debt by 0.97. This means that the default is triggered when A_T falls below $0.97 \cdot B_T$ (see: Ronn and Verma, 1986; Allen and Saunders, 1993).

15.3 Brief Review of the ZPP Model

We briefly review below the ZPP model, following closely Fantazzini *et al.* (2008, 2010) and Fantazzini (2009).

This model aims to overcome the poor reliability of accounting data by using stock prices only. In addition, unlike the KMV-Merton model, the ZPP model easily allows us to describe the features of stock prices such as leptokurtosis and hetero-skedasticity. In this regard, we remind the reader that increasing volatility and leptokurtosis can be read as a signal of informed trading (for recent surveys about market microstructure studies, see Biais *et al.*, 2005; Hasbrouck, 2007).

Let us consider the following two financial identities based on the "true" accounting data at time T.

According to the situation faced by the firm, E_T and E_T' have different financial meanings and signs (see Table 15.1). We

Table 15.1. Financial meaning and signs of E_T and E_T'

	$E_T = A_T - B_T$	$E_T' = A_T$
OPERATIVE	Equity belonging to shareholders (>0)	Asset value (>0)
DEFAULTED	Loss given default for debtholders (≤ 0)	Equity belonging to debtholders (>0)

remark that E_T is negative when the firm defaults as it represents the loss given default for debt holders, while it is positive when the firm is operative representing the equity belonging to shareholders instead. A negative value for E_T is a direct consequence of the limited liability now in place in all modern western legislations. In addition, losses can be theoretically unlimited like profits—just think of the effects of the 11 September 2001 attacks on airline companies or of the mad cow and bird flue diseases on agriculture companies. Therefore, we can resort to probability density functions with negative domain as well.

Fantazzini *et al.* (2008) showed that we can estimate the distance to default simply by using E_T, so that the default probability is given by $\Pr[E_T \leq 0]$, as the firm's defaults when E_T is zero or negative. Furthermore, given that E_T is the product of the quoted stock price P_T with the number of shares, the default probability of a firm can be retrieved by estimating $\Pr[P_T \leq 0]$, i.e. by using ZPP. While the quoted price P_T is a truncated variable which cannot be negative, the quantity E_T has no lower bound, as it has a different financial meaning whether the firm is operative or defaulted (see Table 15.1); in the former case E_T is computed daily in financial markets, whereas in the latter case the loss given default is computed in bankruptcy courts.

It is well-known that stock prices are non-stationary $I(15.1)$ variables: Given that we are interested in finding $\Pr[P_T \leq 0]$, we can do that by considering a conditional model for the differences in prices levels $X_t = P_t - P_{t-1}$, instead of differences in log-prices. An analytical closed-form solution for $\Pr[P_T \leq 0]$ is available in special cases only; otherwise, simulation methods are required. The following algorithm (ZPP estimation algorithm) allows to estimate the probability that the default occurs by time T:

Step 1 Consider a generic conditional model for the differences of prices $X_t = P_t - P_{t-1}$, allowing for negative values, given the filtration at time t, F_t:

$$\begin{cases} X_t = E[X_t|F_t] + \varepsilon_t \\ \varepsilon_t = H_t^{1/2}\eta_t, \quad \eta_t \sim \text{i.i.d.}(0,1) \end{cases} \tag{15.3}$$

where $H_t^{1/2}$ is the conditional standard deviation.

Step 2 Simulate a high number N of price trajectories up to time T, using the estimated time series model (15.3) at Step 1.
Step 3 The default probability is simply the ratio n/N, where n is the number of times out of N when the price touched or crossed the barrier along the simulated trajectory.

15.4 Empirical Analysis

We compared the PDs using the list of acquired or bankrupt banks in the financial crisis of the late 2000s, available at Wikipedia. From this list, we excluded the banks not listed in the stock market or with extremely illiquid stock prices that did not allow any algorithm to converge. The stocks that we finally analyzed are reported in Table 15.2.

Table 15.2. List of acquired or defaulted banks analyzed

Ticker	Name	Country	Currency
NRK LN equity	Northern Rock	GB	GBP
2942331Q US equity	Bear Stearns Companies LLC	US	USD
CFC US equity	Countrywide Financial Corp.	US	USD
AL/LN equity	Alliance & Leicester PLC	GB	GBP
ROSK DC equity	Roskilde Bank	DE	DKK
MER US equity	Merrill Lynch & Co. Inc.	US	USD
AIG US equity	American International Group	US	USD
LEHMQ US equity	Lehman Brothers Holdings Inc.	US	USD
HBOS LN equity	HBOS PLC	GB	GBP
WAMUQ US equity	Washington Mutual Inc.	US	USD
BB/LN equity	Bradford & Bingley PLC	GB	GBP
WB US equity	Wachovia Corp.	US	USD
LAIS IR equity	Landsbanki Islands HF	IC	ISK
KAUP IR equity	Kaupthing Bank	IC	ISK
CBH US equity	Commerce Bancorp Inc./NJ	US	USD
ANGL ID equity	Anglo Irish Bank Corp Ltd	IR	EUR
RBS LN equity	Royal Bank of Scotland Group	GB	GBP
NTBKQ US equity	Netbank Inc.	US	USD
FBTXQ US equity	Franklin Bank Corp/Houston	US	USD
MSBK US equity	Main Street Banks Inc.	US	USD

The models we considered are:

- ZPP model, with $N = 5000$, estimated using an AR(1)-Threshold-GARCH(1,1) model with Skewed-t innovations (for more details, see Fantazzini, 2008 and references therein). For Roskilde and Bradford & Bingley normal innovations were used, since the Skewed-t model failed to converge.
- Classic Merton model with $\mu_A = r$, total debt, public investor perspective (i.e. the total debt amount is known *only* at the end of the year).
- Merton model with Student-GARCH(1,1) volatility, $0.97 *$ (total debt), public investor perspective.
- Moody's credit ratings: We used the PDs implied in the assigned credit rating, by using the S&P 1-year global corporate default rates by credit rating category, 1981−2008.
- Merton model with $\mu_A = r$, total debt, public investor perspective, estimated with an iterative procedure, like KMV and Bharat and Shumway (2008).
- Merton model with $\mu_A = r$, total debt, top management perspective (i.e. contrary to model 2, the classic Merton model, the total debt amount is already known at the beginning of the year), estimated with an iterative procedure.
- Merton model with $\mu_A = r$, net debt (i.e. short- and long-term debts, but with all the cash and quasi-cash excluded), public investor perspective, estimated with an iterative procedure.
- Merton model with $\mu_A = r$, net debt (i.e. short- and long-term debts, but with all the cash and quasi-cash excluded), top management perspective, estimated with an iterative procedure.

For all cases, the required estimations are performed using a 500 working days sliding time window.

For sake of interest and space, we report below only the results relative to first four models (the full set of results is available from the authors upon request).

In order to best summarize the capacity of each considered model to be a proper credit default early warning system, we report in Table 15.3 the number of days before the default (or bailout) when the estimated one-year ahead PD was higher than 1%.

Table 15.3 clearly highlights the superiority of the ZPP model, for which the estimated PDs were higher than 1% in 19 out of 20 analyzed banks more than 100 days before the default/bailout, while for 15 out of 20 banks this had already taken place more than one year in advance. On the opposite side of the spectrum, Moody's ratings and its implied PDs performed the worst, with only two (very small) banks that had

Table 15.3. **Number of days before the default (or bailout) when the estimated PD was higher than 1%**

Bank	ZPP	Merton classic total debt (public investor perspective)	Merton-GARCH 0.97 ∗ total debt (public investor perspective)	Moody's ratings (EDR)
NRK	155	93	154	0
BS	144	77	185	0
CFC	343	229	320	0
AL	392	0	389	0
ROSK	706	45	706	0
MER	317	64	322	0
AIG	706	13	291	0
LEHMAN	409	181	403	0
HBOS	317	0	303	0
WAS	331	207	407	0
BB	226	81	226	0
WB	301	168	420	0
LAIS	704	0	703	53
KAUP	704	0	473	53
CBH	0	0	121	0
ANGL	482	168	414	0
RBS	579	0	265	0
NTB	633	161	333	0
FBT	477	281	462	0
MSBK	150	0	0	0

the assigned (implied) PDs higher than 1% approximately 50 days before the credit event.

Merton models performed in between these two extreme cases. However, we can observe that the Merton-GARCH model does much better than the classic Merton models with constant volatilities—for most of the considered banking stocks, the Merton-GARCH model delivered early warnings very close to the ZPP. The average number of days for the early warning is 403.8 for the ZPP model and 344.85 for the Merton-GARCH model, while it is only 88.4 for the classic Merton model and a poor 5.3 value for the Moody's rating system.

Therefore, the possibility to model the persistence in stock volatility using GARCH-type models seems to be one of the major requirements to obtain robust early warning systems for credit defaults, well in advance of the credit event.

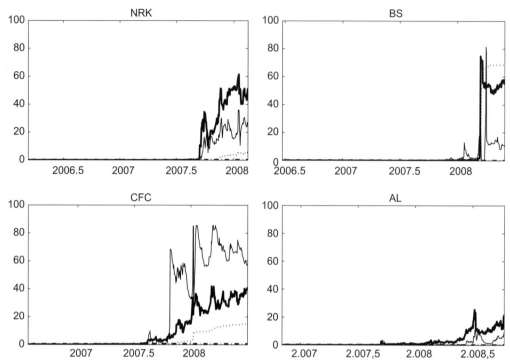

Figure 15.1 PDs: ZPP model (solid, bold), Merton model (dotted), Merton-GARCH (solid) and Moody's EDR (dash-dotted).

Figures 15.1–15.5 show the estimated PDs using the ZPP model, the classic Merton model, the Merton-GARCH model and Moody's ratings [expected default rate (EDR)]. In the vast majority of cases the ZPP tends to jump to values higher than 10% rather early and a similar behavior is also shown by the Merton-GARCH model. The classical Merton model tends to rise quite late and with low PDs, while the implied PDs by credit ratings are almost always close to zero.

The comparison between the Merton model and the Merton-GARCH model shows that the use of market time series to obtain information about the equity volatility increases the performance of the latter model, but at the cost of rather unstable PDs. This depends on the solution of the system of Equations (15.1) and (15.2), which is sensitive to small changes in stock volatility, particularly for high-leverage firms (as banks are). The Merton-GARCH early warning ability is comparable to that of ZPP, but the ZPP PDs are much smoother. For this reason, the ZPP model seems a better tool than Merton models. Moreover, since the ZPP model does not use balance sheet information, it is not

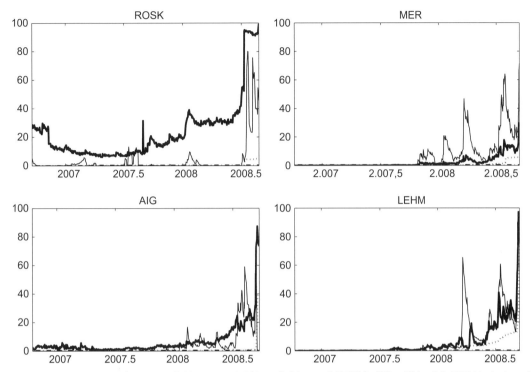

Figure 15.2 PDs: ZPP model (solid, bold), Merton model (dotted), Merton-GARCH (solid)and Moody's EDR (dash-dotted).

influenced by the discontinuity introduced by periodical accounting updating.

Interestingly, the ZPP and the Merton-GARCH models reacted to some relevant events. In this regard, we report below some examples. On 14 September 2007, the Bank of England provided a liquidity support facility to Northern Rock whereby the estimated ZPP started to increase significantly two days before this event and on 14 September 2007 it was equal to 10.76%. The Merton-GARCH PD started to increase on 14 September 2007, but keeping lower values than the ZPP. Although the classic Merton model also yielded increasing PDs, these were higher than 1% only two months later and then remained below 6%. The following nationalization of Northern Rock in February 2008 produced a clear increase in the estimated ZPP and Merton-GARCH PDs for Bradford & Bingley as well. In 2006, NetBank started to restructure the company trying to resume profitability: Only the ZPP model reacted to those problems;—in 2007, Net-Bank recognized the failure of the restructuring attempt and announced the beginning of the shutdown. This event caused

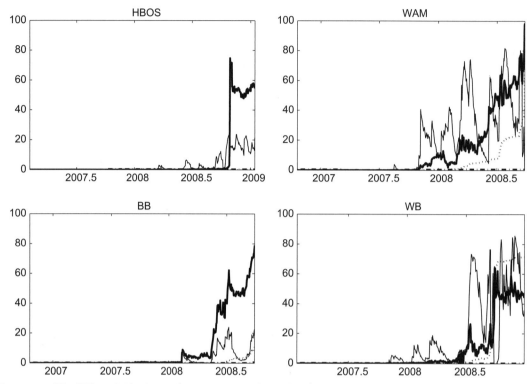

Figure 15.3 PDs: ZPP model (solid, bold), Merton model (dotted), Merton-GARCH (solid) and Moody's EDR (dash-dotted).

a sudden rise of the Merton-GARCH PD and, only later, of the Merton PD. Finally, we note that the estimated ZPP for AIG was higher than 1% already at the beginning of 2006 and remained higher until its bailout in September 2008, thus already highlighting some underlying problems; the Merton-GARCH model PDs started to increase above 1% only in January 2008, while the classic Merton PDs only in September 2008.

15.5 Conclusion

Structural Merton-type models for firm values allow us to compute default probabilities using both market and accounting figures. These types of models are widely used, but recent studies have proposed other approaches to deal with this issue. In this chapter, we analyzed the performance of Merton and ZPP models in the case of acquired (bailout) or defaulted banks during the global financial crisis of 2007–2009.

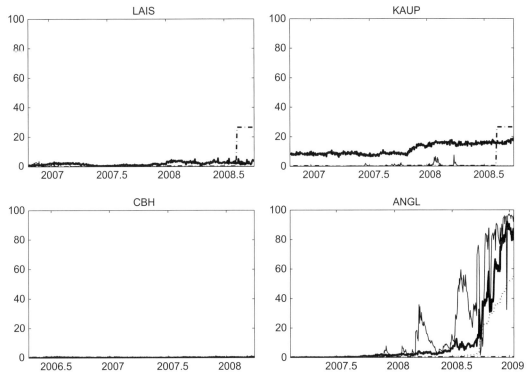

Figure 15.4 PDs: ZPP model (solid, bold), Merton model (dotted), Merton-GARCH (solid) and Moody's EDR (dash-dotted).

Our results show that early warning systems based on Merton-KMV or Moody's ratings are not effective in predicting bank failures. The default probabilities obtained by these models are very small and eventually increase only with a very short period of time just before the default.

In our opinion, there is the need to incorporate a more accurate analysis of market volatility and its persistence into these models. We used GARCH models to describe the volatility, and we applied them to a Merton model together with a Student-GARCH(1,1) and to a ZPP model with a Skewed-t-TGARCH(1,1). The results delivered by these models clearly outperformed those by the classic Merton-KMV and Moody's ratings, both in terms of early warning delay and of reliability of the estimated default probabilities. In particular, the ZPP model delivered much better and stable results.

Therefore, we can conclude that with the arrival (and the continuation) of the recent global financial crisis, the need for new models to evaluate banks solvency is clear. In this regard, an

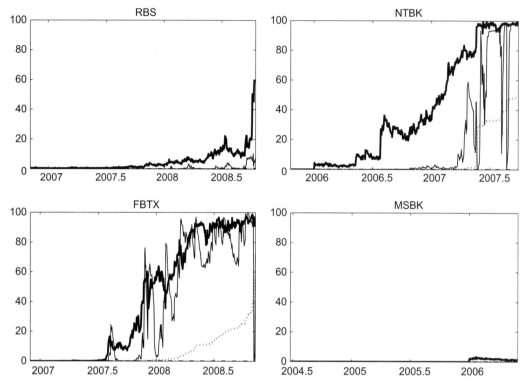

Figure 15.5 PDs: ZPP model (solid, bold), Merton model (dotted), Merton-GARCH (solid) and Moody's EDR (dash-dotted).

accurate volatility analysis is relevant, both to refine standard models and to build new approaches.

References

Allen, L., Saunders, A., 1993. Forbearance and valuation of deposit insurance as a callable put. Journal of Banking and Finance 17 (4), 629–643.

Bharath, S., Shumway, T., 2008. Forecasting default with the Merton distance to default model. Review of Financial Studies 21 (3), 1339–1369.

Biais, B., Glosten, L., Spatt, C., 2005. Market microstructure: a survey of microfoundations, empirical results and policy implications. Journal of Financial Markets 8 (2), 217–264.

Crosbie, P., Bohn, J., 2001. Modeling default risk. KMV Technical Document. Moody's, New York.

Crossen, C., Qu, S., Zhang, X., 2011. Validating the Public EDF Model for North American Corporate Firms. Moody's Analytics, New York.

Fantazzini, D., 2008. Dynamic copula modelling for value at risk. Frontiers in Finance and Economics 5 (2), 72–108.

Fantazzini, D., 2009. Forecasting default probability without accounting data: evidence from Russia. In: Gregoriou, G. (Ed.), Stock Market Volatility. Chapman Hall-CRC/Taylor & Francis, Boca Raton, FL, pp. 535–556.

Fantazzini, D., Maggi, M., De Giuli, E., 2008. A New Approach for Firm Value and Default Probability Estimation beyond Merton Models. Computational Economics 31 (2), 161–180.

Fantazzini, D., Kudrov, A., Zlotnik, A., 2010. Dangers and Opportunities for the Russian Banking Sector: 2007–2008. In: Gregoriou, G. (Ed.), Banking Crisis Handbook. Chapman & Hall/CRC Finance, Boca Raton, FL, pp. 383–405.

Hovhannisyan, R., 2010. Understanding fixed income quantitative analysis: an introduction to Mertonian Models. Metwest, Los Angeles, CA.

Hasbrouck, J., 1988. Trades, quotes, inventories and information. Journal of Financial Economics 22 (2), 229–252.

Hasbrouck, J., 2007. Empirical Market Microstructure. Oxford University Press, Oxford.

Hasbrouck, J., Sofianos, G., 1993. The trades of market makers: an empirical analysis of NYSE specialists. Journal of Finance 48 (5), 1565–1593.

Ingersoll Jr., J.E., 1987. Theory of Financial Decision Making. Rowman & Littlefield, Lanham, MD.

Madhavan, A., Smidt, S., 1991. A Bayesian model of intraday specialist pricing. Journal of Financial Economics 30 (1), 99–134.

Madhavan, A., Sofianos, G., 1997. An empirical analysis of the NYSE specialist trading. Journal of Financial Economics 48 (2), 189–210.

Mason, S., Merton, R.C., 1985. The role of contingent claims analysis in corporate finance. In: Altman, E., Ubrahmanyam, M. (Eds), Recent Advances in Corporate Finance. R.D. Irwin, Homewood, IL.

Merton, R.C., 1977. On the pricing of contingent claims and the Modigliani–Miller theorem. Journal of Financial Economics 15 (2), 241–250.

Miller, M.H., Modigliani, F., 1958. The cost of capital, corporation finance and the theory of investment. American Economic Review 48 (3), 261–297.

Miller, M.H., Modigliani, F., 1961. Dividend policy, growth, and the valuation of shares. Journal of Business 34 (4), 411–433.

Ronn, E.I., Verma, A.K., 1985. pricing risk-adjusted deposit insurance: an option-based model. Journal of Finance 41 (4), 871–895.

Su, E., Huang, S., 2010. Comparing firm failure predictions between Logit, KMV, and ZPP models: evidence from Taiwanese electronics industry. Asia-Pacific Financial Markets 17 (3), 209–239.

16

DISCOUNT RATES, DEFAULT RISK AND ASSET PRICING IN A REGIME CHANGE MODEL

Pu Chen* and Willi Semmler**

*The New School for Social Research, New York, and Center for Empirical Macroeconomics Bielefeld
**Dept of Economics, New School for Social Research, NY, USA

CHAPTER OUTLINE

16.1 Introduction

In the United States, recent expansions and contractions of the macroeconomy have taken the form of boom—bust regimes. The performances of stock markets, credit and bond markets are related to such regimes. Much research has attempted to show that there is a comovement of financial variables with economic regimes, and the comovements with output are postulated to hold, for example, for the stock market, housing prices and real estate sector, the credit market and banking system, the degree of leverage of firms and households, and so on.[1] Moreover, there is,

---

[1] See Chen *et al.* (2006), Reinhard and Rogoff (2008), and Semmler (2011, Chapters 18—20).

Rethinking Valuation and Pricing Models. http://dx.doi.org/10.1016/B978-0-12-415875-7.00016-6

as many have argued, a strong comovement of expansions and contractions with risk premia and discount rates in such regimes.[2] Our chapter will, in particular, focus on the linkages of regimes of the macroeconomy to discount rates, risk premia and asset prices.

There is a long tradition in financial economics that has focused on risk premium and asset pricing, but it takes asset prices as exogenous.[3] Yet, these types of models assume that the asset value of the firm is exogenously given by a Brownian motion when the debt, e.g. corporate liabilities, is priced. One usually refers here to the well-known adding-up theorem, i.e. $V = S + B$, where V is the asset value, S is the value of stocks and B is the value of bonds, where V is independent of the leverage ratio.[4]

Recently another theory has been developed that relates risk premia and asset prices more to the real side of the economy. This theory works with the so-called financial accelerator. Central here is the work by Bernanke *et al.* (1999). It is argued that when the financial market or financial intermediaries evaluate default risk and revise lending standards for economic units (households or firms) this is based on net worth representing the agents's creditworthiness. Creditworthiness rises in an economic expansion and falls in a contraction. In this school of thought[5] the default premium is called the finance premium, the size of which is determined by the cost of screening and monitoring of the borrower. Thus, here risk premia depend on endogenous asset prices, but risk premia do not feedback to asset prices.

Here, we do not want to address the issue of comparability of the above two theories. This has been done elsewhere.[6] For our purpose it is sufficient to assume that there is a strong comovement between those two causes of credit spreads that seems to be supported by empirical evidence.

[2] This is in particularly expressed in a recent work by Cochrane (2011) who explicitly states that in some sense asset price studies were misguided by focusing too much on the variation in expected payoffs and not enough on the variation of the discount rates.
[3] This literature goes back to Black and Scholes (1973) and Merton (1974) where liabilities, e.g. commercial bonds, are modeled in terms of credit derivatives. Here, it is assumed that there is an entire risk structure of interest rates in the commercial bond market whereby for each type of bond the risk premium is determined by the leverage and the volatility of the underlying asset.
[4] Note that what is needed is to assume that two firms undertake the same investment, regardless of different leverage ratios (for details, see Merton, 1974).
[5] For a further survey, see Semmler (2011, Chapters 4 and 19–21).
[6] See Gomez *et al.* (2002).

In this chapter, we want to link asset prices to risk premia (and discount rates) in an endogenous way.[7] We show that there is a strong comovement in a real variable and risk premia by estimating a Markov regime switching model (MRSM) in output and risk premia. These empirical results are then, in a second step, employed to build-up a dynamic decision model—in the context of a firm—where we show that risk premia, proxying discount rates, can impact asset value.[8]

An important issue in this context is then how to compute the asset value of the firm. The consumption-based asset pricing theory would argue that the objective of the firm is to deliver a stream of dividends for the equity holder. The optimization problem of the firm would then be to maximize the present value of dividends to the shareholders, using the the growth rate of marginal utilities as a discount factor. For asset pricing with all equity finance of firms, see Gruene and Semmler (2007). As has long been argued, in the case of an all-equity financed firm the optimization problem of the firm and the one from the consumption-based asset pricing theory should give the same results[9] to price the dividend stream. However, as Cochrane (2011) has recently argued that in the theory of asset pricing there was too much emphasis on payoffs and less on the volatility of the discount rates. The latter has become the focus of recent research.

As our problem is set up we will assume a dynamic decision problem of the firm, which is compatible with the consumption-based asset pricing model, in the case the agents have log utility in their objective function. Yet, what is important in our formulation of the dynamic decision problem is that the asset value of the firm will be affected by risk premia and endogenous discount rates. This is difficult to solve since both the discount rate and the asset prices will be endogenous.

---

[7] Cochrane has recently argued that "Discount rates vary over time... 'Discount rate,' 'risk premium,' and 'expected return' are all the same thing... High expected returns (low prices) correspond to securities that pay off poorly when consumption is low... Thus one can tie ... discount-rate variation to macroeconomic data." (Cochrane, 2011).

[8] Numerous empirical approaches have been pursued to infer from time series data on equity value the asset value of the firm (e.g., see Duan, *et al.*, 2002). There a survey of empirical methods is given of how to estimate the asset value of the firm from time series of its equity value.

[9] For asset pricing with all equity finance of firms, see Gruene and Semmler (2007). As has long been argued, in the case of an all-equity financed firm the optimization problem of the firm and the one from the consumption-based asset pricing theory should give the same results.

Since we are dealing here with a complicated decision model in a rather complex setting we cannot solve the model analytically. We thus make use of a numerical algorithm with adaptively refined grids and a set-oriented algorithm to solve the different model variants.[10]

The remainder of the chapter is organized as follows. Section 16.2 presents measures and empirical results on state-dependent risk premia, as proxies for discount rates, in a MRSM. Section 16.3 employs the Merton model with exogenously given asset value, through a Brownian motion. This leads to the well-known Distance-to-Default model, which is also known as the KMV model. Section 16.4 presents the dynamic decision model and a theoretical measure of our endogenous risk premium, as proxy for the discount rate, and spells out the asset value implications. Section 16.5 presents the numerical results of our procedure to solve the different model variants. Sections 16.6 concludes the chapter. An unpublished appendix provides some technical derivations on the numerical methods.[11]

16.2 Proxy for Discount Rates from a Regime Change Model

Risk perception and risk premia are not easy to measure with accuracy. Much is, as already pointed out by Keynes,[12] psychology, which can be considered one of the driving forces in the expansions and contractions. In times of recovery optimism prevails and the risk perception becomes low, while in times of contraction, pessimism prevails and the risk perception becomes high. If this hypothesis is true we should be able to observe the comovement between risk perception, measured by some metric, and the business cycle. Chen *et al.* (2006) have used many measures as variables for determining risk premia. Among them, on the one side, are diverse leverage ratios and, on the other, the most promising are credit spreads. Here, we simply use the measure of credit spread between commercial loans for BAA_t and AAA_t companies. After a number of econometric tests on comovement with business cycles this measure is found to be the

[10] In this chapter deterministic as well as stochastic versions of a dynamic programming algorithm are used (for details, see Gruene and Semmler, 2004, 2005, 2007; Gruene *et al.*, 2008).
[11] The Appendix with a Hamilton–Jacobi–Bellman (HJB) equation to illustrate the non-standard case as well as the algorithm to solve asset prices with state-dependent risk premia are available upon request.
[12] See Keynes (1937, pp. 161–162).

most convincing in indicating the perception of risk. Relative credit spread, measuring risk in economic expansions and contractions, is depicted in Figure 16.1.

A proper measure to study the relation between risk perception and contraction is not the spread itself, but the relative spread $r_t = (BAA_t - AAA_t)/AAA_t$. The magnitude of the relative spread measures the extent to which the risk is perceived at respective economic regimes (Figure 16.1).

We observe clearly that during economic contractions the yield spread between BAA and AAA increases. This reflects that in the period of an economic contraction pessimism overweighs optimism and risk perceptions are increasing, while in the period of a recovery optimism prevails and risk perception and risk premia are decreasing. This observation leads to a hypothesis that the relative spread during the contractions is positive, while the relative spread is negative during the non-contraction periods. To test this hypothesis for the two regimes we separate the total sample according to the National Bureau for Economic Research (NBER) dating of the economic contractions into two subsamples: contraction and non-contraction. Then we estimate the

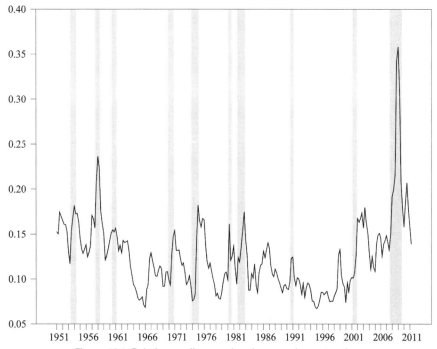

Figure 16.1 Relative credit spread and economic contractions.

average rate of change of the relative spread in the following simple regression model:

$$\Delta r_t = \overline{\Delta r}_c + \varepsilon_t \text{ for } t \text{ during contraction periods} \tag{16.1}$$

$$\Delta r_t = \overline{\Delta r}_{nc} + \varepsilon_t \text{ for } t \text{ during non-contraction periods,} \tag{16.2}$$

where ε_t is the disturbance, and $\overline{\Delta r}_c$ and $\overline{\Delta r}_{nc}$ are the expected rates of change of the relative spread during the contraction and non-contraction periods, respectively. The hypothesis under test is that $\overline{\Delta r}_c > 0$ and $\overline{\Delta r}_{nc} < 0$. We estimate the expected rate of changes of the spread in the two subsamples and test for their opposite signs. The following summarizes the estimation and test results:

$$\overline{\Delta r}_c = 0.10419(2.77253)$$

$$\overline{\Delta r}_{nc} = -0.02066(-2.37366).$$

The two equations above show the estimated mean growth rate of risk premia in the contraction and non-contraction periods, respectively. The numbers in parentheses are the respective t-statistics. The regression result shows that in the 39 quarters of the economic regime of contraction the average rate of change of the relative spread is significantly positive, while the rate of change during the 202 quarters of non-contractions is significantly negative. This implies that during the periods of contraction the risk perception and risk premia are overall increasing, while during the non-contraction periods the risk perception and risk premia are decreasing. Thus, we can observe two distinctive types of risk premia, and thus discount rates, for the two distinctive regimes.

The comovement between the spread and the contraction suggests that the series of the relative spread may be useful in identifying the regime of contraction. If we use a consecutive cumulative increase over 7% within one year as a criterion to characterize the state the economy, this leads to an astonishing correspondence between NBER contraction dating and the state expressed by risk perception and risk premia (Figure 16.2).

The consecutively cumulated increase of the relative spread can identify eight of the total of 10 economic contractions after World War II. We note that there are two outliers according to the 7% criterion. Yet, overall our studies show that the risk perception and risk premia described by the relative spread contains useful information on the regimes of the economy, but not complete information.

Since the relative spread is informative for economic contractions, we want to put the relationship represented by the descriptive statistics above on a more solid model basis. To this

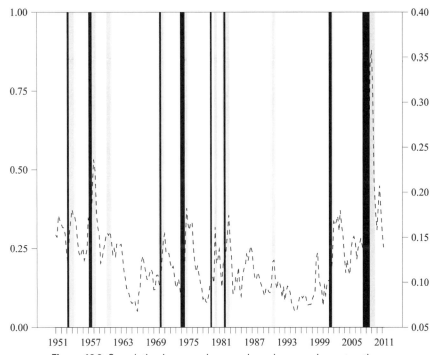

Figure 16.2 Cumulative increase in spreads and economic contractions.

end we fit a Markov switching model to the data.[13] We assume that there are two unobservable states of the economy: contraction and non-contraction. The series of the relative spreads follow an autoregressive process that has two regimes corresponding to the two states and the transition from one state to the other is Markov, i.e. the transition probability depends on the past only through the most recent regime:

$$r_t - \mu_{s_t^*} = \phi_1 \left(r_{t-1} - \mu_{s_{t-1}^*} \right) + \phi_2 \left(r_{t-2} - \mu_{s_{t-2}^*} \right) + \phi_3 \left(r_{t-3} - \mu_{s_{t-3}^*} \right)$$
$$+ \phi_4 \left(r_{t-4} - \mu_{s_{t-4}^*} \right) + \varepsilon_t,$$

(16.3)

with $\varepsilon_t \sim$ i.i.d. $N(0, \sigma^2)$ and with s_t^* presumed to follow a two-state Markov chain process with transition probability p_{ij}^*, $i = 1, 2$ are indicators for non-contraction and contraction, respectively. The maximum likelihood estimation results are presented in Table 16.1.[14]

---

[13] See Hamilton (2005, Chapter 22) for more details of a Markov switching model.

[14] In the estimation of the model we truncate the data series r_t at a maximum of 0.25 in order to avoid the extreme influence of outliers on the estimation.

Table 16.1. Maximum likelihood estimation of parameters for Markov switching model of relative spread (t-statistics in parentheses)

$\hat{\mu}_1 = 0.115$ (32.00)	$\hat{\mu}_2 = 0.152$ (42.45)	$\hat{p}_{11} = 0.96$ (70.87)	$\hat{p}_{22} = 0.74$ (6.18)	$\hat{\sigma}^2 = 0.012$ (19.30)
$\hat{\phi}_1 = 1.178$ (42.15)	$\hat{\phi}_2 = -0.381$ (−13.64)	$\hat{\phi}_3 = 0.066$ (2.48)	$\hat{\phi}_4 = 0.041$ (1.60)	

The inference about the state s_t^* for each period t is obtained by summing the relevant joint probabilities. The probability for s_t^* to be in the state of contraction at period t is calculated:

$$P\left\{s_t^* = 2 \middle| r_t, r_{t-1}, ..., r_{t-4}; \hat{\theta}\right\}$$

$$= \sum_{i=1}^{2} \sum_{j=1}^{2} \sum_{k=1}^{2} \sum_{l=1}^{2} P\left\{s_t^* = 2, s_{t-1}^* = i, s_{t-1}^* = j, s_{t-1}^* \right.$$

$$= k, s_{t-1}^* = l \middle| r_t, r_{t-1}, r_{t-2}..., r_{t-4}; \hat{\theta}\},$$

where $\hat{\theta}$ summarizes all the parameters estimated by the maximum likelihood method. We plot the series of the calculated probability to be in contraction in Figure 16.3. The model fits seven of the nine contractions with a relatively high probability. $p_{11} = 0.96$ indicates that the probability to stay in a non-contraction state is high and the average duration of non-contraction is $1/(1 - p_{11}) = 25$ quarters. The probability to stay in contraction is $p_{22} = 0.74$, which implies an average duration of contraction is $1/(1 - p_{22}) = 4$ quarters.

In Section 16.4 we will employ this information about risk premia in the different regimes, and the regime switching in output and risk premia in a dynamic model with endogenous discount rates. However, before that we want to discuss the standard theory.

16.3 Leveraging, Risk Premia and Asset Prices using Brownian Motions

The traditional model assumes an exogenous stochastic process—a Brownian motion. Traditionally, the asset price is taken as exogenous (see Merton, 1974; Modigliani and Miller, 1958). This model assumes that the capital structure does not

(a)

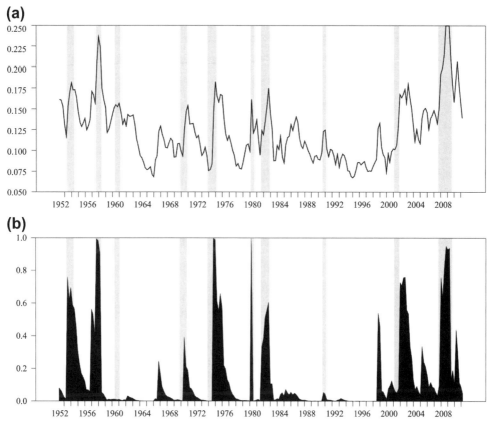

(b)

Figure 16.3 Forecast of the probability of contraction. (a) Relative spread and economic contraction. (b) Probability of economy being in contraction.

affect the firm's asset value. In this tradition the asset value is split up into stocks and bonds, but the asset value is independent of the capital structure.

In the evaluation of firm's debt using option pricing along the line of Merton, (1974), the security price of bonds depends on the value of an underlying asset, the (not observable) asset value of the firm. Following Merton (1974) and defining the value of the firm's asset value by V and the option value of debt by B, we have $B = F(V, t)$. On the maturity date T, one needs to have $V - \overline{B} > 0$, with $\overline{B}$ being the promised payment, otherwise the firm will default. Thus, the debt payment at maturity date T is:

$$F(V, T) = \min(V, \overline{B}),$$

where V is obtained from a Brownian motion. The stochastic process for V can be obtained by using Ito's lemma.[15]

We define as maximum debt capacity $B^* = V$. This will, however, be different for endogenous risk premia where the risk premia may depend on the extent to which the firm is levered. Then, as shown in Section 16.4, we will have $B^* = F(V(B^*))$, which is a more difficult problem to solve.

A practical implementation has been developed that comes with solutions to this problem. The most well-known model of this type is the KMV model,[16] named after the founders Kealhover, McQuown and Vasicek (Keahover, 2003).[17] It models credit risk and the default probability of a firm as follows. The model states that there are three main elements determining the default probability of a firm: (i) The value of assets—the market value of the firm's assets, (ii) the asset risk—the uncertainty or risk of the asset value, and (iii) the leverage—the extent of the firm's contractual liabilities. It is the book value of liabilities relative to the market value of assets.

In our considerations above, the default risk of the firm increases when the value of the assets approaches the book value of the liabilities. The firm defaults when the market value of the assets is smaller than the book value of the liabilities. Not all the firms that reach the point where the asset value goes below the book value of their liabilities default. There are many that continue and serve their debt. The reason for this can be found in the long-term liabilities that enable the firms to continue their business until the debt becomes due. The firms may also have credit lines at their disposal, which may vary with lending standards.

Crosbie and Bohn (2003) show that the default point, i.e. the asset value at which the firm will default, generally lies somewhere between total liabilities and short-term liabilities. The relevant net worth of the firm is therefore defined as:

$$[\text{Market Net Worth}] = [\text{Market Value of Assets}]$$
$$- [\text{Default Point}]. \quad (16.4)$$

If the market net worth of a firm is zero, the firm is assumed to default. To measure the default risk, one can combine all three elements determining the default probability in a single measure

---

[15] See Merton (1974) and Schoenbucher (2006, Chapter 9).

[16] For more details on the KMV model, see Semmler (2011, Chapter 19).

[17] See Footnote 9. A further practical method of computing firm value is proposed in Benninga (1998, Chapters 2 and 3).

of default risk, the Distance-to-Default:

$$[\text{Distance-to-Default}] = \frac{[\text{Market Net Worth}]}{[\text{Size of One Standard Deviation of the Asset Value}]} \quad (16.5)$$

$$= \frac{[\text{Market Value of Assets}] - [\text{Default Point}]}{[\text{Asset Volatility}]}. \quad (16.6)$$

The Distance-to-Default is the number of standard deviations the asset value is away from default. The default probability can then be computed directly from the Distance-to-Default if the probability distribution of the asset value is known. For an illustration, see Figure 16.4.[18]

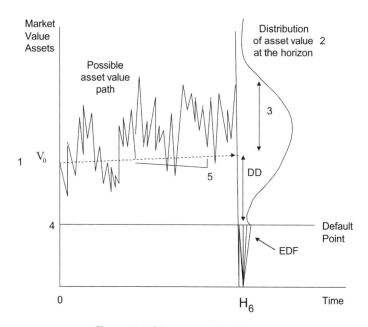

Figure 16.4 Distance-to-Default model.

[18] Crosbie and Bohn (2003) give six variables that determine the default probability of a firm over some horizon, from now until time H (see figure 16.4): (1) The current asset value, (2) the distribution of the asset value at time H, (3) the volatility of the future assets value at time H, (4) the level of the default point, i.e. the book value of the liabilities, (5) the expected rate of growth in the asset value over the horizon and (6) the length of the horizon, H.

Those relationships can be developed in quantitative terms. According to the Merton and the Black–Scholes models, the market value of the firm's underlying assets is described by the following stochastic process:

$$dV_A = \mu V_A dt + \sigma_A V_A dz, \qquad (16.7)$$

where V_A and dV_A are the firm's asset value and change in asset value, μ and σ_A are the firm's asset value drift rate and volatility, and dz is the increment of a Wiener process. The probability of default that the market value of the firm's assets will be less than the book value of the firm's liabilities by the time the debt matures:

$$
\begin{aligned}
p_t &= \Pr[V_A^t \leq X_t | V_A^0 = V_A] \\
&= \Pr[\ln V_A^t \leq \ln X_t | V_A^0 = V_A],
\end{aligned} \qquad (16.8)
$$

where p_t is the probability of default by time t, V_A^t is the market value of the firm's assets at time t and X_t is the book value of the firm's liabilities due at time t. The change in the value of the firm's assets is described by (16.8), so the value at time t, V_A^t, given that the value at time 0 is V_A, is:

$$\ln V_A^t = \ln V_A + \left(\mu - \frac{\sigma_A^2}{2}\right)t + \sigma_A \sqrt{t}\varepsilon, \qquad (16.9)$$

where μ is the expected return on the firm's asset and ε is the random component of the firm's return. Equation (16.9) describes the asset value path shown in Figure 16.4. Combining (16.8) and (16.9), one can write the probability of default as:

$$p_t = \Pr\left[\ln V_A + \left(\mu - \frac{\sigma_A^2}{2}\right)t + \sigma_A \sqrt{t}\varepsilon \leq \ln X_t\right], \qquad (16.10)$$

or:

$$p_t = \Pr\left[-\frac{\ln\dfrac{V_A}{X_t} + \left(\mu - \dfrac{\sigma_A^2}{2}\right)t}{\sigma_A\sqrt{t}} \geq \varepsilon\right]. \qquad (16.11)$$

Since the Black-Scholes model assumes that ε is normally distributed, one can write the default probability as:

$$p_t = N\left[-\frac{\ln\dfrac{V_A}{X_t} + \left(\mu - \dfrac{\sigma_A^2}{2}\right)t}{\sigma_A\sqrt{t}}\right].$$

Since the Distance-to-Default measure is nothing else than the number of standard deviations that the firm is away from default, one can write this measure with the Black–Scholes notation as:

$$[\text{Distance-to-Default}] = \frac{\ln \frac{V_A}{X_t} + \left(\mu - \frac{\sigma_A^2}{2}\right)t}{\sigma_A \sqrt{t}}. \qquad (16.12)$$

In practice, this Distance-to-Default measure is adjusted to include several other factors that play a role in measuring the default probability.

From the Distance-to-Default we also can obtain the risk premium:[19]

$$r_b = r^f + \left(r_{V_A} - r^f\right)N(1 - DD\sigma_e)b, \qquad (16.13)$$

with DD the Distance-to-Default, σ_e expressing the volatility of the equity of the firm and r_{V_A} the return on the asset of the firm. Note that the equation reveals that the smaller the distance to default, the greater will be the spread and the risk premium for the firm on the bond market. Yet, the asset value of the firm and its volatility is given exogenously.

Overall, we want to stress that although the value approach to default risk and asset value is theoretically intriguing, it might be empirically difficult to estimate firm value. Theoretically, it appears to be more sound to build up an asset pricing model by determining the asset value endogenously using a dynamic decision model rather than formulating the asset price dynamics as Brownian motion. This will be done next, using results of Section 16.2.

16.4 Discount Rates, Risk Premia and Asset Prices in a Dynamic Model

As the above citation from Cochrane (2011) indicated, risk premia can be taken as a proxy for discount rates. Discount rates are high when risk premia are high and asset prices are low, and thus when expected returns are high.

Given a stochastic discount factor m_{t+1} we can write for an asset price:

---

[19] For the derivation, see Chou (2005).

$$p_t = E_t m_{t+1}(p_{t+1} + d_{t+1}),$$

where p_t is the asset price at time t and $E_t m_{t+1}(p_{t+1} + d_{t+1})$ is the discounted expected payoff, with p_{t+1} the asset price at period $t+1$ and d_{t+1} the dividend payment. The issue is what is a good model for the discount rate.

Taking the log on both sides we can approximately write:

$$\ln p_t - \ln(p_{t+1} + d_{t+1}) = \ln E_t m_{t+1}.$$

We could argue along the line of Araujo and Issler (2004) that any factor (or factors) modeling the dynamics of the left-hand side of the above equation can serve as a discount factor.[20] Thus, it does not have to be the growth rate of marginal utilities as derived from the consumption capital asset pricing model (CCAPM) to give us the stochastic discount factor.[21]

Following the reasoning of Cochrane (2011, p. 23) that "'Discount rate,' 'risk premium' and 'expected return' are all the same thing" we take the risk premia as a proxy for the discount rates. As we have shown in Section 16.2 risk premia, proxying discount rates, may follow regime switsches and large swings and thus they might not be very smooth.

One theoretical approach to justify this in terms of theory maybe Bernanke *et al.* (1999). They make the risk premium endogenous by making risk dependent on net worth of the borrower, as collateral for borrowing. Uncollateralized borrowing is assumed to pay a larger premium than collateralized borrowing or self-financing. In this context, the premium arises from the threat of bankruptcy, i.e. by the cost constituted by auditing, accounting, legal costs, as well as loss of assets arising from asset liquidation.[22]

---

[20] Note that here we have a discrete-time model, therefore we refer to the discount factor. Araujo and Issler (2004) use a linear combination of different asset returns to explain the discount factor. Using a simplification in their derivations, the discount factor is equal to the mean return plus the half of the variance of the asset return—higher variance raises the discount rate, a standard result. Their approach does not depend on any parametric assumptions about preferences, as usual estimations of the stochastic discount factors (SDF) have to do, and there is no risk of mis-specification in choosing an inappropriate functional form for the estimation of the SDF. Thus a major benefit of their approach is that they are able to study intertemporal asset pricing without using consumption data. For another way to largely bypass consumption data, see the application of loss aversion to asset pricing in Gruene and Semmler (2009).

[21] The CCAPM assumes that $m_{t+1} = \beta u'(c_{t+1})u'(c_t) > 0$, where the latter is the growth rate of marginal utility from consumption and β is the subjective discount rate.

[22] This literature originates in the seminal work by Townsend (1979).

Empirically, in terms of observable variables, we suggest to use the results of Section. 16.2, i.e. the empirical data on credit spreads, presuming that the spread is arising from some risk premia as evaluated by the financial market.[23] Such premia drive a wedge between the expected return of the borrower and the risk-free interest rate. The premium is likely to be positively related to the default cost and inversely related to the borrower's, net worth. Net worth is defined as the firm's collateral value of the (illiquid) capital stock less the agent's outstanding obligations.

One way to formalize this is to follow Bernanke *et al.* (1999) and to measure the inverse relationship between the risk premium (default premium) and net worth in a function such as:

$$H(k(t), B(t))) = \frac{\alpha_1}{\left(\alpha_2 + \dfrac{N(t)}{k(t)}\right)^{\mu}} \, \theta B(t), \qquad (16.14)$$

where $H(k(t), B(t))$ represents the risk premium, depending on net worth, $N(t) = k(t) - B(t)$, with $k((t)$ as capital stock and $B(t)$ as debt. The parameters are $\alpha_1, \alpha_2, \mu > 0$ and θ is the risk-free interest rate. In the analytical and numerical study of the model below we presume that the risk premium will be zero for $N(t) = k(t)$ and thus, in the limit, for $B(t) = 0$, the borrowing rate is the risk-free rate. Borrowing at a risk-free rate will be considered here as a benchmark case.[24] Note that we want to employ here a monotonic function for the risk premia as proxy for the discount rate, and not just two-state risk premia and discount rates as we would get from Section 16.2. Although the risk premium and discount rate as above stated are also state dependent, but they do not jump, as they would do, following our regime change model of Section 16.2. Our simplification here is done because of computational reasons.

Next, we first specify a dynamic model of a firm with constant discount rate. Here, we focus on the firm's intertemporal optimal investment where debt can be continuously issued and retired. In each period the firm does not have to pay attention to the maturity structure of its debt and it does not face one period

---

[23] As Gomes *et al* (2002) show for a large class of models one can expect the external finance premium indeed to be equal to the premium necessary to compensate lenders for the default risk. Gomes *et al* (2002) measure the default risk by the spread of corporate bonds and T-bills. Another proxy is the relative size of external finance to capital, see Gomes *et al.* (2002).

[24] Another way to state the risk premium, and thus the risk structure of interest rates if there is debt with different maturity, is $R(\tau) - \theta$ with $R(\tau)$ the yield to maturity τ, see Merton (1974). Hereby $R(\tau)$ is then implicitly defined as $e^{-R(\tau)\tau} = F(V, \tau)/\overline{B}$.

borrowing constraints. Yet, there can be intertemporal debt constraints. If the interest rate $\theta = H(k, B)/B$ is constant, we have a benchmark case and it is easy to see that the asset value, $V(k)$, is in fact the present value of k:

$$V(k) = \underset{j}{\text{Max}} \int_0^\infty e^{-\theta t} f(k(t), j(t)) dt, \qquad (16.15)$$

$$\dot{k}(t) = j(t) - \sigma k(t), \quad k(0) = k, \qquad (16.16)$$

$$\dot{B}(t) = \theta B - f(k(t), j(t)), \quad B(0) = B_0. \qquad (16.17)$$

The firm's net income:

$$f(k, j) = ak^\alpha - j - j^\beta k^{-\gamma}, \qquad (16.18)$$

is generated from capital stock, through a production function, Ak^α, and investment, j, is undertaken so as to maximize the present value of net income of Equation (16.15) given the adjustment cost of capital $\varphi(k, j) = j^\beta k^{-\gamma}$. Note that $\sigma > 0, \alpha > 0, \beta > 1, \gamma > 0$, are constants. Equation (16.16) represents the equation for capital accumulation and Equation (16.17) the evolution of debt of the firm. Since net income in (16.18) can be negative, the temporary budget constraint requires further borrowing from credit markets and if there is positive net income debt can be retired.[25] For $k(0)$ and $B(0)$, the initial value of k and B. For any value of debt, B, below $B^* = V$, it holds that $V - B > 0$ and the residual remains as equity of the firm.

A more complicated case arises when the risk premia and discount rates are endogenous as given by Equation (16.14). Employing the above measure of finance or risk premia, as proxy for discount rates, we can now study the following constrained dynamic decision problem of the firm:

$$\dot{k}(t) = j(t) - \sigma k(t), \quad k(0) = k, \qquad (16.19)$$

$$\dot{B}(t) = H(k(t), B(t)) - f(k(t), j(t)), B(0) = B_0. \qquad (16.20)$$

As above in Equation (16.20), we assume now that the risk premium $H(k, B)$ is state dependent, depending on the capital stock k and the level of debt B with $H_k < 0$ and $H_B > 0$.

Our more general model (16.19)–(16.20) represents a decision problem of a firm facing a risk premium. The problem to be

---

[25] The model can also be interpreted as written in efficiency labor, therefore σ can represent the sum of the capital depreciation rate, and rate of exogenous technical change. Note that a consumption stream could be included, see Gruene *et al.* (2004).

solved is how to compute $V(k)$, thus the more general case when there is an endogenous risk premium as proxy for the discount rate. Pontryagin's maximum principle is not suitable to solve the problem with endogenous risk premium and endogenous net worth, and we thus need to use special numerical methods to solve for the present value and investment strategy of a levered firm.

This turns out to be a controllability problem. The issue is now at what investment strategy and endogenous risk premia do the trajectories stay within a bounded set?[26] Employing our general form of a risk premium[27] $H(k, B) \geq \theta B$, the creditworthiness $B^*(k)$ relates to the asset value of the firm for $B(t) \leq B^*(k(t))$ as follows. Consider the equation:

$$\dot{B} = H(k, B) - f(k, j).$$

Multiplying by $e^{-\theta t}$ and using partial integration we find

$$\int_0^T e^{-\theta t} f(k, j) dt = B(0) - e^{-\theta T} B(T) + \int_0^T e^{-\theta t} (H - \theta B) dt.$$

Let us define the present value of the external finance premium, with initial value (k, B), by:

$$\int_0^\infty e^{-\theta t} (H - \theta B) dt = V_H(k, B),$$

where we use the optimal investment rate j. Then for $T \to \infty$ we find:

$$V(k) = B(0) - \lim e^{-\theta T} B(T) + V_H(k, B).$$

Note that we permit $B(t)$ to be negative. The term $V_H(k, B)$ would be equal to zero for the case $H(k, B) = \theta B$.[28]

In particular, if $B(0) = B^*(k)$ we have:

$$V(k) = B^*(k) + V_H(k, B^*(k)).$$

---

[26] Our numerical procedure, and an example, for a simple case of a state-dependent risk premium, using the HJB equation, is given in, an unpublished Appendix available upon request.

[27] For more details of the subsequent derivations, see Gruene et al. (2004).

[28] Note that in practice the discount rate θ is often approximated by taking a weighted average cost of capital (WACC) composed of the weighted average of equity return and bond return, see Benninga (2000, Chapter 2).

We want to point out how to compute $V(k)$ and its component parts. We can use the above statement to compute the solution to the optimal investment problem. (i) Compute $B^*(k)$, thereby find the optimal path $(k(t), B(t))$ that satisfies $B(t) = B^*(k(t))$. (ii) Compute:

$$V_H(k, B) = \int_0^\infty e^{-\theta t}(H(k(t), B(t)) - \theta B(t))dt.$$

(iii) Compute:

$$V(k) = B^*(k) + V_H(k, B^*(k)). \qquad (16.21)$$

In sum, the above three steps allow us to compute the creditworthiness, for the case of $H(k, B^*(k))$, the creditworthiness will be less than $V(k)$. However, as we will show, the firm's asset value may also be affected by the risk premium.

16.5 Results of the Numerical Study

Next, we present numerical results for our debt control problem obtained for our case with a risk-free interest rate and the case of a default premium. For both cases we specify the firm's technology parameters to be the same i.e. $\sigma = 0.15$, $a = 0.29$, $\alpha = 0.7$, $\beta = 2$, $\gamma = 0.3$ and $\theta = 0.1$. The distinct results that we obtain should therefore solely arise from the issuance of the firm's risky debt.

16.5.1 Deterministic case: Debt and asset value

In our benchmark case, debt is issued, but with zero default premium paid by the firm, so that we have as credit cost $H(k, B) = \theta B$. In this case we can use the dynamic programming algorithm to solve the problem (16.15)—(16.18). Figure 16.5 shows the corresponding optimal value function representing the present value curve, $V(k)$. The present value curve represents the asset value of the firm for initial conditions $k(0)$.

There is no impact of the a regime-dependent risk premium on the asset value, and thus the firm is creditworthy whenever debt is bounded by the firm's asset value, so that we have $V - B \geq 0$. The optimal investment strategy is not constrained and thus the asset value V, which represents the maximum debt capacity B^*, is obtained by a solution for an unconstrained optimal investment strategy, represented by the value function in Figure 16.5.

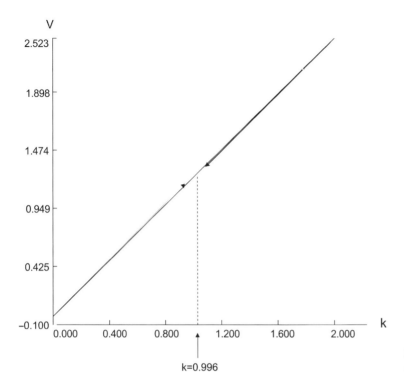

Figure 16.5 Asset price at constant interest rate.

Figure 16.5 also implies a sequence of investment decisions, in a neighborhood of the threshold for the given initial capital stock. We denote, with k^+ ($= 0.996$), the steady state. Investment of a firm to the left of k^+ is lower than σk and makes the capital stock shrink, whereas investment of a firm to the right of k^+ is larger than σk and lets the capital stock increase.

For the model with a risk premium (16.14), proxying the discount rate, i.e. net worth, is now an additional constraint on the optimization problem. Equation (16.14) represents different alternative variants for the risk premium. The steepness of the risk premium is defined by the parameter α_2. For the above risk premium (16.14) we specify $\mu = 2$. The limit case should be the risk-free interest rate: Thus $\alpha_1/(\alpha_2 + 1)^2 = 1$ for $\alpha_1 = (\alpha_2 + 1)^2$. Note that for $\alpha_2 \to \infty$ one obtains $H(k, B) = \theta B$.

Figure 16.6 shows the respective present value curves $V(k) = B^*(k) + V_H(k, B)$ for $\alpha_2 = 100, 10, 1, \sqrt{2} - 1$ (from top to bottom) and the corresponding $\alpha_1 = (\alpha_2 + 1)^2$.

For $\alpha_2 = 100$ firm's asset value, the trajectory for $V(k)$ is almost the same as in Figure 16.5, for a constant interest rate. Then, for the other trajectories it holds that the asset value is smaller the larger the risk premia. The debt capacity curve, B^*,

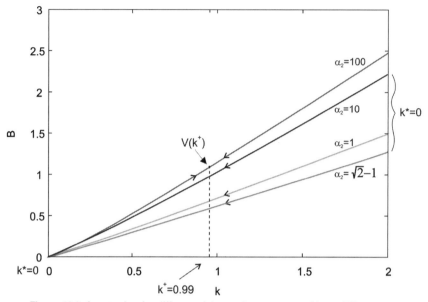

Figure 16.6 Asset price for different risk premia, represented by a different α_2.

moves down due to greater default risk and it becomes optimal to decrease the capital to zero. Thus, Figure 16.6 shows, as predicted in Section 16.4, the maximum claim to the firm $V(k)$ moves down with a higher risk premium (16.14), which gives rise to a larger loss $V_H(k, B^*)$ in Equation (16.21).

Decreasing α_2 in (16.14)—higher risk premium—we compute the component parts of $V(k)$. In Table 16.2, the values are given for $k_0 = 2$. The last row represents the $V(k)$ for linear function θB, the other rows represent the case $H(k, B)$. There is a considerable loss in asset value due to a rising risk premia and discount rate: if the risk premium becomes larger, $V_H(k, B^*(k))$ rises, reducing available asset value for collateral; the asset value $V(k)$ itself is reduced.

Thus, the asset value of the capital stock that can be divided up into bond and equity value is reduced. For any actual $B(k)$ here it

Table 16.2. Numerical results

α_2	100	10	$\sqrt{2}-1$
$V_H(k, B^*(k))$	0.041	0.274	1.140
$B^*(k)$	2.477	2.214	1.273
$V(k)$	2.518	2.488	2.410
$V(k)$ for θB	2.523	2.523	2.523

Table 16.3. Increase of risk premia versus. decrease of value V

α_2	Increase of interest rate (%)	Decrease of V (%)
100	1.24	0.16
50	2.45	0.20
10	11.67	1.38
3	30.55	5.51

holds again that the value of stocks is $S(k) = V(k) - B(k)$, but asset value itself is reduced. The reduction of a firm's asset value in those cases comes from the fact that firms now face a constrained optimization problem, through which, since their sequence of optimal investment strategy is constrained, asset value is reduced.[29]

Note, however, that the dependence between all these values is highly non-linear. In order to give an intuition about the relationship between these quantities, for selected values of α_2 and $k = 2$ in Table 16.3 we show the increase of the interest rate i.e., the relation $H(k, B)/(\theta B)$ and the decrease of the value $V(k)$.

Table 16.3 shows the numerical results on the percentage fall in value $V(k)$ with an increase of risk premia, for a fixed value of the capital stock $k = 2$. The percent increase in interest rate of 1.24% in Table 16.3, for example, means that the default risk causes the interest rate to rise from $\theta = 0.1$, the risk-free interest rate, to $H(k, B) = 0.1124$, causing a fall of the asset value of the firm by 0.16 %. The cases shown in Table 16.3 represent, for example, an increase of the risk premium from $\alpha_2 = \infty$ with a credit cost $\theta = 0.1$, to $\alpha_2 = 3$, with a credit cost of 0.13055. Yet, in the latter case the asset value of the firm is predicted to fall by 5.51%.

Overall, if there is a sudden regime shift, as we have discussed in Section 16.2, let us say from the case of $\alpha_2 = 100$ to $\alpha_2 = 3$ and thus a considerable rise of the risk premium (and discount rate), asset value will not only be lost, but a larger fraction will have to be paid out as dead weight loss for risk premia.[30]

---

[29] Note that this effect could not be seen in Merton (1974) and Modigliani and Miller (1958), since the firm's asset value in their studies is exogenously given.

[30] As we can see, this could set in motion a vicious cycle on risk premium, discount rates and asset value—an important issue not only for firms, but also for bank and sovereign borrowing.

16.5.2 The Stochastic case: Probability of default and asset value

Next, we will elaborate on an extension that brings our model of asset valuation on debt dynamics closer to empirical work and the KMV as discussed in Section 16.3. The main extension we undertake here pertains to a stochastic feature of our model. The stochastic version of our model can be written, with additive disturbances, as:

$$\dot{k}(t) = (j(t) - \sigma k(t))\mathrm{d}t + \delta_k k(t)\mathrm{d}w(t), \qquad (16.22)$$

$$\dot{B}(t) = (H(k(t), B(t))) - f(k(t), j(t))\mathrm{d}t, \qquad (16.23)$$

where $H(k(t), B(t))$ is defined as Equation (16.14), δ_k is the standard deviation and $\mathrm{d}w(t)$ is the increment in Brownian motion. With $\delta_k = 0$ we recover the deterministic dynamics (16.19) and (16.20). The problem of asset and debt valuation as well as the controllability problem then becomes to steer the system (16.22) and (16.23) to the set $B \leq 0$, i.e. to debt bounded in the long run. We use again our standard parameters of Sections 16.5.1 and 16.5.2, but $\alpha_2 = 100$, $\alpha_1 = (\alpha_2 + 1)^2$ and $\mu = 2$.

Figure 16.7 shows the numerical results for $\delta_k = 0.1$ and 0.5. The case $\delta_k = 0$ corresponds to our deterministic version of Section 16.5.1, where the probability of no controllability and thus bankruptcy is just 0 or 1. As Figure 16.7 shows in the stochastic cases $\delta_k = 0.1$ and $\delta_k = 0.5$ the line of critical debt B^* moves down, i.e. debt capacity without going bankrupt shrinks and a non-zero probability of going bankrupt arises earlier. Overall, the stochastic model (16.22) and (16.23) demonstrates

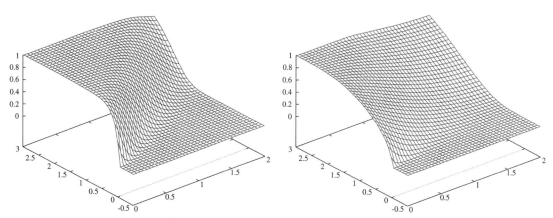

Figure 16.7 Numerically determined probabilities for $\delta_k = 0.1$ (left) and $\delta_k = 0.5$ (right).

the economic intuition that in a stochastic environment the likelihood of bankruptcy increases due to unexpected negative income shocks and shrinking creditworthiness.[31]

16.5.3 Implications for bond and equity premium

This last section expresses more of a conjecture on asset pricing and credit derivatives. If there is a feedback effect of credit and default risk on asset pricing, as we have shown above, then the value of the underlying asset for credit derivatives and the equity premium, which is usually studied under the assumption of all-equity finance, is likely to be affected. According to the line of research, starting with Merton (1974), on the pricing of firms' debt, the default premia for commercial bonds arise from two factors. One factor is the ratio of the discounted promised payments $\overline{B}$, at the date of maturity, to the value of the assets and the other is the volatility of the asset, δ_A. Let τ be the time to maturity, we then have according to this literature:

$$B(V, \tau) = \overline{B}e^{-\theta\tau}\phi(d, \delta_A, \tau), \qquad (16.24)$$

where $\phi(d, \delta_A, \tau)$ is a function of d, δ_A and τ, with $d = \overline{B}e^{-\theta\tau}/V$ and δ_A the volatility of the value of the underlying asset. Summarizing this in one term, in $R(\tau)\tau$, the yield of the bond, given by the right-hand side of (24), we have:

$$e^{-R(\tau)\tau}\overline{B} = B(V, \tau). \qquad (16.25)$$

Equations (16.24) and (16.25) show[32] the relation of the value of the bond and the bond premium. As we have shown, both the value and volatility of the assets of firms are not independent of the default risk of bonds. Our deterministic and stochastic model of Section 16.5.2 of asset value and debt valuation suggests the conjecture that there is thus a considerable extent to which the risk premium affects the asset value, the equity price and the equity premium.

The problem has been addressed empirically in a thorough study by Vassalou and Xing (2003). They show that although previous empirical studies of the effect of default risk on equity returns were not conclusive, their new study computes default likelihood indicators measuring default probabilities and relates these to equity returns. Although, in general, as one would expect,

---

[31] Further elaborations on a stochastic model, but with more heterogeneity among firms, with correlated risk and default correlation can be found in Gruene *et al.* (2008).
[32] For details, see Merton (1974) and the empirical application in Duan *et al.* (2004).

the relationship needs to be conditioned on firm size and book-to-market value ratios, their study shows that default risk indeed has a quantitatively important effect on asset prices and equity returns.[33] Those issues may, however, be subject to future research.

16.6 Conclusions

In this chapter, we study in a MRSM the interaction between growth regimes and default risk and risk premia that are tied to some macroeconomic fundamentals. Following Cochrane (2011), we hereby obtain a proxy for the regime switch of discount rates. Firms, as they are set up here, can borrow and leverage their activities, and can face a default arising from losing their credit-worthiness and thus face a state-dependent risk premium. We start with a Merton-type model where the asset price is given exogenously through a Brownian motion, demonstrated in the KMV model. We then build on a production-oriented asset pricing model and we show that leveraging impacts the firm's risk premia (and discount rates) and the firm's asset value. If risk premia, debt capacity (creditworthiness) and asset value are endogenous, then the asset value of firms cannot be taken as exogenous when securities such as stocks and bonds are priced. We use computational methods to solve the intertemporal decision problem and to compute the asset value of firms with endogenous risk premia. We also explore the impact of different shapes of the risk premium function, as proxy for discount rates, on firm value and creditworthiness. We employ numerical methods and a set-oriented algorithm[34] to solve the complicated dynamics of the asset value of the firm. We also extend the model to a stochastic version where we show, as in the KMV model, that the probability of default increases when the firm moves closer to its borrowing capacity.

Our study suggests not only implications for the issue of the equity premium puzzle, but also for monetary policy. As many researchers have recently argued, monetary authorities should, beside focusing on inflation and output, also consider asset markets. The movement of risk premia—and possible regime switsches of them—are crucial for monetary policy. If interest rates are reduced, this, in principle, moves down the risk

---

[33] Other studies find a strong relationship between firm-level volatility and cross-sectional variation in bond yield, see Campbell and Taksler (2003).

[34] For details, see Grune *et al.* (2008).

structure of interest rates and this might improve the willingness to lend by banks and to purchase risky asset by investors. Yet, if at the same time the perception of default risk increases and asset prices fall, as the interest rate decreases, the expected positive effect on financial market and real activity will not arise, but one might rather observe adverse effects in real and financial markets.[35]

References

Benninga, S., 2000. Financial Modeling. Cambridge, MIT Press, MA.

Bernanke, B., Gertler, M., Gilchrist, S., 1999. In: Taylor, J., Woodford, M. (Eds.), The financial accelerator in a quantitative business cycle framework. Handbook of Macroeconomics, Volume 1. Amsterdam, North-Holland, pp. 1341–1393.

Bernanke, B., 2007. Speeches of the Governor of the Federal Reserve System. US Federal Reserve, Washington, DC. www.federalreserve.gov.

Campbell, J., Taksler, G.B., 2003. Equity volatility and corporate bond yields. Journal of Finance 58, 2321–2350.

Chen, L.P., Collin-Dufresne, Goldstein, R.S., 2006. On the relation between the credit spread puzzle and the Equity Premium Puzzle. State University of Michigan, East Lancing, MI.

Cochrane, J., 2011. Presidential Address: Discount Rates. University of Chicago, Chicago, IL.

Crosbie, P., Bohn, J., 2003. Modeling Default Risk. Moody's, New York. http://www.modyskmv.com.

Duan, J.C., Gauthier, G., Simonato, J., Zaanoun, S., 2002. Estimating Merton's model by maximum likelihood with survivorship consideration. working paper. Rotman School of Management. University of Toronto, Toronto.

Gomes, J.F., Yaron, A., Zhang, L., 2002. Asset pricing implications of firms financing constraints, working paper, The Wharton School. University of Pennsylvania.

Gruene, L., Semmler, W., Sieveking, M., 2004. Creditworthiness and thresholds in a credit market model with multiple equilibria. Economic Theory 25, 287–315.

Gruene, L., Semmler, W., 2004. Using dynamic programming with adaptive grid scheme for optimal control problems in economics. Journal of Economic Dynamics and Control 28, 2427–2456.

Gruene, L., Semmler, W., 2005. Default risk, asset pricing, and debt control. Journal of Financial Econometrics 3, 79–106.

Gruene, L., Semmler, W., 2007. Asset pricing with dynamic programming, Computational Economics. (Special issue on Advances in Asset Pricing and Dynamic Portfolio Decisions) 29 (3–4), 233–265.

Gruene, L., Semmler, W., Bernard, L., 2008. Firm value, diversified capital assets and credit Risk: Towards a theory default correlation. Journal of Credit Risk 3, 81–109.

---

[35] This is a situation that the US Federal Reserve faced in the second half of 2007 and the beginning of 2008, see Bernanke (2007) and this is also the situation that the European Central Bank in the European Union faced in the years 2011–2012.

Hamilton, J.D., 2005. Time Series Analysis. Princeton University Press, Princeton, NJ.

Kealhofer, H., 2003. Quantifying credit risk I, default prediction. Financial Analyst Journal, January/February, 30–43.

Keynes, J.M., 1967. The General Theory of Employment, Interest and Money. Macmillan, London.

Merton, R.C., 1974. On the pricing of corporate debt: the risk structure of interest rates. Journal of Finance 2, 449–470.

Semmler, W., 2011. Asset Prices, Booms and Recessions. Springer. New York.

Semmler, W., Sieveking, M., 2000. Critical debt and debt dynamics. Journal of Economic Dynamics and Control 24, 1121–1144.

Sieveking, M., Semmler, W., 1997. The present value of resources with large discount rates. Applied Mathematics and Optimization 35, 283–309.

Townsend, R., 1979. Optimal contracts and competitive Markets with costly state verification. Journal of Economic Theory 21, 265–293.

Vassalou, M., Xing, Y., 2004. Default risk in equity return. Journal of Finance LIX (2), 831–868.

A REVIEW OF MARKET RISK MEASURES AND COMPUTATION TECHNIQUES

Kasirga Yildirak* and Cumhur Ekinci**

*Trakya University, **Istanbul Technical University

CHAPTER OUTLINE

17.1 Introduction

Market risk is a major concern for all types of traders and investors. This chapter concisely presents the widely used risk measures and the way they are implemented, particularly in the banking industry. Market risk refers to the risk of financial assets whose prices are determined exogenously in financial markets. If an instrument is held until maturity, then it is not subject to market risk.

There are various concerns and criticisms in measuring market risk. These include the choice of the appropriate holding period, backtesting issues, the problems with association measures, reporting and putting limits on trading activities, and so forth. Any other question brings a new assumption into the risk model, causing the model to drift from reality. This raises an even bigger concern. In reality, is the cash amount reported by

Rethinking Valuation and Pricing Models. http://dx.doi.org/10.1016/B978-0-12-415875-7.00017-8

the risk calculation a value or just a kind of index helping managers develop a rough idea on their risky positions? Apparently, we need some additional mapping effort or a fine-tuning for the reported risk value to reflect the real amount of money to be lost.

This chapter focuses on the most popular definitions of risk and risk computation methods as well as the technical details practitioners have to consider, through specific examples.

17.2 Market Risk, Portfolio Value and Returns

Market risk is the term for defining the uncertainty associated with future changes of the portfolio value,[1] mostly in monetary terms. The change in the portfolio value, profit and loss (P&L), is the difference between the current value (at time t) of the portfolio and its future value (at time $t + h$), where h is the *holding period*, discounted to time t. The length of the holding period usually is one day, one week, 10 days, one month or one year. The reporting frequency and horizon vary depending on the type of portfolio. In banking, daily measures are common, and there are shorter holding periods such as one, five or 10 days. For portfolio management companies, both the reporting frequency and the holding period are around one month.

Risk is associated with the variations in portfolio value. Hence, we start by defining these variations and returns in mathematical terms.

The value of a portfolio at time t, PV_t, is defined as follows:

$$PV_t = \Phi_{1,t}S_{1,t} + \Phi_{2,t}S_{2,t} + \ldots + \Phi_{n,t}S_{n,t},$$

where $\Phi_{i,t}$ is the *amount* and $S_{i,t}$ is the *value* of the ith instrument in the portfolio at time t. The total amount $\Phi_{i,t}S_{i,t}$ is known as the *position* associated with the ith instrument at time t. Likewise, the *realized value* of the portfolio at the end of the holding period (i.e. at time $t + h$) is the linear combination of the positions:

$$PV_{t+h} = \Phi_{1,t+h}S_{1,t+h} + \Phi_{2,t+h}S_{2,t+h} + \ldots + \Phi_{m,t+h}S_{m,t+h}.$$

As seen from the equation, there are three uncertain items at time $t + h$: Amounts, asset values, and number of financial instruments kept within and/or added to the portfolio. This creates a

---

[1] Although market risk is not limited to portfolios, our focus point will be the portfolio rather than individual assets throughout this chapter.

higher-dimensional problem for risk engineers. Traditional risk measures assume that amount Φ and assets that constitute the portfolio at time t remain the same during the holding period. Under these assumptions, the realized value of the portfolio at time $t + h$ becomes:

$$PV_{t+h} = \Phi_{1,t}S_{1,t+h} + \Phi_{2,t}S_{2,t+h} + \ldots + \Phi_{n,t}S_{n,t+h}.$$

Discounted portfolio value at time t, DPV_t, is obtained by discounting PV_{t+h} with continuously compounded *risk-free rate* of h-day (alternatively h-month or h-year) maturity, $f(t,t+h)$ (see Alexander, 2009). For $t = 0$, this is usually the observed spot money market rate (Libor) with h-day maturity, $r(h)$:

$$DPV_t(h) = PV_{t+h}e^{-r(h)\cdot\left(\frac{h}{360}\right)}.$$

Profit and/or loss value, ΔPV_t, is then the difference between the discounted value and the current value of the portfolio:

$$\Delta PV_t(h) = DPV_t(h) - PV_t.$$

As the mathematics and the interpretation of returns have advantages over change in levels, financial computations are done generally in terms of returns. First, return is a better tool for comparing the performance of two or more assets. Moreover, statistical assumptions such as identicalness, independency or normality are easier to assign to returns than to levels. In terms of return,[2] R, the change in the portfolio value, for an h-day holding period is represented as:

$$\Delta PV_t(h) = R(h) * PV_t,$$

where:

$$R(h) = \frac{DPV_t(h) - PV_t}{PV_t}.$$

Market risk computations for the banking industry usually do not take discounted value into consideration, as the holding period is too small to deal with. Then, the h-day actual return becomes:

$$R(h) = \frac{PV_{t+h} - PV_t}{PV_t}.$$

[2] Notice that these are "excess" returns.

Since the mathematics is easier in continuous time, the actual return is approximated by logarithmic return:

$$R(h) = \log\left(\frac{PV_{t+h}}{PV_t}\right).$$

Again, this is not harmful since h is chosen to be very small in the banking system.

For the rest of this chapter, $R(h)$ will represent the h-day return independent of how it is computed.

17.3 Market Risk Factors and Portfolio Value

Market risk factors, denoted by f_k, with $k = 1, 2, \ldots, K$, showing each factor, are the underlying elements that determine the market price or value of a financial product, e.g. interest rate, commodities, foreign currencies, assets or indices (for derivative instruments).[3] For instance, the value of a cross-currency swap is a function of the spot price of the currencies that are swapped and the spot interests of these currencies for given maturities, the price of a bond is a function of interest rate, and so on. On the other hand, the prices of some products such as currencies and assets are just their observed prices.

The change in the portfolio value can be approximated by the Taylor expansion with respect to the values of risk factors up to the first derivative (assuming linearity in the risk factors):[4]

$$\Delta PV_t(h) = \frac{\partial PV}{\partial S_1} \sum_k \frac{\partial S_1}{\partial f_k} \Delta f_k + \frac{\partial PV}{\partial S_2} \sum_k \frac{\partial S_2}{\partial f_k} \Delta f_k + \ldots$$
$$+ \frac{\partial PV}{\partial S_n} \sum_k \frac{\partial S_n}{\partial f_k} \Delta f_k.$$

Let us first write the change in the value of the portfolio in terms of the h-day return of risk factors:

$$\Delta PV_t(h) = \Phi_{1,t} \sum_k f_{k,t} * R_{f_k}(h) * \frac{\partial S_1}{\partial f_k} + \ldots$$
$$+ \Phi_{n,t} \sum_k f_{k,t} * R_{f_k}(h) * \frac{\partial S_n}{\partial f_k}.$$

---

[3] It is a general convention to assume that the prices or values of risk factors are determined exogenously in the market.

[4] This assumption is made to simplify the representation. However, the relationship between derivatives or fixed-income securities prices and their risk factors is usually non-linear. Linearity assumption may imply inadequate explanation for market price behavior, but non-linearity requires additional computation and may be problematic for price functions without closed-form solution.

As the amount $\Phi_{i,t}f_{k,t}$ is constant at time t, it can be denoted by a time-independent symbol π_{ik}. Notice that this is the position associated with the kth risk factor, and brought into the portfolio by ith instrument. $\partial S_i/\partial f_k$ is the sensitivity of the ith asset's price with respect to the kth risk factor (delta, modified duration, vega, and so on).

The first moment of $\Delta PV_t(h)$ is the mean under an assumed probability law P:

$$E^P[\Delta PV_t(h)] = \Phi_{1,t}\sum_k f_{k,t} * E^P\left[R_{f_k}(h)\right] * \frac{\partial S_1}{\partial f_k} + \cdots$$
$$+ \Phi_{n,t}\sum_k f_{k,t} * E^P\left[R_{f_k}(h)\right] * \frac{\partial S_n}{\partial f_k}.$$

In matrix form:

$$E^P[\Delta PV_t(h)] = \Pi'E^P[R_F(h)] = \Pi'\mu_{R_F} = \mu_{PV},$$

where Π is the $\mathbf{K}\times 1$ column vector of sum of π_{ik} times the sensitivities on k and $R_f(h)$ is the $\mathbf{K}\times 1$ vector of h-day factor returns.

The variance under the same probability law is then:

$$\text{var}P[\Delta PV_t(h)] = \Pi'\sum_{R_F}^P(h)\Pi,$$

where $\sum_{R_F}^P(h)$ is the covariance matrix of the h-day factor returns. Notice that the probabilities and quantiles of any normal distribution can be computed from the standard normal distribution, if the first two moments are known.

The qth normal quantile of returns is the value R_q defined by:

$$q = P(R \le R_q) = F(R_q),$$

where $F(R)$ denotes the cumulative normal distribution function of returns. It is easy to compute the qth quantile of the return for a given factor f, by Z-score transformation, as:

$$\frac{R_q - \mu_{R_f}}{\sigma_{R_f}} = Z_q.$$

17.4 Major Market Risk Measures and Their Computation Methods

There are various approaches to measuring market risk. A common feature of these approaches is that they mostly rely on statistical concepts. Here, we will cover such risk measures as capital asset pricing model (CAPM) beta, quantile-based [value at risk (VaR) and expected shortfall (ES)] and volatility-based measures among others.

17.4.1 CAPM beta

Beta, a central element of CAPM, is considered one of the early measures of market risk. Developed and advocated by Sharpe (1964) and Lintner (1965) among others, CAPM suggests that asset returns (alternatively portfolio returns) are in relation with market returns. This relation is given by the security market line (SML) equation as:

$$E[R_i] = R_f + \beta(E[R_m] - R_f),$$

where R_i is the asset return, R_m is the market return and R_f is the risk-free rate of interest.

The last portion of this equation, $(E[R_m] - R_f)$, is called the market risk premium, showing the expected market return in excess of what a riskless asset yields. Hence, the CAPM assumes that asset i's returns are associated with market returns and β amplifies or reduces the effect of market risk premium on asset i's return. As such, it shows how the asset i is positioned *vis-à-vis* the market and how much it is sensitive to market trends.

In most calculations, interest rates of short-term government securities (such as treasury bills) are used to proxy risk-free rate and stock market index is used to proxy market return R_m. Then, β is defined as the covariance between the asset i's returns and the market returns, divided by the variance of market returns, i.e.:

$$\beta = \frac{\sigma_{R_i R_m}}{\sigma_{R_m}^2}.$$

When the SML equation is considered in vector form, it is also a practical convenience to regress R_i on R_m to obtain β, which is simply the regression coefficient.

Portfolio β is analogous to asset β. We can find it simply by replacing asset returns by portfolio returns in the SML equation.

17.4.2 VaR and ES

VaR is one of the most widely used risk measures in the financial industry, particularly in banking. The reason is quite compelling: It is easy to implement and report. By definition,

VaR reports a quantile[5] for a given holding period as the quantity of risk. The confidence level is usually 99%. In this case, VaR gives us the cutoff point such that this very loss will not happen with a probability greater than 99%.

In order to better see this notion of VaR, let us consider the following examples.

EXAMPLE 1: DELTA-NORMAL VaR

Suppose a portfolio holds only one foreign exchange (FX) position of 1000 monetary units of domestic currency. Assume that the daily return time series of FX follows a normal distribution with mean 0.005 and standard deviation 0.025. Given that the holding period is one day and the confidence level is 99%, what is the VaR of portfolio?

A practitioner first must decide what the risk factor(s) is (are), and what kind of function would determine the relation between the price of the instrument and the value of the risk factor. In this example, the pricing function that explains the price of the asset in terms of the value of the risk factor is the identity function, as for the spot FX position, risk factor is level of the FX price itself. The portfolio value at time t can be written as:

$$PV_t = \Phi S_t.$$

For a spot FX position, the functional relation between the price of the asset and the risk factor is linear. The change in the portfolio value with respect to risk factor level by the Taylor expansion is:

$$\Delta PV_t(1) = \frac{\partial PV_t}{\partial S_t}\frac{\partial S_t}{\partial f_t}\Delta f_t = \Phi S_t R_{S_t}.$$

Notice that since $S_t = f_t$ for a spot FX position, the sensitivity $\partial S_t/\partial f_t = 1$ and all we need to know is the distribution of FX return. The term ΦS_t is nothing but the FX position, which is 1000 monetary units in domestic currency. Then, $\mu_{PV} = 100 * 0.005 = 5$ and $\sigma_{PV} = 100 * 0.025 = 25$. Z-score transformation for the given confidence level $(1 - 0.99 = 0.01)$ is:

$$\frac{VaR - \mu_{PV}}{\sigma_{PV}} = \Phi^{-1}(0.01) = -2.3263.$$

where Φ indicates the cumulative distribution function of the standard normal distribution. Then, the VaR is found to be:

$$VaR = 5 - 2.3263 * 25 = -53.1575.$$

In practice, the VaR is usually reported as a positive number. That is why Z-score transformation is done by absolute values.

---

[5] Determined by the regulator or internal needs driven by economic capital, in which case the confidence levels may differ.

As seen from the example, the practitioner assumes there is only one risk factor associated with the portfolio value: The market price of FX. This assumption is valid as long as the portfolio holder is able to buy/sell the asset in the market without a liquidity constraint. When the liquidity constraint is an issue, then either the pricing model or the risk model should be revised. For the spot FX example, there is nothing we can do to change the pricing relation as it is the identity function. However, risk computation can be re-engineered to cover illiquidity situations. One way of doing it is to assume that illiquidity happens at extraordinary times and creates jumps.

EXAMPLE 2: JUMP PROCESS AND MIXED NORMAL DISTRIBUTION

Suppose that logarithmic spot FX returns follow a jump process as:

$$\mathrm{d}\log S_t = \mu \mathrm{d}t + \sigma \mathrm{d}W_t + \mathrm{d}J_t.$$

The solution of the stochastic differential equation for S_T is:

$$S_T = S_0 \exp\left\{\left(\mu - \frac{\sigma^2}{2}\right)T + \sigma W_T\right\} \prod_{j=1}^{N(T)} Y_j,$$

where W_t is the Wiener process, J_t is the jump component of the stochastic process, N is the number of jumps at an interval and Y is the size of the jumps. One can write the discrete time analogy of the solution as (Glasserman, 2003):

$$X_{t_{i+1}} = X_{t_i} + \mu(t_{i+1} - t_i) + \sigma(W_{t_{i+1}} - W_{t_i}) + \sum_{j=N_{t_i}+1}^{N_{t_{i+1}}} \log Y_j,$$

where $X_t = \log S_t$, $(W_{t_{i+1}} - W_{t_i}) \sim N(0, (t_{i+1} - t_i))$, $N_{t_{i+1}-t_i} \sim$ Poisson $(\lambda(t_{i+1} - t_i))$ and $Y \sim N(\alpha, \beta^2)$. It is extremely difficult to estimate the parameters α, β and N when $N > 1$. Then, the best solution is to assume that returns follow a mix of two Gaussian distributions:

$$R \sim pN(\alpha_1, \sigma_1) + (1-p)N(\alpha_2, \sigma_2).$$

As VaR for Gaussian distribution is a direct function of volatility, jump detection should be done over the volatility modeling. For instance, jump levels can be detected by the realized volatilities that exceed the values estimated by such models as generalized autoregressive conditional heteroskedasticity (GARCH) or exponentially weighted moving average (EWMA).[6]

It is always possible to use alternative distributions to the normal ones. However, especially for discrete-time distributions, VaR can be problematic. Indeed, VaR has been criticized for not guaranteeing the satisfaction of the subadditivity condition—an issue raised by Artzner *et al.* (1999). That is to say, VaR, as a risk measure, does not necessarily support portfolio diversification—a situation that is intolerable for most financial investors. However, as long as the distribution is elliptical, the VaR measure is coherent, mathematically speaking. In the industrial applications of market risk, it is very rare to go with distributions that are not elliptical.

A more severe criticism states that VaR is a point estimate rather than the estimate of an area that carries more information within. In words, VaR only indicates a quantile, but does not tell us anything about what happens if the realized loss exceeds the estimated quantile. In this case, one needs to know the area behind the quantile. Another risk measure, called the ES, has been proposed to overcome this serious problem, as shown as:

$$ES_q = -E^P[X|X \leq VaR_q].$$

For a normally distributed tail (when P is Gaussian), ES is just the plain average of the values that exceed VaR_q.

Financial risk literature and experiences have shown that most asset returns follow leptokurtic distributions violating the normality assumption. Below are two examples of widely used risk computation methods on returns with non-Gaussian distributions.

EXAMPLE 3: STUDENT'S *t*-DISTRIBUTION AND VaR

One way to calibrate the VaR result obtained in Example 1 to the leptokurtic world is to introduce a Student's *t*-distribution with degrees of freedom v. The easiest way to estimate v is the method of moments in which the empirical kurtosis value is matched with theoretical kurtosis:

$$\text{kurtosis} = \frac{3v - 6}{v - 4}, \quad v > 4.$$

For instance, if the empirical kurtosis is found to be 5, then the degrees of freedom would be 7. Instead of the Z value, inverse of the t distribution with degrees of freedom 7 is used to find the quantile. Accordingly, $F^{-1}(0.01|v = 7) = -2.998$. Then, the VaR will be -69.949.

---

[6] See the definitions of these volatility models in Section 17.4.3.

EXAMPLE 4: GENERALIZED PARETO DISTRIBUTION AND THE VaR/ES

There exist other distributions that model fat tails, such as the family extreme value distributions. The generalized Pareto distribution (GPD) is the most suitable one for portfolio VaR computations. It employs the peaks-over-threshold method in which all points above a certain threshold are extracted (see Embrechts *et al.*, 1997). Under the GPD assumption, the parametric VaR formula at confidence level q is:

$$VaR_q = u + \frac{\sigma}{\xi}\left\{\left(\frac{N}{N_u}q\right)^{-\alpha} - 1\right\},$$

where α is the tail index, ξ is the shape parameter of GPD, N is the sample length, N_u is the number of the observations exceeding u and u is the predetermined threshold level. α and ξ are estimated by maximum likelihood method. Similarly, the ES formula for GPD is:

$$ES_q = \frac{VaR_q + \xi - \sigma u}{1 - \xi}.$$

The computational methods given above are mostly parametric. There are alternative approaches for calculating quantile-based risk. These include simulation methods. Two of them are particularly popular: Historical simulation and Monte Carlo (MC) simulation.

Historical simulation is the easiest way to compute the portfolio risk. It assumes that past returns (historical returns) may repeat themselves and, thus, they are natural candidates for the returns in holding period. Steps to compute historical simulation-based VaR are the following.

(i) Obtain $(T-h) \times N$ factor returns for the given holding period by $R_t(h) = \ln\left(\frac{S_{t+h}}{S_t}\right)$, $t = 0, 1, \cdots T$ for stocks and $\Delta r_t(h) = r_{t+h} - r_t, t = 0, 1, ..., T$ for interest rates.

(ii) Update the values of risk factors by $S_{T+h} = S_T e^{R_t}$ for stocks, and $r_{T+h} = r_T + \Delta r_t(h)$ for interest rates.

(iii) Price the simulated future values of instruments by Price $= f(S_{T+h}, r_{T+h})$.

(iv) Obtain $(T-h) \times 1$ simulated portfolio values PV_{T+h}.

(v) Compute the change in the portfolio value by $\Delta PV_T(h) = PV_{T+h} - PV_T$.

(vi) Report αth percentile as the VaR number.

In this methodology, the ES is just the average (or weighted average if a distribution is assigned to the tail) of the values exceeding the VaR number.

Historical simulation can easily be criticized as its space is limited to historical realizations of the factor prices. Although there are bootstrap and mirrored sampling algorithms available for increasing the size of the sample, the performance of the historical simulation algorithm can still be inadequate as it is slow to adjust for market dynamics. Filtered historical simulation (Barone-Adesi *et al.*, 2002) and EWMA weighted historical simulation (Boudoukh *et al.*, 1998) are the most widely used extensions attempting to improve the performance of traditional historical simulation.

MC simulation is a method that uses the stochastic process[7] to generate many paths for the factor prices or values. The key point to the MC simulation is the parameterization of the process and the selection of the suitable probability distribution assigned to the selected process. By generating many numbers from the distribution process, a practitioner can simulate possible future prices. The methods based on distribution functions to produce random numbers invert the cumulative distribution function (CDF) for a given probability.

When working on the Monte Carlo simulation, there are two challenges facing both academics and practitioners: Generating random numbers for α on (0,1) and finding the inverse of the CDF.

The most common way of generating a random number in financial software programs is through a pseudo-random number generator, also known as a deterministic bit generator. The pseudo-random number generator is usually based on a physical phenomenon such as the clock of a computer. That is why it is likely to repeat itself after some point. Moreover, these methods do not mimic the probability distributions. Another way of generating random numbers is through computational methods such as a linear congruential generator and middle-square methods.

Inversion of the CDF is available for some distribution functions. Nevertheless, in practice, it may still be computationally expensive for some probability distributions. There are methods that help decrease the computation time, such as the Box–Muller method.

---

[7] See the Appendix for a description of stochastic processes in finance.

A version of MC simulation, called *quasi-MC* (*QMC*), is also popular among practitioners. Usually the portfolio of a bank consists of thousands of different instruments to be priced at any moment. This means thousands of area computations requiring a very long time for generating random numbers. Accordingly, QMC makes use of sequences, such as Halton or Sobol, to compute α. This method is a lot faster and has a better convergence rate than MC, and inversion is also smoother (see Bratley *et al.*, 1992).

EXAMPLE 5: CORRELATED RANDOM NUMBER GENERATION AND SIMULATING MULTIDIMENSIONAL GEOMETRIC BROWNIAN MOTION PATHS

Consider the following N-dimensional geometric Brownian motion (GBM):[8]

$$R_t = \mu\Delta t + A\sqrt{\Delta t Z_t}, \quad t = 1, 2, ..., T,$$

where R_t is $N \times T$, μ is $N \times 1$ and repeated T times, A is $N \times N$, and Z_t is $N \times T$. If A is found by Cholesky decomposition then it is a lower triangle matrix. Notice that $variance(R_t) = E(A\sqrt{\Delta t}Z_t Z_t'\sqrt{\Delta t}A') = \sum \Delta t$.

[8] See the Appendix.

Steps to compute the MC-based portfolio VaR are:
  (i) Obtain a discrete time approximation of stochastic differential equation (SDE).
 (ii) Estimate the parameters of the SDE.
(iii) Generate multivariate random numbers for stochastic processes from the assigned distributions.
 (iv) Evaluate $R_t(h)$ and $\Delta r_t(h)$ given S_T and r_T.
  (v) Evaluate S_{T+h} and r_{T+h}.
 (vi) Evaluate Price $= f(S_{T+h}, r_{T+h})$.
(vii) Obtain simulated portfolio values PV_{T+h}.
(viii) Compute the change in the portfolio value by $\Delta PV_T(h) = PV_{T+h} - PV_T$.
 (ix) Repeat steps (iii)−(viii) by N times.
  (x) Report the αth percentile as the VaR number.

17.4.3 Volatility

Volatility is probably one of the most important figures of financial risk assessment. In the simplest terms, it shows price fluctuation. Volatility itself is used as a risk measure, since, by

definition, it measures the deviation from the expected value. There are mainly three types of volatility:
- Realized volatility.
- Implied volatility.
- Model volatility.

Realized volatility is the square root of the sum of squared returns. More commonly, realized variance is computed for high-frequency data such as the squared intra-day returns for a particular day. Realized variance is one of the estimators of quadratic variation of a stochastic process. The realized volatility between times t and T, $rv(t,T)$, is:

$$rv(t, T) = \left[\frac{1}{T-t} \sum_{i=1}^{T-t} r_i^p \right]^{\frac{1}{p}},$$

where r is the return on asset. When the exponent $p = 2$, rv is the standard deviation about zero. As seen from the equation, real-ized volatility is computed from historical data and is also called *historical volatility*.

Implied volatility is the volatility implied by the market price of a derivative. It is computed by solving an inverse problem when the market price is observed and the pricing function includes a volatility parameter. For instance, for a European call option, the Black–Scholes pricing equation is (see Hull, 2008):

$$c = S_0 N(d_1) + K e^{-rT} N(d_2)$$

$$d_1 = \frac{\ln\left(\frac{S_0}{K}\right) + \left(r + \frac{\sigma^2}{2}\right)^T}{\sigma \sqrt{T}}$$

$$d_2 = d_1 - \sigma\sqrt{T},$$

where S_0 is the spot price of underlying, K is the strike price, r is the risk free rate, T is the maturity and σ is the volatility. There exists one σ to satisfy this relation when other parameters are given. Indeed, all other parameters are observed and σ is the only one to be estimated. This function is not invertible, so σ cannot be analytically expressed as a function of other parameters, $\{S_0, K, r, T, c\}$. However, a numerical procedure is available to compute implied σ.

EXAMPLE 6: MATLAB COMMAND: *blsimpv*

Computation of implied function for a given pricing function is a standard application in many software applications. For instance, the MATLAB command *blsimpv* computes the implied volatility for Black–Scholes formula:

$$\text{Volatity} = blsimpv\,(S_0,\ K,\ r,\ T,\ c)$$
$$\text{Volatity} = blsimpv\,(100,\ 105,\ 0.05,\ 1,\ 5) = 0.1240.$$

Model volatility refers to the variation measure of a given parametric model usually with a particular probability distribution. The best known examples are constant volatility (CV), EWMA, autoregressive conditional heteroskedasticity/GARCH family and stochastic volatility (SV).

Let us explain each volatility model with an example.

Suppose (in the Examples 7–10) that asset return R_t on time t evolves over time as follows:

$$R_t = \sigma_t Z_t,$$

where $Z_t \sim N(0,1)$ and, thus, as volatility is constant, returns are distributed normally,

$$R_t \sim N\left(0, \sigma_t^2\right).$$

EXAMPLE 7: CV

The CV model for R_t can be expressed as:

$$R_t = \sigma Z_t.$$

Notice that this is the discrete-time representation of GBM without the drift parameter and $\Delta t = 1$. For the multivariate case:

$$R_t = A Z_t,$$

where $AA' = \Sigma$ is the $N \times N$ covariance matrix of $N \times T$ matrix of returns on N different assets.[9]

[9] In the language of RiskMetrics this method is called the "Equally Weighted Volatility Estimator."

EXAMPLE 8: EWMA

Having a CV is not a good assumption for financial assets, as recent events have again raised question about market stability. Then, assigning larger weights to the near past, i.e. attributing a greater emphasis on recent events, can be an alternative. When these weights are decreasing exponentially, the EWMA model is obtained to explain the time-varying feature of volatility (RiskMetrics, 1996). For an arbitrary constant λ, $0 < \lambda < 1$, the weight on volatility at time $t-1$ is:

$$\frac{\lambda_{t-1}}{\sum_{j=1}^{T} \lambda^{j-1}}.$$

Since λ is between 0 and 1, as T goes to infinity, the denominator is equal to $1/(1-\lambda)$ in the limit. Then, the EWMA estimator for variance about zero mean is:

$$\sigma_t^2 = (1-\lambda) \sum_{t=1}^{T} \lambda^{t-1} r_t^2.$$

This expression can be written in a recursive form as:

$$\sigma_t^2 = \lambda \sigma_{t-1}^2 + (1-\lambda) r_{t-1}^2.$$

For the multivariate case, the EWMA covariance at time t between two returns r_1 and r_2 is:

$$\sigma_{12,t} = \lambda \sigma_{12,t-1} + (1-\lambda) r_{1,t-1} r_{2,t-1}.$$

As the left-hand side of the equation is constant at time $t-1$, $\sigma_{12,t}$ is conditionally constant at time $t-1$. Therefore, although volatility is time-varying, returns are still normally distributed.

EXAMPLE 9: GARCH

Suppose that conditional variance σ_t^2 evolves over time as:

$$\sigma_t^2 = K + \sum_{i=1}^{P} \alpha_i \sigma_{t-i}^2 + \sum_{j=1}^{Q} \beta_j r_{t-j}^2,$$

where:

$$K > 0, \quad \alpha_i \geq 0, \quad \beta_i \geq 0,$$

and

$$\sum_{i=1}^{P} \alpha_i + \sum_{j=1}^{Q} \beta_i < 1.$$

Then, conditional variance σ_t^2 is said to follow a GARCH(P,Q) process. Assuming that variance is conditionally constant in between $t-1$ and t, the maximum likelihood estimator (MLE) is available to estimate the parameters of the model. The estimation is done by various iterative numeric algorithms, hence different package programs result in different values for the parameters. When modeling a multidimensional GARCH process, estimation becomes very hard since the likelihood gets flatter as dimension increases. That is why orthogonal GARCH or GARCH−EWMA mixed applications are often preferred in practice. Orthogonal GARCH makes use of principal component analysis in order to avoid complex covariance matrix estimation. The GARCH–EWMA mixed approach obtains the diagonal elements of the covariance matrix from individual univariate GARCH models and fills in the off-diagonal elements by EWMA for a given λ.

EXAMPLE 10: SV

SV is different from CV, EWMA and GARCH models, as it contains a stochastic error term in its representation:

$$d\sigma_t^2 = \alpha(S,t)dt + \beta(S,t)dW_t.$$

As is clear from the equation, variance is a normally distributed random variable, not a constant. The stochastic term in conditional mean equation Z_t is also normally distributed. However, the product of two normally distributed random variables is not necessarily normal. In fact, most of the time, it is not. In order to obtain a closed-form solution for an option price or to estimate the parameters of the process by MLE, unlike CV, EWMA and GARCH models, we need to make assumptions on the distribution of this product. Markov chain MC Gibbs sampling algorithms along with the WinBUGS program are widely used to estimate the parameters of SV in a Bayesian setup.

For the Examples 7–10, non-Gaussian distributions could also be used for risk computation purposes. In particular, the GARCH family covers several models with different types of distributions and various parameterizations.

17.5 Backtesting of Market Risk Computation Methods

Any model ultimately needs validation and perhaps calibration depending on its real-time performance. Backtesting is a procedure where actual profits and losses are systematically compared to corresponding VaR estimates. It is equally important for monitoring agencies, as all these agencies do nothing but watch the validation performance of the model. They cannot intervene in a bank's model choice or specification. What they can do is to give a penalty based on the backtesting performance of the model.

EXAMPLE 11: NUMBER OF HITS AND BASEL II ZONE CLASSIFICATION

For regulatory capital, the Market Risk Amendment imposes a multiplier on the VaR depending on the number of backtesting exceptions the bank experiences. For some specific number of violations within a year, the financial authority penalizes banks by increasing regulatory capital with a multiplier. Banks are allowed to have four violations and this keeps them in the green zone where the multiplier is 3. The yellow zone is where the number of hits is five to nine, and multipliers are 3.4, 3.5, 3.65, 3.75 and 3.85, respectively. Finally, the last zone is red and the multiplier is 4. Banks in the red zone are required to build a developed model. This method is known as the *traffic light approach* and is proposed by the Bank of International Settlements (BIS).

There are also some statistical tests that examine the failure rates, such as Kupiec's POF (proportion of failures) test and TUFF (time until first failure) test (see Kupiec, 1995).

17.6 Conclusion

This chapter aims at providing a brief introduction to market risk. After defining market risk, portfolio values and returns, it establishes the link between portfolio value and risk factors. Then, it reviews basic risk measures such as CAPM beta, VaR, ES and volatility. In addition, it describes computation methods such as parametric methods, historical simulation and MC simulation through examples in an attempt to cover the tools most widely used by market professionals. Our objective was to provide a compact presentation of risk measurement methods rather than long mathematical or computational details and mostly from a practitioner's perspective. Certainly, the interested reader can find detailed documentation on each of these concepts.

Appendix: Stochastic Processes Used in Finance

There are various types of stochastic processes used in asset pricing and risk computations. The Wiener process (also called

Brownian motion) is the main process employed by both scholars and practitioners. It is a continuous-time stochastic process named after Norbert Wiener. The Wiener process W_t is characterized by three properties:

- $W_0 = 0$.
- The function $t \to W_t$ is almost surely continuous.
- W_t has independent, stationary increments with $dW_t \sim N(0, dt)$.

EXAMPLE A.1: GBM

A stochastic process S_t is said to follow a GBM if it satisfies the following SDE:

$$dS_t = \mu S_t dt + \sigma S_t dW_t,$$

where W_t is a Wiener process, and μ and σ are constants. Let S_t be the price of an asset at time t. Given the initial value of the asset, the analytic solution of the SDE is obtained by the Ito formula:

$$S_t = S_u e^{\left[\mu - \frac{\sigma^2}{2}\right](t-u)+\sigma(W_t - W_u)}.$$

Let holding period h equal $t - u$, then h-day logarithmic return $R_t(h)$ is:

$$R_t(h) = \left[\mu - \frac{\sigma^2}{2}\right]h + \sigma(W_t - W_u).$$

By method of moments, constants are estimated as:

$$\hat{\mu} = \frac{\text{mean}(R_t(h))}{h} + \frac{\hat{\sigma}^2}{2}$$

$$\hat{\sigma} = \frac{\text{var}(R_t(h))^{0.5}}{h^{0.5}}.$$

EXAMPLE A.2: ORNSTEIN–UHLENBECK PROCESS AND VASICEK SHORT RATE MODEL

Another widely used continuous-time stochastic process is Ornstein–Uhlenbeck (OU) process named after Leonard Ornstein and George Eugene Uhlenbeck. This process is used to model short-term interest rates rather than stock prices, as, over time, it tends to drift towards its long-term mean (mean-reverting property). The Vasicek short rate model is one of the well-known models that follow the OU process. The main problem in interest rate modeling is to build the term structure of interest rates given the short rate process. By making use of the Vasicek model (Vasicek, 1977), a closed-form solution can be obtained for yields. Let r_t be the short rate and assume that it follows the following stochastic process:

$$dr_t = \Theta(\mu - r_t)dt + \sigma dW_t,$$

where θ is the speed of adjustment, μ is the long-run mean of the interest rate and σ is the diffusion constant. Vasicek obtains the following expression for yields given short rate:

$$R(t,T) = R(t, \infty)$$
$$+ \frac{1}{\Theta(T-t)\left[(R(t,T) - r(t))(1 - e^{-\Theta(T-t)}) - \frac{\sigma^2}{4\Theta^2}\left(1 - e^{-\Theta(T-t)}\right)^2\right]},$$

where:

$$R(t, \infty) = \mu - \frac{\sigma^2}{\Theta^2}.$$

As seen from the equation, by updating $r(t)$ to $r(t + h)$ for some holding period h, one can obtain future scenarios of the yield curve and do pricing accordingly. Parameter estimation is done by either estimating the time series model (short rate process) or calibrating the term structure. Both should give the same results for stationary ergodic data.

References

Alexander, C., 2001. Market Models: A Guide to Financial Data Analysis. Wiley, New York.

Alexander, C., 2009. Market Risk Analysis: Value at Risk Models. Volume IV. Wiley, New York.

Artzner, P., Delbaen, F., Eber, J.M., Heath, D., 1999. Coherent measures of risk. Mathematical Finance 9 (3), 203–228.

Barone-Adesi, G., Giannopoulos, K., Vosper, L., 2002. Backtesting derivative portfolios with filtered historical simulation (FHS). European Financial Management 8 (1), 31–58.

Boudoukh, J., Richardson, M., Whitelaw, R., 1998. The best of both worlds: a hybrid approach to calculating value at risk. Risk 11 (5), 64–67.

Bratley, P., Fox, B.L., Niederreiter, H., 1992. Implementation and tests of low-discrepancy sequences. ACM Transactions on Modeling and Computer Simulation 2 (3), 195–213.

Embrechts, P., Kluppelberg, C., Mikosch, T., 1997. Modelling Extremal Events for Insurance and Finance. Springer, Berlin.

Glasserman, P., 2003. Monte Carlo Methods in Financial Engineering. Springer, Berlin.

Hull, J., 2008. Options, Futures and Other Derivative Securities, 7th edn. Prentice Hall, Upper Saddle River, NJ.

Kupiec, P., 1995. Techniques for verifying the accuracy of risk management models. Journal of Derivatives 3 (2), 73–84.

Lintner, J., 1965. The valuation of risk assets and selection of risky investments in stock portfolios and capital budgets. Review of Economics and Statistics 47 (1), 13–37.

RiskMetrics, 1996. RiskMetrics™—Technical Document. J.P. Morgan, New York.

Sharpe, W., 1964. Capital asset prices: a theory of market equilibrium under conditions of risk. Journal of Finance 19 (3), 425–442.

Vasicek, O., 1977. An equilibrium characterization of the term structure. Journal of Financial Economics 5 (2), 177–188.

18

HIGH-FREQUENCY PERFORMANCE OF VALUE AT RISK AND EXPECTED SHORTFALL: EVIDENCE FROM ISE30 INDEX FUTURES

Cumhur Ekinci*, Kasirga Yildirak** and Ali Sabri Taylan***

*Istanbul Technical University, **Trakya University, ***Turkish Derivatives Exchange (TURKDEX) and Dokuz Eylül University

CHAPTER OUTLINE

18.1 Introduction

Risk shows the limits of unwanted occurrences. In finance, as in many other disciplines, measuring risk is an important area of research. Risk measurement is widely used by banks and financial institutions as well as portfolio managers and professional investors. Among many measures of risk are the standard deviation of returns, the gap between the maximum and minimum values, sum (or average) of absolute or squared returns, capital asset pricing model (CAPM) beta, value at risk (VaR), and expected shortfall (ES).

Rethinking Valuation and Pricing Models. http://dx.doi.org/10.1016/B978-0-12-415875-7.00018-X

Although considerable effort has been devoted in the finance industry to measuring market risk, it is not obvious how much these measures are capable of warning against future losses. In fact, these measures are extensively questioned just after crashes. Moreover, research mostly concentrates on daily aggregates, whereas intra-day evidence is more and more looked for by frequently trading investors. Motivated by this lack of obviousness, this chapter attempts to assess the intra-day performance of two major quantile-based risk measures.

The remainder of the chapter is organized as follows. Section 18.2 reviews the literature about risk measures. The market and data are described in Section 18.3, and methodology is given in Section 18.4. Then, empirical findings are presented and discussed in Section 18.5. We conclude in Section 18.6 by emphasizing major findings and indicating possible improvements.

18.2 Literature

Quantile-based risk measures have been widely used by market participants and widely discussed in the literature. One of the first of these measures, VaR, which determines the maximum amount of loss not exceeded by a certain probability within a defined holding period, has been a standard tool for risk management (RiskMetrics, 1996; Duffie and Pan, 1997; Dowd, 1998; Jorion, 2006). This trend has been supported by risk measurement requirements settled in 1996 by the Basel Committee on Banking Supervision at the Bank of International Settlements (BIS).

A few methods have emerged for the calculation of VaR: the "historical simulation" approach that relies on past occurrences to tell about future risks, the "parametric" approach (also called the variance–covariance method) that uses standard deviation of returns[1] and the "Monte Carlo" (MC) approach—a simulation technique used for integration.

Even if VaR has been largely used in practice, it sometimes imposes severe assumptions—such as normality and constant volatility—that bring about criticisms. In fact, it is quite usual to observe skewness, excess kurtosis or fat tails in return series of various assets. Moreover, VaR has been criticized for not

---

[1] The simplest version of the parametric method assumes returns follow a normal distribution that implies a constant volatility and equal weights for each observation, but other parametric methods do exist. For instance, the exponentially weighted moving average (EWMA) model that attributes higher weights to the recent past (suggesting a conditional variance) has gained importance recently. It this chapter, we employ both of these parametric methods.

addressing the issue of what would happen when extreme events occur (see, e.g. Danielsson, 2002; Krause, 2003; Stulz, 2008). Furthermore, Artzner *et al.* (1999), among others, state that VaR is not coherent and does not satisfy some essential properties such as subadditivity, implying, for instance, that diversification does not necessarily yield lower risk. As a consequence, the authors suggest an alternative measure called ES or conditional VaR (CVaR) that satisfies the basic criteria needed by a good risk measure. Hence, this alternative measure has gained popularity over VaR.[2]

Despite the extensive use of quantile-based risk measures, relatively little research has been devoted to backtesting these methods, especially at the intra-day level. For instance, Yamai and Yoshiba (2005) check the validity of VaR, and compare VaR and ES methods. They state that VaR may be seriously misleading for investors and warn against its unconditional use. Nieppola (2009) investigates various backtest models for VaR, and evaluates their results on equity, fixed-income and equity option portfolios. Contreras (2010) questions the usefulness of VaR in volatile markets. Specifically, he shows that major US investment banks had a higher number of VaR exceptions during 2007 and 2008. In a series of papers, Wong (2008, 2009, 2010) argues a saddle-point technique to backtest trading risk using ES which gives more accurate and powerful results than VaR, even in a small sample case.

More recently, Colletaz *et al.* (2011) developed a tool for backtesting VaR models. They take into account the number and magnitude of VaR exceptions, define "super exceptions," and show how to estimate them. However, almost all these studies are based on daily measures of risk.[3] Dionne *et al.* (2009), in their turn, investigate the use of tick-by-tick data for market risk measurement. They propose an intra-day VaR (IVaR) at different horizons with irregularly spaced high-frequency data, and based on MC simulation and a UHF-generalized autoregressive conditional heteroskedasticity (GARCH) model. They argue that this approach yields a reliable measure of risk. Similarly, Colletaz *et al.* (2007) propose a market risk measure defined in price event time and a suitable backtesting procedure for irregularly spaced data.

---

[2] For applications of CVaR to portfolio optimization problems, see, e.g. Rockafellar and Uryasev (2000, 2002), Andersson *et al.* (2001), Alexander *et al.* (2004), Alexander and Baptista (2004), and Rockafellar *et al.* (2006).

[3] Although there are some papers analyzing intra-day data, their main focus is assessing daily risk. See, e.g. Mendis and Rosen (1999) and Lang (2000).

18.3 Market and Data

Our dataset, obtained by the Turkish Derivatives Exchange (TURKDEX), covers transactions data of ISE30 index futures contracts. ISE30 is the blue chip index of the Istanbul Stock Exchange (ISE) and futures contracts on ISE30 index account for a large majority of the overall turnover at TURKDEX.[4] Usually, contracts are issued bimonthly (i.e. six contracts are issued yearly) and the liquidity of the contract with the nearest maturity date is considerably higher than any other. Consequently, we analyze 11 subsequent contracts (with maturities from December 2009 to August 2011) for a period of 457 business days,[5] each one for the period of two months at which it was the most liquid (e.g. the period analyzed was from 1 July to 31 August for the August 2011 contract).

From the transactions data mentioned above, we prepare regularly spaced (close-to-close) return series. Five-minute frequency appears to be optimal for the analysis since this particular length provides a considerable amount of observations in each interval (and keeps at a minimum the intervals without transaction[6]) and is short enough to capture intra-day sensitivity. Alternatively, 25-minute intervals are constructed. A typical day consists of 100 five-minute and 20 twenty five-minute intervals. Hence, the overall dataset consists of 45,700 five-minute and 9140 twenty five-minute intervals.

18.4 Methodology

In order to assess how much risk measures are capable of predicting unexpected losses, we simply calculate VaR and ES with three alternative methods, i.e. parametric method assuming normality, parametric method by EWMA and historical simulation, based on historical data of 40 (alternatively 20) prior business days.[7] After determining how effective these measures are in

---

[4] According to our calculation from the data on TURKDEX's website, in 2011 almost 90% of the overall derivatives trading volume (in TL) was performed on ISE30 futures contracts.

[5] We omitted 5 of 462 business days in the dataset since they did not have full data for the whole day.

[6] As these index futures are quite liquid, there were no intervals without transactions in the whole dataset.

[7] At every step, we take the last 4000 (alternatively 2000) intra-day observations to calculate the VaR and ES for the next 5 minutes, and 800 (alternatively 400) intra-day observations to calculate the VaR and ES for the next 25 minutes. Note that this method does not take into account intra-day seasonality.

detecting future losses, we make comparisons between measures, methods, frequencies, data periods and buy–sell sides.

Specifically, we test the following (null) hypotheses:

H-1   Quantile-based risk measures are good at forecasting the next period's loss (i.e. the next period's loss is less than the calculated VaR or ES).

H-2   VaR and ES have the same failure rates in detecting losses.

H-3   The parametric method with normality assumption, parametric method with EWMA and historical simulation method yield the same failure rates in detecting losses.

H-4   Failure rates are the same for downside and upside risks (i.e. in predicting positive returns, risk measures are as successful as they are in predicting negative returns[8]).

We use Kupiec's proportion of failures (POF) test[9] (Kupiec, 1995) for backtesting risk measures (H-1) and difference tests (two-proportion z-test) for other hypotheses (H-2, H-3 and H-4).

18.5 Empirical Results

Table 18.1 shows failure rates of quantile-based risk measures in predicting the subsequent period's loss. Accordingly, the VaR calculated at 1% confidence interval with the data of 4000 (2000) latest 5-minute intervals, i.e. over the past 40 days (20 days), fails to catch losses 2.1% (2%) of the time while the ES calculated with the same dataset fails to catch losses 1.5% (1.4%) of the time. Similarly, when looked at horizontally, the VaR calculated with the data of 800 (400) latest 25-minute intervals, i.e. over the past 40 days (20 days), fails to catch losses 2.3% (2.2%) of the time while the ES calculated with the same dataset fails to catch losses 1.5% (1.4%) of the time.

As for the 5% confidence interval, we see that the VaR calculated with the data of 4000 (2000) latest 5-minute intervals fails to catch losses 4.4% (4.2%) of the time while the ES calculated with the same dataset fails to catch losses 2.7% (2.6%) of the time. Similarly, the VaR calculated with the data of 800 (400) latest 25-minute intervals fails to catch losses 5.4% (5.3%) of the time while the ES calculated with the same dataset fails to catch losses 3.2% (3%) of the time.

---

[8] This makes sense since in futures market, an investor can easily be short as well as they can be long. If they are short, then any price increase means a loss for them.

[9] This test is pretty common among backtesting methods. Specifically, by looking at the frequency of failures, it attempts to determine if the reported VaR/ES has been violated. The test statistic is compared to the χ^2-value. For simplicity, we directly present p-values.

Table 18.1. Failure rates

Method	Risk measure	Confidence interval (%)	5-minute		25-minute	
			40-day	20-day	40-day	20-day
Parametric (normal)	VaR	1	0.021	0.020	0.023	0.022
		5	0.044	0.042	0.054	0.053
		95	0.042	0.040	0.044	0.045
		99	0.017	0.016	0.019	0.018
	ES	1	0.015	0.014	0.015	0.014
		5	0.027	0.026	0.032	0.030
		95	0.024	0.023	0.027	0.025
		99	0.012	0.011	0.012	0.012
Parametric (EWMA)	VaR	1	0.019	0.019	0.021	0.027
		5	0.043	0.042	0.052	0.061
		95	0.040	0.040	0.045	0.053
		99	0.016	0.016	0.016	0.024
	ES	1	0.013	0.013	0.014	0.018
		5	0.025	0.025	0.029	0.035
		95	0.023	0.023	0.024	0.032
		99	0.010	0.011	0.010	0.016
Historical simulation	VaR	1	0.012	0.012	0.013	0.012
		5	0.055	0.053	0.057	0.056
		95	0.055	0.053	0.053	0.053
		99	0.012	0.011	0.012	0.011
	ES	1	0.004	0.004	0.006	0.006
		5	0.020	0.019	0.022	0.021
		95	0.018	0.018	0.021	0.021
		99	0.004	0.004	0.005	0.004
Number of observations			41700	43700	8340	8740

The rows with 99 and 95% confidence intervals in Table 18.1 show the failure rates of VaR and ES in detecting positive returns (upside risk) compared to 1 and 5% confidence intervals, which show the failure rates in detecting negative returns (downside risk). According to Table 18.1, as for the upside risk, the VaR calculated at 1% confidence interval with the data of 4000 (2000) latest 5-minute intervals fails to catch losses 1.7% (1.6%) of the time while the ES calculated with the same dataset fails to catch losses 1.2% (1.1%) of the time. Similarly, the VaR calculated with the data of 800 (400) latest 25-minute intervals fails to catch losses

1.9% (1.8%) of the time while the ES calculated with the same dataset fails to catch losses 1.2% (1.2%) of the time.

Critical observations in Table 18.1 can be summarized as follows. When risks are measured by the parametric method assuming normality (and more apparently at 1% confidence interval), failure rates are higher in catching negative returns (downside risk) than in catching positive returns (upside risk) (e.g. 2.1 versus 1.7% for VaR at 1%), but this evidence is less pertinent when risks are measured by parametric (EWMA) and almost vanishes when historical simulation is employed. On the other hand, failure rates are higher for VaR than for ES. Similarly, they are slightly higher when the frequency is 25 minutes (rather than 5 minutes) and the analysis is based on 20 prior days (rather than 40 prior days). Generally speaking, historical simulation is the most successful among alternative methods.

Table 18.2 provides (Kupiec's POF) test results about the significance of failure rates. In Table 18.2, most statistics are close to zero, meaning that quantile-based risk measures at various frequencies or confidence intervals and by various computation methods are not capable of detecting the subsequent period's losses at the desired level of confidence (H-1 is rejected). A few exceptions include the estimation of upside risk by ES with parametric methods and by VaR with historical simulation.

Tables 18.3, 18.4 and 18.5 give the results of the tests comparing the failure rates of VaR and ES, alternative methods of calculation, and in the cases of downside and upside risk, respectively. From Table 18.3, it is clear that ES provides a much more reliable risk estimation than VaR does since the test statistics are all close to zero (and all the failure rates are lower for ES than for VaR in Table 18.1), meaning a strong rejection of the null hypothesis of equal failure rates (H-2).

Test statistics in Table 18.4 are more heterogeneous. All test statistics are zero in the middle and lower parts for the 5-minute analysis, showing that parametric (normal) and historical simulation—but also parametric (EWMA) and historical simulation—methods yield different success rates (H-3 is rejected). From Table 18.1, it follows that historical simulation has the lowest failures rates of all.

Interestingly, although historical simulation offers much better risk estimation results than both parametric methods at a 1% confidence interval (for both VaR and ES), this finding is inversed for VaR at 5% confidence interval [e.g. from Table 18.1, for 5-minute analysis, failure rates are 4.4 and 4.3% for parametric (normal) and parametric (EWMA) methods, respectively, while it

Table 18.2. Test results for the significance of failures

Method	Risk measure	Confidence interval (%)	5-minute		25-minute	
			40-day	20-day	40-day	20-day
Parametric (normal)	VaR	1	0.0000	0.0000	0.0000	0.0000
		5	0.0000	0.0000	0.0000	0.0000
		95	0.0000	0.0000	0.0000	0.0000
		99	0.0000	0.0000	0.0000	0.0000
	ES	1	0.0000	0.0000	0.0000	0.0001
		5	0.0000	0.0000	0.0000	0.0000
		95	0.0000	0.0000	0.0000	0.0000
		99	0.0008	0.0142	0.0375	0.1029
Parametric (EWMA)	VaR	1	0.0000	0.0000	0.0000	0.0000
		5	0.0000	0.0000	0.0000	0.0000
		95	0.0000	0.0000	0.0000	0.0000
		99	0.0000	0.0000	0.0000	0.0000
	ES	1	0.0000	0.0000	0.0002	0.0000
		5	0.0000	0.0000	0.0000	0.0000
		95	0.0000	0.0000	0.0000	0.0000
		99	0.4059	0.2941	0.8607	0.0000
Historical simulation	VaR	1	0.0000	0.0003	0.0053	0.0253
		5	0.0000	0.0000	0.0000	0.0000
		95	0.0000	0.0000	0.0000	0.0000
		99	0.0002	0.0083	0.1179	0.3105
	ES	1	0.0000	0.0000	0.0000	0.0000
		5	0.0000	0.0000	0.0000	0.0000
		95	0.0000	0.0000	0.0000	0.0000
		99	0.0000	0.0000	0.0000	0.0000
Number of observations			41700	43700	8340	8740

is 5.5% for historical simulation]. No difference seems to exist between parametric methods as most statistics are far from zero (except a few cases in the last column). Although the results are similar for both frequencies, they are less obvious for the 25-minute analysis when the confidence interval is 5%.

Finally, Table 18.5 depicts the test results comparing the failure rates in measuring downside and upside risks. Since almost all the failure rates in measuring downside risks—as shown in Table 18.1—are greater in absolute terms than those in

Table 18.3. Test results for the equality of failure rates of VaR and ES

Method	Confidence interval (%)	5-minute		25-minute	
		40-day	20-day	40-day	20-day
Parametric (normal)	1	0.0000	0.0000	0.0005	0.0004
	5	0.0000	0.0000	0.0000	0.0000
	95	0.0000	0.0000	0.0000	0.0000
	99	0.0000	0.0000	0.0019	0.0028
Parametric (EWMA)	1	0.0000	0.0000	0.0011	0.0003
	5	0.0000	0.0000	0.0000	0.0000
	95	0.0000	0.0000	0.0000	0.0000
	99	0.0000	0.0000	0.0023	0.0005
Historical simulation	1	0.0000	0.0000	0.0000	0.0000
	5	0.0000	0.0000	0.0000	0.0000
	95	0.0000	0.0000	0.0000	0.0000
	99	0.0000	0.0000	0.0000	0.0000
Number of observations		41700	43700	8340	8740

measuring upside risks, any significance in Table 18.5 means failure is higher in negative returns (bearish market) than in positive returns (bullish market). From Table 18.5, it is obvious that for parametric methods at 5-minute analysis, failure in detecting downward returns is higher (H-4 is rejected) as test statistics are close to zero while at 25-minute analysis results are more ambiguous. However, the null hypothesis (H-4) cannot be rejected for the historical simulation method.

By analyzing all the tables, one can assert that taking a dataset of 40 prior days or 20 prior days for risk computation only matters slightly and rarely alters the qualitative results.

18.6 Conclusion

This paper questions the predictability of financial risk through its most widely used quantile-based measures, i.e. VaR and ES. More specifically, it asks the following questions: How reliable are these measures in detecting future losses? Are there any differences of performance between VaR and ES, computational methods (such as the parametric method assuming normality or EWMA and historical simulation) or in bearish and

Table 18.4. Test results for the equality of failure rates of parametric (normal and EWMA) and historical simulation methods

Methods compared	Risk measure	Confidence interval (%)	5-minute		25-minute	
			40-day	20-day	40-day	20-day
Parametric (normal) versus parametric (EWMA)	VaR	1	0.1234	0.2713	0.2930	0.0473
		5	0.2698	0.3989	0.3138	0.0295
		95	0.2889	0.3930	0.3889	0.0237
		99	0.1638	0.3185	0.1562	0.0031
	ES	1	0.0223	0.1070	0.3382	0.0564
		5	0.1024	0.1702	0.1917	0.0540
		95	0.1909	0.3819	0.2227	0.0045
		99	0.0853	0.2469	0.1669	0.0126
Parametric (normal) versus historical simulation	VaR	1	0.0000	0.0000	0.0000	0.0000
		5	0.0000	0.0000	0.2551	0.2585
		95	0.0000	0.0000	0.0113	0.0278
		99	0.0000	0.0000	0.0006	0.0007
	ES	1	0.0000	0.0000	0.0000	0.0000
		5	0.0000	0.0000	0.0001	0.0002
		95	0.0000	0.0000	0.0121	0.0683
		99	0.0000	0.0000	0.0000	0.0000
Parametric (EWMA) versus historical simulation	VaR	1	0.0000	0.0000	0.0001	0.0000
		5	0.0000	0.0000	0.1043	0.1600
		95	0.0000	0.0000	0.0201	0.3980
		99	0.0000	0.0000	0.0312	0.0000
	ES	1	0.0000	0.0000	0.0000	0.0000
		5	0.0000	0.0000	0.0061	0.0000
		95	0.0000	0.0000	0.1165	0.0000
		99	0.0000	0.0000	0.0001	0.0000
Number of observations			41,700	43,700	8340	8740

Table 18.5. Test results for the equality of failure rates in measuring downside and upside risks

Method	Risk measure	Confidence interval (%)	5-minute		25-minute	
			40-day	20-day	40-day	20-day
Parametric (normal)	VaR	1	0.0001	0.0002	0.0431	0.0469
		5	0.0949	0.0913	0.0047	0.0257
	ES	1	0.0002	0.0005	0.0910	0.1361
		5	0.0087	0.0016	0.0439	0.0454
Parametric (EWMA)	VaR	1	0.0003	0.0003	0.0107	0.2399
		5	0.1086	0.0648	0.0476	0.0318
	ES	1	0.0018	0.0040	0.0194	0.2867
		5	0.0264	0.0277	0.0573	0.2209
Historical simulation	VaR	1	0.3507	0.3129	0.2810	0.2801
		5	0.3978	0.3889	0.1814	0.2504
	ES	1	0.1847	0.3133	0.2498	0.2254
		5	0.1842	0.2152	0.3245	0.3989
Number of observations			41,700	43,700	8340	8740

bullish markets? We argue that although these measures are widely used by market professionals, their validity is not questioned enough. To the best of our knowledge, this is the first study to ask these questions in this manner.

The main results are as follows. Both VaR and ES fail to predict losses at more than tolerable levels, ES performs better than VaR, historical simulation seems to be the most reliable among various methods, and when parametric methods are employed at 1% confidence interval, failure rates are higher in detecting losses in bearish periods than in bullish periods.

This study, that starts by asking very basic questions about risk measurement, can be improved and extended in many ways. For instance, intra-day filtering can be inserted into the analysis to see the intra-day performance of these measurements. Moreover, we are interested in the risk of a single asset (futures contract) that is by nature a leveraged one. Thus, measuring portfolio risk or taking account of margin trading may bring other challenges to the analysis. Interval-high or interval-low data can be used to calculate returns instead of using close-to-close returns. Similarly, irregularly spaced data can be employed instead of 5- or

25-minute intervals. All these points are potentially areas for future research.

Notes

Any opinions expressed in this chapter are those of the authors and may not necessarily reflect the opinions of Turkish Derivatives Exchange (Vadeli İşlem ve Opsiyon Borsası AŞ).

References

Alexander, G.J., Baptista, A.M., 2004. A comparison of VaR and CVaR constraints on portfolio selection with the mean-variance model. Management Science 50 (9), 1261–1273.

Alexander, S., Coleman, T.F., Li, Y., 2004. Derivative portfolio hedging based on CVaR. In: Szego, G. (Ed.), Risk Measures for the 21st Century. Wiley, New York, pp. 339–363.

Andersson, F., Mausser, H., Rosen, D., Uryasev, S., 2001. Credit risk optimization with conditional value-at-risk, Mathematical Programming. Series B. 89, 273–291.

Artzner, P., Delbaen, F., Eber, J.-M., Heath, D., 1999. Coherent risk measures. Mathematical Finance 9, 203–228.

Colletaz, G., Hurlin, C., Perignon, C., 2011. The risk map: a new tool for backtesting value-at-risk models. Available at http://ssrn.com/abstract=1824984 or http://dx.doi.org/10.2139/ssrn.1824984.

Colletaz, G., Hurlin, C., Tokpavi, S., 2007. Irregularly spaced intra-day value at risk (ISIVaR) models: forecasting and predictive abilities. Working Papers halshs-00162440. Available at http://halshs.archives-ouvertes.fr/docs/00/16/24/40/PDF/ISIVAR.pdf.

Contreras, P., 2010. Is VAR a useful tool in volatile markets? Risk 23 (10), 66–69.

Danielsson, J., 2002. The emperor has no clothes: limits to risk modelling. Journal of Banking and Finance 26 (7), 1273–1296.

Dionne, G., Duchesne, P., Pacurar, M., 2009. Intra-day value at risk (IVaR) using tick-by-tick data with application to the Toronto Stock Exchange. Journal of Empirical Finance 16 (5), 777–792.

Dowd, K., 1998. Beyond Value at Risk: The New Science of Risk Management. Wiley, New York.

Duffie, D., Pan, J., 1997. An overview of value-at-risk. Journal of Derivatives 4 (3), 7–49.

Jorion, P., 2006. Value at Risk: The New Benchmark for Managing Financial Risk. McGraw-Hill, New York.

Krause, A., 2003. Exploring the limitations of value at risk: how good is it in practice? Journal of Risk Finance 4 (2), 19–28.

Kupiec, P., 1995. Techniques for verifying the accuracy of risk measurement models. Journal of Derivatives 3 (2), 73–84.

Lang, T.M., 2000. Is value-at-risk (VaR) a fair proxy for market risk under conditions of market leverage? Master's Thesis. Virginia Polytechnic Institute, Blacksburg, VA.

Mendis, J., Rosen, D., 1999. An empirical study of mark-to-future for measuring risk intra-day. Algo Research Quarterly 2 (4), 9–26.

Nieppola, O., 2009. Backtesting value-at-risk models, Master's Thesis. Helsinki School of Economics.

RiskMetrics, 1996. RiskMetrics™. Technical Document. J.P. Morgan, New York.

Rockafellar, R.T., Uryasev, S., 2000. Optimization of conditional value-at-risk. Journal of Risk 2 (3), 21–41.

Rockafellar, R.T., Uryasev, S., 2002. Conditional value-at-risk for general loss distributions. Journal of Banking and Finance 26 (7), 1443–1471.

Rockafellar, R.T., Uryasev, S., Zabarankin, M., 2006. Master funds in portfolio analysis with general deviation measures. Journal of Banking and Finance 30 (2), 743–776.

Stulz, R., 2008. Risk management failures: what are they and when do they happen? Journal of Applied Corporate Finance 20 (4), 39–48.

Wong, W.K., 2008. Backtesting trading risk of commercial banks using expected shortfall. Journal of Banking and Finance 32 (7), 1404–1415.

Wong, W.K., 2009. Backtesting the tail risk of VaR in holding US dollar. Applied Financial Economics 19 (4), 327–337.

Wong, W.K., 2010. Backtesting value-at-risk based on tail losses. Journal of Empirical Finance 17 (3), 526–538.

Yamai, Y., Yoshiba, T., 2005. Value-at-risk versus expected shortfall: a practical perspective. Journal of Banking and Finance 29 (4), 997–1015.

19

A COPULA APPROACH TO DEPENDENCE STRUCTURE IN PETROLEUM MARKETS

Riadh Aloui,* Mohamed Safouane Ben Aïssa* and Duc Khuong Nguyen**

*University of Tunis El Manar, **ISC Paris School of Management

CHAPTER OUTLINE

19.1 Introduction

While time series properties and volatility of petroleum prices have been examined by several past studies (see, e.g. Choi and Hammoudeh, 2009; Arouri *et al.*, 2012, and references therein), little is known about their comovement. Understanding the way petroleum prices move together is of paramount importance for policy makers. Indeed, policy makers can, based on the obtained results, analyze how and what market conditions, regulations and policies affcct the prices of petroleum products. The close comovement of these prices will imply that they cannot be analyzed separately from each other as the occurrence of a market event on a particular product is likely to impact upon the prices of other products as well. A study of petroleum price comovement is also useful for risk management and hedging issues for petroleum producers, consumers and investors

Rethinking Valuation and Pricing Models. http://dx.doi.org/10.1016/B978-0-12-415875-7.00019-1

because the relationships between different petroleum prices are vital for the definition of risk measures and management tools.

This chapter extends the extant literature on the dynamics of petroleum prices by examining their conditional dependence structure. We make use of a copula-generalized autoregressive conditional heteroskedasticity (GARCH) approach to analyze both the degree and type of dependence between three main petroleum products—crude oil, gasoline and heating oil. This approach also allows us to gauge the potential of joint extreme variations of petroleum prices through tail dependence coefficients of various copulas. Furthermore, it permits us to capture non-linearities in the petroleum price relationships as well as some empirical stylized facts of return distributions (Chan-Lau *et al.*, 2004; Aloui *et al.*, 2011), while avoiding the drawbacks of linear measures of interdependence.

Using daily spot data of WTI (West Texas Intermediate) crude oil, gasoline and heating oil, we find a significant dependence structure between these prices and that the Student-t copula is the best model for modeling their comovement. Moreover, this dependence structure is found to be symmetric. Overall, the proposed copula-GARCH model leads to an improvement of market risk accuracy for an equally weighted portfolio of three petroleum products.

The remainder of this chapter is structured as follows. Section 19.2 describes the empirical methodology and estimation strategy. Section 19.3 presents the data used and discusses our empirical results. Section 19.4 concludes the chapter.

19.2 Empirical Methodology

This section first introduces copula models and dependence measurement, and then present the estimation procedure.

19.2.1 Copulas and dependence

Copulas are functions that link multivariate distributions to their univariate marginal functions. They can be defined as follows (Joe, 1997; Nelsen, 1999):

Definition 1. *A d-dimensional copula is a multivariate distribution function C with standard uniform marginal distributions.*

Theorem 1. *Sklar's theorem. Let $X_1, \ldots, X_d$. be random variables with marginal distribution $F_1, \ldots, F_d$ and joint distribution H, then there exists a copula C: $[0, 1]^d \rightarrow [0, 1]$ such that:*

$$H(x_1, \ldots, x_d) = C(F_1(x_1), \ldots, F_d(x_d)).$$

Conversely if C is a copula and $F_1, ..., F_d$ are distribution functions, then the function H defined above is a joint distribution with margins $F_1, ..., F_d$.

Copula functions offer an efficient way to create distributions that model correlated multivariate data. As far as the measure of interdependence matters, one can construct a multivariate joint distribution by first specifying marginal univariate distributions and then choosing an appropriate copula to examine the dependence structure between the variables. Bivariate distributions as well as distributions in higher dimensions are possible. Copulas can also be used to characterize the dependence in the tails of the distribution by means of two measures of tail dependence, commonly known as the upper and the lower tail dependence coefficients (i.e. the probability of the joint occurrence of market booms and crashes).

Let X, Y be random variables with marginal distribution functions F and G. Then the coefficient of lower tail dependence λ_L is:

$$\lambda_L = \lim_{t \to 0^+} \Pr\left[Y \leq G^{-1}(t) | X \leq F^{-1}(t)\right],$$

which quantifies the probability of observing a lower Y assuming that X is lower itself. In the same way, the coefficient of upper tail dependence λ_U can be defined as:

$$\lambda_U = \lim_{t \to 1^{--}} \Pr\left[Y > G^{-1}(t) | X > F^{-1}(t)\right].$$

The dependence structure is symmetric if the lower tail dependence coefficient equals the upper one, otherwise it is asymmetric. The tail dependence coefficient provides a way for ordering copulas. Copula C_1 is said to be more concordant than copula C_2 if λ_U of C_1 is greater than λ_U of C_2.

The copula models we consider in this chapter allow us to investigate both the symmetric or asymmetric structure of extreme dependence between variables. They fall into two families of copulas: Elliptical copulas (normal and Student-t) and Archimedean copulas (Gumbel, Frank and Clayton).

The bivariate *normal copula* is defined by:

$$C(u,v) = \phi_\theta\left(\phi^{-1}(u), \phi^{-1}(v)\right)$$
$$= \int_{-\infty}^{\phi^{-1}(u)} \int_{-\infty}^{\phi^{-1}(v)} \frac{1}{2\pi\sqrt{1-\theta^2}} \exp\left(-\frac{s^2 - 2\theta st + t^2}{2(1-\theta^2)}\right) ds dt,$$

where ϕ_θ is the standard bivariate normal distribution with linear correlation coefficient θ restricted to the interval $(-1, 1)$, ϕ represents the univariate standard normal distribution function.

The bivariate *Student*-t *copula* is defined by:

$$C(u,v) = \int\limits_{-\infty}^{t_v^{-1}(u)} \int\limits_{-\infty}^{t_v^{-1}(v)} \frac{1}{2\pi\sqrt{1-\theta^2}} \left(1 + \frac{s^2 - 2\theta st + t^2}{v(1-\theta^2)}\right)^{-\frac{v+2}{2}} ds dt,$$

where $t_v^{-1}(u)$ denotes the inverse of the cumulative distribution function of the standard univariate Student-t distribution with υ degrees of freedom.

The *Gumbel copula* (Gumbel, 1960) is an asymmetric copula with higher probability concentrated in the right tail. It is given by:

$$C(u,v) = \exp\left\{-\left[(-\ln u)^\theta + (-\ln v)^\theta\right]^{1/\theta}\right\},$$

where the dependence parameter θ can take any value in $(1, +\infty)$.

The *Frank copula* (Frank, 1979) is defined as:

$$C(u,v) = -\frac{1}{\theta} \ln\left(1 + \frac{(\exp(-\theta u) - 1)(\exp(-\theta v) - 1)}{\exp(-\theta) - 1}\right),$$

where the dependence parameter θ can take any value in $(-\infty, +\infty)$.

The *Clayton copula* (Clayton, 1978) is expressed as:

$$C(u,v) = \left(u^{-\theta} + v^{-\theta} - 1\right)^{-1/\theta}, \quad \theta \in [-1, \infty) \setminus \{0\}.$$

19.2.2 Empirical procedure

To investigate the interdependence in petroleum markets, we combine the copula functions described above with a GARCH-type model of conditional heteroskedasticity. This combination is advantageous in that it permits to separately model the margins and association structure of different variables. A univariate GARCH(1,1) model of Bollerslev (1986) is used and it is expressed as:

$$y_t = c + \varepsilon_t$$
$$\sigma_t^2 = \omega + \alpha\varepsilon_{t-1^2} + \beta\sigma_{t-1}^2,$$

where y_t refers to the financial return series. σ_t^2 is the conditional variance of return series at time t, which depends on both past return innovations and past conditional variance. The GARCH model works like a filter in order to remove any serial dependency from return series.

We estimate the parameters of the copula using a semiparametric two-step estimation method—the canonical maximum likelihood (CML) (Cherubini *et al*, 2004). In the first step, we estimate the marginals F_X and G_Y non-parametrically via their empirical cumulative distribution functions (ECDFs) $\hat{F}_X$ and $\hat{G}_Y$ defined as:

$$\hat{F}_X(x) = \tfrac{1}{n}\sum_{i=1}^{n} 1\{X_i < x\} \quad \text{and} \quad \hat{G}_Y(y) = \tfrac{1}{n}\sum_{i=1}^{n} 1\{Y_i < y\}.$$

In the implementation, $\hat{F}_X$ and $\hat{G}_Y$ are rescaled by $n/(n+1)$ to ensure that the first-order condition of the log-likelihood function for the joint distribution is well defined for all finite n. We then transform the observations into uniform variates using the ECDF of each marginal distribution and we estimate the unknown parameter θ of the copula as:

$$\hat{\theta}_{\text{CML}} = \arg\max_{\theta} \sum_{i=1}^{n} \ln c\Big(\hat{F}_X(x_i), \hat{F}_Y(y_i); \theta\Big).$$

Under suitable regularity conditions, the CML estimator $\hat{\theta}_{\text{CML}}$ is consistent, asymptotically normal and fully efficient at independence. In order to check the overall quality of the fit, we use the goodness-of-fit test of Genest *et al.* (2005), which is based on a comparison of the distance between the estimated (C) and the empirical copula (C_0):

$$C_n = \sqrt{n}\big(C_n - C_{\theta_n}\big).$$

The test statistic considered is based on a Cramér–Von Mises distance:

$$S_n = \int C_n(u)^2 \mathrm{d}C_n(u).$$

Large values of the statistic S_n lead to the rejection of the null hypothesis that the copula C belongs to a class C_0. In practice, we require knowledge about the limiting distribution of S_n, which depends on the unknown parameter value θ. To find the p-values associated with the test statistics we use a multiplier approach as described in Kojadinovic and Yan (2011). The highest p-values thus indicate that the distance between the estimated and empirical copulas is the smallest, and that the copula in use provides the best fit to the data.

19.3 Data and Results

19.3.1 Data and stochastic properties

Our data contains daily closing spot prices of WTI crude oil index and two refined products (gasoline and heating oil) over the period from 3 January, 2005 to 20 December, 2011. The price series are obtained from the US Energy Information Administration, and expressed in US dollars per barrel for crude oil and per gallon for gasoline and heating oil. The time variations of spot prices are plotted in Figure 19.1.

We compute the returns on the individual series by taking the difference in the logarithm of the two successive daily prices. The time paths of return series over the study period are plotted in Figure 19.2. It is observed that daily returns were fairly stable during the period preceding the start of the recent global financial crisis (January 2005 to the third quarter of 2008). After that, all return series exhibit higher instability.

Descriptive statistics and distributional characteristics of return series are reported in Table 19.1. All the returns series have asymmetric distributions as shown by the skewness statistics and exhibit excess kurtosis. This finding indicates that returns are not normally distributed. In particular, the probability of observing extremely negative returns is thus higher than that in a normal distribution. The departure from normality is confirmed by the

Figure 19.1 Time variations of crude oil, gasoline and heating oil prices.

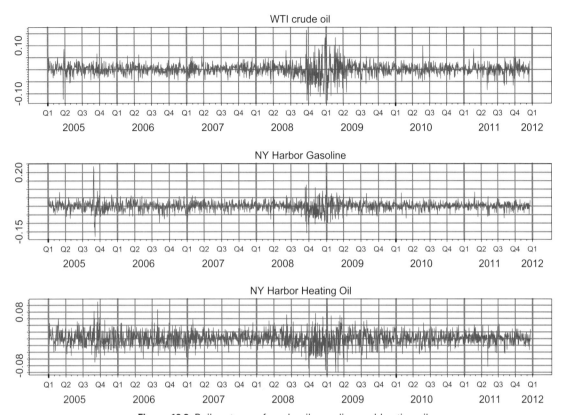

Figure 19.2 Daily returns of crude oil, gasoline and heating oil.

Jarque–Bera test and the *QQ*-plots of the returns against the normal distribution. The Ljung–Box *Q*-statistics of order 12 show the existence of return autocorrelations for all the series, except for the heating oil. The Ljung–Box statistics of order 12 applied to squared returns are highly significant. The results of the Lagrange multiplier tests point to the presence of ARCH effects in the return data, thus supporting our decision to use GARCH model to filter returns.

19.3.2 Empirical results from GARCH-based copula models

Recall that the GARCH-based copula approach requires the estimation of a GARCH-type model to remove any serial dependency from the return. Once the estimates of the GARCH(1,1) model become available, we turn to estimate the dependence structure between the individual series. For this purpose, we consider the vector of standardized residuals $(x_{1t}, x_{2t}, ..., x_{nt})_{t=1}^{\mathrm{T}}$ from the GARCH(1,1) model and transform it into a vector of

Table 19.1. Descriptive statistics of daily crude oil, gasoline and heating oil returns

	Minimum	Mean	Maximum	Standard devintion	Skewness	Excess kurtosis	$Q(12)$	$Q^2(12)$	JB	ARCH(12)
Crude oil	−0.128	4.767e-04	0.164	0.026	0.023	4.603	52.056***	999.020***	1536.881***	317.822***
Gasoline	−0.179	4.852e-04	0.235	0.029	0.223	6.814	20.273*	743.88***	3382.903***	440.570***
Heating oil	−0.099	5.081e-04	0.110	0.023	−0.010	1.387	4.393	251.506***	139.098***	134.252***

The sample period is from 3 January, 2005 to 20 December, 2011. $Q(12)$ and $Q^2(12)$ are the 12-order Ljung–Box statistics for serial correlation in returns and squared returns. JB is the empirical statistics of the Jarque–Bera test for normality. ARCH is the Lagrange multiplier test for autoregressive conditional heteroskedasticity. Asterisks indicate the rejection of the null hypothesis of no autocorrelation, normality and homoscedasticity at the *10, **5 and ***1% levels, respectively.

uniform variates, $(u_{1t}, u_{2t}, ..., u_{nt})_{t=1}^{T}$, using the probability-integral transformation. Figure 19.3 shows a scatterplot of each pair of variables transformed into its rank using $U_t = \dfrac{rank(X_t)}{T+1}$ and $V_t = \dfrac{rank(Y_t)}{T+1}$, where T is the sample size. The joint behavior of the returns supports the idea of extreme comovement since the observations appear to be concentrated in the lower-left and upper-right quadrant. Moreover, the dependence structure seems to be symmetric, which suggests the Student-t copula as a possibly best dependence model.

We now investigate the dependence of petroleum markets in a bidirectional manner. For each pair, the estimated parameters of the best copula model as well as the values of the lower and upper tail dependence coefficients are reported in Table 19.2. Selection of the best copula fit is based on the goodness-fit test discussed in Section 19.2. The results are ordered according to the value of their tail dependence coefficients.

As expected, the Student-t copula provides the best fit to the data as it yields the smallest distance between the estimated and the empirical copulas. The estimates of the dependence

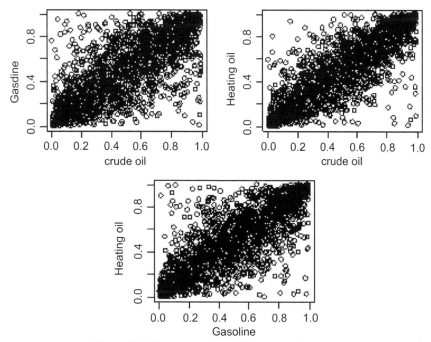

Figure 19.3 The scatterplot of different market pairs.

Table 19.2. Copula parameter estimates and tail dependence coefficients (TDC) for the considered pairs

Pairs	Copula estimates (standard errors)	TDC
Crude oil–heating oil	Student-t $\theta = 0.820$, d.f. $= 4.879$ $(0.008)^*$ $\quad\quad\quad (0.604)^*$	$\lambda_l = \lambda_u = 0.475$
Gasoline–heating oil	Student-t $\theta = 0.775$, d.f. $= 4.526$ $(0.010)^*$ $\quad\quad\quad (0.571)^*$	$\lambda_l = \lambda_u = 0.437$
Crude oil–gasoline	Student-t $\theta = 0.730$, d.f. $= 4.740$ $(0.011)^*$ $\quad\quad\quad (0.596)^*$	$\lambda_l = \lambda_u = 0.382$

Standard errors are given in parenthesis. An asterik indicates that the associated coefficients are significant at the 1% level.

parameter are positive and highly significant for all considered pairs. Accordingly, an increase in the price of crude oil leads to an increase in the price of gasoline and heating oil. Table 19.2 also reports the values of the lower and the upper tail dependence coefficients, obtained from the best-fitting copula model. As we can see, the hypothesis of comovement in the tails of distributions between petroleum prices cannot be rejected. However, the dependence structure is symmetric in bear and bull markets because lower and upper tail dependence coefficients are exactly equal. The degree of extreme comovement with the crude oil market is highest for heating oil and lowest for gasoline.

19.3.3 Value at risk forecasting with a three-dimensional Student-t copula

We now examine the usefulness of the copula-GARCH approach in managing the market risk of an equally weighted portfolio that is composed of crude oil, gasoline and heating oil. We first compare the three-dimensional empirical distribution of the petroleum returns, the distribution of a trivariate normal sample of the same size and the distribution of the Monte Carlo simulated sample, obtained from a three-dimensional Student-t copula with unstructured dispersion matrix. The results are given in Figure 19.4. It is obvious from the plots that the empirical distribution is better reproduced by the simulated returns from the Student-t copula. The trivariate normal distribution fails in

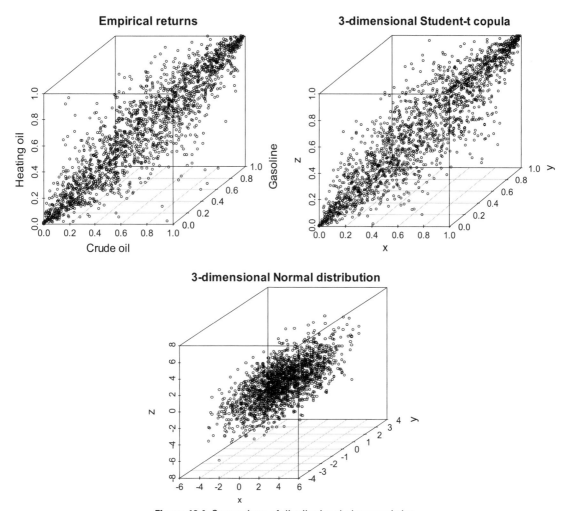

Figure 19.4 Comparison of distributional characteristics.

capturing the isolated points appearing in the upper and lower tails. This is a clear indication that returns are not normally distributed and assuming normality will therefore lead to an underestimation of the extreme risk.

Suppose that the value at risk (VaR) is used to measure the market risk of our portfolio, a backtesting procedure can be implemented to assess the accuracy of VaR estimates from the copula-GARCH model (Aloui *et al.*, 2010). First, we estimate the whole Student-t copula-GARCH model using data up to time t_0 only. We then simulate innovations from the Student-t copulas and transform them into standardized residuals by inverting the marginal cumulative distribution function of each series. Finally,

Table 19.3. Out-of-sample performance of the copula-GARCH model

Model	$\alpha = 0.10$	$\alpha = 0.05$	$\alpha = 0.01$	$\alpha = 0.005$
Normal	88	58	23	18
Student-t copula	86	41	8	3

VaR backtesting results obtained from the trivariate normal and trivariate Student-t copula models. A model that is said to be best suited for calculating VaR refers to the one with the number of exceedances closest to the expected number of exceedances. The latter are 87, 43, 8 and 4 for 90, 95, 99 and 99.5% confidence levels, respectively.

we calculate the returns by reintroducing the GARCH volatilities and the conditional mean term observed in the original return series, and recompute the value of the portfolio. This procedure can be repeated until the last observation and we compare the estimated VaR with the actual next-day value change in the portfolio. The whole process is repeated only once in every 50 observations owing to the computational cost of this procedure and because we do not expect to see large modifications in the estimated model when only a fraction of the observations is modified. However, at each new observation the VaR estimates are modified because of changes in the GARCH volatility and the conditional mean.

More concretely, we estimate the whole model using the first half of the data. Then, we simulate 3000 values of the standardized residuals, estimate the VaR and count the number of losses that exceeds these estimated VaR values. In Table 19.3, we display the out-of-sample proportions of portfolio returns which are lower than the 10, 5, 1 and 0.5% quantile values for both the trivariate normal model and the Student-t copula models. Our results thus suggest that the Student-t copula model outperforms the trivariate normal model by providing more accurate estimates of the VaR amount for extreme rare values.

19.4 Conclusion

This chapter investigates the comovement in petroleum markets using a copula-GARCH approach. We first employ a standard GARCH(1,1) process to model the margins of the return distributions. Various copula models are then fitted to standardized residuals from the marginal models. Our results show that the Student-t copula is the best model for modeling the dependence structure of petroleum prices. This dependence structure is also found to be identical for both bearish and bullish market periods. Finally, our portfolio simulations show that the copula-GARCH model provides more accurate VaR forecasts than the commonly-used multivariate normal models.

References

Aloui, R., Ben Aïssa, M., Nguyen, D.K., 2011. Global financial crisis, extreme interdependences, and contagion effects: the role of economic structure? Journal of Banking and Finance 35, 130–141.

Arouri, M., Lahiani, A., Nguyen, D.K., 2012. Forecasting the conditional volatility of oil spot and futures prices with structural breaks and long memory models. Energy Economics 34, 283–293.

Bollerslev, T., 1986. Generalized autoregressive conditional heteroskedasticity. Journal of Econometrics 31, 307–327.

Chan-Lau, J.A., Mathieson, D.J., Yao, J.Y., 2004. Extreme contagion in equity markets. IMF Staff Papers 51, 386–408.

Cherubini, U., Luciano, E., Vecchiato, W., 2004. Copula methods in finance. Wieley, New York.

Clayton, D.G., 1978. A model for association in bivariate life tables and its application in epidemiological studies of familial tendency in chronic disease incidence. Biometrika 65, 141–152.

Frank, M.J., 1979. On the simultaneous associativity of $F(x,y)$ and $x + y - F(x,y)$. Aequationes Mathematicae 19, 194–226.

Genest, C., Ghoudi, K., Rivest, L.-P., 1995. A semiparametric estimation procedure of dependence parameters in multivariate families of distributions. Biometrika 82, 543–552.

Gumbel, E.J., 1960. Bivariate exponential distributions. Journal of the American Statistical Association 55, 698–707.

Joe, H., 1997. Multivariate Models and Dependence Concepts. Chapman & Hall, Landon.

Kojadinovic, I., Yan, J., 2011. A goodness-of-fit test for multivariate multiparameter copulas based on multiplier central limit theorems. Statistics and Computing 21, 17–30.

Nelsen, R.B., 1999. An Introduction to Copulas. Springer, NewYork.

20

MISTAKES IN THE MARKET APPROACH TO CORRELATION: A LESSON FOR FUTURE STRESS-TESTING

Massimo Morini

Banca IMI

CHAPTER OUTLINE

20.1 Introduction

Most of the blame about the weaknesses of financial models during the recent credit crunch has focused on the Gaussian copula model for credit derivatives. The problems of Gaussian copulas were usually attributed to the fact that this model is "Gaussian"—a bad choice since the Gaussian distribution has no fat tails and the derived Gaussian copula has no extreme tail

Rethinking Valuation and Pricing Models. http://dx.doi.org/10.1016/B978-0-12-415875-7.00020-8

331

dependency. As a solution, models based on alternative, and usually much more complex, approaches to modeling default correlation were proposed.

In this chapter, we take a different route. We start from analyzing those feature of the Gaussian copula model and of its typical application that could really have a material role in generating the situation that led to the crisis. We perform a stress test of the model based on this analysis and show that the real problems of Gaussian copulas were not related so much to the Gaussian distribution assumption, but to other features of the model (e.g. the fact of being a copula) or to specific, extra-model extensions (e.g. mapping for bespoke portfolios). Once these issues are exposed, we suggest solutions that have the same level of complexity as the Gaussian copula or are even simpler. This seems to us a good start for a rethink of our valuation approach, considering that lack of comprehension of model complexities from model users has been mentioned by quantitative researchers as one of the reasons behind the poor use of models, while the excessive conceptual and computational complexity of some really superior approaches was the fundamental reason that inhibited their use and favored suboptimal choices.

In our first test, we address the supposed impossibility of a Gaussian copula to fit the market evidence. We show that actually the Gaussian nature of the distribution used in the market approach was compatible with a realistic representation of risk and also with the skew quoted in the collateralized debt obligation (CDO) market. However, to obtain these two goals one needs a total rethink of the approach to correlations. Second, we show that the choice of a copula framework—any copula—implied some unrealistic scenarios in terms of the probability of losses clustered in a short period of time, like those that fuelled the crisis. Such problems can be avoided solely using models with a structural representation of default events. Third, the approach used in the market to map correlations from quoted indices to bespoke deals was bounded to underestimate the risk of bespoke products. This can be detected only by subjecting the methods to the appropriate scenario analysis and can be solved only by introducing more exogenous information in the methods. The three problems are dissected through a stress-testing approach that can be applied also to other pricing approaches, and based on the results of stress-testing we propose alternative methods free of the flaws just detected.

We can consider the above work as an example of stress-testing of the different features of a market model, and we hope it can give useful suggestions for the evolution of this important aspect of model analysis and validation. Thus, in Section 20.5 we review the steps we followed incorporating them in a general framework for efficient stress-testing.

20.2 From Flat Correlation towards a Realistic Approach

The typical reference about Gaussian copulas when applied to credit portfolio derivatives like CDOs is Li (2000). A description can be found also in Morini (2011). Here, we start by considering one crucial aspect of the application of the model: The standard market parameterization of the Gaussian copula for CDOs was based on keeping correlations as one flat parameter, even if the underlying names to correlate were usually more than 100. This unique number was then changed every time one considered a different tranche of the same CDO. In fact, the model with the above parameterization could not fit the real quoted tranche correlations skew and the correlation needed to be changed for every different tranche if one wanted to replicate the market price of all of them. This showed the model to be inconsistent with market reality, and made the link between the reality and the implied correlation rather weak and not intuitive.

The Gaussian assumption was usually deemed to be the reason for the inconsistency with market reality. Here, however, we notice that the market approach to CDO is not only a Gaussian copula, it also has a strong constraint: The correlation parameters are all kept equal. May the existence of a correlation skew be somehow related to the difference between such a flat correlation and a more realistic correlation matrix? This would appear the first thing to check, but neither the scientific community nor the market pursued this line before the crisis. We now investigate the issue and the findings are somewhat surprising.

How could we model credit loss correlation with a financially more meaningful parameterization? Let us borrow from experienced loan professionals: "The loans with the highest predictable losses have the lowest sensitivity to macroeconomic conditions. Conversely the lowest risk loans have the highest sensitivity to macroeconomic conditions" (Breeden, 2006).[1]

This concept, when translated in our modeling framework, implies that correlation should be a function of default risk. This

---

[1] This is the application to the financial reality of a concept that we can find expressed, in general terms, by Leo Tolstoy in the incipit of *Anna Karenina*: "Happy families are all alike, every unhappy family is unhappy in its own way" (I thank Marcos Costa Santos Carreira for pointing out to me this analogy during a conference on derivatives).

is not unusual. Often, names with different *levels* of credit risk are often associated to different *types* of credit risk: The risk of subinvestment-grade borrowers usually comes from idiosyncratic, or firm-specific, risk factors, while the risk of senior borrowers usually comes from the risk of more systemic crisis. There are obviously many exceptions to this: Senior names can become fallen angels, i.e. companies that jump from being considered very reliable to default in a short period of time, even without a systemic crisis. Enron or Parmalat defaults were such cases. However, in spite of these exceptions, the link between low probability of default and higher correlation to systemic risk factors seems a fundamental pillar, as confirmed by the 2007–2009 crisis. This suggest that correlation must be a decreasing function of the names' default risk.

20.2.1 Correlation parameterization for the market skew

We can implement this principle using the simplest possible Gaussian correlation framework—a one-factor Gaussian copula. We define the *n*-variate Gaussian distribution as:

$$X_i = \rho_i M + \sqrt{1 - \rho_i^2} Y_i \quad i = 1, ..., n,$$

where M and $Y_i i = 1, ..., n$ are all mutually independent standardized Gaussians, so that:

$$\rho_{ij} = Corr(X_i X_j) = \rho_i \rho_j.$$

However, now we do not assume that the individual correlation parameters ρ_i are all the same like in market practice, but instead we make them a function of individual intensities or spreads:

$$\rho_i = f(Spread_i).$$

What is the effect on ρ_{ij} of the parameterization of ρ_i? Notice that if ρ_i and ρ_j are high, then ρ_{ij} will also be high, with the limit case:

$$\rho_i = \rho_j = 1 \Rightarrow \rho_{ij} = 1,$$

while if either ρ_i or ρ_j is low, the resulting correlation of the two names will be lower, and very low when both $\rho_i \approx 0$ and $\rho_j \approx 0$, e.g.:

$$\rho_i = \rho_j = 0.03 \Rightarrow \rho_{ij} = 0.0009.$$

If we build a decreasing parameterization:

$$Spread_i < Spread_j \Rightarrow \rho_i = f(Spread_i) > \rho_j = f(Spread_j),$$

we obtain the financial effect we want: When a senior name "meets" another senior name in computing $\rho_i \rho_j$, their resulting correlation ρ_{ij} will be high; when a junior name meets another junior name the correlation will be low, with a slightly higher correlation for mixed meetings.

An approach similar to the one above is mentioned in Andersen and Sidenius (2005), long before the crisis, but in that work it is rejected *a priori* on the basis of some of its features and not tested. On the other hand, this approach is underpinned by some quantitative results. Glasserman *et al.* (2007) show analytically that it is not true that in a Gaussian copula the tails of the loss decay exponentially, as one would expect due to lack of tail dependence. This is true for low default probabilities, but when default probabilities grow the Gaussian copula produces a heavier tail, suggesting a difference in the dependence induced by the Gaussian copula for sets of high-quality credits (exponential decay of the tail) and low-quality credits (power-law decay of the tail). Therefore, in a Gaussian copula model with flat correlation, senior names are, in practice, less correlated than junior names, even if the correlation parameter is the same. In our approach we contrast effectively this model behavior by increasing the correlations for more senior names. Glasserman *et al.*(2007) conclude that higher implied correlations for names with lower default risk may, in part, offset the diminished dependence in the Gaussian copula at low default probabilities, keeping an acceptable amount of dependency.

We have to choose now a functional form for the parameterization:

$$\rho_i = f(Spread_i).$$

We want the function to depend on few parameters, but also be sufficiently general to allow for correlation factors as high as $\rho_i = 1$ and as low as $\rho_i = 0$. A simple parameterization of this kind is a three-parameter constrained polynomial chosen in Duminuco and Morini (2008). We take the 125 market spreads of the components of the iTraxx index on 15 February 2008 and we calibrate the default intensities of our portfolio to their market spreads. Then, we run an optimization on the three parameters in order to replicate as much as possible the quotation of the five-year iTraxx tranches on the same day. The resulting shape of f as a function of spreads is shown in Figure 20.1.

There are a few parameters ρ_i set to 0 and some set to 1. The effect of this parameterization on the elements ρ_{ij} is summarized by the three-dimensional picture of the resulting correlation matrix given in Figure 20.2. On the x-and y-axes there are i and j for the 125 names; on the z-axis there are correlations ρ_{ij}.

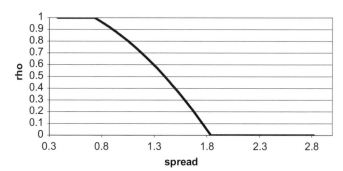

Figure 20.1 Correlation parameterization: parametric correlation factor ρ_i as a function of spreads (iTraxx).

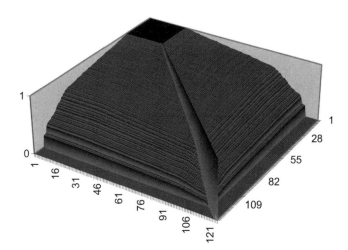

Figure 20.2 Correlation matrix resulting from the parameterization.

We can see that there is a small area of names with unit correlation, representing the risk of systemic events, and an area of zero correlation names, capturing purely idiosyncratic risk. What is the agreement of this correlation matrix with the quoted tranche prices, i.e. the market correlation skew? This correlation implies the rather realistic correlation skew that we see in Figure 20.3 together with the market correlation skew of the same day.

Considering that we only have three parameters and that we are still in the one-factor Gaussian copula, the fit appears surprisingly good. It is not very precise, but it captures very well the shape of the skew and this is a good result for a model that was supposed to admit no skews or skews with no relations with market reality.[2]

[2] This specific calibration day was chosen as an example of the model behavior because in those days of the crisis calibration was particularly difficult since recovery expectations had fallen while the market still used, as we did, the approach of keeping recovery at 40%.

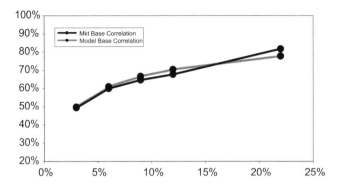

Figure 20.3 Correlation skew resulting from the parameterization.

The implied loss distribution can be easily computed and it has a "fat tail" multimodal structure, with bumps in the tails similar to those visible in realistic loss distributions coming from more complex models like Hull and White (2005), which are able to fit exactly the market correlation skew. See Figure 20.4.

However, here we obtain all these elements of consistency with the market *without abandoning the Gaussian copula framework*. We just eliminate its most unrealistic feature, i.e. flat correlation. The message is clear: To avoid the model weaknesses often put in relation with the crisis, before inventing new over-complex models we have still to learn to use the simple models applied by practitioners better.

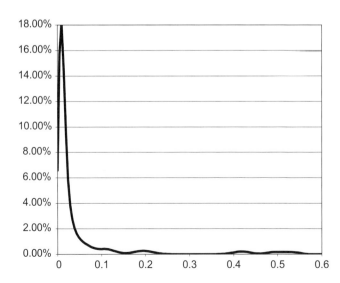

Figure 20.4 Loss density resulting from the parameterization.

20.3 Payoff Stress and the Liquidity Mistake

As mentioned in Section 20.2, the Gaussian copula has been attacked mainly for being "Gaussian." Thus, it lacks tail dependency and the implied loss of a credit portfolio that has a distribution that does not feature fat tails, underestimating the risk of big losses around the size of the entire portfolio. These criticisms appear to be misled. (i) We have seen in Section 20.2 that this problem can be tackled without abandoning the Gaussian distribution, but just taking a different approach to the parameterization of correlation. (ii) The crisis was not started by credit losses that wiped out entire portfolios, but by a liquidity crunch generated by few credit losses in different portfolios that were however concentrated in a short period of time.

This is an important point to ponder. Before the crisis, market players chose the Gaussian copula as a model for assessing the risk of having a high concentration of losses in a single portfolio, over a horizon of some years from now such as five or ten years. In fact these were the usual maturities of CDOs and this aspect of default correlation risk was considered the core risk involved in CDO investments. The problems that led to the credit crunch came instead from losses that were not so high in a single portfolio, being split among more equity tranches of a number of CDOs in the books of a bank and its related vehicles, but were concentrated in a short period of time, creating panic and liquidity difficulties. The recent crisis has shown that a bank, under the liquidity risk point of view, looks like a senior "temporal tranche." A standard senior tranche in a CDO is a product that suffers losses when *the losses concentrated in one portfolio, over a relatively long time horizon, are higher than a given threshold*. Analogously and yet differently, a bank exposed to the structured credit market runs into liquidity problems, either directly due to the losses or indirectly through the withdrawal of investors, when *the losses concentrated in a relatively short period of time, over all of its portfolios, are higher than a given threshold*.

Thus, it seems that "losses concentrated in time" were more relevant to understand the crisis than "losses concentrated in a portfolio." Let us see if the Gaussian copula was suitable for modeling this sort of losses. We consider a bank that, after the credit crunch, wants to protect itself against this liquidity risk. Suppose it is exposed towards the default of two different investments. The two investments are one more senior and one more risky, with default intensities:

$$\lambda_1 = 0.03, \lambda_2 = 0.2.$$

The bank is not very worried that one of the two names will default, because it knows it has sufficient liquidity to face such an event. Even if they both default, but the two defaults are not very close, e.g. they are five years apart, the bank believes it can cope with this without running out of liquidity. The real worry is that the two investments both default in the same, short period of time. In particular, we suppose now that the bank knows that the worst period under a liquidity point of view will be between three and five years from now, because of some planned future expenses (later we will generalize this case). How may the bank protect itself against this event, which can make the difference between survival and bankruptcy of the bank itself?

The natural choice is to buy protection on a last-to-default, but not a standard one with a start date equal to today. The bank needs a forward start last-to-default, paying protection only if both names default in the specific period of time that worries it, i.e. a product with payoff:

$$\text{LGD at } \hat{\tau} = \max(\tau_1, \tau_2) \text{ if } 3 \leq \tau_1 \leq 5, 3 \leq \tau_2 \leq 5, \qquad (20.1)$$

where LGD represents the loss given default. The value of the protection on the last-to-default in (20.1) depends on the probability of the two names to default together exactly in that short period of time:

$$\Pr(3 \leq \tau_1 \leq 5, 3 \leq \tau_2 \leq 5).$$

We may expect this probability of loss to be higher when correlation is higher, as always happens with last-to-default. The higher the default correlation, the higher the probability risk that the names both default in the same period of time.

However, in Figure 20.5 we see the relation and the behavior is opposite than expected.

The probability of joint default *decreases* with correlation, different from what one expects and from what happens with a standard, spot-starting last-to-default. This fact is surprising, but it can be easily explained mathematically. Consider the case of flat default intensity. We know that:

$$\tau_1 = \frac{\varepsilon_1}{\lambda_1}, \tau_2 = \frac{\varepsilon_2}{\lambda_2}, \ldots, \tau_n = \frac{\varepsilon_n}{\lambda_n},$$

where the ε_is are unit exponential variables. Setting all correlations equal to one implies that the ε_is not only have the same distribution, but they are even the same random variable, i.e.:

$$\varepsilon_1 = \varepsilon_2 = \ldots = \varepsilon_n = \varepsilon.$$

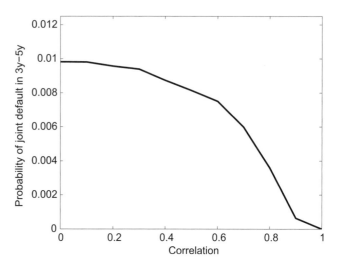

Figure 20.5 Probability of concentrated losses for different correlations.

Instead, the deterministic components of the default times, which are the intensities λ_is, are set by the credit default swap (CDS) market and can be very different from each other. Thus, we have:

$$\tau_1 = \frac{\varepsilon}{\lambda_1}, \tau_2 = \frac{\varepsilon}{\lambda_2}, ..., \tau_n = \frac{\varepsilon}{\lambda_n}. \qquad (20.2)$$

When the correlation is zero, the probability that the two investments default together is:

$$\Pr(3 \le \tau_1 \le 5, 3 \le \tau_2 \le 5) =$$
$$\Pr(3 \le \tau_1 \le 5) \times \Pr(3 \le \tau_2 \le 5) =$$
$$= 0.053 * 0.181 = 0.0096.$$

When the correlation is one, instead, $\tau_1 = \frac{\varepsilon}{\lambda_1} = \frac{\varepsilon}{0.03}$ and $\tau_2 = \frac{\varepsilon}{\lambda_2} = \frac{\varepsilon}{0.2}$, so $3 \le \tau_1 \le 5$ means $0.09 \le \varepsilon \le 0.15$, while $3 \le \tau_2 \le 5$ means $0.6 \le \varepsilon \le 1$. The two ε intervals do not overlap, so the probability:

$$\Pr(3 \le \tau_1 \le 5, 3 \le \tau_2 \le 5).$$

that the two default events happen jointly is zero. For intermediate levels of correlation, the probability of joint default goes down between these two extremes.

The result is surprising because the market wisdom is that the risk of last-to-defaults, like senior tranches, goes up with correlation. Unfortunately, in the Gaussian copula this is guaranteed only for a last-to-default which is spot-starting, e.g. the one that pays when both names default between today and two years from now. In fact, in this case we have, under independence:

$$\Pr(0 \le \tau_1, \tau_2 \le 2) =$$
$$\Pr(0 \le \tau_1 \le 2) \times \Pr(0 \le \tau_2 \le 2) =$$
$$= 0.058 * 0.330 = 0.019.$$

When the correlation is one, we have now that $0 \le \tau_1 \le 2$ means $0 \le \varepsilon \le 0.06$, while $0 \le \tau_2 \le 2$ means $0 \le \varepsilon \le 0.4$. The two ε intervals now overlap and the both inequalities hold true when the first one holds true, thus:

$$\Pr(0 \le \tau_1, \tau_2 \le 2) =$$
$$\Pr(0 \le \tau_1 \le 2) = 0.058 > 0.019,$$

and the probability of joint defaults goes up between these two extremes.

Thus, we have shown numerically and explained mathematically that the relationship between the only parameter of the model and the financial risk we are really interested in, i.e. the risk of having defaults in the same period of time, tends to invert in moving from a period of time that starts now to a period of time located in the future. The relation is clearly increasing for the zero to two years period and clearly decreasing for the three to five years interval. In between we can have intervals where there is almost no relation between correlation and risk, and cases where the relation is not monotonic. This makes the behavior of the relation between model parameter and financial risk unstable and irregular.

Different from expectations of the theory of copulas, the copula parameter ρ does not allow us to control neatly the risk of default dependence, which is of real financial interest: The risk of defaults happening near in time. Now we show, even more in contrast with what one would expect from the theory of copulas, that this risk is strongly influenced by a change in the default intensities instead, i.e. the marginal distributions of the default times. Suppose that we keep the total probability of default equal to the above example, where $\lambda_1 + \lambda_2 = 0.03 + 0.2 = 0.23$, but we redistribute this risk evenly among the two names, setting:

$$\lambda_1 = \lambda_2 = \frac{0.23}{2} = 0.115.$$

In this case, when correlation is zero the probability of joint default is:

$$\Pr(3 \le \tau_1 \le 5) \times \Pr(3 \le \tau_2 \le 5) =$$
$$= 0.146 * 0.146 = 0.021.$$

while the probability that the two events happen together when $\rho = 1$ is simply $\Pr(3 \leq \tau_1 \leq 5) = 0.146$. The pattern for intermediate values is given in Figure 20.6.

This redistribution of risk between the investments has two effects. (i) It allows for higher probability of joint defaults in the same period of time. (ii) It alters the relation between correlation and financial risk again, which goes back to being increasing and therefore consistent with our intuition. It seems that capturing the temporal aspect of "correlation risk" is related more to credit spreads than to the Gaussian copula correlation ρ. The copula has not allowed us "to analyze the dependence structure of multivariate distributions without studying marginal distributions" and does not give us a parameter that has a clear relation with the most relevant financial risk associated to default correlation.

20.3.1 Dynamic value at risk

The above example can be made even more realistic. We have assumed above that a bank is able to predict precisely what the worst period for having the joint default of the two names is, assuming a period of two years starting in three years for now. More likely, a bank will not be able to make such a prediction, but will know that it would enter in a liquidity crisis whenever the two investments default close together. For example, it may be enough that the distance between the two defaults is less than

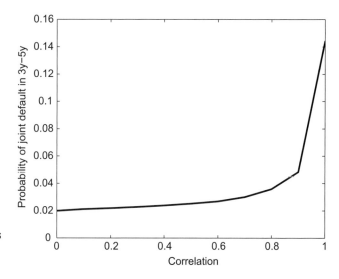

Figure 20.6 Probability of concentrated losses for different correlations. The case of names with the same default risk.

three months for not being able to cover the losses and be led to default. Thus, in the following we compute:

$$\Pr(|\tau_1 - \tau_2| < 3m), \qquad (20.3)$$

and analyze how this probability behaves with correlation, limiting the analysis to a 10-year horizon, i.e. $\tau_1 < 10$ years, $\tau_2 < 10$ years. This is a much more general case than above, and also includes the spot three-month period that starts now. It is also similar to a standard risk management computation. The probability in (20.3) can be rewritten as a standard credit value at risk problem:

$$\Pr(Loss([t, t + 3m]) > 500mn).$$

The behavior of the probability as a function of correlation is shown in Figure 20.7.

Now the relation starts increasing, but suddenly it reverts to decreasing. This is particularly dangerous in stress-testing. Suppose a risk manager wants to see what the price would be in the worst possible financial scenario. For the risk of two names happening together, it likely that the poor risk manager chooses $\rho = 1$ as the worst-case scenario. Unfortunately, here $\rho = 1$ is not the *most pessimistic* case, but the *most optimistic* one. Even worse, the most pessimistic case corresponds to $\rho \approx 0.7$. How could one have guessed it *a priori*? There is no way—one must always compute (numerically or analytically when possible) the probability of losses for all levels of correlation to find out which correlation really maximizes the risk and can be used for a stress test.

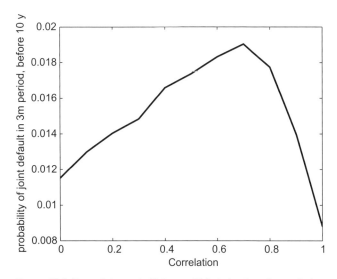

Figure 20.7 Test of dynamic Value at Risk: behavior of correlation.

20.3.2 Conclusions

In this section, we have tested the Gaussian copula for modeling the risk of losses concentrated in time. Unfortunately, we find that the Gaussian copula can easily lead to a wrong estimation of the probability of joint credit losses from different investments in a short period of time, since the relation between this risk we want to capture and the correlation parameter of the Gaussian copula is:

(i) Unstable, in the sense that it changes dramatically for small changes in the features of the events we analyze.

(ii) Irregular, since this relation is not even monotonic, making it difficult to control the risk and understand, for example, what level of correlation maximizes risk.

These unpleasant features do not appear crucially related to the model being "Gaussian," but, unlike most other critics, we point the finger at the model being "a copula." Our results suggest that one central fact about copulas is not true. Enthusiasts of the application of copulas in finance claim that copulas allow for the separate the modeling of the interdependence between financial variables from the modeling of individual variables,[3] so that we can *first* set the individual marginal distributions (e.g. in credit we fix them in the single name CDS market), and *then* we can give them the dependency structure we like through the copula function and its parameters. Unfortunately, this may be true when we use a purely mathematical definition of dependence—functional dependence—but it is not true anymore when we consider the meaning of dependency, which is more relevant in credit modeling: Losses happening in the same period of time. Copulas do not allow control of this dependency independently from the individual distributions. The level of dependency in copulas can be limited by the individual distributions.

Can we find alternative approaches to default correlation that do not suffer from the problems of the Gaussian copula? The tests in Minucci (2010) and Morini (2011) suggest also that other copulas suffer from the same problem, while structurally founded models like the Marshall and Olkin (1967) model allow avoidance of similar issues. A solution to this problem is moving away from the framework of copulas, that in a credit application behave like a mathematical black box, and using instead a model with

---

[3] For example, Bouyé *et al.* (2000), in one of the first popular papers that introduced copulas in finance, claim that copulas provide "a way to analyze the dependence structure of multivariate distributions without studying marginal distributions."

structural foundations and an easy interpretation as a physical model for default times.

20.4 Testing with Historical Scenarios and the Concentration Mistake

In the market model based on the Gaussian copula with flat correlation, in order to price a CDO on a portfolio an investor requires the level of the spreads of the components of the portfolio and a correlation skew (a relation between detachments of equity options and implied correlations) specific for the portfolio. When the portfolio is bespoke (i.e. unique with no associated derivatives quotes), we have surely no market information on correlations. In the best case, we only know the single name spreads. Here, *mapping* used to enter the picture.

The idea behind mapping is that there is some stable relation between the portfolio composition (the spreads) and the portfolio correlation skew. We can capture this relation on a quoted index portfolio, for which we know spreads and market correlation, and then apply it to the bespoke portfolio, of which we only know the spreads. The mapping literature assumes that the level of correlation ρ_K associated to a tranche $[0, K]$ is a function of one fundamental characteristic of the tranche, called *invariant*. We can look at the information available on the index in order to understand what this map $f(\cdot)$ is, giving the tranche correlation as a function of the tranche invariant:

$$\rho_K^{\text{Index}} = f(\text{Invariant}_K^{\text{Index}}).$$

In other words, we are using the information available on the index portfolio to calibrate the relation between the invariant and the correlations. This calibration gives the function $f(\cdot)$. Then we apply $f(\cdot)$ to the level of the invariant computed for the tranches of the bespoke, obtaining as an output the right bespoke correlations:

$$\rho_{\bar{K}}^{\text{Bespoke}} = f(\text{Invariant}_{\bar{K}}^{\text{Bespoke}}).$$

The first choice to make is to decide what the invariant is. Many proposals have been made in the market. Surprisingly enough, none of these proposals is underpinned by a structured financial reasoning. For more details, see, e.g. Baheti and Morgan (2007) and Turc *et al.* (2006).

(i) *Tranche detachment (TD) or no mapping.* The first example of invariant we can think of is a trivial one. If the correlation skew that is correct for CDOs on the index portfolio was deemed to be correct also for CDOs written on any bespoke portfolio, then the invariant would be just the detachment K of the tranche, leading to:

$$\rho_K^{\text{Index}} = f^{\text{TD}}(K), \quad \rho_{\bar{K}}^{\text{Bespoke}} = f^{\text{TD}}(\bar{K}).$$

Once we devise a way to test the mapping methods, no mapping will be used as a benchmark to assess if the other non-trivial mapping methods described below are really useful: If they do as good as "no mapping," or even worse, clearly the non-trivial mapping methods are useless or even harmful and the whole idea behind mapping should be questioned.

(ii) *Expected loss (EL).* This second method was largely used in the market. It was implemented by the vast majority of financial software and even now it is probably the most widespread approach to "marking-to-market" CDOs on bespoke portfolios. Here, the invariant is the normalized detachment $\dfrac{K}{\mathbb{E}[L^{\text{Index}}]}$, where L indicates the portfolio loss at the maturity of interest. Thus, one must detect from the index the map:

$$\rho_K^{\text{Index}} = f^{\text{EL}}\left(\frac{K}{\mathbb{E}[L^{\text{Index}}]}\right),$$

and then one can apply it to the bespoke, so that:

$$\rho_{\bar{K}}^{\text{Bespoke}} = f^{\text{EL}}\left(\frac{\bar{K}}{\mathbb{E}[L^{\text{Bespoke}}]}\right).$$

(iii) *Expected tranched loss (ETL).* This third method was considered an improvement on the EL method, although it was similar in spirit. The invariant is in fact the expected tranched loss:

$$\frac{\mathbb{E}[L_K]}{\mathbb{E}[L]},$$

where L_K is:

$$\frac{L - (L - K)^+}{K}.$$

20.4.1 Historical scenarios to test mapping methods

The mapping methods have been tested in a Lehman Research Paper by Baheti and Morgan (2007). The test is based on a simple reasoning. Mapping methods claim that correlation is just a function of the invariant and the function is the same for all portfolios in the market. If this is true, one can detect this function from any index with quoted tranches, e.g. the CDX Investment Grade, which is the index of the American "senior" names. The function can then be applied to the spreads of another index with quoted tranches, such as i-Traxx Main, which is the index of the European senior names, or CDX High Yield, which is the index of the American "junior" names, with higher spreads and lower rating. This will return a correlation skew for either index. If mapping works, these correlation skews will be similar to the corresponding correlation skews quoted in the market.

The results of the Lehman tests are puzzling. Only one day of data is used. On that day mapping seems to work in the most complex exercise (guessing European correlation from the American correlation) and fails in the easiest test (guessing American high-yield correlation from the American senior correlation). The real point is that it is hard to give a judgement on mapping methods based on tests that use portfolios that are very different from each other.

It would be better, for a validation, to apply mapping to portfolios that are similar, but have some specific differences that must be easy to detect and interpret, so that we can check if the effect of such a difference on the correlation skew is captured by mapping. Consequently, we suggest in the following an alternative use of our information about the indices that provides us with portfolios that are similar, but differ for some specific features that are easy to detect. We suggest to use not *different portfolios at the same time*, like in the Lehman test, but *the same portfolio at different times*. We can consider two different days, let us say yesterday and today. We treat the spreads and the skew of yesterday as the spreads and the skew of the index. Then, the spreads of today are treated as the spreads of the bespoke. By applying a mapping method to these three inputs we obtain a guess for the correlation skew of today (our bespoke) that can be compared with the actual correlation skew quoted in the market for today. The test will be even more relevant if we take two dates that are a few days apart and such that in-between some relevant market facts have happened, changing the index portfolio in a limited and clear way.

Every mapping method is based on assuming a relation between the spreads of a portfolio and its correlation skew. The above test allows us to see if such a relation implied by the mapping method is at least consistent with the historical spread—correlation relationship. The test is a relatively easy task for the mapping methods, because we consider two portfolios that are still very similar, since they are composed of the same names and separated apart only by the changes that happened to the spreads in a few trading days. If a mapping method works well in this simple test, it may work also in a real bespoke mapping. If it does not work here, it is even more dubious to apply it to more complex situations like bespoke mapping.

Here, we perform the historical testing of mapping methods explained above. Each one of these tests is based on two dates—the "index date" used for kind of calibrating the mapping method and the "bespoke date" whose correlation skew needs to be guessed. The two dates used to come just before and just after an important event or relevant crisis that happened in the past. In this case the interpretation of the difference between the pre-crisis portfolio and the post-crisis portfolio is easier because the market operators have already analyzed and interpreted the crisis with hindsight.

We concentrate on only two pairs of days, but we have selected periods during which we are sure that the market went through relevant changes. The first event study looks at what happened in the so-called "May 2005 Correlation Crisis." On 5 May 2005 Standard & Poor's downgraded General Motors and Ford to junk status, provoking a sharp increase in the credit spreads of all companies related to the auto sector, both in Europe and in the United States. The second event study focuses on July 2007, when CDS spreads, after years of impressive calm and low volatility broken only by occasional turmoils like the May 2005 event, suddenly rocketed with an increase never seen before. It was the beginning of the systemic crisis that led to the credit crunch. Consistently, together with the growth of the CDS spreads of almost all names, implied default correlation also increased sharply.

20.4.1.1 Idiosyncratic crisis: May 2005

We consider the period between 4 May 2005 and 17 May 2005. In-between these two days the iTraxx Main index spread increased strongly, while the correlation skew decreased as much as shown in Table 20.1. In Table 20.1, we see also the results of applying the two mapping methods explained (EL and ETL) to the skew of 5 May (the index day) and the five-year spreads of 5 May and 17 May (the bespoke day), to see how mapping would have guessed the correlation skew of 17 May. In Table 20.1, we report the correlation one would obtain with no mapping, which obviously equals the correlation of 5 May (Market initial ρ) and the correlations guessed by EL and ETL for 17 May (EL/ETL

Table 20.1. **Correlations (%)**

	0–3%	0–6%	0–9%	0–12%	0–22%
Market initial ρ	19.38	30.43	39.75	47.45	64.72
EL mapping final ρ	17.22	26.22	34.55	41.72	57.66
ETL mapping final ρ	17.17	26.62	35.58	43.47	61.65
Market final ρ	9.66	24.73	35.74	43.78	60.88

mapping final ρ), to be compared with the true market correlation on 17 May (Market final ρ).

Figure 20.8 shows graphically the four correlation skews: The one by no mapping, the skews guessed by the mapping methods and the true, realized skew.

The errors associated to the three guessed skews are given in Table 20.2.

The mapping methods work definitely well. The error is very low, particularly for ETL, confirming that this more complex method is better than simple EL. Let us now see how the mapping methods perform in an opposite situation—the systemic crisis.

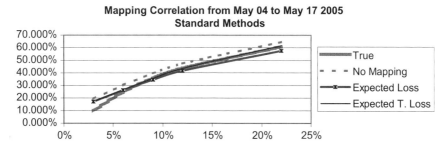

Figure 20.8 Mapping correlation from May 4 to May 17, 2005.

Table 20.2. **Correlation errors (%)**

	0–3%	0–6%	0–9%	0–12%	0–22%
No mapping	−9.7	−5.7	−4.0	−3.7	−3.8
EL mapping	−7.6	−1.5	+1.2	+2.1	+3.2
ETL mapping	−7.5	−1.9	+0.2	+0.3	−0.8

20.4.1.2 The Systemic crisis: July 2007

From 20 July 2007 and 27 July 2007, we have a large increase in spreads, which affects almost all names, associated with a movement in the correlation skew. We have selected this period since both the increase in the index spread and the movement of the correlation skew are comparable in size to the one seen in the May 2005 test. In both cases spreads have increased, but for the correlation skew the two moves followed opposite directions. The mapping results compared to the market movements are shown in Table 20.3 and in Figure 20.9.

This time the behavior of the mapping methods is wrong. The true final correlation is much higher than the initial correlations, but the mapping methods predict instead a decrease in correlation, leading to a bigger error than using no mapping. Table 20.4 below shows the size of the correlation errors.

Among the mapping methods ETL is slightly better than EL, but in any case both lead to an error larger than using no mapping.

Table 20.3. Correlations (%)

	0–3%	0–6%	0–9%	0–12%	0–22%
No mapping final ρ	19.61	28.93	36.76	43.38	60.70
EL mapping final ρ	16.81	23.33	29.71	35.18	49.26
ETL mapping final ρ	17.61	25.26	32.57	39.11	56.61
Market final ρ	24.92	36.37	44.93	52.09	69.34

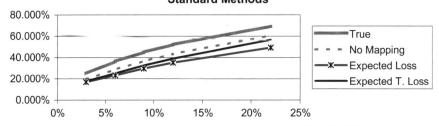

Figure 20.9 Mapping correlation from July 20 to July 27, 2007.

Table 20.4. **Correlation errors (%)**

	0–3%	0–6%	0–9%	0–12%	0–22%
No mapping	+5.31	+7.44	+8.17	+8.71	+8.64
EL mapping	+8.11	+13.04	+15.22	+16.91	+20.08
ETL mapping	+7.31	+11.11	+12.36	+12.98	+12.73

20.4.2 Limits of Mapping and the Management of Model Risk

The mapping methods have correctly interpreted the idiosyncratic crisis (an increase of spreads concentrated on a small minority of the names), decreasing correlation when spreads have increased, but unfortunately they have the same behavior also in the systemic crisis (an increase of spreads that affects a large majority of the names in the portfolio), when correlation should instead be increased. Notice that "systemic" must be intended at a portfolio level: What makes an increase of risk to be systemic, from the point of view of mapping, is the fact that it affects the majority of the names *in the portfolio*.

The evidence from these tests leads to a relevant observation. Let us consider the mechanism underlying EL mapping. It is clear that every time the bespoke is more risky than the index the entire correlation skew is shifted to the right. Due to the fact that, in the market, we have always seen an increasing correlation skew, this always translates into a reduction of correlation.

Let us see this analytically. According to the mapping principle, the correlation ρ_K^{Bespoke} given to the bespoke tranche with detachment K must be the correlation ρ_K^{Index} given to the index tranche with detachment K' such that:

$$\frac{K}{\mathbb{E}[L^{\text{Bespoke}}]} = \frac{K'}{\mathbb{E}[L^{\text{Index}}]}.$$

If $\mathbb{E}[L^{\text{Bespoke}}] > \mathbb{E}[L^{\text{Index}}]$, we must have $K' < K$. Since the correlation skew is increasing:

$$K' < K \Rightarrow \rho_{K'}^{\text{Index}} < \rho_K^{\text{Index}}.$$

Given that $\rho_{K'}^{\text{Index}} = \rho_K^{\text{Bespoke}}$, we have that:

$$\rho_K^{\text{Bespoke}} < \rho_K^{\text{Index}}.$$

Thus, as far as EL is concerned, the wrong behavior in the test is not due to a one-off error associated with the fine details of this test. The EL mapping is bound to lower the correlation every time we move to a bespoke that is more risky, thus making a mistake every time this increase of risk is, on the contrary, systemic. The ETL method, which replaces K at the numerator of the invariant with $\mathbb{E}[L_K]$, has a less trivial behavior, since it depends also on moments of the distribution of the loss, which are higher than the first moment $\mathbb{E}[L]$, but the backbone of the movement it imposes to the correlation skew remains the same as EL, as confirmed by the above tests.

This rigidity and predictability of standard mapping methods outlined by these tests is surprising for two reasons. (i) Such a fact has never been remarked in the literature in spite of the widespread use of this method, confirming that in the years before the crisis there was little analysis of the practical implications of such methods. (ii) It is obvious that this method leads, in some common practical cases, to painful errors with mathematical certainty. Suppose we are given a bespoke that is more risky than the index because all names in the bespoke belong to the same sector, which is now in a crisis. Intuitively, a CDO on this portfolio should be priced with rather high correlation skew. The mapping, instead, will always lower the correlation skew.

20.4.2.1 Introducing dispersion as a benchmark for model risk

Is this the end of the mapping illusion? Probably it is. A simple algorithm like mapping is too rigid to express sensible relations between the composition of a portfolio and its correlation skew. However, it is interesting to point out that it is not difficult to improve on the standard methods proposed before the crisis. In the following, we propose a method that captures the behavior of the correlation skew both when the increase in risk is systemic and when it is idiosyncratic, recognizing the two different situations and adapting itself to give a realistic outcome. The idea of this method was suggested to us not by complex mathematical considerations, but by the market experience learned from expert tranche traders. Such traders usually looked at the movements of a market indicator called the *spread dispersion index*. It is the ratio between the spread standard deviation and its maximum value:

$$s^* = \frac{\hat{s}}{\max \hat{s}} = \frac{\hat{s}}{\bar{s}\sqrt{(n-1)}},$$

where:

$$\bar{s} = \frac{1}{n}\sum_{i=1}^{n} s_i, \quad \hat{s} = \sqrt{\frac{1}{n}\sum_{i=1}^{n}(s_i - \bar{s})^2}.$$

It captures how dispersed the risk in a portfolio is, rescaling standard deviation by the average risk of the portfolio. When $s^* = 1$ we have the maximum dispersion we can get given the average portfolio risk expressed by $\bar{s}$.

The two indicators usually looked at by traders are $\bar{s}$ and s^*. The information conveyed by $\bar{s}$ is very close to the information conveyed by $\mathbb{E}[L]$, which is the invariant of EL. Instead the information conveyed by s^* is not considered by EL. It could be somewhat included in ETL, but the tests above have shown that the behavior of ETL is rather similar to EL. Thus, we create a new invariant based on s^*, whose information appears left out by standard methods. The functional form we choose for this invariant is simply:

$$K^{s^*}.$$

From 20 to 27 July 2007, the dispersion index has moved from $s^*_{20/7} = 11.28\%$ to $s^*_{27/7} = 8.40\%$, i.e. the dispersion has reduced. This is what one expects in a systemic crisis because increasing the risk of all names by similar amounts redistributes the risk among all names. In Table 20.5 we add the results of using K^{s^*} as a mapping invariant (dispersion mapping) to the errors made by mapping methods in the systemic crisis test.

The dispersion mapping works well in explaining this systemic crisis. What makes this method more interesting than the methods seen previously is that not only does it work well in explaining the systemic crisis of July 2007, but it also explains well the other case study, i.e. the idiosyncratic crisis of May 2005.

Table 20.5. Correlation errors (%)

	0–3%	0–6%	0–9%	0–12%	0–22%
No mapping	+5.31	+7.44	+8.17	+8.71	+8.64
EL mapping	+8.11	+13.04	+15.22	+16.91	+20.08
ETL mapping	+7.31	+11.11	+12.36	+12.98	+12.73
Dispersion	−1.84	−1.51	−0.68	+0.31	+5.98

In the idiosyncratic crisis the dispersion index moved in a direction opposite to the systemic crisis: It increased from $s^*_{4/5} = 5.70\%$ to $s^*_{17/5} = 6.15\%$. This is consistent with intuition: A crisis concentrated on a few names raises the dispersion by increasing one or few spreads, while the others are almost unaffected. The results of dispersion mapping in the May 2005 test are shown in Table 20.6.

The dispersion mapping works as well in explaining the idiosyncratic crisis (that was explained also by the standard methods) as for explaining the systemic crisis (that was missed by the standard methods).

20.4.3 Conclusions

We found, in the previous analysis, that standard mapping methods treat any increase in risk as an idiosyncratic increase. This way when we consider senior tranches, which represent the majority of the tranches bought by institutional investors before the crisis, mapping has the effect of watering down increases of risk, due to higher spreads in the bespoke compared to the index, by diminishing the correlation at the same time. The underestimation may have affected also the pricing of CDOs on mortgage-related securities that, as revealed clearly by the crisis, were strongly subject to systemic risk. When mapping was used to price very risky CDOs, the senior tranches had their risk reduced by the lower correlation imposed by mapping methods. This matched the underestimation of risk typical of the rating agency methods based on historical correlations.

Was it impossible to devise mapping methods able to recognize a systemic increase of risk? No, as we have shown by displaying the performance of a simple method based not on complex mathematical considerations, but on an indicator, the dispersion index, that was well-known to practitioners in the

Table 20.6. Correlation errors (%)

	0–3%	0–6%	0–9%	0 12%	0–22%
No mapping	−9.7	−5.7	−4.0	−3.7	−3.8
EL mapping	−7.6	−1.5	+1.2	+2.1	+3.2
ETL mapping	−7.5	−1.9	+0.2	+0.3	−0.8
Dispersion	−7.2	−1.3	+0.8	+1.1	+0.4

field. This method we introduced is not proposed as a solution to the problems of mapping methods, because all mapping methods, including the dispersion mapping, appear too simple for the task they are supposed to perform. More information about the bespoke portfolio should be used in attributing a correlation skew to the portfolios and a more structural analysis of the behavior of the different credit markets should be the foundation for the design of algorithms used to price bespoke. Simple mathematical recipes with no structural foundation should not be relied upon as much as was done before the crisis.

20.5 Lessons for Future Stress-Testing

The analysis of this chapter, focused on model improvement in the field of credit derivatives, can be seen also as a useful case study to reason about stress-testing. It covers both meanings of stress-testing of interest to quant analysts: Portfolio stress-testing (assessing how a portfolio or derivative would perform in an adverse financial scenario) and model stress-testing (subjecting the model's inputs to extreme values for understanding when a model breaks down).

The first problem we addressed is that the Gaussian copula, used in the market as quotation system by changing its parameter for each different strike, is not only inconsistent with the skew, but also, more importantly, difficult to use and to understand. Since it is not one consistent model, but a collection of several inconsistent models, it is unfit, for example, to stress-test a portfolio in order to understand its value in a crisis. This pricing framework does not allow one to easily express a financial scenario in terms of model parameters, and this is an important element of model risk. Suppose, for example, that we decide to shock the correlation on the most senior tranche up by 10%. Is it meaningful to assume such a stress keeping the other correlations fixed? It may not even be arbitrage-free and in any case it is very difficult to figure out what such a stress means. On may decide to shift all correlations up by 10%. Notice that now such an increase will have a profoundly different effect on different tranches that have different sensitivities to correlations (some negative, some positive). What is the real-world situation to which this stress corresponds? It is very hard to say.

A first improvement would be to eliminate the need to change the parameter set when pricing a different tranche. There are many models much more complex than the Gaussian copula that can fit consistently the tranche market. However, none of these models impacted market practice. Thus, in the practical example of Section 20.2, we remained in a Gaussian copula, but we just give it a more reasonable correlation matrix. The surprise is that this allows an approximate but consistent fit to the correlation skew, and gives results that can be interpreted and can give useful insight. In such an approach stress-testing becomes feasible: Increasing the size of the subset of names with unit correlation, for example, has a direct positive effect on senior tranches, while increasing the size of the subset with zero correlation has a direct positive effect on the riskiness of equity tranches. Even more interestingly, increasing the slope can increase the riskiness of both senior and equity tranches. In any case, all stresses one can perform to the parameterization result in an arbitrage-free model with a viable correlation matrix.

In the first example we addressed a property that is a pre-requisite for stress-testing. In the second example, where we stressed the model capability to represent the risk of losses concentrated in time, we had examples of the pitfalls we can meet in portfolio stress testing. Due to the irregular relation between model parameter and real risk, it was extremely difficult to understand which value of the parameter represents a real stress test. Expressing a financial scenario through a quantitative model is a very delicate task, since models are difficult to understand when applied in domains that are not fully standard (in this example the non-standard application is the fact of considering future intervals of time). Our intuition can fail us and models can have a misleading behavior, leading us to consider apparent worst-case scenarios that actually are best-case scenarios.

We saw in Section 20.3 that the problems of the Gaussian copula with the estimation of losses concentrated in time can be associated to the fact that the model admits some very unrealistic behavior. For example, for maximum correlation the model implies that the default of a company causes with certainty the default of another one, but the default of this second one can happen many years later, even decades later in some cases. This is an unrealistic feature, for whatever application of the copula. However, for a period of time starting now, or when the spreads of the different companies in a portfolio are very similar, this feature does not affect the value of the tranche so much: It does not reduce dramatically the range of possible values that the model can give.

For an evaluation in a future period of time, and for heterogenous spreads, this unrealistic feature becomes relevant, leading to nonsensical results. This is a typical example of model stress-testing: Detecting the situations, in terms of market configuration (the level of the spreads) or in terms of payoff features (the possibility that the period where losses are estimated is forward-start), where we have implausible and bizarre consequences from the same model assumptions that were considered reasonable in more basic situations.

Finally, we test the mapping methods used to move from copula parameters of liquid CDOs to copula parameters of illiquid CDOs. By definition, we do not have liquid quotes to assess their fitting capability or to perform a backtest on their validity. Therefore, here we have to devise another, more elaborate, type of model stress test. We do not simply move forward the start date, or move the spreads away from a common value, or increase the correlation. We design different financial scenarios and apply mapping methods to them, to see if, in all of these scenarios, the model has a reasonable behavior.

How do we construct these scenarios and how can we know which behavior is reasonable? We take the scenarios from relevant events that really happened in the past, but we use them in a way very different from backtesting. In fact we carried out a "rotation" from the time axis to the "space axis," or the axis of different portfolios. This cannot guarantee that methods are right, but, as stress test should do, it can tell us if they have problems; in fact, it detects that standard mapping methods *cannot represent* the behavior observed historically. After getting this hint from the stress test, in the above example we were able to confirm it also by mathematical analysis.

Notes

This paper express the views of its authors and does represent the opinion of Banca IMI, which is not responsible for any use which may be made of its contents.

References

Andersen, L., Sidenius, J., 2005. Extensions to the Gaussian copula: random recovery and random factor loadings. Journal of Credit Risk 1, 29–70.

Baheti, P., Morgan, S., 2007. Base correlation mapping. Quantitative Credit Research Quarterly, 2007–Q1, 3–20.

Breeden, D.T., Litzenberger, R.H., 1978. Prices of state-contingent claims implicit in option prices. Journal of Business 51, 621–651.

Duminuco, C., Morini, M., 2008. Correlation parameterizations for calibrating the market skew. Banca IMI Internal Report. Banca IMI, Milan.

Glasserman, P., Kang, W., Shahabuddin, P., 2007. Large deviations in multifactor portfolio credit risk. Mathematical Finance 17, 345–379.

Hull, J., White, A., 2005. The perfect copula: the valuation of correlation-dependent derivatives using the hazard rate path approach. Working Paper, Rotman School of Management, Toronto.

Li, D.X., 2000. On default correlation. A copula function approach. Working Paper 99-07. RiskMetrics, New York.

Marshall, A.W., Olkin, I., 1967. A multivariate exponential distribution. Journal of the American Statistical Association 2, 84–98.

Minucci, F., 2010. Gaussian copula and joint default probability estimation. MSc Thesis. Politecnico di Milano, Milan.

Morini, M., 2011. Understanding and Managing Model Risk. A Practical Guide for Quants, Traders and Validators. Wiley Finance, New York.

Turc, J., Very, P., Benhamou, D., 2005. Pricing CDO with a Smile. Société Generale Credit Research, New York.

21

ON CORRELATIONS BETWEEN A CONTRACT AND PORTFOLIO AND INTERNAL CAPITAL ALLIOCATION

Sergei Esipov
Quant Isle Ltd.

CHAPTER OUTLINE

21.1 Introduction

Modern financial contracts and insurance deals are characterized by swap-like positive and negative volatile cash flows. A company expecting such flows prepares itself in advance by setting aside a certain amount of capital for a specified period of time even if the net expected value of these cash flows is positive. Subsequently, this capital is either released over time, for profitable deals, or further increased, otherwise. The entire proccss of managing internal capital across contracts or deals, booked or prospective, constitutes the internal capital allocation. This definition is linked to the loss tail of a company's profit and loss (P & L) and it is not reducible to the so-called "capital allocation line"—a one-factor classical capital asset pricing model (CAPM) relation between the return and its standard deviation. Capital

Rethinking Valuation and Pricing Models. http://dx.doi.org/10.1016/B978-0-12-415875-7.00021-X

allocation represents a fundamental managerial task, which is regarded as one of the key ingredients of the company capital budgeting for assets and liabilities (Perold, 2005). In this chapter, we address the calculation of the risk capital needed for a deal, or for a rated company bounded by a high-quantile or value at risk (VaR), and the calculation of the return on such capital. For modern complex correlated deals and portfolios this problem could be quantitatively demanding even in a single-period setting.

Over the past few decades, the works of rating agencies, whose ultimate goal is to *quantify* investors' knowledge about the capital solvency of companies and the defaults of structured liabilities under extremely adverse scenarios, have influenced the capital allocation process and led to a division of managerial labor where company risk managers play increasingly important roles. Evolution of modern contracts (Fabozzi, 2008; BBC News, 2003) makes the work of risk managers increasingly demanding. Risk management is commoditized by vendors of risk-monitoring products, which compete in sophistication with modern market contracts and with rating agency models.

Competition in complexity between modern contracts and risk management is tested at the times of multistage economic crises, including the latest crisis, unfolding since 2007. This crisis and subsequent public criticism of the approaches used by rating agencies (*Wall Street Journal*, 2009) manifests itself, among other things, in accelerated model revisions and in incorporating counterparty credit considerations and exchange credibility. The amount of research published by rating agencies has grown considerably over the last decade.

Using adaptive approaches, rating agencies form expectations regarding balance sheets and income statements of their clients, and make use of their internal proprietary rating models. The connection between rating and default probabilities is stated semi-quantitatively (see, e.g. Standard & Poors, 2011); however, it is diligently backtested (Adelson *et al.*, 2009). Comparison of historical default rates and spreads of credit default swaps has become one of the important benchmarks of judging market and rating efficiencies. Based on statistical properties of historical defaults of similarly rated companies, an estimate of a company's default probabilities for a given time horizon, and even a list of such horizons, can be determined. It then becomes a quantitative benchmark for the company's internal risk management. In response, companies have developed a procedure where probabilities of large losses are accessed and capital is allocated to offset losses in extreme cases using quantiles of P&L distributions (Jorion, 2006).

The quantile-linked source of external constraints (in addition to risk–return considerations and importance and pressure of credit ratings) is enforced by the market or government regulators. These regulations gradually grow in sophistication, as can be seen in the development of Basel recommendations I, II, and III for banks. On the road to improving risk management they have migrated from non-quantitative recommendations, through weighted averages, to quantiles and VaRs. While the premise of these regulations is very clear, some of them come with hidden complications. It is shown in this chapter that the popular internal capital allocation method, which aims to leave a given high quantile unchanged, shifts the focus of deal analysis to deal–portfolio analysis, and does it to such an extent that the result becomes supremely sensitive to very fine and rarely addressed properties of the company's P&L distribution. The list of these properties includes high-order derivatives of a company's P&L distribution, and high-order cross-cumulants between the deal and the portfolio. These findings support the importance of hedging in risk management by means of structuring, collateralization, finite risk and reinsurance.

This chapter is organized as follows. In Section 21.2, addition of individual deals to a company portfolio is analyzed in the simplest single-horizon setting. An example for power-law distributions is given in Section 21.3. A formula for portfolio quantile shift is derived in Section 21.4. This formula is then revisited in the presence of secondary uncertainty (frequency–severity models) in Section 21.5. Section 21.6 is devoted to studying the change of a company's average shortfall below a given quantile. This measure is important since it is more conservative and considerably less sensitive that the quantile shift. In Section 21.7, we consider long-term effects of portfolio aggregation based on the quantile shift formula and establish that the quantile shift formula leads to an asymptotically normal portfolio. Section 21.8 is devoted to the return on capital calculation. Section 21.9 contains a brief discussion.

21.2 Adding a Deal to a Company Portfolio

Suppose the company-wide P&L distribution density of future cash flows, $P_c(x)$ and deal-specific P&L distribution density of future cash flows, $P_d(x')$, are both known. The cash flows are discounted to present-day currency units. The joint distribution function, $P(x, x')$, is seldom known in detail. It has marginal distributions $P_c(x) = \int dx' P(x, x')$ and $P_d(x') = \int dx P(x, x')$.

Statistically speaking, only the marginal cumulants are available, along with the lowest-order cross-cumulant:

$$c_{11} = \langle (x - \langle x \rangle)(x' - \langle x' \rangle) \rangle = \rho \sigma_c \sigma_d, \qquad (21.1)$$

based on the lowest-order pair-wise correlation coefficient between the deal and the company portfolio, ρ. Here $\langle x \rangle$ and $\sigma^2 = \langle (x - \langle x \rangle)^2 \rangle$ are the mean and marginal standard deviations of the deal (index d) and the company portfolio (index c). The rest of the correlation structure, i.e. the entire family of higher-order cross-cumulants, $c_{n,m}$ is left unspecified. Instead, *ad hoc ansätze* are employed, leaving the issue of high-order correlation aside. The copula-based risk management is the typical example; it is characterized by a gallery of joint distribution tails, as explained by Mikosch (2006). Alternatively, a Poisson event decomposition is used, with uncontrolled quantile-to-quantile severity linkage.

Let us introduce marginal generating functions:

$$G_{c,d}(J) = \int dx e^{ixJ} P_{c,d}(x), \quad P_{c,d}(x) = \int \frac{dJ}{2\pi} e^{-ixJ} G_{c,d}(x), \quad (21.2)$$

and first address the simplest case when all higher-order cross-cumulants are equal to zero. Then, the joint generating function is given by:

$$G(J,J') = G_c(J) G_d(J') e^{-c_{11} J J'}. \qquad (21.3)$$

For the net P&L, $X = x + x'$, one can write with the help of (21.3):

$$
\begin{aligned}
P(X) &= \int dx dx' \delta(x + x' - X) P(x, x') \\
&= \int \frac{dx dx' dJ dJ'}{(2\pi)^2} \delta(x + x' - X) G(J,J') e^{-ixJ - ix'J'} \\
&= \int \frac{dx dx' dJ dJ'}{(2\pi)^2} \delta(x + x' - X) G_c(J) G_d(J') e^{-ixJ - ix'J' - c_{11} J J'},
\end{aligned}
\qquad (21.4)
$$

where integration over $dx dx'$ could be carried out, leading to:

$$P(X) = \int \frac{dJ dJ'}{2\pi} \delta(J - J') G_c(J) G_d(J') e^{-iXJ' - c_{11} J J'} \qquad (21.5)$$

$$= \int \frac{dJ dx dx'}{2\pi} P_c(x) P_d(x') e^{ixJ + ix'J - iXJ - c_{11} J^2}. \qquad (21.6)$$

Next, integration over $dJ dJ'$ could be performed and the net P&L probability distribution is given by a simple convolution formula:

$$P(X) = \int \frac{dx dx'}{\sqrt{4\pi |c_{11}|}} P_c(x) P_d(x') e^{-\frac{(x + x' - X)^2}{4 c_{11}}}, \qquad (21.7)$$

which contains a Gaussian kernel.

21.3 Example: Correlated Power-Law Distributions

Correlated t-distributions provide a relevant example based on their asymptotic Pareto-like decay: the probability density vanishes as $q(x) \propto x^{-2\alpha}$, where $\alpha = (\nu + 1)/2$. Parameter ν is the number of degrees of freedom. One can correlate two t-distributions using formula (21.7):

$$P(X) = \int \frac{dx_1 dx_2}{\sqrt{4\pi\rho\sigma_1\sigma_2}} q_1(x_1) q_2(x_2) \exp\left[-\frac{(x_1 + x_2 - X)^2}{4\rho\sigma_1\sigma_2}\right],$$

(21.8)

where:

$$q_n(x) = \frac{\Gamma(\alpha_n)}{\sigma_n \Gamma\left(\alpha_n - \frac{1}{2}\right)\sqrt{\pi(2\alpha_n - 3)}}\left[1 + \frac{(x - \mu_n)^2}{\sigma_n^2(2\alpha_n - 3)}\right]^{-\alpha_n}.$$

(21.9)

This method of correlating marginal t-distributions is different from the so-called elliptical distribution or copulas (see Kotz and Nadarajah, 2004). If we are only interested in the asymptotic dependence of $P(X)$ at large $|X|$, $|X| \gg \mu_{1,2}, \sigma_{1,2}$, then by introducing the sum and difference of integration variables, $y = x_1 + x_2$, $z = x_1 - x_2$, one can make use of the saddle-point approximation for y-integral and obtain:

$$P(X) \simeq \int_{-\infty}^{\infty} dz\, q_1\left(\frac{X}{2} + \frac{z}{2}\right) q_2\left(\frac{X}{2} - \frac{z}{2}\right).$$

(21.10)

At large X the integrand has two maxima, at $z = \pm X$, and the integral converges around each of them, separately, leading to:

$$P(X) \simeq q_1(X) + q_2(X).$$

(21.11)

If $\alpha_1 \neq \alpha_2$, only one term should be retained here, with $\min(\alpha_1, \alpha_2)$. In the saddle-point approximation, the distribution for the sum of correlated t-variables is independent of the correlation coefficient ρ. To improve upon this approximation one has to expand the product $q_1(y/2 + z/2)q_2(y/2 - z/2)$ in powers of $y - X$ in the vicinity of saddle point $y = X$. The term linear in $y - X$ vanishes due to symmetry and the leading correction to (21.11) comes from the quadratic term. Integration of $(y - X)^2$ with the Gaussian kernel over y gives its second cumulant, $2\rho\sigma_1\sigma_2$, and then integration over z is again carried out

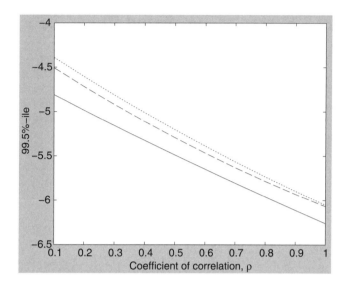

Figure 21.1 Dependence of 99.5%-ile on the seed correlation coefficient, ρ. Dotted line is the case of a normal copula, dashed line is t-copula and solid line is Formula (21.8). The number of degrees of freedom, $\nu = 12$, or $2\alpha = 13$.

using separate convergence of the integral around the maxima $z = \pm X$. One finds:

$$P(X) \simeq \left(1 + \frac{\rho\sigma_1\sigma_2}{4}\frac{d^2}{dX^2}\right)[q_1(X) + q_2(X)]. \qquad (21.12)$$

Numerical analysis shows close to linear residual ρ-dependence (Figure 21.1). Over a wide range of parameter ν the distribution (21.8) has a heavier tail as compared to correlated t-distributions obtained by means of either a normal copula or t-copula: Formula (21.8) dominates when the number of degrees of freedom, $\nu > 3$.[1] Note that, by construction, Formula (21.8) contains no high-order cross-cumulants. Therefore, it cannot be established without case-specific studies whether or not even this formula has a more conservative tail as compared to correlated power-law distributions encountered in practice. It also follows from here that usage of a t-copula as a substitute for normal copula is neither necessary nor sufficient.

21.4 Formula for the Quantile Shift

This section is devoted to the analytical properties of the quantile shift caused by adding a deal. It is assumed here that the

---

[1] In the rarely used case $\nu = 3$ the quantiles cross, such that at large ρ copulas dominate. At $\nu < 3$ the variance of t-distribution is infinite.

scale of the deal, L_d, is much smaller than the scale of the company portfolio L_c, $L_d/L_c \ll 1$, so that the company is not betting its fate on just one deal. The company quantile, X_q, (typically, a large negative P&L value), is defined as:

$$\int^{X_q} P_c(X)\mathrm{d}X = 1 - q, \tag{21.13}$$

with q being the corresponding probability. For example, the Solvency II regulation requires annual capital adequacy at the level of $q = 0.995$ or 99.5%. To derive a formula for a quantile shift when a deal is added, we make a change of variable in (21.7), $x'' = X - x$, and expand $P_c(X - x'')$ in po:wers of x''. Substituting this expansion into integral (21.7) and exchanging the order of summation and integration, one finds:

$$P(X) = \sum_{n=0}^{\infty} \frac{(-1)^n}{n!} \frac{\mathrm{d}^n P_c}{\mathrm{d}X^n} \langle\langle (x'')^n \rangle\rangle, \tag{21.14}$$

where:

$$\langle\langle (x'')^n \rangle\rangle = \int \frac{\mathrm{d}x'\mathrm{d}x''}{\sqrt{4\pi|c_{11}|}} P_d(x')(x'')^n e^{-\frac{(x'-x'')^2}{4c_{11}}}, \tag{21.15}$$

are Gaussian moments of x'' further averaged over the marginal distribution P_d. Direct integration gives:

$$\langle\langle x'' \rangle\rangle = \langle x' \rangle, \tag{21.16}$$

$$\left\langle\left\langle \left(x''\right)^2 \right\rangle\right\rangle = \left\langle (x')^2 \right\rangle + 2c_{11}, \tag{21.17}$$

where $\langle (x')^n \rangle$ are moments of P_d. Third and higher moments will not be needed: they are multiplied by progressively higher derivatives of P_c and could be omitted based on the parameter $L_d/L_c \ll 1$. One obtains:

$$P(X) = P_c(X) - \langle x' \rangle \frac{\mathrm{d}P_c}{\mathrm{d}X} + \frac{\left\langle (x')^2 \right\rangle + 2c_{11}}{2} \frac{\mathrm{d}^2 P_c}{\mathrm{d}X^2}. \tag{21.18}$$

This expansion could be integrated between negative infinity (or the left limit) and the new quantile X_q^*. The terms $\int^{X_q^*} P(X)\mathrm{d}X$ on the left-hand side and part of the integral $\int^{X_q} P_c(X)\mathrm{d}X$ on the right-hand side are both equal to $1 - q$ and cancel. We are left with:

$$0 = \int_{X_q}^{X_q^*} P_c(X)\mathrm{d}X - \langle x' \rangle \, P_c\left(X_q^*\right) + \frac{\left\langle (x')^2 \right\rangle + 2c_{11}}{2} \frac{\mathrm{d}P_c}{\mathrm{d}X}\Big|_{X=X_q^*}. \tag{21.19}$$

Next, we expand $P_c(X)$ under the integral around the point X_q^*. Since the difference $X_q^* - X_q$ is or order L_d, this expansion is in powers not exceeding L_d/L_c. Other terms in (21.19) are of no higher than first order in L_d/L_c and we conclude that to the same order of precision in L_d/L_c the integral here can be replaced by its lowest approximation, $P_c(X_q^*)(X_q^* - X_q) = P_c(X_q^*)\Delta X_q$. To the same order in L_d/L_c all arguments could now be set to X_q. Thus, the change of quantile is given by:

$$\Delta X_q = \langle x' \rangle - \left(\rho\sigma\sigma_c + \frac{\sigma^2}{2} \right) \frac{\mathrm{dln}P_c}{\mathrm{d}X} \Big|_{X=X_q}. \tag{21.20}$$

In the simplest case, where the company portfolio is normally distributed and correlation is not small, $\rho\sigma_c \gg \sigma^2$, (20) is reduced to:

$$\Delta X_q = \langle x \rangle - \xi_1 \rho\sigma, \tag{21.21}$$

with $\xi_1 = \Phi^{-1}(q)$ being the inverse cumulative normal distribution computed at the quantile q. This last formula was used in our work (Esipov and Guo, 1999).

Although the assumption above provides a small parameter, it *does not*, in general, control the precision of the formula (21.20) for an arbitrary analytic joint distribution of the deal's P&L and the P&L of the company portfolio. However, this formula does contain the correct first terms of the regular expansion of the quantile shift in terms of the cumulants of the joint distribution $P(x, x')$. It will be shown in Section 21.7 that formula (21.20) is consistent with the central limit theorem.

We are now in a position to consider arbitrary higher-order cross-cumulants, satisfying the condition, $c_{n,m} \sim L_d^n L_c^m \ll L_c^{n+m}$. Given the small parameter $L_d/L_c \ll 1$, one can show that only the cumulants of the first order in x', i.e. $c_{1,n} = \langle x' x^n \rangle_c$, should be retained and the quantile shift is:

$$\Delta X_q = \frac{1}{P_c(X_q)} \sum_{n=0}^{\infty} \frac{(-1)^n c_{1,n}}{n!} \frac{\mathrm{d}^n P_c}{\mathrm{d}X^n} \Big|_{X=X_q}. \tag{21.22}$$

For example, the third-order cross-cumulant here is

$$c_{1,2} = \langle xX^2 \rangle_c = \langle xX^2 \rangle - 2\rho\sigma\sigma_c\langle x \rangle - \sigma_c\langle x \rangle - \langle x \rangle\langle X \rangle^2.$$

Formulae (21.20) and (21.22) have implications for risk management. In order to be able to rely on the pair-wise lowest-order correlation coefficient, ρ, the risk manager should check the validity of the strong inequalities $c_{1,n} \ll c_{11}L_c^{n-1}$ or, as an absolute minimum, check the third and fourth cross-cumulants. If these inequalities are met, one could replace portfolio simulations with formula (21.20). However, even in the absence of high-order cross-cumulants the change of quantile is sensitive to the slope and amplitude of the company P&L distribution at the quantile position. Such fine details of the tail of company P&L distribution are seldom available with precision. Formula (21.20) casts a shadow on the entire percentile maintenance and/or default probability approach, since they lead to sensitivity and simulation instabilities.[2]

21.5 Quantile Shift Under Secondary Uncertainty

Suppose the P&L probability distribution of the deal, P_d, is itself a random function, governed by a distribution Q. One important practical example of this situation is the frequency–severity model of the deal, when P_d is the severity applied with Poisson frequency p. Then (21.7) is modified:

$$P(X) = \left\langle \int \frac{\mathrm{d}x\mathrm{d}x'}{\sqrt{4\pi|c_{11}|}} P_c(x)P_d(x')\mathrm{e}^{-\frac{(x+x'-X)^2}{4c_{11}}} \right\rangle_Q , \qquad (21.23)$$

however, the subsequent derivation is very similar to Section 21.4. The formula for the quantile shift (21.20) remains valid, assuming that the average and standard deviation entering this formula are given by:

$$\langle x' \rangle \to p\langle x' \rangle ,$$
$$\rho\sigma\sigma_c + \frac{\sigma^2}{2} \to \frac{p}{2}\left\langle (x')^2 \right\rangle + \rho\sigma_c \sqrt{p\left\langle (x')^2 \right\rangle - p^2 \langle x' \rangle^2} . \qquad (21.24)$$

Usually, the variability of the deal by far exceeds its expected profit, $\langle (x')^2 \rangle \approx \sigma^2$, and the second substitution above is reduced to:

$$\rho\sigma\sigma_c + \frac{\sigma^2}{2} \to \rho\sigma\sigma_c \sqrt{p} + \frac{p\sigma^2}{2} . \qquad (21.25)$$

---

[2] In order to cope with the sensitivity stemming from simulations, some practitioners make use of the normal approximation, i.e. work with (21.21). It has a steeper slope as compared to typical homogeneous fat-tailed distributions, leading to conservative allocation. Formula (21.21) has another attractive feature: for a given deal, not only is the result almost insensitive to the statistical properties of the company's P&L distribution (thus decoupling portfolio maintenance and deal modeling), but the remaining coupling, to the lowest order in cumulant expansion, is solely controlled by the lowest-order correlation with the company portfolio, ρ.

For small enough Poisson frequencies this term is dominated by the first addend, $\rho\sigma\sigma_c\sqrt{p}$. In the normal case, $\Delta X_q = p\langle x'\rangle - \xi_1\rho\sigma\sqrt{p}$.

21.6 Capital Allocation by Average Shortfall

The undesirable sensitivity of capital allocation to the amplitude and slope of the portfolio probability distribution function at the high quantile position can be addressed by "integrating" the definition, by allocating capital using average shortfall below a certain quantile:

$$Y_q = \frac{1}{1-q}\int^{X_q} dXXP_c(X).$$ (21.26)

The derivation of Section 21.5 can be similarly carried out for such average shortfall. To accomplish this, we return to (21.18), multiply it by X, then integrate it, as before, between negative infinity and the new quantile position X_q^*, and carry out integration by parts:

$$\int^{X_q^*} dXXP(X) = \int^{X_q} dXXP_c(X)$$

$$+ \int_{X_q}^{X_q^*} dXXP_c(X) - \langle x'\rangle\left[X_q^*P_c\left(X_q^*\right) - \int^{X_q^*} dXP_c(X)\right]$$

$$+ \frac{\langle(x')^2\rangle + 2c_{11}}{2}\left[X_q^*\frac{dP_c}{dX}_{|X=X_q^*} - \int^{X_q^*} dX\frac{dP_c}{dX}\right].$$ (21.27)

To the leading order in L_d/L_c one finds:

$$(1-q)(\Delta Y_q - \langle x'\rangle) = P_cX_q(\Delta X_q - \langle x'\rangle)$$
$$+ \left(\rho\sigma\sigma_c + \frac{\sigma^2}{2}\right)\left(-P_c + X_q\frac{dP_c}{dX}_{|X=X_q}\right).$$ (21.28)

Substituting the quantile shift given by (21.20) and simplifying, we obtain the shift of the average shortfall:

$$\Delta Y_q = \langle x'\rangle - \left(\rho\sigma\sigma_c + \frac{\sigma^2}{2}\right)\frac{P_c(X_q)}{1-q}.$$ (21.29)

This shift is no longer sensitive to the slope of company probability distribution. However higher-order cumulants, if present, come with sensitivity to higher-order derivatives of the portfolio P&L distribution function at the selected quantile.

If the company portfolio is normally distributed and correlation is not small, $\rho\sigma_c \gg \sigma^2$, (29) is reduced to:

$$\Delta Y_q = \langle x' \rangle - \xi_2 \rho\sigma, \quad \xi_2 = \frac{1}{(1-q)\sqrt{2\pi}} \exp -\frac{\left[\Phi^{-1}(q)\right]^2}{2}. \quad (21.30)$$

While this formula is very similar to (21), the shift of the average shortfall is larger than the shift of quantile. For example, at the above-mentioned quantile $q = 0.995$, one finds $\xi_1 = \Phi^{-1}(0.995) = 2.5758$ and $\xi_2 = 2.8919$. This allocation is more robust than quantile allocation.

21.7 Evolution of Quantiles in Portfolio Aggregation

Suppose a company has a regular deal flow, where new deals are added and old deals mature. We consider the limit of many small deals. Using (18), the company distribution P_c after adding a deal with index n evolves as:

$$\frac{\partial P_c}{\partial n} = \langle x_n \rangle \frac{\partial P_c}{\partial X} + \rho_n \sigma_n \sigma_c \frac{\partial^2 P_c}{\partial X^2}, \quad (21.31)$$

This equation is highly non-linear, since $\sigma_c^2 = \int dX (X - \langle X \rangle)^2 P_c$. Nevertheless, the drift and diffusion coefficients are only functions of the index n and the equation could be integrated. One can see that the company P&L distribution evolves to a normal or Gaussian one, with the average value given by:

$$\langle X(n) \rangle = \int^n \langle x_m \rangle dm, \quad (21.32)$$

and variance:

$$\tilde{\sigma}_c(n)^2 = 2 \int^n \rho_m \sigma_m \sigma_c(m) dm. \quad (21.33)$$

Differentiating (21.33) with respect to n, one finds that self-consistency, $\tilde{\sigma}_c = \sigma_c$, is maintained by:

$$\frac{d\sigma_c}{dn} = \rho_n \sigma_n. \quad (21.34)$$

To reiterate, even if one begins with a non-normal distribution of the company P&L, the portfolio aggregation based on the risk load in proportion to correlation times standard deviation above allows one to reconstruct the deal evolution of the portfolio aggregation, as long as the mean values, correlations and standard deviations are available. The net result is a normally distributed portfolio with the mean value (21.32) and standard deviation:

$$\sigma_c(n) = \int^{n} \rho_m \sigma_m dm. \tag{21.35}$$

This derivation is simply a version of the central limit theorem, as applied to a sequence of deals with the mean vector $\{\langle x_m \rangle\}$ and covariance matrix (amongst the vector components) replaced by a sequence of individual variances and pair-wise correlations between the next component and the intermediate accumulated sum $\{\rho_m, \sigma_m\}$. The central limit theorem states that the normal distribution is established as long as certain (Lindeberg) conditions are satisfied. Extreme cases with multiscale unbounded Pareto- or Lévy-distributed deals are not considered here, as the risks are assumed to be finite (see the assumption $L_d \ll L_c$ above).

The derivation given in this section shows that by working with many small moderately correlated deals, one can enormously simplify the company-wide risk management simulations and focus on deal modeling and portfolio hedging, instead of portfolio aggregation.

One can also see that the incremental contribution of a given deal is dependent on the order of aggregation (sic!) and this eventually leads to an issue for individual deal managers. It is a conventional practice to perform portfolio aggregation by simulation and then simulate the portfolio without a booked/ proposed deal to access the "incremental" risk–return of that deal on a "portfolio basis." Managers whose deals are added at later stages of risk management modeling could be unfairly penalized for smaller profit-to-volatility ratios, as compared to the same deals aggregated earlier.

21.8 Static and Dynamic Capital Allocation

In the classical external CAPM-based capital allocation the risks of capital lending and borrowing are analyzed in the mean--variance framework (Brealy and Myers, 1988) or, more realistically, with the use of multiple regressions, such as to book-to-market equity ratio and company size (Fama and French, 1992). This analysis is static, in the sense that allocation is performed in a single time-step setting. As mentioned in Section 22.1, the company's internal capital allocation is quite different—it is related to the tail risk and returns have to be computed based on the quantile capital (instead of pledged capital).

To preserve a given quantile after adding a deal, one has to ensure that the company allocates the amount of capital:

$$C = -\Delta X_q, \tag{21.36}$$

where the quantile change ΔX_q is given by (21.20) or (21.21), if normal approximation is used. We will not modify the formulae here with borrowing costs and lending benefits, this could be done following Perold (2005).

The period return μ of the deal could be obtained from:

$$C(1 + \mu T) = (C + \langle x \rangle)(1 + rT), \tag{21.37}$$

where T is the deal duration and r is the reference rate. By construction, this period return is risk-adjusted and with the help of, for example, (21.21) one finds:

$$\mu = \frac{\langle x \rangle + rT\xi\rho\sigma}{T(-\langle x \rangle + \xi\rho\sigma)}. \tag{21.38}$$

Suppose, now, that the results of economic analysis of an added deal allow us to determine the time profile of volatile cash flows of the deal. Then, at any point in time, t, between inception and maturity, $0 \leq t \leq T$, we could compute the expected *remaining* P&L along with the remaining $\langle\langle x(t, T) \rangle\rangle$ and remaining standard deviation $\langle \sigma(t, T) \rangle$, where one averaging is performed between t and T, while the second, external averaging, is performed between 0 and t, using simulation results in both cases. All quantities are available as known at the inception point, 0, and refer to the remaining time interval between t and T. Then there is no reason to keep the allocated capital static (other than *reallocation costs*, which are not considered here) and one could introduce a time-dependent capital $C(t)$.

Between the times t and $t + dt$ the left-hand side of (21.37) is expected to grow by $\mu C(t)dt$ while the right-hand side changes by $r[C(t) + \langle x(t, T) \rangle]dt$. Over the entire time interval one obtains:

$$\mu \int_0^T dtC(t) = r \int_0^T dt(C + \langle x \rangle), \tag{21.39}$$

or, by using (21.36) and (21.21):

$$\xi\rho(\mu - r) \int_0^T dt\langle \sigma(t, T) \rangle = \langle x(0, T) \rangle + \mu \int_0^T dt\langle x \rangle, \tag{21.40}$$

and:

$$\mu = \frac{\langle x(0, T)\rangle + r\xi\rho \int_0^T \langle \sigma(t, T)\rangle \mathrm{d}t}{\int_0^T \mathrm{d}t[- \langle x(t, T)\rangle + \xi\rho\langle \sigma(t, T)\rangle]}, \qquad (21.41)$$

which is reducible to (38) for time-independent mean and variance.

The rationale for the dynamic case is based on the assumption that the standard deviation, $\langle \sigma(t, T)\rangle$, is usually a decreasing function of time, implying smaller allocated capital and smaller required expected profit for a given rate of return. The main problem with this approach is that, unlike delta-hedging, it does not factor in any future revisions. The corresponding analysis will be published elsewhere.

One could consider capital allocation for even shorter time horizons, deferring it until losses are developed. This approach harbors the risk of cumulative credit squeeze and such risk should be quantified before addressing any "by period" allocations, as in the recent case of Martin (2011). The credit squeeze may quickly lead to a company's default.

21.9 Conclusion

As financial and insurance industries improve quantitative risk management, following rating agency and governmental requirements, and adjusting to the evolving contract types, the capital allocation procedure becomes progressively more sophisticated. A transition from simple ratios, such as in Basel 8% capital adequacy ratio, to P&L quantiles as in EU Solvency II and Basel III is now underway. Multiple constraints on quantiles are further complicated by the term structure of correlations for driving factors and prices, where risk managers are forced to perform large-scale simulations.

In this study we have shown how to allocate capital for a contract to keep a selected tail quantile of the company portfolio unchanged. This allocation was then translated to returns and to the portfolio aggregation process. Detailed analysis for multiperiod time-dependent deals and portfolios will be presented elsewhere.

We have shown that the portfolio default probability is a demanding measure of risk, that its changes are sensitive to the slope and even higher-order derivatives of company P&L probability distribution function. We suggest to replace them, as a minimum, by loss-based values, such as average loss in tail loss cases. The overall situation with "tail risk" reflects the depth of market resilience to analysis and control. On the one hand, a risk manager is expected to develop models computing a high-order quantile of the company portfolio. On the other hand, the deal aggregation is usually performed while ignoring all except mean and variance of the joint distribution function. Under these conditions, high quantiles remain intractable. Since these high quantiles represent the backbone of rated paper and government regulations, we are forced to conclude that this source of market instabilities and crises continues its work. Regulations that target quantiles are making the work of risk managers progressively more complex. A qualitatively similar process is taking place in the regulations of derivatives and it has been termed the "morass of uncertainty" in the media (Eisinger, 2011). The entire array of default parameters and tail quantiles imposed on the companies results in calculations that are computationally challenging while refocusing the managers from the level of portfolio aggregation to the level of discussing poorly parametrized and mostly hypothetical conditional distribution tails, which are much better addressed by classical hedging, including structured collateralization, finite risk approach and traditional reinsurance.

References

Adelson, M., Ravimohan, R., Griep, C.M., Jacob, D., Coughlin, P., Bukspan, N., Wyss, D., 2009. Understanding Standard & Poor's Rating Definitions. Standard & Poors RatingsDirect, New York.

BBC News, 2003. Buffett warns on investment time bomb, 4 March. From the article: The derivatives market has exploded in recent years, with investment banks selling billions of dollars worth of these investments to clients as a way to off-load or manage market risk. But Mr Buffett argues that such highly complex financial instruments are time bombs and 'financial weapons of mass destruction' that could harm not only their buyers and sellers, but the whole economic system.

Brealy, R., Myers, S.C., 1988. Principles of Corporate Finance. McGraw-Hill, New York.

Eisinger, J., 2011. Reform adds more twists to a convoluted derivatives world. The New York Times,16 November.

Esipov, S., Guo, D., 1999. Portfolio based risk pricing: pricing long term put options with GJR-GARCH(1,1)/jump diffusion process Available at http://ssrn.com/abstract%3D141588.

Fabozzi, F. (Ed.), 2008. Handbook of Finance, Financial Markets and Instruments, Wiley Hoboken, NJ.

Fama, E.F., French, K., 1992. The cross-section of expected stock returns. Journal of Finance 47 (2), 427—465.

Jorion, P., 2006. Value at Risk: The New Benchmark for Managing Financial Risk, 3rd edn. McGraw-Hill, New York.

Kotz, S., Nadarajah, S., 2004. Multivariate t Distributions and Their Applications. Cambridge University Press, Cambridge.

Martin, A., 2011. Kodak stock dives after credit line is tapped. The New York Times, 26 September.

Mikosch, T., 2006. Copulas: tales and facts. Extremes 9, 3–20 and 55–62.

Perold, A., 2005. Capital allocation in financial firms. Journal of Applied Corporate Finance 17 (3), 110–118.

Standard & Poor's, 2011. Credit ratings definitions & FAQs. Are credit ratings absolute measures of default probability? Available at: http://www. standardandpoors.com/ratings/definitions-and-faqs/en/us\#def_4. From the webpage: Since there are future events and developments that cannot be foreseen, the assignment of credit ratings is not an exact science. For this reason, Standard & Poor's ratings opinions are not intended as guarantees of credit quality or as exact measures of the probability that a particular issuer or particular debt issue will default. Instead, ratings express relative opinions about the creditworthiness of an issuer or credit quality of an individual debt issue, from strongest to weakest, within a universe of credit risk. The likelihood of default is the single most important factor in our assessment of creditworthiness. For example, a corporate bond that is rated "AA" is viewed by Standard & Poor's as having a higher credit quality than a corporate bond with a 'BBB'rating. But the "AA" rating isn't a guarantee that it will not default, only that, in our opinion, it is less likely to default than the 'BBB' bond.

Wall Street Journal, 2009. A triple-A idea—ending the rating oligopoly, 15 April. Available at: http://online.wsj.com/article/SB123976320479019717.html.

A MAXIMUM ENTROPY APPROACH TO THE MEASUREMENT OF EVENT RISK

Marco Bee
University of Trento

CHAPTER OUTLINE

22.1 Introduction

Geometric Brownian motion (GBM) has played a key role in finance since the introduction of continuous-time pricing models by Black and Scholes (1973) and Merton (1973). If prices follow GBM in continuous time, logarithmic returns are normally distributed and this provides a theoretical justification for the use of the normal distribution as a model for log-returns. In addition, the mathematical tractability of the normal distribution is a considerable advantage from the practictioners' point of view.

On the other hand, several empirical studies have shown that the log-returns of security prices do not satisfy, in general, some of the properties implied by GBM. In particular, at least for moderate- to high-frequency data, the normality assumption is typically rejected, because the data exhibit skewness, excess kurtosis, serial correlation, jumps and time-varying volatility (for a review, see Cont, 2001). Nonetheless, the risk management community has continued using the normal distribution for many years, because, for not too high confidence levels (say, 95% or less), the risk measures used to be reasonably accurate.

In the last few years, given the high volatility caused by the severe market turmoil that stemmed from the subprime mortgage crisis, the extent of loss underestimation due to

Rethinking Valuation and Pricing Models. http://dx.doi.org/10.1016/B978-0-12-415875-7.00022-1

non-standard features of the return distributions has increased. Thus, finding models that explicitly take into account fat tails and jumps has become more and more urgent.

In terms of parametric risk measurement, two possible statistical solutions to this problem are *ad hoc* assumptions or extreme value theory (EVT), if the focus is on the tail of the distribution. Both ways of proceeding are not completely satisfactory.

The first, mainly based on the Student-*t* or the generalized error distribution (Nelson, 1991), lacks generality and is justified only by empirical considerations to be checked on a case-by-case basis. A more advanced way of proceeding with desirable theoretical and empirical properties consists in resorting to the family of generalized hyperbolic distributions (Eberlein and Keller, 1995); however, estimation and simulation of these distributions is rather difficult (McNeil *et al.*, 2005, section 3.2).

EVT does not estimate the whole distribution; moreover, estimation procedures are very sensitive to the threshold where the tail begins, whose determination is far from straightforward and somewhat arbitrary (McNeil *et al.*, 2005, Chapter 7).

As the distributions of financial log-returns are often "far from standard," non-parametric techniques are a viable alternative. In this chapter, we propose a non-parametric approach to the estimation of the true data-generating process (DGP) based on the concept of entropy maximization. The maximum entropy (ME) method aims at obtaining a probability distribution that is consistent with the information in the data and "expresses maximum uncertainty with respect to all other matters" (Jaynes, 1957; for a comprehensive treatment, see Kapur, 1989). The available information is assumed to be entirely incorporated in the first k empirical moments, which are used as constraints in the estimation process.

A basic feature of non-parametric statistics consists of being more flexible and data-driven than parametric statistics, and ME makes no exception. However, with respect to other non-parametric methods, its major advantage is that the best density can be found using a general methodology that does not require any arbitrary specification of input variables by the user.

22.2 Theory and Methods

The ME density is the density that maximizes Shannon's information entropy:

$$W = \int -f(x)\log(f(x))\mathrm{d}x, \qquad (22.1)$$

under constraints that impose the equality of the first k theoretical and empirical moments. The constraints are usually the arithmetic or geometric moments, respectively given by $\mathbf{E}(X^i) = \int x^i f(x)\mathrm{d}x$ and $\mathbf{E}(\log(X)^i) = \int \log(x)^i f(x)\mathrm{d}x$, $i = 0, 1, ..., k$. They are called characterizing moments (Kapur, 1989).

Using a more general notation, let $\mu^i = \mathbf{E}[T(x)^i]$ and $\hat{\mu}^i = \frac{1}{n}\sum_j T(x_j)^i$ be, respectively, the ith theoretical and empirical characterizing moment; note that the arithmetic and geometric moments are recovered by taking, respectively, $T(x) = x$ and $T(x) = \log(x)$. The ME approach entails the maximization of W under the constraints $\mu^i = \hat{\mu}^i$, which can be solved by means of $k + 1$ Lagrange multipliers λ_i $(i = 0, ..., k)$, so that the solution (i.e. the ME density) takes the form $f(x) = \mathrm{e}^{-\sum_{i=0}^{k}\lambda_i T(x)^i}$.

Most distributions in the exponential family are encompassed by the ME distribution. In particular, the Pareto distribution is an ME density with $k = 1$, whereas the lognormal is ME with $k = 2$; for both distributions, the characterizing moments are the logarithmic ones. If we use arithmetic moments instead, we obtain the exponential (when $k = 1$) and the normal (when $k = 2$) distribution. The functions relating the parameters of the original and the ME distributions are summarized in Table 22.1.

Despite its interesting properties, the method has found limited application in economics and finance (Buchen and Kelly, 1996; Stutzer, 1996; Hawkins, 1997). One reason is that (22.1) cannot be solved analytically for $k \geq 2$ and the Newton–Raphson algorithm is very sensitive to the choice of the initial values,

Table 22.1. Parameters of the ME density for some commonly used distributions with logarithmic and arithmetic characterizing moments

Distribution	Moments	λ_0	λ_1	λ_2
Pareto	logarithmic	$-\log(\alpha c^\alpha)$	$\alpha + 1$	—
Lognormal	logarithmic	$2\dfrac{\mu^2}{\sigma^2} - \dfrac{1}{2}\log\left(\dfrac{1}{2}\sigma^2\right) + \dfrac{1}{2}\log(\pi)$	$1 - \dfrac{2\mu}{\sigma^2}$	$\dfrac{1}{2\sigma^2}$
Exponential	arithmetic	$-\log(\alpha)$	α	—
Normal	arithmetic	$\log\left(\sqrt{2\pi}\sigma\right)$	0	$\dfrac{1}{2\sigma^2}$

even for moderately large k. However, Wu (2003) has developed a generalization of the algorithm that works much better: Noting that it is not necessary to impose all the moment constraints simultaneously, the algorithm uses the constraints sequentially, for $i = 0, ..., k$, and updates the ME density accordingly, every time a new constraint is taken into account. This procedure has two advantages: (i) The maximization subject to few moment constraints can be easily carried out with a standard Newton–Raphson, and (ii) the moments are not independent, so that the estimates of the first k parameters will typically be little changed when considering the ME density of order $k + 1$ and can therefore be used as starting values for the $(k + 1)$-order problem.

Having solved the estimation problem, the most important practical concern in ME estimation is the choice of k. A larger number of constraints results in a more precise approximation, but also in a tailormade model with more parameters. Thus, the advantage of a better fit must be balanced against the noise caused by the estimation of a more complicated model. Keeping in mind this tradeoff, there are at least two ways of making a decision concerning the optimal value of k (k^*, say).

Since the maximized log-likelihood is equal to $-N\sum_{i=0}^{k}\lambda_i\hat{\mu}^i$ (where N is the number of observations), we can compute a log-likelihood ratio (LLR) test of the null hypothesis $k = k^*$ against $k = k^* + 1$ as:

$$\text{LLR} = -2N\left(\sum_{i=0}^{k^*+1}\hat{\lambda}_i\hat{\mu}^i - \sum_{i=0}^{k^*}\hat{\lambda}_i\hat{\mu}^i\right).$$

Standard limiting theory guarantees that, asymptotically, the LLR follows a χ_1^2 distribution (Cox and Hinkley, 1974; Wu, 2003). Thus, the first procedure is based on the following steps: (i) Estimate sequentially the ME density with $k = 1, 2, ...$, (ii) perform the test for each value of k, and (iii) stop at the first value of k (k_0, say) such that the hypothesis $k = k_0$ cannot be rejected and conclude that $k^* = k_0$.

However, this method does not fully account for cases where the estimation of more parameters introduces further instability without substantially increasing the likelihood and the explanatory power of the model. A strategy that considers this issue, borrowed from the econometric literature (Greene, 2003; Koop, 2003), employs an information criterion, such as the Akaike (AIC) or Bayesian (BIC) Information Criterion, which penalizes the maximized likelihood using a function of the number of parameters. Therefore the second procedure, which is particularly well-suited when it is deemed important to avoid overfitting, differs from the first one only as it concerns the stopping rule: The algorithm terminates at the value k^* such that either the LLR test cannot reject the hypothesis $k = k^*$ or the numerical value of $\text{AIC}(k^* + 1)$ [or $\text{BIC}(k^* + 1)$] is larger than the numerical value of $\text{AIC}(k^*)$ [or $\text{BIC}(k^*)$].

So far, we have stressed the advantages of the ME approach from the point of view of its statistical properties, in particular in terms of its goodness of fit. It is also worth noting that the methodology can be employed to find risk-neutral probability distributions (Stutzer, 1996), and therefore has a strong potential for both risk management and pricing applications.

For comparison purposes, in addition to ME, we use two other methods:

(i) As a benchmark, we consider the standard market risk approach based on the normal distribution. This is known to be inadequate, in particular in turbulent periods, but has the advantage of simplicity.

(ii) We fit the tail of the distribution by means of the generalized Pareto distribution (GPD), which is a very precise way of estimating the tail of a distribution using only the observations above a predefined threshold and finds a strong theoretical justification (Embrechts *et al.*, 1997, theorem 3.4.13) in the asymptotic theory of extreme order statistics (EVT). The maximum likelihood estimators cannot be computed in closed form, but numerical maximization of the log-likelihood function is relatively straightforward. In practice, a more difficult problem consists in choosing the optimal threshold. However, as the GPD-based approach is not the focus of this work, we will not expand on it; the interested reader is referred to Embrechts *et al.* (1997, Chapter 6) or to McNeil *et al.* (2005) for a full account of the GPD, and to McNeil (1999) for details about risk management applications.

22.3 Empirical Analysis

The empirical analysis aims at fitting the optimal ME density and using it for computing tail probabilities. Parameter estimation is carried out by means of the sequential algorithm proposed by Wu (2003). The ME cumulative distribution function (CDF) is not available in closed form, but tail probabilities can be readily computed by standard numerical integration of the optimal ME density.

In order to assess the performance of the method for two different categories of assets, we consider the time series of the returns of the EUR/USD exchange rate and of the JPMorgan Chase stock, both for the period 4 January 2000 to 4 January 2012. These assets are expected to represent two types of DGPs commonly observed in finance. The EUR/USD distribution is "not far from the normal," with moderately heavy tails, as witnessed by an empirical kurtosis equal to 5.48 (see also Figure 22.1 below). On the other hand, the JPMorgan Chase DGP is strongly leptokurtic (the kurtosis is equal to 14.10) and the presence of some very large returns suggests the existence of a jump component (Gibson, 2001). This is not surprising, considering that, in general, the stocks of the financial sector showed tremendous variability during the subprime mortgage crisis. Thus, the first asset exemplifies the behavior, commonly observed in relatively quiet periods, of a not very volatile, yet definitely non-normal, DGP, whereas the second represents a more extreme benchmark, being the realization, in unprecented market conditions, of a highly volatile DGP, possibly given by a contaminated distribution.

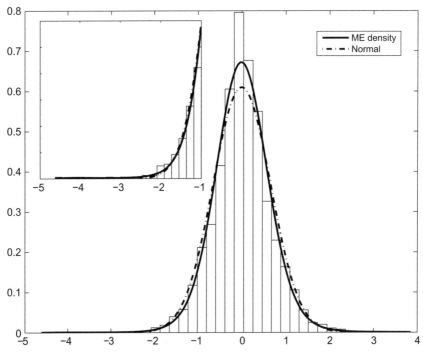

Figure 22.1 EUR/USD percentage returns, fitted normal density and optimal ME density ($k = 6, \alpha = 0.05$).

In both cases we fit the distribution of the percentage log-returns and compute value at risk (VaR) measures by means of the ME density, the normal distribution and the GPD. As for the choice of k in the ME approach, we use the second strategy outlined above, i.e. stop when either the LLR test cannot reject the hypothesis $k = k^*$ or AIC($k^* + 1$) is larger than AIC(k^*). Throughout, the analysis uses a 5% significance level for the LLR test.

As concerns the exchange rate data, Figure 22.1 shows the normal and optimal ME densities estimated from the data superimposed on the histogram of the percentage log-returns, whereas the inset shows the data and the two estimated densities for $r_t < -1\%$, i.e. the relevant range for risk management purposes. Table 22.2 contains detailed numerical results. All the criteria suggest that the optimal value of $k = 6$, although the LLR is marginally significant when $k = 4$.

In any case, the normal distribution is not appropriate. From the graph in Figure 22.1 it is clear that the ME(6) density gives a better fit, particularly in the tails.

To assess the impact on risk measures of the difference between the two fitted distributions, Table 22.3 reports tail probabilities $P(r < c)$ computed from the ME, the normal and the GPD distribution for various c as well as the observed percentages $(\#\{r < c\}/N) \cdot 100$. The probabilities for the ME density are computed by means of standard numerical integration techniques; for the GPD, we use for estimation the observations smaller than -1.2%, a criterion that provides a sample of size 109.

For the most extreme values of c, the tail probabilities estimated from the ME density are much larger, and much closer to the observed percentages, than the normal tail probabilities, which grossly underestimate the potential losses. The GPD-based

Table 22.2. EUR/USD: Estimation results

Log-likelihood	AIC	BIC	LLR	p-value
−6648.4	13301	13313	—	—
−3113.3	6233	6251	7070.17	0
−3108.6	6225	6249	9.38	0.002
−3042.9	6096	6126	131.3	0
−3041.1	6094	6131	3.66	0.047
−3033.7	6081	6124	14.83	<0.001
−3033.2	6082	6131	0.99	0.319

Table 22.3. EUR/USD: Percentage tail probabilities $P(r<c)$ and observed relative frequencies for various thresholds c

| | c | | | | | | |
	-1	-1.25	-1.5	-1.75	-2	-2.25	-2.5
ME	5.48	2.59	1.24	0.64	0.38	0.26	0.20
Normal	6.45	2.87	1.12	0.39	0.12	0.03	<0.01
GPD	–	2.95	1.41	0.77	0.45	0.29	0.19
Observed	5.78	2.84	1.56	0.77	0.42	0.26	0.19

tail probabilites are very similar to ME; in particular, they are almost identical for the largest values of c.

Figure 22.2 and Tables 22.4 and 22.5 report the outcomes of the same analysis for the JPMorgan Chase stock. The LLR and the BIC displayed in Table 22.4 indicate that the optimal value of k should be equal to 6, whereas the AIC suggests $k = 7$. We fitted both the ME(6) and ME(7) distributions and got essentially the

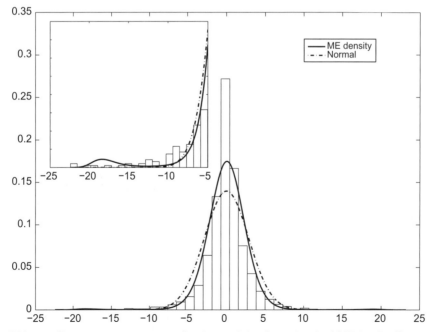

Figure 22.2 JPMorgan Chase percentage returns, fitted normal density and optimal ME density ($k = 6, \alpha = 0.05$).

Table 22.4. JPMorgan Chase: Estimation results

Log-likelihood	AIC	BIC	LLR	*p*-value
−11960	23924	23936	–	–
−7727	15460	15478	8465.86	0
−7707.2	15422	15447	39.67	<0.001
−7439.6	14889	14920	535.11	0
−7437.1	14886	14923	5.02	0.025
−7310.6	14635	14678	252.98	0
−7309	14634	14682	3.34	0.0674

same results, so that we decided to use the most parsimonious model, i.e. the ME(6).

Figure 22.2 shows that the ME density is not unimodal in this case, as it has a small local mode around −18%. This is not surprising, according to the peculiar features of the JPMorgan Chase DGP, which seems to contain a jump component taking into account few observations that may be too extreme to be generated by the same DGP as the bulk of the observations. Roughly speaking, in this case, the data "suggest" a density function that explicitly models the possible presence of a low-probability component distribution with a large negative mean, which therefore accommodates a few very large negative observations. Such observations are so large (in absolute value), that a unimodal distribution tends to assign them a too small probability.

Table 22.5. JPMorgan Chase: Percentage tail probabilities $P(r<c)$ and observed relative frequencies for various thresholds c

	c						
	−4	−7	−10	−13	−15	−17	−19
ME	2.44	0.85	0.51	0.45	0.40	0.30	0.10
Normal	8.01	0.70	<0.001	<0.001	<0.001	<0.001	<0.001
GPD	–	1.79	0.72	0.32	0.19	0.12	0.08
Observed	5.30	1.76	0.64	0.32	0.19	0.16	0.13

Estimated tail probabilities again show that the normal distribution dramatically underweights large losses, whereas probabilities computed by means of the ME density are not far from the observed percentages. For intermediate to large c, the GPD-based probabilities are, on an average, slightly closer to the observed frequencies than the ME-based probabilities. The difference is that the latter includes a jump component that increases the estimated probabilities for $c = -13$, -15 and -17%. In any case, both methods are very precise for $c = -19\%$. Although an explicit model of the jump is suggested by the ME method, the GPD provides a good fit as well. Thus, it is difficult to make a final decision about the inclusion of a jump using only the available empirical evidence; financial models of equity prices may be of some help.

A word of caution is in order as concerns the problem of overfitting, in particular in presence of outliers, as an ME density with very large k tries to approximate every single observation, resulting in a density whose generality would be questionable. In this respect, we stress again the importance of using a stopping rule based not only on the llr test but also on one or more information criteria. In addition, even when the criteria do give a clear-cut answer, it is highly recommended to visually inspect the estimated densities to assess their features and the goodness-of-fit.

22.4 Conclusions

In this chapter, we have proposed the ME density as a model for financial returns, with the goal of capturing their non-standard features and measuring event risk. Two empirical applications to foreign exchange and equity data have shown that the approach is computationally feasible and fits extreme events very well, both when the distributions are moderately and very heavy-tailed, because of the possible presence of jumps. In both cases, the ME approach performs much better than the normal-based VaR methodology, and similarly to the GPD suggested by EVT. However, with respect to the latter, it has the advantage of providing an estimate of the entire distribution.

References

Black, F., Scholes, M., 1973. The pricing of options and corporate liabilities. Journal of Political Economy 81, 637–654.

Buchen, P., Kelly, M., 1996. The maximum entropy distribution of an asset inferred from option prices. Journal of Financial and Quantitative Analysis 31, 143–159.

Cont, R., 2001. Empirical properties of asset returns: stylized facts and statistical issues. Quantitative Finance 1, 223–236.

Cox, D., Hinkley, D., 1974. Theoretical Statistics. Chapman & Hall, London.

Eberlein, E., Keller, U., 1995. Hyperbolic distributions in finance. Bernoulli 1, 281–299.

Embrechts, P., Klüppelberg, C., Mikosch, T., 1997. Modelling Extremal Events for Insurance and Finance. Springer, Berlin.

Gibson, M.S., 2001. Incorporating event risk into value-at-risk. FEDS Discussion Paper 2001-17. Federal Reserve, Washington, DC. Available at http://ssrn.com/abstract=268849.

Greene, W.H., 2003. Econometric Analysis, 5th ed. Prentice Hall, Englewood Cliffs, NJ.

Hawkins, R., 1997. Maximum entropy and derivative securities. Advances in Econometrics 12, 277–301.

Jaynes, E.T., 1957. Information theory and statistical mechanics. Physics Review 106, 620–630.

Kapur, J., 1989. Maximum Entropy Models in Science and Engineering. Wiley, New York.

Koop, G., 2003. Bayesian Econometrics. Wiley, New York.

McNeil, A.J., 1999. Extreme value theory for risk managers. In: Internal Modelling and CAD II. Risk Books, London, pp. 93–113.

McNeil, A., Frey, R., Embrechts, P., 2005. Quantitative Risk Management: Concepts, Techniques, Tools. Princeton University Press, Princeton, NJ.

Merton, R., 1973. Theory of rational option pricing. Bell Journal of Economics and Management Science 4, 141–183.

Nelson, D., 1991. Conditional heteroskedasticity in asset returns: a new approach. Econometrica 59, 347–370.

Stutzer, M., 1996. A simple nonparametric approach to derivative security valuation. Journal of Finance 51, 1633–1652.

Wu, X., 2003. Calculation of maximum entropy densities with application to income distribution. Journal of Econometrics 115, 347–354.

23

QUANTIFYING THE UNQUANTIFIABLE: RISKS NOT IN VALUE AT RISK

Carsten S. Wehn*

DekaBank, Frankfurt

CHAPTER OUTLINE

23.1 Introduction and Motivation

23.1.1 Scope of risks not in value at risk

Market risk refers typically to the impact of market risk factors on the gains and losses associated with a portfolio of investments.

---

* All opinions expressed herein are the authors' and should not be cited as being those of their affiliated institutions. None of the methods described herein is claimed to be in actual use at DekaBank

Rethinking Valuation and Pricing Models. http://dx.doi.org/10.1016/B978-0-12-415875-7.00023-3

These risk factors might be, for example, interest rates, equity prices, foreign exchange rates or implied volatilities. For many risk factors, market risk factors are readily observable. The measurement of market risk is preceded by a prediction of the distribution of the future (and therefore unknown) gains and losses. Several building blocks mark the derivation of a predictive distribution for portfolio gains and losses (for a more mathematical quotation and introduction, see Wehn, 2010):

(i) Identification of relevant, i.e. most important, risk factors driving gains and losses (such as interest rates for different maturities and rating classes, equity indices or equity prices, exchange rates, implied volatilities, etc.) is required.

(ii) One has to choose a relevant multivariate distribution for the risk factor returns, which can be done empirically or be based on parametric distributions. This distribution has to incorporate the empirically observable stylized facts of the respective time series.

(iii) Risk models usually make assumptions concerning the relationship (mapping) between risk factors (or risk factor returns, respectively) and the portfolio gain and loss function (e.g. sensitivities and "Greeks," full valuation, present value grids, and so on).

Most risk models show statistics of the distribution of the portfolio's gains and losses, such as a quantile for the value at risk (VaR) or conditional means for the expected shortfall (ES). Financial institutions commonly reserve economic capital for risks such as market risk and hence are interested in reserving an adequate amount to these risks.

Despite the fact that models for market risk measurement have been readily available for years, they, by construction, rely on the building blocks drafted above (e.g. the selection of adequate risk factors is highly dependent on the availability of data for estimating a respective distribution). Due to different reasons that will be explained in detail below there might exist market risks (e.g. potential losses due to movements of market risk factors) in a financial institution that are reflected (neither fully nor, in some cases, even in part) in the portfolio model and thus not in the overall risk measure. These risks are defined as "risks not in VaR."

23.1.2 Reasons for risks not in VaR

The reasons for a market risk model not reflecting some risks are manifold. Among others, they comprise:

- Necessary reduction of risk factors/model complexity. By construction, not all risk factors can be incorporated completely into the model (e.g. interest rate curves are continuous; the model will limit this to relevant maturities, hence discretizing the curves to driving buckets, and so on). Also, the reduction of risk factors is necessary to give meaningful results of risk analysis and the efficient computational calculation of risk.

- Sometimes valuation parameters are already adequately reflected by other risk factors in the model (e.g. one may think about highly correlated interest rate key rates or alike).
- There exist valuation parameters that are not directly observable and where there is no market dataset available for modeling (i.e. for estimating a daily return distribution). Other valuation parameters are given implicitly by respective valuation models.
- Approximate procedures for the mapping between risk factor returns and gains and losses are sometimes necessary [*cf.* building block (iii) above] due to the highly complex and computationally intensive valuation functions/procedures.

As every model can only be an approximation to reality, we have to judge whether the approximations we make, by neglecting some valuation parameters, are acceptable or not.

In the rest of this chapter, I first outline the recent regulatory developments in this context and the current requirements for approved internal market risk models (Section 23.2). I then give some examples for different products and risk factors affected in this context (Section 23.3). Next, I try to approach the quantification of risks not in VaR in Section 23.4 and then consider issues arising from risks not in VaR in the risk management context in Section 23.5, before concluding in Section 23.6.

23.2 Regulatory Developments and Requirements

The history of market risk models in a regulatory context dates back to 1996, when, with the Market Risk Amendment, banks were first allowed to use their internal market risk models for regulatory purposes upon approval by the respective supervisory authorities. Due to the necessity of an approval and in-depth examination of the model, the respective requirements were more of a qualitative nature and were not very detailed. They were taken over to the Basel II framework by the Basel Committee on Banking Supervision (2006). For example, it is required that:

An important part of a bank's internal market risk measurement system is the specification of an appropriate set of market risk factors, i.e. the market rates and prices that affect the value of the bank's trading positions. The risk factors contained in a market risk measurement system should be sufficient to capture the risks inherent in the bank's portfolio of on- and off-balance sheet trading positions.

Under the pressure of the recent financial crisis, the Basel II framework was and still is under substantial review, and thus regulators have forced (among others) banks to consider risks not in VaR (Basel Committee on Banking Supervision, 2010) that expanded the scope of the Basel II framework (Basel Committee on Banking Supervision, 2006) in the following manner:

Factors that are deemed relevant for pricing should be included as risk factors in the value-at-risk model. Where a risk factor is incorporated in a pricing model but not in the value-at-risk model, the bank must justify this omission to the satisfaction of its supervisor. In addition, the value-at-risk model must capture nonlinearities for options and other relevant products (e.g. mortgage-backed securities, tranched exposures or n-th-to-default credit derivatives), as well as correlation risk and basis risk (e.g. between credit default swaps and bonds). Moreover, the supervisor has to be satisfied that proxies are used which show a good track record for the actual position held (i.e. an equity index for a position in an individual stock).

The Basel Committee on Banking Supervision (2010) also explains the rationale behind these strengthened requirements:

The improvements in the Basel II Framework concerning internal value-at-risk models in particular require banks to justify any factors used in pricing which are left out in the calculation of value-at-risk.

Besides this, regulators are defining additional qualitative requirements and also special requirements for illiquid positions.

Currently, the complete structure of the former Basel regulations is under review (so-called "fundamental review"). A consultative document has been lately (May 2012) issued. Concerning the risks not in VaR, a discussion paper by the Financial Supervisory Authority (2010) gives some ideas of current regulatory concerns:

Firms are already required to capture all material risks for positions within the scope of their model approval. To improve implementation of the current framework, we have been working with firms in the UK to ensure that they have in place risk management processes to regularly and systematically evaluate whether their VaR models capture all material risk factors. Where this is not the case, we have been requiring firms to hold capital buffers against missing or poorly captured risk factors. We believe this promotes and enhances proactive risk management, which is clearly desirable. We will continue to promote this more systematic approach to capturing what we currently refer to as Risks Not In VaR (RNIV). In addition, when the [Basel Committee on Banking Supervision (2010)] package is introduced, firms will have to ensure that all risk factors used in their pricing models are also included in their VaR model. This may necessitate an extension of the RNIV framework.

We observe that regulators are very well aware of what I defined above as risks not in VaR and within the storm of regulatory strengthening it will only be a matter of time before risks not in VaR will come even more into the focus of further regulatory requirements.

23.3 Examples of Different Products and Risk Factors

Here, I give some impressions of different products and risk factors affected by risks not in VaR.

23.3.1 Dividends

Dividends and dividend estimations play a certain role for dividend futures, equity-linked products, (plain vanilla) derivatives and also within the repo business. Losses might occur due to a change in the amount of the dividends as well as the timing of the dividend payout. Dividends are measured as dividend yield or dividend cash flow, depending on the respective product. One might further distinguish between declared and undeclared dividends. Whereas the first category reflects a dividend payout already declared by the board of a company and will only very seldom be changed later on, the second category reflects a higher uncertainty.

Dividend payouts are commonly only once *per annum*, and thus jumps in dividends are not well modeled on a day-to-day basis and are only rarely observable.

23.3.2 Implied volatilities and implied correlations

The present value of complex derivatives usually depends on implied volatilities and/or implied correlations. These can be seen as prototypical examples of "derived market data" in the sense that they will be quoted by a certain market convention on a pricing model (e.g. Black–Scholes implied volatilities or base correlations via a Gaussian copula). The model in use to value the complex derivative might be different and take the implied volatility or correlation as an input, i.e. as a basis for its calibration and, hence, replication and hedging strategies.

Commonly, market quotes are quite liquid for at-the-money options and certain maturities. If the bank faces the issue to value an option far in- or out-of-the-money or with a rather long-term maturity, then the smile or skew of the volatility surface has to be considered. For risk modeling purposes, these points are more challenging to model as quotes might be illiquid and, thus, other procedures to derive the respective market data could be employed. Parametric models are often used to fit the volatility surface, but these parameters cannot generally be assumed to be deterministic or otherwise independent identically distributed random variables and thus their usefulness for the risk model might be limited. A further point of interest is the mapping of single stock volatilities to a (more liquid) market volatility, i.e. volatility spread risks, which have drawn the close attention of risk managers and regulators in the aftermath of the credit crunch.

For equity basket or quanto products as well as for basket credit derivatives, the implied correlation plays an important role. Here, similar questions arise concerning an adequate derivation of the respective valuation parameter and its modeling within a stochastic context. Even for standard tranches of CDX or iTraxx, a reliable modeling of implied or base correlations is still in its infancy, as was clearly demonstrated by the problems that arose after the bankruptcy of Lehman Brothers due to vanishing market liquidity.

23.3.3 Interest rate curves and spread curves

As already highlighted in other chapters of this book by different authors (e.g. Chapter 9 by Mercurio), the crisis has questioned in-depth what was meant to be already understood in the past, i.e. the "correct" or at least adequate discount curve for valuing derivative products. Nowadays, the respective tenor of the curve and its constituents, i.e. the credit quality of the (panel) banks providing the basis for its calculation, is highly important and thus there exist a variety of basis risks that are arbitrage-free materializing nowadays that were readily observable before, but of much less importance (*cf.* Tuckman and Porfirio, 2003).

Figure 23.1 shows the development of the one-year EUR swap rate versus different tenors since 2006. Where before the crisis the

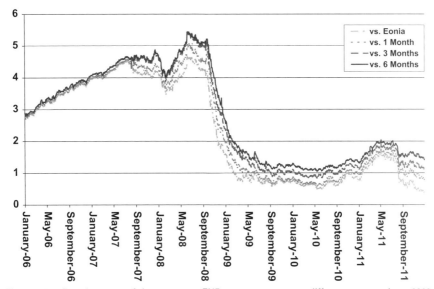

Figure 23.1 Development of the one-year EUR swap rate versus different tenors since 2006.

basis swap spreads were almost not measurable, nowadays they play a distinct role in the discounting of cash flows and thereby also for risk measurement purposes.

The mapping of even plain vanilla interest rate derivatives to their adequate "risk-free" interest rate curve has to be questioned. This also plays a distinct role for foreign exchange products like cross-currency swaps and alike via the so-called cross-currency basis spread or foreign exchange basis spread risks, which are also well-known to have been a significant source of losses for several financial institutions during the beginning of the financial crisis in 2007/08.

A further point that arose as a consequence of the debt crisis of the EUR member states is the adequate spread curve associated with a country's government and municipal bonds. As ratings are changed quite often and the instruments (bonds) used to "build" the corresponding spread curves are likely to change according to this stochastic as well, the adequate mapping of bonds to the respective spread curves has to be validated. For example, only a short time ago, countries with a similar rating issuing bonds in the EUR faced quite similar spreads. Nowadays, the spreads are more country-specific and differ significantly again; however, there is no further jump in the spread observable, once a rating is changed by one of the big rating agencies.

23.3.4 Higher-order risks

Complex products often bring up the issue of highly time-consuming valuation functions. Here, approximations like sensitivities of the first- and second-order or present value grids come into place. As the aim of the market risk model, in a broader sense, is to provide information about the tail behavior of the portfolio's gains and losses (e.g. by VaR), the adequacy of these approximations has to be assessed.

It should be mentioned that the difference between real revaluation and approximation might be significantly less important in a portfolio context, where some products might offset the differences of others (given a more or less balanced mix of, for example, long and short positions). Even under the impression that there remain differences at a single-product level, approximate valuation functions might, in practice, be adequate in a market risk model under a portfolio perspective.

23.3.5 Other risks

Other products affected by risks not in VaR can comprise (among others):
- Prepayment risks, i.e. embedded options that allow the investor to cancel or close out a transaction, like a loan, with or without a special charge.
- Rating migration risks that can affect, for example, rating-linked notes, where the payoff profile explicitly depends on the issuer rating.
- Recovery risks that can affect credit derivatives and require the recovery rate as a discretely observable market data object.

This list is not exhaustive and is highly dependent on the portfolio under review.

23.4 Approaches to Quantifying Risks not in VaR

23.4.1 Scenario analysis

Some of the products introduced in Section 23.3 allow measuring the change in value by varying the valuation parameter in question by either:
- The sensitivity with respect to the parameter, i.e. the first (or higher)-order derivative of the valuation formula. This is, to some extent, best market practice for dividends (referring to the so-called dividend-phi), for implied volatilities

(so-called vegas, vonnas, volgas, etc.) and correlations (so-called Corr01), recovery rates (so-called RR01), etc., and gives us a good impression of the materiality when changing the parameter slightly. Clearly, these sensitivity analyses should be done in a full-valuation context to measure the total impact of risks not covered in VaR according to the single parameter or risk factor as well as possible.

- Eventually scenarios including relevant valuation parameters can be derived to give a measure comparable to the VaR measure under certain assumptions like probability (confidence level) and holding period. This is of importance in order to include and to quantify the impact of dependencies to other driving risk factors, which can be obtained, for example, in a simple way applying spot-vol matrices. To derive scenarios, more complex models for the stochastic process for the respective valuation parameter can also be used, such as jump processes (see, e.g. McNeil *et al.*, 2005). Also, scenarios can be derived by expert estimation. Scenario valuation can also be a good means to quantify risks in a situation where the different valuation parameters come from a parametric model, e.g. in a context for implied volatility surfaces.
- A principal component analysis can lead to insights into the behavior of similarly behaving valuation parameters, e.g. in the context of volatility surfaces, and help to reduce complexity to the necessary minimum number of risk factors.
- Direct introduction of new risk factors. This might be possible for the category where risk factors that used to behave with a correlation around one now tend to behave differently, e.g. for the above-mentioned basis risks and spread curve risks. Here, data is readily available and a tentative calculation can be eventually preceded within the risk model itself.
- Stress testing, i.e. applying extreme market movements to valuation parameters or opaque risk factors to capture and calculate the impact of these on the valuation and, hence, on the risk measures under consideration, should be mentioned as particular scenario analyses. These results can also be used to reserve capital for model risks or calculate or verify certain valuation adjustments, which should also be related to model risks and parameter uncertainties usually not captured in risk measures like VaR.

23.4.2 Other means

For other categories of the above-mentioned assumptions, alternative also means come to mind. In order to judge, for example, the adequacy of the use of sensitivities instead of a full valuation, test calculations preceded on exemplary dates with a full valuation instead of the approximation can lead to insights into the adequacy of the assumptions. Here, it should be distinguished between a calculation on the product level, where the error might be not negligible (e.g. for barrier options), and on the portfolio level, where different approximation errors might offset one each other. In general, when preceded on a mark-to-market profit and loss time series or even on a dirty profit and loss time series, backtesting can help identify potential shortcomings in this regard (see, e.g. Wehn, 2010).

23.5 Treatment within the Internal Capital Adequacy Process

Once we observe risks of any kind, we will be in a situation to include them into risk management circles and in the internal capital adequacy process (ICAAP) as well. The inclusion in the risk management circle might be easier when we are able to quantify the amount of risk in the sense above (scenario analysis or sensitivity with respect to the given valuation parameter). I now present a few ideas of how to incorporate risks not in VaR into the ICAAP under a groupwide fiction of confidence level and a holding period.

23.5.1 Materiality concerns

The starting point for ICAAP is the amount of capital available to cover potential losses due to the different aspects of risk. This amount is defined under a fiction for the business, e.g. going-concern or gone-concern, and we must now determine whether the risks not reflected by the common risk measure are negligible or not. Intuitively, we would take a starting point to define materiality from the available amount of capital for risks.

23.5.2 Stand-alone and interaction with other market risks

Whenever a quantification of the risks not in VaR is possible, we can first calculate the risk (under the probability/confidence level and the holding period relevant for the ICAAP) on a stand-alone basis, i.e. the risk of the specific risk category. If this quantification exceeds the barrier defined by the available amount of capital, we potentially have to re-engineer the market risk model or include the risk in question by other means, e.g. a certain scenario that should again be compatible with the ICAAP assumptions.

The issue arising here is that we typically make a very conservative assumption about the treatment of risks not in VaR. In a portfolio context, we need to assume a certain interaction with the other market risks already measured by the model. Under assumptions of correlation, we are then able to pose the question of the additional effect by including the specific risk category.

23.6 Conclusion and Outlook

By construction of a risk model, it is clear that not all valuation parameters might be incorporated in the same manner. There exist some types of risk factors that are hard to model and sometimes even hard to quantify. When constructing or validating a market risk model, these risks have to be questioned and it has to be decided whether they are indeed negligible or not. This might also concern further approximations of the risk model, e.g. the valuation function.

Regulatory requirements have strengthened in this regard. Sometimes methods to quantify these risks are readily available and inclusion in the risk management circle as well as in the ICAAP is possible; sometimes the risk model itself has to be re-engineered.

Notes

All opinions expressed herein are the author's and should not be cited as being those of his affiliated institutions. None of the methods described herein is claimed to be in actual use at DekaBank

References

Basel Committee on Banking Supervision, 2006. International Convergence of Capital Measurement and Capital Standards. Basel Committee on Banking Supervision, Basel.

Basel Committee on Banking Supervision, 2010. Revisions to the Basel II Market Risk Framework. Basel Committee on Banking Supervision, Basel.

Financial Services Authority, 2010. The prudential regime for trading activities—a fundamental review. Discussion Paper. Financial Services Authority, London.

McNeil, A.J., Frey, R., Embrechts, P., 2005. Quantitative Risk Management: Concepts, Techniques, and Tools. Princeton University Press, Princeton, NJ.

Tuckman, B., Porfirio, P., 2003. Interest rate parity, money market basis swaps, and cross-currency basis swaps. Fixed income liquid markets research, Lehman Brothers White Paper. Lehman Brothers, New York.

Wehn, C.S., 2010. Evaluating the adequacy of market risk models. In: Gregoriou, G.N., Hoppe, C., Wehn, C.S. (Eds.), The Risk Modeling Evaluation Handbook: Rethinking Financial Risk Management Methodologies in the Global Capital Markets. McGraw-Hill, New York, pp. 419–438.

ACTIVE PORTFOLIO CONSTRUCTION WHEN RISK AND ALPHA FACTORS ARE MISALIGNED

Ralph Karels and Michael Sun

MSCI Consultants

CHAPTER OUTLINE

24.1 Introduction

When looking at active portfolio optimization, there are three main ingredients: The portfolio manager's return forecasts (alphas), a portfolio risk forecast and a risk aversion parameter.

In an ideal world, one factor model should account for both risk and return forecasts. In practice, however, portfolio managers use different models to forecast risk and alpha—in general not necessarily including mutually exclusive but overlapping or related factors such as variations of a momentum factor. These discrepancies may lead to unintended biases in optimized portfolios as the optimizer tends to exploit inconsistencies between the risk and alpha factors resulting in inadvertent bets. Technically, we are talking about risk and alpha factor misalignment when alpha cannot be written as a linear combination of the risk factors. Therefore, there is an alpha part aligned

Rethinking Valuation and Pricing Models. http://dx.doi.org/10.1016/B978-0-12-415875-7.00024-5

with the risk factors and a residual alpha part that is orthogonal to the aligned alpha part. Depending on the portfolio managers' interpretation of the misalignment, it must be treated differently: Residual alpha may contain only noise or may incur risk and return, and hence a positive information ratio. In the first case, residual alpha has to be penalized; in the second case, it has to be managed. It can be shown from an analytical decomposition of alpha into its aligned and residual parts that the optimizer favors residual over aligned alpha in an unconstrained active optimization problem. In principle, there are three ways of mitigation for alpha and risk factor misalignment, distinguished by their focus: (i) Focus on the risk model, (ii) focus on the optimization process or (iii) focus on adding an additional (alpha) factor. We will show that the alpha factor approach creates an unclear risk forecast setting, and furthermore penalizes everything outside the common factor space and thus in particular over-rides the specific risk model; it is not recommended. There is no need to penalize anything other than residual alpha and we will use this approach in the following. We will conclude with three case studies on the penalizing residual alpha approach.

24.2 Framework for Active Portfolio Construction

In general, the goal of active portfolio information is to turn information like expected returns (alphas) into "good" portfolios. The well-accepted portfolio construction theory (Bender, 2008) identifies the relationships between forecast returns, realized returns and portfolio holdings shown in Figure 24.1.

The information coefficient (*IC*) describes the correlation between forecasts and realized returns. The transfer coefficient (*TC*) outlines the correlation between constructed and ideal

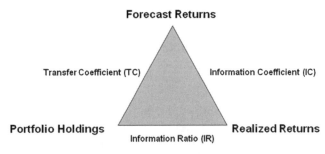

Figure 24.1 Triangle of portfolio construction (Bender, 2008).

(unconstrained) portfolios. The information ratio (*IR*) describes the risk-adjusted returns. In formula terms we thus have:

$$IR_{PF} = TC \cdot IR_{Opt}$$
$$IR_{PF} = TC \cdot IC \cdot \sqrt{Breadth}.$$

The *IR* of the optimal, unconstrained portfolio is the product of the *IC* and the square root of the number of independent bets. It translates into the *IR* of the actual, constrained portfolio by scaling with the transfer coefficient *TC*. Active portfolio construction with return forecasts is characterized by the quadratic optimization problem of the form when the goal is to maximize utility or risk-adjusted return (Grinold and Kahn, 2008):

$$U = \underbrace{r'w}_{\text{Expected Return}} \underbrace{- w'(\lambda_{CF}X^{T}FX + \lambda_{AS}D)w}_{\text{Cost of Risk}} \rightarrow \max_{w},$$

$$\underbrace{\phantom{U = r'w - w'(\lambda_{CF}X^{T}FX + \lambda_{AS}D)w}}_{\text{Risk Adjusted Return}}$$

where the risk term $X^{T}FX + D$ stems from a classic multifactor model approach:

$$r_k = x_{k,1} \cdot \hat{f}_1 + x_{k,2} \cdot \hat{f}_2 + \dots + x_{k,n} \cdot \hat{f}_n + \hat{u}_{k,\text{Spec}},$$

or in matrix form:

$$r = Xf + u,$$

where the excess asset returns *r* are modeled as a linear combination of the weighted factor returns *f* plus an idiosyncratic part *u*. By assuming independence between *f* and *u*, and between the individual components of *u*, we can easily deduce:

$$\text{cov}(r) = X^{T}FX + D,$$

with *X* as the matrix of asset exposures to the risk factors *f*, *F* as the covariance matrix of risk factor returns and *D* as the diagonal matrix of volatilities of the asset specific returns *u* by assumption. Hence, the risk term in this setting is divided into a common factor risk block $X^{T}FX$ and an asset specific (idiosyncratic) risk block *D*. By specifying the risk aversion parameters λ_{CF} and λ_{AS} for the respective risk blocks, the portfolio manager can incorporate his/her specific risk and return profile into the optimization process. After specifying an initial portfolio, a benchmark (optional), an asset universe (optional), constraints (optional), expected returns on asset level, and transaction costs (optional) and penalties (optional) the optimization case is complete. If, in the presence of additional constraints, the optimization problem is feasible, the optimizer returns the optimal portfolio with portfolio weights w^* as optimization result.

24.3 Misalignment of Risk and Alpha Models

Active portfolio optimization requires a forecast for both portfolio volatility and exceptional return. In theory, the same factor model would forecast risk and alpha, but in practice different models are used to forecast risk and alpha as portfolio managers intend to incorporate proprietary information not found in the risk model into their alpha forecasts to outperform the market. Mostly the factors used as alpha components or descriptors are not entirely different to the risk model factors, but somewhat overlapping. For instance, different versions or definitions of a momentum, earnings yield, value or growth factor may be used for risk and alpha. Bender *et al.* (2009) show that there is, however, the possibility that these discrepancies between risk and alpha factors may create unintended bets or biases in the optimized portfolios. Before we present a case study of the effects of such a risk and alpha misalignment, let us formalize the meaning of different factor models for risk and alpha by a portfolio manager:

$$r = X_R f_R + u_R$$

$$r = X_A f_A + u_A$$

$$\Sigma_R = X_R F_R X_R^T + D_R$$

$$\alpha = X_A w.$$

Both models above, for excess return r, attribute returns towards specific factors f and an idiosyncratic part u. Moving from returns to risk and incorporating the standard factor model assumptions we obtain:

$$\text{cov}(f, u) = \text{cov}(u, u) = 0.$$

As we have already stated, optimizers tend to exploit inconsistencies between risk and alpha models, resulting in inadvertent and unwanted bets. Lee and Stefek (2008) look at a manager that is betting on a 12-month price momentum factor strategy lagged one month that differs slightly from the momentum factor in the risk model used which has no lag (Figure 24.2).

The alpha model hence includes the return from 13 months ago, but the risk model does not. As a conclusion when optimizing, the optimizer sees return but no factor risk in month 13 and places a large bet. On the other hand, the risk model includes

Figure 24.2 Different momentum factors in the risk and alpha model (Lee and Stefek, 2008).

return from one month ago, but the alpha model does not. Similarly, the optimizer sees factor risk but no return for one-month momentum and places a negative bet here. The combination of these two effects is probably not what the manager had in mind when designing his alpha model. When the risk and alpha models match their definition of momentum, the exploitation of these inconsistencies by the optimizer resulting in concentrated bets disappears.

Let us now have a closer look at the meaning of risk and alpha factor misalignment. Per definition, risk and alpha factors are aligned if alpha is spanned entirely by the risk factors, i.e. alpha can be written as a linear combination of the risk factor exposures:

$$\alpha = \sum_j \gamma_j X_{R_j}.$$

If alpha on the other hand cannot be written as a linear combination of the risk factors, then there is a residual part of alpha that is orthogonal to the alpha part that is aligned with the risk factors. In a stylized graphical representation, the alpha decomposition looks like Figure 24.3. The question arising now is: Is alpha and risk misalignment to be avoided generally? Since the alpha part not aligned with the risk model may contain not only noise, but also may incur return and risk and hence a positive information ratio *IR*, the answer to this question is no. There are

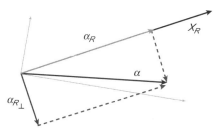

Figure 24.3 Decomposition of alpha into a part aligned with the risk model and a part orthogonal to it.

in fact cases where the return–risk tradeoff of the non-aligned alpha should be managed.

Let us now look closer into the analytical decomposition of alpha along the lines of the sketch above. When regressing alpha against the risk factor exposures, the fit from the regression is represented by the spanned alpha α_R and the residual is represented by the orthogonal alpha $\alpha_{R_\perp}$. Therefore the managers' alpha may be decomposed into a part that is spanned by the risk factor exposures and a part that is orthogonal to them (Bender et al., 2009):

$$\alpha = X_R\left(X_R^T X_R\right)^{-1} X_R^T \alpha + \left(I - X_R\left(X_R^T X_R\right)^{-1} X_R^T\right)\alpha$$
$$\qquad = \alpha_R \qquad\qquad\qquad = \alpha_{R_\perp}.$$

Note that the components of alpha are viewed differently by the risk model:

$$X_R^T \alpha_R = X_R^T X_R \left(X_R^T X_R\right)^{-1} X_R^T \alpha = X_R^T \alpha$$

$$X_R^T \alpha_{R_\perp} = X_R^T \left(I - X_R\left(X_R^T X_R\right)^{-1} X_R^T\right)\alpha = 0.$$

A tilt in the direction of α_R incurs a factor risk but a tilt in the direction of $\alpha_{R_\perp}$ incurs no factor risk since the orthogonal alpha is outside the risk factor space.

24.4 Portfolio Optimization with Alpha Decomposition

Let us now examine the effects of the alpha decomposition above on an unconstrained active portfolio optimization problem:

$$\alpha^T w - \frac{\lambda}{2} w^T \left(X^T F X + D\right) w \to \max.$$

Since there are no constraints involved here, the optimal portfolio is easy to obtain:

$$w^* = \frac{1}{\lambda}\left(X^T F X + D\right)^{-1}\alpha.$$

If we further assume for simplicity reasons that all assets have the same specific risk σ_s and use the alpha decomposition derived in the previous section, we obtain (Lee and Stefek, 2008):

$$\Sigma = X_R F_R X_R^T + \sigma_s I$$

$$w^* = \frac{1}{\lambda\sigma_s^2}\left[\alpha_{R_\perp} + \left(1 - X_R\left(X_R^T X_R + \sigma_s^2 F_R^{-1}\right)^{-1} X_R^T\right)\alpha_R\right].$$

Close inspection of the optimal portfolio weights above reveals that the optimizer favors $\alpha_{R_\perp}$ over α_R. While the orthogonal alpha is only scaled to adjust for specific risk, the spanned alpha is also scaled to adjust for specific risk but additionally twisted and shrunk to adjust for common factor risk. In the special case of a risk model with just one single factor f_R with volatility σ_{f_R} this phenomenon becomes even more obvious. Since the matrices $F_R = (\sigma_{f_R})$ and $X_R = (x_R)$ now are 1×1, the necessary inversions are easy to calculate and we obtain:

$$w^* = \frac{1}{\lambda\sigma_s^2}\left[\alpha_{R_\perp} + \left(\frac{\sigma_s^2}{n\sigma_{f_R}^2 + \sigma_s^2}\right)\alpha_R\right].$$

The equation suggests the following. (i) Since the ratio in brackets is always smaller than 1, $\alpha_{R_\perp}$ always has a greater weight than α_R. (ii) As the number of assets n and the factor volatility σ_{f_R} increases, the weight in the part of alpha spanned by the risk factor exposures decreases even more, thus increasing the size of the unwanted bets in the optimal portfolio. There are several ways to mitigate this effect, focusing on the risk model or the optimization itself. We will explore those in Section 24.5.

24.5 Mitigation for Alpha and Risk Factor Misalignment

One way to mitigate the effects of alpha and risk factor misalignment is to focus on the risk model. We will assume for now that risk and alpha factors are not mutually exclusive, but more a like in practice, related to each other as shown in the momentum example in Section 24.3. Those risk model factors resembling alpha model factors are called related risk factors. The following approaches (Lee and Stefek, 2008) may be applied in order to reduce misalignment between alpha factors and their risk model counterparts with increasing steps of complexity.

  (i) Drop the related risk factors from the model by setting all asset exposures to those factors to zero.
  (ii) Modify the risk model by swapping all related risk factors by their alpha factor counterparts and retain all other risk factors. That implies building and estimating a new risk model including the new alpha factors.

(iii) Alter the risk model by swapping the related risk factor exposures X_{R_i} with the alpha factor exposures X_{A_i}.

(iv) The portfolio manager may use his/her risk model to emulate the new risk model obtained in (ii). The idea here is to approximate the covariance matrix of a risk model based on the portfolio managers' alpha factors and the retained risk factors. The emulated model would be of the form $\Sigma = X_C F_C X_C^T + \Delta_R$, where F_C represents the approximation of the covariance matrix of the new model's factor returns and X_C are the exposures to the retained risk and alpha factors. The diagonal matrix of specific return volatilities Δ_R stems from the managers' risk model.

Another way to mitigate issues arising from misaligned risk and alpha factors is to focus on the optimization process itself. The idea is to penalize the portion of the alpha not related to the risk factors (the orthogonal alpha α_R) to counteract the tendency of the optimizer to over allocate this part (Bender *et al.*, 2009). This technique is called "penalizing residual alpha" and implies adding a quadratic penalty term for residual alpha and an adjustment parameter ϑ to the utility function in the optimizer:

$$\alpha^T w - \frac{\lambda}{2} w^T \Sigma w - \vartheta \left(w^T \alpha_{R_\perp} \right)^2 \rightarrow \max.$$

The parameter ϑ allows the portfolio manager to control the importance of the penalty term similarly to λ adjusting for the importance of the risk term. How should this parameter be chosen? We consider two cases:

(i) The residual alpha is essentially noise. This is the case when the managers' alpha and the risk model factors capture essentially the same properties, but measure them slightly differently (the momentum case). Then the manager should choose ϑ sufficiently large to avoid any tilt towards $\alpha_{R_\perp}$.

(ii) There is some factor return and risk associated with a tilt towards the residual alpha. In this case, the manager should choose $\vartheta \sim \lambda \sigma^2_{\alpha_{R_\perp}}$ to achieve an optimal risk–reward tradeoff. Choosing ϑ like this associates the proper risk penalty with a bet on the orthogonal alpha $\alpha_{R_\perp}$. We assume here that residual alpha return is uncorrelated with the risk model factor returns.

A third way of possible mitigation of alpha and risk factor misalignment is to add an additional factor to the risk model and penalize it (Saxena and Stubbs, 2011):

$$\alpha^T w - \frac{\lambda}{2} w^T \Sigma w - \vartheta w^T \left(I - P_{X_R} \right) w \rightarrow \max.$$

With $P_{X_R} := X_R(X_R^T X_R)^{-1} X_R^T$ and $w_\perp := (I - P_{X_R})w$ we easily observe symmetry and idempotency:

$$P_{X_R}^T = P_{X_R}$$

$$(I - P_{X_R})^2 = I - P_{X_R},$$

and therefore can rewrite the utility optimization problem:

$$\alpha^T w - \frac{\lambda}{2} w^T \Sigma w - \vartheta w_\perp^T w_\perp \to \max.$$

The so-called alpha factor $I - P_{X_R}$ represents the orthogonal part of implied alpha. Now there are two risk terms in the utility function that we cannot combine—hence the risk setting in this approach is unclear. Also, the meaning of the penalty parameter ϑ and how to calibrate it are not straightforward. Furthermore, this approach penalizes everything outside the common factor space and would thus especially over-ride the specific risk part that cannot be desired by the portfolio manager. There is no need to penalize anything other than residual alpha. Thus, we do not recommend this mitigation of alpha and risk factor approach. If there is doubt about the risk model missing factors with high explanatory power, the factors should be added directly to the model. If the missing factor is the orthogonal alpha $\alpha_{R_\perp}$, the penalizing residual alpha approach adds the missing factor directly to the risk model as desired. When we introduce $\alpha_{R_\perp}$ as a new column to the exposure matrix X_R and rename it Y and also adjust the factor return covariance matrix F_R according to (Stefek, 2007):

$$Y = \begin{bmatrix} X_R & \alpha_{R_\perp} \end{bmatrix} \qquad F = \begin{bmatrix} F_R & 0 \\ 0 & \dfrac{\theta}{\lambda} \end{bmatrix},$$

we obtain as the new enhanced utility maximization problem:

$$\alpha^T w - \frac{\lambda}{2} w^T (YFY^T + \Delta)w \to \max.$$

Simple matrix algebra now shows that this translates into:

$$\alpha^T w - \frac{\lambda}{2} w^T (X_R F_R X_R^T + \Delta)w - \vartheta(w^T \alpha_{R_\perp})^2 \to \max,$$

which represents exactly the penalizing residual alpha approach. This shows not only that contrary to the alpha factor approach discussed above, the risk forecast $YFY^T + \Delta$ in this setting is clearly defined, but also that if the missing factor in the risk model is the orthogonal alpha, penalizing residual alpha is a superior approach to the alpha factor approach.

24.6 Case Studies

In a recent paper, Bender *et al.* (2009) illustrated how penalizing the residual alpha in portfolio optimization may improve a portfolio's exposures and *ex ante* information ratio. We will briefly discuss this result as a modifying objective function by including a penalty term on the residual alpha that helps to mitigate the mismatch between alpha and the risk by assigning a suitable penalty to the residual alpha.

In Figure 24.4 we plot four portfolios' exposures to the spanned and residual alphas. It is immediately clear that the parameter θ affects the portfolio's tilt on the spanned ($\boldsymbol{h}^T \alpha_R$) and residual alpha ($\boldsymbol{h}^T \alpha_{R_\perp}$). When the penalty term is neglected the resulting portfolio has a significant tilt on residual alpha. Gradually increasing the value of θ will tilt the optimal portfolio's exposure away from residual alpha until there is no exposure left, e.g. in the case of when $\theta = 0.01$.

The authors further analyzed the cases where the residual alpha is a noise, and contains return and risk (Figure 24.5). In the former case where alpha (momentum alpha, which is defined as $\alpha_t = r_{t-2} + r_{t-3} + \ldots + r_{t-13}$) is the "true" alpha and by assumption the risk model is estimated without error (within which the momentum risk factor is defined as $X_t = r_{t-1} + r_{t-2} + \ldots + r_{t-12}$), tilt on the momentum factor only contributes risk but generates no return. Figure 24.5 demonstrates that increasing θ for penalizing the residual alpha helps the optimized portfolio to achieve a higher information ratio.

In Figure 24.6 we again look at the same alpha and risk model, but assume the residual alpha contains return and risk. In this

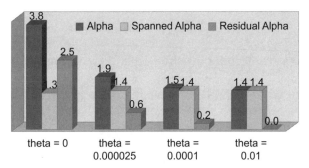

Figure 24.4 Exposure to alpha components.

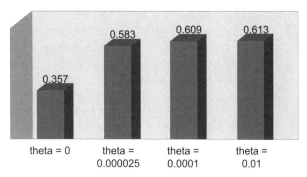

Figure 24.5 Information ratio when residual alpha is noise.

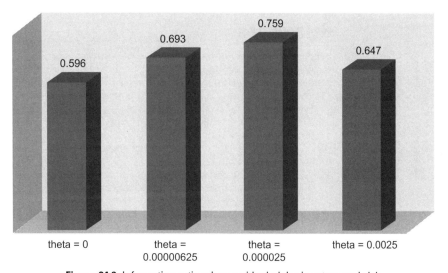

Figure 24.6 Information ratio when residual alpha is return and risk.

chart we plot the information ratio of the optimized portfolio, the information ratio is maximized when $\theta = 0.000025$, approximately equal to $\lambda \sigma^2_{\alpha_{R_\perp}}$, where $\sigma^2_{\alpha_{R_\perp}}$ is the variance of the return to the residual alpha. The portfolio will achieve the highest risk–reward tradeoff when θ associates the proper risk penalty with a bet on residual alpha. If θ is too big or too small, the volatility of the residual alpha will be over- or underestimated, resulting in a suboptimal portfolio.

24.7 Conclusion

Portfolio managers use different factor models for alpha and risk, and misalignment of those factors is a common phenomenon. Alpha can be decomposed into a part spanned by the risk model and a part orthogonal to it (the so-called orthogonal or residual alpha). Mitigation of alpha and risk factor misalignment may be approached at various levels. Alteration of the risk model, adjusting the optimization process and adding additional risk factors were some of the opportunities discussed. The tendency of optimizers to favor residual alpha is addressed by adding a penalty term to the utility function. We also showed that should the risk model be missing the orthogonal alpha as a risk factor, penalizing residual alpha is a superior mitigation for risk and alpha factor misalignment than the alpha factor approach.

References

Bender, J., 2008. Measuring the efficiency of portfolio construction. MSCI Barra Research Insights MSCI, New York.

Bender, J., Lee, J., Stefek, D., 2009. Refining portfolio construction when alphas and risk factors are misaligned. MSCI Barra Research Insights MSCI, New York.

Grinold, R.C., Kahn, R.N., 2008. Active *Portfolio Management*. McGraw-Hill Professional, New York.

Lee, J., Stefek, D., 2008. Do risk factors eat alphas. The Journal of Portfolio Management 34 (4), 12–25.

Saxena, A., Stubbs, R., 2010. Alpha alignment factor: a solution to the underestimation of risk for optimized active portfolios. Axioma Research Paper 15 Axioma, New York.

Saxena, A., Stubbs, R., 2011. Pushing the frontiers (literally) with the alpha alignment factor. In: Axioma Research Paper 22, Axioma, New York.

Stefek, D., 2007. Getting the most out of portfolio optimization—guarding against estimation error. MSCI Research Conference, New York.

25

MARKET VOLATILITY, OPTIMAL PORTFOLIOS AND NAIVE ASSET ALLOCATIONS

Massimiliano Caporin* and Loriana Pelizzon**

*University of Padova, **University Ca' Foscari Venice

CHAPTER OUTLINE

25.1 Introduction

Over the past 30 years we have seen a long debate on the performance of various asset allocation strategies when the investor cares only about the mean and the variance of static portfolio returns. In a recent paper, De Miguel *et al.* (2009b) show that the $1/N$ asset allocation rule typically has a higher out-of-sample Sharpe ratio, a higher certainty-equivalent value and a lower turnover than several static and dynamic optimal asset allocation policies for different datasets.

As already highlighted by other authors (Hodges and Brealey, 1978; Michaud, 1989; Best and Grauer, 1991; Litterman, 2003; Jagannathan and Ma, 2003) this result is mostly due to the estimation error problem. This problem could be related, as stressed by Merton (1980), to the difficulties in estimating the expected returns precisely or to the uncertain estimates of the variance–covariance matrix (Green and Hollifield, 1992; Jagannathan and Ma, 2003).

Rethinking Valuation and Pricing Models. http://dx.doi.org/10.1016/B978-0-12-415875-7.00025-7

This issue has been addressed in the literature by the use of Bayesian approaches (Barry, 1974; Bawa *et al.*, 1979; Jobson and Korkie, 1980; Jorion 1985, 1986; Pastor, 2000; Pastor and Stambaugh, 2000), non-Bayesian approaches based on moment restrictions and optimal combination of portfolios (Goldfarb and Iyengar, 2003; Garlappi *et al.*, 2006; Kan and Zhou, 2005; MacKinlay and Pastor, 2000; Best and Grauer, 1992; Chan *et al.*, 1999; Ledoit and Wolf, 2004) and portfolio rules that impose constraints on portfolio weights (Frost and Savarino, 1988; Chopra, 1993; Jagannathan and Ma, 2003; De Miguel *et al.*, 2009a).

However, the analysis of De Miguel *et al.* (2009b) shows that 13 strategies that try to overcome the estimation problem based on Bayesian approaches, moment restrictions and optimal combination of portfolios, and portfolio rules that impose constraints on portfolio weights are not able, out-of-sample, to perform statistically better than the $1/N$ strategy.

As in De Miguel *et al.* (2009b), the objective of this chapter is to understand the conditions under which mean-variance optimal portfolio models can be expected to perform better than $1/N$ even in the presence of estimation risk. The perspective that we investigate in this paper is the role of predictability and mean reversion in allowing mean-variance optimal portfolio models to perform better than $1/N$ in the short term. We also add a further purpose, by verifying if the introduction of predictability or mean reversion has an impact on strategy preference during market turmoil.

For this purpose, we investigate whether improving the estimation of the expected returns through the use of predictable variables, mean reversion or both, mean-variance optimal portfolio strategies are able to perform statistically better than the $1/N$ portfolio. We concentrate on four mean-variance allocation strategies and on five equity datasets. We considered three models of mean forecast: (i) Historical moment, (ii) mean forecast based on different predictor variables (the dividend yield, the short term rate, the term spread and the credit spread; we consider each separately or all of them jointly; we call this model "predictability") and (iii) VAR(1) that captures mean reversion. The performances are evaluated using the Sharpe ratio and the inference in the Sharpe ratio follows the approach of Ledoit and Wolf (2008).

Our analysis shows that, even for the short-term horizon, exploiting the mean reversion and predictability feature present in some of the datasets allows mean-variance strategies to perform statistically better than the $1/N$ strategy. Differently to

De Miguel *et al.* (2009b) we also analyze the preference relation across strategies on a rolling approach (the paper by De Miguel *et al.* (2009b) can be considered a full sample static comparison). We investigate whether this result is strictly related to the ability of our prediction models to explain the returns of the single assets. The analysis of the R^2 shows that the ability of the model to explain the dynamic of the single asset return is very poor. However, by performing a rolling window analysis of the Sharpe ratio we detected periods where the mean-variance strategies perform statistically better and others where they are not statistically different. The interesting fact is that mean-variance strategies are not statistically different than the $1/N$ during crisis periods. There are potentially two different reasons for this result: (i) The predictability power of the predictor variables disappears during these periods as well as mean-reversion effects and (ii) the data are more noisy, the volatility is higher as well as the estimation errors. In general, we have the theory that the data generating process that characterizes the dynamic of financial assets returns changes during crisis periods. On the other hand, we may have that simply the $1/N$ weights are not so different from the optimal weights that arise from the mean-variance strategies. In order to try to investigate this result we determined the implicit mean that, given the variance–covariance matrix we estimate, makes the $1/N$ portfolio the optimal mean-variance portfolio. We compared these means with those of our forecasts. We find that when the differences among these parameters are large, the mean-variance strategy performs statistically better than the $1/N$; in the other cases, the difference is not statistically significant. The practical implications of our results are that when the mean-reversion model produces a forecast for the mean that is significantly different than the one implied by the $1/N$ model, it is worth implementing the optimization strategy, in the other cases it is preferable to adopt the $1/N$ strategy.

The chapter is organized as follows. Section 25.2 presents the models we use to forecast the mean and the variance–covariance matrix. Section 25.3 describes the investment sets considered. Section 25.4 shows the performance evaluation method used. Section 25.5 presents the results from the full sample and Section 25.6 those from the rolling window analysis. Section 25.7 concludes.

25.2 Mean and Variance Forecasts

We determine optimal portfolios on a monthly basis using several strategies. Most of the strategies we implement determine next-month optimal portfolios using the one-month-ahead forecasts of the assets means and variances.

We denote by X_t the n-dimensional vector of monthly log-returns for the assets we monitor, by $E_t[\cdot]$ and $Var_t[\cdot]$ the expectation and variance for the relevant quantity made at time t, and with m we indicate the length of the estimation window used. In our analysis we use $m = 60$ for the main results, whereas the case where $m = 120$ is considered for a robustness check.

We compute the next-month mean and variance forecasts using four different approaches:

(i) Sample means and sample variances over the last m months computed as $\mu_{t+1} = \frac{1}{m}\Sigma_{j=t-m+1}^{t}X_j$ and $\Sigma_{t+1} = \frac{1}{m}\Sigma_{j=t-m+1}^{t}(X_j - E_t[X_{t+1}])^2$.

(ii) Mean forecast from a regression model with explanatory variables and variance forecasts from mean model residuals:
$\mu_{t+1} = \hat{\alpha} + \hat{\beta}Z_t$ and $\Sigma_{t+1} = \frac{1}{m}\Sigma_{j=t-m+2}^{t}(X_j - \hat{\alpha} - \hat{\beta}Z_{j-1})^2$,
where α and β have been estimated from a linear regression of X_t on the k-dimensional vector of predicting variables Z_t.

(iii) VAR(1) model (mean reversion only) for the mean forecasts and variances arising from model residuals:
$\mu_{t+1} = E_t[X_{t+1}] = \hat{\alpha} + \hat{\beta}X_t$ and $\Sigma_{t+1} = \frac{1}{m}\Sigma_{j=t-m+2}^{t}$
$(X_j - \hat{\alpha} - \hat{\beta}X_{j-1})^2$, where α and β have been estimated using a least squares method with robust standard errors.

(iv) VARX(1) model (mean reversion and predictability) for the mean forecasts and variances arising from model residuals:
$\mu_{t+1} = E_t[X_{t+1}] = \hat{\alpha} + \hat{\beta}Z_t + \hat{\delta}X_t$ and $\Sigma_{t+1} = \frac{1}{m}\Sigma_{j=t-m+2}^{t}$
$(X_j - \hat{\alpha} - \hat{\beta}Z_{j-1} - \hat{\delta}X_{t-1})^2$, where α, β and δ have been estimated using a least squares method with robust standard errors.

25.2.1 Asset allocation strategies

Following Campbell and Viceira (1999, 2001), we use data expressed in log-returns to extract expectations about next-period mean and variances, while we focus on an allocation problem where the strategy evaluation makes use of percentage returns. Given that we use a mean-variance utility function or a certainty equivalent satisfaction index (Meucci, 2005), we can optimize portfolios solving a problem expressed in log-returns, but correcting the objective function. The correction makes the results approximately equal to those we could obtain by solving the allocation problem in percent returns. Following this approach, the maximization problem depends on the expected portfolio mean and variances with the following expressions:

$$\tilde{\mu}_{t+1} = \omega' \mu_{t+1} + \frac{1}{2}\omega'(\text{diag}(\Sigma_{t+1}) - \Sigma_{t+1}\omega)$$

$$\tilde{\Sigma}_{t+1} = \omega' \Sigma_{t+1}\omega. \tag{25.1}$$

Portfolio mean and variances are then used within a set of alternative allocation problems.

The first set of strategies that we consider comes from the classical mean-variance optimization. We maximize a mean-variance utility function with the risk-aversion coefficient set to 1, 2, 3, 5, 8, 15, 20 and 50. The strategy labels are MV-(A), where (A) identifies the risk-aversion level. All these strategies do not allow for short selling and weights are determined solving the maximization problem:

$$\max_{\omega} \tilde{\mu}_{t+1} - \frac{R_A}{2}\tilde{\Sigma}_{t+1}$$

$$\text{s.t. } \omega'1 = 1, \quad \omega \geq 0. \tag{25.2}$$

The second strategy set considers variations of the global minimum variance portfolio. The first is the general global minimum variance portfolio (GMV), where the strategy weights are determined solving the problem:

$$\min_{\omega} \tilde{\Sigma}_{t+1}$$

$$\text{s.t. } \omega'1 = 1. \tag{25.3}$$

The second is the global minimum variance with no short selling (GMVB), where the strategy weigths are determined solving the problem:

$$\min_{\omega} \tilde{\Sigma}_{t+1}$$

$$\text{s.t. } \omega'1 = 1, \quad \omega \geq 0.$$

The third and fourth are the global minimum variance with no short selling and upper bound over weights set at q% with q equal, respectively, to 50 and 33% (GMVB50 and GMVB33):

$$\min_{\omega} \tilde{\Sigma}_{t+1}$$

$$\text{s.t. } \omega'1 = 1, \quad 0 \leq \omega \leq q. \tag{25.4}$$

25.3 Investment Sets

In the empirical comparison of the allocation strategies we considered the following datasets from the website of Kenneth French. The first dataset is characterized by five industry portfolios in the US market: consumer, manufacture, hi-tech, healthcare and others. The second dataset is composed of six asset portfolios sorted by size and book-to-market. The portfolios, which are constructed at the end of each June, are the intersections of two portfolios formed on size [market equity (ME)] and three portfolios formed on the ratio of book equity to market equity (BE/ME). The size breakpoint for year t is the median NYSE market equity at the end of June of year t (small, big). BE/ME for June of year t is the book equity for the last fiscal year end in $t - 1$ divided by ME for December of $t - 1$. The BE/ME breakpoints are the 30th and 70th NYSE percentiles (value, neutral, growth). The third is composed of six asset portfolios sorted by size and short-term reversal. The portfolios, which are constructed monthly, are the intersections of two portfolios formed on size (ME) and three portfolios formed on prior $(1-1)$ return. The monthly size breakpoint is the median NYSE market equity (small, big). The monthly prior $(1-1)$ return breakpoints are the 30th and 70th NYSE percentiles (high, medium and low). The fourth is characterized by six asset portfolios sorted by size and momentum. The portfolios are the intersections of two portfolios formed on size (ME) and three portfolios formed on prior $(2-12)$ return. The monthly size breakpoint is the median NYSE market equity (small, big). The monthly prior $(2-12)$ return breakpoints are the 30th and 70th NYSE percentiles (high, medium and low). The last dataset is composed by six asset portfolios sorted by size and long-term reversal. The portfolios, which are constructed monthly, are the intersections of two portfolios formed on size (ME) and three portfolios formed on prior $(13-60)$ return. The monthly size breakpoint is the median NYSE market equity. The monthly prior $(13-60)$ return breakpoints are the 30th and 70th NYSE percentiles.

The portfolios constructed each month include NYSE, AMEX and NASDAQ stocks with prior return data. All these dataset have been collected in the range from April 1953 to December 2010 (693 observations).

In the robustness check of our results, we make use of the same datasets previously described, but with a finer market decomposition. The six assets portfolios have been generalized to the 25-asset case by considering intersections between five categories for company size, boot-to-market, short-term reversal, momentum and long-term reversal. In this case the breakpoints have been fixed according to Fama and French to the equally spaced 20% quantiles. Furthermore, the industry portfolio has been generalized to the 10-asset sectoral decomposition: consumer non-durables, consumer durables, manufacturing, energy (oil, gas and coal extraction and production), hi-tech, telecommunications, retail, healthcare, utilities and others.

We then consider the following predicting variables: The dividend yield over the US stock market index (composite index of NYSE, NASDAQ and AMEX) obtained by difference from the value-weighted index with and without dividends; the credit spread determined from Moody's AAA and BAA corporate issues; the term spread between the 10-year Treasury Bond and the three-month Treasury Bills yields to maturity; and the short-term rate defined as the Treasury Bills yield. Finally, in order to translate the returns into real terms, we used as a proxy of the inflation the Consumer Price Index (CPI) index for all consumer goods obtained from the Federal Reverse online database (FRED).

All datasets include equity indices computed on a value-weighted base at a monthly frequency. The industry portfolios and the size and book-to market datasets are similar to those considered by De Miguel *et al.* (2009b). The main differences are: (i) Longer sample period, (ii) different combination of asset portfolios (we consider both the two- and five-group decompositions proposed by Fama and French) and (iii) use of a rolling approach for comparing the strategy preference across time.

The other portfolios are included in the analysis for completeness and given the objective of the paper, i.e. that exploiting the mean reversion and predictability feature present in some of the datasets allows mean-variance strategies to perform statistically better than the $1/N$ strategy. Furthermore, the introduction of momentum and short-term reversal is interesting given the purpose of evaluating strategy preference during large market movements (market turmoil), since those portfolios would have a faster reaction compared to portfolios based on industries or on long-term reversal.

25.4 Performance Evaluation

The performance evaluation methodology we use is the same as that adopted by De Miguel *et al.* (2009b). (i) We choose a window for estimating the parameter based on 60 months (in the robustness section we consider also a window of 120 months). (ii) We estimate the parameters over the estimation window for the particular mean and variance forecast model we consider; let indicate m indicate a particular mean and variance forecast method with $m = 1, 2, 3$. (iii) Using the estimated parameters we calculate the weights of the asset allocation strategy considered. Let k indicate one of the 13 strategies considered. (iv) We calculate the return $R_t^{m,k}$ from holding the portfolio with these weights over the next period, t (i.e. out-of-sample). (v) We repeat this procedure for the next period, using a "rolling-window" approach (i.e. by including the data for the new date and dropping the data for the earliest). We repeat this procedure until the end of the dataset is reached. At the end for each strategy and each mean and variance forecast methodology we have the time series of the T returns determined out-of-sample that we represent with the vector $\underline{R^{m,k}}$. The initialization of the procedure creates a reduction in the sample dimension (60 months are needed in order to obtain the first out-of-sample forecast). All strategies and models provide an evaluation sample with length $T = 633$ (when dealing with the 120 months window, the sample size reduces to $T = 573$ observations).

The performance evaluation is based on two different analyses: (i) the T out-of-sample observation and (ii) on a rolling window of the out-of-sample portfolio returns with a size of M months.

In the first case, from the out-of-sample return vector $\underline{R^{m,k}}$ we calculate the mean $\mu_T^{m,k}$ and the standard deviation $\sigma_T^{m,k}$ for all the T out of sample returns. The corresponding out-of-sample Sharpe ratio is determined as $SR_T = \mu_T^{m,k}/\sigma_T^{m,k}$. In the second case we determined a time series of the out-of-sample Sharpe ratio based on a window of M months. The corresponding out-of-sample Sharpe ratios are determined as $SR_M = \mu_M^{m,k}/\sigma_M^{m,k}$. The inference on the Sharpe ratio follows the approach of Ledoit and Wolf (2008). Given two Sharpe ratios, we test the null hypothesis of equivalence computing the test statistic p-values by a block-bootstrap approach. The bootstrap p-values are based on 1000 simulations and a block size of six months.

25.5 Results from the Full Sample-Analysis

Here, we present the Sharpe ratio and the p-values of the test of the null hypothesis that the Sharpe ratio of the $1/N$ and those of the asset allocation strategies are the same. The analysis is performed on the full sample (therefore on $T = 633$ or $T = 573$).

The first result is that in most of the cases the Sharpe ratio based on the mean-variance strategy for the different size-based datasets is larger than the one of the $1/N$ strategy when we focus on mean-variance. Differently, the results of constrained global minimum variance strategies are very close to the performances of the $1/N$ case. The results are opposite for the industry dataset where mean-variance strategies provide lower performances compared to the equally weighted allocation. The results are confirmed if we focus on 60 or 120 estimation windows, or if we modify the risk-aversion value. However, when we analyze for a given dataset if the Sharpe ratios of a given strategy are statistically different than the $1/N$ strategy, we have that for the industry database the null hypothesis is accepted for both the 60- and 120-month estimation window. Differently, for the other datasets, the results are influenced by the estimation strategy. If we consider sample moments, we have limited evidence (at the 5% confidence level) for mean-variance strategies beating the $1/N$ for the size and momentum and size and short-Term reversal datasets (the result is valid for 60- and 120-month estimation periods, and somewhat stronger for size and momentum with the longer estimation period). Results for the model with predictability are similar and include also some cases (still at the 5% confidence level) for the size and book-to-market dataset. However, there is much stronger evidence for a preference of mean-variance strategies compared to the equally weighted ones when we focus on the model with mean reversion. Such a result is particularly evident for size and momentum and size and short-term reversal datasets. Again, this is confirmed by varying the estimation sample size. Finally, if we include both mean reversion and predictability, only for the datasets including momentum and short-term reversal do we note a statistical preference for mean-variance strategies with respect to $1/N$.

This indicates that mean-variance strategies are preferred when the asset allocation is based on size, momentum and short-term reversal, i.e. in the presence of mean reversion. This suggests that the predictability effect is less relevant and also points out that the introduction of a larger number of parameters creates an increase of the estimation error that might affect the benefits coming from the mean-reversion component of the model. In conclusion, is preferable to exploit the mean-reversion effect and the use of predictor variables has the negative effect of increasing the estimation error.

All the previous results are confirmed if we consider the Fama–French datasets composed of 25 portfolios instead of six portfolios. However, overall, we have as in De Miguel *et al.* (2009b) that there is no strategy among all the different datasets that always performs better than $1/N$ with many cases of strategy equivalence. Moreover, the predictability component plays only a limited role, while the possible presence of mean reversion seems to be more relevant.

The results on the mean reversion are, however, quite surprising and we investigate the reason for this. We first investigate the relevance of the mean-reversion in the full-sample estimation of the models. If we consider the size and book-to-market sample we have that the portfolio-specific R^2 is very low: It ranges from 3.50 to 5.93%. If we consider the industry dataset, the R^2 is quite similar, it ranges from 2.52 to 6.31%. If we consider the R^2 evaluated on rolling samples of 60 or 120 months, the relevance of predictability and mean-reversion sensibly change over time. Figure 25.1 reports an example. Furthermore, if we analyze the number of coefficients that are statistically significant in the mean-reversion specification, we find that they largely depend on the period considered. In fact, there are sample periods where almost half of the coefficients are statistically significant and others where this number is zero. These results indicate that there are sample periods where there is a possibility of exploiting the mean-reversion feature, even if this feature is not so relevant in the full sample. Moreover, when such a feature is stronger, the model estimation error is reduced and optimal mean-variance strategies over-perform the $1/N$ naive strategy.

In summary, one key aspect of our result is that it is not only the number of observations in the sample period considered that

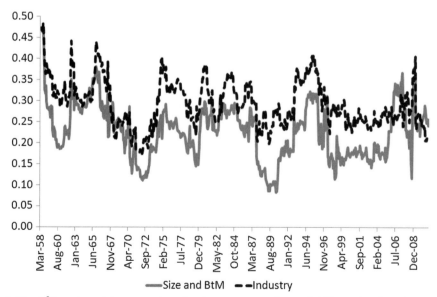

Figure 25.1 Rolling R^2 for selected datasets referred to the mean-reversion model. The estimation window has a size of 60 months. BtM, book-to-market.

is relevant, as stressed by De Miguel *et al.* (2009b), but also the period considered.

25.6 Rolling Performance Evaluation and Market Volatility

In order to identify the reasons for the previous result, we repeat the Sharpe ratio test for a rolling window of five and 10 years. For each sample we performed the robust test of Ledoit and Wolf (2008) for the equivalence of the Sharpe ratios of the $1/N$ strategy and of an optimized strategy. Using a rolling approach on 60 months, we have a time series of $T = 525$ evaluations points. In this case our analysis is implicitly biased toward accepting the null hypothesis. In fact, the estimation errors increase when the number of observations is lower.

As we expect, the strategy preference (or equivalence) is influenced by several factors: the indices used, the model adopted and the estimation of window size. As an illustrative example, Figure 25.2 reports the p-values for the test of Ledoit and Wolf (2008); p-values lower than 10% suggest a preference for the

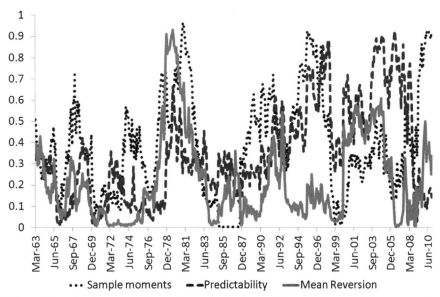

Figure 25.2 Robust Sharpe testing across forecasts: *p*-value for testing the equivalence of the mean-variance strategy without short selling and of the equally weighted portfolio. We consider the size and momentum portfolios, the risk aversion has been set to three, and the mean and variance forecasts have been set equal to the sample moments, to the model with predictability and to the one with mean reversion. Results are based on a 60-month rolling window. BtM, book-to-market.

optimized strategies, while p-values larger than 90% suggest a preference for the equally weighted portfolio. Table 25.1 summarizes the frequency of strategy preference across datasets, strategies and estimation window size. In general, we observe that in most cases there is a preference for either the $1/N$ or the optimized strategy in less than 50% of the estimates. However, if we compare results across the optimized strategies, we note the following elements: In most cases the frequency of preference for optimized strategies is larger than that of the equally weighted portfolio; the introduction of mean reversion sensibly increases the frequency of preference for mean variance strategies and only marginally affects the preference for global minimum variance strategies; as a consequence of this second element, the preference for the equally weighted portfolio decreases when mean reversion is included in the model. Moreover, results also differ across datasets. The preference for optimized strategies is larger for the size and book-to-market and for the size and momentum cases. In the size and short-term reversal, results are quite different from the others when considering the global minimum variance portfolio. We motivate this finding by the fact that the French indices are created taking into account the previous-month returns, thus something strongly related to the mean reversion. Therefore, it is not surprising that $1/N$ is quite frequently preferred here.

In order to further relate the strategy preference to the entire equity market volatility, we evaluate the strategy preference relations when the equity market is in the high-volatility state. We determined the occurrence of high volatility by means of a simple two-state Markov switching model (with switching mean and variance) fitted on the Fama–French market factor from January 1960 to December 2010. The identified high-volatility periods are the following: from March to December 1962, from February 1969 to September 1970, from March 1973 to January 1976, from June 1978 to November 1982, from May 1986 to January 1988, from January 1990 to February 1991, from April 1998 to April 2003 and from November 2007 to December 2010. The identified periods are reasonable and correspond to known high-volatility occurrences in the equity market. We thus report in Table 25.1 the percentage of strategy preference over the last high-volatility period and over all the other high-volatility periods. The results indicate that, during the recent financial crisis, the large market volatility strongly affected the model estimation, leading to a large estimation error, i.e. to a very large uncertainty about the mean and variance forecasts. Therefore, in most cases, the performances of the $1/N$ strategy and of the optimized strategies turn out to be statistically

Table 25.1. Frequency of strategy preference across datasets and sample periods, and with different sizes of the evaluation window

Size and:	Preference	Window	Full sample Mean-variance			GMV		
			SM	PR	MR	SM	PR	MR
Book-to-market	Equally weighted	60	2.61	0.35	0.52	4.18	5.92	2.96
	Indifferent		86.41	85.89	63.59	64.29	59.58	62.89
	Column		10.98	13.76	35.89	31.53	34.49	34.15
	Equally weighted	120	4.47			12.84	13.23	11.28
	Indifferent		77.82	75.49	49.22	54.28	52.92	55.64
	Column		17.70	24.51	50.78	32.88	33.85	33.07
Momentum	Equally weighted	60	2.09	0.17	0.35	9.41	8.71	10.45
	Indifferent		78.05	82.93	68.29	71.08	72.47	70.73
	Column		19.86	16.90	31.36	19.51	18.82	18.82
	Equally weighted	120	1.56	3.31	0.39	4.28	4.47	4.09
	Indifferent		78.40	76.65	37.74	82.30	79.96	81.32
	Column		20.04	20.04	61.87	13.42	15.56	14.59
Long-term reversal	Equally weighted	60	12.02		6.97	2.79	0.35	1.05
	Indifferent		68.47	81.36	78.75	85.02	89.55	82.58
	Column		19.51	18.64	14.29	12.20	10.10	16.38
	Equally weighted	120	16.93	4.09	1.17	4.09	5.45	3.89
	Indifferent		64.40	69.07	66.15	81.91	81.52	81.71
	Column		18.68	26.85	32.68	14.01	13.04	14.40
Short-term reversal	Equally weighted	60	0.17	8.01		20.91	23.34	23.00
	Indifferent		83.28	48.26	53.14	61.67	59.23	58.71
	Column		16.55	43.73	46.86	17.42	17.42	18.29
	Equally weighted	120	0.39	1.56		21.60	21.40	20.43
	Indifferent		81.32	68.48	45.53	57.59	57.20	53.89
	Column		18.29	29.96	54.47	20.82	21.40	25.68
Industry	Equally weighted	60	0.13	0.11	0.25	0.06	0.06	0.25
	Indifferent		0.76	0.87	0.62	0.84	0.82	0.62
	Column		0.11	0.02	0.13	0.10	0.12	0.13
	Equally weighted	120	0.05	0.01	0.06	0.06	0.04	0.04
	Indifferent		0.92	0.98	0.77	0.81	0.83	0.82
	Column		0.02	0.01	0.17	0.13	0.13	0.13

(continued)

November 2007–December 2010

Size and:	Preference	Window	Mean-variance			GMV		
			SM	PR	MR	SM	PR	MR
Book-to-market	Equally weighted	60						
	Indifferent		0.18	0.87	0.68	0.63	0.79	0.68
	Column		0.82	0.13	0.32	0.37	0.21	0.32
	Equally weighted	120						
	Indifferent		1.00	1.00	1.00	0.26	0.26	0.29
	Column					0.74	0.74	0.71
Momentum	Equally weighted	60						
	Indifferent		0.32	1.00	1.00	0.92	0.87	1.00
	Column		0.68			0.08	0.13	
	Equally weighted	120						
	Indifferent		0.76	0.76	0.66	0.66	0.66	0.68
	Column		0.24	0.24	0.34	0.34	0.34	0.32
Long-term reversal	Equally weighted	60						
	Indifferent		0.39	1.00	1.00	1.00	1.00	1.00
	Column		0.61					
	Equally weighted	120						
	Indifferent		0.26	0.55	0.71	0.95	0.95	0.95
	Column		0.74	0.45	0.29	0.05	0.05	0.05
Short-term reversal	Equally weighted	60						
	Indifferent		0.03	1.00	0.89	0.82	0.89	0.89
	Column		0.97		0.11	0.18	0.11	0.11
	Equally weighted	120						
	Indifferent		0.87	0.74	0.08	0.89	0.92	0.95
	Column		0.13	0.26	0.92	0.11	0.08	0.05
Industry	Equally weighted	60						
	Indifferent		0.71	0.18	1.00	1.00	1.00	1.00
	Column		0.29	0.82				
	Equally weighted	120						
	Indifferent		1.00	1.00	1.00	0.34	0.34	0.32
	Column					0.66	0.66	0.68

Size and:	Preference	Window	Mean-variance			GMV		
			SM	PR	MR	SM	PR	MR
Book-to-market	Equally weighted	60	0.02		0.01	0.08	0.15	0.01
	Indifferent		0.79	0.87	0.61	0.63	0.59	0.61
	Column		0.19	0.13	0.38	0.28	0.27	0.38
	Equally weighted	120	0.11			0.26	0.27	0.23
	Indifferent		0.69	0.70	0.59	0.55	0.54	0.58
	Column		0.20	0.30	0.41	0.19	0.19	0.19
Momentum	Equally weighted	60	0.86	0.94	0.00	0.19	0.19	0.00
	Indifferent		0.14	0.06	0.71	0.70	0.70	0.71
	Column		0.00		0.28	0.11	0.11	0.28
	Equally weighted	120		0.02		0.11	0.11	0.10
	Indifferent		0.77	0.77	0.41	0.78	0.76	0.78
	Column		0.22	0.21	0.59	0.12	0.13	0.12
Long-term reversal	Equally weighted	60	0.07		0.10	0.03		0.10
	Indifferent		0.72	0.75	0.69	0.85	0.92	0.69
	Column		0.20	0.25	0.21	0.12	0.08	0.21
	Equally weighted	120	0.57	0.66	0.01	0.10	0.14	0.09
	Indifferent		0.23	0.34	0.62	0.72	0.70	0.72
	Column		0.20		0.37	0.18	0.17	0.19
Short-term reversal	Equally weighted	60	0.02	0.11	0.40	0.11	0.11	0.40
	Indifferent		0.88	0.85	0.50	0.86	0.85	0.50
	Column		0.10	0.04	0.09	0.03	0.04	0.09
	Equally weighted	120	0.01	0.00	0.46	0.36	0.36	0.36
	Indifferent		0.73	0.60	0.54	0.47	0.47	0.47
	Column		0.26	0.40		0.17	0.17	0.17
Industry	Equally weighted	60	0.02	0.11	0.40	0.11	0.11	0.40
	Indifferent		0.88	0.85	0.50	0.86	0.85	0.50
	Column		0.10	0.04	0.09	0.03	0.04	0.09
	Equally weighted	120	0.03	0.02	0.14	0.11	0.10	0.10
	Indifferent		0.91	0.96	0.68	0.84	0.85	0.84
	Column		0.06	0.02	0.18	0.05	0.05	0.06

The first column reports the dataset combining size with book-to-market, momentum, long-term reversal and short-term reversal. As a further case we consider the industry dataset. The second column identifies the strategy preference for equally weighted for the column strategy or the indifference between equally weighted and the column strategies. The third column denotes the size of the evaluation window (60 or 120 months). The remaining columns report frequencies of preference over the full sample, the range November 2007—December 2010 or over other crisis periods.
SM, sample moments, PR, predictability, MR, mean reversion.

equivalent. This is due to both the increase of the estimation error, potentially harming the performances of the optimized strategies, as well as to the large market volatility, which influences the asymptotic properties of the test statistic.

If we compare the strategy preference over the last high-volatility period to that observed over previous high-volatility occurrences, results are mixed, but the most common outcome is related to an increase in the preference for $1/N$ portfolios for an increase in the equivalence across portfolio performances. Such a result points to the effect of model estimation errors that induce poor performance on optimized strategies. As a result, during turbulent market periods, equally weighted portfolios seem to be a good compromise between the need for diversification and the search of performance.

25.7 Conclusions

Our analysis shows that exploiting the mean reversion and predictability feature present in some of the datasets allows mean-variance strategies to perform statistically better than the $1/N$ strategy. Our investigation on the R^2 shows that this result is not strictly related to the significant ability of the model to explain the dynamics of the single asset return. The key determinant is the presence of prediction that implies weights largely different than the $1/N$ weights. When these differences are not so large, optimal mean-variance strategies do not perform statistically better than the naive strategy based on equally weighted portfolios. The rolling-window analysis of the Sharpe ratio shows that there are periods where the mean-variance strategies perform statistically better and others where they are not statistically different. This means that there are only some periods where mean reversion really matters for asset allocation strategies. The practical implication of our results is that when the mean-reversion model is producing a forecast for the mean that is significantly different from the one implied by the $1/N$ model, it is worth implementing the optimization strategy; in the other cases, it is preferable to perform the $1/N$ strategy. Sadly, crisis periods are usually those where mean-variance optimal strategies, given the large estimation errors, present optimal weights that are very similar to the $1/N$ naive strategy.

References

Barry, C.B., 1974. Portfolio analysis under uncertain means, variances, and covariances. Journal of Finance 29, 515–522.

Bawa, V.S., Brown, S., Klein, R., 1979. Estimation Risk and Optimal Portfolio Choice. North-Holland, Amsterdam.

Best, M.J., Grauer, R.R., 1991. On the sensitivity of mean-variance-efficient portfolios to changes in asset means: some analytical and computational results. Review of Financial Studies 4, 315–242.

Best, M.J., Grauer, R.R., 1992. Positively weighted minimum-variance portfolios and the structure of asset expected returns. Journal of Financial and Quantitative Analysis 27, 513–537.

Campbell, J.Y., Viceira, L.M., 1999. Consumption and portfolio decisions when expected returns are time varying. Quarterly Journal of Economics 114, 433–495.

Campbell, J.Y., Viceira, L.M., 2001. Who should buy long-term bonds? American Economic Review 91, 99–127.

Chan, L.K.C., Karceski, J., Lakonishok, J., 1999. On portfolio optimization: forecasting covariances and choosing the risk model. Review of Financial Studies 12, 937–974.

Chopra, V.K., 1993. Improving optimization. Journal of Investing 8, 51–59.

De Miguel, V., Garlappi, L., Nogales, F., Uppal, R., 2009a. A generalized approach to portfolio optimization: improving performance by constraining portfolio norms. Management Science 55, 798–812.

De Miguel, V., Garlappi, L., Uppal, R., 2009b. Optimal versus naive diversification: how inefficient is the $1/N$ portfolio strategy? The Review of Financial Studies 22, 1915–1953.

Frost, P.A., Savarino, J.E., 1986. An empirical Bayes approach to efficient portfolio selection. Journal of Financial and Quantitative Analysis 21, 293–305.

Garlappi, L., Uppal, R., Wang, T., 2007. Portfolio selection with parameter and model uncertainty: a multi-prior approach. The Review of Financial Studies 20, 41–81.

Goldfarb, D., Iyengar, G., 2003. Robust portfolio selection problems. Mathematics of Operational Research 28, 1–38.

Green, R., Hollifield, B., 1992. When will mean-variance efficient portfolios be well diversified. Journal of Finance 47, 1785–1809.

Hodges, S.D., Brealey, R.A., 1978. Portfolio selection in a dynamic and uncertin world. In: Lorie, J.H., Brealey, R.A. (Eds), Modern Developments in Investment Management, second ed. Dryden Press, Hinsdale, IL.

Jagannathan, R., Ma, T., 2003. Risk reduction in large portfolios: why imposing the wrong constraints helps. Journal of Finance 58, 1651–1684.

Jobson, J.D., Korkie, R., 1980. Estimation for Markowitz efficient portfolios. Journal of the American Statistical Association 75, 544–554.

Jorion, P., 1985. International portfolio diversification with estimation risk. Journal of Business 58, 259–278.

Jorion, P., 1986. Bayes–Stein estimation for portfolio analysis. Journal of Financial and Quantitative Analysis 21, 279–292.

Kan, R., Zhou, G., 2005. Optimal estimation for economic gains: portfolio choice with parameter uncertainty. Working Paper. University of Toronto, Toronto.

Ledoit, O., Wolf, M., 2004b. Honey, I shrunk the sample covariance matrix. Journal of Portfolio Management 30, 110–119.

Ledoit, O., Wolf, M., 2008. Robust performance hypothesis testing with the Sharpe ratio. Journal of Empirical Finance 15, 850–859.

Litterman, R., 2003. Modern Investment Management: An Equilibrium Approach. Wiley, New York.

MacKinlay, A.C., Pastor, L., 2000. Asset pricing models: implications for expected returns and portfolio selection. Review of Financial Studies 13, 883–916.

Merton, R.C., 1980. On estimating the expected return on the market: an exploratory investigation. Journal of Financial Economics 8, 323–361.

Michaud, R.O., 1989. The Markowitz optimization enigma: is optimized optimal. Financial Analysts Journal 45, 31–42.

Pastor, L., 2000. Portfolio selection and asset pricing models. Journal of Finance 55, 179–223.

Pastor, L., Stambaugh, R.F., 2000. Comparing asset pricing models: an investment perspective. Journal of Financial Economics 56, 335–381.

HEDGING STRATEGIES WITH VARIABLE PURCHASE OPTIONS

Manuel Moreno* and Javier F. Navas**

*University of Castilla La-Mancha, **Pablo de Olavide University

CHAPTER OUTLINE

26.1 Introduction

Nowadays, many firms have difficulties obtaining the funds needed for their investment projects and their operations. Internally generated funds have decreased because of the economic crisis and lower growth rates. At the same time, external financing sources have become scarce. Many banks are unwilling to lend money because of liquidity problems and firms find it expensive to issue new equity as shares prices are low. In this scenario, firms may be interested in using securities such as variable purchase options (VPOs), which guarantee the success of future equity issues.

Assume that a certain firm knows it will need a certain amount of money at some date in the future. This amount of money can be related to future expansion activities that are being planned today, payments to be done at maturity of certain fixed-income assets issued previously by this firm, and so on. One way to obtain this money would be to raise new equity capital on that future day. What can this company do today to guarantee the

Rethinking Valuation and Pricing Models. http://dx.doi.org/10.1016/B978-0-12-415875-7.00026-9

success of this future issue of equity capital? The answer to this question depends on the time frame. If the new capital is scheduled for the near future, the company can agree with a certain financial intermediary to act as an underwriter providing the necessary guarante. The problem arises if this new capital issue is scheduled for a distant future time as finding this guarantee can be a hard task. This guarantee is precisely the goal of VPOs—a security traded in the Australian Stock Exchange since 1992.

More concretely, a VPO is a European call option issued by a corporation on a stochastic number of shares of the issuer. The optionholder has the right (but not the obligation) to buy shares of the underlying stock at maturity at a fixed discount. Thus, this option is always in-the-money at maturity and will be exercised for sure by rational investors.

The VPO can have additional features, like upper and lower bounds (caps and floors) on the number of shares underlying the option. In fact, most VPOs are usually bounded. Moreover, in some cases, the VPO can have Asian characteristics if its payoff is based on average stock prices. The motivation for this feature is that Asian options (i) are cheaper than the corresponding European options, as the average price is less volatile than the terminal asset price, and (ii) constitute an adequate hedging instrument for investors who trade very frequently over certain time periods. Moreover, Asian options prevent possible manipulations of the underlying asset price at the maturity option. This fact is recognized explicitly in Turnbull and Wakeman (1991, p. 377) who indicate that "average options by their design reduce the significance of the closing price at the maturity of the option. This reduces the effects of any possible abnormal price movements at the maturity of the option."

Despite their interesting attributes, VPOs have not received much attention in the literature. On the theoretical side, Handley (2000) describes VPOs and prices them using standard option pricing techniques, and Moreno and Navas (2008) value a security related to Asian VPOs (they name it Australian options). On the empirical side, the only work that we are aware of is Handley (2003), which studies the performance of his theoretical model extended with discrete dividends. He uses a sample of five VPOs traded on the Australian Stock Exchange during the six-year period from May 1992 to May 1998 and finds that his model systematically overprices VPOs.[1]

---

[1] However, he shows that the mispricing almost disappears using different estimates of the risk-free rate and the volatility of the stock price.

Another gap in the literature is the analysis of the hedge parameters (Greeks) of VPOs. This is crucial for a proper management of the risk exposures of portfolios containing VPOs for issuers and investors alike. Computation of these Greeks is relevant because, as shown in Carr (2001), these amounts can be interpreted as the values of certain quantoed contingent claims and, as this author recognizes, "this interpretation allows one to transfer intuitions regarding values to these Greeks and to apply any valuation methodology to determine them."

The literature on hedging derivatives risks is very rich. Black and Scholes (1972) use discretely adjusted delta hedges to cover derivatives risks and find that the variance of the excess hedge return decreases as the rebalancing frequency increases. Similar findings are obtained by Boyle and Emanuel (1980). Other studies on hedging derivatives risk are Bhattacharaya (1980) and Leland (1985). Galai (1983) is generally recognized as the first study of model risk. He decomposes the return from discrete delta hedging into three parts. Ross (1997) considers the problem of hedging long-run commitments under temporal incompleteness of the futures contract market. Ahn *et al.* (1999) investigate the optimal hedging strategies for mis-specified volatility processes. Additionally, Rasmussen (2002) studies the hedging performance of the Black–Scholes model in an economy driven by the constant elasticity of variance (CEV) model.

In this chapter, we review the valuation of VPOs, and study their sensitivities with respect to changes in the stock price, time, volatility and interest rate. The rest of the chapter is organized as follows. In section 26.2, we present briefly the characteristics of bounded VPOs. In Section 26.3, we provide the pricing formulas and we study the sensitivity of the VPO price to changes in the variables that determine its value. Finally, Section 26.4 summarizes and concludes.

26.2 Description of the Product

As mentioned before, a VPO is just a European call option on the shares of the issuer company. If there are no other features, this asset is known as a standard VPO. Here, the number of underlying shares at maturity, T, is:

$$N_S = \frac{k}{S_T(1-d)}, \tag{26.1}$$

where k is the fixed exercise price of the option, S_T is the stock price at time T and d represents the fixed exercise discount, expressed as a proportion.

Therefore, the optionholder pays an effective price per share equal to:

$$\frac{k}{N_S} = S_T(1-d).$$

The pay off at maturity of this option is $F_T = \max\{0, N_S S_T - k\}$, which, using (26.1), can be rewritten as:

$$F_T = \max\left\{0, \frac{k}{1-d} - k\right\} = \frac{kd}{1-d},$$

which is also known as the VPO discount.

In general, the optionholder buys the underlying shares at maturity at a $(d \times 100)\%$ discount to the stock price at maturity and gains $d \times S_T$ dollars on each of the N_S shares. The total gain is the VPO discount, which is constant. Thus, the standard VPO is just a pure discount bond that matures at time T, with a face value equal to the VPO discount.

Looking at (26.1), it is clear that, in a standard VPO, the number of shares that can be bought at maturity can take any positive value. To make this product more interesting, typically, the number of underlying shares is restricted to be in a certain interval $[f, c]$, in the following way:

$$N_S = \begin{cases} c & S_T < x_c \\ \dfrac{k}{S_T(1-d)} & x_c \leq S_T < x_f \\ f & x_f \leq S_T, \end{cases} \qquad (26.2)$$

where, respectively, f and c are the floor and cap levels, and $x_f = \dfrac{k}{f(1-d)}$ and $x_c = \dfrac{k}{c(1-d)}$ are the floor and cap prices. The values of x_c and x_f are chosen to guarantee the continuity of N_S as a function of S_T.

With this restriction, we obtain what is known as a bounded VPO. In this case, the optionholder cannot buy more than c shares when the stock price at time T is "small enough" (below the cap price, x_c). Analogously, the floor operates when S_T is "large enough" (higher than the floor price, x_f). Now, the holder can buy f shares. For intermediate values of S_T (between the cap and the floor prices), the option holder buys N_S shares, as given by (26.1). This constraint on the upper and lower number of shares underlying the VPO is one of its most typical and common features.

It is clear (see Handley, 2000) that the pay off for a bounded VPO is given by:

$$F_T = \begin{cases} 0 & S_T < x_c(1-d) \\ cS_T - k & x_c(1-d) \le S_T < x_c \\ \dfrac{kd}{1-d} & x_c \le S_T < x_f \\ fS_T - k & x_f \le S_T. \end{cases} \qquad (26.3)$$

Therefore, the bounds imply that the bounded VPO will not be always exercised at maturity. In fact, the VPO will be exercised if and only if the stock price at maturity is higher than the minimum price, $x_c(1-d)$.

26.3 Pricing and Hedging Bounded VPOs

Here, we value the VPOs under the classical assumptions of the Black–Scholes economy and we provide the tools needed for hedging risk exposures.

We can interpret the bounded VPO in two ways:

(i). As a combination of three positions, as seen in Expression (26.3):
- Long f calls with strike x_f.
- Short c calls with strike x_c.
- Long c calls with strike $x_c(1-d)$.

(ii). As a combination of four positions:
- Long one bond with face value $kd/(1-d)$.
- Long f calls with strike x_f.
- Short c puts with strike x_c.
- Long c puts with strike $x_c(1-d)$.

Thus, it is straightforward to derive the next Proposition.

Proposition 1. *The price of a bounded VPO is given by:*

$$F_t = S_t[f\Phi(n_1) - c[\Phi(n_3) - \Phi(n_5)]] \\ - \frac{k}{1-d}e^{-r(T-t)}[\Phi(n_2) - \Phi(n_4) + (1-d)\Phi(n_6)], \qquad (26.4)$$

which can be rewritten as:

$$F_t = \frac{kd}{1-d}e^{-r(T-t)} + f\left[S_t\Phi(n_1) - x_f e^{-r(T-t)}\Phi(n_2)\right] \\ - c\left[x_c e^{-r(T-t)}\Phi(-n_4) - S_t\Phi(-n_3)\right] \\ + c\left[x_c(1-d)e^{-r(T-t)}\Phi(-n_6) - S_t\Phi(-n_5)\right], \qquad (26.5)$$

where r is the risk-free interest rate and:

$$n_1 = \frac{\ln(S_t/x_f) + \left(r + \dfrac{1}{2}\sigma_S^2\right)(T-t)}{\sigma_S\sqrt{T-t}} \qquad (26.6)$$

$$n_3 = \frac{\ln(S_t/x_c) + \left(r + \frac{1}{2}\sigma_S^2\right)(T-t)}{\sigma_S\sqrt{T-t}} \tag{26.7}$$

$$n_5 = \frac{\ln(S_t/(x_c/(1-d))) + \left(r + \frac{1}{2}\sigma_S^2\right)(T-t)}{\sigma_S\sqrt{T-t}} \tag{26.8}$$

$$n_j = n_{j-1} - \sigma_S\sqrt{T-t}, j = 2, 4, 6 \tag{26.9}$$

Here, σ_S is the volatility of the underlying asset, $\Phi(.)$ denotes the distribution function of a standard normal variable, and c, f, x_c and x_f are given in (26.2).

As expected, the expression (26.5) is the same as that obtained by Handley (2000). When comparing the price of the bounded VPO and f standard call options, it can be shown (see Figure 26.1) that, for a certain stock price, the bounded VPO is always more expensive than f standard calls and that the difference between both values remains constant.

As seen in Proposition 1, the VPO value depends on the same variables as the option price in the Black–Scholes framework. Both issuers and investors will be interested in knowing the

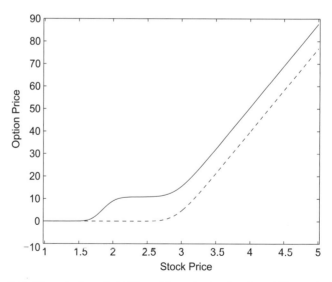

Figure 26.1 Price of a bounded VPO and f standard call options. This graph shows the price of a bounded VPO (solid line) in comparison with that of f standard call options (dashed line). These prices are given by Equation (26.5) and the Black–Scholes formula, respectively. The parameters used are $c = 500/9$, $f = 1000/27$, $k = 100$, $d = 0.1$, $x_c = 2$, $x_f = 3$.

sensitivity of the VPO value to changes in each of these variables, so that they can assess and hedge their market risk. We next study these effects by taking partial derivatives of the VPO value [as given by (26.4) or (26.5)] with respect to each variable, that is by computing the Greeks of the VPO. Although this is a trivial exercise, this is something that has not been done before in the literature.

26.3.1 Delta of the bounded VPO

Delta measures the sensitivity of the bounded VPO to small changes in the share price. It is given by the partial derivative of the VPO price with respect to the stock price:

$$\Delta_{\text{VPO}}(S_t) = f\Delta_C(n_1, n_2) - c\Delta_C(n_3, n_4) + c\Delta_C(n_5, n_6) \quad (26.10)$$
$$= f\Phi(n_1) - c[\Phi(n_3) - \Phi(n_5)].$$

As $n_3 < n_5$, we get $\Delta_{\text{VPO}}(S_t) > f\Phi(n_1) > 0$ and, then, an increase in the stock price increases the VPO price. Another result is that the delta of a VPO is higher than that of f calls with strike x_f. Moreover, we have $\Delta_{\text{VPO}}(0) = 0, \Delta_{\text{VPO}}(\infty) = f$. See Figure 26.2.

We compute the maximum of $\Delta_{\text{VPO}}(S_t)$ for the particular (simple) case in which n_1 is large (and negative) enough and,

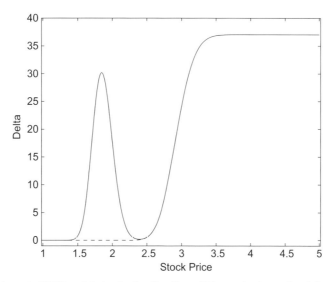

Figure 26.2 Delta of a bounded VPO and f standard call options. This graph shows the delta of a bounded VPO [$\Delta_{\text{VPO}}(S_t)$, solid line] in comparison with that of f standard call options [$\Delta_{\text{standard}}(S_t)$, dashed line]. These hedge ratios are given by $\Delta_{\text{VPO}}(S_t) = f\Phi(n_1) + c[\Phi(n_5) - \Phi(n_3)]$ and $\Delta_{\text{standard}}(S_t) = f\Phi(n_1)$, respectively, with $n_i, i = 1, 3, 5$ as given by expressions (26.6)–(26.8). The parameters used are $c = 500/9, f = 1000/27, d = 0.1, x_c = 2, x_f = 3, r = 0.05, \sigma_s = 0.1, T-t = 0.5$.

then, $\phi(n_1) = 0$. In this case, the highest delta corresponds to the minimum of $\Phi(n_3) - \Phi(n_5)$. Differentiating with respect to S_t, we have:

$$\frac{\partial[\Phi(n_3) - \Phi(n_5)]}{\partial S_t} = \frac{1}{S_t \sigma_S \sqrt{T-t}} \frac{1}{\sqrt{2\pi}} \left[\exp\left\{-\frac{1}{2}n_3^2\right\} - \exp\left\{-\frac{1}{2}n_5^2\right\} \right].$$

This expression is equal to zero iff $n_5 = -n_3$, which implies that:

$$S_t^* = x_c \sqrt{1-d} \exp\left\{ -\left(r + \frac{1}{2}\sigma_S^2 \right)(T-t) \right\}.$$

For this value, we obtain:

$$n_1^* = \frac{\ln\left((1-d)x_c/x_f\right)}{2\sigma_S\sqrt{T-t}}, \quad n_3^* = \frac{\ln(1-d)}{2\sigma_S\sqrt{T-t}}, \quad n_5^* = -n_3^*,$$

and $\Delta_{\text{VPO}}(S_t^*) = c[2\Phi(n_5^*) - 1]$.

A delta-hedged portfolio of VPOs will be neutral with respect to stock price movements for very small stock price changes. For large stock price changes, the portfolio may not be completely hedged as the delta can change rapidly. The risk of the delta changing too fast is captured by the gamma of the VPO.

26.3.2 Gamma of the bounded VPO

Gamma is the sensitivity of the delta of the VPO to the stock price. It can be obtained by computing the partial derivative of the delta of the VPO with respect to the stock price or, what is the same, the second partial derivative of the VPO value with respect to the share price.

When the gamma of the VPO is small, delta changes slowly, so that it is relatively easy to maintain the VPO delta-hedged. However, if gamma is large in absolute terms, the delta will change quickly and frequent rebalancing will be needed to keep the VPO position delta-neutral. Thus, the hedging requirement can be decreased by following a gamma-neutral strategy:

$$\Gamma_{\text{VPO}}(S_t) = f\Gamma_C(n_1, n_2) - c\Gamma_C(n_3, n_4) + c\Gamma_C(n_5, n_6)$$

$$= \frac{1}{S_t \sigma_S \sqrt{T-t}} [f\Phi'(n_1) - c(\Phi'(n_3) - \Phi'(n_5))] \tag{26.11}$$

In Figure 26.3 we see that the gamma of a bounded VPO is negative around x_c (when the minimum gamma is reached) and it equates the gamma of f standard calls for some stock prices. For stock prices smaller than x_c, the delta of the bounded VPO is more sensitive to the underlying price than the delta of f standard calls.

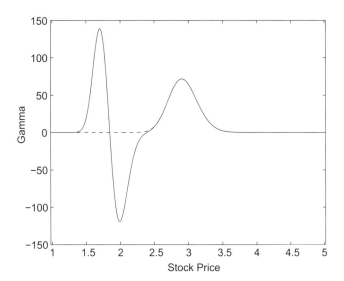

Figure 26.3 Gamma of a bounded VPO and f standard call options. This graph shows the gamma of a bounded VPO [$\Gamma_{\text{VPO}}(S_t)$, solid line] in comparison with that of f standard call options [$\Gamma_{\text{standard}}(S_t)$, dashed line]. These measures are given by $\Gamma_{\text{VPO}}(S_t) = 1/(S_t\sigma_S\sqrt{T-t})[f\Phi'(n_1) - c(\Phi'(n_3) - \Phi'(n_5))]$ and $\Gamma_{\text{standard}}(S_t) = 1/(S_t\sigma_S\sqrt{T-t})$ $\Phi'(n_1)$ with $n_i, i = 1, 3, 5$ as given by Expressions (26.6)–(26.8). The parameters used are $c = 500/9$, $f = 1000/27$, $x_c = 2$, $x_f = 3$, $r = 0.05$, $\sigma_s = 0.1$, $T-t = 0.5$.

Moreover, we have that ...

$$\Gamma_{\text{VPO}}(0) = \Gamma_{\text{VPO}}(\infty) = 0.$$

From the previous expressions, we can write:

$$\Gamma_{\text{VPO}}(S_t) - f\Gamma_{\text{C}}(n_1, n_2)$$
$$= \frac{c}{\sqrt{2\pi}}\frac{1}{S_t\sigma_S\sqrt{T-t}}\exp\left\{-\frac{1}{2}n_3^2\right\}\left(\exp\left\{\frac{\ln(1-d)}{2\sigma_S\sqrt{T-t}}(n_5 + n_3)\right\} - 1\right).$$

Then, $\Gamma_{\text{VPO}}(S_t) - f\Gamma_{\text{C}}(n_1, n_2) > 0$ iff $n_5 + n_3 < 0$, which implies that:

$$S_t < x_c\sqrt{1-d}\exp\left\{-\left(r + \frac{1}{2}\sigma_S^2\right)(T-t)\right\}.$$

Hence, we can state that for "small" (large) values of the stock price, the delta of the VPO is more (less) sensitive to changes in the stock price than that of f call options exercisable at the floor price x_f.

26.3.3 Theta of the bounded VPO

Theta measures the sensitivity of the value of the VPO to the passage of time. It indicates the time decay of the VPO holding. Theta can be computed by taking the partial derivative of the price of the bounded VPO with respect to time.

$$\Theta_{VPO}(S_t) = f\Theta_C(n_1, n_2) - c\Theta_C(n_3, n_4) + c\Theta_C(n_5, n_6)$$

$$= -\frac{S_t\sigma_S}{2\sqrt{T-t}}[f\Phi'(n_1) - c(\Phi'(n_3) - \Phi'(n_5))]$$

$$-\frac{k}{1-d}re^{-r(T-t)}[\Phi(n_2) - \Phi(n_4) + (1-d)\Phi(n_6)].$$

It can be seen that the theta of a bounded VPO is positive between x_c and x_f, it is specially negative before x_c and it tracks quite closely the theta of f standard calls after x_f, as shown in Figure 26.4.

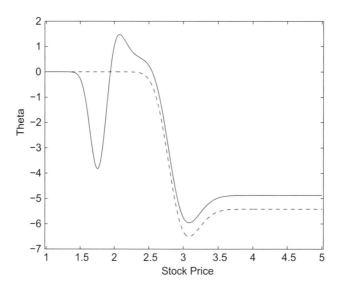

Figure 26.4 Theta of a bounded VPO and f standard call options. This graph shows the theta of a bounded VPO [$\Theta_{VPO}(S_t)$, solid line] in comparison with that of f standard call options [$\Theta_{standard}(S_t)$, dashed line]. These measures are given by $\Theta_{VPO}(S_t) = -S_t\sigma_S/(2\sqrt{T-t})[f\Phi'(n_1) - c(\Phi'(n_3) - \Phi'(n_5))] - k/(1-d)\cdot re^{-r(T-t)}[\Phi(n_2) - \Phi(n_4) + (1-d)\Phi(n_6)]$ and $\Theta_{standard}(S_t) = -S_t\sigma_S/(2\sqrt{T-t})\Phi'(n_1) - x_f re^{-r(T-t)}\Phi(n_2)$ with $n_i, i = 1, ..., 6$ as given by Expressions (26.6)–(26.9). The parameters used are $c = 500/9, f = 1000/27, k = 100, d = 0.1, x_c = 2, x_f = 3, r = 0.05, \sigma_s = 0.1, T-t = 0.5$.

Moreover, we have that $\Theta_{\text{VPO}}(0) = 0$ and $\Theta_{\text{VPO}}(\infty) = (1-d)f\Theta_{\text{standard}}(\infty)$.

26.3.4 Vega of the bounded VPO

Vega is the sensitivity of the VPO value to changes in the volatility of the share price. Vega is given by the partial derivative of the VPO price with respect to the volatility. If the volatility of the underlying stock changes, the VPO price can change substantially, even without movements in the stock price:

$$\nu_{\text{VPO}}(S_t) = f\nu_{\text{C}}(n_1, n_2) - c\nu_{\text{C}}(n_3, n_4) + c\nu_{\text{C}}(n_5, n_6)$$
$$= S_t\sqrt{T-t}[f\Phi'(n_1) - c(\Phi'(n_3) - \Phi'(n_5))].$$

Looking at (26.11), we see that $\nu_{\text{VPO}}(S_t) = S_t^2 \sigma_S(T-t)\Gamma_{\text{VPO}}(S_t)$.

Then, the behavior of vega is similar to that of gamma, as shown in Figure 26.5.

As an additional result, we have that $\nu_{\text{VPO}}(0) = \nu_{\text{VPO}}(\infty) = 0$.

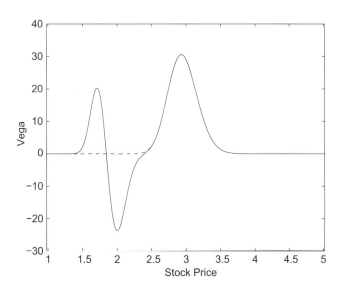

Figure 26.5 Vega of a bounded VPO and f standard call options. This graph shows the vega of a bounded VPO [$\nu_{\text{VPO}}(S_t)$, solid line] in comparison with that of f standard call options [$\nu_{\text{standard}}(S_t)$, dashed line]. These measures are given by $\nu_{\text{VPO}}(S_t) = S_t\sqrt{T-t}[f\Phi'(n_1) - c(\Phi'(n_3) - \Phi'(n_5))]$ and $\nu_{\text{standard}}(S_t) = S_t\sqrt{T-t}\Phi'(n_1)$ with $n_i, i = 1, 3, 5$ as given by Expressions (26.6)–(26.8). The parameters used are $c = 500/9$, $f = 1000/27$, $x_c = 2$, $x_f = 3$, $r = 0.05$, $T-t = 0.5$.

From the previous expressions, we can write:

$$\nu_{\mathrm{VPO}}(S_t) - f\nu_C(n_1, n_2)$$

$$= \frac{c}{\sqrt{2\pi}} S_t \sqrt{T-t}\, \exp\left\{-\frac{1}{2}n_3^2\right\}\left(\exp\left\{\frac{\ln(1-d)}{2\sigma_S\sqrt{T-t}}(n_5+n_3)\right\}-1\right).$$

Then, $\nu_{\mathrm{VPO}}(S_t) - f\nu_C(n_1, n_2) > 0$ iff $n_5 + n_3 < 0$, the same condition as that obtained for the VPO gamma.

26.6.5 Rho of the bounded VPO

Rho measures rate of change of the value of the VPO with respect to the interest rate. It can be obtained by computing the partial derivative of the VPO price with respect to the instantaneous interest rate:

$$\rho_{\mathrm{VPO}}(S_t) = f\rho_C(n_1, n_2) - c\rho_C(n_3, n_4) + c\rho_C(n_5, n_6)$$

$$= (T-t)\frac{k}{1-d}\mathrm{e}^{-r(T-t)}[\Phi(n_2) - \Phi(n_4) + (1-d)\Phi(n_6)]. \tag{26.12}$$

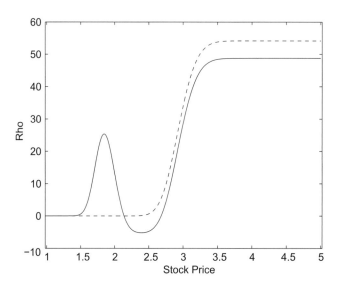

Figure 26.6 Rho of a bounded VPO and f standard call options. This graph shows the rho of a bounded VPO [$\rho_{\mathrm{VPO}}(S_t)$, solid line] in comparison with that of f standard call options [$\rho_{\mathrm{standard}(S_t)}$, dashed line]. These measures are given by $\rho_{\mathrm{VPO}}(S_t) = (T-t)\frac{k}{1-d}\mathrm{e}^{-r(T-t)}[\Phi(n_2) - \Phi(n_4) + (1-d)\Phi(n_6)]$ and $\rho_{\mathrm{standard}}(S_t) = (T-t)x_f\mathrm{e}^{-r(T-t)}\Phi(n_2)$ with $n_i, i = 2, 4, 6$ as given by Expressions (26.6)–(26.9). The parameters used are $c = 500/9$, $f = 1000/27$, $k = 100$, $d = 0.1$, $x_c = 2$, $x_f = 3$, $r = 0.05$, $\sigma_s = 0.1$, $T-t = 0.5$.

It is easy to see that the rho of a bounded VPO is negative in a certain interval between x_c and x_f, and that it is similar to the theta of f standard calls for stock prices greater than x_f. For stock values close to x_c, the bounded VPO is more sensitive to changes in interest rates than f standard calls. These facts are shown in Figure 26.6.

Moreover, we have that $\rho_{\text{VPO}}(0) = 0$ and $\rho_{\text{VPO}}(\infty) = (1-d)f\rho_{\text{standard}}(\infty)$. Looking at (12), we can write $\rho_{\text{VPO}}(S_t) - f\rho_C(n_1, n_2) = c(T-t)x_c e^{-r(T-t)}[(1-d)\Phi(n_6) - \Phi(n_4)]$ whose sign depends on that of $h(S_t) = (1-d)\Phi(n_6) - \Phi(n_4)$. This function starts at 0, attains a maximum (positive) value at

$$S_t^* = x_c\sqrt{1-d}\exp\left\{-\left(r + \frac{1}{2}\sigma_S^2\right)(T-t)\right\}$$ and then decreases,

converging asymptotically to $-d$. Hence, we get the maximum difference between ρ_{VPO} and $f\rho_C(n_1, n_2)$ for S_t^*.

Both issuers and investors will try to rebalance their portfolios containing VPOs frequently so that the portfolio is hedged and its Greeks have values close to zero. In practice, this will not be possible, and the portfolio will be delta-hedged but not gamma-, theta-, vega-, or rho-hedged. However, it is important to know the value of these Greeks so that when they are too large (in absolute terms) actions are taken to reduce them and to manage the risk of the portfolio.

26.4 Conclusions

The current economic crisis is affecting how many companies obtain financing. Internally generated funds have been reduced, and bank financing has become more difficult and more expensive. At the same time, uncertainty about future growth opportunities has increased. In this scenario, a firm that is interested in raising money in the future (e.g. to repay a debt loan) may be interested in issuing securities like VPOs. A VPO is a European call option issued by a corporation on a stochastic number of shares of the issuer that will end in-the-money at maturity and, then, should be exercised by rational investors. The VPO can have additional features like bounds on the number of shares underlying the option or Asian characteristics.

Despite its interesting attributes, pricing of VPOs has not received much attention in the literature. Another gap in the literature is the analysis of the hedge parameters of VPOs. This chapter has reviewed the main features and valuation of VPOs, and studied their sensitivities with respect to changes in the different variables that affect these option prices. This is crucial for managing adequately the risk exposures of portfolios containing VPOs for issuers and investors.

Acknowledgments

The authors acknowledge the financial support from the grants P08-SEJ-03917 and JCCM PPII11-0290-0305. The usual caveat applies.

References

Ahn, H., Muni, A., Swindle, G., 1999. Optimal hedging strategies for misspecified asset price models. Applied Mathematical Finance 6, 197–208.

Bhattacharya, M., 1980. Empirical properties of the Black–Scholes formula under ideal conditions. Journal of Financial and Quantitative Analysis 15, 1081–1105.

Black, F., Scholes, M., 1973. The pricing of options and corporate liabilities. Journal of Political Economy 81, 637–654.

Boyle, P.P., Emanuel, D., 1980. Discretely adjusted option hedges. Journal of Financial Economics 8, 259–282.

Carr, P., 2001. Deriving derivatives of derivative securities. Journal of Computational Finance 4, 5–29.

Galai, D., 1983. The components of the return from hedging options against stocks. Journal of Business 56, 45–54.

Handley, J.C., 2000. Variable purchase options. Review of Derivative Research 4, 219–230.

Handley, J.C., 2003. An empirical test of the pricing of VPO contracts. Australian Journal of Management 28, 1–22.

Leland, H.E., 1985. Option pricing and relation with transaction costs. Journal of Finance 40, 1283–1301.

Moreno, M., Navas, J.F., 2008. Australian options. Australian Journal of Management 33, 69–93.

Rasmussen, N.S., 2002. Hedging with a Misspecified Model, Centre for Analytical Finance. Aarhus Universitet.

Ross, S.A., 1997. Hedging long run commitments: exercises in incomplete market pricing. Economic Notes 2, 385–420.

Turnbull, S.M., Wakeman, L.M., 1991. A quick algorithm for pricing European average options. Journal of Financial and Quantitative Analysis 26, 377–389.

27

ASSET SELECTION USING A FACTOR MODEL AND DATA ENVELOPMENT ANALYSIS— A QUANTILE REGRESSION APPROACH

David E. Allen, Abhay Kumar Singh and Robert J. Powell
Edith Cowan University

CHAPTER OUTLINE

27.1 Introduction

The main objective of asset selection for any portfolio manager is to select stocks that can form a portfolio with higher expected returns for given risk levels. The level of risk associated with the assets, stocks in our case, becomes a major deciding factor when choosing stocks from the ever-expanding universe of available stocks in the market. Markowitz (1952), used stock return variance as a primary measure of risk in the determination of stock selection to construct efficient portfolios. Treynor (unpublished manuscript), Sharpe (1964), Lintner (1965) and Mossin (1966) independently proposed the capital asset pricing model (CAPM) to quantify the relationship between beta of an asset and its corresponding return, given a comprehensive set of

Rethinking Valuation and Pricing Models. http://dx.doi.org/10.1016/B978-0-12-415875-7.00027-0

443

assumptions, which simplified Markowitz portfolio selection theory by reducing the number of parameters required for asset selection to a set of linear ones.

The single factor used to capture risk in the CAPM maybe an oversimplification of a complex market. Fama and French (1992, 1993) developed the Fama–French three-factor model, which included "value" and "size" as significant factors, in addition to market risk, for explaining the riskiness of stock portfolios. These three factors, beta, *SMB* (for size effect), *HML* (for value), are better proxies for risk than beta alone. The usual approach adopted for estimating the model is ordinary least squares regression (OLS), which assumes a linear relationship around the mean of the distribution to capture the quantification of risk across the distribution. A new and more robust alternative to OLS is quantile regression, first developed by Koenker and Basset (1978), which has the capability of modeling the conditional quantiles across the distribution. Modeling the whole distribution becomes important when the return distribution becomes skewed in adverse market conditions, such as the recent global financial crisis, and the difficulties inherent to OLS in quantifying behavior in the lower tails of the distribution may lead to inaccurate asset selection or weighting, which will then lead to greater losses.

Data envelopment analysis (DEA) (Charnes *et al.*, 1978; Banker *et al.*, 1984) is a powerful technique adopted from the operational research area. DEA is used for evaluating and comparing the performances of organizational units in multiattribute and multidimensional environments by determining the relative efficiency of a productive unit by considering its closeness to an efficiency frontier.

In this chapter, we use the Fama–French factor model coefficients as calculated from quantile regression as an input to DEA for the asset selection process. We show by a comparative analysis of assets selected using OLS and assets selected using quantile regression that the assets selected by the latter method give better returns when combined in a equally weighted portfolio. We also show that these assets selected using quantile regression not only give better returns in normal market conditions, but also in situations of extreme financial distress.

The rest of the chapter is organized as follows. Section 27.2 gives more insight into the Fama–French three-factor model, quantile regression and DEA. Section 27.3 discusses the research method employed, Section 27.4 presents the major results and, finally, Section 27.5 concludes.

27.2.1 Fama—French three-factor model

Treynor (unpublished manuscript), Sharpe (1964), Lintner (1965) and Mossin (1966) independently proposed CAPM to quantify the risk/return relationship. CAPM, given a sweeping set of assumptions, suggests that only one risk factor is required: beta. Modeling the CAPM using OLS assumes that the relationship between return and beta is linear, as given in:

$$r_A = r_F + \beta_A(r_M - r_F) + \alpha + e, \qquad (27.1)$$

where r_A is the return on the asset, r_M is the return on the market, r_F is the risk-free rate of return, α is the intercept of the regression and e is the standard error of the regression. Fama and French (1992, 1993) extended the basic CAPM to include size and book-to-market effects as explanatory factors in explaining the cross-section of stock returns. *SMB* ("small minus big") gives the size premium, which is the additional return received by investors from investing in companies having low market capitalizations. *HML* ("high minus low") gives the value premium, which is the return provided to investors for investing in companies having high book-to-market values.

SMB is a factor measuring "size risk," which comes from the view that small companies (companies with low market capitalization) are expected to be relatively more sensitive to various risk factors as a result of their undiversified nature and their inability to absorb negative financial events. *HML*, on the other hand, is a factor that proposes an association of higher risk with "value" stocks (high book-to-market values) as compared to "growth" stocks (low book-to-market values). This is intuitively justified given that firms or companies ought to attain a minimum size in order to enter an initial public offering (IPO). The three-factor Fama—French model is written as:

$$r_A = r_F + \beta_A(r_M - r_F) + s_A SMB + h_A HML + \alpha + e, \qquad (27.2)$$

where s_A and h_A capture the security's sensitivity to these two additional factors.

Portfolio formation using this model requires the historical analysis of returns based on the three factors using regression measures, which provide estimates of the coefficients attached to the three risk variables involved in the model, i.e. β_A, s_A and h_A, and the usual regression analysis using OLS gives us the estimates around the means of the distributions of the historical returns. It can be argued that this procedure does not efficiently quantify the behavior in the area of the tails. The modeling of the behavior of factor models using quantile regression gives us the added advantage of capturing the relationships across the tail values as well as efficiently analyzing the median values. The coefficients obtained from the lower quantiles (5% or lower) represent the lower tail risk in the return distribution of every stock, which is of interest when it comes to efficient asset selection for portfolio selection purposes.

27.2.2 Quantile regression

Linear regression represents the dependent variable, as a linear function of one or more independent variable, subject to a random "disturbance" or "error" term. It estimates the mean value of the dependent variable for given levels of the independent variables. For this type of regression, where we want to understand the central tendency in a dataset, OLS is the accepted method. OLS loses its effectiveness when we try to go beyond the mean value or towards the extremes of a dataset.

Koenker and Bassett (1978) introduced quantile regression as an extension of the classical OLS estimation of conditional mean models to the estimation of an ensemble of models for conditional quantile functions for a data distribution. The central special case is the median regression estimator that minimizes a sum of absolute errors. The remaining conditional quantile functions are predicted by minimizing an asymmetrically weighted sum of absolute errors, weights being the function of quantile of interest. This makes quantile regression a robust technique even in the presence of outliers. Taken together, the ensemble of estimated conditional quantile functions offers a much more complete view of the effect of covariates on the location, scale and shape of the distribution of the response variable.

Quantiles refer to the generalized case of dividing a conditional distribution into parts. The technique of quantile regression extends this idea to build models that express the quantile of the conditional distribution of the response variable as a function of observed covariates.

A linear regression coefficient represents the change in the response variable produced by a one unit change in the predictor variable associated with that coefficient. Quantile regression coefficients give the change in a specified quantile of the response variable produced by a one unit change in the predictor variable.

Quantile regression as proposed by Koenker and Bassett (1978) can be defined via an optimization problem. Similar to the problem of defining the fitting of a line via the sample mean as the solution to the problem of minimizing the sum of squared residuals (as done in OLS regression), the median quantile (0.5) is defined through the minimization of sum of absolute residuals. The symmetrical piecewise linear absolute value function assures the same number of observations above and below the median of the distribution.

The other quantile values can be obtained by minimizing a sum of asymmetrically weighted absolute residuals, (giving different weights to positive and negative residuals). Solving:

$$\min_{\xi \in R} \sum \rho_\tau(y_i - \xi), \tag{27.3}$$

where $\rho_\tau(\cdot)$ is the tilted absolute value function as shown in Figure 27.1; this gives the τth sample quantile with its solution. Taking the directional derivatives of the objective function with respect to ξ (from left to right) shows that this problem yields the sample quantile as its solution.

After defining the unconditional quantiles as an optimization problem, it is easy to define conditional quantiles similarly. Taking the least squares regression model as a base to proceed, for a random sample $\{y_1, y_2, ..., y_n\}$ we solve:

$$\min_{\mu \in R} \sum_{i=1}^{n} (y_i - \mu)^2, \tag{27.4}$$

which gives the sample mean, an estimate of the unconditional population mean, EY. Replacing the scalar μ by a parametric function $\mu(x, \beta)$ and then solving:

$$\min_{\mu \in R^P} \sum_{i=1}^{n} (y_i - \mu(x_i, \beta))^2, \tag{27.5}$$

gives an estimate of the conditional expectation function $E(Y|x)$.

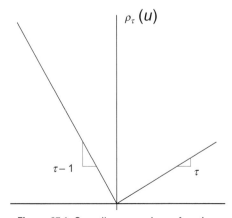

Figure 27.1 Quantile regression ρ function.

Koenker and Bassett (1978) propose to proceed exactly the same way in quantile regression. To obtain an estimate of the conditional median function, the scalar ξ in the first equation is replaced by the parametric function $\xi(x_t, \beta)$ and τ is set to $1/2$. The estimates of other quantile functions are obtained by replacing absolute values by $\rho_\tau(\cdot)$ and solving:

$$\min_{\xi \in R^p} \sum \rho_\tau(y_i - \xi(x_i, \beta)), \tag{27.6}$$

The resulting minimization problem, when $\xi(x, \beta)$ is formulated as a linear function of parameters, can be solved very efficiently by linear programming methods. Further insight into this robust regression technique can be obtained from Koenker's (2005) monograph.

Quantile regression coefficients can be combined by certain weighting schemes to yield more robust measurements of sensitivity to the factors across the quantiles, as opposed to single OLS estimates around the mean. Chan and Lakonishok (1992) originally proposed this approach in their work, which demonstrated by simulations the applicability of quantile regression in beta estimation. We will use a symmetric weighting scheme to combine the coefficients obtained from each of the quantile levels (5, 25, 50, 75 and 95%) to get a single coefficient for each of the three factors, which will be set as a input in the DEA model. The resulting estimators have weights that are the linear combination of quantile regression coefficients:

$$\beta_t = 0.05\beta_{0.05,t} + 0.2\beta_{0.25,t} + 0.5\beta_{0.5,t} + 0.2\beta_{0.75,t} + 0.05\beta_{0.95,t}$$
$$\tag{27.7}$$

$$s_t = 0.05s_{0.05,t} + 0.2s_{0.25,t} + 0.5s_{0.5,t} + 0.2s_{0.75,t} + 0.05s_{0.95,t} \tag{27.8}$$

$$h_t = 0.05h_{0.05,t} + 0.2h_{0.25,t} + 0.5h_{0.5,t} + 0.2h_{0.75,t} + 0.05h_{0.95,t}. \tag{27.9}$$

27.2.3 DEA

DEA was originally introduced by Charnes *et al.* (1978) as a non-parametric linear programming approach, capable of handling multiple inputs as well as multiple outputs (Charnes *et al.*, 1994; Cooper *et al.*, 2000). DEA measures the efficiency of the decision making unit (DMU) by comparison with the best producer in the sample to derive compared efficiency.

DEA generates subjective measures of operational efficiency via the number of homogenous entities compared with each other, through a number of the sample's units that together form a performance frontier curve that envelopes all observations, and hence this approach is called DEA. Consequently, DMUs that lie on the curve are efficient in distributing their inputs and producing their outputs, whilst DMUs that do not lie on the curve are considered to be inefficient.

Performance measurement using the DEA method consists of determining the relative efficiency of a productive unit by considering its proximity to an efficiency frontier. DEA efficiency is not the same as mean-variance efficiency in the Markowitz model where mean and variance are the only two parameters for optimization. In the DEA approach, efficiency is the objective function value of a multicriteria linear programming model. The objective of the DEA is to determine relative performance indicators amongst productive units, considering specific groups of inputs and outputs. It is a multifactor productivity analysis model for measuring the relative efficiencies of a homogenous set of DMUs. The efficiency score in the presence of multiple input and output factors is defined as:

$$Efficiency = \frac{Weighted\ sum\ of\ outputs}{Weighted\ sum\ of\ Inputs}. \qquad (27.10)$$

In the current analysis, the Fama–French three factor coefficients for the securities are used as an input to the DEA and the expected returns are the output. Assuming that there are n DMUs, each with m inputs and s outputs, the relative efficiency score of a test DMU p is obtained by solving the following model proposed by Charnes *et al.* (1978):

$$\max \frac{\sum_{k=1}^{s} v_k y_{kp}}{\sum_{j=1}^{m} u_j x_{jp}}$$

$$\text{s.t.:} \ \frac{\sum_{k=1}^{s} v_k y_{ki}}{\sum_{j=1}^{m} u_j x_{ji}} \leq \forall i$$

$$u_k, u_j \geq 0 \forall k, j. \qquad (27.11)$$

where $k = 1, ..., s, j = 1, ..., m, i = 1, ..., n$, y_{ki} is the amount of output k produced by DMU i, x_{ji} is the amount of input j utilized by DMU i, v_k is the weight given to output k and u_j is the weight given to input j. The fractional program shown in (27.11) can be converted to a linear program as:

$$\max \sum_{k=1}^{s} v_k y_{kp}$$

$$\text{s.t.:} \sum_{j=1}^{m} u_j x_{jp} = 1$$

$$\sum_{k=1}^{s} v_k y_{ki} - \sum_{k=1}^{s} v_k y_{ki} < 0 \forall i$$

$$u_k \cdot u_j \geq 0 \forall k \cdot j. \tag{27.12}$$

To identify the relative efficiency scores of all the DMUs the above problem is run n times. Each DMU selects input and output weights that maximize its efficiency score.

DEA has been proven to have satisfactory applicability in finance in a variety of settings; these include the evaluation (*ex post*) of investment funds (e.g. Morey and Morey, 1999; Gregoriou, 2003; Haslem and Scheraga, 2003), although its initial applications had been predominantly to public organizations (e.g. Avkiran 2001; Calhoun, 2003; Zhu, 2003; Shen *et al.*, 2005). Chen (2008), used DEA for stock selection to form portfolios and compare them against the benchmark market portfolio, using the size effect in the model. Lopes *et al.* (2008) applied DEA to the Brazilian stock market using risk measures like variance and beta as inputs, and quarterly returns as outputs. Singh *et al.* (2010) used DEA to form efficient portfolios in their comparative analysis. In spite of these various applications, DEA has never been tested in contrasting market situations, such as the period before the financial crisis and during the financial crisis (2007–2008).

27.3 Data and Methodology

The study uses daily prices of the 30 Dow Jones Industrial Average stocks for a period from January 2005 to December 2008, along with the Fama–French factors for the same period, obtained from French's website to calculate the Fama–French coefficients.

Table 27.1 presents the 30 stocks tracked in the Dow Jones Industrial Average and used in this study.

The methodology adopted in this research can be summarized in the following steps:

   (i) Calculate Fama–French Coefficients using quantile regression (5, 25, 50, 75 and 95% quantiles) and OLS, by using daily log returns for each stock along with the daily factors.

Table 27.1. Dow Jones Industrial Average 30 stocks used in the study

3M	El Du Pont de Nemours	Kraft Foods
Alcoa	Exxon Mobile	McDonalds
American Express	General Electric	Merck & Co.
AT&T	General Motors	Microsoft
Bank of America	Hewlett-Packard (HP)	Pfizer
Boeing	Home Depot	Procter & Gamble
Caterpillar	Intel	United Technologies
Chevron	International Business Machines (IBM)	Verizon Communications
Citigroup	Johnson & Johnson	Wal Mart Stores
Coca Cola	JP Morgan Chase & Co.	Walt Disney

(ii) Use the symmetric weighting scheme (Equations 27.7–27.9) to combine the coefficients calculated from quantile regression to get a single measure for each of the three coefficients.

(iii) Standardize the coefficients and the annualized returns to make them positive to be used as deciding input and output parameters in the DEA model, using the following relation:

$$RZ_{ij} = \text{Abs}(\min Z_j) + Z_i, \qquad (27.13)$$

where RZ_{ij} is the rescaling for each j attributes for stock i, Min Z_j is the minimum of all the values of jth attribute for all stocks and Z_i is the value of attribute j for stock i. Finally all the attributes for all the stocks are divided by respective maximums, as:

$$MRZ_{ij} = \frac{RZ_{ij}}{Column\ Maximum}, \qquad (27.14)$$

where MRZ_{ij} is the final rescaled value for each attribute for a stock.

(iv) We drop the stock having the minimum rescaled annualized return, which was zero in every case. The asset selection using the three factors for the rest of the 29 stocks is done for both OLS and quantile regression measures.

(v) The coefficients are chosen as inputs to the variable return to scale input-oriented DEA model and the annualized returns as the output, which minimizes the inputs (three risk factors) for a given level of output (return). Stocks having an efficiency score of 100% are chosen to form an equally weighted portfolio.

(vi) The resulting portfolios obtained for both the regression techniques are evaluated based on their return after a hold-out period of one year.

(vii) All the steps are repeated for the three-year data period (2005–2007), resulting in three different asset sets selected during different time periods representing different market conditions, which included the period of the global financial crisis.

GRETL, an open-source software, is used for OLS and quantile regression, and another open-source software, called Efficiency Measurement System (EMS), is used for calculating the DEA model.

27.4 Discussion of Results

Table 27.2 gives the stocks selected using the factor coefficients calculated from OLS; it also gives the return that the set of selected stocks provide when combined into an equally weighted portfolio after a hold-out period of one year. Table 27.3 presents the stocks selected using factor coefficients calculated for different quantiles using quantile regression together with the hold-out period equally weighted portfolio return. As evident from the results in Tables 27.2 and 27.3, the stocks selected using quantile regression estimates give better hold-out period returns than those selected using OLS. The method not only gives better results in normal market conditions, but also gives a better performance at the time of the recent financial crisis (years 2007–2008).

Table 27.2. Asset selected from DEA by using OLS estimates

Year	Stocks	One-year hold-out return
2005	Boeing, HP, Intel, Johnson & Johnson, Kraft Foods, Pfizer, Procter & Gamble	12.03333
2006	AT&T, General Motors, HP, IBM, Johnson & Johnson, Kraft Foods, Merck & Co., Walt Disney	4.181735
2007	Boeing, Chevron, Coca Cola, HP, Intel, IBM, Johnson & Johnson, McDonalds, Merck & Co., Procter & Gamble	−43.0281

Table 27.3. Asset selected from DEA by using quantile regression estimates

Year	Stocks	One-year hold-out return
2005	Boeing, HP, Intel, IBM, Johnson & Johnson, Kraft Foods, Merck & Co., Pfizer, Procter & Gamble	14.414368
2006	AT&T, General Motors, HP, IBM, Johnson & Johnson, Kraft Foods, Merck & Co., Microsoft	5.259369
2007	AT&T, Chevron, Coca Cola, HP, Intel, IBM, Johnson & Johnson, McDonalds, Microsoft, Procter & Gamble	−39.1764

The stocks selected based on quantile regression estimates using DEA perform better, as the quantile measures provide an efficient quantification of the tail risk involved with the return distribution, which is not possible with OLS. Figure 27.2 gives the distribution of fitted values obtained for one of the sample stocks from the factor model using OLS and the 5 and 95% quantile regressions. The fitted values show that OLS is incapable of capturing the tail values and hence less efficient for the quantification of the overall risk.

27.5 Conclusion

The Fama–French three-factor model captures the dependence of asset returns on three factors: The market return, the size factor and the value factor; however, the traditional technique used for the estimation of the model, OLS, is incapable of describing the extremes of the distribution. In this study, we used the robust technique of quantile regression that efficiently describes the required quantiles and hence gives better estimates of the risk described by the factors. The research gives a new dimension to the use of factors in DEA analysis for selecting efficient assets by means of quantile regression. The empirical results suggest that the assets selected by DEA perform better when quantile estimates are used and they also show that the quantile based estimates help to shield the investor from extreme losses to a degree in times of unpredictable financial distress.

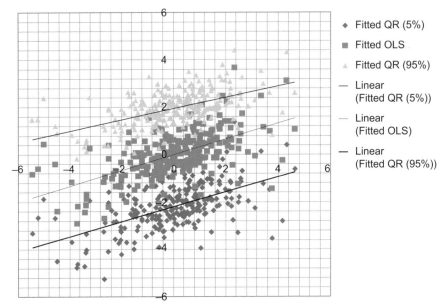

Figure 27.2 Fitted values obtained from OLS and quantile regression (5 and 95%).

Quantile regression techniques are now more widely used in quantitative finance and also in specialized financial fields such as financial econometrics. Further work can be done to apply this robust tool in combination with other optimization algorithms to test the capabilities and applicability of this technique.

References

Allen, D.E., Gerrans, P., Singh, A.K., Powell, R., 2009. Quantile regression and its application in investment analysis. The Finsia Journal of Applied Finance (JASSA) 4, 7–12.

Banker, R.D., Charnes, R.F., Cooper, W.W., 1984. Some models for estimating technical and scale inefficiencies in data envelopment analysis. Management Science 30, 1078–1092.

Barnes, M., Hughes, A.W., 2002. A quantile regression analysis of the cross section of stock market returns Available at http://ssrn.com/abstract=458522.

Black, F., 1993. Beta and return. Journal of Portfolio Management 20, 8–18.

Charnes, A., Cooper, W.W., Rhodes, R., 1978. Measuring the efficiency of decision making units. European Journal of Operational Research 2, 429–444.

Chan, L.K.C., Lakonishok, J., 1992. Robust measurement of beta risk. Journal of Financial and Quantitative Analysis 27, 265–282.

Chen, H.-H., 2008. Stock selection using data envelopment analysis. Journal of Risk Finance 108 (9), 1255–1268.

Fama, E.F., French, K.R., 1992. The cross-section of expected stock returns. Journal of Finance 47, 427–486.

Fama, E.F., French, K.R., 1993. Common risk factors in the returns on stocks and bonds. Journal of Financial Economics 33, 3−56.

Gregoriou, G.N., 2003. Performance appraisal of hedge funds using data envelopment analysis. Journal of Wealth Management 5 (4), 88−95.

Haslem, J.A., Scheraga, C.A., 2003. Data envelopment analysis of Morningstar's large-cap mutual funds. Journal of Investing, Winter 12 (4), 41−48.

Hsu, C.-C., Chou, R.K., 2003. Robust measurement of size and book-to-market premia. EFMA 2003 Helsinki Meetings Available at http://ssrn.com/abstract=407726.

Koenker, R.W., 2005. Quantile Regression. Cambridge University Press, Cambridge.

Koenker, R.W., Bassett Jr., G.T., 1978. Regression quantiles. Econometrica 46, 33−50.

Lintner, J., 1965. The valuation of risk assets and the selection of risky investments in stock portfolios and capital budgets. Review of Economics and Statistics 47, 13−37.

Lopes, A., Lanzer, E., Lima, M., da Costa Jr., N., 2008. DEA investment strategy in the Brazilian stock market. Economics Bulletin 13 (2), 1−10.

Markowitz, H.M, 1952. Portfolio selection. Journal of Finance 7, 77−91.

Markowitz, M.H., 1991. Foundations of portfolio theory. Journal of Finance 46, 469−477.

Sharpe, W., 1963. A simplified model for portfolio analysis. Management Science 9, 277−293.

Sharpe, W.F., 1964. Capital asset prices: a theory of market equilibrium under conditions of risk. Journal of Finance 19, 425−442.

Singh, A.K., Sahu, R., Bharadwaj, S., 2010. Portfolio evaluation using OWA-heuristic algorithm and data envelopment analysis. Journal of Risk Finance 11, 75−88.

28

TAIL RISK REDUCTION STRATEGIES

Lerby M. Ergun* and Philip A. Stork**

*Duisenberg School of Finance and Erasmus University of Rotterdam,
**VU University Amsterdam

CHAPTER OUTLINE

28.1 Introduction

This chapter combines two strands of literature: (i) The measurement of tail risk with extreme value theory (EVT) and (ii) the use of technical analysis or systematic trading rules. The first strand, on EVT, is gaining popularity rather quickly. We refer to Novak and Beirlant (2006) for a recent article on the use of EVT to predict the size of a stock market crash. They estimate value at risk (VaR) and expected shortfall (ES) from dependent heavy-tailed data, using a non-parametric approach.

EVT is well-suited to analyze extremely large falls in asset prices. Prevention of such major losses is what should be of most concern for risk managers and investors. From a risk management perspective, the more common returns centered around the mean are of less relevance. A standard VaR approach, assuming normally distributed returns, underestimates the downside tail investment risks. EVT, on the other hand, focuses on the tail returns only. Under certain rather weak assumptions, the shape of the entire tail may be estimated even if only very few extreme observations are available. For seminal papers on EVT, we refer to Mandelbrot (1963), Hill (1975) and Daníelsson *et al.* (2006).

The second strand of literature concerns the use of technical analysis, which dates back to the 1800s. As Brock *et al.* (1992) discuss, it was probably used as the main method of investment analysis before corporate and other financial information became more and more disclosed. The literature is divided on the use of technical analysis. Park and Irwin (2007) find that the more recent studies indicate that consistent abnormal excess returns are generated with technical trading strategies. However, they also indicate that several of the existing studies can be criticized because of problems in their testing procedures, like data snooping, *ex post* selection of trading rules or search methodologies and difficulties in estimation of risk or transaction costs. Faber (2007) shows how simple moving average trading rules may be used to reduce investment risk, without reducing expected returns. He shows that during bull markets a trend-following model (such as the one in this chapter) tends to underperform a Buy-and-Hold strategy. More importantly, the longer and deeper bear markets are likely to be avoided, as the trend-following Timing strategy is likely to exit the market in the beginning of the down period.

Several papers try to link market price dynamics to trading rules. Brock *et al.* (1992) study the profitability of technical trading rules and investigate the use of simple autoregressive (AR) or generalized autoregressive conditional heteroskedasticity (GARCH) models. Although they find that their sample of technical trading rules is quite profitable, they do not succeed in linking the stock price dynamics to the success of the trading rules. Trading strategies that compare a long- and short-term moving average have been linked to the reversal of correlation as the return horizon increases (LeBaron, 1992; Sentana and Wadhwani, 1992; Nam *et al.*, 2006). De Long *et al.* (1990) have attributed the reversal to the presence of feedback traders, i.e. traders who use previous price movements for trading. Positive feedback trading may be caused by extrapolative expectations, the use of stop-loss orders, purchases on margin that are liquidated when the price falls, or dynamic trading strategies such as portfolio insurance or derivatives hedging. A more detailed discussion may be found in Sentana and Wadhwani (1992), Koutmos (1997), and Park and Irwin (2007).

In this chapter, we empirically analyze the risk–return characteristics of a simple systematic trading rule. We compare these characteristics to those of a Buy-and-Hold investment strategy. We first focus on the US equity markets, represented by the S&P

500 Index, for the period 1926–2010. Next, we extend our analysis to six other markets, including bonds, real estate and gold, for the period 1990–2010. We use a set of advanced risk measurement techniques, which enables us to determine the level of risk, including tail risks. Overall, our results indicate that in the Timing strategy all measures of risk are strongly reduced. At the same time average holding period returns stay the same or even increase marginally. This result is relevant for portfolio managers, risk managers, treasurers, individual investors and other capital market participants.

28.2 Data and Methodology

Daily data are taken from the CRSP (Center for Research in Security Prices) database for the value-weighted S&P 500 Index, for the period 1 July 1926–31 December 2010. For the stock markets of Germany, Hong Kong and the United Kingdom we obtain daily total return indices from Datastream for the period 2 January 1990–31 December 2010. For this same period, we use daily Datastream total return index series for gold, Real Estate Investment Trust (REIT) and 10-year bonds. Stock market returns are calculated as the relative percentage differences in the respective stock market index. The interest rate we use is the one-month US Treasury bill rate, attained from the website of Kenneth R. French (http://mba.tuck.dartmouth.edu/pages/faculty/ken.french/data_library.html).

This chapter uses the EVT framework to study the tail of the distribution of investment returns and various risk management measures. The EVT framework facilitates, through the use of the limiting distribution of the maxima, the modeling of the tail of the distribution. It is assumed that the tail is regularly varying and that it satisfies the following expansion:

$$F(-x) = 1 - F(x) = Ax^{-\alpha}[1 + Bx^{-\beta} + o(x^{-\beta})],$$

where α is the shape parameter and A is the scale parameter of the distribution. Further, B and β are, respectively, the scale and shape parameters of the second-order expansion. We work with the first term of the expansion for calculating the quantiles, as the second and third terms are of lesser importance. The most important parameter of the analysis is the tail index α. This parameter is estimated by the Hill estimator (Hill, 1975). It is also called the shape parameter of the cumulative distribution function (CDF) as it determines how fat the tail is.

Using EVT methodology, we calculate the VaR and the ES for the Buy-and-Hold strategy and for the systematic trading rule. The VaR is calculated by inverting the CDF for the tail as:

$$1 - F(x) = P(X > x) = Ax^{-\alpha} \Rightarrow \left(\frac{A}{P(X > x)}\right)^{\frac{1}{\alpha}} = x = VaR.$$

The scaling coefficient A is determined at the threshold level of the Hill estimator:

$$P(X > x_k) = Ax_k^{-\alpha_k} \Rightarrow A = P(X > x_k)x_k^{\alpha_k},$$

where k is the number of observations used for the Hill estimator and P is the empirical CDF, which has value k/n.

The ES is a measure of the expected return, given that a certain threshold is crossed. This threshold is often set at the VaR level that is chosen. The ES can alternatively be described by the conditional expectation of the random variables, thus:

$$E(X|X > VaR) = \int_{VaR}^{\infty} \frac{xf(x)}{1 - F(VaR)} dx = \frac{\alpha}{\alpha - 1} VaR.$$

The above formula shows that once the value of VaR is calculated, the value of ES is derived easily as well.

28.3 Empirical Results

In this section, we describe the main empirical results. Figure 28.1 depicts the natural logarithmic value of two investment strategies on the S&P 500 Index. The first line shows a simple Buy-and-Hold strategy's cumulative return index and the second line reflects the Timing strategy based on two moving averages. This second strategy is fully invested in the S&P 500 when the one-month moving average of the level of the index [MA(1M)] exceeds the 10-month moving average of the level of the index [MA(10M)]. Note that we use true end-of-month days, which are the dates on which an investor is assumed to take his or her investment decision (when using the Timing strategy). Thus, we do not use a 20- or 200-day approximation, but we are being more precise in our approach. The long position is sold and changed into short-term Treasury bonds when the MA(1M) is below the MA(10M) at the last trading day of the month only. Taxes, commissions and slippage are ignored, although these may all be expected to be of modest size, due to the high liquidity of the S&P 500 contracts in, for example, futures or trackers.

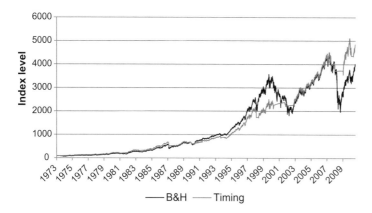

Figure 28.1 S&P investment strategies. The graph shows the normalized natural logarithmic value of two investment strategies for the period 2 January 1973–31 December 2010. The Buy-and-Hold line reflects the results for a simple strategy in which the S&P 500 value-weighted index is bought and held for the entire period. In the Timing strategy the investor is long in the stock market if the 10-month moving average exceeds the one-month moving average of the index level, otherwise the money is invested in short-term Treasury notes. All timing decisions are made at the last trading day of the month and real calendar-monthly periods are used, not 20- or 200-day approximations.

Figure 28.1 shows that for the last nearly four decades, the Timing strategy generated slightly higher cumulative returns. More interestingly, the Buy-and-Hold strategy's return index exhibits larger volatility than the Timing strategy. On several occasions, the magnitude of the Buy-and-Hold indexes' downward moves clearly exceed those generated by the Timing strategy. The latter avoids several of the largest and most protracted bear markets, like the post-Internet-bubble years of 2001–2002 and the Credit Crisis period of 2007–2008. The difference between the investment risks, especially concerning the extremely negative returns, is of most interest to investors. To further analyze the two strategies' performance, Table 28.1 documents the return statistics.

Table 28.1 shows that for the full sample period 1926–2010, the Buy-and-Hold strategy yields somewhat higher annualized holding period returns. The annualized difference equals 0.07% ($= 9.62\% - 9.55\%$), which economically is of little consequence. In contrast, the Buy-and-Hold strategy's standard deviation clearly exceeds that of the Timing strategy. The relative difference equals 39% ($= (1.07 - 0.77)/0.77$) for the full 1926–2010 period, which underscores the greater risk that is generated by the Buy-and-Hold strategy. For the 1973–2010 period, the Timing

Table 28.1. Statistics of two investment strategies

	Period 1926–2010		Period 1973–2010	
	Buy-and-Hold	**Timing**	**Buy-and-Hold**	**Timing**
Holding period return (%)	9.62	9.55	10.44	11.01
Standard deviation (%)	1.07	0.77	1.06	0.76
Skewness	−0.13	−1.24	−0.57	−1.57
Kurtosis	19.92	38.93	18.91	38.68
Sharpe ratio	3.54	6.39	4.02	7.62
Maximum absolute drawdown (%)	55.59	21.25	55.59	21.25
Maximum relative drawdown (%)	83.74	51.06	55.59	32.12
Best annual return (%)	56.96	50.51	40.09	33.47
Worst annual return (%)	−43.18	−20.63	−38.63	−13.11
VaR 2.5% (%)	1.99	1.42	2.01	1.52
VaR 1.0% (%)	2.94	2.04	2.79	2.01
VaR 0.5% (%)	3.95	2.67	3.59	2.48
ES 2.5% (%)	3.46	2.34	3.14	2.18
ES 1.0% (%)	5.11	3.35	4.37	2.89
ES 0.5% (%)	6.86	4.39	5.61	3.57

Basic statistics of two investment strategies on the equally weighted S&P 500 Index: a Buy-and-Hold strategy and a Timing strategy. In the latter strategy, the investor is long in the stock market if the 10-month moving average exceeds the one-month moving average of the index level, otherwise the money is invested in short-term notes. Daily data between 1 July 1926 and 31 December 2010 are used.

strategy's holding period returns exceed those of the Buy-and-Hold (11.01% versus 10.44%), whereas the standard deviation again is around 40% lower. As a result, for both periods, the Timing strategy's Sharpe ratio is nearly twice the size of the Buy-and-Hold strategy's Sharpe ratio. Note that the Sharpe ratio is calculated as the average daily return divided by the standard deviation of the daily returns, without correcting for the risk free rate.

Further, two maximum drawdown measures are calculated. The first is an absolute drawdown, which uses the absolute levels and absolute differences. The second is a relative drawdown, which uses relative differences. Both drawdowns of the Buy-and-Hold strategy far exceed those of the Timing strategy. This finding is in line with the much deeper troughs that are depicted in Figure 28.1. The VaR and ES estimates confirm that, for both the full and the shorter period, the Timing strategy's tail risks are markedly lower than in the case of the Buy-and-Hold strategy.

Apparently, the Timing strategy succeeds in strongly reducing the return distribution's left tail.

Next, Table 28.2 reports the results of several risk-return models. A standard capital asset pricing model (CAPM) is estimated on monthly returns. For the 1926–2010 sample for the Buy-and-Hold strategy, alpha equals zero and beta equals one. For the Timing strategy, alpha has a positive value of 0.0023, which is significant at a 1% confidence level. This amounts to an annualized abnormal return of 2.8%. For the sample 1973–2010, the alpha is of similar size, but significant at a 7% confidence level. The positive level of alpha reflects the improved risk-return relationship discussed in this chapter. The value of beta, reported in the second column, equals 0.49 and 0.58, depending on the period investigated. Thus, the systematic risk of the Timing strategy is much lower than that of the Buy-and-Hold strategy.

Columns (3) and (4) in Table 28.2 further strengthen the notion that the Timing strategy succeeds in reducing investment risk. The strategy's returns are divided into two separate samples: One sample contains the higher than average returns, whereas the other sample contains the lower than average returns. Subsequently, the CAPM is re-estimated for both subsamples. The resulting upside and downside betas thus measure the strategy's exposure to (relative) upward and downward market movements. Table 28.2 shows that for the Timing strategy, both the upside beta (= 0.24 or 0.44) and the downside beta (= 0.44 or 0.51) equal a value clearly lower than 1.00. Downward market moves are mirrored somewhat more strongly by the Timing strategy than is the case for upward market moves, although the difference is rather small in the 1973–2010 period. Finally, Table 28.2 shows that the extreme downside and upside betas are estimated to have levels that are similar to their regular, non-extreme counterparts.

28.3.1 Robustness test

Next, to analyze the robustness of the Timing strategy's results, we change the number of days used in the calculation of the moving averages. Instead of using only the MA(200), Table 28.3 below also reports results for MA(x), in which $x = 250$, 150, 100 and 50 days. In Table 28.3, the shorter moving average metric is left unchanged at MA(1M), thus using one full calendar month.

Table 28.3 shows that average returns exhibit a consistent, decreasing pattern. The overall compounded investment return tends to decrease with the length of the period used in the moving

Table 28.2. Timing strategy analysis

Period	CAPM alpha	CAPM beta	Downside beta	Upside beta	Extreme downside beta	Extreme upside beta
1925–2010	0.0023 (0.01)	0.4864 (0.00)	0.4391 (0.00)	0.2391 (0.00)	0.4480 (0.00)	0.3122 (0.00)
1973–2010	0.0022 (0.06)	0.5792 (0.00)	0.5059 (0.00)	0.4413 (0.00)	0.3298 (0.00)	0.2553 (0.00)

Results of several model estimations of the Timing strategy. Both the full sample period (1 July 1926–31 December 2010) and the subsample period (2 January 1973–31 December 2010) are investigated. The investor is long in the stock market if the 10-month moving average exceeds the 1-month moving average of the index level, otherwise the money is invested in short-term Treasury notes. A standard CAPM model is estimated, using OLS on monthly return data:

$$R_t^T - r_t = \alpha + \beta \left(R_t^{BH} - r_t \right) + \varepsilon_t.$$

In this formula, variables R_t^T and R_t^{BH} represent the Timing and Buy-and-Hold strategy's returns at time t, respectively. Variable r_t represents the risk-free rate and ε_t is an error term. For all estimates, p-values are reported in brackets. To arrive at downside betas β^- and upside betas β^+, the returns are separated into two subsamples. The first sample contains the returns that exceed the average Buy-and-Hold return. The second sample contains the returns that are lower than the average. Paired observations are used in estimating the downside and upside betas:

$$\beta^- = \frac{\text{cov}\left(R^T, R^{BH} | R^{BH} < \mu^{BH} \right)}{\text{var}\left(R^{BH} | R^{BH} < \mu^{BH} \right)}, \quad \beta^+ = \frac{\text{cov}\left(R^T, R^{BH} | R^{BH} \geq \mu^{BH} \right)}{\text{var}\left(R^{BH} | R^{BH} \geq \mu^{BH} \right)}.$$

Variable μ^{BH} represents the Buy-and-Hold strategy's mean return. Extreme up and downside betas are estimated with a non-parametric copula, calculated by counting the number of extreme observations of the Timing strategy, given that the Buy-and-Hold strategy return reaches an extreme level. This calculation is done for both the downside and upside. An observation is considered 'extreme' when it belongs to the 1% quantile.

Table 28.3. Timing strategy statistics using different moving averages

	Buy-and-Hold	250-Day	200-Day	150-Day	100-Day	50-Day
Holding period return (%)	9.60	9.78	8.98	8.86	8.56	7.65
Standard deviation (%)	1.07	0.77	0.76	0.75	0.74	0.75
Skewness	−0.13	−1.21	−1.23	−1.13	−1.11	−0.59
Kurtosis	19.89	38.00	39.03	40.36	40.56	28.13
Sharpe ratio	3.53	6.40	6.09	6.25	6.11	5.49
Maximum absolute drawdown (%)	55.59	15.67	20.72	15.33	24.91	28.22
Maximum relative drawdown (%)	83.74	51.06	55.65	55.88	62.24	51.78
Maximum annual return (%)	56.96	50.51	50.51	50.51	50.51	50.51
Minimum annual return (%)	−43.18	−20.63	−21.94	−21.21	−34.33	−20.73
VaR 2.5% (%)	1.99	1.44	1.42	1.39	1.40	1.42
VaR 1.0% (%)	2.94	2.06	2.02	1.99	1.99	2.07
VaR 0.5% (%)	3.95	2.70	2.64	2.61	2.61	2.74
ES 2.5% (%)	3.47	2.36	2.31	2.29	2.28	2.40
ES 1.0% (%)	5.12	3.38	3.30	3.27	3.26	3.48
ES 0.5% (%)	6.88	4.43	4.31	4.29	4.26	4.62
CAPM alpha		0.0025	0.0020	0.0020	0.0017	0.0007
CAPM beta		0.4924	0.4727	0.4610	0.4686	0.5110
Downside beta		0.4401	0.4333	0.3915	0.4011	0.4214
Upside beta		0.2493	0.1979	0.2350	0.2680	0.4230
Extreme downside beta		0.4525	0.4434	0.4027	0.3891	0.4434
Extreme upside beta		0.3258	0.3032	0.3032	0.2986	0.3484

Statistics of a Buy-and-Hold strategy and a number of Timing strategies, each using a different combination of two moving averages. The investor is long in the stock market if the x-day moving average exceeds the one-month moving average of the index level, otherwise the capital is invested in short-term notes. The duration of the first moving average varies from 50 days (column "50-Day") to 250 days (column "250-Day"), whereas the second duration stays unchanged. Investment decisions are taken on the last day of each calendar month only. A standard CAPM model is estimated using OLS on monthly return data. For brevity, we refer to the text under Table 28.2 that describes how we estimate the various CAPM parameters reported in Table 28.3.

average rule. Interestingly, no such conclusion may be drawn with regard to the other statistics, where no clear pattern emerges. These other metrics, like the standard deviation, skewness, kurtosis and Sharpe ratio, do not clearly favor one Timing strategy over another and the main qualitative conclusions are not affected. Only the maximum and absolute drawdowns appear to document a trend: The drawdown increases for the shorter moving average rules. This finding is intuitive; as the moving average period reduces, the results become more volatile and reflect the market more closely. Further, as in Table 28.1, the VaR and ES estimates confirm that the Timing strategy's tail risks are considerably lower than for the Buy-and-Hold strategy. Table 28.3 shows that this finding holds for all moving average durations used.

Also, we find that the alphas are positive and significant at a 5% confidence level, for all moving average durations. The only exception is the MA(50), where alpha is insignificant. Further, the downside beta clearly exceeds the upside beta for all combinations of moving average durations. Hence, not only are many of the downside movements avoided, but even more upside bull markets are missed out. However, in spite of asymmetry in beta estimates, the average compounded return is close to the one that is generated by the Buy-and-Hold strategy.

28.3.2 Empirical tests on other markets

Next, we move our focus from the S&P 500 Index to several other markets. Table 28.4 shows that for six out of the seven indices, holding period returns for the Timing strategy exceed those of the Buy-and-Hold strategy. The difference between the Timing and Buy-and-Hold strategies ranges from −0.85% for the United Kingdom to 3.22% for Hong Kong. For all series, we find that the standard deviation that is generated by the Timing strategy is below that of the Buy-and-Hold strategy. As a consequence, the Timing strategy's Sharpe ratio comes out markedly higher. The other risk metrics (drawdown, VaR and ES) paint a picture that is quite similar to the results found for the S&P 500 Index in previous tables. The risk metrics tend to be substantially lower for the Timing strategy than for the Buy-and-Hold strategy. For the real estate index (REIT) this difference is highest, where for instance the 0.5% ES of the Buy-and-Hold strategy equals 19.99%, which is four times as high as for the Timing strategy (equal to only 4.98%). For the 10-year bond index, the relative difference is much smaller, as the risk metrics are only slightly lower for the Timing strategy. Further, all alpha

Table 28.4. Investment strategy statistics

	United Kingdom		Germany		Hong Kong		10-year bonds		REIT		Gold	
	Buy-and-Hold	Timing	Buy-and-Hold	Timing	Buy-and-Hold	Timing	Buy-and-Hold	Timing	Buy-and-Hold	Timing	Buy-and-Hold	Timing
Holding period return (%)	9.24	8.39	8.11	10.85	14.33	17.55	7.41	7.51	15.08	17.05	6.76	7.66
Standard deviation (%)	1.14	0.75	1.44	0.92	1.57	1.15	0.36	0.32	1.63	0.80	0.96	0.79
Skewness	0.03	−0.12	0.02	−0.57	0.15	−0.12	−0.39	−0.47	0.44	−0.04	0.05	−0.35
Kurtosis	9.87	7.60	8.66	11.00	12.48	22.10	9.78	13.01	31.30	13.03	10.57	13.32
Sharpe ratio	3.55	4.50	2.80	4.74	4.05	5.95	7.83	8.76	4.11	7.95	3.09	3.98
Maximum absolute drawdown (%)	44.79	23.35	72.68	20.56	63.80	27.79	7.68	6.38	74.58	23.53	29.74	22.25
Maximum relative drawdown (%)	48.29	23.35	72.68	31.30	63.80	45.28	10.19	7.49	74.58	23.53	39.13	22.25
Maximum annual return (%)	28.77	29.51	47.11	47.11	127.66	118.53	18.46	18.40	61.83	44.00	31.78	31.78
Minimum annual return (%)	−28.55	−16.29	−43.94	−17.21	−48.38	−18.11	−7.13	−2.17	−39.00	−9.43	−21.70	−5.12
VaR 2.5% (%)	2.22	1.55	2.77	1.90	3.07	2.36	0.70	0.65	2.76	1.65	1.90	1.63

(continued on next page)

Table 28.4 (continued)

	United Kingdom		Germany		Hong Kong		10-year bonds		REIT		Gold	
	Buy-and-Hold	Timing	Buy-and-Hold	Timing	Buy-and-Hold	Timing	Buy-and-Hold	Timing	Buy-and-Hold	Timing	Buy-and-Hold	Timing
VaR 1.0% (%)	3.10	2.09	3.81	2.51	4.26	3.23	0.92	0.85	4.88	2.35	2.72	2.28
VaR 0.5% (%)	3.98	2.61	4.85	3.10	5.47	4.09	1.13	1.05	7.52	3.07	3.57	2.93
ES 2.5% (%)	3.49	2.29	4.25	2.73	4.78	3.59	1.00	0.93	7.33	2.68	3.12	2.56
ES 1.0% (%)	4.86	3.08	5.84	3.61	6.64	4.90	1.30	1.22	12.97	3.82	4.46	3.57
ES 0.5% (%)	6.24	3.85	7.43	4.46	8.52	6.21	1.60	1.51	19.99	4.98	5.85	4.58
CAPM alpha	0.0012		0.0039		0.0062		0.0004		0.0066		0.0016	
CAPM beta	0.5438		0.4907		0.5420		0.8847		0.4137		0.6196	
Upside beta	0.4629		0.2972		0.4484		0.8692		0.1662		0.5192	
Downside beta	0.3525		0.4848		0.5018		0.9945		0.3492		0.6238	
Extreme upside beta	0.1698		0.1321		0.4906		0.7925		0.0566		0.7736	
Extreme downside beta	0.1698		0.1698		0.3962		0.7358		0.0943		0.5472	

Investment return statistics of both a Buy-and-Hold strategy and a Timing strategy, executed over the period 2 January 1990—31 December 2010. To generate these results, we use the same procedures as were used to generate Tables 28.1 and 28.2. Hence, to save space, for calculation details we refer to the footnotes of those tables.

estimates are positive. We find that some alphas are significant and others are not, possibly due to the short sample period. The betas are of a similar level as the one documented for the S&P 500 Index, thus equal to around 0.50. The only exception is the beta documented for the 10-year bond index, which equals 0.88 and thus is substantially higher than the other betas. Finally, both the regular and extreme upside and downside betas confirm that many of the market movements are not mirrored in the Timing strategy. Both up- and downward markets are often avoided, as is evidenced by the betas that equal levels considerably below 1.00.

28.4 Conclusion

The empirical results in this chapter show that a simple systematic trading rule, based on two moving averages, succeeds in reducing investment risks. Using EVT, we find that VaR and ES measures are strongly reduced when applying such a Timing strategy. Moreover, this reduction in tail risk is realized without any loss in compounded returns, which even show an increase for most of the assets studied. Apart from these tail risk measures, other risk metrics such as drawdowns and standard deviations further strengthen the conclusion that investment risk is markedly reduced.

Even though the empirical results are strong and consistent across all assets and periods investigated, it is yet unclear what the cause for this finding may be. Possible explanations may lie in behavioral finance (e.g. overconfidence or momentum) or in technical market dynamics (e.g. the presence of stop-loss orders, the use of margins and derivatives-hedging techniques) or otherwise. In future research, we intend to delve deeper into the potential reasons behind the apparent risk-reduction success of the trading rules investigated.

References

Brock, W., Lakonishok, J., Lebaron, B., 1992. Simple technical trading rules and the stochastic properties of stock returns. Journal of Finance 47 (5), 1731–1764.

Daníelsson, J., Jorgensen, B.N., Sarma, M., de Vries, C.G., 2006. Comparing downside risk measures for heavy tailed distributions. Economics Letters 92 (2), 202–208.

De Long, B.J., Shleifer, A., Summers, L.H., Waldmann, R.J., 1990. Positive feedback investment strategies and destabilizing rational speculation. Journal of Finance 45 (2), 379–395.

Faber, M., 2007. A quantitative approach to tactical asset management. Journal of Wealth Management 9 (4), 69–79.

Hill, B., 1975. A simple general approach to inference about the tail of a distribution. The Annals of Statistics 3 (5), 1163–1173.

Koutmos, G., 1997. feedback trading and the autocorrelation pattern in stock returns: further empirical evidence. Journal of International Money and Finance 16 (4), 625–636.

LeBaron, B., 1992. Some relations between volatility and serial correlations in stock market returns. The Journal of Business 65 (2), 199–219.

Mandelbrot, B., 1963. The variation of certain speculative prices. The Journal of Business 36 (4), 394–419.

Nam, K., Kim, S., Arize, A., 2006. Mean reversion of short-horizon stock returns: asymmetry property. Review of Quantitative Finance and Accounting 26 (2), 137–163.

Novak, S.Y., Beirlant, J., 2006. The magnitude of a market crash can be predicted. Journal of Banking and Finance 30 (2), 435–462.

Park, C., Irwin, S.H., 2007. What do we know about the profitability of technical analysis. Journal of Economic Surveys 21 (4), 786–826.

Sentana, E., Wadhwani, S., 1992. Feedback traders and stock return autocorrelations: evidence from a century of daily data. Economic Journal 102 (411), 415–425.

IDENTIFICATION AND VALUATION IMPLICATIONS OF FINANCIAL MARKET SPIRALS

Pankaj K. Jain, Ajay K. Mishra and Thomas H. McInish
University of Memphis

CHAPTER OUTLINE

29.1 Introduction

Liquidity is a critically important factor for financial market stability and efficiency. Reduced liquidity played a crucial role in exacerbating the 1987 stock market crash, and in causing the near collapse of both financial markets and the real economy in 2007–2008. According to Brunnermeier's (2008) theoretical framework, market illiquidity was potentially one of the prime causes of the 2007–2008 crisis. In a follow-up study, Brunnermeier and Pedersen (2009) show that a loss spiral can arise if speculators with large initial positions in a security incur losses that force them to sell, driving down prices and forcing them to sell even more. These authors also show that speculators' funding problems can cause illiquidity spirals in which small changes in fundamentals can lead to a large jump in illiquidity. These loss and illiquidity spirals reinforce each other. Figure 29.1 shows the variation in

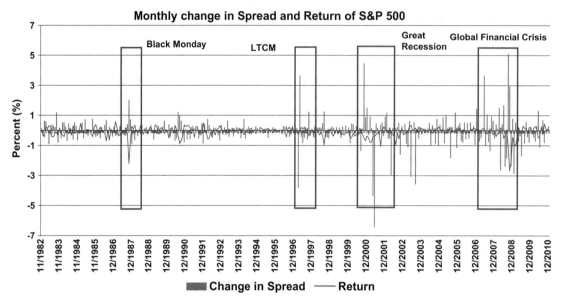

Figure 29.1 Monthly change in spread and return for S&P 500 Index. We present changes in average monthly returns and change in average monthly spread of S&P 500 firms. Change in spread is $100 * \ln(Spread_t / Spread_{t-1})$. A decrease in spread indicates improved market efficiency and decrease in trading cost.

average monthly returns and change in quoted spread of S&P 500 Index stocks. Security returns fall steeply during crisis periods while change in bid-ask spreads widen, reflecting the fact that loss and illiquidity spirals go hand-in-hand.

We address two main issues: (i) We extend Brunnermeier and Pedersen's (2009) theoretical framework by rigorously defining loss spirals and illiquidity spirals and (ii) we investigate the role of market illiquidity on the valuation of assets.

The remainder of the chapter is organized as follows. In Section 29.2, we briefly discuss the related literature and provide a summary of studies looking into the role of liquidity on security prices. Our study differs from earlier studies by presenting evidence for the role of illiquidity spirals in asset valuation. Section 29.3 provides a description of the data and our definitions of illiquidity measures. Section 29.4 presents our results. Section 29.5 presents our conclusions.

29.2 Literature Review

29.2.1 Market Illiquidity Spirals

Early models of market microstructure have hinted at the dynamic nature of stock market liquidity based on returns distribution, market maker inventory, informational events and risk management. (i) Grossman and Miller (1988) predict that exogenous liquidity events coupled with the risk of delayed trade create a demand for immediacy. Market makers supply immediacy by their continuous presence and willingness to bear risk during the time period between the arrival of final buyers and sellers. They conclude that the lower the autocorrelation in rates of return, the higher the equilibrium level of liquidity. (ii) The inventory paradigm of Demsetz (1968), Stoll (1978), and Ho and Stoll (1981) suggests that liquidity depends on factors that influence the risk of holding inventory. Extreme events like the recent financial crisis provoke order imbalances and, thereby, cause inventory overload. (iii) The informed speculation paradigm (Kyle, 1985; Admati and Pfleiderer, 1988) suggests that marketwide changes in liquidity are closely related to previous informational events such as major macro announcements about the state of the economy. (iv) Garleanu and Pedersen (2007) show that a feedback mechanism exists between risk management practices and market liquidity. This study points to a feedback effect—tighter risk management reduces liquidity, which, in turn, leads to tighter risk management. Their findings explain why crises cause sudden drops in liquidity. They also conclude that the resultant market illiquidity ultimately creates pressure on prices. Brunnermeier and Pedersen (2009) present a formal theoretical framework to analyze the liquidity behavior and illiquidity spirals during the periods of crisis. Their model links an asset's market liquidity (i.e. the ease with which it is traded) and traders' funding liquidity (i.e. the ease with which they can obtain funding). Traders provide market liquidity and their ability to do so depends on their access to funding. Conversely, traders' funding, i.e. their capital and margin requirements, depends on the assets' market liquidity. These authors predict that margins are destabilizing, and market liquidity and funding liquidity are mutually reinforcing, leading to illiquidity spirals. One of the main contributions of our paper is to develop empirical measures of illiquidity and loss spirals.

29.2.2 Market Liquidity and Security Valuation

The literature that analyzes the impact of market liquidity on asset valuation can be divided into two categories. The first branch examines the role of market structure and its participants on the valuation of financial assets (e.g. Stoll, 2000; Easley and O'Hara, 2010). Amihud and Mendelsen (1986) argue that if investors value securities based on the trading costs involved, they expect a higher return and assign a lower valuation for securities having the higher bid–ask spread, in order to compensate for their higher cost of trading. The second branch follows the traditional asset-pricing approach (e.g. Fama and French, 1992, 1993, 1995; Fama and MacBeth, 1973) by adding liquidity as a systematically priced factor. Pastor and Stambaugh (2003) find that expected stock returns are related cross-sectionally to the sensitivities of returns to fluctuations in aggregate liquidity. We conjecture that a financial crisis can aggravate the negative implications of illiquidity on asset valuation. Hameed *et al.* (2010) argue that market liquidity can suddenly dry-up during large-scale market declines because market participants engage in panic selling (a demand effect), financial intermediaries withdraw from providing liquidity (a supply effect) or both. Yeyati *et al.* (2008) also predict that during crisis, the secondary market liquidity comes under stress; both trading volume and trading costs increase. Thus, we hypothesize a negative relation between a stock's vulnerability to illiquidity spirals and its valuation.

29.2.3 Studies Motivating our Control Variables

Apart from illiquidity spirals, valuation can be affected by expected future growth rate, leverage, size, dividend policy, required future return and dividend policy (Pastor and Veronesi, 2003). Thus, we include these variables in our regressions.

29.3 Data and Descriptive Statistics

We extract daily closing bid and ask prices, trading volume, ticker symbol, daily closing prices, market capitalization, and permanent company code (PERMCO) for firms in the and S&P 500 (US) for the entire period from November 1982 to December 2010 from the Center for Research in Security Prices (CRSP) database. We gather the price-to-book ratio (data item mnemonic *PTBV*), dividend per share (*DPS*), total assets (*TA*), return on equity (*ROE*), S&P 500 market value (*MV*), and S&P 500 price-to-earnings (*P/E*) from Datastream International.[1] Our final sample comprises observations for 476 firms with data available throughout our sample period for the variables presented in Table 29.1.

---

[1] Total assets and return on equity are the variables *DWTA* and *DWRE*, respectively, from Datastream.

Table 29.1. Descriptive statistics for data sample and proxy variables

Variable label	Number of non-missing observations	Mean	Standard deviation	Minimum	25th Percentile (lower quartile)	50th Percentile (median)	75th Percentile (upper quartile)	Maximum
Price-to-earnings	1550914	26.24	25.11	0.7	14.6	19.8	28.4	146.2
PTBV	848074	3.74	10.64	−422.19	1.85	2.85	4.52	26.07
MV (million $)	2015260	16479	36070	9.88	2523.11	5938.93	14222.08	188086
Return on equity	1667167	16.92	184.21	−71.67	9.48	15.29	21.75	104.13
TA (millions $)	1688046	30.37	123.08	0	2.29	6.44	18.51	538.09
S&P 500 MV (billion $)	1674380	9097.8	3013	1966	7513	10052	11259	13569
S&P 500 return (%)	1704907	0.02	1.26	−22.83	−0.52	0.06	0.6	3.53
Price	2015260	43.63	39.32	0.22	25	37.38	53.38	141.5
Spread (%)	2015260	0.67	1.03	−6.45	0.05	0.28	0.96	4.71
Return (%)	2014214	0	3.49	−353.08	−1.07	0	1.13	7.57
Threshold price	1967420	44.09	38.49	1.59	25.88	38.15	54.06	893.48
Outstanding shares (in '000)	2015260	409.77	950.62	0.32	72.15	160.87	361.41	5141.51
Total volume (in '000)	2015256	3193.5	13602.2	0.1	268.5	912.9	2691.1	36292.5
Dividend per share	1700699	0.54	0.89	0	0	0.28	0.8	2.8

We present summary statistics for our panel of trading data for 476 common stocks that are included in the S&P 500 Index for the entire period November 1982—December 2010. The spread is 100 * (ask price—bid price)/mid-quote. Mid-quote is 0.5 * (bid + ask).

29.3.1 Spiral Measures: Illiquidity Spiral and Loss Spiral

Our illiquidity spiral measure is based on changes in the bid–ask spread and our loss spiral is based on changes in stock prices. The spirals are calculated in two steps. We begin with the description of the illiquidity spiral. In the first step, we assess whether a stock's liquidity on a given day is improving, unchanged or deteriorating based on two joint conditions. As shown in Equation (29.1), a stock day is assigned a value of -1, which indicates improving liquidity, if the spread on the given day is not only less than the spread on the previous day, but is also less than the previous year's benchmark spread by at least half standard deviation. Analogously, a stock day is assigned a value of $+1$ for increasing spread see Equation (29.2), which indicates deteriorating liquidity, if the spread on the given day is more than the spread on the previous day as well as more than the previous year's average spread benchmark by half standard deviation. If the two joint conditions are not met as described above, the stock day is assigned a value of 0 for unchanged liquidity.

If $Spread_{t,\mathrm{yr}} < Spread_{(t-1),\mathrm{yr}}$ and $Spread_{t,\mathrm{yr}} < (Av.\ Sprd_{t,(\mathrm{yr}-1)}$

$- 0.5 * \sigma_{i,\mathrm{av}(\mathrm{yr}-1)})$

then $S_{\mathrm{spiral}} = -1$ \hfill (29.1)

if $Spread_{t,\mathrm{yr}} > Spread_{(t-1),\mathrm{yr}}$ and $Spread_{t,\mathrm{yr}} > (Av.\ Sprd_{t,(\mathrm{yr}-1)}$

$+ 0.5 * \sigma_{i,\mathrm{av}(\mathrm{yr}-1)})$

then $S_{\mathrm{spiral}} = +1$ \hfill (29.2)

otherwise, $S_{\mathrm{spiral}} = 0.$ \hfill (29.3)

In the above equations, $\sigma_{i,\mathrm{av}(\mathrm{yr}-1)}$ is defined as the previous year's standard deviation of spread for the ith stock. The indicator variable S_{spiral} represents the direction of the daily change in illiquidity. In the second step of defining the length of illiquidity spiral, we sum S_{spiral} for 10 day overlapping windows:

$$S_{\mathrm{spiral},10} = \sum_{t=0}^{-9} S_{\mathrm{spiral}}. \hfill (29.4)$$

$S_{\mathrm{spiral},10}$ is the moving sum of S_{spiral} for the last 10 days and captures the strength of the illiquidity spiral in terms of how long it is sustained for each individual stock. A value of -10 for $S_{\mathrm{spiral},10}$ indicates very liquid markets, whereas $+10$ indicates extremely poor liquidity.

Next, we turn our attention to loss spirals, which is similar to that for computing illiquidity spirals. First, we assess whether a stock's value on a given day is increasing, unchanged or decreasing in a statistically significant manner, based on two joint conditions. A stock day is assigned a value of -1 on the day when its price advances if the stock's price is also above the midpoint of the previous year's high and low prices by at least half standard deviation. Analogously a stock day is assigned a value of $+1$ on the day when its price declines if stock's price on the given day is also below the midpoint of the previous year's high and low prices by at least half standard deviation. If the two joint conditions are not met, the stock day is assigned a value of 0 for no significant losses or gains. To summarize, a stock day is categorized in one of the four price loss categories as follows:

If $Price_{t,\mathrm{yr}} < Price_{t-1,\mathrm{yr}}$ and $Price_{t,\mathrm{yr}} < (Midpoint_{(\mathrm{yr}-1)}$
$- 0.5 * \sigma_{i,\mathrm{av}(\mathrm{yr}-1)})$
then $P_{\mathrm{spiral}} = +1$ $\qquad(29.5)$

if $Price_{t,\mathrm{yr}} > Price_{t-1,\mathrm{yr}}$ and $Price_{t,\mathrm{yr}} > (Midpoint_{(\mathrm{yr}-1)}$
$+ 0.5 * \sigma_{i,\mathrm{av}(\mathrm{yr}-1)})$
then $P_{\mathrm{spiral}} = -1$ $\qquad(29.6)$

$$\text{otherwise, } P_{\mathrm{spiral}} = 0. \qquad(29.7)$$

Our loss spiral measure is defined as the sum of the price decline indicators over the previous 10 consecutive days:

$$P_{\mathrm{spiral},10} = \sum_{t=0}^{-9} P_{\mathrm{spiral}}. \qquad(29.8)$$

In our definition of spirals, -10 for $P_{\mathrm{spiral},10}$ indicates a strong bull market, which is usually not alarming for market participants and regulators. However, a loss spiral of $+10$ is associated with severe bear market conditions and would likely be alarming.

We present summary statistics for our panel of trading data for 476 common stocks in Table 29.1. Our sample comprises 1,550,914 stock-day observations for the price-to-earnings (P/E) ratio, and 848 074 observations for the price-to-book (PTBV) ratio. Our key valuation variables P/E and PTBV have mean values of 26.24 and 3.74, respectively. The standard deviation for P/E is 25.11 and its value ranges from 0.7 to 146.2. The standard deviation for PTBV is 10.64 and its value varies from 3.74 to 26.07. We obtain 1,688,046 observations for each firm's total assets and 1,674,380 observations for the S&P 500 market value control variable. The average value of total asset of firms is $30.37 million with standard deviation of 123.08. The mean price of the sample stocks is $43.63 and the average value of the daily spread is 0.67.

In Table 29.2, we present the frequency distribution counts for illiquidity spiral and loss spirals. We adopt two different approaches to quantify the spiral measures. For the sigma illiquidity spiral measure, we follow Equations (29.1) and (29.2). In the alternative approach, we relax the condition regarding the half standard deviation by ignoring the $0.5 * \sigma_{i,\text{av(yr}-1)}$ term and simply compare the spreads on day t with the stock's average spread in the previous year and with its spread on the previous day. Similarly, for the loss spirals, the sigma measure follows

Table 29.2. **Spiral measures computation**

Frequency	Sigma illiquidity spiral measure	Alternative illiquidity spiral measure	Sigma loss spiral measure	Alternative loss spiral measure
−10	15	41	509	592
−9	253	856	6381	7215
−8	3143	7880	33,726	37,901
−7	25,324	46,635	102,021	113,595
−6	96,460	152,715	189,855	210,433
−5	189,715	271,280	242,098	265,114
−4	225,945	303,289	216,172	232,329
−3	206,800	266,360	140,671	144,014
−2	185,460	217,172	74,685	67,873
−1	183,545	176,264	45,670	32,438
0	293,262	136,569	146,501	23,852
1	168,463	106,237	45,618	31,096
2	132,206	84,036	66,830	60,281
3	106,779	73,726	116,283	120,950
4	90,621	71,049	169,625	187,656
5	66,734	59,435	181,347	205,849
6	31,482	31,316	137,599	158,543
7	7965	8953	71,322	82,699
8	1014	1334	23,563	27,332
9	61	99	4466	5133
10	3	4	308	355

Number of spread and loss spirals. Column 1 shows the frequency, which is cumulative spiral count. Column (1) indicates the direction and strength of spirals. The higher the frequency count, the higher the intensity of spirals. Column (2) presents the number of illiquidity spiral counts of 10 days duration based on the calculation done in Equations (29.2) and (29.4). Column (3) shows the number of illiquidity spirals, ignoring the variations in the spread series of the previous year. Our computation for this variable is similar to the sigma illiquidity spiral measure except we do not assume that $\sigma_{i,\text{av(yr}-1)} = 0$. We computed sigma loss spirals using Equation (29.4). To compute this measure, we followed the condition described in Equations (29.1), (29.2), (29.5) and (29.8). The last column indicates loss spirals without assuming that $\sigma_{i,\text{av(yr}-1)} = 0$.

Equations (29.3) and (29.4), and the alternative measure relaxes the condition regarding standard deviation. The density of observation at count zero for the spirals indicates that the majority of time markets behave normally. Spiral counts of 10 are rare, but can be observed in the data.

Figure 29.2 presents the plots for frequency distribution for illiquidity spiral and loss spirals. For the loss spiral measures, note the bimodal nature of the distribution, which indicates that zero returns or unchanged prices are not as common as unchanged liquidity.

29.4 Results

29.4.1 Spiral Measures and Asset Valuation

Here, we analyze the impact of our spiral measures on the security valuations. We estimate the following regression model with *PTBV* of S&P 500 constituent securities as the dependent

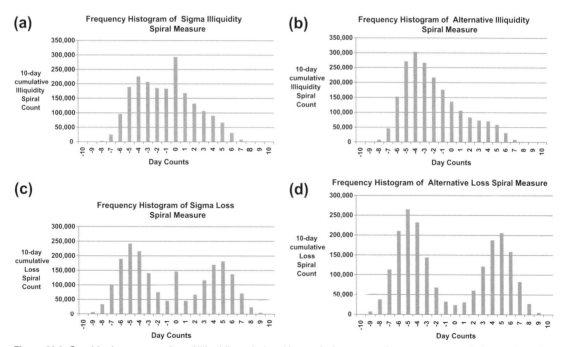

Figure 29.2 Graphical representation of illiquidity spiral and loss spiral measures frequency counts during study period (1982–2010). (a) Frequency histogram of sigma illiquidity spiral measure. (b) Frequency histogram of alternative illiquidity spiral measure. (c) Frequency histogram of sigma loss spiral measure. (d) Frequency histogram of alternative loss spiral measure.

variable and our new spiral measures, $P_{\text{spiral},10}$ and $S_{\text{spiral},10}$, as the key independent variables, as follows:

$$PTBV = \beta_0 + \beta_1\, P_{\text{spiral},10} + \beta_2\, S_{\text{spiral},10} + \beta_3\, PTBV_{\text{S\&P 500}}$$
$$+ \beta_4\, Excess\ Return + \beta_5\, TA + \beta_6\, ROE + \beta_7\, DPS\ Dummy$$
$$+ \varepsilon,$$

$$(29.9)$$

where, $P/E_{\text{S\&P 500}}$, *Excess Return*, *TA* and *ROE* are defined above, and *Excess Return* is the difference between the S&P 500 Index return and the risk-free rate obtained from the Fama–French data library. *DPS Dummy* is a dummy variable that equals one on the ex-dividend date and zero otherwise.

Table 29.3. Multivariate regression: impact of spirals on *PTBV*

Independent variables	Dependent variable: PTBV		
	Model 5.1	Model 5.2	Model 5.3
Intercept	3.72**	2.79**	3.18**
	(303.19)	(70.93)	(89.21)
$P_{\text{spiral},10}$ (loss spiral)	−0.034**	−0.030**	−0.032**
	(−13.22)	(−11.67)	(−15.30)
$S_{\text{spiral},10}$ (illiquidity spiral)	−0.003	−0.008*	−0.049**
	(−0.77)	(−2.00)	(−15.56)
$PTBV_{\text{S\&P 500}}$		0.001**	0.002**
		(24.53)	(66.66)
Excess Return		0.041**	0.021**
		(4.43)	(2.86)
TA			−0.58**
			(−95.87)
ROE			0.004**
			(98.12)
DPS Dummy			−0.63**
			(−27.35)
Number of observations	848,064	848,064	834,231
R^2	0.0002	0.001	0.0306

We estimate the following ordinary least squares model using panel data: $PTBV = \beta_0 + \beta_1\, P_{\text{spiral},10} + \beta_2\, S_{\text{spiral},10} + \beta_3\, PTBV_{\text{S\&P 500}} + \beta_4$ *Excess Return* $+ \beta_5\, TA + \beta_6\, ROE + \beta_7\, DPS\ Dummy + \varepsilon$, where $P_{\text{spiral},10}$ is the loss spiral measure for each firm calculated using Equation (29.8) and $S_{\text{spiral},10}$ is illiquidity spiral calculated using Equation (29.4). $PTBV_{\text{S\&P 500}}$ is the daily price-to-book value for the S&P 500 index. *Excess Return* is the difference between the return on the S&P 500 Index and the risk-free rate. In Model 5.3, we include the natural log of total assets in millions $ (*TA*), return on equity (*ROE*) and *DPS Dummy*, which equals one if a firm pays a dividend and zero otherwise. *t*-statistics are reported in parentheses. Significance at the *0.05 and **0.01 levels, respectively.

Table 29.4. Multivariate regression: impact of spirals on *P/E*

	Dependent variable: P/E ratio		
Independent variables	**Model 6.1**	**Model 6.2**	**Model 6.3**
Intercept	25.62**	25.55	35.41
	(1202.3)	(763.56)	(743)
$P_{spiral,10}$ (loss spiral)	−0.33**	−0.33**	−0.36**
	(−73.41)	(−73.18)	(−80.04)
$S_{spiral,10}$ (illiquidity spiral)	−0.37**	−0.37**	−0.33**
	(−54.64)	(−54.16)	(−48.88)
$P/E_{S\&P\ 500}$		0.002**	0.015**
		(2.53)	(16.68)
Excess Return		0.13**	0.11**
		(7.83)	(7.17)
TA			−1.36**
			(−106.78)
ROE			−0.004**
			(−29.37)
DPS Dummy			−10.13**
			(−205.36)
Number of observations	1550,914	1550,914	1525,707
R^2	0.008	0.008	0.06

We estimate the following ordinary least squares model using panel data. $P/E = \beta_1 + \beta_1\ P_{spiral10} + \beta_2\ S_{spiral10} + \beta_3\ P/E_{S\&P\ 500} + \beta_4$ *Excess Return* $+ \beta_5\ TA + \beta_6\ ROE + \beta_7\ DPS\ Dummy + \varepsilon$, where $P_{spiral,10}$ is the loss spiral measure for each firm calculated using Equation (29.8) and $S_{spiral,10}$ is illiquidity spiral calculated using Equation (29.4). $P/E_{S\&P\ 500}$ is the daily price-to-earning value for the S&P 500 index. *Excess Return* is the difference between the return on the S&P 500 Index and the risk-free rate. In Model 5.3, we include the natural log of total assets in millions $ (*TA*), return on equity (*ROE*) and *DPS Dummy*, which equals one if a firm pays a dividend and zero otherwise. t-statistics are reported in parentheses. Significance at the *0.05 and **0.01 levels, respectively.

Table 29.3 presents the results of our estimations of three subset of model based on Equation (29.9). The results for all three models confirm that the loss spirals and illiquidity spirals affect *PTBV*. The coefficients for both the loss spiral and the illiquidity spiral are negative and statistically significant at the 1% level. Thus, valuations are lower for stocks that are more vulnerable to spirals. Positive contemporaneous returns serve to enhance a stock's valuation. The negative coefficient for *TA* indicates that *PTBV* is lower for bigger firms and higher for smaller firms. *PTBV* is higher for firms with higher returns on *PTBV* because investors are willing to pay more for high *ROE* firms. The coefficient of *PTBV*$_{S\&P\ 500}$, marketwide *PTBV* ratio, is positive as expected, indicating that overall market sentiment affects individual stock valuations. The coefficient of *DPS Dummy* is negative because the payment of dividends can signal a lack of growth opportunities. Dividends may also have adverse tax treatment relative to capital gains resulting from the earnings retention alternative. These reasons may justify lower valuations for dividend payers than for non-payers. Overall, the regression results imply that after controlling for several potential determinants of valuation, loss spiral and illiquidity spiral stand out as important determinants of valuation and they adversely affect a stock's *PTBV*.

Next, using *P/E* of individual securities as a measure of asset valuation, we examine the impact of loss and illiquidity spirals on valuation by estimating the following regression:

$$P/E = \beta_0 + \beta_1 \, P_{\text{spiral,10}} + \beta_2 S_{\text{spiral,10}} + \beta_3 \, P/E_{\text{S\&P 500}}$$
$$+ \, \beta_4 \, Excess \, Return + \beta_5 \, TA + \beta_6 \, ROE + \beta_7 \, DPS \, Dummy$$
$$+ \, \varepsilon.$$

$$(29.10)$$

Table 29.4 presents the results, which are largely consistent with our earlier results for the *PTBV* models. The signs of the coefficients of $P_{\text{spiral,10}}$ and $S_{\text{spiral,10}}$ are negative and statistically significant at the 0.01 level, which confirms the adverse impact of spirals on valuation. The coefficient of $P/E_{\text{S\&P 500}}$, marketwide *P/E* ratio, is positive as expected, suggesting that overall market sentiment affects individual stock valuations.

29.5 Conclusion

We define and investigate illiquidity spirals, which measure the number of consecutive days on which: (i) The closing bid–ask spread for a firm is above average and (ii) the firm's liquidity is worsening. Loss spirals measure the number of consecutive days on which: (i) A stock's price is below average and (ii) is declining. Although spirals are rare, they cause significant damage during periods of financial crisis and market downturns. In regressions with valuation ratios as dependent variables, and controlling for several other determinants of valuations, we find that our measures of firm valuation are significantly and negatively related to the presence of spirals. Stocks that are more vulnerable to illiquidity and loss spirals have lower price-to-earning and market-to-book ratios, suggesting that spirals play an important role in determining asset valuations.

References

Admati, A.R., Pfleiderer, P., 1988. A theory of intraday patterns: volume and price variability. Review of Financial Studies 1 (1), 3–40.

Amihud, Y., Mendelson, M., 1986. Liquidity and stock returns. Financial Analysts Journal 42 (3), 43–48.

Brunnermeier, M.K., 2008. Deciphering the liquidity and credit crunch 2007–08. NBER Working Paper 14612. NBER, Cambridge, MA.

Brunnermeier, M.K., Pedersen, L.H., 2009. Market liquidity and funding liquidity. Review of Financial Studies 22 (6), 2201–2238.

Demsetz, H., 1968. The cost of transacting. Quarterly Journal of Economics 82 (1), 33–53.

Easley, D., O'Hara, M., 2010. Liquidity and valuation in an uncertain world. Journal of Financial Economics 97 (1), 1–11.

Fama, E.F., French, K., 1993. Common risk factors in the returns on bonds and stocks. Journal of Financial Economics 33 (1), 3–56.

Fama, E.F., French, K., 1992. The cross-section of expected stock returns. Journal of Finance 47 (2), 427–465.

Fama, E.F., French, K., 1995. Size and book-to-market factors in earnings and returns. Journal of Finance 50 (1), 131–155.

Fama, E.F., MacBeth, J., 1973. Risk, return and equilibrium: empirical tests. Journal of Political Economy 81 (3), 607–636.

Garleanu, N.B., Pedersen, L.H., 2007. Liquidity and risk management. NBER Working Paper 12887. NBER, Cambridge, MA.

Grossman, S.J., Miller, M.H., 1988. Liquidity and market structure. Journal of Finance 43 (3), 617–633.

Hameed, A., Kang, W., Viswanathan, S., 2010. Stock market declines and liquidity. Journal of Finance 65 (1), 257–293.

Ho, T., Stoll, H.R., 1981. Optimal dealer pricing under transactions and return uncertainty. Journal of Financial Economics 9 (1), 47–73.

Kyle, A.S., 1985. Continuous auctions and insider trading. Econometrica 53 (6), 1315–1335.

Pastor, L., Veronesi, P., 2003. Stock valuation and learning about profitability. Journal of Finance 58 (5), 1749–1789.

Pastor, L., Stambaugh, R.F., 2003. Liquidity Risk and expected stock returns. Journal of Political Economy 111 (3), 642–685.

Stoll, H.R., 1978. The supply of dealer services in securities markets. Journal of Finance 33 (4), 1133–1151.

Stoll, H.R., 2000. Friction. Journal of Finance 55 (4), 1479–1514.

Yeyati, E.V., Schmukler, S., Van, H.N., 2008. Emerging market liquidity and crises. Journal of the European Economic Association 6 (2–3), 668–682.

30

A RATING-BASED APPROACH TO PRICING SOVEREIGN CREDIT RISK

Marco Rossi and Gabriele Zinna
International Monetary Fund

CHAPTER OUTLINE

30.1 Introduction

Assessing credit risk is key to evaluating the adequacy of a lender's prudential balances, in informing its loan pricing policies, and in developing internal rating systems and risk management processes. In practice, credit risk can be assessed by first estimating transition matrices and then developing credit rating models. However, sovereign ratings seem to behave differently from corporates. Specifically, sovereign ratings have been traditionally more stable, as sovereigns have generally displayed a lower probability of downgrade than corporates. In fact, sovereign defaults tend to cluster on major regional events and are largely the outcome of political decisions (Duffie and Singleton, 2003).

Although rating agencies generally publish sovereign transition matrices estimated at a yearly frequency, this chapter relies on the homogeneous hazard rate (HHR) method to estimate rating

Rethinking Valuation and Pricing Models. http://dx.doi.org/10.1016/B978-0-12-415875-7.00030-0

transition matrices on *continuously* observed sovereign rating histories from Moody's. Such a continuous-time method achieves a better performance than the discrete multinomial estimator traditionally used by rating agencies. In particular, the HHR method efficiently exploits all the information available. For example, it detects the presence of "rare events" (e.g. the default of an Aa-rated sovereign) and provides point estimates of the default probabilities. By estimating conditional transition matrices, we find evidence of negative correlation between the international business cycle and sovereign default probabilities. Using transitions matrices estimated over a timespan sufficiently long to capture a broad range of credit events remains, however, preferable for risk management applications. The risk is that the estimation of conditional matrices over short periods and over a small panel, as the sovereign one, raises concern about the precision of the estimates, while neglecting the presence of rare events.

We then calibrate the estimated transition matrices to the eurodollar bonds and develop a rating-based term structure model, using two alternative methodologies: A numerical technique proposed by Kijima and Komoribayashi (1998) and a framework proposed by Lando (1998, 2001), which allows us to control for the business cycle effect.

After having calibrated the transition probabilities using the method proposed by Kijima and Komoribayashi (1998), spread option prices are derived. Such options are particularly useful in quantifying potential liquidity risks for a lender. For instance, by purchasing a put spread option a sovereign acquires the right to sell its own debt at a predetermined spread over a reference rate, say the interest rate on US Treasuries. If the same sovereign is borrowing from a specific lender at a certain spread, the sovereign is likely to pay back this lender once the market spread falls below the spread on the loan. In this regard, the probability of a put spread option being exercised helps the lender quantifying its liquidity risk. Equally important, we test the robustness of Kijima and Komoribayashi's results by pricing spread options for different recovery rates.

Finally, in order to control for the business cycle effect, and following Lando (1998), this chapter uses the US interest rate as the driver of sovereign risk-neutral transition matrices and, ultimately, of credit spreads. The business cycle effect was first detected by Nickell *et al.* (2000) for corporates; there are significant differences in the estimates of transition matrices according to different states of the business cycle (peak, normal and trough). Moreover, our pricing is also consistent with a vast literature on sovereign credit spreads detecting the existence of a systematic global factor driving sovereign credit spreads, which is ultimately linked to the US economy.

The remainder of the chapter is organized as follows. Section 30.2 reviews the relevant literature and presents the methodology. Section 30.3 describes the data, while Section 30.4 reports the estimated transition matrices and investigates the presence of a business cycle effect. Section 30.5 derives credit-spread option and defaultable bond prices, after having calibrated the estimated transition matrices to market data, using two alternative techniques. Section 30.6 concludes.

30.2 Literature Review and Methodology

The empirical literature on credit risk is extensive. A pioneering study on transition matrix estimation is Nickell *et al.* (2000), which implements both a discrete multinomial and ordered probitive approach, arguing the necessity of conditioning the transition matrices on several factors (industry, country and business cycle). Lando and Skodeberg (2002) improves the estimation in a continuous-time setting, whereas Christensen *et al.* (2004) introduces a technique to bootstrap confidence sets and a continuous-time hidden Markov chain model to handle non-Markov effects. Comparably little attention has, however, been given to sovereigns—the few exceptions being Hu *et al.* (2002), Wei (2003), and Fuertes and Kalotychou (2007).

The financial literature looks at credit risk by using either structural or reduced-form models. Structural models identify the default event with the time the asset value of the firm falls below the value of its liabilities. This assessment can occur at a specific point in time or on a continuous basis as in *first-passage models*. By contrast, reduced-form models directly model the stochastic intensity of a default, with the default event given by the first arrival time of a Poisson process and the intensity of default by its mean. Structural and reduced-form models represent the natural framework to price risky securities and manage portfolio risk.

Rating-based models, in which a finite state space Markov process determines the evolution of migration and default intensities for a generic issuer, belong to the family of reduced-form models. Among others, Jarrow *et al.* (1997) propose a Markov model for the term structure of credit risk spreads, such that issuers' credit ratings are the exclusive drivers of the likelihood of default.

Markov chains represent the natural framework to cast credit migration probabilities and are usually distinguished into discrete-time versus continuous-time Markov chains. The discrete multinomial or cohort method is widely used across practitioners (Moody's, 2007). Such method assumes that credit rating migrations are modeled according to a multinomial distribution. There are $K-1$ possible outcomes of migrating from state i to $j = 1, ..., K$ $(i \neq j)$ with probability p_{ij}; there are N sovereigns and T discrete periods $(t = 0, 1, 2, ..., T)$. The discrete multinomial estimator, however, neglects the exact date of the transition and constrains the analysis to multiples of the basic period length (one year).

By contrast, the continuous-time HHR estimator efficiently uses the information on the time a sovereign spends in a certain rating class. This estimator assumes independent durations (or migrations) and time homogeneity. The intensity estimator trades off the number of transitions from i to j, $N_{ij}(T)$, and the number of sovereigns in rating class i in time s, $Y_i(s)$, such as

$$\hat{\lambda}_{ij} = N_{ij}(T) / \int_0^T Y_i(s) \, ds.$$ Intuitively, the intensity estimator scales the number of transitions from i to j, $(i \neq j)$, over the period $[0; T]$ by the overall time spent in rating class i. Estimates of the intensities $\lambda(t)_{ij}$, i.e. the probability of moving from state i to state j conditional of the sovereign survival up to time t, are the building blocks of any rating-based term structure model.

The HHR method attaches probabilities different from zero to rare events, even if they are not observed. For instance, if a sovereign transits through an A rating moving from an Aaa to a Baa rating within the period of one year, the continuous estimates of the intensities incorporates this information, while the discrete estimator would read it as a direct transition from Aaa to Baa.

The use of the HHR estimator also allows us simply to simulate fake rating histories and derive bootstrapped confidence intervals. The bootstrap exercise consists of using the estimated intensities to simulate a number of fake monthly datasets, each with the same structure as the original, and estimating the statistic of interest for each dataset (see, e.g. Fuertes and Kalotychou, 2007). Such an exercise is particularly important as in several risk management applications the entire distribution of the probability of default is required. The pricing of financial securities may also require the use of simulated rating histories (e.g. pricing financial securities with credit triggers requires information about the probability of migrating to non-default states).

Besides bootstrapping the probabilities of default there is a second important issue. Far migrations (reflecting rare and severe events such as defaults) have higher economic and financial impact than near migrations. These issues are looked at with a mobility index, which quantifies the amount of probability mass distributed over the off-diagonal entries, and represents a statistical tool to compare different transition matrices and estimators. Different mobility indexes can be constructed depending on the objective (e.g. risk management, pricing etc.). As for risk management, Jafry and Schuermann (2004) propose the *distribution discriminatory criterion*, which is sensitive to the distribution of the off-diagonal mass. This statistic is *the average of the singular values of the mobility matrix* and provides a picture of distribution of the off-diagonal probability mass (but no information about how far the probabilities are concentrated from the main diagonal). The higher the index, the higher the probability mass spread over the off-diagonal entries. The difference of the mobility indices calculated for different samples provides a statistical comparison of the degree of mobility.

30.3 Dataset

The dataset consists of sovereign bond rating histories published by Moody's Investor Service (2007) in June 2007 (*Sovereign Default and Recovery Rates, 1983–2006*) and updated through July 2007. The overall sample covers monthly sovereign long-term bond rating histories in the period July 1984 to July 2007. In case of multiple ratings, the lowest is considered the most representative indicator of a country's likelihood of defaulting. Sovereigns are rated from low to high credit risk as: Aaa, Aa, A, Baa, Ba, B, Caa, Ca, C, plus numerical modifiers 1, 2 and 3 (for ratings Aaa to Caa) to further differentiate across sovereigns' creditworthiness. In this exercise, we use eight categories: Aaa, Aa, A, Baa, Ba, B, C and default (D). If a country fully cures "default" within a specified grace period, then Moody's dataset excludes these events from the default list. The whole dataset therefore covers 102 sovereigns. Taking into account withdrawn ratings ($n = 5$) and defaulted countries ($n = 9$) that re-entered the sample, the study considers 116 issuers.

30.4 Transition Matrices Estimation

Rating migration matrices describe the evolution of credit quality over time and provide a complete picture of the credit risk associated with each rating class. Sovereign transition matrices are stable (most of the mass is concentrated on the main diagonal), reflecting the likelihood of a country to finish the year with the same rating it had at the beginning of the year. The amount of mobility depends on the off-diagonal entries; the upper (lower) triangle reflects transition to lower (higher) credit standing classes within a one-year horizon.

The HHR estimates weight the transitions observed in the sample window (1984−2007) between classes i and j by the time spent in the starting rating class i (Table 30.1). The elements on the main diagonal of the generator, λ_{ii}, describe the probability that the sovereign moves to another rating over an infinitesimal time step (one month in this study). The probability of observing a transition increases as the credit standing deteriorates, except for classes Ba and B ($\lambda_{Ba} > \lambda_B$).

Moving to the credit migration matrix (by taking the exponential of the generator) one can observe that, unlike in the

Table 30.1. HHR

Generator/intensity matrix								
	Aaa	**Aa**	**A**	**Baa**	**Ba**	**B**	**C**	**Default**
Aaa	−2.32	2.32	—	—	—	—	—	—
Aa	5.03	−5.94	0.91	—	—	—	—	—
A	—	3.74	−6.08	2.34	—	—	—	—
Baa	—	—	9.39	−13.35	3.96	—	—	—
Ba	—	—	—	7.67	−15.83	7.19	—	0.96
B	—	—	—	—	4.70	−14.68	7.05	2.94
C	—	—	—	—	—	25.11	−50.21	25.11
Default	—	—	—	—	—	—	—	—
Transition probability matrix								
	Aaa	**Aa**	**A**	**Baa**	**Ba**	**B**	**C**	**Default**
Aaa	97.76	2.23	0.01	0.00	0.00	0.00	0.00	0.00
Aa	4.83	94.30	0.86	0.01	0.00	0.00	0.00	0.00
A	0.09	3.52	94.22	2.12	0.04	0.00	0.00	0.00
Baa	0.00	0.16	8.53	87.73	3.42	0.12	0.00	0.02
Ba	0.00	0.00	0.32	6.64	85.64	6.20	0.19	1.00
B	0.00	0.00	0.00	0.16	4.05	87.17	5.14	3.48
C	0.00	0.00	0.00	0.01	0.45	18.31	61.13	20.09
Default	—	—	—	—	—	—	—	100.00

The top panel presents the empirical generator, estimated with the HHR method over the full sample size, from August 1984 to July 2007. The bottom panel shows the empirical transition probability matrix. Note that "−" denotes zeros, whereas "0.00" denotes particularly small numbers.

discrete multinomial case (not reported), the HHR transition matrix has all the entries different from zero, i.e. the probability mass is spread over all entries. The HHR estimator attaches a positive probability, although extremely small, even to defaults from investment grade classes. Again, the reason is that the continuous estimator assigns probabilities different from zero to direct transitions that are not observed in sample. Also, the probability of default from the C rating class (20.1%) is considerably higher since the discrete method neglects a transition in C before default. Moreover, the continuous-time estimator provides accurate estimates of the default probabilities for any credit rating.

30.4.1 In-sample analysis: Business cycle effect

The estimated transition matrix for the sample period 1997–2007 (not reported) is similar to the full sample one. The main difference relates to the slightly higher probabilities of default and a higher probability of leaving the Aa class. A further exercise consists of splitting the period into subperiods of equal size, 1997–2001 and 2002–2007. We find that the two transition matrices are extremely different. The 1997–2001 matrix shows higher probability of defaults over all the rows than the 2002–2007 matrix. The latter is lower triangular, portraying a period with a high probability of improving the credit standing.

Figure 30.1 presents the yearly mobility index (with bootstrapped confidence intervals) and the business cycle. The cycle has been separated from the trend by means of the

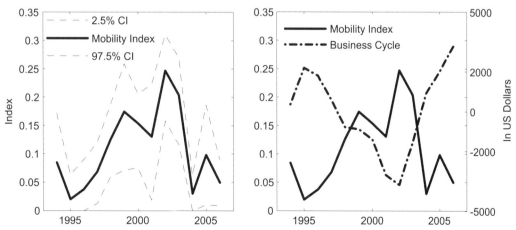

Figure 30.1 Mobility index and business cycle. (Left) Mobility index with the bootstrapped confidence intervals, 2.5 and 97.5%. (Right) Mobility index (left y-axes) and business cycle in US dollar (right y-axes).

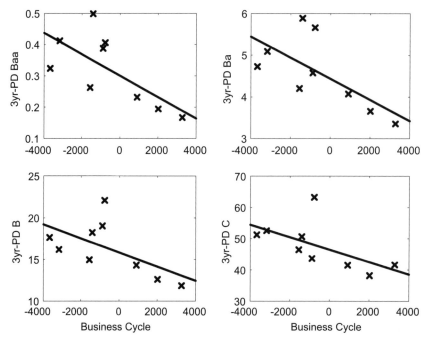

Figure 30.2 Probability of default versus the business cycle. Three-year probabilities of default are plotted against the business cycle (in US dollars) for the period 1998–2007.

Hodrick–Prescott filter. The mobility index varies through time and is negatively correlated with the business cycle. The correlation between the mobility index and the cycle time series ranges from a minimum of −0.49 for the period 1985–2007 to the maximum negative correlation of −0.9 for the period 2002–2007.

Figure 30.2 shows that the probability of default is negatively correlated with the business cycle, irrespective of the rating class. The negative correlation increases when only the most recent years in the sample are considered, ranging from −0.57 for the C class to −0.82 for the Aa class.

The presence of a business cycle effect has important asset pricing implications. In theory, agents should demand a premium above the expected default losses to hold defaultable securities that co-move with the business cycle. Risk adverse agents prefer to hold securities that provide insurance against downturns.

30.5 Asset Pricing

The credit migration matrices estimated from the sovereign rating histories are defined under the objective (or historical) probability measure. While these matrices are directly used in risk management applications, they need to be risk adjusted to be used to price securities or credit derivatives as a risk-neutral probability measure is required. The risk-neutral probability measure reflects agents' aversion to (the uncertainty of) the timing of default. For this reason, we would expect higher probabilities of default under the risk-neutral measure than under the historical measure. In practice, moving from one probability measure to the other requires extracting risk premia from market data.

In order to extract (risk-neutral) probabilities of default from market data, we first need to assume a model to price defaultable bonds. In particular, we assume that (i) the risk-free interest rate and the default process are independent, (ii) the recovery rate (δ) is known, and (iii) the survival probability is rating dependent, where $Q_i(\tau > T)$ denotes the probability of surviving until time T for a sovereign with rating i. It follows that, the bond price for a sovereign rated i is $v_i(t, T) = v_0(t, T)\delta + v_0(t, T)(1 - \delta) Q_i(\tau > T)$, where $v_0(t,T)$ denotes the price at time t of a default-free bond with maturity T. The risk-neutral probability of survival can then be recovered.

We use the US Sovereign Strips as the default free benchmark term structure from 1 to 10 years. We then use daily yields on 36 actively traded eurodollar bonds from Bloomberg covering 25 sovereigns as proxies for the yields on sovereign debt. Yield term structures are sorted by the sovereign rating and averaged. Table 30.2 reports the term structure of discount bonds (estimated as of

Table 30.2. Eurodollar bond term structure

	1 Year	2 Years	3 Years	5 Years	7 Years	10 Years
US Strip	4.26	4.30	4.35	4.42	4.52	4.83
Aaa	4.87	4.67	4.73	5.02	5.12	5.20
Aa	5.10	4.94	5.01	5.27	5.39	5.52
A	5.19	5.07	5.15	5.38	5.54	5.69
Baa	5.34	5.27	5.38	5.60	5.78	5.96
Ba	5.76	5.77	5.90	6.16	6.35	6.58
B	6.64	6.79	6.93	7.30	7.45	7.80
C	8.21	8.55	8.70	9.28	9.31	9.86

Term structure of discount yields per rating class against a maturity from 1 to 10 years on 14 August 2007. The US Strip is assumed the risk-free interest rate. The yields have been extracted from on the run eurodollar bonds quoted on Bloomberg LP.

14 August 2007). We use two methods to risk adjust the estimated transition probability matrices. Each method assumes a specific parameterization of the dependence of the risk-neutral transition matrix on the risk premiums.

30.5.1 A first calibration technique: Pricing spread options

A first approach consists of adjusting all entries of the generator, except for the absorbing state ones. The idea is that the risk premium varies with the starting rating class. This framework was proposed initially by Jarrow *et al.* (1997), and then refined by Kijima and Komoribayashi (1998) assuming that the risk premium adjustment is independent of the migration state *only if* it is not the default one.

Table 30.3 shows the estimated risk premium adjustments for the generator matrix for the full sample 1985–2007. A number of results follow. First, for classes from Aaa to Ba, the risk adjustments are smaller than one. Risk adjustments below one stem from the (risk-neutral) spread-based estimate of default probability being higher than the (objective) ratings-based estimate: The higher the difference, the lower the risk adjustment. Consistent with numerical results in the literature, a lower recovery rate implies higher *risk premium* adjustments (Figure 30.3). Overall, the higher the recovery rate, the more volatile the risk premium adjustment.

We then use the calibrated matrices to price European spread options written on the yield spread and test the robustness of the results to different recovery rates. A put spread option gives the

Table 30.3. **Risk premium adjustments**

	1 Year	2 Years	3 Years	4 Years	5 Years	6 Years	7 Years	8 Years	9 Years	10 Years	UB
Aaa	0.994	0.999	0.996	0.990	0.993	0.995	0.995	1.000	1.000	1.000	1.000
Aa	0.992	0.996	0.993	0.989	0.988	0.993	0.989	0.995	0.995	0.995	1.000
A	0.991	0.994	0.992	0.990	0.987	0.990	0.989	0.997	0.996	0.994	1.000
Baa	0.990	0.992	0.989	0.987	0.986	0.985	0.987	0.996	0.993	0.985	1.000
Ba	0.996	0.997	0.995	0.990	0.993	0.990	0.992	0.995	0.992	0.974	1.010
B	1.013	1.012	1.011	1.005	1.016	1.014	1.029	1.036	1.036	1.036	1.036
C	1.206	1.192	1.183	1.129	1.154	1.160	1.054	0.776	0.730	0.090	1.252

The risk premium adjustments for 1–10 years estimated over the whole sample 1984–2007. The numerical algorithm follows Kijima and Komoribayashi (1998). The last column "UB" denotes the upper bound. The risk adjustment is restricted to not exceeding this number.

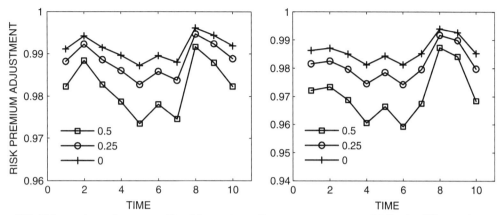

Figure 30.3 Risk premium adjustments. The risk premium adjustments are computed following Kijima and Komoribayashi (1998). (Left) Risk premium adjustment against time (years) for rating A for different recovery rate assumptions: 0, 25 and 50%. (Right) The same for rating Ba.

right to buy a sovereign bond at a given spread (say 2%) to the US Treasury. The put option price is computed as the risk-neutral expectation, conditional on the current rating i, of the future discounted payoffs.[1]

Figure 30.4 presents the prices of a series of put options with a 2% strike rate and maturity date fixed at $T = 10$. The time paths of the put prices vary with the rating class. For high credit rating classes, the credit spread increases with time because of a higher probability of migrating to lower credit quality classes. Accordingly, the option premium falls over time. Low-grade issuers' spreads tend to be lower in the future, the reason being that the probability of default is higher in the first years. Ultimately, this implies an increasing put premium.

A theoretical analysis of the impact of the recovery rate assumption on put option prices is complicated by contrasting effects of the recovery rate on (i) the option intrinsic value and (ii) risk-neutral probabilities. It therefore remains an empirical question. We find that *only* for sufficiently long maturities can option prices significantly depend on the recovery rate. In particular, the put option premium is particularly high for very low recovery rates. Figure 30.4(B) shows that the risk-neutral probability of exercising the option decreases with maturity for

---

[1] Given a strike yield K and the underlying yield spread $\Delta_j(t, T)$, with the date of option maturity t and of the bond maturity T, the option price is $Put_i = v_0(0, t)E_i^Q[\{K - \Delta_{\eta_t}(t, T)\}_+]$, where the risk-neutral expectation (E_i^Q) depends on the initial rating i at time zero (e.g. $i = $ Aa at time t $= 0$).

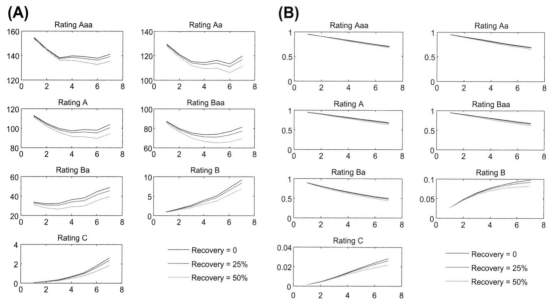

Figure 30.4 Spread put option premium. (A) Premia (in basis points) of put options with maturity from one to seven years and strike price K equal to 2%. Prices are computed for all rating classes assuming three recovery rates: 0%, 25% and 50%. (B) Probability of exercising the put options with maturity from one to seven years and strike price K equal to 2%.

ratings from Aaa to Ba, unlike for ratings B and C. As for the recovery rate assumption, the difference across different probabilities is higher for investment rate classes.

30.5.2 A second calibration technique: Pricing defaultable bonds

A second calibration method proposed by Lando (1998, 2001) gives an explicit solution to the risk premium adjustment. Assuming that the generator matrix allows an eigenvector/ eigenvalue decomposition, the eigenvalues can then be multiplied by the risk adjustment matrix. In this way the risk-adjusted generator becomes time dependent. In addition, such a framework can be extended so that the transition intensities can be driven by underlying factors such as the business cycle.

In this framework, multiperiod transition probability matrices are conditional on the continuous path of the underlying factor. By simulating random paths of the underlying factor, and averaging over the conditional transition matrices, one can recover the unconditional transition matrix. Here, we model the stochastic factor as the one-year US strip interest rate, again

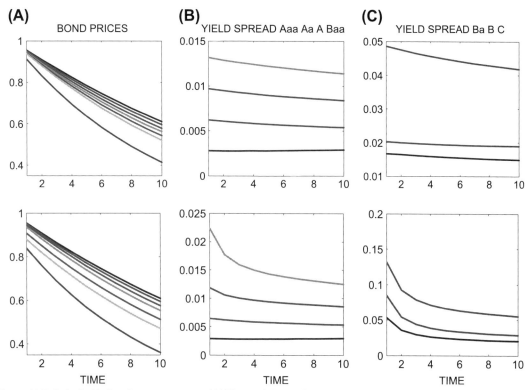

Figure 30.5 Defaultable bond term structures. (A) The top left panel presents the defaultable bond price term structure for maturities 1–10 years. The highest curve belongs to sovereign Aaa and the lowest to sovereign C (thereby in all the other curves, the higher the credit standing, the higher the curve). The remaining two plots in (A) show the credit spread term structure. (B) Bond prices assuming a loss different from 100%. The lower the credit rating, the higher the risk neutral expected loss, i.e. L = (0.4, 0.45, 0.5, 0.55, 0.6, 0.8, 0.85, 0.9).

assuming the US interest rate as a proxy for the "world" business cycle. We conveniently assume (i) a *Vasicek* risk-neutral process for the US interest rate and (ii) an affine dependence of the intensity matrix eigenvectors on the interest rate. Such assumptions allow for the computation of *defaultable bond* prices.[2]

The top of panels Figure 30.5 presents the 10-year *defaultable bond* term structure and the credit spread term structure, assuming a 100% loss in case of default (zero recovery rate). The intensity matrix estimated with the HHR over the period 1984–2007 is the same as in Table 30.1. The dependence

---

[2] This approach may generate negative transition intensities, even for small fluctuation of the interest rate. However, this can be fixed by maintaining the non-default intensities constants and modeling the default probabilities as functions of the interest rate (Huge and Lando, 1999).

parameters are calibrated to the term structure of sovereign credit spreads on 14 August 2007. Finally, the Vasicek parameters are estimated using the historical data on the US Sovereign Strip over the period 1997–2007. We find that the credit spread term structure is slightly decreasing over time.

The defaultable bond term structure is then calibrated assuming different recovery rates per rating class.[3] In short, we construct an "artificial" intensity matrix by adjusting the default probabilities of the original (estimated) intensity matrix for the fractional loss of market value upon default and the risk-free rate (Huge and Lando, 1999; Duffie and Singleton, 2003). In this way we can price defaultable bonds as if they were risk free. As shown in the bottom panels of Figure 30.5, such adjustment for the recovery rate yields complex effects on bond prices. In particular, speculative ratings experience an increase in the level of interest rates combined with an increase of the curvature at short horizons.

30.6 Conclusions

This study provides a rating-based framework to manage portfolio sovereign credit risk, and to price sovereign risky securities and credit derivatives.

Estimating sovereign transition matrices is an important component for both risk management and rating-based pricing models. The choice of the estimation technique is a delicate issue. This chapter argues that, despite the presence of heterogeneity in sovereign ratings, the HHR estimator efficiently pools all the information available, yielding precise estimates. This estimator captures "rare events," featuring a broad range of possible credit events. Then, by means of the intensity matrix we are able to bootstrap artificial rating histories, deriving the entire distribution of default probabilities. The results underscore the need for financial applications to use transitions matrices estimated over timespans sufficiently long to capture a broad range of credit events. This study also addresses the issue of calibrating empirical transition matrices to eurodollar bond data, showing that numerical problems arise for long maturities and that the assumption on the recovery rate is a non-trivial one.

---

[3] This is particularly important as ratings not only indicate the probability of default, but also the expected loss given a default. The evidence shows that the loss given default increases as we move from high to low ratings. Our loss rates are therefore chosen to match such evidence.

From a risk management perspective, the term structure of the implied probability of a spread option being in the money has important implication for the assessment of the lender liquidity risk as it shows the evolution through time of the borrower's probability of default. The results in this chapter suggest that this probability varies with the borrower's rating; for sovereigns rated B or C, the prospect of a future upgrade determines a higher probability of paying back the loan in the future.

The pricing of defaultable bonds shows that systematic global factors, mostly explained by spillovers from the US economy, drive sovereign credit risk as reported by Longstaff *et al.* (2011). Even though this framework is economically appealing, the calibration procedure may further be improved by specifying more accurate stochastic processes for the interest rate and by using empirical estimated sensitivities for the credit spreads. To understand the sources of sovereign credit risk it is key to balance the contribution of idiosyncratic versus systematic components. The surge in sovereign default swap market provides a useful vantage point (data) to isolate credit risk from other components such as liquidity and taxes.

Notes

The views expressed herein are those of the authors and should not be attributed to the International Monetary Fund, its Executive Board or its management.

References

Duffie, D., Singleton, K.J., 2003. Credit Risk. Princeton University Press, Princeton, NJ.

Fuertes, A.-M., Kalotychou, E., 2007. On the sovereign credit migration: small-sample properties and rating evolution. Computational Statistics and Data Analysis 51, 3448–3483.

Hu, Y.-T., Kiesel, R., Perraudin, W., 2002. the estimation of transition matrices for sovereign credit ratings. Journal of Banking and Finance 26, 1383–1406.

Jafry, Y., Schuermann, T., 2004. Measurement, estimation and comparison of credit migration matrices. Journal of Banking and Finance 28, 2603–2639.

Jarrow, R.A., Lando, D., Turnbull, S.M., 1997. A Markov model for the term structure of credit risk spreads. Review of Financial Studies 10, 481–523.

Kijima, M., Komoribayashi, K., 1998. A Markov chain model for valuing credit risk derivatives. The Journal of Derivatives, Fall, 97–108.

Lando, D., 1998. Cox processes and credit-risky securities. Review of Derivatives Research 2, 99–120.

Lando, D., 2001. Some elements of rating-based credit risk modeling, published. In: Jegadeesh, N., Tuckman, B. (Eds), Advanced Fixed-Income Valuation Tools. Wiley, New York, 193–215.

Lando, D., Skodeberg, T.M., 2002. Analyzing rating transitions and rating drift with continuous observations. Journal of Banking and Finance 26, 423–444.

Longstaff, F., P., Jun, P., Lasse, H., Singleton, K.J., 2011. How sovereign is sovereign credit risk? American Economic Journal: Macroeconomics 3, 75–103.

Moody's Investor Service, 2007. Sovereign Default and Recovery Rates, 1983–2006. Moody's, Boston, MA (Special Comment June).

Nickell, P., Perraudin, W., Varotto, S., 2000. Stability of rating transitions. Journal of Banking and Finance 24, 203–227.

Wei, J.Z., 2003. A multi-factor, credit migration model for sovereign and corporate debts. Journal of International Money and Finance 22, 709–735.

31

OPTIMAL PORTFOLIO CHOICE, DERIVATIVES AND EVENT RISK

Matthias Muck and Stefan Weisheit

University of Bamberg

CHAPTER OUTLINE

31.1 Introduction

In September 2008, the US administration decided not to rescue Lehman Brothers—one of the country's biggest investment banks. According to the views of many practitioners and academics this event fostered the financial crises that was triggered by the US subprime mortgage crises. In the aftermath, markets experienced an unseen dry-out of liquidity in interbank markets since banks started to dramatically mistrust each other. Another problem with the Lehman's bankruptcy was that the bank was a major counterparty in the over-the-counter derivatives market, putting the positions of many market participants into jeopardy.

Major risk factors to be considered in the context of portfolio choice include daily volatility as well as shocks or "event risks," which have deep impacts and happen unexpectedly. In this chapter, we provide an event study and analyze the impact of the Lehman default on portfolio choice. We argue that before the

Rethinking Valuation and Pricing Models. http://dx.doi.org/10.1016/B978-0-12-415875-7.00031-2

collapse many investors had believed that Lehman was simply "too big to fail." For this reason, investors had to reassess this risk since the possibility of potential bank breakdowns was demonstrated to investors quite plainly. In general, there are two possible effects: (i) Investors might become more "aware" of event risk and price it differently (i.e. there are changes in preferences) or (ii) they might also assume that markets will be destabilized in the future and thus events become more likely under the empirical probability measure. Of course a mixed case is also possible. Nevertheless, both effects should lead to increases in risk-neutral event probabilities, resulting in adjustments of optimal portfolios held by investors.

Starting with Markowitz (1952) and Merton (1969, 1971, 1973), portfolio choice is certainly one of the most intensively studied problems in finance. Modern approaches consider dynamic portfolio choice when there is jump risk. These jumps can capture event risks like the Lehman debacle. This issue is addressed by Liu *et al.* (2003). Liu and Pan (2003) include derivatives in portfolio choice. When there is event risk the market can be completed by making derivatives available for trade. Branger *et al.* (2008) examine the case when volatility is stochastic and subject to jump risk. The model presented by Muck (2010) considers portfolio choice when there are several stocks and investors have full, partial or no access to the derivatives market.

Our chapter provides several contributions. (i) We estimate the model for the German market. To assess the impact of Lehman Brothers' bankruptcy we determine the risk-neutral jump intensities from DAX option prices before and after the event. We find that this intensity increased substantially. (ii) We investigate utility improvements from adding derivatives to investors' portfolios before and after the event. We consider three scenarios. In one scenario the price of jump risk increases. In another one the empirical intensity increases and the jump risk premium remains constant. Furthermore, as a special case we also assume the sum of diffusion and jump risk premium remains constant (with the jump risk premium increasing and the diffusion risk premium decreasing). For all scenarios it turns out that investors' utility improves significantly in case of availability of derivatives. (iii) We provide optimal stock and derivative positions. For the cases under consideration, derivatives are mainly used in order to reduce (and thus hedge) exposure to event risk.

The remainder of this chapter is organized as follows. Section 31.2 introduces the model and contains the solution to the investment problem used to analyze the effects of Lehman Brothers' bankruptcy. Section 31.3 presents the parameter estimation. In Section 31.4, we analyze optimal portfolios. Section 31.5 concludes.

31.2 Model

We assume an economy with two securities that are available for trade: A risk-less bond that pays a constant interest rate r and a risky stock being representative for the whole stock market. Under the data generating measure P the dynamics of the stock price S are given by the stochastic process:

$$\mathrm{d}S_t = \left[r + \eta\sigma^2 + \mu(\lambda^P - \lambda^Q)\right]S_t\mathrm{d}t + \sigma S_t\mathrm{d}B_t^P + \mu S_{t-}\left(\mathrm{d}N_t^P - \lambda^P\mathrm{d}t\right),$$

$$(31.1)$$

where B_t is a standard Wiener process, scaled by a constant factor $\sigma > 0$. This is the diffusion part of the process. Furthermore, N_t represents a Poisson-jump process with constant arrival intensity $\lambda^P > 0$. Intuitively, the probability of a jump over the next small time interval Δt is approximately $\lambda^P\Delta t$. Given that a jump occurs, i.e. N_t takes on value 1, the stock price jumps by a constant $\mu > -1$ (case of $\mu = -1$ total ruin).

In practice, jumps (or events) happen unexpectedly and they cannot be forecasted from everyday market changes. For this reason, we make the (standard) assumption that the risk factors B_t and N_t are independent of each other. The equity risk premium depends on the amounts of jump and diffusion risk as well as the market prices of risk. The market price of diffusion risk is constant $(\eta\sigma)$ and the diffusion risk premium follows as $\eta\sigma^2$ (market price of risk times exposure to diffusion risk). Moreover, the pricing of jump risk follows from jump intensities under the empirical and risk neutral probability measures P and Q. These intensities are denoted by λ^P and λ^Q. The market price of jump risk is characterized by the constant $\xi = \dfrac{\lambda^Q}{\lambda^P} - 1$. Hence, the jump risk premium is $\mu(\lambda^P - \lambda^Q) = \mu(\lambda^P - \lambda^P(\xi - 1)) = \mu\lambda^P\xi$. It is the expected jump (amount of risk) multiplied by the market price of jump risk. Intuitively, the pricing of jump risk is performed by varying the jump intensity when moving from the empirical to the risk-neutral measure. The Model (31.1) is similar to Liu and Pan (2003). We consider constant intensities instead of stochastic ones though.

31.2.1 Investment problem with derivatives

In contrast to a Black and Scholes (1973) economy, the market considered in this chapter is incomplete.[1] In order to complete the market we need derivatives that provide specific exposures to risk factors B_t and N_t. We follow Liu and Pan (2003) and specify the pricing kernel endogenously. The kernel is the link to the risk neutral pricing measure Q under which each security (that can be traded) is expected to earn the risk-free rate of interest r. According to (31.1) the pricing kernel is:

$$\mathrm{d}\pi_t = -\pi_t(r\mathrm{d}t + \eta\sigma\mathrm{d}B_t) + \xi\pi_{t-}(\mathrm{d}N_t - \lambda^P\mathrm{d}t), \qquad (31.2)$$

where the market prices of risk η and ξ are the sensitivities of the kernel to risk factors B_t and jump risk N_t, respectively. Moreover, it holds $\pi_0 = 1$.

Given the market prices of risk we introduce derivatives as a function of time and the stock price S_t, i.e. $O_t = g(S_t, t)$. The stochastic process of derivatives follows from an application of Itô's lemma and the pricing kernel:

$$\frac{\mathrm{d}O_t}{O_t} = r\mathrm{d}t + \frac{g_S S_t}{O_t}\left(\eta\sigma^2\mathrm{d}t + \sigma\mathrm{d}B_t\right) + \frac{1}{O_t}\Delta g\left[\mathrm{d}N_t - \lambda^Q\mathrm{d}t\right], \quad (31.3)$$

where g_S is short-hand notation for the partial derivative with respect to the stock price S_t and $\Delta g = g[S_t(1+\mu), t] - g[S_t, t]$ is the price change in case of a jump. A derivative with $g_S \neq 0$ and/or $\Delta g \neq 0$ provides exposure to the risk factors B_t and N_t, respectively. This market requires two non-redundant securities in order to be complete. More precisely, an investment in the risky stock provides exposure to both diffusion and jump risk. An additional option written on to the stock is able to separate both risks and thus allows us to create specific exposures to diffusion and jump risk.

Assume that investors have full access to the derivatives market and that the market is therefore dynamically complete. Thus, there are no restrictions to trade the risk-less bond, the stock and derivatives. Consider an investor with an initial endowment W_0, and let ϕ_t and ψ_t represent the fractions of wealth invested in the stock and the derivative security, respectively. Then the dynamics of wealth turn out to be:

$$\mathrm{d}W_t = rW_t\mathrm{d}t + \theta_t^B W_t\left(\eta\sigma^2\mathrm{d}t + \sigma\mathrm{d}B_t\right) + \theta_t^N W_{t-}\left(\mathrm{d}N_t - \lambda^Q\mathrm{d}t\right), \qquad (31.4)$$

[1] In the Black and Scholes (1973) world the market is dynamically completed through investments in the stock and a bond.

where:

$$\theta_t^B = \phi_t + \psi_t \frac{g_S S_t}{O_t} \qquad (31.5)$$

$$\theta_t^N = \mu\phi_t + \psi_t \frac{1}{O_t}\Delta g.$$

In the following we call θ_t^B and θ_t^N the factor exposures with respect to the diffusion and the jump factor. Note that under regularity conditions these factors are disentangled and can be chosen independently from each other.[2]

The investor's objective is to maximize expected utility of terminal wealth at time $T > 0$. Suppose that the investor has constant relative risk aversion (CRRA). Let the objective function be:

$$\max_{\theta_t^{(\cdot)},0\le t\le T} \mathbb{E}\left[\frac{W_T^{1-\gamma}}{1-\gamma}\right], \qquad (31.6)$$

where $0 < \gamma \neq 1$ is the coefficient of relative risk aversion. The case $\gamma = 1$ represents the log-investor. The solution to the investment problem is obtained according to Merton (1971), i.e. through an application of the principle of stochastic control. We determine the indirect utility function of wealth and solve the relevant Hamilton–Jacobi–Bellman equation. Note, however, that in contrast to Merton (1971) we do not maximize expected utility with respect to portfolio weights of stocks (ϕ_t) and derivatives (ψ_t). Instead, we address factors exposures θ_t^B and θ_t^N directly. These factor exposures can be turned into portfolio weights according to (31.5). The next proposition provides the solution to the optimization problem.

Proposition 1. *Let stock price and pricing kernel evolve according to (31.1) and (31.2). Then the investor's indirect utility function is given by:*

$$\mathcal{J}(t, W_t) = \frac{W_t^{1-\gamma}}{1-\gamma}e^{\gamma h(t)}, \qquad (31.7)$$

where function h solves:

$$h(\tau) = \frac{1-\gamma}{\gamma}\tau r + \frac{1-\gamma}{2\gamma^2}\tau\eta^2\sigma^2 + \lambda^Q\tau\left[\left(\frac{\lambda^P}{\lambda^Q}\right)^{1/\gamma}\frac{1}{\gamma}\left(1 - \frac{\lambda^P}{\lambda^Q}\right) - 1\right],$$

$$\qquad (31.8)$$

---

[2] For example, we must ensure that the jump exposure $\theta_t^N > -1$ in order to avoid ruin with positive probability.

with $\tau = (T - t)$. The optimal exposures to the risk factors are:

$$\theta_t^{B*} = \frac{\eta}{\gamma}$$

$$\theta_t^{N*} = \left(\frac{\lambda^P}{\lambda^Q}\right)^{1/\gamma} - 1. \tag{31.9}$$

Proof. See Liu and Pan (2003) and the generalized Proposition 1 in Muck (2010).

31.2.2 Investment problem without derivatives

In contrast to the previous section, we consider a situation where derivatives are not available for trade, i.e. an investor's opportunity set that contains the risky stock and the risk-less bond only. A similar model is analyzed by Liu *et al.* (2003). However, we focus on constant jump intensities $\lambda^{(\cdot)}$. Let again ϕ_t be the fraction of wealth invested in the risky stock then the stochastic process for wealth follows by:

$$dW_t = rW_t dt + \phi_t(\eta\sigma^2 dt + \sigma B_t) + \phi_t W_{t-}\mu(dN_t - \lambda^Q dt). \tag{31.10}$$

Note that given this opportunity set factor exposures cannot be chosen independently of each other. Instead, the stock is exposed to both jump and diffusion risk at the same time. Hence, an investor who buys the stock accepts both risk factors according to the "package" that is offered by this security.

The optimization problem is similar to (31.6). However, in this case only one parameter (ϕ_t) can be optimized. The solution to the portfolio optimization problem can be obtained as before. The result is summarized in the following proposition.

Proposition 2. *Given the price dynamics according to (31.1), the optimal position in the risky security is obtained from:*

$$\phi_t^* = \frac{\eta}{\gamma} + \frac{\mu\lambda^P}{\gamma\sigma^2}\left[(1 + \phi_t^*\mu)^{-\gamma} - \frac{\lambda^Q}{\lambda^P}\right]. \tag{31.11}$$

The indirect utility function is defined as in (31.7) in Proposition 1 with:

$$h(\tau) = \frac{1 - \gamma}{\gamma}\tau(r + \phi_t^*\eta\sigma^2 - \phi_t^*\mu\lambda^Q) - \frac{1}{2}(1 - \gamma)\tau\sigma^2(\phi_t^*)^2$$
$$+ \frac{\lambda^P}{\gamma}\tau\left[(1 + \phi_t^*\mu)^{1-\gamma} - 1\right]. \tag{31.12}$$

Proof. See Liu and Pan (2003) and the generalized Proposition 2 in Muck (2010).

Equation (31.11) cannot be solved analytically; however, we can apply standard numerical methods to find suitable solutions for given parameter settings. Once optimal stock positions have been determined the solution to function h can be obtained from Equation (31.12).

31.3 Parameter Estimation

In this section, we examine the impact of Lehman Brothers' bankruptcy on the portfolio selection of a German investor.[3] The Lehman event took place on 15 August, 2008. First of all we need a robust parametrization of the model presented in Section 31.2. We approximate the market portfolio by the German stock market index DAX, which consists of the 30 largest German companies. As a performance index the DAX assumes that dividends are reinvested. Therefore, we do not have to address them explicitly in our estimation. All data on the DAX is retrieved from Datastream.

The expected equity return is necessary to derive risk premiums for diffusion and jump risk. We estimate the excess stock return based on annual returns over one-year German government bonds. It is well known that excess returns are historically time-varying. For this reason we take into account only 11 years prior to the event. Ignoring tax-related issues the excess return during this period is 7.37%.

The diffusion volatility σ, the jump amplitude μ and the jump intensity λ^P are determined using nearly 44 years of DAX data (the longest time series available). We do so because volatility is known to be more stable over time. Furthermore, jumps are rare events and therefore we want to include as much information as possible. Diffusion volatility σ is estimated as the standard deviation of monthly log-returns and annualized.[4] Moreover, similar to Liu *et al.* (2003), we assume that jumps are all those events when DAX returns fall by more than three standard deviations. Altogether we identify five historical events. The jump amplitude μ is therefore set equal to the mean of these five events. Moreover, given five events in nearly 44 years the frequency of a jump is approximately one jump per 8.73 years.

---

[3] For simplicity we assume that investors invest on the home market (Germany in this case) only. For international portfolio choice, the problem becomes much more involved as discussed, for example, by Adler and Dumas (1983).

[4] In order to estimate diffusion risk we need to correct for jumps. For technical details, see Navas (2003).

Option prices contain information on jump intensities under the risk-neutral (pricing) measure Q. The price dynamics defined by (31.1) allow to derive prices for European-style call and put options. The pricing formulas follow as a special cases of Merton (1976) with zero jump volatility. Assuming the market reflects the model parameters correctly, the model is calibrated to options written on the DAX prior to as well as after Lehman Brothers' bankruptcy.[5] More precisely, we use EUREX DAX call and put options for a variety of exercise prices ranging from 4000 up to 8500 which were obtained from Datastream. Maturities of the options are on 19 December 2008 and 20 March 2009.[6] The whole sample consists of 122 and 120 market prices, respectively. Some of the option prices were excluded based on the standard criteria of Bakshi *et al.* (1997).

The calibration is carried out by minimizing the sum of squared errors between model-implied prices and those observed on the market. Following again, for example, Bakshi *et al.* (1997),[7] let C_i be the price of the ith option traded in the market and let $\tilde{C}_i$ be the corresponding price implied by the model. Then, for I options the sum of squared error terms is determined by:

$$SSE = \sum_{i=1}^{I} (C_i - \tilde{C}_i)^2. \tag{31.13}$$

Since we focus on event risk we fix the parameters determined by historical data. The only coefficient allowed to vary is the intensity λ^Q. We find that λ^Q increased remarkably after the default of Lehman Brothers, namely from 0.441 (12 September) to 0.565 (15 September). In technical terms this implies that under the risk-neutral measure Q bad states become more likely, leading to fatter left tails of the distribution. Thus, investors expect more jumps under the risk-neutral measure. As already discussed by, for example, Ingersoll (1987) risk neutral (jump) probabilities follow from both empirical probabilities and investors' preferences. Recall again the definition of the market price of jump risk.

[5] Especially short-term volatility smiles can be explained by jump risk. For this reason we mainly use short-term options for calibration purposes. Long-term smiles can mainly be explained by stochastic volatility, (see, e.g. Heston, 1993; Bates, 2000; Christoffersen *et al.*, 2008).
[6] Note that one could argue to consider the most short-term September 2009 options as well. However, time to maturity would be less than 10 days and may therefore cause liquidity-related biases.
[7] Potential biases such like overweighted in-the-money (ITM) options are ignored here.

Table 31.1. **Calibrated parameters**

r	σ^2	μ	η	λ^P	λ^Q before	λ^Q after
0.043	0.178	−0.211	0.152	0.115	0.441	0.565

Estimated parameters, where "λ^Q before" and "λ^Q after" denote the risk-neutral intensities before and after the event.

Given the definition of ξ it holds that:

$$\lambda^Q = \lambda^P(\xi + 1). \tag{31.14}$$

One explanation for an increase of λ^Q is that ξ increased as well. Hence, investors changed their preferences to jump risk due to the Lehman event and thus increased the market price of jump risk. Alternatively, it is also possible that investors assume a constant ξ and simply considered a higher jump intensity under the empirical measure. Finally, and perhaps most likely, a mixture of both cases is of course possible as well. Table 31.1 provides an overview of historical parameters relevant for portfolio choice. It also contains an estimate for the short rate, which is the Euro Over Night Index Average (EONIA) Swap Index that is frequently used for derivatives pricing.

31.4 Optimal Portfolios

Unfortunately, no information is available on the future stock price risk premium that follows from jump and diffusion risk. Therefore, in order to investigate the impact of the Lehman event on portfolio choice we consider three scenarios. In Scenario 1, we assume that investors reassess the jump risk premium ξ. Moreover, the diffusion risk premium remains constant. Since risk-neutral intensities increased during the event this leads to an increase of the stock price risk premium. In Scenario 2, we assume the special case that the overall stock price risk premium remains constant while the jump risk premium increases as in Scenario 1. This implies a decrease in the risk premium for diffusion risk.[8] A constant market price of jump risk is analyzed in Scenario 3. Risk-neutral intensities increase due to higher empirical intensities, while the market price of jump risk ξ as well as diffusion risk η

---

[8] Given the dataset provided here, η becomes negative. This is due to the after-event jump risk premium that increased above the level of the initial equity premium. The scenario must therefore be regarded as an extreme case.

remain constant. Thus, the stock earns a higher risk premium because it is exposed to more jump risk. In particular, Scenarios 1 and 3 can be seen as rather extreme scenarios. The true change of the equity risk premium very likely is an intermediate case. We consider an investment horizon of one year since we assume that the Lehman event has an impact on medium-term investment decisions at least.

31.4.1 Optimal exposures

Here, we determine optimal exposures according to Section 31.2. These optimal factor exposures are obtained from Propositions 1 and 2. Figure 31.1 provides a comparison of exposures before and after the bankruptcy of Lehman Brothers for different levels of risk aversion in Scenario 1. Obviously, optimal exposures mainly reflect myopic demand, i.e. re-adjustments after the event result more or less from increases in the market price for jump risk ξ. Furthermore, optimal exposures decrease in the level of risk aversion (in absolute terms).

If derivatives are available for trade the exposure θ_t^B remains unchanged after the event. This result follows directly from Proposition 1 since $\theta_t^B = \eta/\gamma$. Thus, the change in the market price of jump risk does not affect the diffusion risk exposure. For the stock-only investor the situation is different: Although the premium for diffusion risk has not been adjusted, a higher amount of wealth is invested in the stock. This is due to the fact that the investor is interested in earning the equity premium

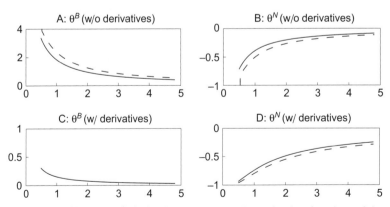

Figure 31.1 Optimal exposures (Scenario 1). Optimal exposures are determined as functions of the risk aversion coefficient γ given that the equity premium increased after the bankruptcy of Lehman. The upper panels provide optimal exposures for stock-only investors, while the lower panels describe the case with derivatives. All panels provide a comparison of the situation before (solid line) and after the event (dashed line).

which is increased by the new jump risk premium. Due to the "packaging" of risk factors this results in an increase of both optimal diffusion and jump exposures. Furthermore, investors with access to the derivatives market increase jump risk exposures to a higher level compared to the stock-only investor (in absolute terms). They use derivatives as a vehicle to disentangle both risk factors from each other.

The situation looks somewhat different when considering the case of a constant equity risk premium after the Lehman default as shown by Figure 31.2 (Scenario 2). When there is no access to the derivatives market, factor exposures are the same after the event. This can best be interpreted by the argument from above: Although there is a change in the attractiveness of specific risk factors, overall risk–return characteristics of the stock remain unchanged. Per definition, the expected return of the stock is the same. Moreover, looking at the risk, neither diffusion volatility nor jump intensity are varied. Thus, investors take positions in stocks (and the risk-less bonds) in order to earn the equity risk premium as a whole that comes in a "package" of diffusion and jump risk. For this reason, they do not adjust the number of stocks to be bought. In contrast, optimal exposures of investors with access to derivatives change substantially after the event. Jump risk becomes relatively more attractive compared to the diffusion risk. The optimal jump factor exposure is expanded (in absolute terms), while the diffusion exposure is reduced. Obviously, the investor seeks for the higher jump risk premium.

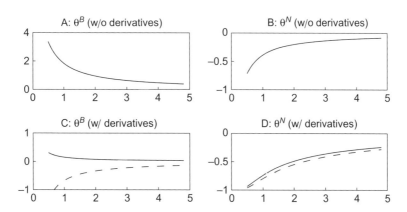

Figure 31.2 Optimal exposures (Scenario 2). Optimal exposures are determined as functions of the risk aversion coefficient γ assuming a constant equity premium after the bankruptcy of Lehman. The upper panels provide optimal exposures for stock-only investors, while the lower panels describe the case with derivatives. All panels provide a comparison of the situation before (solid line) and after the event (dashed line).

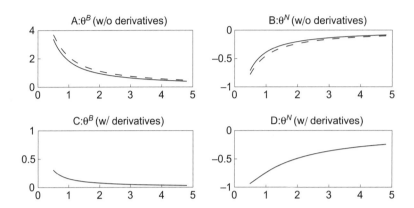

Figure 31.3 Optimal exposures (Scenario 3). Optimal exposures are determined as functions of the risk aversion coefficient γ assuming that the market price of risk remain unchanged. The upper panels provide optimal exposures for stock-only investors, while the lower panels describe the case with derivatives. All panels provide a comparison of the situation before (solid line) and after the event (dashed line).

Figure 31.3 shows optimal exposures for Scenario 3 with constant market price of jump risk ξ. Investors who have access to derivatives do not adjust their factor exposures after the Lehman default. This is due to the fact that diffusion and jump risk premiums persist at the prior event level and optimal exposures with derivatives are chosen according to specific factor premiums. However, as empirical intensities become larger, the amount of jump risk increases. As a consequence, the stock is exposed to "more" jump risk although the market price of risk ξ (i.e. the price "per unit of risk") is the same. Hence, the overall equity premium which consists of jump and diffusion risk premium is higher. For this reason the stock-only investor expands both diffusion and jump factor exposure by buying more stocks.

31.4.2 Portfolio improvement

Here, we examine the usefulness of derivatives. As derivatives allow investors to choose factor exposures independently from each other, the utility of wealth of an investor with access to derivatives should be higher than for an investor trading in the stock alone. In order to analyze the improvement created by derivatives we follow Liu and Pan (2003) and introduce a performance measure in terms of the annualized, continuously compounded return in certainty equivalent wealth (CEW). Let:

$$W^{\mathrm{CEW}} = W_0 \exp\left[\frac{\gamma}{1-\gamma}h(\tau)\right], \qquad (31.15)$$

be the certainty equivalent wealth of an investor who has access to derivatives. Then the portfolio improvement is measured by:

$$\mathcal{R} = \frac{\ln W^{\text{CEW}} - \ln W_{\text{no}}^{\text{CEW}}}{\tau}, \tag{31.16}$$

with $W_{\text{no}}^{\text{CEW}}$ being the certainty equivalent wealth for a stock-only investor.

Figure 31.4 shows improvements from making derivatives available for trade for different levels of risk aversion (γ). After Lehman Brother's default utility improvements from derivatives are higher. For Scenario 1 and 2 this is due to the fact that the market price for jump risk increased, making jump risk more attractive to investors. Derivatives are used to disentangle diffusion and jump risk. In order to earn higher jump risk premiums investors increase their jump factor exposures. In contrast, the stock-only investor is interested in earning jump risk premiums as well. However, this jump risk only comes in "packages" with diffusion risk. Therefore the stock-only investor's utility (in terms of certainty equivalent wealth) is lower than the utility given that derivatives are available.

In Scenario 2, diffusion risk is particularly unattractive making trading in derivatives even more interesting. A stock-only investor can get exposure to jump risk only by investing in low priced diffusion risk at the same time. With derivatives both factor exposures can be disentan'gled again, i.e. the diffusion risk factor exposure can be reduced while the jump risk factor exposure is increased. This implies utility improvements for the investor. In contrast, the stock-only investor's certainty equivalent wealth does not change at all. For this reason, including derivative securities in the portfolio becomes even more valuable and improvements in Scenario 2 are higher than in Scenario 1.

Finally, for Scenario 3 the results are similar as for Scenarios 1 and 2. Derivatives still improve portfolios to a larger extent after the Lehman event. However, utility gains are smaller. This is due to the fact that the packaging of risk offered to stock-only investors becomes more attractive compared to investors who have full access to the derivatives market.

31.4.3 Demand for derivatives and stock

In the next step we analyze optimal stock and derivatives position derived from optimal exposures. We focus on Scenario 1. According to (31.5), the exposures are linear combinations of

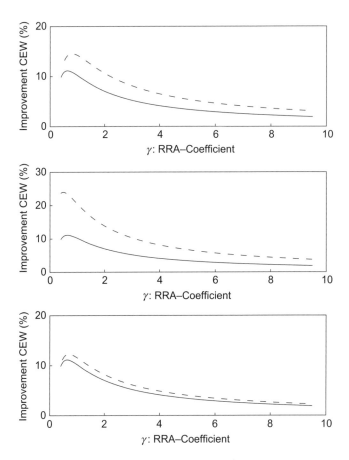

Figure 31.4 Portfolio improvement. The improvement from including derivatives to the portfolio is measured in terms of certainty equivalent wealth. All panels compare portfolio improvements prior to (solid line) and after (dashed line) the Lehman event. The upper panel assumes Scenario 1, the middle panel Scenario 2 and the lower panel Scenario 3.

stock and derivative investments. Optimal positions in the risky stock and the derivative follow from:

$$\phi_t^* = \frac{\eta}{\gamma} - \psi_t^* \frac{g_S S_t}{O_t}$$

$$\psi_t^* = \left(\frac{\Delta g}{\mu O_t} - \frac{g_S S_t}{O_t}\right)^{-1} \left(\frac{1}{\mu}\left[\left(\frac{\lambda^P}{\lambda^Q}\right)^{1/\gamma} - 1\right] - \frac{\eta}{\gamma}\right). \tag{31.17}$$

Deep out-of-the-money put options are known to be highly sensitive to large changes in the stock price. We consider a put with a strike price of 6000 and expiry of one month. Thus, the

Table 31.2. Demand for stock and derivatives (Scenario 1)

γ	λ^Q/λ^P	Stock only	Stock and put	
			ϕ	$\psi(\%)$
0.5	3.85	3.35	4.4	0.36
	4.93	4.73	4.53	0.21
1	3.85	1.84	3.49	0.29
	4.93	2.38	3.77	0.18
3	3.85	0.64	1.71	0.14
	4.93	0.85	1.95	0.09
5	3.85	0.38	1.11	0.09
	4.93	0.51	1.29	0.06
7	3.85	0.28	0.83	0.07
	4.93	0.37	0.96	0.05
10	3.85	0.19	0.59	0.05
	4.93	0.26	0.7	0.03
12	3.85	0.16	0.5	0.04
	4.93	0.22	0.59	0.03

Portfolio compositions of a stock-only investor as well as of an investor with access to the derivatives market for Scenario 1. The upper rows show portfolio weights before the event, the lower rows those after the event.

strike is close to the level of the DAX after the event (6064).[9] Nevertheless, it should be stressed that any derivative can be used as long as it has non-zero exposure to both risk factors. Table 31.2 reports optimal stock and derivative positions. In addition, the stock-only investor's optimal position is also provided.

After the default of Lehman Brothers the premium for jump risk rises due to an increase in the risk-neutral intensity parameter λ^Q. As we argue that this causes an increase in the overall equity premium the stock-only investor will expand her stock position in order to earn the equity premium, since she has no means to trade jump risk separately.

This is also true when derivatives are available for trade. Before the Lehman default for all levels of risk aversion optimal stock positions are higher compared to the ones of the stock-only investor. However, stock positions do not seem to be increased as aggressively. Derivatives are used to hedge partially against jump risk: investors buy put options that offer protection against

[9] Before the event the DAX was 6234.

downward jumps. Moreover, note that investors with access to the derivatives market invest huge fractions of their wealth in stocks (depending on the risk aversion the amount exceeds 100% of their wealth). This risk is also hedged by put options.

The results for Scenarios 2 and 3 are similar.[10]

31.5 Conclusion

This chapter addresses asset allocation in the presence of jumps in a constant volatility and intensity framework. We discuss the solution for the investment problem in both incomplete and complete markets. Furthermore, the model parameters are estimated from DAX time series and options data. We find a substantial increase in risk-neutral jump intensities after the event. This has implications on portfolio choice. It turns out that the utility of derivatives increases after the event. Finally, we provide stock and derivative positions derived from the optimal exposures to the risk factors. Results indicate that investors use derivatives to hedge their larger stock positions after the increase in market price of jump risk.

In the context of our study we made a couple of simplifying assumptions. (i) We do not consider stochastic volatility. Certainly, volatility was affected by the Lehman debacle as well. (ii) There is evidence that jump intensities are not constant but are linked to (stochastic) volatility. This effect might also be taken into account. (iii) Another direction for future research might also be to address other stock market indices or international portfolios.

References

Adler, M., Dumas, B., 1983. International portfolio choice and corporate finance. Journal of Finance 38, 925–984.

Bakshi, G., Cao, C., Chen, Z., 1997. Empirical performance of alternative option pricing models. Journal of Finance 52, 2003–2049.

Bates, D.S., 2000. Post-'87 crash fears in S&P 500 options. Journal of Econometrics 94, 181–238.

Black, F., Scholes, M., 1973. The pricing of options and corporate liabilities Journal of Political Economy 81, 637–654.

Branger, N., Schlag, C., Schneider, E., 2008. Optimal portfolios when volatility can jump. Journal of Banking and Finance 32, 1087–1097.

Christoffersen, P.F., Heston, S., Jacobs, K., 2008. The shape and term structure of the index option smirk: why multifactor stochastic volatility models work so well. Management Science 55, 1914–1932.

---

[10] For sake of brevity results are not reported in detail here.

Heston, S., 1993. A closed-form solution for options with stochastic volatility with applications to bond and currency options. Review of Financial Studies 6, 327–343.

Ingersoll, J.E., 1987. Theory of Financial Decision Making. Rowman & Littlefield, Totowa, NJ.

Liu, J., Pan, J., 2003. Dynamic derivative strategies. Journal of Financial Economics 69, 401–430.

Liu, J., Longstaff, F.A., Pan, J., 2003. Dynamic asset allocation with event risk. Journal of Finance 58, 231–259.

Markowitz, H.M., 1952. Portfolio selection. Journal of Finance 7, 77–91.

Merton, R.C., 1969. Lifetime portfolio selection under uncertainty: the continuous time case. Review of Economics and Statistics 51, 247–257.

Merton, R.C., 1971. Optimum consumption and portfolio rules in a continuous-time model. Journal of Economic Theory 3, 373–413.

Merton, R.C., 1973. An intertemporal capital asset pricing model. Econometrica 41, 867–887.

Merton, R.C., 1976. Option pricing when underlying stock returns are discontinuous. Journal of Financial Economics 3, 125–144.

Muck, M., 2010. Trading strategies with partial access to the derivatives market. Journal of Banking and Finance 34, 1288–1298.

Navas, J.F., 2003. Calculation of volatility in a jump-diffusion model. Journal of Derivatives 11, 66–72.

32

VALUATION AND PRICING CONCEPTS IN ACCOUNTING AND BANKING REGULATION

Christopher Kullmann
Nomura Bank Deutschland

CHAPTER OUTLINE

32.1 Introduction

Valuation of assets and liabilities is a key component of both financial and regulatory reporting. Apart from revenues generated out of the operative business of a company it is the valuation of a company's assets and liabilities that has the highest potential to significantly impact its earnings and capital position. This has become particularly apparent during the financial crisis that started in 2007. In particular, for financial services firms, whose

Rethinking Valuation and Pricing Models. http://dx.doi.org/10.1016/B978-0-12-415875-7.00032-4

assets mainly consist of financial instruments, the biggest financial risks lie in the need for depreciation of their assets.

Both accounting standard setters and regulators are aware of the importance of asset and liability valuation for financial services firms. A number of guiding documents have been issued on the correct valuation and pricing concepts to be used by financial services firms by various bodies—ranging from international bodies such as the International Accounting Standards Board (IASB) and the Basel Committee on Banking Supervision (BCBS) to national accountancy bodies such as the Institute of Chartered Accountants in England and Wales, the American Institute of Certified Public Accountants or the Institute of Public Auditors in Germany (Institut der Wirtschaftsprüfer). The guidance provided by these bodies differs based on the subject of the valuation (i.e. fixed asset, financial asset or liability, etc.), aim of holding valuation subject (e.g. trading, investment, etc.) and purpose of valuation (i.e. accounting, regulatory treatment, transaction pricing, and so on).

The goal of this chapter is to show the different valuation and pricing concepts used in accounting and financial services regulation. The focus lies on the valuation of financial instruments as these are the most relevant category of assets for financial services firms. Similarities and differences will be highlighted and, where possible, explained.

32.2 Accounting

32.2.1 International Financial Reporting Standards (IFRS)

In May 2011, the IASB issued *IFRS 13: Fair Value Measurement* (International Accounting Standards Board, 2011). Prior to the publication of IFRS 13 the term fair value was defined in each individual standard using the term. Some of these standards contained limited guidance on how to measure fair value, while other gave extensive guidance. Furthermore, the guidance provided was not always consistent across those standards. IFRS 13 aims to remedy that situation and thereby to increase the comparability of information across different financial statements. Also, IFRS 13 was developed jointly with the Financial Accounting Standards Board (FASB)—the accounting standards setter for US generally accepted accounting principles (GAAP).[1]

---

[1] IFRS 13.BC3–BC7.

32.2.1.1 Definition of fair value

According to IFRS 13.9, fair value is defined as "the price that would be received to sell an asset or paid to transfer a liability in an orderly transaction between market participants at the measurement date." This definition consists of several components:

- *The asset or liability.* Fair value may be determined on the basis of an individual asset or liability, a portfolio of assets or liabilities, or a group of assets and liabilities (e.g. a business). In all cases the condition, the location and any potential restrictions on the sale or use of the asset or liability need to be taken into account, if they have an impact on the price a third party would be willing to pay or expecting to receive in exchange for the asset or liability.[2]
- *The transaction.* The assumed transaction for the determination of an asset's or liability's fair value is observed in the principal market for that asset or liability. The principal market is defined as "the market with the greatest volume and level of activity for the asset or liability."[3] Where no principal market exists, the transaction should be assumed to take place in the most advantageous market for the asset or liability.[4] Where a principal market exists, the IASB believes that it provides the most representative input for a fair value measurement due to the liquidity of that market. In most cases, the principal market and the most advantageous market will likely be the same.[5] In any case, the selected market must be a market that the reporting entity has access to. Therefore, two different entities may view different markets as the principal market for a given asset or liability.[6]
- *Market participants.* When determining fair value, entities should take into account all assumptions and methods that market participants would use when pricing the asset.[7] This is particularly relevant in cases where no observable market prices exist and valuation models are used. Market participants have to be active in the relevant market (as defined above), have to be independent of each other, knowledgeable regarding the asset or liability, and have to be able and willing to enter into a transaction.[8]

---

[2] IFRS 13.11−14.
[3] IFRS 13, appendix A.
[4] IFRS 13.16.
[5] IFRS 13 Fair Value Measurement—Project Summary and Feedback Statement.
[6] IFRS 13.19.
[7] IFRS 13.22.
[8] IFRS 13, appendix A.

- *The price.* The relevant price for determining fair value is an exit price. Transaction costs should not be taken into account when determining fair value. However, where relevant, the price should be adjusted for transportation costs (e.g. for a commodity) to the principal or most advantageous market.[9]

32.2.1.2 Valuation techniques

Valuation techniques used to derive fair value must be appropriate in the circumstances, and must maximize the use of relevant observable inputs and minimize the use of unobservable inputs. In general, all valuation techniques used must be consistent with one or more of three approaches: "market approach," "cost approach" and "income approach."[10]

The *market approach* includes all techniques that use prices and other relevant information generated by market transactions involving identical or comparable assets or liabilities. In its most basic form this approach consists of identifying the principal market for an asset or liability and using the price the asset or liability is traded for on that market. If no direct market price is available, other techniques with the market approach include valuation using market multiples and matrix pricing.[11]

Using the *cost approach*, an asset's fair value is determined as the amount that would be required currently to replace the service capacity of the asset. This current replacement cost reflects the amount a buyer would pay for a different asset that offers the same service capacity. This then needs to be adjusted for obsolescence. The cost approach is most often used to measure the fair value of tangible assets.[12]

In the *income approach* future income and expenses (or cash flows) are converted into one current amount. In this approach the fair value measurement reflects current market expectation about future income or expenses. The most relevant valuation techniques within the income approach are present value techniques (i.e. estimating and discounting future cash flows) and option pricing models (e.g. the Black—Scholes—Merton formula). Apart from estimation of future cash flows, the key inputs to be considered in present value techniques are the variability of future cash flows as well as risk-free interest rates and risk premiums for relevant risks.[13]

---

[9] IFRS 13.24—26.
[10] IFRS 13.61—66.
[11] IFRS 13.B5—B7.
[12] IFRS 13.B8—B9.
[13] IFRS 13.B10—13.

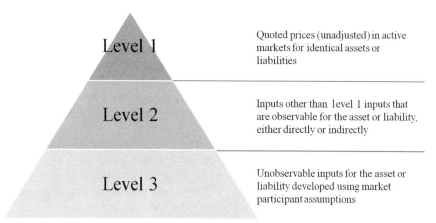

Figure 32.1 Fair value hierarchy under IFRS 13.

32.2.1.3 Hierarchy of inputs

Ideally, the IASB would like reporting entities to use observable market prices for every fair value determination. However, in many cases, observable market prices are not readily available. Therefore, the IASB defined a fair value hierarchy that is based on the available inputs to valuation techniques as shown in Figure 32.1.

The highest priority is given to Level 1 inputs. These are "quoted prices (unadjusted) in active markets for identical assets or liabilities that the entity can access at the measurement date."[14] This first level in the fair value hierarchy will be applicable to many financial assets and liabilities as these are often traded in active markets. In cases where an entity holds a large number of identical assets or liabilities (e.g. a large number of shares in a single company) the fair value of that asset or liability will be determined by multiplying the observable market price of that asset or liability with the quantity held by the entity. This remains the case even if the quantity held by the entity is so significant that an attempt to sell the total position would exceed the normal trading volume and might affect the quoted price.[15]

If no direct market prices are observable, other directly or indirectly observable input parameters should be used to determine an asset's or liability's fair value (Level 2 inputs). These include, but are not limited to, quoted prices for similar assets or liabilities in active markets or for identical assets or liabilities in

[14] IFRS 13.76.
[15] IFRS 13.76–80.

non-active markets, interest rates and yield curves, implied volatilities and credit spreads. These inputs may need to be adjusted depending on factors specific to the asset or liability (e.g. the extent to which inputs relate to comparable items or the volume or level of activity in the observed markets). If the required adjustments are significant and those adjustments use unobservable inputs, the entire measurement may be reclassified into Level 3.[16]

Lastly, if observable input parameters are not sufficient to determine fair value, unobservable inputs may be used (Level 3). This will often be the case in illiquid markets. In those cases, assumptions should be used, reflecting the assumptions market participants would use for pricing, including assumptions about risk. This includes both risk inherent to the asset or liability and model risk. In order to use robust assumptions, entities should use all information about market participant assumptions that are reasonably available.[17] Examples for unobservable inputs include historical market data (e.g. if current market data is not available because of limited market activity) or internal risk assessments (if third parties would use the same or similar methods to assess risks).

32.2.2 Differences between IFRS and selected national accounting standards

32.2.2.1 US GAAP

IFRS 13 is the result of a joint project between the IASB and the FASB to develop common requirements for measuring fair value and for disclosing information about fair value measurements. Therefore, IFRS 13 is largely identical to the fair value guidance of US GAAP (Financial Accounting Standards Board, 2011). However, a few minor differences remain. Apart from wording and spelling differences, these are:

- *Investment in investment companies.* Under US GAAP these can be measured at the reported net asset value without adjustments under certain circumstances. Under IFRS the investment company needs to control its underlying investments (Financial Accounting Standards Board, 2011). Since publishing IFRS 13/Topic 820 the IASB has published an exposure draft (Exposure Draft ED/2011/4 Investment Entities) aiming at exempting investment companies from

---

[16] IFRS 13.81–85.
[17] IFRS 13.86–90.

consolidating their financial statements with that of a subsidiary. Instead, the investment company would carry all investments at fair value through profit and loss.

- *Deposit liabilities.* Under US GAAP the fair value of a deposit liability is measured as the amount payable on demand at the reporting date. Under IFRS 13 the fair value of such a liability cannot be less than the present value of the amount payable on demand (Financial Accounting Standards Board, 2011).
- *Disclosure requirements.* Differences in the disclosure requirements between US GAAP and IFRS relating to fair value measurement include differences due to the differences in gross or net presentation of derivatives, sensitivity analyses for financial instruments measured at fair value within Level 3 of the fair value hierarchy and disclosure requirements for non-public entities (Financial Accounting Standards Board, 2011).

32.2.2.2 German GAAP

Generally, fair value is not as relevant for German GAAP preparers as it is under other accounting regimes. Due to the prudent businessman principle, which calls for a cautious valuation of assets, most assets may not be valued higher than amortized cost. However, current assets must be carried at fair value if fair value is below amortized cost.

An exception exists for banks' current assets. These need to be carried at fair value regardless of acquisition cost. However, the fair value must be reduced by a risk discount.[18] German GAAP does not include any guidance on how this risk discount is to be determined. The prevailing view is that a value at risk (VaR)-based determination of the discount would meet the requirements. If a bank does not calculate VaR for its trading book, other methods may also be applicable, as long as these methods comply with regulatory risk management requirements (Scharpf and Schaber, 2009, Chapter 4.4.2.4.2).

Under German GAAP the fair value is defined as the market price or, if no market price from a sufficiently active and liquid market is available, as a value calculated according to commonly accepted valuation methods.[19]

Which valuation methods qualify as commonly accepted is not regulated in German GAAP. According to the prevailing view,

---

[18] Section 340e, paragraph 3, HGB (Handelsgesetzbuch, German Commercial Code).
[19] Section 255, paragraph 4, HGB.

discounted cash flow models and option pricing models (such as Black–Scholes–Merton or binomial models) belong to the commonly accepted valuation methods (Ellrott *et al.*, 2010).[20] Generally speaking, fair value models which are relevant under IFRS should also be relevant under German GAAP.

32.3 Banking Regulation

32.3.1 Links between accounting and banking regulation

Pricing and valuation concerns impact banking regulation in two distinct ways. On the one hand, the different valuation concepts in accounting frameworks affect the regulatory position, as accounting figures form the calculation basis for both capital and risk positions. On the other hand, a number of regulatory requirements directly make reference to fair values, some of those providing their own requirements to pricing and valuation methods.

Fair value accounting has a procyclical effect on banks' capital positions by weakening capital in times of weakening financial markets. This trend was particularly visible during the beginning of the financial crisis in 2007–2008. In a working paper from 2009 (Novoa *et al.*, 2009), the International Monetary Fund (IMF) comes to the conclusion that fair value accounting nevertheless is the preferred accounting framework from a regulatory perspective. Some of the recommendations made by the IMF, such as a countercyclical capital buffer and more forward-looking provisioning, have since been implemented by international regulatory and accounting bodies.

32.3.2 Capital requirements

The capital requirements for positions held in a bank's trading book as well as for certain counterparty exposures are calculated based on those positions' fair value. The BCBS[21] has outlined guidance for prudent valuation, which consists of the components valuation methodologies, systems and controls, and valuation adjustments or reserves.

---

[20] Section 255, HGB, Rn 519.

[21] The BCBS is a committee of international banking supervisors aiming to the enhance understanding of key supervisory issues and to improve the quality of banking supervision worldwide.

In terms of valuation methodologies the BCBS differentiates between marking-to-market and marking-to-model. The BCBS defines marking-to-market as "at least daily valuation of positions at readily available close out prices that are sourced independently." This is the preferred valuation methodology—banks must use it whenever possible. Significant market makers may use mid-market prices, all others must use the more prudent side of bid/offer (Basel Committee on Banking Supervision, 2010, paragraph 693 *et seq.*).

When banks are marking-to-model (i.e. benchmarking, extrapolating or otherwise calculation prices from market inputs) the BCBS expects them to apply an extra degree of conservatism. No specific guidelines as to the choice of valuation models are given. Similar to the fair value hierarchy under IFRS and US GAAP (see above), wherever possible market inputs should be sourced in line with the requirements set out for market prices. Also, senior management and risk management should be aware of the uncertainty produced by valuation models and of their weaknesses (Basel Committee on Banking Supervision, 2010, paragraph 695).

After determining market prices the banks must apply valuation adjustments/reserves, where applicable. At a minimum the following valuation adjustments/reserves need to be considered: Unearned credit spreads, close-out costs, operational risks, early termination, investing and funding costs, future administrative costs, and, where appropriate, model risk. These valuation adjustments/reserves must impact Level 1 regulatory capital. Where they exceed those adjustments/reserves made under financial accounting standards, they must be specifically deducted from capital when calculating the bank's regulatory capital position (Basel Committee on Banking Supervision, 2010, paragraph 698 *et seq.*).

32.3.3 Liquidity requirements

As a part of the Basel III Framework, new minimum liquidity standards were defined by the BCBS. These standards require banks to hold a liquidity buffer consisting of high-quality, highly liquid assets. As these assets need to be highly liquid, they cannot be marked to model, but must be marked to market (Basel Committee on Banking Supervision, 2010).

The proposed implementation of the new liquidity standards within the European Union includes some more guidance on the valuation of liquid assets. Specifically, the market value should be adjusted to reflect the duration as well as credit and liquidity risk for the asset. Also, typical repo haircuts in periods of general market stress should be applied.[22]

32.4 Critical Assessment

When comparing the different valuation and pricing requirements in the various accounting and regulatory frameworks it becomes apparent that there are many similarities. All frameworks prefer valuations on the basis of market prices over valuation models. However, all frameworks also accept the fact that market inputs will not always be available, in those cases allowing valuation models. When models are used, the addressees of the reports using model prices (e.g. readers of financial statements, management or supervisors) should be informed about the limitations and potential shortcomings of the models used. This trend towards transparency regarding the basis of market prices has picked up momentum significantly since the financial crisis.

Even though the general concepts in terms of valuation and pricing requirements are very similar across the different frameworks, some differences in the details do exist. These differences are mainly due either to different reporting concepts (e.g. the prudent businessman principle of German GAAP versus the true and fair view approach of IFRS) or to different addressees (e.g. financial analysts versus banking supervisors). As a result, while banks may be able to use the same valuation routines as a basis for a number of reporting requirements, individual adjustments will be necessary for the different reports.

Even though the use of fair values in accounting (and subsequently regulatory reporting) is generally accepted to have procyclical impacts, no compelling alternative has been identified so far. All other concepts (e.g. historical cost or amortized cost) significantly deteriorate transparency. As could be observed during certain phases of the financial crisis, a lack in transparency can have significantly more destabilizing influence on financial markets than carrying assets at fair value.

---

[22] European Commission: Proposal for a Directive of the European Parliament and of the Council on the access to the activity of credit institutions and the prudential supervision of credit institutions and investment firms and amending Directive 2002/87/EC of the European Parliament and of the Council on the supplementary supervision of credit institutions, insurance undertakings and investment firms in a financial conglomerate.

32.5 Conclusion

Different definitions of fair value exist in different accounting and regulatory frameworks. However, the definitions converge and thereby differences are minimized. The most notable example of this trend is the common definition of fair value in IFRS and US GAAP, which recently replaced the separate definitions existing previously.

In all accounting and regulatory frameworks observable market prices are the preferred source of input for the determination of fair values. Valuation models are allowed where observable market prices are not available. In most regulatory frameworks no detailed guidance for the methodology to be used by valuation models is given. Rather, the models should use valuation routines which are generally accepted as market standard.

As both market prices and accepted valuation models are by and large independent of the individual accounting or regulatory framework, market participants can usually use the same valuation routines for all accounting and regulatory frameworks they fall under. However, differences may exist in the scope of assets and liabilities for which fair values need to be determined and certain adjustments to be made to the determine fair values under individual standards.

References

Basel Committee on Banking Supervision, 2006. International Convergence of Capital Measurement and Capital Standards: A Revised Framework. Basel Committee on Banking Supervision, Basel.

Basel Committee on Banking Supervision, 2010. International Framework for Liquidity Risk Measurement, Standards and Monitoring. Basel Committee on Banking Supervision, Basel.

Ellrott, N., Förschle, G., Hoyos, M., Winkeljohann, N. (Eds), 2010. Beck'scher Bilanz-Kommentar, 7th edn). Beck, Munich.

Financial Accounting Standards Board, 2011. Accounting Standards Update 2011-04 "Fair Value Measurement" (Topic 820). Financial Accounting Standards Board, Norwalk, CT.

International Accounting Standards Board, 2011. IFRS 13: Fair Value Measurement. International Accounting Standards Board, London.

Novoa, A., Scarlata, J., Solé, J., 2009. Procyclicality and fair value accounting. IMF Working Paper WP/09/39. International Monetary Fund, Washington, DC.

Scharpf, P., Schaber, M., 2009. Handbuch Bankbilanz, 3rd edn). Beck, Munich.

33

REGULATION, REGULATORY UNCERTAINTY AND THE STOCK MARKET: THE CASE OF SHORT SALE BANS

Abraham Lioui* and Michelle Sisto**

*EDHEC Business School, **International University of Monaco

33.1 Introduction

Short sales play an important role in capital markets as they can be used for multiple purposes: To profit from declining prices, for market-making activities and for hedging strategies. In addition, short selling enhances revenue for long-only investors as they can earn fees by lending out securities. In the public eye, however, short selling remains controversial, especially during times of market stress, as short sellers profit from declining prices, an idea generally morally reprehensible to the public at large, and are often accused of putting undue downward pressure on

Rethinking Valuation and Pricing Models. http://dx.doi.org/10.1016/B978-0-12-415875-7.00033-6

531

prices, thereby exacerbating negative price moves. Regulation aimed at reducing the potentially negative effects of short sales differs across countries and the financial crisis brought heightened scrutiny of the practice, spurring a round of regulatory action and public debate about the role of short selling in financial markets. While the academic literature tends to support a view of short sellers as rational, informed participants who maintain market quality and efficient price discovery, politicians, regulators, CEOs and the public lean toward a more skeptical view.

As stock prices were declining in the summer of 2008, regulatory agencies across many countries quickly intervened, instituting emergency temporary bans on short sales in certain financial companies. The duration and specificities of these policies varied and since then subsequent actions by individual countries have diverged.[1] The stated intent of the Securities and Exchange Commission (SEC) ban, as stated in a SEC News Release, was to restore equilibrium to the markets.[2] While recognizing that in normal market conditions short selling contributes to price efficiency and adds liquidity to the markets, the regulators stated in the same SEC News Release that: "At present, it appears that unbridled short selling is contributing to the recent, sudden price declines in the securities of financial institutions unrelated to true price valuation." The bans offered researchers a unique experimental opportunity to explore the effects of short sale constraints on prices and on market efficiency and to confront the empirical data with the classical models

In this chapter, Section 33.2 reviews the classical models of short sale constraints while Section 33.3 examines empirical evidence prior to the financial crisis. Section 33.4 provides empirical findings from the short sale bans of the financial crisis and Section 33.5 looks toward future challenges in creating models that broaden the classical models in order to include the political uncertainty that so often surrounds regulatory decision making.

---

[1] Currently, the European Council and European Parliament are working to coordinate a uniform policy across member states. On 17 May 2011, the EU Economic and Financial Affairs Council (Ecofin) released a draft proposal to increase transparency and ensure coordination on short selling and credit default swaps. See http://register.consilium.europa.eu/pdf/en/11/st10/st10334.en11.pdf.

[2] SEC News Release 2008-211, 19 September 2008, http://www.sec.gov/news/press/2008/2008-211.htm.

33.2 Classical Models: Theoretical Models of Constraining Short Sales

33.2.1 Overvaluation models

Several classical models make predictions about the impact of short sale constraints on asset prices and market efficiency. Miller's seminal work (Miller, 1977) on overvaluation considers the effects of short sale constraints when investors hold heterogeneous opinions about the underlying value of a security. Under binding constraints, the pessimists are essentially kept out of the market and prices become overvalued as they reflect the opinions of the optimists rather than of all potential investors. The model therefore predicts an upward bias in prices when binding short sale constraints are in place and a higher degree of overvaluation is to be associated with greater dispersion in investor opinion. Harrison and Kreps (1978) also assume investors with heterogeneous beliefs about asset value and suggest that overvaluation may be even more than that suggested by Miller. In their model, investors have access to the same information but may arrive at differing subjective valuation assessments based on the information. They show that restricting short sales may lead the price to exceed the valuation of even the most optimistic investor at a given time as investors anticipate that someday another investor may be even more optimistic and therefore the asset's price reflects both the investor's fundamental value plus some resale value. Bai and Chang (2004) propose a rational expectations model in which short sale restrictions have two competing effects on prices—they drive prices up due to undermining market liquidity and they drive prices down by reducing the informativeness of market prices. The net effect is a slight upward bias in prices.

Several researchers consider the impact of the behavioral component of investor overconfidence on effects of short sale constraints. Hong and Stein (2003) examine the effect of short sale constraints with heterogeneous agents, focusing on the mechanism of the difference of opinion. Their model does not predict upward bias, but rather that returns will be more negatively skewed, conditional on high trading volume when short sale constraints are binding and with wider dispersion in opinion. In a model with two investors, each with a private signal and importantly each paying stronger attention to his own signal even when the signal of the other investor is revealed, they predict a higher frequency of extreme negative returns when short sale constraints are binding. In essence, each investor is overconfident about his own signal and we only learn about the bearish investor's signal once the price has fallen sufficiently for the bearish investors to step in as support buyers. In addition, Scheinkman and Xiong (2003) also suggest that disagreement in the value of an asset may be due to investor overconfidence and that overweighting their own information relative to someone else's can lead to overpricing, and therefore short sale constraints may even lead to bubbles and later crashes.

In a dynamic model of asset valuation, Duffie *et al.* (2002) suggest price inflation under short sale constraints may be due to the capitalization of future lending fees. The search frictions that short selling imposes by requiring borrowers to search for security lenders and bargain over the lending fee may lead to overvaluation.

33.2.2 Alternative models—Informational efficiency

As opposed to the overvaluation effects discussed previously, Diamond and Verrecchia (1987) argue that under short sales restrictions prices will not be biased upward, but rather the speed at which negative information is incorporated into prices through trading will be slowed. In their model, investors differ in information, not beliefs, and market participants understand that those with negative information cannot trade under short sale constraints so lower levels of trading will lead investors to infer that there may be negative information and will lead to a reduction in price. However, since low-level trading is a weaker signal than selling, constraints make the transmission rate of negative information into a slow in prices.

Bai *et al.* (2006) propose a more general rational expectations model based on two trading motives of investors—allocational for risk sharing or informational based on speculation from private information. In contrast to overvaluation models, in their model, imposing short sale constraints could cause prices to fall. As constraints impede trades by negatively informed investors, there is a loss of informational efficiency that may tend to push prices up; however, the loss of informational efficiency increases price uncertainty in the eyes of uninformed investors, thereby reducing allocation to these assets (by requiring a higher risk premium), which tends to push prices down. The two motives affect the demand for the asset and the net effect of constraints depends on which motive is stronger.

Whereas the bulk of models suggest that restricting short sales renders markets less efficient, several address the possible justifications for imposing restrictions. Goldstein and Guembel (2008) see some justification for restricting short sales in their model in which they show that, in the case when short sellers can force prices down by selling a large number of shares, the lower stock price may affect management's opinion of prospects a company and thereby decision-making potentially causing passing up of a profitable investment. They propose that making short selling costly is preferable to prohibiting short selling, as short selling is typically more profitable for those with real negative information.[3] In a similar vein, Khanna and Mathews (2012) examine the conditions under which government intervention may be justifiable. The authors consider the role and ability of long term blockholders to counter potential bear raids, by studying under what conditions the price effect of short sellers can affect a firm's fundamental value. They conclude that intervention measures should be targeted to those companies for whom blockholdings may be insufficient. In a general equilibrium model with incomplete markets and potential financial innovation, Allen and Gale (1991) propose that allowing unlimited short sales may be detrimental to the market as short sales appear to be incompatible with efficiency and price-taking behavior when the possibility of financial innovation exists.

While all models suggest that constraining short sales may affect the efficiency of markets, none address the manner in which constraints are put into place and the possible effects of regulatory action and uncertainty about regulatory action on asset prices.

33.3 Empirical Evidence Prior to the 2008 Financial Crisis

33.3.1 Evidence of overvaluation hypothesis—Price effects

Over the years, considerable empirical work has been carried out regarding Miller's overvaluation hypothesis and the results have been mixed. Miller's model hypothesizes overvaluation when stocks are both subjected to short sale constraints and there

---

[3] Note that current regulation effectively does this by the less favorable tax status of short sale profits as income rather than capital gains and restrictions on naked shorting.

is heterogeneity in investor beliefs. One strand of testing tended to focus on the first condition by looking at the effect of short sale constraints on overvaluation. Another strand examined effects of investor dispersion of opinion on overvaluation. A key challenge in testing how short sale constraints affect prices lies in determining how to measure the extent to which constraints are binding. As proxies for short sale constraints, researchers have used relative short interest (RSI) levels,[4] short stock rebate rates,[5] option status,[6] institutional ownership[7] and failures to delivery, security lending transactions, and shorting flow measures.[8] Proxies for investor dispersion include the standard deviation of analyst earnings/share forecasts,[9] average daily turnover and firm volatility.

Evidence about the effect of short sales constraints on prices is mixed. Figleweski (1981) looks at RSI as a proxy for the level of short sale constraints and finds some evidence that heavily shorted stocks underperform those with lower levels of shorting, although the differences are not statistically significant, whereas Asquith and Meulbroek (1995) find statistically significant underperformance for heavily shorted firms. Lamont and Thaler (2003) examine overvaluation facilitated by difficulty in short selling in the case of technology stocks Palm and 3Com, and show that while there was clear mispricing it could not be arbitraged away due to the difficulty in borrowing Palm shares, concluding that constraints on borrowing may have contributed to the technology bubble frenzy of the late 1990s.

With regard to investor dispersion of opinion, Diether *et al.* (2002) use dispersion in analysts' forecasts as a proxy for breadth of heterogeneity in investors' beliefs and show that firms with wider dispersion subsequently tend to earn lower future returns than control firms, thereby offering evidence of overvaluation at

[4] Figleweski (1981) was the first to introduce RSI = shares held short/shares outstanding, arguing that higher RSI indicates shares that are more difficult to short, thus more binding constraints.

[5] Short rebate rates are difficult data to obtain due to the opacity of the lending market, but are used by D'Avolio (2002), Jones and Lamont (2002), and Cohen *et al.* (2007).

[6] Firms with traded options are considered less short sale constrained than those without traded options as options make it possible to take a short position without directly short selling the security. See Figleweski and Webb (1993) and Danielsen and Sorescu (2001).

[7] Institutional ownership or breadth of ownership as a proxy for lendable supply of shares—the reasoning being that the lower the institutional ownership, the more binding the constraints as shares harder to borrow. See Asquith *et al.* (2005), Chen *et al.* (2002), D'Avolio (2002) and Nagel (2005).

[8] Boehmer *et al.* (2008).

[9] Diether *et al.* (2002), Danielsen and Sorescu (2001), and Boehme *et al.* (2006).

the time of the forecasts. However, they find that this effect is stronger in the 1980s than in the 1990s. Again consistent with Miller's hypothesis, Chang *et al.* (2007) use the unique situation of short sale practices in the Hong Kong market to examine price effects on stocks when they are added to the official list of securities that can be sold short, and find that binding constraints tend to cause overvaluation and that the overvaluation is more pronounced for stocks with wider dispersion in investor opinion.

Combining both levels of short sale constraints and degrees of investor heterogeneity, Boehme *et al.* (2006) find evidence in support of Miller's overvaluation hypothesis when both conditions are met, but do not find evidence of systematic overvaluation when only one condition is met (either short sale constraints or differences of opinion). They suggest that the lack of consistent overvaluation evidence in previous studies is due to focusing on only one of the two conditions.

While many researchers investigate the implications of high levels of shorting on subsequent returns, in an interesting twist Boehmer *et al.* (2010) examine the information contained in low levels of shorting. Rather than asking the traditional question whether high short interest leads to negative abnormal returns, they investigate whether low short interest is informative about future returns, and find that portfolios of low short interest stocks have economically and statistically significant positive abnormal returns. Their findings have implications on existing theories of short sale constraints, in that not only do constraints prevent negative information from being incorporated into prices but also positive information. In addition, the empirical evidence indicates that the undervaluation of lightly shorted stocks is concentrated in smaller stocks, whereas traditional theory would suggest that smaller stocks should be harder to short and therefore have a tendency to be overvalued.

33.3.2 Evidence on market efficiency

If short sellers are informed traders and contribute to price efficiency, then constraining short sales should affect market efficiency.

Empirical support for Diamond and Verrecchia's model of slower incorporation of negative information into prices under short sale constraints comes from Bris *et al.* (2007). By carrying out a country-level analysis of 46 equity markets around the world with differing regulations, they show that negative information is incorporated into prices more slowly in countries with more impediments to short selling, thereby lending support to idea that shorting constraints decrease efficiency.

Historically, the SEC imposed some impediments to short selling in US equities through the "uptick rule."[10] Regulation SHO, implemented on 3 January 2005 and the first update to shorting regulation since 1938, included a pilot program to suspend sale price tests (uptick rule) on a set of 1000 stocks from the Russell 3000. The pilot ran from May 2005 through July 2007 at which point the SEC repealed the uptick rule.[11] Boehmer *et al.* (2008) study changes in shorting activity, effects on share prices and changes in effective spreads associated with the repeal. They found an increase in shorting for both pilot and non-pilot stocks following the repeal, but no significant price effects. One reason may be that at time of creation of Rule 10a the price tick was 12.5 cents, whereas in 2001 it was only one cent, making the uptick rule far from a binding constraint. Critically, Boehmer *et al.* (2008) argue that if short sellers were manipulative, the repeal of the uptick rule should have allowed them to carry out bear raids leading to a drop in price for heavily shorted shares, followed by a later rise to some fundamental value. The empirical tests showed no evidence of such reversals.[12]

In a series of articles using a large panel of daily short sale orders on the NYSE, Boehmer and his coauthors investigated whether short sellers are informed market participants (Boehmer *et al.*, 2008), the sources of short sellers' informational advantage (Boehmer *et al.*, 2012), and the link between short selling and the price discovery process (Boehmer 2012). They find that short sellers account for over a fifth of trading volume and are considered as traders with value-relevant information similar to that of analysts; with institutional investors, Boehmer and Wu use daily shorting flow to document whether short sellers enhance the informational efficiency of prices at short horizons. They find that increased daily shorting flow is associated with efficiency across all four dimensions of efficiency levels studied.[13] Therefore, the evidence indicates that short sellers are informed

---

[10] Securities and Exchange Act of 1934, Rule 10a-1.

[11] Announced 13 June 2007, effective 6 July 2007. See Diether *et al.* (2009) for a study showing that piloted stocks returns and volatility were not affected by lifting of the price tests.

[12] Empirical method: Sort stocks into quintiles based on past week's short sales (normalized by volume) and examine difference in cumulative return on most heavily shorted quintile less least heavily shorted quintile.

[13] The four measures of efficiency are: High-frequency transaction-based measure, low-frequency price delay measure, post-earnings announcement drift anomaly, and short selling around large price movements and price reversals.

participants and play an important role in the price discovery process.

33.4 Empirical Evidence from and Since the Financial Crisis of 2008

In response to the financial crisis of 2008, several regulatory agencies across differing countries instituted short sale bans and restrictions of varying degrees and duration. These bans provided researchers with unique experimental opportunities to empirically test the impact of short sale constraints. One particular advantage of studies over the ban period is that there is no need to develop proxies for short sale constraints as the bans were clear and binding.[14]

33.4.1 Impact of bans on stocks

Researchers investigated the impact of the bans on arbitrage, market efficiency, price impacts, the equity options market and across countries.

Gagnon and Witmer (2010) investigate the extent to which short sale restrictions impede market efficiency from the point of view of arbitrage. The Ontario Securities Commission and the US SEC both instituted temporary bans on short sales for stocks of cross-listed Canadian financial issuers for the same period. Gagnon and Witmer (2010) compare price differentials and trading volume of the banned cross-listed stocks with cross-listed non-financial Canadian stocks not subjected to the ban. The ban period showed Canadian shares subject to the ban trading at a premium of 74 basis points to the US share prices and a migration of trading volume to Canada, whereas no significant difference arises for non-banned stocks. These results lend support to Miller's price optimism theory, showing the critical role of short selling in avoiding arbitrage across markets.

Boehmer *et al.* (2012) use the SEC emergency order ban of September 2008 as an opportunity to study the impact of short sale constraints on prices and market quality of banned stocks as compared to a matched group of control stocks.[15] Although they find some evidence of a brief positive price impact to prices of banned stocks, this effect is hard to disentangle from the troubled

---

[14] Note that the SEC ban excludes market makers.
[15] Matching based on market capitalization, exchange listing, options listings and dollar trading volume.

asset relief program (TARP) bail-out announcements made on the same day and the positive impact is not seen in stocks added to the ban in the days following the initial list of banned stocks. However, the ban is associated with severe market degradation as evidenced by significant and negative impacts on liquidity measures and daily volatility. In addition, the rate of short selling, as measured by the number of shares shorted as a percentage of trading volume, declines significantly during the ban period as expected, but does not return to pre-ban levels after the ban. This may be due to the ban on naked shorting that remained in place after the 9 October expiration of the shorting ban. The authors conclude that the shorting ban did reduce shorting activity in the banned stocks, but at the high cost of reducing their liquidity and market quality.

Autore *et al.* (2009) take advantage of the US three-week short sale ban in September/October 2008 to test how binding short sale constraints affect stock valuation. While other authors matched banned stocks to a control set of stocks, Autore *et al.* focus only on the banned stocks and examine the effects on stocks with higher versus lower dispersion of investor opinion as well as those that experience greater or less market deterioration. Their study lends support to Miller's overvaluation hypothesis as they found greater overvaluation for those stocks with greater heterogeneity in investor opinion;[16] however, when the ban is lifted the dispersion effect disappears. This is inconsistent with Chang *et al.*'s (2007) finding that abnormal returns are more negative for firms with greater investor dispersion when short sale constraints are removed. Autore *et al.* also consider the effects of the ban on market quality as measured by relative quoted spreads around the ban and observe a greater decrease in valuation among banned stocks that undergo more severe market quality deterioration. Whereas the dispersion affect disappears over the three weeks following the ban, the ban has a lasting consequence with respect to market deterioration.

Battalio and Schultz (2010) study the impact of the confusion and regulatory uncertainty surrounding the September 2008 ban on the equity options market. By matching banned and control stocks they found no significant migration to the options market from the stock market by investors seeking short exposure to the banned stocks, that the cost of trading in banned stocks increased

---

[16] Autore *et al.* (2009) measure investor dispersion using two proxies—residual standard deviation using market model during 60 days prior to ban, with more divergence being associated with greater residual volatility, and also analyst earnings forecast dispersion.

significantly relative to the control group, and that as uncertainty reduced with clarifications in the week following the initial restrictions they observed a narrowing of spreads and convergence of actual and synthetic prices.

Several researchers examine bans in varying countries. Marsh and Niemer (2008) examine the return distributions of restricted stocks in 17 countries and find no strong evidence of an impact of restrictions on the behavior of returns, in particular no strong effect on skewness, which the classical models would expect to see become more positive. Berber and Pagano (2011) carry out a large study of restrictions across 30 countries, and find that the bans imposed during the financial crisis are associated with a statistically and economically significant liquidity disruption, that the bans do diminish price discovery, and importantly that they are not associated with stronger stock price performance.

33.4.2 Spillover effects of bans

As broad indices are underlying assets of derivative markets, and as such are important to the asset management and hedge fund industries, Lioui (2011) examines the impact of the 2008–2009 short sale bans on a selection of leading market indices and financial indices in the United States, France, United Kingdom and Germany.[17] Lioui investigates changes in higher moments of these indices in the period preceding and during the financial crisis, the ban periods and the post-ban periods across the countries, and finds that the bans had a systematic positive impact on the daily volatility of indices, and an even stronger impact on the financial indices. However, he does not observe a systematic effect on skewness, indicating that the ban did not reduce downward pressure in a significant manner.

On the whole, recent empirical research from the financial crisis strongly suggests that the intervention of regulatory agencies imposing short sale restrictions during the financial crisis did not consistently stem downward pressure on prices, as would be predicted by classical models, but that the bans negatively impacted market quality and efficiency. In addition, the bans may engender unintended consequences in broader market indices.

---

[17] United States (S&P 500, NASDAQ, S&P North American Financial Services Sector Index, NASDAQ Financial 100), France (CAC 40, CAC Financials), United Kingdom (FTSE 100) and Germany (DAX 40).

33.5 Future Challenges

Since the beginning of the financial crisis, there has been a strong push toward greater regulation of the financial markets by regulators and the public. According to most classical models of short sale constraints, restrictions should provide upward pressure on prices, albeit with potentially negative effects on market efficiency. In an effort to attenuate the negative movement in financial stocks during the summer of 2008, regulators imposed bans across many countries. However, the empirical evidence surrounding these short sale bans casts doubt on the wisdom of these regulatory interventions. Nonetheless, in the summer of 2011, as share prices of several European banks declined rapidly, regulators once again resorted to imposing short sale constraints on a group of financial stocks.

Several questions arise:

- Why do the restrictions not provide upward bias in prices as many classical models predict?
- What is missing in the classical models?
- Why do regulators continue to impose restrictions despite their questionable ability to stem declining prices?

The classical models essentially look at the effect of short sale constraints under investor heterogeneity or asymmetric information. However, none include the regulatory risk of loosening/ tightening constraints or make imposing constraints endogenous to the model. As regulators have clearly become important market participants, on occasion changing the rules of the game suddenly, and their actions impact the market, a promising new direction in asset pricing models incorporates uncertainty about government policy.

Pastor and Veronesi (2010) propose a theoretical general equilibrium model in which the government must make a policy decision that impacts stock prices. Their model incorporates two sources of uncertainty, political uncertainty regarding the political cost or benefit of changing policy and policy uncertainty regarding the impact on stock prices of a change in policy. Two empirical predictions of the model are that on average stock prices should fall at the announcement of policy changes and the fall should be greater the larger the uncertainty about the policy. Falling rather than rising prices with the imposition of short sale bans may be consistent with their model. In addition, political pressure on regulators to act in times of market stress may bring sufficient "political" benefits to outweigh the negative effects on the market, providing some insight into why regulators continue to impose short sale bans in times of stress.

Therefore, a promising direction of future research is a model of short sale constraints explicitly incorporating regulatory uncertainty to provide greater insight into the potential positive and negative impacts of short sale bans and better inform regulators the world over.

References

Asquith, P., Meulbroek, L., 1995. An empirical investigation of short interest. Harvard University Working Paper. Harvard University, Cambridge, MA.

Autore, D., Billingsley, R., Kovacs, T., 2011. The 2008 short sale ban: liquidity, dispersion of opinion, and the cross-section of returns of US financial stocks. Available at http://ssrn.com/abstract=1422728. http://dx.doi.org/10.2139/ssrn.1422728. or.

Bai, Y., Chang, E., Wang, J., 2006. Asset prices under short-sale constraints. University of Hong Kong and MIT Working Paper. MIT, Cambridge, MA.

Battalio, R., Schultz, P., 2011. Regulatory uncertainty and market liquidity: the 2008 short sale ban's impact on equity option markets. Journal of Finance 66, 2013–2053.

Berber, A., Pagano, M., 2011. Short-selling bans around the world: evidence from the 2007–09 crisis. CSEF Working Paper 241. CSEF, Naples.

Boehme, R., Danielsen, B., Sorescu, S., 2006. Journal of Financial and Quantitative Analysis 41, 455–487.

Boehmer, E., Wu, J., 2012. Short selling and the price discovery process. Forthcoming: Review of Financial Studies.

Boehmer, E., Jones, C., Zhang, X., 2008. Which shorts are informed? Journal of Finance 43, 498–521.

Boehmer, E., Jones, C., Zhang, X., 2009. Unshackling short sellers: The repeal of the Uptick Rule. Working paper, Edhec Business School. Available at: http://www0.gsb.columbia.edu/whoswho/more.cfm?&uni=cj88&pub=3231.

Boehmer, E., Jones, C., Zhang, X., 2012. Shackling short sellers: The 2008 shorting ban. Working Paper, Edhec Business School. Available at: http://papers.ssrn.com/sol3/papers.cfm?abstract_id=1412844.

Boehmer, E., Jones, C., Zhang, X., 2012. What do short sellers know? Working Paper, Edhec Business School. Available at: http://faculty-research.edhec.com/research/edhec-publications/2012/what-do-short-sellers-know–166422.kjsp?RH=1295357439915.

Boehmer, E., Huszar, Z., Jordan, B., 2010. The good news in short interest. Journal of Financial Economics 96, 80–97.

Bris, A., Goetzmann, W., Zhu, N., 2007. Efficiency and the bear: short sales and markets around the world. Journal of Finance 62, 1029–1079.

Chang, E., Cheng, J., Yu, Y., 2007. Short-sales constraints and price discovery: evidence from the Hong Kong Market. Journal of Finance 62, 2097–2121.

Danielsen, B., Sorescu, S., 2001. Why do option introductions depress stock priccs? A study of diminishing short-sale constraints. Journal of Financial and Quantitative Analysis 36, 451–484.

Diamond, D., Verrecchia, R., 1987. Constraints on short-selling and asset price adjustment to private information. Journal of Financial Economics 18, 277–311.

Diether, K., Malloy, C., Scherbina, A., 2002. Differences of opinion and the cross section of stock returns. Journal of Finance 57, 2113–2141.

Duffie, D., Gârleanu, N., Pedersen, L., 2002. Securities lending, shorting and pricing. Journal of Financial Economics 66, 307–339.

Figleweski, S., 1981. The informational effects of restrictions on short sales: some empirical evidence. Journal of Financial and Quantitative Analysis 16, 463–476.

Figleweski, S., Webb, G., 1993. Options, short sales, and market completeness. Journal of Finance 48, 761–777.

Gagnon, L., Witmer, J., 2010. Short changed? The market's reaction to the short sale ban of 2008. Available at http://ssrn.com/abstract=1569114 or http://dx.doi.org/10.2139/ssrn.1569114

Goldstein, I., Guembel, A., 2008. Manipulation and the allocational role of prices. Review of Economic Studies 75, 133–164.

Harrison, M., Kreps, D., 1978. Speculative investor behavior in a stock market with heterogeneous expectations. Quarterly Journal of Economics 92, 323–336.

Hong, H., Stein, J., 2003. Differences of opinion, short-sales constraints and market crashes. Review of Financial Studies 16, 487–525.

Khanna, N., Mathews, R., 2012. Doing battle with short sellers: the conflicted role of blockholders in bear raids. Forthcoming: Journal of Financial Economics

Lamont, O., Thaler, R., 2003. Can the market add and subtract? Mispricing in tech carve-outs. Journal of Political Economy 111, 227–268.

Lioui, A., 2011. Spillover effects of counter-cyclical market regulation: evidence from the 2008 ban on short sales. Journal of Alternative Investments 13, 53–66.

Marsh, I., Payne, R., 2010. Banning Short Sales and Market Quality: The U.K.'s Experience. Working paper, Cass Business School. Available at: http://papers.ssrn.com/sol3/papers.cfm?abstract_id=1645847.

Miller, E., 1977. Risk, uncertainty and divergence of opinion. Journal of Finance 32, 1151–1168.

Nagel, S., 2005. Short sales, institutional investors and the cross-section of stock returns. Journal of Financial Economics 78, 277–309.

Pastor, L., Veronesi, P., 2010. Uncertainty about government policy and stock prices. Chicago Booth Research Paper 10–25 Fama–Miller Working Paper Series. Booth School of Business, Chicago, IL.

Scheinkman, J., Xiong, W., 2003. Overconfidence and speculative bubbles. Journal of Political Economy 111, 1183–1219.

34

QUANTITATIVE EASING, FINANCIAL RISK AND PORTFOLIO DIVERSIFICATION

Modena Matteo, Lossani Marco and Borello Giuliana
Catholic University of Milan

CHAPTER OUTLINE

34.1 Introduction

After the financial crisis broke out in autumn 2008, the US monetary authority engaged in an unprecedented expansion of the money supply. The federal funds rate and the short-term yields quickly approached the zero lower bound. Despite this, the level of resource utilization has remained unsatisfactorily low. In December 2008, the Federal Reserve announced the intention of purchasing large quantities of agency debt and mortgage-backed securities; moreover, it was disclosed that a team of economists were analyzing the potential benefits of purchasing long-term Treasury securities. A few months later, in April 2009, the quantitative easing (QE) strategy was further detailed. In this respect, Gagnon *et al.* (2011) point out that the Federal Reserve increased the size of its balance sheet by an amount twice the magnitude of total Federal Reserve assets prior to 2008.

In this chapter, we assess the extent to which the aforementioned changed monetary conditions have affected the relationship between financial markets and some leading macro-finance indicators. In the first part, we thus examine the financial markets dynamics before and after February 2006. We find evidence

Rethinking Valuation and Pricing Models. http://dx.doi.org/10.1016/B978-0-12-415875-7.00034-8

supporting the view that the macro-finance foundation of market movements has changed substantially in the Bernanke period. If real interest rates could explain markets' performance in the second part of the Greenspan tenure, the stochastic discount factor (SDF) seems to be the only factor capable of explaining financial markets movements after 2006. In the second part, we relate our findings to the extraordinary growth of money supply determined by the Federal Reserve's choice of expanding its balance sheet by purchasing long-term Treasury securities. In addition, rather than focusing exclusively on money supply, we explore the role of the risk premium that seems to lie beneath the different outcome characterizing the Bernanke sample. Gagnon *et al.* (2011), in fact, find that the flattening of the yield curve is mostly due to declining term premia. Our empirical findings are in line with the achievements of modern macro-finance theory, according to which asset pricing is explained by time-varying risk aversion and the cyclical movements of term premia (Campbell and Cochrane, 1999; Brandt and Wang, 2003; Wachter, 2006; Li, 2007; Mele, 2007). In particular, we argue that risk premia are related to changes in both unemployment and risk aversion, finding evidence that the weak discounting process implied by high levels of risk aversion can explain the cyclical behavior of assets prices.

A number of studies have recently analyzed the effects of the large-scale assets purchases (LSAPs) on the US term structure. Gagnon *et al.* (2011) argue that LSAPs have been successful in lowering long-term rates through significant reduction of the risk premia. Hamilton and Wu (2012) estimate the effects on the term structure exerted by an eventual maturity swap, i.e. selling short-term debt and using the proceeds to retire long-term Treasury securities. They find that such a swap could have reduced long-term rates by about 13 basis points. In a similar vein, Swanson (2011) highlights the similarities between QE and Operation Twist (or Operation Nudge) carried out in the 1960s. D'Amico and King (2010) find a much larger drop of long rates (50 basis points), probably due to the greater market segmentation (Gürkaynak and Wright, 2011) associated with the unusual monetary conditions. However, Stroebel and Taylor (2009) find evidence that a negligible effect could be ascribed to QE; in particular, they show that the mortgage-backed securities purchase program had insignificant or little impact after controlling for prepayment and default risks. Thornton (2009) points out that the yield curve flattening that followed the Federal Open Market Committee announcement in March 2009 vanished after a few weeks. Finally, Doh (2010) discusses the efficacy of unconventional monetary policy in a preferred-habitat term structure framework. He sustains that changes in the supply of bonds affect yields provided investors have preferences for the specific maturity spectrum hit by the central bank's action.

Although it happened with some delay, at the end the extraordinary expansion of the M1 aggregate was successful in reducing long-term rates (Figure 34.1a). As a matter of fact, it seems that the diminishing trend of long-term rates started much before the 2008–2009 crises; it actually began in 2000. In addition, the relatively high volatility of the 10-year yield between 2008 and 2011 may well lead LSAP analysis to significantly different results depending on the timespan.

As mentioned above, a lot of empirical research has focused on LSAPs with the aim of determining whether QE has been effective. Different methods have been employed to estimate the impact of LSAPs on the long end of the yield curve. However, little attention has been paid to the macro-finance foundations of asset pricing in the era of unconventional monetary policy. This chapter aims at bridging such a gap, analyzing whether QE data evidence is consistent with the most recent achievements in the macro-finance literature. Results show that the changing perception of risk across the business cycle significantly accounts for the cyclical variation of asset prices.

A visual inspection of Figure 34.1(b) makes clear where our interest in the risk premium originates from. Essentially, our attention is captured by the fact that the premium dynamics

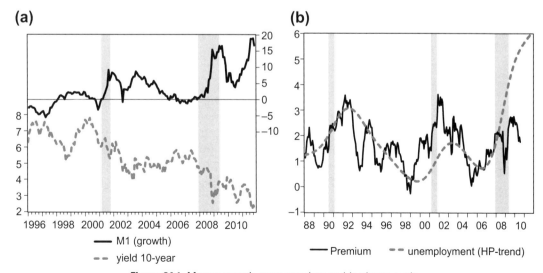

Figure 34.1 Money growth, term premium and business cycle.

reproduces quite closely the cyclical fluctuations of unemployment (the shaded areas represent the National Bureau of Economic Research recession dates). Backus and Wright (2007) have emphasized the positive correlation between the nominal forward premium and the rate of unemployment. Although the premium series exhibits relatively high volatility, while the unemployment is more persistent, the movements of the two variables seem determined by a common drift. In addition, we give emphasis to the opposite movements followed by the 10-year yield (Figure 34.1a) and the risk premium (Figure 34.1b) just before the recent recession commenced (December 2007). On the one hand, falling long-term rates were reflecting expectations of expansionary monetary policy; on the other hand, rocketing risk premia were mirroring market participants' mounting risk aversion.[1]

The risk premium displays an unquestionable countercyclical pattern (Fama and French, 1989; Ferson and Harvey, 1991). The analysis carried out in this chapter moves from the additional assumption that such behavior of the term premium can be viewed as a consequence of the changing perception of risk resulting in time-varying risk aversion. In particular, the idea that risk aversion drives premia across states of nature (Cochrane, 2005) can be generalized along the time dimension since the volatility of investors' marginal utilities increases during recessions (Campbell and Cochrane, 1999). Hence, countercyclical risk aversion provides an argument in favor of a rational response of agents to investment opportunities (Constantinides, 1990). Accordingly, Wachter (2006) finds that time-varying risk aversion can explain the predictability of both stock returns and the price movements of long-term bonds. In a similar fashion, Li (2007) shows how time-varying risk aversion affects risk premia. Lettau and Ludvigson (2001) find that fluctuations of consumption relative to aggregate wealth can be a good predictor of future stock returns. More interestingly, volatility of returns is related to asymmetric changes in the risk premium over the business cycle (Mele, 2007). In particular, large variations of risk premia in bad times and small changes in good times can explain countercyclical stock market volatility. In this chapter, we provide further evidence relating asset pricing and risk aversion. In particular,

[1] The typical determinant of the risk premium (inflation) was not driving the premium dynamics. Despite that inflation expectations could temporarily explain the rise of risk premia in late 2007 and early 2008, when the oil price was also rising and the risk of a supply shock was perceived as a threat, the upward trend of the term premium (between 2005 and 2009) seems a more general issue.

there is evidence that countercyclical risk premia may result from a weaker discounting process applied by agents in regimes characterized by high risk aversion.

Figure 34.1(b) also provides an interesting explanation of QE. After the US economy fell into the liquidity trap, the Federal Reserve not only realized that the federal funds rate reductions were ineffective in revitalizing the credit market, but also observed the abnormal deviation of the unemployment rate from what could be considered its natural track, i.e. the term premium. Common trends in Figure 34.1(b) thus find a rationalization in the idea that low labor income, associated with high unemployment, makes agents more risk averse. For instance, Lettau and Ludvigson (2001) explain fluctuations in the aggregate consumption/wealth ratio with the deviations in the shared trend among consumption, asset wealth and labor income. When the long-lasting connection between the premium and the unemployment rate broke down, the Federal Reserve was forced to explore further options to tackle an unprecedented economic distress. In particular, the aim of reducing term premia by managing the supply of long-term bonds can be interpreted as an attempt to drive unemployment down in order to re-establish the broken link. However, such an effort could work provided the direction of causality runs from the premium to unemployment and not *vice versa*. If this is not the case, reversing the direction of causality between two variables becomes a far more complex goal to be achieved.

The rest of the paper is organized as follows. In Section 34.2, we examine the relationship between financial markets and some key macro-finance drivers. Section 34.2 also contains a brief discussion regarding the implications for strategic portfolio diversification. The effects of QE and the role of the risk premium are analyzed in Section 34.3. Section 34.4 concludes.

34.2 Financial Markets and Macro-Finance Indicators Before and After 2006

In this chapter, we examine the dynamics of financial markets within a two-stage approach. This section contains the first step of the analysis which is merely preliminary to the core part of the empirical work reported in Section 34.3. First, we split the sample into two subperiods. The first subperiod (Sample 1) ranges between 1996 and 2006, and it covers approximately the second half of the Greenspan era. The second subsample (Sample 2) goes from February 2006 to November 2011; it thus starts when Ben Bernanke became the chairman of the Federal Reserve. The Chow breakpoint test supports the choice of splitting the sample in early 2006.

In this section, we investigate whether the relationship between financial markets and some potential drivers, i.e. acknowledged macro-finance variables, has changed after 2006. The empirical findings outline a very different picture before and after February 2006. This outcome encourages a deeper investigation, which is carried out in Section 34.3, where we take into account the non-linear effects of QE giving particular emphasis to the role of the risk premium.

We start the analysis by estimating Equation (34.1). It captures the relationship between the first principal component (PC) of the annual returns of some representative US stock market indexes[2] ($\Delta XX^{\text{PC},1}$) and the core macro-finance drivers:

$$\Delta XX_t^{\text{PC},1} = \phi_0 + \phi_1 x_{t-h} + v_t, \tag{34.1}$$

where x_t represents the macro-finance variables, such as the real interest rate, the SDF and the yield spread. In particular, the real interest rate is built as the log difference between the nominal rate, either the one-year yield or the federal funds rate (Bekaert *et al.*, 2010), and expected inflation.[3] The SDF is a theoretical measure of the marginal rate of substitution (parameterization as in Campbell and Cochrane, 1999). The yield spread is the difference between the 10-year and the three-month yields. With the choice of explaining the actual dynamics of stock markets using lagged values of the macro-finance drivers we assume that the direction of causality runs from the macro-finance drivers to the stock markets. The Granger test supports this choice since the lagged values of the SDF help predict market dynamics, but not *vice versa*. In this respect, the adopted strategy also allows avoiding the endogeneity problem. As a further check, we have estimated Equation (34.1) imposing as dependent variable the returns series of each single stock index, achieving results that are similar to those presented in Table 34.1.

As expected, the evidence reported in the left panel of Table 34.1 highlights a significant inverse correlation between stock

---

[2] S&P 500, Dow Jones Industrial Average (DJIA), Wilshire 5000 and Russell 2000. The first PC summarizes markets' returns quite accurately; in the entire sample it captures about the 95% of stock market variability, while two components explain almost 99% of markets' dynamics.

[3] Expected inflation is the core consumer price index (CPI; all items less food and energy) forecast from a backward-looking Phillips curve in which actual inflation responds to its lagged quarterly average and to the Hodrick–Prescott detrended unemployment rate.

Table 34.1. Equations (34.1) and (34.2)

| | | | | | Dependent variable | | | | | |
| | | | | | US stock markets | | | | | |
Sample	Lag	Real FFR	R^2	AIK	SDF	R^2	AIK	Spread	R^2	AIK
1996–2006	$t-1$	1.315 (0.025)	0.17	3.65	−4.151 (0.000)	0.22	3.58	−0.394 (0.102)	0.11	3.72
	$t-3$	1.109 (0.061)	0.12	3.70	−4.973 (0.000)	0.32	3.45	−0.353 (0.153)	0.08	3.74
	$t-6$	0.776 (0.206)	0.06	3.77	−4.691 (0.000)	0.28	3.50	−0.279 (0.261)	0.05	3.78
2006–2011	$t-1$	1.197 (0.176)	0.09	4.52	−2.046 (0.004)	0.17	4.47	0.147 (0.640)	0.01	4.60
	$t-3$	0.884 (0.325)	0.05	4.56	−2.838 (0.001)	0.34	4.23	0.263 (0.357)	0.02	4.58
	$t-6$	0.292 (0.724)	0.01	4.61	−3.908 (0.000)	0.64	3.60	0.369 (0.178)	0.05	4.56
					Hedge funds returns					
1996–2006	$t-1$	1.713 (0.000)	0.27	3.59	0.169 (0.907)	0.01	3.90	−0.463 (0.023)	0.13	3.76
	$t-3$	1.658 (0.001)	0.25	3.61	−0.867 (0.552)	0.01	3.89	−0.450 (0.043)	0.13	3.77
	$t-6$	1.458 (0.005)	0.19	3.69	−1.730 (0.196)	0.03	3.87	−0.449 (0.057)	0.13	3.77
2006–2011	$t-1$	1.700 (0.041)	0.16	4.49	−2.003 (0.007)	0.14	4.66	−0.086 (0.783)	0.01	4.67
	$t-3$	1.412 (0.099)	0.11	4.56	−2.905 (0.001)	0.31	4.14	0.074 (0.802)	0.01	4.68
	$t-6$	0.833 (0.323)	0.04	4.64	−4.106 (0.000)	0.62	3.75	0.209 (0.444)	0.01	4.66

The dependent variable is the US stock markets' first PC in the left panel, while it is the first PC of the annual change of some hedge funds return indexes in the right panel. Lag identifies the lag of the independent variable. Although significant in some cases, the estimation of the intercept is not reported here. Spread is the difference between the 10-year and the 3-month yields. p-values in parentheses. FFR is the federal funds rate, R^2 is the goodness-of-fit and AIK is the Akaike information criterion.

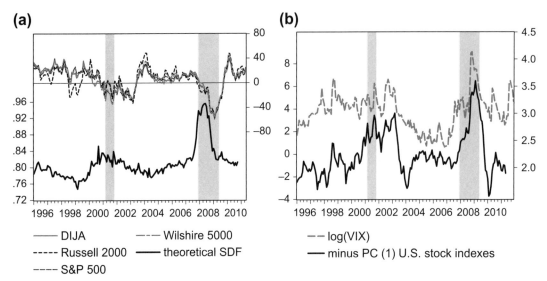

Figure 34.2 Financial markets, volatility and SDF.

market movements and the SDF since larger discounts applied to the future dividend stream imply a weaker stock market rush. Importantly, during the Bernanke tenure, the SDF can account for over 50% of the stock market fluctuations.[4] Figure 34.2(a) suggests this result may not be surprising since the sharp increase of the SDF occurs before the recession starts; in addition, the SDF peak precedes the 2008 stock market collapse. More interesting, the SDF reduction promoted by QE has had a positive impact on stock markets and hedge funds returns.

Focusing on the Japanese case, Kimura and Small (2006) find that QE has increased the risk premium on assets characterized by procyclical returns, i.e. typically equities. In this respect, our results outline a similar effect, since the drop of the SDF reinforced by the Federal Reserve's QE action has driven the stock markets along a temporary upward path in 2009. The real interest rate effect on markets is either marginal or absent. Consistent with our findings, recent evidence suggests that the stance of monetary policy has not triggered asset prices and it has not been

---

[4] As an additional experiment, we analyzed the predictability of the S&P 500 future movements over the three- and six-month horizons. Hence, the future realizations of the stock index have been regressed onto the actual level of the macro-finance drivers. Results show that the SDF carries a significant predictive power, while the real interest rates and the yield spread do not. In particular, the SDF captures the future evolution of the S&P 500 Index with a relatively high goodness-of-fit in the second subsample (0.50). In the first subsample, the goodness-of-fit is only 0.22.

at the origin of the housing bubble before the crisis broke out (Del Negro and Otrok, 2007; Bernanke, 2010).

The right panel of Table 34.1 shows the results for the hedge funds industry. After extracting the PCs from the annual returns of some hedge funds indexes,[5] we have estimated the following regression:

$$\Delta \mathrm{HF}_t^{\mathrm{PC},1} = \gamma_0 + \gamma_1 x_{t-h} + u_t. \tag{34.2}$$

The variance proportion explained by the first PC is relatively small, i.e. smaller than that obtained for the stock markets. This is due to the greater heterogeneity of hedge funds indexes, which may be either little or negatively correlated one another. For instance, market-neutral investments, macro strategies or short-biased hedging display peculiar features; such investment approaches generate returns that do not track conventional market movements. Estimations of Regression (2) suggest that traditional macro-finance variables (the real interest rate and the yield spread) can only explain the hedge funds returns in Sample 1. However, the returns in the hedge funds industry seem independent from the past realizations of both the real rate and the spread after 2006. As it happens for the stock markets, the lagged values of SDF significantly capture the hedge funds dynamics[6] in the second sample.

We estimate Equation (34.3) to see whether the macro-finance drivers can explain the evolution of the log(VIX) index over time. The VIX index is an indicator of expected (implied) volatility derived from options on the S&P 500, and it is regarded as a measure of financial risk. Upward spikes of the VIX index are usually interpreted as signals of incoming bouts of market turmoil:

$$\log(\mathrm{VIX}_t) = \varphi_0 + \varphi_1 x_{t-h} + \varsigma_t. \tag{34.3}$$

Figure 34.2(b) shows that volatility substantially increased after 2006; hence, we expect empirical evidence to be significantly different in the two subsamples. Results are striking in this sense. Between 1996 and 2006, volatility cannot be explained by past values of the macro-finance variables,[7] while, periods

---

[5] The PCs have been obtained using the group composed by the following hedge fund research representative indexes: macro, distressed, event driven, merger arbitrage, relative value, market neutral and short bias.

[6] Evidence reported in the right panel of Table 34.1 is also confirmed when the dependent variable is the returns series of the hedge funds return total index, rather than the first PC of the hedge fund indexes.

[7] Results for Subsample 1 are not reported in Table 34.2. In Sample 1, the goodness-of-fit is very low (approximately zero) and the coefficients multiplying the macro-finance drivers are not statistically significant.

Table 34.2. Equation (34.3)

Sample	Lag	Real rate	R^2	AIK	Real FFR	R^2	AIK	SDF	R^2	AIK	Spread	R^2	AIK
2006–2011	t − 1	−0.425 (0.000)	0.29	0.80	−0.435 (0.000)	0.37	0.67	0.338 (0.049)	0.14	1.09	0.087 (0.105)	0.09	1.05
	t − 3	−0.379 (0.001)	0.23	0.88	−0.388 (0.001)	0.29	0.79	0.475 (0.014)	0.29	0.87	0.088 (0.076)	0.09	1.05
	t − 6	−0.365 (0.003)	0.21	0.91	−0.335 (0.005)	0.21	0.90	0.633 (0.000)	0.52	0.43	0.091 (0.037)	0.09	1.04

The dependent variable is the log(VIX) index. Lag identifies the lag of the independent variable. Although significant in some cases, the estimation of the intercept is not reported here. Spread is the difference between the 10-year and the three-month yields. p-values in parentheses. FFR is the federal funds rate, R^2 is the goodness-of-fit and AIK is the Akaike information criterion.

characterized by high volatility seem to have a macro-finance rationalization since the lagged values of the drivers significantly explain actual volatility levels. In Sample 2, real rates are inversely correlated with stock market volatility. Coefficient estimates suggest that decreasing real rates boosts expected volatility. Although a direct link between monetary policy and the housing bubble has been mitigated by recent evidence (Del Negro and Otrok, 2007; Bernanke, 2010), our results could be interpreted in line with Rajan (2006). He points out that low real rates encourage investors to buy risky assets and potentially illiquid securities. The worse the quality of held portfolios the more they turn into high volatility and illiquid trade because subsequent portfolio readjustments are difficult due to lack of demand for toxic assets.

Table 34.2 shows clear evidence of a positive relationship between volatility and lagged values of the SDF. Heavy discount applied to future assets payoffs results in lower stock prices and higher volatility; both the inverse correlation between stock market returns and volatility, and the countercyclical pattern of volatility are corroborated in a number of empirical studies (Schwert, 1989; Brandt and Kang, 2004; Giot, 2005). Brandt and Kang (2004) find that the correlation between (the innovations to) the conditional mean and volatility is negative and statistically significant. Giot (2005) provides evidence of an inverse correlation between the returns of the S&P 100 and the NASDAQ 100 indexes and their corresponding implied volatility indexes. A clear inverse relationship between the US stock markets first PC and the log(VIX) index can be seen in Figure 34.2(b) where peaks in expected volatility mainly occur in bear markets.

So far, empirical evidence seems to suggest that post-2006 stock market volatility could be fairly anticipated by looking at the evolution of simple macro-financial indicators. Hence, two issues arise. (i) The deep financial crisis can be interpreted as the consequence of self-fulfilling prophecies so long as markets participants' awareness of potential financial fragility may have encouraged important short trade and led to a massive way-out outcome. In such a context, a relatively weak idiosyncratic negative shock could have produced devastating effects. (ii) If asset managers were aware of the incoming distress on financial markets, they could have thought of alternative trading strategies to tackle the situation. There is evidence supporting a canny portfolio substitution effect since asset managers have recently given a greater weight to the investment in commodities and commodity futures. In particular, this phenomenon can be ascribed to hedge funds managers whose strategic view is free to contemplate a great variety of investment opportunities, such as structured finance instruments, commodities and commodity derivatives. When stock market indexes follow a downward trend, in fact, fund managers find it convenient to shift resources from financial securities to commodities in order to limit negative returns of their equity portfolios. Jensen *et al.* (2000) investigate the role of commodity futures in diversified portfolios. In periods characterized by tight monetary policy, they observe that commodity futures play an important role in efficient portfolios, allowing significant superior returns at any risk level. Modena (2011b) argues that the price dynamics of agricultural commodities has a rationalization that goes beyond the mere interaction between supply and demand. Robust evidence corroborates a significant inverse correlation between financial markets' returns and the movements of food commodity prices that emerged, in particular, during the recent financial crisis. Cheung and Miu (2010) provide evidence concerning the diversification benefits of adding commodities to equity portfolios. In a similar vein, Edwards and Park (1996) emphasize the positive effects of adding actively managed commodity futures to conventional equity portfolios.

Before moving to Section 34.3, we look at the bond market represented by the latent factors of the term structure of interest rates: level, slope and curvature. First, we analyze the relationship between the factors and their theoretical (financial) equivalents.[8]

[8] Nelson and Siegel (1987), as well as Diebold and Li (2006), argue that the level reflects a long-term component, i.e. the 10-year yield. The slope is a measure of the yield spread, i.e. the difference between the 10-year and the three-month yields. Curvature, or the butterfly factor, is computed as twice the two-year yield minus the sum between the 10-year and the three-month yields.

In this respect, our findings suggest consistency before and after 2006. A marginal exception is the larger response of the level to the 10-year yield in Sample 2. This is consistent with the policy aim of managing the long end of the yield curve during QE. Then, inspired by recent developments in the literature (Ang and Piazzesi, 2003; Rudebusch and Wu, 2008; Dewachter and Lyrio, 2006; Modena, 2011a), we examine the extent to which the factors track their macroeconomic counterparts. Rudebusch and Wu (2008) associate the level with a measure of inflation (the rate of inflation targeted by the central bank) and the slope with the policy rate implied by a Taylor rule (Rudebusch *et al.*, 2006). However, the implicit positive correlation between the slope and the policy rate in their interpretation contrasts with the conventional view that low values of the spread reflect the expectations of a tight stance of monetary policy. If long-term rates are persistent, in fact, a rise in the policy rate flattens the yield curve. Hence, tight policy implies a drop of the yield spread and a reduction of the slope. Consistent with this view, an inversion of the yield curve indicates an incoming slowdown in economic activity (Estrella and Hardouvelis, 1991). In the Greenspan era we find a significant inverse correlation between the federal fund rate changes and the slope (Modena, 2010); however, this relationship is definitely weak in Sample 2. Short nominal rates at the zero lower bound coupled with long-maturity Treasury curve management provide a rationale for this outcome.

Following the seminal paper by Stock and Watson (1989), a lot of the empirical research has confirmed that the yield spread is a leading indicator. In particular, a large spread is usually welcomed because it is a signal of faster economic growth. High values of the spread, in fact, reflect expectations of easy monetary policy: If the monetary authority reduces the policy rate, the impact on the short end of the yield curve is larger than the effect on the long end and the spread widens. It is worth noticing that the aforementioned mechanism is inverted during QE, because yield curve movements are exclusively driven by long-term rates. After 2006 we find evidence that the slope factor is related to the quarterly change in the 10-year yield.

The right panel of Table 34.3 highlights the relationship between curvature and real activity (Modena, 2011a). Results are approximately the same in both subsamples; the R^2 reduction is due to the greater volatility affecting both variables after 2007.

We now summarize the main results emerged so far:
- The theoretical SDF, rather than the other drivers, has had a major role in explaining the evolution of financial markets.

Table 34.3. Latent Factors of the Term Structure

| | | Dependent variable | | | | | |
| | | *Term structure level* | | | | | |
Sample	Lag	Yield (120 months)	R^2	AIK	Core CPI	R^2	AIK
1996—2006	*t*	1.757 (0.000)	0.84	2.36	2.923 (0.000)	0.34	3.81
	t − 1	1.724 (0.000)	0.81	2.57	2.754 (0.000)	0.31	3.86
2006—2011	*t*	1.957 (0.000)	0.90	2.06	2.824 (0.000)	0.62	3.43
	t − 1	1.976 (0.000)	0.88	2.23	2.825 (0.000)	0.62	3.44
		Term structure slope					
1996—2006	*t*	−0.631 (0.000)	0.48	0.58	0.314 (0.000)	0.90	−1.00
	t − 1	−0.665 (0.000)	0.52	0.49	0.299 (0.000)	0.81	−0.42
2006—2011	*t*	−0.128 (0.109)	0.10	1.07	0.282 (0.000)	0.90	−1.15
	t − 1	−0.155 (0.039)	0.15	1.01	0.256 (0.000)	0.75	−0.23
		Term structure curvature					
1996—2006	*t*	0.820 (0.000)	0.61	−2.26	1.908 (0.000)	0.66	3.15
	t − 1	0.685 (0.000)	0.42	−1.87	1.938 (0.000)	0.69	3.06
2006—2011	*t*	0.816 (0.000)	0.52	−2.03	1.238 (0.000)	0.44	3.81
	t − 1	0.522 (0.000)	0.22	−1.54	1.262 (0.000)	0.46	3.77

The dependent variables are the term structure level, slope and curvature. Lag identifies the lag of the independent variable. Although significant in some cases, the estimation of the intercept is not reported here. Spread is the difference between the 10-year and the three-month yields. NS is the theoretical curvature *à la* Nelson—Siegel. TCU is the (log) total capacity utilization. *p*-values in parentheses. FFR is the federal funds rate, R^2 is the goodness-of-fit and AIK is the Akaike information criterion.

In this regard our results are consistent with recent literature (Lettau and Ludvigson, 2001; Wachter, 2006).
- Evidence in Sample 2 displays features that can be related to the QE strategy.
- It seems that recent financial markets movements have not been completely unpredictable.

Section 34.3 provides further evidence that the relationship between financial markets and macro-finance indicators has changed substantially during the QE; in particular, we emphasize the role of risk aversion that affected financial markets through the risk premium.

34.3 Risk Aversion, Risk Premia and the Discounting Process

In this section, we investigate the extent to which the dynamics of the macro-finance drivers is due to pure monetary policy actions or to the risk premium. Then, we look at risk aversion and risk premia more deeply, and examine the implications for asset pricing. A lot of emphasis has recently been attributed to the role of the risk premium in the macro-finance literature (Rudebusch *et al.*, 2007; Li, 2007; Mele, 2007; Bekaert *et al.*, 2009; De Graeve *et al.* 2010); then the financial crisis gave a further stimulus to continue in that direction. Adrian and Shin (2010) introduced the notion of macro risk premium. Adrian *et al.* (2010) have explored this further. We agree that the analysis of the risk premium is crucial to understanding the relationship between macroeconomics and finance. The correct determination of the risk premium allows fair asset pricing; in turn, with efficient markets, asset prices, alias the price of risk, are informative about the economic conjuncture (Hamilton and Kim, 2002; Favero *et al.*, 2005; Ang *et al.*, 2006).

Although many reasons underlie the determination of the term premium,[9] we believe that the attitude towards risk is the prevailing motive in bad times. A visual inspection of Figure 34.1(b) seems to support our conjecture. There is clear evidence that the premium reproduces the cyclical fluctuation of

---

[9] It captures the level of uncertainty perceived by market participants. Long-term investors require a premium to be compensated for postponing consumption. The premium reflects the unanticipated stance of monetary policy or the unexpected movements in long-term yields (Campbell and Shiller, 1991). An inflationary risk premium typically explains the upward-sloping shape of the nominal yield curve (Buraschi and Jiltsov, 2005; Ang and Bekaert, 2008). More generally, the term premium reflects macroeconomic uncertainty (Bekaert *et al.*, 2009).

unemployment because aggregate risk aversion increases in bad times and decreases in good times. Consistently, investors prefer assets whose payoffs are inversely correlated with the business cycle (Cochrane, 2005) and require higher premia in bad states. The Granger test suggests that the direction of causality moves from unemployment to the risk premium. In addition, as shown later, the effect exerted by an increase in the term premium on the non-linear relationship between the SDF and financial markets is analogous to that generated by a rise in the rate of unemployment (see Table 34.6 below).

As mentioned above, Figure 34.1(b) provides an appealing explanation of QE. After observing the remarkable deviation of the unemployment trend from the risk premium (in 2008), reducing the term premium (intermediate target), with the hope of reversing the direction of causality between unemployment and the premium, was the only feasible option for the Federal Reserve. Hence, the final goal of QE of achieving a socially acceptable level of resource utilization has been pursued through the aim of re-establishing the above-mentioned link.

The estimation of Equation (34.4) introduces the second part of our analysis. The risk premium is the average across maturity of excess (log) bond returns as in Cochrane and Piazzesi (2005). We assume money supply and the premium to be separate sources of economic influence. In this respect, M1 represents money supply (the traditional monetary policy tool) and the premium reflects agents' risk aversion.

$$\Delta x_t = \delta_0 + \delta_1 \Delta M1_t + \delta_2 \Delta M1_{t-6} + \delta_3 pr_{t-1} + \varepsilon_t, \qquad (34.4)$$

where x_t represents each of the macro-finance drivers. Equation (34.4) is estimated by ordinary least squares. However, to capture the contemporaneous effect of the term premium on the macro-finance drivers, we use the generalized method of moments (GMM) to estimate a slightly different version of Equation (34.4), where the first lag of the premium (pr_{t-1}) is replaced by its actual value (pr_t). In the latter case the first lag of each regressor is used as the instrument. Results are reported in Table 34.4.

In both samples there is evidence of a real *liquidity effect*. An increase in money supply, in fact, leads to lower real interest rates; this occurs because short rates decrease and expected inflation eventually rises. The magnitude of the estimated δ_2 coefficient is greater in Sample 1 than in Sample 2 since real rates are computed using short-term nominal rates whose fluctuations were actually limited by the zero bound in the second sample. After 2006, the risk premium is inversely correlated with both the real interest rate and the SDF. The premium affects the real interest rate through

Table 34.4. Equation (34.4)

Sample	Dependent variable	Newey–West				GMM (IV)			
		$\Delta M1_t$	$\Delta M1_{t-6}$	pr_{t-1}	R^2	$\Delta M1_t$	$\Delta M1_{t-6}$	pr_t	R^2
1996–2006	real FFR	−0.664	−0.505	−0.148	0.61	−0.579	−0.617	−0.170	0.61
		(0.001)	(0.005)	(0.412)		(0.010)	(0.003)	(0.384)	
	SDF	−0.076	0.079	0.408	0.45	−0.142	0.155	0.445	0.45
		(0.334)	(0.368)	(0.000)		(0.176)	(0.113)	(0.000)	
	spread	2.155	0.729	1.129	0.63	2.028	0.921	1.226	0.65
		(0.000)	(0.114)	(0.022)		(0.001)	(0.077)	(0.018)	
2006–2011	real FFR	−0.663	−0.264	−0.607	0.77	−0.625	−0.304	−0.749	0.75
		(0.000)	(0.023)	(0.065)		(0.000)	(0.037)	(0.050)	
	SDF	0.144	−0.533	1.827	0.52	0.180	−0.608	2.294	0.57
		(0.125)	(0.000)	(0.000)		(0.070)	(0.000)	(0.000)	
	spread	0.570	1.753	1.072	0.78	0.523	1.850	1.351	0.80
		(0.009)	(0.000)	(0.163)		(0.015)	(0.000)	(0.123)	

Although significant in some cases, the estimation of the intercept is not reported here. Δ indicates the annual rate of growth. p-values in parentheses. FFR is the federal funds rate and R^2 is the goodness-of-fit.

the inflation expectations component. However, this effect is negligible between 1996 and 2006 because inflation was not a threat (the CPI inflation average was approximately 2.5%). Although supply-side shocks did not hit the US economy in the 1990s, Mankiw (2001) points out that discretionary monetary policy was successful and interest rate reaction to inflationary pressures were prompt. In the Bernanke sample, the negative correlation between the premium and the real rate is determined by opposite movements of the two variables. Immediately before the recession, the inverse correlation is explained by the premium's escalation, while, especially during QE2, the relationship is governed by a gentle upward trend of inflation.

The empirical evidence suggests that the effect of money supply[10] on the yield spread has been roughly the same before and after 2006. This seems to cast a shadow on the efficacy of QE pursuing the above-mentioned intermediate target. However, as a matter of fact, the reduction of long rates followed policy intervention with some delay. What emerged by a visual inspection of Figure 34.1(a) is confirmed by the estimate of the δ_2 coefficient, which is definitely much larger in the second sample. In the Greenspan sample, variations in the M1 aggregate have an immediate effect on the yield spread; while, in the Bernanke period, money supply affects long-term rates with some delay.

The key result in Table 34.4 concerns the effect of QE on the SDF. Before 2006, variations in the supply of money are ineffective; the estimated coefficients (δ_1 and δ_2) are not statistically significant. Importantly, we obtain the same outcome if the first sample is extended backward as to cover the overall Greenspan era. On the contrary, in Sample 2 the M1 influence on the SDF is significant. The predominant effect is negative and occurs with a six-month delay. The negative sign of the coefficient is consistent with the results discussed in Section 34.3. An easy stance of monetary policy induces investors to reduce the discounting measures applied to future payoffs so as to have higher asset prices in the future. We emphasize that the influence of the premium on the SDF is much larger in the second sample; these results coupled with the empirical findings of Section 34.3 encourage exploring non-linearities.

[10] Actually, if the contemporaneous and the lagged effect of M1 are jointly considered, the overall effect of M1 on the yield spread is larger in Sample 1. However, if we extend Sample 1 backward to cover the entire Greenspan tenure, the coefficient multiplying the lagged growth rate of M1 becomes statistically not significant. The coefficient capturing the contemporaneous influence remains significant with an estimated value of 1.85.

To have a clearer picture of the QE effect we investigate eventual asymmetries in the relationship between financial markets and the key macro-finance indicator (SDF). In particular, we check whether the SDF informative content depends upon the supply of money and assess the extent to which the discounting process implicit in asset pricing is contingent to the economy's monetary conditions. We recall that the SDF reflects agents' savings preferences by weighting the relative value of future to present consumption. In light of that, the Federal Reserve's decision to increase the size of its balance sheet by purchasing assets with medium and long maturities has been welcomed by market participants as an effective way to provide markets with short-term liquidity. In addition, fixed-income investors have benefited from the price effect associated with the reduction of long-term rates. The following threshold model is used to test the non-linear effect of QE on the relationship between financial markets and the discount factor:

$$
\begin{cases}
z_t = \alpha_1 + \beta_1 \, \mathrm{SDF}_{t-1} + e_{1,t} & \Delta \mathrm{M1}_{t-2} \leq \widehat{\mathrm{THR}} \\
z_t = \alpha_2 + \beta_2 \mathrm{SDF}_{t-1} + e_{2,t} & \Delta \mathrm{M1}_{t-2} > \widehat{\mathrm{THR}},
\end{cases}
\tag{34.5}
$$

where z_t is either the first principal component of the US stock market returns, the log(VIX) index or the factor capturing the dynamics of the hedge funds returns. Hence, z_t represents the same dependent variables as in Equations (34.1), (34.2) and (34.3), respectively. The Hansen (2000) test suggests that the relationship between z_t and the SDF is strongly non-linear. The null hypothesis of linearity, "absence of threshold," is rejected at the highest significance level. Threshold estimations are reported in Table 34.5. The number of observations within each regime depends on the optimization involved by the threshold technique. Regime 1 (below the ΔM1 estimated threshold) includes periods characterized by moderate growth of money supply, while the rate of growth of M1 is relatively high in Regime 2. Therefore, Regime 2 is more closely associated to the monetary conditions prevailing during the QE windows (QE1 and QE2). There is clear-cut evidence supporting the asymmetric relationship between the SDF and financial markets. In Regime 2, the magnitude of the estimated β coefficients is significantly larger than in Regime 1. These results provide us with an explanation of the unusual volatility exhibited by financial markets during the recent crisis as long as the impact on asset prices implied by the discounting process has been much greater for a given variation of the SDF. The joint-R^2 indicates much better fit in the two-regime framework than in the single regime hypothesis.

Table 34.5. Threshold Estimation of Model (34.5)

Dependent variable	SDF_{t-1}	R^2	N	Reg.	SDF_{t-1}	R^2	N	Joint-R^2
ΔXX_t	−2.305 (0.000)	0.21	179	1	−1.681 (0.000)	0.20	140	0.39
				2	−9.013	0.54 (0.000)	39	
$Log(VIX_t)$	0.211 (0.067)	0.06	179	1	0.078 (0.153)	0.02	117	0.27
				2	1.336	0.64 (0.000)	62	
ΔHFR_t	−2.025 (0.002)	0.13	179	1	−2.017 (0.000)	0.33	89	0.40
				2	−2.995	0.20 (0.000)	90	

Dependent variable	SDF_{t-3}	R^2	N	Reg.	SDF_{t-3}	R^2	N	Joint-R^2
ΔXX_t	−2.815 (0.000)	0.31	179	1	−2.175 (0.000)	0.41	88	0.44
				2	−4.400	0.41 (0.000)	91	
$Log(VIX_t)$	0.297 (0.027)	0.11	179	1	0.082 (0.166)	0.01	108	0.32
				2	1.013	0.61 (0.000)	71	
ΔHFR_t	−2.651 (0.000)	0.23	179	1	−2.391 (0.000)	0.40	90	0.46
				2	−3.920	0.34 (0.000)	89	

Although significant in some cases, the estimation of the intercept is not reported here. ΔXX is the first PC of the US stock market returns. VIX is the volatility index. ΔHFR is the first PC of the hedge funds indexes returns. Lagged values of the SDF are the regressors. The appropriate lag of the money supply growth is the threshold variable. p-values in parentheses. Linearity, "no threshold," is the null hypothesis of the THR test. Regime (Reg.) 1 means below the estimated threshold value. N indicates number of observations.

So far the empirical evidence corroborates the basic assumption of modern finance, i.e. the monetary stimulus induces investors to ask for higher premia when they feel poor and consumption levels are relatively low. The observations clustered in Regime 2 reflect, in fact, periods of expansionary monetary policy implemented to tackle weak aggregate demand when the economy does not face any inflationary pressure. In such a macroeconomic context the desire for higher returns on assets is rational and aims at offsetting the declining labor income due to the disturbing rise of unemployment. Kimura and Small (2006) find that QE increased risk premia on assets with cyclical returns, generating a positive effect on equity prices in Japan.

A related issue is the role of changing risk aversion across different phases of the business cycle. In this respect, rising unemployment and falling labor income make agents upset. Risk aversion increases both at the individual and at the aggregate level. Time-varying risk aversion has been examined in the literature as a determinant of asset prices predictability (Campbell and Cochrane, 1999; Wachter, 2006). In a similar vein, Li (2007) shows that countercyclical risk aversion may result in procyclical risk premium. Mele (2007) analyzes countercyclical stock volatility. He argues that it does not merely depend upon countercyclical risk premia as he suggests volatility being asymmetrically linked to swings in risk premia. Mele (2007) finds that larger risk premia required by investors when the economy departs from good states may cause volatility peaks in bad states.

Instead of focusing on time-varying risk aversion, we release the assumption of time continuity and estimate a threshold model in which the level of the risk premium discriminates between regimes. We thus analyze how the relationship between financial markets and the SDF is related to the level of uncertainty reflected in risk premia. To address this issue we perform a sensitivity analysis exploiting the features of the threshold methodology rather than estimating a conventional threshold model. We estimate Equations (34.1) and (34.2) using the risk premium and the unemployment rate to discriminate between regimes:

$$
\begin{cases}
z_t = \alpha_1 + \beta_1 \mathrm{SDF}_{t-1} + e_{1,t} & pr_{t-2,\,t-4} \le \widehat{\mathrm{THR}} \\
z_t = \alpha_2 + \beta_2 \mathrm{SDF}_{t-1} + e_{2,t} & pr_{t-2,\,t-4} > \widehat{\mathrm{THR}}
\end{cases}
. \qquad (34.6)
$$

In Model (34.6) z_t is either $\Delta XX^{\mathrm{PC},1}$ or $\Delta \mathrm{HF}^{\mathrm{PC},1}$. Results are reported in Table 34.6. In the left panel the dynamic threshold variable is the (rescaled) average of the risk premium over the previous quarter. The threshold (THR) value in Model (34.6) is discretely increased in order to assess the sensitivity of markets movements to the SDF conditional on the level of the premium. The non-linear framework, in fact, allows clustering observations on the basis of the level of the (lagged) term premium. In this case

Table 34.6. Sensitivity Analysis Based on the Threshold Model (34.6)

THR variable: risk premium (Regime 2)

		$\Delta XX^{PC,1}$				$\Delta HF^{PC,1}$	
THR	N (reg. 2)	Coefficient estimates	R^2	THR	N (reg. 2)	Coefficient estimates	R^2
0.10	125	−2.275	0.19	0.27	86	−2.225	0.20
0.12	116	−2.243	0.18	0.30	79	−2.213	0.20
0.15	112	−2.173	0.17	0.32	71	−2.026	0.18
0.17	109	−2.159	0.17	0.35	67	−2.009	0.18
0.20	104	−2.042	0.15	0.37	61	−2.077	0.22
0.22	95	−1.867	0.14	0.40	54	−2.319	0.24

THR variable: unemployment (Regime 1)

		$\Delta XX^{PC,1}$		$\Delta HF^{PC,1}$	
THR	N (reg. 1)	Coefficient estimates	R^2	Coefficient estimates	R^2
0.05	91	−2.189	0.36	−2.281	0.32
0.10	109	−2.215	0.32	−2.022	0.23
0.15	123	−2.211	0.30	−1.912	0.19
0.20	129	−2.185	0.29	−1.875	0.18
0.25	141	−2.182	0.28	−1.838	0.16
0.30	145	−2.157	0.27	−1.816	0.15

The dependent variables are the first PC of the US stock markets and the first PC of the hedge funds indexes. The explanatory variable is the average of the rescaled risk premium over the previous quarter (left panel) only Regime 2 estimations are reported, while when the threshold variable is cyclical unemployment (right panel) only Regime 1 estimations are reported. Although significant in some cases, the estimation of the intercept is not reported here. Newey—West p-values are always zero (not reported). N indicates number of observations.

our attention is restricted to Regime 2 (high term premia), which mainly includes bad times data (immediately before, or during, the recession).

As the term premium increases, i.e. as Regime 2 includes "riskier" observations, the discounting process becomes weaker and weaker. The absolute value of the estimated coefficients decreases when moving down along the columns in the left panel of Table 34.6. Hence, recent high levels of term premia induce investors to command higher premia in the future, since a weak discount implies soaring asset prices. This evidence is also consistent with the self-fulfilling prophecies hypothesis proposed in Section 34.3. When the risk increases, i.e. investors become more risk averse, they require higher premia; generally, they prefer holding assets delivering good payoffs in states like a recession to offset the diminishing levels of consumption associated with low labor income. It is worth noting that hedge funds investors face higher threshold value to obtain excess returns on their investments. This is consistent with the principle governing investments in the "hedging" sector: Hedge funds investors seek important excess returns and, correspondingly, hedge funds managers offer absolute returns to the fund owners thanks to the freedom they have to adopt any sort of trading strategy.

Another argument in this paper is that risk aversion is closely related to the unemployment rate (Figure 34.1b). In this regard, the right panel of Table 34.6 gives a picture consistent with the results in the left part of Table 34.6. Equation (34.6) is also estimated using the (rescaled) lagged value of cyclical unemployment as the dynamic threshold. Focusing on Regime 1 only, we analyze the results when the unemployment rate increases (down the columns of the right panel in Table 34.6). In principle, Regime 1 (below the threshold) includes "good" observations, i.e. data corresponding to relatively low levels of unemployment. As the threshold value rises and Regime 1 starts including periods characterized by higher level of unemployment, the estimated coefficient decreases. Thus, in states of the world featuring high risk aversion investors apply low discount and ask for higher premia.

34.4 Concluding Remarks

In the last decade two major events have reshaped US monetary policy: The end of the Greenspan era and the appointment of Ben Bernanke at the helm of the Federal Reserve.

The outbreak of the major financial crisis after the end of World War II pushed the US monetary policy into uncharted waters. The policy measures adopted to tackle the crisis culminated in the implementation of the zero interest rate policy and QE.

Although many empirical works have recently focused on the effectiveness of the Federal Reserve's large-scale asset purchases, little attention has been paid to the macro-finance determinants of asset pricing during the QE. In this chapter, we thus examine whether the relationship between financial markets and some macro-finance variables changed after Bernanke was appointed as Chairman of the Federal Reserve. We relate our results to the changing behavior of risk aversion across different phases of the business cycle. In this respect, we find that cyclical variation in risk aversion can explain the dynamics of asset prices over time since it governs the discounting process implicit in asset pricing. In particular, there is significant evidence that the effect on asset pricing determined by the cyclical fluctuations of unemployment is similar to the effect generated by the countercyclical movements of risk premia.

Empirical evidence suggests that the SDF, rather than the other macro-finance drivers, plays a major role in explaining the dynamics of financial market returns in the Bernanke sample. In this regard, our findings are consistent with recent results in the literature on consumption-based representative agent models (Campbell and Cochrane, 1999; Lettau and Ludvigson, 2001; Wachter, 2006; Li, 2007). In addition, we highlight that the joint dynamics of the term structure latent factors and macroeconomic variables display features that can be related to the QE. In particular, in the second half of the Greenspan era we find a significant inverse correlation between the slope and changes of the federal funds rate, but this relationship is definitely weak in Sample 2. The zero lower bound on short rates coupled with long-maturity Treasury curve management may lie beneath such an outcome.

Finally, evidence tends to support that the recent movements of financial markets have not been completely unpredictable. Predictability of future market movements may have encouraged investors to accomplish strategic portfolio diversification. When asset managers lose confidence in the possibility of generating satisfactory returns on equity markets, they find it convenient to diversify their portfolios in order to limit losses in bear markets. In particular, hedge fund managers seem to have considered commodities and commodity futures as valid investment opportunities (Edwards and Park, 1996; Jensen *et al.*, 2000; Cheung and Miu, 2010; Modena, 2011b). Macro-oriented allocations, directional strategies and commodity-based investments have, in fact, neutralized the negative effects on returns related to the financial crisis.

References

Adrian, T., Hyun, S.S., 2010. Financial intermediaries and monetary economics. In: Friedman, B.M., Woodford, M. (Eds), Handbook of Monetary Economics, Volume 3. Elsevier, Amsterdam, pp. 601–650.

Adrian, T., Moench, E., Shin, H.S., 2010. Macro risk premium and intermediary balance sheet quantities. IMF Economic Review 58, 179–207.

Alvarez, F., Jermann, U.J., 2000. Efficiency, equilibrium, and asset pricing with risk of default. Econometrica 68, 775–797.

Ang, A., Piazzesi, M., 2003. A no-arbitrage vector autoregression of term structure dynamics with macroeconomic and latent variables. Journal of Monetary Economics 50, 745–787.

Ang, A., Bekaert, G., Wei, M., 2008. The term structure of real rates and expected inflation. Journal of Finance 63, 797–849.

Ang, A., Piazzesi, M., Wei, M., 2006. What does the yield curve tell us about GDP growth? Journal of Econometrics 131, 359–403.

Backus, D.K., Wright, G.H., 2007. Cracking the conundrum. Brookings Papers on Economic Activity 1, 293–329.

Bekaert, G., Engstrom, E., Xing, Y., 2009. Risk, uncertainty, and asset prices. Journal of Financial Economics 91, 59–82.

Bekaert, G., Hoerova, M., Lo Duca, M., 2010. Risk, uncertainty and monetary policy. CEPR Discussion Paper 8154. CEPR, London.

Bernanke, B., 2010. Monetary policy and the housing bubble. Presented at the *Annual Meeting of the American Economic Association*, January 3, GA, Atlanta.

Buraschi, A., Jiltsov, A., 2005. Inflation risk premia and the expectations hypothesis. Journal of Financial Economics 75, 429–490.

Campbell, J.Y., Shiller, R.J., 1991. Yield spreads and interest rate movements: a bird's eye view. Review of Economic Studies 58, 495–514.

Campbell, J.Y., Cochrane, J.H., 1999. By force of habit: a consumption-based explanation of aggregate stock market behavior. Journal of Political Economy 107, 202–251.

Cheung, C.S., Miu, P., 2010. Diversification benefits of commodity futures. Journal of International Financial Markets, Institutions and Money 20, 451–474.

Cochrane, J.H., 2005. Asset Pricing. Princeton University Press, Princeton, NJ.

Cochrane, J.H., Piazzesi, M., 2005. Bond risk premia. American Economic Review 95, 130–160.

Constantinides, G., 1990. Habit-formation: a resolution of the equity premium puzzle. Journal of Political Economy 98, 519–543.

De Graeve, F., Dossche, M., Emiris, M., Sneessens, H., Wouters, R., 2010. Risk premiums and macroeconomic dynamics in a heterogeneous agent model. Journal of Economic Dynamics and Control 34, 1680–1699.

Del Negro, M., Otrok, C., 2007. 99 Luftballons: monetary policy and the house price boom across U.S. states. Journal of Monetary Economics 4, 1962–1985.

Dewachter, H., Lyrio, M., 2006. Macro factors and the term structure of interest rates. Journal of Money, Credit, and Banking 38, 119–140.

Doh, T., 2010. The efficacy of large-scale asset purchases at the zero lower bound. Economic Review. Fed of Kansas City, 2nd quarter 2010, pp. 5–34.

Diebold, F.X., Li, C., 2006. Forecasting the term structure of government bond yields. Journal of Econometrics 130, 337–364.

Edwards, F.R., Park, J.M., 1996. Do managed futures make good investments? Journal of Futures Markets 16, 475–517.

Estrella, A., Hardouvelis, G.A., 1991. The term structure as a predictor of real economic activity. Journal of Finance 46, 555–576.

Favero, C.A., Kaminska, I., Soderstrom, U., 2005. The predictive power of the yield spread: further evidence and a structural interpretation. CEPR Discussion Paper 4910.

Fama, E.F., French, K.R., 1989. Business conditions and expected returns on stocks and bonds. Journal of Financial Economics 25, 23–49.

Ferson, W., Harvey, R., 1991. The variation of economic risk premiums. Journal of Political Economy 99, 385–415.

Gagnon, J., Raskin, M., Remache, J., Sack, B., 2011. The financial market effects of the Federal Reserve's large-scale asset purchases. International Journal of Central Banking 7, 3–43.

Giot, P., 2005. Relationships between implied volatility indexes and stock index returns. The Journal of Portfolio Management 31, 92–100.

Gürkaynak, R.S., Wright, J.H., 2011. Macroeconomics and the term structure. CEPR Discussion Paper 8018. CEPR, London.

Hamilton, J.D., Kim, D.H., 2002. A reexamination of the predictability of economic activity using the yield spread. Journal of Money, Credit and Banking. Blackwell Publishing. vol. 34(2), 340–360.

Hamilton, J.D., Wu, J.C., 2012. The effectiveness of alternative monetary policy tools in a zero lower bound environment. Journal of Money, Credit, and Banking 44, 3–46.

Hansen, B., 2000. Sample splitting and threshold estimation. Econometrica 68, 575–603.

Jensen, G.R., Johnson, R.R., Mercer, J.M., 2000. Efficient use of commodity futures in diversified portfolios. Journal of Futures Markets 20, 489–506.

Kimura, T., Small, D.H., 2006. Quantitative monetary easing and risk in financial asset markets. The B.E. Journal of Macroeconomics 6, 1–54.

Lettau, M., Ludvigson, S., 2001. Consumption, aggregate wealth, and expected stock returns. Journal of Finance 56, 815–849.

Li, G., 2007. Time-varying risk aversion and asset prices. Journal of Banking and Finance 31, 243–257.

Mankiw, G.N., 2001. U.S. Monetary policy during the 1990s. NBER Working Paper.

Mele, A., 2007. Asymmetric stock market volatility and the cyclical behavior of expected returns. Journal of Financial Economics 86, 446–478.

Modena, M., 2010. A macroeconometric analysis of the unobservable components of the term structure: evidence from US and Canada. PhD Thesis. University of Glasgow, Glasgow.

Modena, M., 2011a. A macroeconometric analysis of the latent factors of the yield curve: curvature and real activity. In: Gregoriou, G.N., Pascalau, R. (Eds.), Financial Econometrics Modeling. Term Structure Models. Palgrave Macmillan, London, pp. 121–146.

Modena, M., 2011b. Agricultural commodities and financial markets. MPRA Working Paper. MPRA, Munich.

Nelson, C.R., Siegel, A.F., 1987. Parsimonious modelling of yield curves. Journal of Business 60, 473–489.

Rajan, R., 2006. Has finance made the world riskier? European Financial Management 12, 499–533.

Rudebusch, G.D., Wu, T., 2008. A macro-finance model of the term structure, monetary policy and the economy. Economic Journal 118 (530), 906–926.

Rudebusch, G.D., Swanson, E.T., Wu, T., 2006. The bond yield conundrum from a macro-finance perspective. Monetary and Economic Studies, Institute for Monetary and Economic Studies, Bank of Japan 24 (S1), 83–109.

Schwert, G.W., 1989. Business cycles, financial crises, and stock volatility. Carnegie–Rochester Conference Series on Public Policy 31, 83–125.

Stock, J.H., Watson, M.W., 1989. New indexes of coincident and leading indicators. In: Blanchard, O., Fischer, S. (Eds), NBER Macroeconomics Annual 4. MIT Press, Cambridge, MA, pp. 351–394.

Stroebel, J.C., Taylor, J.B., 2009. Estimated impact of the Fed's mortgage-backed securities purchase program. NBER Working Paper 15626. NBER, Cambridge, MA.

Thornton, D., 2009. The effect of the Fed's purchase of long-term treasuries on the yield curve. Economic Synopses. Federal Reserve of St Louis, St Louis, MO.

Wachter, J.A., 2006. A consumption-based model of the term structure of interest rates. Journal of Financial Economics 79, 365–399.

35

REVISITING INTEREST RATE PRICING MODELS FROM AN INDIAN PERSPECTIVE: LESSONS AND CHALLENGES

Rituparna Das* and Michael C.S. Wong**

*National Law University, **City University of Hong Kong

CHAPTER OUTLINE

35.1 Introduction

Two of the primary purposes that the Indian debt market reform started with were: (i) Inducing the government to borrow at the market rate and therefore (ii) helping the evolution of benchmark rates. However, in an emerging economy, the debt market in its initial stage requires support in price discovery from institutions like banks, and primary dealers because government security as paper for long-term risk-free investment is not as popular as equity. Again, in a framework of fixed-income pricing by the market, the regulator expects the government security market to provide the macroeconomic information contained in

Rethinking Valuation and Pricing Models. http://dx.doi.org/10.1016/B978-0-12-415875-7.00035-X

the yield curve.[1] This chapter highlights the major challenges in building the yield curve of government securities in the Indian market.

35.2 Success and Lessons

The success of the government debt market reform process includes, *inter alia*, the emergence of a yield curve in a situation of online auction and full subscription with the help of primary dealers, and encouraging insurance and corporate sectors to participate therein. The lessons learnt from the reform process are given below.

35.2.1 Demand for Repo in Corporate Bonds

Government security (G-sec) is one of the assets held by banks, financial institutions and corporates. Non-bank financial institutions and corporates do not have "statutory liquidity ratio" (SLR) obligations. Hence, they do not need to hold G-sec in situations like continuous portfolio depreciation during a prolonged inflationary regime. In addition, entities with a high-risk appetite like to supplement/substitute G-Sec with equity and corporate bonds in their portfolio for diversification purposes. During the post-crisis period that featured a series of stock market crashes and successive monetary policy rate hikes, India's largest private sector company, Reliance Industries Limited (RIL), reduced its stock market exposure where its ordinary unquoted non-subsidiary equity portfolio fell from around INR 45 cr to INR 27 cr and looked towards fixed-income products.[2] However, within the fixed-income category in its investment portfolio, it replaced the G-sec quoted, which came down from around INR 373 cr at the end of FY 2008–2009 to a little above INR 5 cr at the end of FY 2009–2010 and then went down below INR 5 cr at the end of FY 2010–2011, and the Treasury bills, which came down from around INR 7 cr at the end of FY 2008–2009 to nil at the end of FY 2009–2010 and remained nil throughout FY 2010–2011, by investments in interest products issued by public sector undertakings, public

---

[1] Zero coupon yield curves: technical documentation, http://www.bis.org/publ/bppdf/bispap25.pdf, accessed 15 August 2011. Paper on NSS yield curve, http://www.ccilindia.com/Lists/DiscussionForum/Attachments/55/Topic-14-03-2005071736.pdf, accessed 15 August 2011.

[2] RIL website; http://ril.com/html; "cr" is the short form of "crore" equal to 10 million – a unit of INR currency used in financial reporting in India.

financial institutions and corporate bonds, which rose from around INR 944 cr at the end of FY 2008−2009 to around INR 3670 cr at the end of FY 2009−2010 and then further to around INR 4630 cr.[3] Hence, there is a demand for Repo (repurchase agreement) products in corporate bonds.

35.2.2 Success of Collateralized Lending and Borrowing Obligations *vis-á-vis* Repo

The inconveniences of traditional Repo products experienced by the banks with regard to the fixity of the due date of squaring up and absence of foreclosure gave rise to the demand for collateralized lending and borrowing obligations (CBLO) as an improvement over Repo; it is also considered instrumental for obtaining access to the money market for non-bank entities prevented from participating in the interbank call money market. The importance of CBLO *vis-à-vis* the Repo of the Reserve Bank of India (RBI),[4] the central bank of India, was reflected in CBLO traded near RBI's Repo rate of 7.50% on demand for funds from banks to meet their funding requirements ahead of RBI's first-quarter monetary policy review on 26 July 2011.[5] Owing to the growing volume of CBLO trading, the eligibility of the CBLO rate to be designated as the benchmark rate for the valuation of floating rate products was examined.[6] A study of the traded volumes on CBLO and Repo on the Clearing Corporation of India (CCIL), an official clearing agency, for the four years up to September 2011 exhibited the following year-to-year properties (Samples 1−4) and also explored for the four

---

[3] RIL Annual Report 2010, pp. 115−116; RIL Annual Report 2011, pp. 114−115. Available at: http://ril.com/html/aboutus/aboutus.html, http://ril.com/rportal1/DownloadLibUploads/1274425260043_AR0910.pdf, accessed 24 September 2011.

[4] Reserve Bank of India (2010) Repo in corporate debt securities (reserve bank) directions, http://www.rbi.org.in/scripts/NotificationUser.aspx?Id=5456&Mode=0, accessed 10 August 2011.

[5] NDTV Profit (2011) CBLO trades near RBI repo rate ahead of RBI July 26 policy review, http://profit.ndtv.com/news/show/cblo-trades-near-rbi-repo-rate-ahead-of-rbi-jul-26-policy-review-165320, accessed 28 September 2011.

[6] *The Financial Express* (2000) RBI may value non-SLR securities above FIMMDA yield curve, http://www.expressindia.com/fe/daily/20001019/fec19076.html, accessed 15 August 2011. *The Financial Express* (2007) Interview: Ashish Nigam price discovery mechanism needed in corporate bond market, http://www.financialexpress.com/news/price-discovery-mechanism-needed-in-corporate-bond-market/220179, accessed 16 August 2011. *The Financial Express* (2011) Benchmark rate for CBLO market proposed, http://www.financialexpress.com/news/new-benchmark-rate-for-cblo-market-proposed/168498, accessed 28 September 2011.

Table 35.1. CBLO and Repo product: drift and standard deviation

Sample number	Period From	Period To	Drift (INR cr) a CBLO	Repo	Standard deviation (INR cr) σ CBLO	Repo	Expected value (INR cr) μ CBLO	Repo
1	09/16/ 2010	09/29/ 2011	193.7	−100	14,268	5939	50,385	15,793
2	08/26/ 2009	09/15/ 2010	−439.12	229.28	19,094	9371.2	54,441	22,066.1
3	07/28/ 2008	08/25/ 2009	195.43	185.69	16,532	7248.2	43942	21,235.3
4	07/13/ 2007	07/25/ 2008	50.639	4043.3	9509.5	5109.6	36,780.4	16,834
Aggregate sample	07/13/ 2007	09/29/ 2011	−10.645	67.513	16,826	8660.8	47,444	19,190

Drift and standard deviations are calculated by using the daily volumes of Repo and CBLO. Data source for Repo: http://ccilindia.com/ SecuritiesSettlement/Pages/DaysStatistics.aspx, accessed 10 November 2011; data source for CBLO: http://ccilindia.com/CBLO/Pages/ StatisticsArchive.aspx, accessed 10 November 2011.

years together in the aggregate sample in Table 35.1 the following findings:

(i) The average traded CBLO volume was more than double its Repo counterpart. It reflected the relative popularity of CBLO.

(ii) The standard deviation of the average traded CBLO volume was more than double its Repo counterpart. This meant participation in CBLO trading was wider than in Repo trading in terms of the risk-taking attitude of the market agents.

(iii) Although both of the variables were found to follow an Ito process, the expected drift in CBLO was more stable.

35.3 Challenges

The challenges of the Indian interest rate market included:

• The shift from the short end of the yield curve to the long end was resisted by continued inflation followed by monetary policy rate hikes.

• Beyond one year there was only a single on-the-run maturity considered to be a benchmark, i.e. the 10-year rate; other maturities were not that liquid. This was reported far back by Mohanty (2002). This is also true today as evident from the cancellation of RBI's auction of 6-year maturity government security on 11 November 2011.[7] We took daily traded G-sec volumes across maturities for over 1000 days from August 2007 to September 2011 and then divided this into four annual samples. The respective averages and standard deviations are given in Table 35.2. It shows that during the post-crisis period there was a gradual shift from short to relatively less volatile long-term maturity, although the bucket containing 10 years was the most liquid.[8] This fact was further corroborated by comparison of the J.P. Morgan measure of volatility of yields on three- and 10-year maturity between the period of six months starting from August 2007 (the onset of crisis) and the most recent six months May–October 2011 (Table 35.3). It revealed that the volatility of the shorter term increased, while its longer-term counterpart decreased. This was in line with the mention of reduction in risk-bearing capacity of low-grade participants in Filardo (2011). There was competition between the bucket containing 10-year maturity and the bucket above 10 years, especially for the maturity a little above 10 years and up to 11 years because of the expected substitution of a security currently in the latter bucket for the benchmark one in the former bucket.

- Owing to continued inflation, there was increasing demand for inflation-indexed bonds other than government securities and connected to the wholesale price index.[9] However, making the issue successful was a challenge as a past attempt had failed to receive the expected market response because of its relatively unpopular property of lower mark-to-market with constant yield, which made it less tradable or saleable at the time of liquidity stress.

- Currently, the CCIL constructs the gilt yield curve using the Nelson–Siegel–Svensson method. However, a self-regulated organization, the Fixed Income Money Market and Derivatives

[7] *The Times of India* (2011) Government borrowing hits rough patch, http://articles.timesofindia.indiatimes.com/2011-11-12/mumbai/30391106_1_crore-bond-auction-yields-cash-management-bills, accessed 15 November 2011.
[8] The trend becomes prominent in the volume differences between the maturity bucket containing 10 years and other buckets, when delineated in graphs.
[9] *Business Standard* (2011) Time ripe for introducing inflation-indexed bonds, say market participants, 27 July 0:43 IST, http://www.business-standard.com/india/news/time-ripe-for-introducing-inflation-indexed-bonds-say-market-participants/443993, accessed 14 August 2011.

Table 35.2. Daily trading volume of G-sec

Sample number	Period		Average (INR cr)			
	From	To	Up to 3 Years	Above 3 Years and up to 7 Years	Above 7 Years and up to 10 Years	Above 10 Years
1	09/21/2010	09/29/2011	191.1489	1426.5288	3686.5728	3974.3853
2	09/04/2009	09/20/2010	952.2949	2577.5851	4828.0285	3001.2964
3	08/07/2008	09/03/2009	795.577	2341.8649	4369.2781	2996.4246
4	08/01/2007	08/06/2008	1064.181	314.50901	2887.7669	1545.0275
Aggregate sample	08/01/2007	09/29/2011	751.7137	1664.689	3942.541	2876.983

Sample number	Period		Standard deviation (INR cr)			
	From	To	Up to 3 Years	Above 3 Years and up to 7 Years	Above 7 Years and up to 10 Years	Above 10 Years
1	09/21/2010	09/29/2011	250.5616	964.69194	3682.484	2135.3994
2	09/04/2009	09/20/2010	807.7178	1681.8726	2447.2419	2633.7252
3	08/07/2008	09/03/2009	599.7235	2036.362	2881.1654	2256.2986
4	08/01/2007	08/06/2008	750.2614	336.49195	1873.2802	1668.4645
Aggregate sample	08/01/2007	09/29/2011	722.4646	1671.912	2888.651	2362.074

The average is obtained by taking the volumes of daily traded securities maturitywise for calculation of average and standard deviation. Data Source: http://ccilindia.com/SecuritiesSettlement/Pages/MaturityWisestatistics.aspx, accessed 10 November 2011.

Table 35.3. Yield volatility of G-sec

	Period		J.P. Morgan volatility measure (%)	
Sample number	From	To	3 years	10 years
1	08/01/2007	01/31/2008	0.000081	0.00016528
2	05/02/2011	10/31/2011	0.0014107	0.0000366754

The yield volatility is obtained by using the handy exponentially weighted moving average formula of the J.P. Morgan volatility measure: $\sigma_n^2 = \lambda\sigma_{n-1}^2 + (1-\lambda)u_{n-1}^2$, where u_i is daily return under continuous compounding, the variance of u_i is σ_n^2 calculated at the end of $n-1$ days; mean of u_i is zero under normal probability distribution assumption, u_{n-1} is the most recent day's return, constant $\lambda = 0.94$. Data source: http://ccilindia.com/SecuritiesSettlement/Pages/MaturityWisestatistics.aspx, accessed 10 November 2011.

Association of India (FIMMDA),[10] collaborates with Reuters,[11] Bloomberg and the Primary Dealers Association of India on building a yield curve based on the cubic spline method. There are differences in spreads across maturities between what is provided by the two entities, and also differences in academic opinions regarding the appropriateness of the parametric method, spline-based method and other methods like the regression method. Deciding on the relative accuracy is a challenge since the RBI recommends FIMMDA rates for banks, while the CCIL claims their data to be extracted by the minimum error method. A comparison may be made for a select segment of the yield curve.

- Construction of a yield curve in the Indian fixed-income market has to allow for the existence of unutilized arbitrage opportunities, e.g. both the zero coupon securities IN002010X028 91 DTB and IN002009Y028 182 DTB have same term to maturity (TTM) or residual maturity of 0.036. However, the fact that they were selling in different segments at the same price of 99.83 refuted the market segmentation theory, but at the same time the fact that IN002010X028 91 DTB and IN002010Y026 182 DTB having the same TTM of 0.1528, were selling at different prices of 99.11 and 99.04, respectively, corroborated the above theory. What follows is a revised version of Das (2011), where in circumstances similar to what is now happening in India, i.e. a series of Repo rate

[10] FIMMDA Database, http://www.fimmda.org/modules/content/?p=1009, accessed 15 August 2011.
[11] Thomson Reuters reference rates for India gilts, http://in.reuters.com/article/2011/08/02/markets-india-gilts-table-idINL3E7J21E220110802, accessed 15 August 2011.

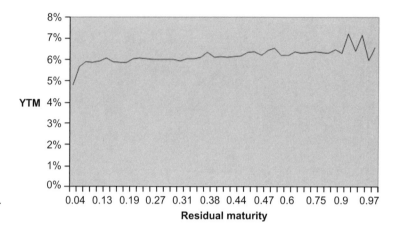

Figure 35.1 Short rate curve: alternative method.

hikes by the RBI to curb inflation, there is evidence of the short end of the yield curve being the most responsive. Hence, the importance of constructing an alternative short rate curve is more profound relative to the importance of constructing the long end and the medium part of the yield curve, when one such is already provided by CCIL. Thus, applying regression and spline methods on the outstanding G-sec as of 20 August 2010, based on the information provided by CCIL, a short rate curve was drawn (Figure 35.1).

- The absolute differences between the CCIL short rates and the rates represented by our curve were found to decrease towards relatively longer maturities (Figure 35.2). Below are given one of each of the occasions where regression and spline were necessary.

35.3.1 Use of Regression

Since there was no rate available for TTM below 0.0194 it was necessary to employ the regression technique using the security IN0020020213 6.57% 2011 (private placement), date of maturity (DoM) 24 August 2010 and next coupon date (NCD) 24 February 2011, i.e. NCD comes after three days or 0.0111 years (Cohen

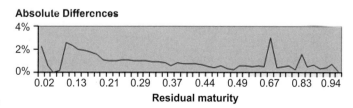

Figure 35.2 Absolute deviations between CCIL short rates and alternative short rates.

et al., 1966). Here, the independent variables are D and $(\log D)^2$, whereas the dependent variable is yield to maturity (YTM); D is the residual maturity in number of days. The regression equation is estimated as:

$$y = -0.00026D + 0.0225(\log D)^2$$
$$(-9.3) \qquad (20.18) \qquad \bar{R}^2 = 0.95.$$

For $D = 3$ days, YTM $= 0.0043$. If a is the YTM of redemption, the last traded price (LTP) is:

$$\text{LTP} = 99.80 = \frac{3.29}{(1 + 0.0043)^{0.0111}} + \frac{103.29}{(1 + a)^{0.5111}},$$

where $a = 0.142899$. Das (2011) interpreted this result in terms of the forward rate mechanism. There are two options for an investor. Assume the investment amount is INR 1: (i) invest for TTM $= 0.5111$ @ 0.142899 or (ii) invest for TTM $= 0.111$ at a forward rate φ such that $(1.142899)^{0.5111} = (1.0043)^{0.0111} \times (1 + \varphi)^{0.5}$ in the no-arbitrage situation. Solving this for φ gives $\varphi = 0.1461$. Hence, 0.142899 is the geometric average of 0.0043 and 0.1461. Since the 0.5111-year short rate 0.14289 is the average rate, the 0.5-year short rate needs to be higher than the average given the fact that the 0.0111-year rate is lower than the average.

A second way of explaining the above forward rate was found in Das (2011) in the line of reasoning offered in Litterman *et al.* (1991). The preceding 0.0111-year short rate was 0.0043. Given the standard deviation of the short rate of 0.003719, following the term premium theory the next 0.5-year short rate could go up to $0.0043 + 0.003719 = 0.0080$ or down to $0.0043 - 0.003719 = 0.0006$ with equal probabilities. Hence, the present value of an investment of INR 1 is:

$$0.5 \times \left(\frac{1}{(1 + 0.0008)^{0.5}} + \frac{1}{(1 + 0.0006)^{0.5}} \right) = 0.9993.$$

Had ζ been the 0.5-year forward rate between 24 February 2010 and 24 August 2010, the following equality should work:

$$(1 + 0.0043)^{0.0111} \times \frac{1}{0.9993} \times (1 + \zeta)^{0.5} = (1 + 0.14289)^{0.5111}.$$

The solution to the above gives $\zeta = 0.1446$, which is higher than 0.14289. This means the yield curve had a hump at maturity point 0.5, and between the points of maturity 0.0111 and 0.5111.

35.3.2 Use of Spline

Interpolation for TTM of 0.186 was imperative in order to find the corresponding yield because of the security IN0019810020 8% 2011 with DoM 27 April 2011, where NCD 27 October 2010, had TTM = 0.186, which was not traded. This maturity point lies between the points 0.172 and 0.192, and the traded maturity points before 0.172 and after 0.192 were, respectively, 0.153 and 0.208. The existence of cubic splines is reflected by a yield curve segment consisting of these maturity points and the respective yields. The securities in the above spline with their respective details collected by Das (2011) are given in Table 35.4 (Choudhry, 2005).

Now interpolation can be performed for TTM = 0.186 with help of the cubic spline function in Microsoft Excel "=CubicSpline(range of TTM values, range of corresponding ZC yields, new TTM value)." The zero coupon (ZC0 yield was 0.05877. The following equality exists for the redemption yield of IN0019810020 8% 2011 with DoM 27 April 2011 and LTP 101.1:

$$LTP = 101.1 = \frac{4}{(1+5.877)^{0.186}} + \frac{104}{(1+c)^{0.686}},$$

where $c = 10.4549\%$. Various possible alternative ways for testing the efficacy of the short rate curve derived in this study were suggested by Das (2011). The simplest one is graphical observation as presented in Figure 35.2. It shows a declining trend in the difference towards longer TTM. A practical question relevant to dealers and treasurers in their daily business relating to the test of the above efficacy is: "What could be the absolute difference between the CCIL rate and the manual rate for an unknown short TTM that is not in the sample?" Das (2011) tried to answer this in the following steps:

 (i) The absolute deviations, i.e. the modulus of the same (d) between CCIL rates and the manual rates, were computed without outliers. As shown in Figure 35.2, these seemed to be slowly reducing towards longer TTM.
 (ii) The volume-weighted average YTMs reported by daily CCIL reports was a bit different than the CCIL rates. Removing outliers and heteroskedasticity in the interest of a suitable combination of R^2 and t resulted in $d = 0.013136 - 0.00875$ TTM + $\hat{e}$. As shown in Figure 35.3, the estimated error term $\hat{e}$ did not exhibit any pattern.
 (iii) Now for any unknown value of TTM, the absolute difference between the CCIL rate and the manual rate could be

Table 35.4. Spline data

International Securities Identification Number	Security	DoM	LTP	YTM (%)	TTM
IN002010X028	91 DTB	15/10/2010	99.11	5.7759	0.1528
IN002010X028	91 DTB	22/10/2010	98.99	5.8239	0.1722
IN002010X028	91 DTB	29/10/2010	98.88	5.8142	0.1917
IN002010X028	91 DTB	05/10/2010	98.75	5.9244	0.2083

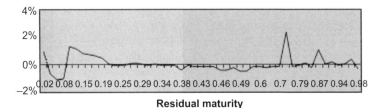

Residual maturity

Figure 35.3 Error estimates.

estimated with equation (1): $d = 0.013136 - 0.00875$ TTM. It was also ascertained that the above difference would decrease as residual maturity became longer and longer.

The final question was workability of the formula in Equation (1) In order to answer this question the primary data of traded government securities of the very next day, 23 August 2010, were taken into consideration.[12] In Table 35.5, the first three securities with the earliest DoM are taken. Their (i) CCIL YTMs Column (6) and manual YTMs, Column (7), (ii) the actual absolute differences, AAD in Column (8) between the CCIL YTMs and manual YTMs, (iii) the estimated absolute differences, EAD in Column (9) corresponding to the TTMs Column (5) as per Equation (1), and (iv) the difference d between (ii) and (iii) were computed, Column (10); this difference was found to be reducing. Hence, the formula worked reasonably well.

Coroneo *et al.* (2008), Christensen *et al.* (2008), Svennson (1994), and Diebold and Rudebusch (2011) are relevant here to implicate that a model of the Nelson–Siegel or Nelson–Siegel-Svensson type in the very beginning presumed an

[12] See http://ccilindia.com/CCIL/DATA/Market%20Statistics/G-Sec%20Settlement/Daily%20Maturity%20wise/CCIL-107-23082010.pdf, accessed 15 December 2010.

Table 35.5. Test of workability

Security	DoS	DoM	LTP	TTM	CCIL	Manual	AAD	EAD	d
91 DTB	23/08/2010	27/08/2010	99.96	0.011111	0.054896	0.036014	0.018882	0.013039	0.005843
92 DTB	23/08/2010	03/09/2010	99.85	0.027778	0.055161	0.054081	0.00108	0.012893	−0.01181
93 DTB	23/08/2010	22/10/2010	99.02	0.163889	0.05716	0.060388	0.003228	0.011702	−0.00847

DoS, date of settlement.

arbitrage-free situation, although its parameter may not be much different compared to a non-arbitrage-free situation. Under this circumstance, this chapter demonstrated how, under the assumption of a non-arbitrage-free state from the very beginning, a short-term yield curve could have been constructed with traded securities. Then, by plugging the gaps with regression and cubic splines on case-by-case basis, which contained market information and gave enough room for scenario analysis for designing portfolio strategies, e.g. if there was wilder yield fluctuation expected in the lower end of the curve, a barbell portfolio was found to work as a lever.

In terms of further research there is scope for running time series regression of short rates on the three-month Mumbai interbank offer rate and one dummy variable for the news of RBI's auction of dated securities. The patterns of spot rates, forward rates and par rates are found to be flat because the market participants did not seem to take any trade decisions as the sample date fell on the eve of the RBI auction and also because of the inflationary information content in the above rates.[13]

35.4 Conclusion

In view of the above challenges, RBI insists upon strengthening the risk management system of banks by means of focusing on stress testing and attracting skilled manpower with quantitative and econometric skills since scarcity of quants is a major constraint in emerging economies like India. Fixed-income product means not only bonds, but also deposits. Inefficacy in deposit pricing may lead to massive outflow due to asset liability mismatch in a liberalized interest rate regime.

[13] The patterns of spot rates, forward rates and par rates are found to be flat because the market participants did not seem to take any trade decisions as the sample date fell on the eve of the RBI auction and also because of the inflationary information content in the above rates Reuters (2011).

Further deposits in state-owned banks are comparable with G-sec in terms of grade, both being considered to be SLR category by RBI. Hence, there is a need to revisit the fixed-income pricing literature.

References

Christensen, J.H.E., Diebold, F.X., Rudebusch, G.D., 2008. An arbitrage-free generalized Nelson–Siegel term structure model. NBER Working Paper 14463. NBER, Cambridge, MA.

Choudhry, M., 2005. The Market Yield Curve and Fitting the Term Structure of interest Rates. In: Fabbozi, F.J. (Ed.), The Handbook of Fixed Income Securities. McGraw-Hill, New York, Chapter 41.

Cohen, K.J., Kramer, R.L., Waugh, W.H., 1966. Regression yield of US government securities. Management Science 13 (4), B168–B175.

Coroneo, L., Nyholm, K., Vidova-Koleva, R., 2008. How arbitrage-free is the Nelson–Siegel model? European Central Bank Working Paper 874. ECB, Frankfurt am Main.

Das, R., 2011. Handbook of Fixed Income Securities. Volume II: Monographs on Term Structure in India Verlag Dr Müller, Saarbrücken.

Diebold, F.X., Rudebusch, G.D., 2013. Yield Curve Modeling and Forecasting The Dynamic NelsoneSiegel Approach. Draft available at. Princeton University Press, Princeton, NJ. Available at: http://www.ssc.upenn.edu/~fdiebold/papers/paper105/EIRL.pdf, accessed 5 September 2012.

Filardo, A., 2011. The Impact of the International Financial Crisis on Asia and the Pacific: Highlighting Monetary Policy Challenges from a Negative Asset Price Bubble Perspective. Bank of International Settlement, Basel. Available at: http://www.bis.org/publ/work356.htm.

Litterman, R., Scheinkman, J., Weiss, L., 1991. Volatility and the yield curve. The Journal of Fixed Income 1 (1), 49–53.

Mohanty, M.S., 2002. Improving Liquidity in Government Bond Markets: What Can Be Done? Bank of International Settlement, Basel. Available at: http://www.bis.org/publ/bppdf/bispap11e.pdf.ac.

Reuters (2011) Analysis Flat emerging yield curves signal hit to growth June 8, http://in.reuters.com/article/2011/06/08/emerging-yieldcurves-idINLDE74U1A420110608

Svensson, L.E.O., 1994. Estimating and interpreting forward interest rates: Sweden 1992–1994. NBER Working Paper 4871. NBER, Cambridge, MA.

36

INVESTMENT OPPORTUNITIES IN AUSTRALIA'S HEALTHCARE STOCK MARKETS AFTER THE RECENT GLOBAL FINANCIAL CRISIS

Jonathan Penm, Betty Chaar and Rebekah Moles
University of Sydney

36.1 Introduction

There has already been widespread use of vector autoregressive (VAR) models and vector error-correction models (VECM) for analyzing dynamic relationships among financial variables. Granger (1981), Sims (1980) and Sargent (1987), who won Nobel Prizes in Economics, advocated the use of full-order VAR modeling to capture the linear interdependencies among multiple time series. Engle and Granger (1987) noted that, for cointegrated systems, the VAR in the first differences will be misspecified. Hence, Engle and Granger suggested that if a time-series system under study includes integrated variables of order 1 and cointegrating relations, then this system will be more appropriately specified as a VECM rather than a VAR.

A problem with these approaches is that they typically examine each series as if they were independent. In practice, we know that financial markets are integrated across sectors and economies, and prices are subject to common drivers and risks.

Rethinking Valuation and Pricing Models. http://dx.doi.org/10.1016/B978-0-12-415875-7.00036-1

Indeed, it is these attributes that make identifying market price movements and volatility behavior so difficult. Traditionally, the issue has been tested by full-order time-series modeling, which was originally introduced to avoid the need to incorporate *a priori* highly uncertain restrictions on the structure of models. As a result, heavy parameterization of vector time-series models has become a major deficiency (Penm and Terrell, 2003). This requires us to examine the dynamic relations by using subset sparse-patterned vector time-series modeling (O'Neill *et al.*, 2007). This sophisticated approach is particularly useful in complex relationships where the relevant financial time series have been generated from structures subject to evolutionary changes in their environment.

In a cointegrated time-series system, VECM has been traditionally used to assess causality and cointegrating relations, as a VECM is equivalent to a VAR in this cointegrated system. The standard approach is to employ a full-order VECM, which assumes non-zero entries in all the coefficient matrices. As indicated previously, the number of elements estimated in these possibly over-parameterized models grows with the square of the number of variables and the degrees of freedom are heavily reduced. Moreover, the statistical and numerical accuracy of the estimates in these full-order models is diminished. Applications of vector time-series models in financial time-series data have revealed that zero entries are indeed necessary. Further, in tests of Granger non-causality and cointegrating relations in a VECM, the efficiency of the causality and cointegration detection is crucially dependent upon finding zero coefficient entries where the true structure does indeed include zero entries. A VECM that makes allowance for possible zero entries in the coefficient matrices is referred to as a sparse-patterned VECM. Penm and Terrell (2003) have previously shown how sparse patterns can be explicitly recognized in a VECM. This feature needs to be extended to incorporate an evolutionary VECM algorithm that allows for a changing profile of parameter estimates, causality strength measures and cointegrating relationships. This linkage between markets is crucial for any practical application. The popularity of these models has been associated with the realization that financial systems and relationships among financial variables are complex, which traditional full-order time-series models have failed to fully capture.

In 2008, the International Pharmaceutical Federation (FIP) hosted the inaugural Global Conference on the Future of Hospital Pharmacy in Basel, Switzerland. This conference represented 98 nations and led to the development of the first international consensus assertions regarding the future of hospital pharmacy, called the Basel Statements. These statements have already been used to guide hospital pharmacy management practices in numerous countries, with results presented at the 69th, 70th and 71st FIP World Congresses. Developing countries involved have found the Basel Statements particularly useful as management guidelines for hospital pharmacy practices, which were limited or non-existent in these areas. As the Basel Statements have a strong concentration on evidenced-based management practices and medication safety, they may also prove to be a valuable tool in assessing and comparing hospital management practices among countries, with a view to the application of good management practices in the hospital pharmacy sector.

This investigation aims to develop a series of research instruments to identify how hospital pharmacy management practices can be assessed in Australia, based on the Basel Statements (Penm *et al.*, 2010). As the implementation of the Basel Statements will lead to improved financial management, strengthened medication safety and optimal patient care in the hospital setting by medical professionals, this study is of critical importance in hospital financial modeling and hospital pharmacy management research. We suggest that an entirely different quantitative sparse-patterned VECM approach to assessing the implementation of the Basel Statements might be considered, drawn from investments theory, including market integration, portfolio diversification and cointegration theory.

The last decade has witnessed massive growth in investment equity markets. Throughout the last decade, investors have paid increased attention to stock markets in emerging sectors such as healthcare, including biotech and medical equipment areas, in their search for new investment opportunities. These sector markets appear to exhibit fundamentally different characteristics from a specific industry that we will compare them with, i.e. the developed banking and finance stock markets. In the late 1990s and early 2000s, these healthcare markets appeared to experience substantial capital net inflows. Part of their appeal was a belief that returns exhibited different characteristics from those in banking and finance stock markets, due to efficient management practices and sophisticated technology breakthroughs, and as the population ages, increasing attention will need to be paid to healthcare and increased expenditure. Investors will perceive that improvements will occur in the mean-variance efficiency of their portfolio because of the weak correlations between the stock market returns of the healthcare equity sector and those of stock markets in traditional banking and finance sectors. In contrast, when share prices exhibit comovements in the same direction (or "unidirectional" comovements), such as identified in cointegrating vector tests, those unidirectional comovement relations indicate reduced benefits from equity portfolio diversification.

Since the implementation of the Basel Statements, the development and growth opportunities in the Western Pacific Region (WPR) attracted the interest of equity investors seeking an expansion of their healthcare investment portfolios. The early 2000s witnessed periods of high returns in the WPR equity markets, including the healthcare sector. However, the most recent financial crisis of 2007–2009 resulted in negative returns and associated net capital outflows in the WPR region. The purpose of this proposed research is to analyze whether the causal relations and the cointegrating relations between the Australian healthcare equity (AHE) markets and the Australian overall stock market changed over this period. Such analysis has important implications as the extent of cointegration between AHE and the Australia's All Ordinaries Index (AOI) markets is a major factor in identifying the benefits of investment diversification in Australian stock markets.

The research will test two hypotheses. The first hypothesis is that following the implementation of the Basel Statements after the recent global financial crisis, the integration level will become more significant between the price movements of AHE and AOI markets. ASX 200 AHE is the price index of one of Australia's most significant stock sectors. This traded share sector represents a significant component of the hospital biotech and medical technology industry sector in Australia. The AOI is the main stock market indicator in Australia. The resulting sparse-patterned vector model will suitably capture the interactions, and quantify the linkages, in this AHE–AOI bivariate system. The findings will indicate the causal relationships and the integration measurement in this system. The outcome will also identify the role of a lead indicator, which will definitely improve the out-of-sample forecasting performance of the system, and identify the benefits of investment diversification in Australian stock markets. The second hypothesis is that after the implementation of the Basel Statements, the returns of AOI will lead to a change in the same direction in the AHE returns as exist in cointegrating relationships. Such identified "unidirectional" comovements indicate increased investments in the healthcare equity sector from stronger AOI market growth or decreased healthcare equity investments from weaker AOI market growth. Identification of such long-term and unidirectional comovements is essential in forecasting equity market growth and volatility movements. Causality and cointegration will be assessed in the sparse-patterned VECM modeling. This issue is complicated by the large number of lagged variables due to market movement expectations and integration and segmentation effects.

This paper is organized as follows. Section 36.2 shows the formulae for evaluating the strength measurement of integration in patterned VECM modeling and presents a proposed algorithm to select the optimal patterned VECM. Section 36.3 presents and discusses the empirical findings of this study. The Section 36.4 contains brief concluding remarks.

36.2 Patterned Vecm Modeling and Causality Measurement

First, as shown below, note that a VECM is identical to a VAR model with unit roots. Consider the following VAR model (36.1):

$$z(t) + \sum_{k=1}^{s} \Psi_k z(t-k) = \Psi^s(L)z(t) = \eta(t), \qquad (36.1)$$

where $\eta(t)$ is a $p \times 1$ independently and identically distributed vector random process with $E\{\eta(t)\} = 0$ and:

$$E\{\eta(t)\eta'(t-k)\} = \Lambda, k = 0$$

$$E\{\eta(t)\eta'(t-k)\} = 0, k > 0,$$

Ψ_k, $k = 1, 2, \ldots, s$ are $p \times p$ parameter matrices and $\Psi^s(L) = I + \sum_{k=1}^{s} \Psi_k L^k$. L denotes the lag operator and the roots of $|\Psi^s(L)| = 0$ lie outside or on the unit circle. Further, $\Psi^s(L)$ can be factorized into:

$$\Psi^s(L) = \Psi^s(1)L + (I - L)\left(I + \sum_{k=1}^{s-1} C_k L^k\right),$$

where these C_ks depend on Ψ_ks. If $z(t)$ contains at least one element which must be differenced before $z(t)$ becomes $I(0)$, $z(t)$ is said to be $I(1)$ (Engle and Granger,1987). Then $z(t)$ is said to be cointegrated of order 1 with the cointegrating vector, γ, if $\gamma'z(t)$ becomes $I(0)$. Further, $z(t)$ has to contain at least two $I(1)$ variables for this to occur. Under this assumption the identical VECM for (36.1) can be described as:

$$\Psi^s(1)z(t-1) + \Psi^{s-1}(L)\Delta z(t) = \eta(t), \qquad (36.2)$$

where $z(t)$ contains both $I(0)$ and $I(1)$ variables, $\Delta = (I - L)$, $\Psi^s(1)z(t - 1)$ is stationary and $\Psi^{s-1}(L) = (I + \sum_{k=1}^{s-1} C_k L^k)$. The first term in (36.2) [i.e. $\Psi^s(1)z(t - 1)$] is the error-correction term, which contains the long-term cointegrating relationships. $\Psi^{s-1}(L)\Delta z(t)$ is referred to as the VAR part of the VECM, describing the short-term dynamics. Because $z(t)$ is cointegrated of order 1, the long-term impact matrix $\Psi^s(1)$ must be singular. As a result $\Psi^s(1) = \alpha\gamma'$, where α and γ are $p \times r$ matrices and the rank of $\Psi^s(1)$ is r, where $r < p$. The columns of γ are the cointegrating vectors and the rows of α are the loading vectors.

To assess the degree of market integration within the framework of a patterned VECM, causality measurements proposed by Geweke (Penm and Terrell, 2003) are extended and then incorporated into the new procedure for patterned VECM modeling. Using causality measures, the procedure can provide quantitative assessment of the degree of market integration arising not only from lagged causal relations between each pair of variable blocks, but also from linear dependence between those pairs. Three steps are presented below for the patterned VECM modeling. First, we consider a bivariate block system where a two block vectors $z(t)$ has been partitioned into an $m \times 1$ vector, $z_1(t)$, and an $n \times 1$ vector, $z_2(t)$, $z'(t) = [z_1'(t) \quad z_2'(t)]$. We then redefine k as τ, then the following VECM system of (36.2) can be shown:

$$
\begin{bmatrix} \Delta z_1(t) \\ \Delta z_2(t) \end{bmatrix} + \sum_{\tau=1}^{s-1} \begin{bmatrix} C_\tau^{11} & C_\tau^{12} \\ C_\tau^{21} & C_\tau^{22} \end{bmatrix} \begin{bmatrix} \Delta z_1(t - \tau) \\ \Delta z_2(t - \tau) \end{bmatrix} + \begin{bmatrix} \alpha_1 \\ \alpha_2 \end{bmatrix} x(t - 1)
$$
$$
= \begin{bmatrix} \eta_1(t) \\ \eta_2(t) \end{bmatrix},
$$

(36.3)

where the $r \times 1$ cointegrated vector, $x(t - 1) = \gamma'z(t - 1)$. We then separate (36.3) into the following $\Delta z_1(t)$ and $\Delta z_2(t)$ equations:

$$
\Delta z_1(t) + \sum_{\tau=1}^{s-1} C_\tau^{11} \Delta z_1(t - \tau) + \sum_{\tau=1}^{s-1} [C_\tau^{12} \quad \alpha_1^\tau] \begin{bmatrix} \Delta z_2(t - \tau) \\ x(t - \tau) \end{bmatrix} = \eta_1(t),
$$

(36.4)

$$
\Delta z_2(t) + \sum_{\tau=1}^{s-1} C_\tau^{22} \Delta z_2(t - \tau) + \sum_{\tau=1}^{s-1} [C_\tau^{21} \quad \alpha_2^\tau] \begin{bmatrix} \Delta z_1(t - \tau) \\ x(t - \tau) \end{bmatrix} = \eta_2(t),
$$

(36.5)

where:

$$\alpha_i^\tau = \begin{cases} \alpha_i & \tau = 1 \\ 0 & \tau > 1 \end{cases}, \text{var}\{\eta_1(t)\} = \Lambda_{11} \text{ and var}\{\eta_2(t)\} = \Lambda_{22}.$$

These disturbances $\eta_1(t)$ and $\eta_2(t)$ are each serially uncorrelated, but may be correlated with each other contemporaneously.

Second, we partition $x(t-1)$ into the form:

$$\begin{bmatrix} x_1(t-1) \\ x_2(t-1) \\ x_3(t-1) \end{bmatrix} = \begin{bmatrix} \gamma'_1 & 0 \\ 0 & \gamma'_2 \\ \gamma'_3 & \gamma'_4 \end{bmatrix} \begin{bmatrix} z_1(t-1) \\ z_2(t-1) \end{bmatrix},$$

where the cointegrated variables for constructing the cointegrated vectors, $x_1(t-1)$ and $x_2(t-1)$, are only the components of $z_1(t-1)$ and $z_2(t-1)$, respectively. The cointegrated vector $x_3(t-1)$ is the linear combination of components of both $z_1(t-1)$ and $z_2(t-1)$. We then specify and test the following three null hypotheses:

H1 No linear dependence between $\Delta z_1(t)$ and $\Delta z_2(t)$.
H2 The variables $\Delta z_2(t)$, $x_2(t)$ and $x_3(t)$ do not lead $\Delta z_1(t)$.
H3 The variables $\Delta z_1(t)$, $x_2(t)$ and $x_3(t)$ do not lead $\Delta z_2(t)$.

Under H1, H2 and H3, the two Equations (36.4) and (36.5) become:

$$\Delta z_1(t) + \sum_{\tau=1}^{s-1} C_\tau^{11} \Delta z_1(t-\tau) + \alpha_a x_1(t-1) = \eta_3(t) \qquad (36.6)$$

$$\Delta z_2(t) + \sum_{\tau=1}^{s-1} C_\tau^{22} \Delta z_2(t-\tau) + \alpha_b x_2(t-1) = \eta_4(t), \qquad (36.7)$$

where $\text{var}\{\eta_3(t)\} = T_1$ and $\text{var}\{\eta_4(t)\} = T_2$.

Third, the causality measurement relations in patterned VECM modeling become:

$$F\{\Delta z_1(t) \leftarrow \Delta z_2(t), x(t)\} = \ln\left(\frac{|T_1|}{|\Lambda_{11}|}\right),$$

which denotes measurement of the impact of the market returns in variable block 2 on the market returns in variable block 1 and:

$$F\{\Delta z_2(t) \leftarrow \Delta z_1(t), x(t)\} = \ln\left(\frac{|T_2|}{|\Lambda_{22}|}\right),$$

which denotes measurement of the impact of the market returns in variable block 1 on the market returns in variable block 2.

Furthermore, the order selection criterion, i.e. the modified Hannan criterion (MHC), could be used to select the optimal sparse-patterned VECM model. MHC is defined as:

$$\text{MHC} = \log\left(\left|\hat{\Lambda}_{s,T}\right|\right) + \left[2 \log \log T/T\right]M,$$

where T is the sample size and M is the number of functionally independent parameters. Consequently, the optimal VECM is the one that result in the minimum value for MHC in the sparse-patterned VECM framework. A search algorithm proposed by Penm and Terrell (2003) to select the optimal sparse-patterned VECM, and the cointegrating and loading vectors without assessing all possible candidate models, including full-order VECMs, is summarized in the following steps:

Step 1 To begin this algorithm we first identify the optimal sparse-patterned VECM using the MHC. A leaps-and-bounds tree-pruning search algorithm is then implemented and undertaken for selecting the optimal patterned VECM, which avoids evaluating all possible candidate patterned VECM models, including full-order VECMs.

Step 2 After the optimal sparse-patterned VECM is identified, the rank of the long-term impact matrix, $\Psi^s(1)$, is then computed using the singular value decomposition method, to identify the number of cointegrating vectors in the system.

Step 3 Another tree-pruning search algorithm without evaluating all candidate vectors is implemented for selecting all acceptable sparse patterns of the cointegrating and loading vectors. The identified candidates of the cointegrating vectors are then estimated by using a triangular ECM algorithm proposed in Penm and Terrell (2003).

Step 4 The associated candidates for the sparse-patterned loading vectors are estimated by using the regression method with linear restrictions.

Step 5 The optimal patterned cointegrating and loading vectors are selected by using the MHC.

For a bivariate cointegrated system, a direct decomposition approach to compute α and γ' is summarized in the following procedures to substitute the above-mentioned Steps 3, 4 and 5:

Step a For the bivariate cointegrated system, both the rank of $\Psi^s(1)$ and the number of cointegrating vectors will be one.

Step b In order to obtain a unique γ', a normalized γ' is selected by setting the value one to the first element, γ_1, of γ'.

Step c A direct decomposition approach will then be conducted to compute α and γ', such that $\alpha\gamma' = \Psi^s(1)$.

The optimal patterned VECM, and the optimal patterned cointegrating and loading vectors, are then used to assess the relations among economic and financial variables involved. The strength of the above-mentioned procedure is that it allows a subset structure with zero coefficients to be incorporated into the VECM. If the long-term impact matrix, $\Psi^s(1)$, contains zero coefficients, then the cointegrating and loading vectors may also contain zero coefficients. The inclusion of these coefficients could enhance the power of inferences for VECMs, especially in finite samples.

36.3 Data and Empirical Vecm Findings

As described in Section 36.1, this research tests the hypothesis that after the implementation of the Basel Statements, the returns of the AOI will lead to a long-term comovement in the same or opposite direction in Australia's ASX 200 AHE equity returns, as detected in existing cointegrating relationships by using the sparse-patterned VECM modeling.

Under the currently popular cointegration theory, when AOI movements and AHE movements are non-stationary as individual variables, but stationary in specific linear combinations, then such an AOI−AHE system is in equilibrium in the long run. To investigate the cointegrating relationships between movements in the AOI and AHE, weekly data on the AOI and the AHE were collected from the ASX official website. Both variables are mean-corrected to build optimal patterned VECMs, as a basis for the detection of cointegrating relations. The mean-corrected variables are $z_1(t) = \log(\text{AHE}_t)$ and $z_2(t) = \log(\text{AOI}_t)$. To examine stationarity for each series, Microfit 4.0 is used to carry out the augmented Dickey−Fuller unit root test. The results show that that both $\log(\text{AHE}_t)$ and $\log(\text{AOI}_t)$ are non-stationary, but both $\Delta\log(\text{AHE}_t)$ and $\Delta\log(\text{AOI}_t)$ are stationary. The outcome confirms that both $\log(\text{AHE})$ and $\log(\text{AOI})$ are $I(1)$ variables.

To examine, after the implementation of the Basel Statements, the cointegrating relations between the AHE and the AOI, the two variables are studied contemporaneously in a stochastic vector $\log(\text{AHE})-\log(\text{AOI})$ system. Weekly data on the AOI and the AHE over the period 6 January 2003 through 9 May 2011 ($T = 435$) were collected from the ASX to undertake cointegration detection. The identification algorithms for sparse-patterned VECM modeling as proposed in Section 36.2 are utilized to select the optimal VECM models and identify the cointegrating relations at $T = 428$, 429, 430, 431, 432, 433, 434 and 435. The eight end weeks correspond to the third and fourth weeks of March 2011, the first, second, third, and fourth weeks of April 2011, and the first and second weeks of May 2011.

To demonstrate the usefulness of the proposed algorithms in a small sample environment, a maximum order, q, of eight is selected to cope with this small sample environment. Following the proposed identification algorithm in Section 36.2, the optimal sparse-patterned VECM models from $T = 428$ to $T = 435$ are selected. The optimal models selected are estimated and shown in Table 36.1. In order to check the adequacy of each model fit, the strategy suggested in Penm and Terrell (2003) is used, with the algorithm in Section 36.2, applied to test the residual vector series. The results support all residual vector series being a white noise process. These models are then used as the benchmark models for analyzing the causal and cointegrating relationships for investment opportunities.

A detailed direct decomposition approach is shown below to detect the cointegrating vectors specified in the identified optimal patterned VECM model for $T = 435$. Identified optimal patterned VECM for $T = 435$, with the standard errors are shown in parentheses, where t-ratio is the estimated coefficient/standard error. In this case:

$$\begin{bmatrix} \Delta\log(\text{AHE}_t) \\ \Delta\log(\text{AOI}_t) \end{bmatrix} = \begin{bmatrix} 0 & 0 \\ 0 & 0.084 \\ & (0.047) \end{bmatrix} \begin{bmatrix} \Delta\log(\text{AHE}_{t-6}) \\ \Delta\log(\text{AOI}_{t-6}) \end{bmatrix}$$

$$+ \begin{bmatrix} -0.012 & 0.016 \\ (0.005) & (0.008) \\ 0 & 0 \end{bmatrix} \begin{bmatrix} \log(\text{AHE}_{t-1}) \\ \log(\text{AOI}_{t-1}) \end{bmatrix} + \eta_t,$$

where the long-term impact matrix, $\begin{bmatrix} 0.012 & 0.016 \\ 0 & 0 \end{bmatrix}$, is a 2×2 matrix ($p = 2$). As this matrix has a zero row, the matrix is not a full rank one. The rank of this matrix is 1 ($r = 1$). Thus, the number of cointegrating vectors is $p - r = 1$. We have $\begin{bmatrix} -0.012 & 0.016 \\ 0 & 0 \end{bmatrix} = \alpha\gamma'$, where α has a dimension 2×1, and γ' has a dimension 1×2 and denotes the transpose of γ. We have $\begin{bmatrix} -0.012 & 0.016 \\ 0 & 0 \end{bmatrix} = \begin{bmatrix} \alpha_1 \\ \alpha_2 \end{bmatrix} [\gamma_1 \quad \gamma_2]$, and $\alpha_1\gamma_1 = -0.012$, $\alpha_1\gamma_2 = 0.016$ and $\alpha_2\gamma_1 = \alpha_2\gamma_2 = 0$. In theory, the possible number of

Table 36.1. Patterned VECMs selected for detecting the cointegrating relationships between AHE and AOI after the implementation of the Basel Statements, using weekly data

Sample size: T	Estimated a_1[a]	$\alpha\gamma'$	Cointegrating relations	Pattern of Granger causality and strength measurements[b,c]
428 weeks (06/01/03—21/03/11)	$\hat{a}_1$: 0.091 (0.048)	$\begin{bmatrix} -0.012 & 0.016 \\ (0.005) & (0.008) \\ 0 & 0 \end{bmatrix}$	log(AHE) = 1.333log(AOI)	log(AHE) ← log(AOI) ln(0.267/0.264) = 0.012
429 weeks (06/01/03—28/03/11)	$\hat{a}_1$: 0.092 (0.048)	$\begin{bmatrix} -0.012 & 0.016 \\ (0.005) & (0.007) \\ 0 & 0 \end{bmatrix}$	log(AHE) = 1.333log(AOI)	log(AHE) ← log(AOI) ln(0.269/0.266) = 0.012
430 weeks (06/01/03—04/11)	$\hat{a}_1$: 0.090 (0.048)	$\begin{bmatrix} -0.012 & 0.016 \\ (0.005) & (0.008) \\ 0 & 0 \end{bmatrix}$	log(AHE) = 1.333log(AOI)	log(AHE) ← log(AOI) ln(0.270/0.267) = 0.011
431 weeks (06/01/03—11/04/11)	$\hat{a}_1$: 0.089 (0.048)	$\begin{bmatrix} -0.012 & 0.016 \\ (0.005) & (0.008) \\ 0 & 0 \end{bmatrix}$	log(AHE) = 1.333log(AOI)	log(AHE) ← log(AOI) ln(0.272/0.268) = 0.012
432 weeks (06/01/03—18/04/11)	$\hat{a}_1$: 0.087 (0.048)	$\begin{bmatrix} -0.012 & 0.016 \\ (0.005) & (0.008) \\ 0 & 0 \end{bmatrix}$	log(AHE) = 1.333log(AOI)	log(AHE) ← log(AOI) ln(0.272/0.269) = 0.012
433 weeks (06/01/03—27/0411)	$\hat{a}_1$: 0.087 (0.048)	$\begin{bmatrix} -0.012 & 0.016 \\ (0.005) & (0.008) \\ 0 & 0 \end{bmatrix}$	log(AHE) = 1.333log(AOI)	log(AHE) ← log(AOI) ln(0.273/0.270) = 0.012
434 weeks (06/01/03—02/05/11)	$\hat{a}_1$: 0.085 (0.048)	$\begin{bmatrix} -0.012 & 0.016 \\ (0.005) & (0.008) \\ 0 & 0 \end{bmatrix}$	log(AHE) = 1.333log(AOI)	log(AHE) ← log(AOI) ln(0.273/0.270) = 0.012
435 weeks (06/01/03—09/05/11)	$\hat{a}_1$: 0.084 (0.047)	$\begin{bmatrix} -0.012 & 0.016 \\ (0.005) & (0.008) \\ 0 & 0 \end{bmatrix}$	log(AHE) = 1.333log(AOI)	log(AHE) ← log(AOI) ln(0.273/0.270) = 0.012

Selected VECM specification: $\Delta z(t) = \begin{bmatrix} 0 & 0 \\ 0 & a_1 \end{bmatrix} \Delta z(t-6) + \alpha\gamma' z(t-1) + \eta(t)$, where $z(t) = [\log(AHE)_t \ (\log(AOI)_t)]'$ and $E\{\eta(t)\eta'(t)\} = \begin{bmatrix} \Lambda_{11} & \Lambda_{12} \\ \Lambda_{21} & \Lambda_{22} \end{bmatrix}$.

[a]Standard errors in parentheses.
[b]In the pattern $w \rightarrow y$: w Granger causes y.
[c]The causal strength measurements: $\ln(T_1/\Lambda_{11})$, where $\Delta z_1(t) = \eta_3(t)$ and $\text{var}\{\eta_3(t)\} = T_1$.

solutions for γ' is infinity (∞). To obtain a set of unique solutions for γ', we can assign a single element of each row of γ' to be 1, in order to achieve a normalized γ'. Thus, $\gamma_1 = 1$, $\alpha_1 = -0.012$, $\gamma_2 = -(0.016/0.012) = -1.333$ and $\alpha_2 = 0$. The cointegrating relation, $\gamma' \begin{bmatrix} \log(\mathrm{AHE}_{t-1}) \\ \log(\mathrm{AOI}_{t-1}) \end{bmatrix}$, is identified as $[1.0 \quad -1.333]$ $\begin{bmatrix} \log(\mathrm{AHE}_t) \\ \log(\mathrm{AOI}_t) \end{bmatrix}$ and is stationary, although both log(AHE) and log(AOI) are non-stationary. The normalized cointegrating vector is $[1.0 \quad -1.333]$ and the cointegrating relation, $\log(\mathrm{AHE}_t) = 1.333\log(\mathrm{AOI}_t)$, becomes stationary in the long run.

Our findings indicate that a long-term positive cointegrating relation between AOI and AHE is identified in the period after the implementation of the Basel Statements. After the implementation of the Basel Statements, the AHE movements reached a new equilibrium state with the AOI movements and are integrated with the AOI movements. The identified positive cointegrating relation, $\log(\mathrm{AHE}_t) = 1.333\log(\mathrm{AOI}_t)$, reveals that in the long run, as AOI rises, so does AHE; if the AOI were to fall, the AHE would also fall.

The patterned VECM selected at all times shows that the log(AOI) variable exists in the log(AHE) equation, which indicates Granger causality from the AOI to the AHE. However, neither the log(AHE) variable nor the Δlog(AHE) variable exists in the Δlog(AOI) equation, which shows Granger no-causality from the AHE to the AOI. This outcome confirms that Australia's whole stock market index, AOI, is influential over movements of Australia's ASX 200 AHE, during the test period after the implementation of the Basel Statements. A change in AOI causes changes in AHE. These results are consistent with both investment theory and prior evidence. Further, the AOI's role as a lead indicator in this system has been identified and confirmed. Analogously, the above test has been undertaken for weekly data on the AOI and the AHE, which are collected from ASX over the period 6 January 2003 to 25 June 2007 ($T = 233$) before the implementation of the Basel Statements. The optimal patterned VECM models selected from $T = 226$ to $T = 233$ are estimated and shown in Table 36.2. Our findings indicates that the long-term cointegrating relation between AOI and AHE has not been found in the period before the implementation of the Basel Statements. Also, the outcome confirms that over the test period, Granger no-causality is shown between the AHE and the AOI. The results demonstrate that, before the implementation of the Basel Statements, the AHE movements are segmented from the AOI movements.

Table 36.2. Patterned VECMs selected for detecting the cointegrating relationships between AHE and AOI before the implementation of the Basel Statements, using weekly data

Sample size: T	Estimated a_1 and a_2 with standard errors in parentheses	Cointegrating relations	Granger causality between AHE and AOI
226 weeks (06/01/03–07/05/07)	$\hat{a}_1$: 0.129 (0.065) $\hat{a}_2$: 0.131 (0.066)	Nil	No causality exists
227 weeks (06/01/03–14/05/07)	$\hat{a}_1$: 0.126 (0.065) $\hat{a}_2$: 0.131 (0.066)	Nil	No causality exists
228 weeks (06/01/03–21/05/07)	$\hat{a}_1$: 0.126 (0.065) $\hat{a}_2$: 0.131 (0.066)	Nil	No causality exists
229 weeks (06/01/03–2805/07)	$\hat{a}_1$: 0.123 (0.064) $\hat{a}_2$: 0.132 (0.065)	Nil	No causality exists
230 weeks (06/01/03–04/06/07)	$\hat{a}_1$: 0.124 (0.064) $\hat{a}_2$: 0.135 (0.065)	Nil	No causality exists
231 weeks (06/01/03–12/06/07)	$\hat{a}_1$: 0.126 (0.064) $\hat{a}_2$: 0.138 (0.065)	Nil	No causality exists
232 weeks (06/01/03–18/06/07)	$\hat{a}_1$: 0.123 (0.064) $\hat{a}_2$: 0.131 (0.065)	Nil	No causality exists
233 weeks (06/01/03–25/06/07)	$\hat{a}_1$: 0.126 (0.064) $\hat{a}_2$: 0.127 (0.065)	Nil	No causality exists

Selected VECM specification: $\Delta z(t) = \begin{bmatrix} 0 & 0 \\ 0 & a_2 \end{bmatrix} \Delta z(t-2) + \begin{bmatrix} a_1 & 0 \\ 0 & 0 \end{bmatrix} \Delta z(t-4) + \alpha\gamma' z(t-1) + \eta(t)$, where $z(t) = [\log(AHE_t) \cdot (\log(AOI)_t)]'$ and $\alpha\gamma' = 0$.

36.4 Conclusion

Our findings indicate that a long-term positive cointegrating relation between AOI and AHE is identified in the period after the implementation of the Basel Statements. However, this cointegrating relation has not been found in the period before the implementation of the Basel Statements. The identified positive cointegrating relation reveals that in the long run, as AOI rises, so does AHE; if the AOI were to fall, the AHE would also fall.

Further, the AOI's role as a lead indicator in this system has been identified and confirmed. The outcome demonstrates and confirms that, before the implementation of the Basel

Statements, the AHE movements were segmented from the AOI movements; after the implementation of the Basel Statements, the AHE movements reached a new equilibrium state with the AOI movements and are integrated with the AOI movements. The results confirm the success of the implementation of the Basel Statements in Australia.

References

Engle, R.F., Granger, C.W.J., 1987. Cointegration and error correction representation, estimation and testing. Econometrica 55, 251−276.

Granger, C.W.J., 1981. Some properties of time series data and their use in econometric model specification. Journal of Econometrics 16, 121−130.

O'Neill, T., Penm, J.H.W., Penm, J., 2007. A subset polynomial neural networks approach for breast cancer. International Journal of Electronic Healthcare 3, 293−302.

Penm, J., Chaar, B., Moles, R., 2010. Developing a validated survey to assess the Basel Statements: the Western Pacific Region's response. International Pharmacy Journal 26, 34−37.

Penm, J.H.W., Terrell, R.D., 2003. Collaborative Research in Quantitative Finance and Economics. Evergreen Publishing, Rivett, ACT.

Sargent, T., 1987. Macroeconomic Theory. Academic Press, New York.

Sims, C.A., 1980. Macroeconomics and reality. Econometrica 48, 1−48.

PREDICTING ASX HEALTH CARE STOCK INDEX MOVEMENTS AFTER THE RECENT FINANCIAL CRISIS USING PATTERNED NEURAL NETWORKS

Jonathan Penm,* Betty Chaar,* Rebekah Moles* and Jack Penm**

*University of Sydney, **Evergreen Publishing and Investment Research

CHAPTER OUTLINE

37.1 Introduction

The Global Conference on the Future of Hospital Pharmacy of 2008 was hosted by the Hospital Pharmacy Section of the International Pharmaceutical Federation (FIP) as part of the 68th Annual Congress of the FIP. The Basel Statements are consensus statements for the future of hospital pharmacy endorsed by 98 nations that met in Basel, Switzerland, on 30 and 31 August 2008. The Basel Statements comprise 75 statements, which successfully reflect the healthcare profession's preferred vision of pharmacy management practices in the hospital setting.

Due to the international scope of the Basel Statements, the research team aims to look both within and outside Australia's border, and eventually assess how the desired hospital pharmacy

Rethinking Valuation and Pricing Models. http://dx.doi.org/10.1016/B978-0-12-415875-7.00037-3

management practices actually influence prescribing outcomes in the whole Western Pacific Region. In order to test the rapid economic and financial changes affecting implementation of the Basel Statements in Australia, further impacted by the most recent global financial crisis, this chapter will investigate the proposition that the success of implementation of the Basel Statements in Australia will rely on the limits of Australia's healthcare budgets. Some have suggested that the implementation of the Basel Statements has not been effective because of the most recent global financial crisis or the reliance on limited healthcare budgets in the healthcare sector of Australia. However, it is not clear that this is the case for either of those reasons (Penm *et al.*, 2010).

Our research will test the following hypothesis as a starting point for assessing the implementation of the Basel Statements, which draws upon investments theory, financial econometrics and artificial intelligence. We propose the integration and segmentation hypothesis, which is that after the implementation of the Basel Statements, the integration level will become more significant among the share price index movements of Australia's ASX 200 Health Care equity sector (AHS) and Australia's All Ordinaries Index (AOI). We will examine whether integrated markets experience common price movements, which in turn will provide better out-of-sample forecasting performance than segmented markets would provide.

The AOI is the main stock market indicator in Australia. The AHS is the price index of one of Australia's most significant stock sectors. The AHS represents a significant component of the hospital, biotech and medical technology industry sector in Australia, and provides investors with investment exposure to two industry subsectors. The first subsector, healthcare equipment and services, includes healthcare services and equipment providers, such as private hospitals, nursing homes, companies involved in the commercialization of medical devices, medical diagnostics, medical practice, and pathology. The second subsector, pharmaceuticals and biotechnology, includes pharmaceutical and biotechnology companies involved in medical research and development, drug discovery, drug manufacture, drug sales, and therapeutic processes.

Subset time-series models are often desirable when observation measurements exhibit some form of periodic behavior as well as when covering a range of different measurement periods. For instance, financial data can be measured in periods of seconds, hours and days, and from time-series systems where periodic variation exists. If the underlying true data-generating process has a subset structure, the suboptimal full-order time-series model specification can produce inefficient estimates and inferior projections. It is also likely that zero coefficients could be present in specified time-series models, particularly when seasonal and periodic responses are possible.

Neural networks (NNs) are a non-linear statistical data modeling tool composed of highly interconnected nodes that can model complex relationships between inputs and outputs. A network that works well in explaining the behavior of a process over a small sample may have to be augmented for a longer data span, which evolves slowly over time due to structural changes. To incorporate such changes, the relevance of multilayered sparse-patterned polynomial NNs (SPNNs) has been extended to more effectively model a greater array of subset time-series situations, including sparse-patterned vector autoregressive (VAR) modeling. A VAR that makes allowance for possible "absent" zero coefficients in the coefficient matrices is referred to as a sparse-patterned VAR. Penm and Terrell (2003) have previously shown how sparse coefficient patterns can be explicitly recognized in a VAR. This SPNN algorithm is applicable to full-order NN cases, allows users to update NNs at consecutive time instants and can show evolutionary changes detected in NN structures (O'Neill *et al.*, 2007). Two types of synapse connection, i.e. excitatory synapses and inhibitor arcs, were thus incorporated into extended NN to increase its modeling power. Excitatory synapses allow for switchable connections with zero or non-zero strength at different points of time between nodes in consecutive layers. Inhibitor arcs indicate unnecessary net connections between nodes in consecutive layers. These innovative SPNNs are particularly useful in complex relationships where the relevant financial time series have been generated from underlying model structures subject to evolutionary changes in their environment.

There has already been widespread use of NNs to undertake price predictions for financial instruments including stocks, interest rates, futures and options. However, few studies have incorporated a forgetting factor, which has the added advantage of improving flexibility and capture non-stationarity. As a result, the forecasts obtained by allocating greater weight to more recent observations and "forgetting" some of the past are more likely to outperform alternatives in which such an allocation is not used. It is desirable to incorporate this forgetting factor approach into the framework of SPNNs for improving the performance of this approach.

Forecasting is an important aid in many areas of healthcare, in particular hospital management, which includes financial management, health services demand, pharmacy forecasting, elective surgery scheduling, bed management and patient admission. In order to evaluate the impact of interaction between market integration and price movements in healthcare stock markets, in this chapter we suggest that an innovative forecasting approach—using the sparse-patterned VAR equivalent SPNNs with a forgetting factor—be used to assess the implementation of the Basel Statements. The outcomes of our investigation will be an improved and upgraded general strategy for taking advantage of the opportunities the most recent global financial crisis presented, i.e. in the current economic and financial conditions, how can we seize investment opportunities that allow us to deliver better returns with lower risk, offer lower volatility of returns and the protection of capital in depressed financial markets. The patterned VAR equivalent SPNN approach with a forgetting factor adopted here focuses on non-linear models, which can better simulate out-of-sample AHS price movements after the implementation of the Basel Statements, as the integration level will become more significant between AHS and AOI after the implementation period than it was before.

This paper is organized as follows. Section 37.2 outlines a construction approach of polynomial NNs using a patterned VAR. Section 37.3 presents and discusses the empirical findings of this study. The Section 37.4 contains brief concluding remarks.

37.2 Construction of a Polynomial Neural Networks Using a Patterned VAR

Consider the following VAR model:

$$\tilde{u}(t) + \sum_{i=1}^{p} H_i \tilde{u}(t-i) = H^p(L)\tilde{u}(t) = \omega(t), \qquad (37.1)$$

where $\omega(t)$ is a $r \times 1$ independently and identically distributed vector random process with $E\{\omega(t)\} = 0$ and:

$$E\{\omega(t)\omega'(t-i)\} = \Omega, \ i = 0$$
$$E\{\omega(t)\omega'(t-i)\} = 0, \ i > 0,$$

and the observation vectors $\tilde{u}(t)$ $\{t = 1, 2, ..., T\}$ are available. H_i, $i = 1, 2, ..., p$ are $r \times r$ parameter matrices with zero and non-zero coefficients, and $H^p(L) = i + \sum_{i=1}^{p} H_i L^i$. L denotes the lag operator and the roots of $|H^p(L)| = 0$ lie outside the unit circle. Full-order VAR models with all non-zero coefficients are included in patterned VAR modeling.

Following the VAR identification approach of Penm and Terrell (2003), a practical strategy for incorporating the value of the forgetting factor $\eta(t)$ into the approach is proposed as:

$$
\begin{aligned}
\eta(t) &= \eta \quad \text{if} \quad 1 \leq t \leq T - 1 \\
\eta(t) &= 1 \quad \text{if} \qquad t = T
\end{aligned}
\tag{37.2}
$$

The coefficients in (1) are estimated to minimize $\left|\hat{\Omega}\right|$, where $\hat{\Omega}$ is the sample estimate of Ω, and denotes:

$$
\sum_{t=1}^{T} \eta^{T-t} \left[\tilde{u}(t) - \sum_{i=1}^{p} H_i \tilde{u}(t-i)\right]\left[\tilde{u}(t) - \sum_{i=1}^{p} H_i \tilde{u}(t-i)\right]'.
$$

Furthermore, the order selection criterion, i.e. the modified Hannan criterion (MHC), could be used to select the optimal VAR model. MHC is defined as:

$$
\text{MHC} = \log\left(\left|\hat{\Omega}_{p,t}\right|\right) + \left[2\text{loglog } N\left(T\right)\big/N\left(T\right)\right]M,
$$

where $N(T) = \sum_{i=1}^{T} \eta^{T-i}$ is the effective sample size and M is the number of functionally independent parameters. Consequently, the optimal VAR is the one that results in the minimum value for MHC in the sparse-patterned VAR framework.

37.2.1 Extended Non-Linear Sparse-Patterned Polynomial NNs

If a mean-corrected neural input vector $\tilde{u}(t)$ includes the first-order and second-order terms $u_1(t)$, $u_2(t)$, $u_1(t)u_2(t)$, u_1^2 (t) and u_2^2 (t), the following predictor form of a thrid-order subset patterned VAR system becomes:

$$
\hat{\tilde{u}}(t) = -H_1 \tilde{u}(t-1) - H_3 \tilde{u}(t-3),
\tag{37.3}
$$

where $\tilde{u}(t) = [\, u_1(t) \quad u_2(t) \quad u_1^2(t) \quad u_2^2(t) \quad u_1(t)u_2(t)\,]'$; $H_2 = 0$; and $H_i = [\, h_1(i) \quad h_2(i) \quad \cdots \quad h_5(i)\,]'$, $i = 1$ and 3; and can be used to construct a three-layered non-linear polynomial NN. Figure 37.1 illustrates the structure of this non-linear polynomial NN with a single hidden layer. The lower layer denotes the input layer and the higher layer denotes the output layer. In order to demonstrate the "presence" and "absence" restrictions on the model coefficients of a system, we incorporate two types of connection (synapse), i.e. switchable synapses and inhibitor arcs, into the polynomial NN. A switchable synapse with an arrowhead at the output node indicates a connection strength, which is switchable between zero and non-zero at any time. An inhibitor arc with a small solid black circle at the output node shows that the associated connection strength is

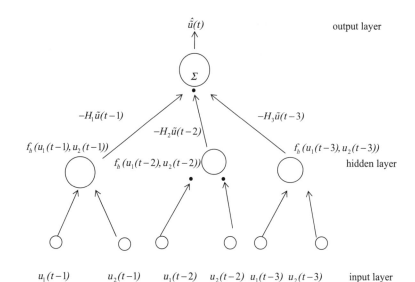

Figure 37.1 A three-layered polynomial NN for the predictor of a VAR model: $\hat{\tilde{u}}(t) = -H_1\tilde{u}(t-1) - H_3\tilde{u}(t-3)$, where $\tilde{u}(t) = [\, u_1(t) \quad u_2(t) \quad u_1^2(t) \quad u_2^2(t) \quad u_1(t)u_2(t)\,]'$ and $H_i = [\, h_1(i) \quad h_2(i) \quad \cdots \quad h_5(i)\,]', i=1$ and 3. The lower layer denotes the input layer and the higher layer denotes the output layer. See text for details.

restricted to zero at all times. Constraints on the connection strength are imposed on the extended polynomial NN structure and these increase its modeling power. The hidden-node transfer function in this NN comprises a quadratic regression polynomial of two variables, $u_1(t)$ and $u_2(t)$. The general connection between the input and output vectors can be expressed as:

$$f_h\big(u_1(t-i), u_2(t-i)\big) = -H_i\tilde{u}(t-i)$$

where the jth row element of $f_h(u_1(t-i), u_2(t-i))$ becomes:

$$h_{j,1}(i)u_1(t-i) + h_{j,2}(i)u_2(t-i) + h_{j,3}(i)u_1^2(t-i)$$
$$+h_{j,4}(i)u_2^2(t-i) + h_{j,5}(i)u_1(t-i)u_2(t-i)$$

where $u_\alpha(t-i)$, $\alpha = 1, 2$, are the input variables, i denotes the time lag index, j denotes the jth Equation in (37.3) and $h_{i,j}(i)$, $k = 1, 2$, ..., 5 are zero or non-zero coefficients of $h_i(i)$. If any $h_{j,k}(i) = 0$, Equation (37.3) becomes a sparse-patterned system. If an input vector, say $\tilde{u}(t-2)$, in Equation (37.3) is missing, Equation (37.3) becomes a subset system. In this case, the hidden unit operating $f_h(u_1(t-2), u_2(t-2))$ becomes inoperative, and the corresponding incoming and outgoing connections become inhibitive.

Each connection to $\hat{\tilde{u}}(t)$ performs a linear transformation determined by the connection strength H_i, so that the total input for the output unit $\hat{\tilde{u}}(t)$ becomes $-H_1\tilde{u}(t-1)-H_2\tilde{u}(t-1)\cdots-H_p\tilde{u}(t-p)$. The $u_1(t)$ equation in the subset VAR of (3) becomes:

$$u_1(t) + h_{1,1}(1)u_1(t-1) + h_{1,2}(1)u_2(t-1) + h_{1,3}(1)u_1^2(t-1)$$
$$+h_{1,4}(1)u_2^2(t-1) + h_{1,5}(1)u_1(t-1)u_2(t-1)$$
$$+h_{1,1}(3)u_1(t-3) + h_{1,2}(3)u_2(t-3) + h_{1,3}(3)u_1^2(t-3)$$
$$+h_{1,4}(3)u_2^2(t-3) + h_{1,5}(3)u_1(t-3)u_2(t-3) = \omega_1(t),$$

where $\omega_1(t)$ is the first element of $\omega(t)$.

The extended polynomial NN provides an update structure setting, which reflects that some synapses interacting between neurons in the input layer and neurons in the output layer switch between the excitatory and inhibitive states. This dynamic pattern illustrates the "presence and absence" restrictions on the coefficients of the time-series system and can update the specification each time a new observation becomes available. This specification is superior to the conventional static one in which all synapses are considered to be excitatory, as no "absence" restrictions are imposed on the coefficients. NNs with inhibitor arcs and switchable connections are intuitively the most direct approach to increase the modeling power of NNs. These extensions provide NNs with an ability to model sequentially changing time-series systems with a sparse-patterned structure. The proposed construction method is simple to use and can be applied to an S-layered polynomial NN with hidden layer nodes in layer $s \in [1, S-2]$.

37.3 Data and Empirical Sparse-Patterned VAR Findings

To demonstrate the usefulness of the proposed algorithm in a small-sample environment, forecasting for period $(T+1)$ is carried out by building sparse-patterned VAR systems on the first T periods, using three-layer polynomial NNs.

To assess out-of-sample forecasting performance after the implementation of the Basel Statements, daily data on the AOI and the AHS were collected from the official website of ASX Limited ABN 98 008 624 691, over the period 4 January 2010 to 23 December 2010. Both variables were mean-corrected to build optimal patterned VARs, as a basis for constructing three-layer

NNs. The mean-corrected variables are $u_1(t) = \log(\mathrm{AHS}_t)$ and $u_2(t) = \log(\mathrm{AOI}_t)$.

We use Microfit 4.0 to undertake forecasting for one-period-ahead $(T+1)$ by building sparse-patterned VAR models on the first T periods, using the sparse-patterned VAR equivalent three-layer NNs. Exponential forgetting is used with a forgetting factor, $\eta = 0.99$. The identification approaches for sparse-patterned VAR modeling as proposed in Section 37.2 are utilized to select the optimal patterned VAR models for $T = 243$ through $T = 250$, where $u_3(t) = u_1^2(t)$, $u_4(t) = u_2^2(t)$ and $u_5(t) = u_1(t)\,u_2(t)$. The estimated AHS equations are provided in Table 37.1. In order to check the adequacy of each model fit, the VAR identification approach suggested in Penm and Terrell (2003) is applied to test the residual vector series. The results support all residual vector series being a white noise process.

For VAR modeling of (37.1), the AHS equation in the VAR has the form:

$$
\log(\mathrm{AHS}_t) + \sum_{i=1}^{p} h_{11}(i)\log(\mathrm{AHS}_{t-i}) + \sum_{i=1}^{p} h_{12}(i)\log(\mathrm{AOI}_{t-i})
$$

$$
+ \sum_{i=1}^{p} h_{13}(i)\log(\mathrm{AHS}_{t-i}^2) + \sum_{i=1}^{p} h_{14}(i)\log(\mathrm{AOI}_{t-i}^2)
$$

$$
+ \sum_{i=1}^{p} h_{15}(i)\log(\mathrm{AHS}_{t-i}\mathrm{AOI}_{t-i}) = \omega_1(t),
$$

where $h_{1k}(i)$, $k = 1,2, \ldots, 5$ are the $(1,k)$th elements of $h_1(i)$. Thus, AHS forecasting for one-period-ahead will be undertaken by using:

$$
\log(\mathrm{A\hat{H}S}_{T+1}) = -\sum_{i=1}^{p} h_{11}(i)\log(\mathrm{AHS}_{T+1-i})
$$

$$
- \sum_{i=1}^{p} h_{12}(i)\log(\mathrm{AOI}_{T+1-i}) - \sum_{i=1}^{p} h_{13}(i)\log(\mathrm{AHS}_{T+1-i}^2)
$$

$$
- \sum_{i=1}^{p} h_{14}(i)\log(\mathrm{AOI}_{T+1-i}^2) - \sum_{i=1}^{p} h_{15}(i)\log(\mathrm{AHS}_{T+1-i}\mathrm{AOI}_{T+1-i}),
$$

where $\mathrm{A\hat{H}S}$ denotes the prediction of AIIS.

Further, we compute the squared error, $[\log(\mathrm{A\hat{H}S}_{T+1}) - \log(\mathrm{AHS}_{T+1})]^2$, for one-period-ahead forecasts outside the observed sample data, these forecasts being generated by the selected optimal sparse-patterned VAR models. A one-period-ahead forecast for daily data is first produced for the trading day, 16 December 2010, using daily data from 4 January 2010 to 15

Table 37.1. One-Period-ahead Forecast Performance of the Estimated AHS Equations in the Sparse-Patterned VARs, after the Implementation of the Basel Statements, as a Basis for Constructing Three-Layer NNs

Trading days in 2010	Sample size	log(AĤS)		Structure of selected patterned AHS equation [estimated non-zero coefficient value[b] (standard error)]
		Forecast value	Forecast error	
16/12	243	9.0958	0.00675	$a_3 = -3.211\ (0.933)$; $a_4 = 6.991\ (1.998)$; $a_5 = -3.738\ (1.069)$; $a_8 = 1.979\ (0.939)$; $a_9 = 2.270\ (1.076)$
17/12	244	9.1013	−0.00243	$a_3 = -3.211\ (0.928)$; $a_4 = 6.998\ (1.995)$; $a_5 = -3.744\ (1.067)$; $a_8 = 1.981\ (0.938)$; $a_9 = 2.272\ (1.075)$
18/12	245	9.0968	−0.00202	$a_3 = -3.216\ (0.931)$; $a_4 = 7.002\ (1.992)$; $a_5 = -3.741\ (1.066)$; $a_8 = 1.982\ (0.935)$; $a_9 = 2.271\ (1.071)$
19/12	246	9.0948	0.00248	$a_3 = -3.219\ (0.930)$; $a_4 = 7.011\ (1.990)$; $a_5 = -3.747\ (1.066)$; $a_8 = 1.987\ (0.935)$; $a_9 = 2.273\ (1.072)$
20/12	247	9.0967	0.00266	$a_3 = -3.221\ (0.928)$; $a_4 = 7.017\ (1.988)$; $a_5 = -3.751\ (1.063)$; $a_8 = 1.988\ (0.933)$; $a_9 = 2.276\ (1.069)$
21/12	248	9.0992	−0.00179	$a_3 = -3.225\ (0.925)$; $a_4 = 7.023\ (1.980)$; $a_5 = -3.755\ (1.061)$; $a_8 = 1.986\ (0.931)$; $a_9 = 2.277\ (1.066)$
22/12	249	9.0967	0.00621	$a_3 = -3.225\ (0.933)$; $a_4 = 7.021\ (1.977)$; $a_5 = -3.753\ (1.058)$; $a_8 = 1.985\ (0.930)$; $a_9 = 2.278\ (1.065)$
23/12	250	9.1022	0.00358	$a_3 = -3.227\ (0.922)$; $a_4 = 7.026\ (1.971)$; $a_5 = -3.757\ (1.051)$; $a_8 = 1.983\ (0.928)$; $a_9 = 2.275\ (1.063)$

RMSE[a] = 0.00915.

The order of each optimal patterned VAR is 2. The full structure of the estimated AHS is: $u_1(t) = a_1 u_1(t-1) + a_2 u_2(t-1) + a_3 u_1^2(t-1) + a_4 u_2^2(t-1) + a_5 u_1(t-1) + a_6 u_1(t-2) + a_7 u_2(t-2) + a_8 u_1^2(t-2) + a_9 u_2^2(t-2) + a_{10} u_1(t-2) - 2) u_2(t-2) + \omega_1(t)$, where $u_1(t) = \log(\text{AHS})$, $u_1(t) = \log(\text{AOI})$.

[a] $\text{RMSE} = \sqrt{\dfrac{1}{8} \sum_{i=1}^{8} \big(\hat{u}_1(242+i) - u_1(242+i)\big)^2}$, where $\hat{u}_i$ and u_i denote the forecast AHS value and the actual AHS price, respectively.

[b] All remaining coefficients in the coefficient set (a_1, a_2, a_6, a_7, a_{10}) are zero coefficients.

Table 37.2. One-period-ahead forecast performance of the estimated AHS equations in the sparse-patterned VARs, before the implementation of the Basel Statements, as a basis for constructing three-layer NNs

Trading days in 2008	Sample size	log(AĤS)		Structure of selected patterned AHS equation [estimated non-zero coefficient value[b] (standard error)]
		Forecast value	Forecast error	
16/04	232	9.1067	0.0152	$a_1 = -2.271$ (1.463); $a_3 = 1.303$ (0.805); $a_6 = 2.519$ (1.458); $a_8 = -1.388$ (0.802)
17/04	233	9.1257	−0.0182	$a_1 = -2.273$ (1.464); $a_3 = 1.304$ (0.806); $a_6 = 2.536$ (1.459); $a_8 = -1.412$ (0.803)
18/04	234	9.1231	−0.0193	$a_1 = -2.257$ (1.459); $a_3 = 1.294$ (0.803); $a_6 = 2.538$ (1.453); $a_8 = -1.399$ (0.799)
21/04	235	9.1224	0.0238	$a_1 = -2.257$ (1.456); $a_3 = 1.295$ (0.801); $a_6 = 2.537$ (1.450); $a_8 = -1.398$ (0.797)
22/04	236	9.1505	0.0075	$a_1 = -2.244$ (1.462); $a_3 = 1.287$ (0.803); $a_6 = 2.548$ (1.456); $a_8 = -1.404$ (0.801)
23/04	237	9.1597	0.0151	$a_1 = -2.337$ (1.448); $a_3 = 1.339$ (0.797); $a_6 = 2.632$ (1.444); $a_8 = -1.450$ (0.798)
24/04	238	9.1775	−0.0241	$a_1 = -2.489$ (1.441); $a_3 = 1.423$ (0.793); $a_6 = 2.705$ (1.443); $a_8 = -1.491$ (0.794)
25/04	239	9.1473	0.0196	$a_1 = -2.081$ (1.425); $a_3 = 1.197$ (0.784); $a_6 = 2.516$ (1.448); $a_8 = -1.388$ (0.795)

RMSE[a] = 0.0185.

The order of each optimal patterned VARD is 2. The full structure of the estimated AHS is: $u_1(t) = a_1 u_1(t-1) + a_2 u_2(t-1) + a_3 u_1^2(t-1) + a_4 u_2^2(t-1) + a_5 u_1(t-1) u_2(t-1) + a_6 u_1(t-2) + a_7 u_2(t-2) + a_8 u_1^2(t-2) + a_9 u_2^2(t-2) + a_{10} u_1(t-2) u_2(t-2) + \omega_1(t)$, where $u_1(t) = \log(\text{AHS}_t)$, $u_2(t) = \log(\text{AOI}_t)$.

[a]RMSE $= \sqrt{\dfrac{1}{8} \sum_{i=1}^{8} (\hat{u}_1(231+i) - u_1(231+i))^2}$, where $\hat{u}_i$ and u_i denote the forecast AHS value and the actual AHS price, respectively.

[b]All remaining coefficients in the coefficient set (a_2, a_4, a_5, a_7, a_9, a_{10}) are zero coefficients.

December 2010. The end trading day of the sample data is rolled forward by one day producing a second daily forecast, covering the period from 4 January 2010 to 16 December 2010. The process is then repeated and so on. The last forecast covers the period from 4 January 2010 to 22 December 2010.

For brevity, the forecast performance outcomes are summarized in Table 37.1. The root mean square error (RMSE) denotes

$$\sqrt{\frac{1}{8}\sum_i [\log(\hat{\text{AHS}}_{T+1})_i - \log(\text{AHS}_{T+1})]^2}$$ and is calculated for the

price variable. The estimated AHS equations for undertaking forecasts in the patterned VARs for selected sample sizes, $T = 243$, 244, 245, 246, 247, 248, 249 and 250, are presented in Table 37.1.

Analogously, the above tests are undertaken for daily data on the AHS and the AOI, being collected from ASX over the period 15 February 2008 to 25 April 2008 before the implementation of the Basel Statements. The estimated AHS equations for undertaking forecasts in the pattered VARs for selected sample sizes, $T = 232$, 233, 234, 235, 236, 237, 238 and 239, are presented in Table 37.2. For one-period-ahead forecasts, the RMSE after the implementation of the Basel Statements is about 0.495 of the RMSE before the implementation of the Basel Statements. The outcome of a superior out-of-sample forecast performance after the implementation indicates that after the implementation of the Basel Statements, the AHS movements reach a new equilibrium state with the AOI movements and are more integrated with the AOI movements than before the implementation of the Basel Statements.

37.4 Conclusion

In Australia, equity growth prospects for the AHS in the long run are positive. Demographic data indicate that about one-quarter of adult Australians are aged between 50 and 69. As an outcome of population growth, the proportion of the population in the age sectors that use health services most intensely and greater sophistication of medical technology indicates that the health sector's expenditure will rise over the long term. In this chapter, the findings have confirmed that, after the implementation of the Basel Statements, investment confidence in the healthcare sector has improved in line with movements of the Australian overall stock market. The outcome of a superior out-of-sample forecast performance after the implementation of the Basel Statements indicates that the AHS movements reach a new equilibrium state with the AOI movements after the implementation and are more integrated with the AOI movements than previously. The results confirm the success of the implementation of the Basel Statements in Australia.

References

O'Neill, T., Penm, J.H.W., Penm, J., 2007. A subset polynomial neural networks approach for breast cancer. International Journal of Electronic Healthcare 3, 293–302.

Penm, J., Chaar, B., Moles, R., 2010. Developing a validated survey to assess the Basel Statements: the Western Pacific Region's response. International Pharmacy Journal 26, 34–37.

Penm, J.H.W., Terrell, R.D., 2003. Collaborative Research in Quantitative Finance and Economics. Evergreen Publishing, Revitt, ACT.

INDEX

Note: Page numbers followed by "f" and "t" indicate figures and tables respectively.